.95

MARXISM, MORALITY, AND SOCIAL JUSTICE

STUDIES IN MORAL, POLITICAL,
AND LEGAL PHILOSOPHY

General Editor: Marshall Cohen

MARXISM, MORALITY, AND SOCIAL JUSTICE

R. G. Peffer

PRINCETON UNIVERSITY PRESS
PRINCETON, NEW JERSEY

Library of Congress Cataloging-in-Publication Data
Peffer, R. G. (Rodney G.), 1952–
Marxism, morality, and social justice / R. G. Peffer.
p. cm.—(Studies in moral, political, and legal philosophy)
Includes bibliographical references.
ISBN 0–691–07789–4—ISBN 0–691–02298–4 (pbk.)
1. Marx, Karl, 1818–1883—Ethics. 2. Marx, Karl, 1818–1883—
Political and social views. 3. Philosophy, Marxist. 4. Communist ethics.
5. Socialist ethics. I. Title. II. Series.
B3305.M74P37   1990
171'.7—dc20   89–38899

This book has been composed in Linotron Palatino

Princeton University Press books are printed on acid-free paper,
and meet the guidelines for permanence and durability of the
Committee on Production Guidelines for Book Longevity of the
Council on Library Resources

Printed in the United States of America
by Princeton University Press,
Princeton, New Jersey
10 9 8 7 6 5 4 3 2 1
(Pbk.)   10 9 8 7 6 5 4 3 2 1

For
S.E.R.
and
D.A.R.P.

The bourgeois period of history has to create the material basis of the new world. . . . Bourgeois industry and commerce create these material conditions of a new world in the same way as geological revolutions have created the surface of the earth. When a great social revolution shall have mastered the results of the bourgeois epoch, the market of the world and the modern powers of production, and subjected them to . . . common control . . . then only will human progress cease to resemble that Hindoo pagan idol, who would not drink the nectar but from the skulls of the slain.

—Karl Marx
New York Daily Tribune
August 8, 1853

CONTENTS

CONTENTS

CONTENTS

ACKNOWLEDGMENTS

First and foremost I would like to thank Sanford G. Thatcher, Kai Nielsen, and Allen E. Buchanan, all of whom have been of invaluable assistance to me in the development of this work. Both my editor, Sandy Thatcher, and Kai Nielsen—whose philosophical work has influenced me since my days as an undergraduate—have supported me in this endeavor since its beginnings in 1978. Without their encouragement and advice my efforts might never have reached fruition. When in 1982 I decided to use the first parts of this manuscript as a dissertation, I was fortunate to have the opportunity to work with Allen E. Buchanan, whose then recently published *Marx and Justice* had a significant impact on its further development. With respect to questions of interpretation and evaluation of Mark's normative views, I came to regard Buchanan's work as Nozick regarded Rawls': either I had to accept his analysis or explain why not. His input has been greatly appreciated.

Three other individuals deserve special mention: Rodger Beehler, Cynthia Caywood, and Marshall Cohen. Professor Beehler—as one of the readers for Princeton University Press—offered valuable comments and criticism. My colleague, Cynthia Caywood, was kind enough to read the penultimate draft in its entirety and offer valuable stylistic suggestions. I would also like to thank Marshall Cohen—the editor of the series of which this work is a part—for his patience and advice.

In addition, the following persons are to be thanked for reading and offering comments on various parts of the manuscript: Joel Feinberg, Ronald Milo, Jules Coleman, Wilfrid Sellars, Jeffrie G. Murphy, William H. Shaw, David Schweickart, Ralph Miliband, Andrew Levine, Robert Brenner, Sharon Lloyd, Les Evans, Nanette Funk, Iris Marion Young, J. Davidson Alexander, Joseph Kupfer, William S. Robinson, G. Darlington Wood, Thomas Leddy, Rita Manning, Dennis Rohatyn, Linda Jenks, Larry Hinman, Mike Wagner, Gregory Trianosky, and Lyle Anderson.

Sharon Ray, W. Dan Koestner, and Robert Pirani were kind enough to proofread various parts of the manuscript in various stages of its development. I also would like to thank the College of Arts and Sciences of the University of San Diego for providing typing services for the final version of the manuscript. Monica Wagner deserves special thanks for doing an expert job of entering it on disk. Finally, I would like to thank Janet Wilson and Lois Krieger for copy editing the manuscript for publication.

The first part of the Introduction and much of chapters 1 through 7 of this work are a revised version of my dissertation, "Marxism, Metaethics, and Morality" (University of Arizona, 1985: copyright Rodney G. Peffer). Chapter 6 is also a revised version of my article, "Morality and the Marxist Concept of Ideology," *Marx and Morality* (Kai Nielsen and Steven C. Patten, eds.), supplementary vol. 7, *Canadian Journal of Philosophy*, 1981. I would like to thank the editors of the *Canadian Journal of Philosophy* for their permission to use this article and Harper & Row for permission to use extensive quotes from Karl Marx, *The Grundrisse* (David McClellan, ed.), Harper & Row, New York, 1971.

MARXISM, MORALITY,
AND SOCIAL JUSTICE

INTRODUCTION

The ultimate goal of this work is to develop at least the outlines of an adequate Marxist moral and social theory. By a "moral and social theory" I mean one that provides a set of moral principles or standards by which to judge social arrangements and, by so doing, provides criteria to decide between competing sets of historically possible social arrangements. Such a theory must contain enough of an empirical, social-scientific theory to determine which sets of social arrangements are real historical possibilities and—of those that are possible which best conform to the moral principles or standards propounded by an adequate moral theory.

By an "adequate" moral and social theory I mean one that is based on a correct set of empirical, social-scientific theories and on an adequate (i.e., correct) moral theory. By an "adequate" or "correct" moral theory I mean one that is most in wide reflective equilibrium with our considered moral judgments. (Whether there is one unique theory that is in wide reflective equilibrium with everyone's judgments or whether morality is in some sense relative is discussed in chapter 7.)

By a "Marxist" moral and social theory I mean one that (1) is informed by the spirit of Marx's radical humanism and egalitarianism; (2) is based on the empirical theses centrally important to the Marxist political perspective (particularly Marx's theory of classes and class struggle and his analysis of capitalism); and (3) attempts to defend the Marxist's basic normative political positions. The first of these positions is that socialism—that is, democratic, self-managing socialism—is morally preferable to any form of capitalism as well as to any other form of society possible under the conditions of moderate scarcity and moderate egoism. The second is that social and/or political revolution, if necessary (and sufficient) to effect the appropriate transformations, is *prima facie* morally justified.

Anyone interested in developing such a theory and showing that it is both a Marxist theory and a plausible moral theory faces two tasks. The first is to interpret Marx's moral views and, if possible, to reconstruct his implicit moral theory.[1] This task is made difficult, of course, by the submerged character of these views. The second task is to answer the charge made by Marxists and non-Marxists alike that Marxism and morality are somehow incompatible. The completion of the first task is necessary if we are to know precisely what it is we are to critique and/or make adequate; the completion of the second is necessary if we are to have a coherent notion of a Marxist morality or a Marxist moral and social theory.

The task of interpreting and reconstructing Marx's implicit moral theory is taken up in part I (chapters 1 through 3). The task of showing the compatibility of Marxism and morality is discussed in part II (chapters 4 through 7). In part III (chapters 8 through 10), I attempt to refute Marx's criticisms of justice and rights and then attempt to provide at least the outlines of an adequate Marxist moral and social theory. In order to accomplish the latter task, I attempt to provide an acceptable theory of social justice, on the one hand, and a minimal set of plausible Marxist empirical, social-scientific theses on the other. Although I view these three parts of the present work as compatible and mutually supportive, I do not claim that the correctness of one part is absolutely dependent on the correctness of the others. For example, one could accept most of the claims within one section of this work and consistently reject most of the claims in the others. Therefore, the adequacy of each of the three sections can and should be judged separately.

To begin the interpretive task, chapter 1 traces the development of Marx's moral views from his earliest published works through the development of his original philosophical system (as expressed in *The Economic and Philosophical Manuscripts* of 1844) to his transitional works (of which *The German Ideology* is the most important) and, then, to his works of maturation (1847–1858) and his fully mature works (1858–1883). *The Grundrisse* and *Capital* are the most important works of these latter two periods. (For my periodization of Marx's works, see the Appendix.)

The major theses propounded in this chapter are that although Marx does not have a fully developed philosophical theory about

[1] I agree with Allen W. Wood's claim that it is "responsible exegetical practice" to distinguish between (1) textual facts, (2) interpretations that can be based on the texts, and (3) speculative extensions that cohere with the texts, even though—as Wood notes—"it is a distinction which cannot always be drawn sharply" ("Justice and Class Interests," p. 10). I shall generally distinguish examples of the third sort from the second by referring to the former as "rational reconstructions." (Works in the Bibliography will be cited by author and title only.)

4

morality, he does have a normative moral perspective, in which there is a fundamental continuity, at least from the formation of his original systematic views in 1844 through his later works. This moral perspective is based on three primary moral values: freedom (as self-determination), human community, and self-realization, as well as on some sort of principle demanding an egalitarian distribution of these goods—or at least the good of freedom. (No effort is made at this point to analyze the exact nature of this principle or Marx's concept and theory of freedom. This task is postponed until chapter 3.) I argue further that the evaluative content of alienation is reducible to or analyzable in terms of these values and principles.

In chapter 2 I review attempts to interpret Marx's overall moral perspective or theory as a species of hedonistic utilitarianism, eudaemonistic utilitarianism, and as some form or other of nonutilitarian consequentialism (e.g., self-realization theory or perfectionism). I argue, in opposition to all of these interpretations, that Marx is a mixed deontologist: he demands not simply the maximization of the primary nonmoral goods of freedom, human community, and self-realization but a radically egalitarian distribution of these goods (or at least the good of freedom). Further, he takes the nonconsequentialist notion of human dignity rather than pleasure, happiness, or human perfection as the ultimate court of appeal in moral reasoning.

In chapter 3 I argue that, in the final analysis, the most fundamental nonmoral good to be promoted, for Marx, is freedom (as self-determination). (The notion of "human dignity" is even more fundamental for him, but it cannot be classified as a nonmoral good because it cannot be specified without using moral terms. It is, in other words, a moral good.) Freedom, the feeling of human community, and the realization of "truly human" potentialities (particularly through the production and "consumption" of higher cultural products) are all intrinsically valuable on Marx's view and, thus, all components of his theory of the good. But it is only his principle of freedom (which must be construed as a principle of equal freedom on my interpretation) that provides grounds for a theory of the right, i.e., a theory of right action, duty, obligation, and/or the rights of individuals. (Although such principles may not be needed in a full-fledged communist society, they are essential in the first stage of communism, even on Marx's view.)

Although Marx did not explicitly defend these views as such, he believed that everyone should be as free and self-determining as possible. He further believed that if this were possible, people would realize their natural propensities for human community and self-realization. On my reconstruction of Marx's moral "theory," the value of freedom is basic because it is the pursuit of a maximum system of equal freedom and opportunity that provides possible grounds for legitimate social coercion, e.g., a system of just laws. The pursuit or maximization of either human community or self-realization does not, on my reconstruction of Marx, provide such grounds. These latter values will be realized to the extent to which a maximum system of equal freedom and opportunity is reached, but their fulfillment does not determine right action or ground obligation. On the Marxist view, of course, a maximum system of freedom and opportunity cannot exist in class-divided societies (more on this presently).

Such a maximum system of freedom and opportunity can be interpreted as an explication of Marx's principle of freedom (as self-determination). This principle is to be interpreted—in my reconstruction of his views—as demanding a maximum system of equal freedom, where "freedom" is taken to designate both negative freedom (i.e., freedom from undue interference in one's personal affairs) and positive freedom (i.e., freedom to control one's own life). Positive freedom, in turn, is taken to consist of two demands (or rights): (1) the right to equal participation in social decision-making processes that affect one's life, and (2) the right to equal access to the means of self-realization (i.e., an equal opportunity to attain the means of self-realization, which, for our purposes, can be taken to consist of Rawls' primary goods, including—most importantly—the good of self-respect).

In the section of this chapter entitled "Morality and Marx's Concept(s) of Exploitation," I first distinguish his general concept of exploitation from his concept and theory of economic exploitation. Second, I distinguish his transhistorical theory of economic exploitation from its applications to various modes of production, e.g., capitalist exploitation. In analyzing economic exploitation I further distinguish between labor theories of exploitation and distributional theories of exploitation, and between force-inclusive definitions and definitions of "exploitation" not including force or coercion as a necessary condition. I argue for a labor theory of exploitation together with a force-inclusive definition such that economic exploitation turns out to be essentially forced, unpaid, surplus labor that is transferred by one mechanism or another from economically productive to economically nonproductive classes.

Exploitation, I argue, violates Marx's principle of maximum equal freedom. On this analysis, economic exploitation is always *prima facie* wrong and, on Marx's empirical assumptions, almost always all-things-considered wrong in actual societies. This analysis, however, leaves open as a logical possibility that economic exploitation is not all-things-considered wrong in particular circumstances—especially circumstances one can think up when producing artificial, hypothetical scenarios. It also leaves open the possibility that economic exploitation can be condemned as bad or wrong in a particular society even when it cannot feasibly be eliminated at that point in time.

But even if it can be shown, through textual exegesis, that Marx's works contain a ubiquitous moral perspective that can even be reconstructed as a full-fledged moral theory, it is difficult to reconcile this fact with his many criticisms of morality and moral theorizing. In chapter 4 I attack the position that has come to be known as "Marx's Anti-Moralism" or "Marxist Immoralism." According to this position, Marx's writings—and, consequently, Marxism—are devoid of moral content. Sometimes this is asserted on the basis that Marxism is completely (and entirely) scientific and thus has no room whatever for morality or normative views. Sometimes it is asserted on the basis that Marx (supposedly) advocates the pursuit of "nonmoral" values such as freedom, human community, or self-realization, but not of moral values such as justice or right. (This is the position of Allen Wood and Richard Miller, for example.) Sometimes it is asserted on the basis that Marx and Marxism reject "morality" in favor of individualistic pursuit of naturalistic inclinations, i.e., in favor of a version of ethical egoism. (Feuer, Skillen, and Collier all argue along these lines.) Needless to say, I argue against these views, all of which I consider pernicious.

Another pernicious claim is that Marx and Marxists are committed, by the nature of their worldview, to the doctrines of moral historicism and/or moral futurism, that is, to the doctrines that whatever social formations have evolved or will evolve are, ipso facto morally justified. While some of Marx's remarks might lead to the belief that he held one or both of these views of morality, I argue that the preponderance of evidence is to the contrary. Further, even if Marx had held these views, there would be no good

7

reason for the contemporary Marxist to do so. This claim is taken up and, I believe, refuted in chapter 5.

In chapters 6 and 7 I consider the problem of justifying a moral principle or theory from a Marxist point of view. Chapter 6 takes up the cluster of issues having to do with the relation between morality and ideology. My contention is that once we become clear about the concepts of morality and ideology, there is no important sense in which morality (as a whole) is ideological and thus no reason—coming from these quarters at any rate—to repudiate morality or moral theory.

Chapter 7 takes up the apparent problem that, as Engels puts it, morality is not "absolute" or "eternal" but relative to particular socioeconomic classes or historical epochs. This brings us squarely up against the problem of moral relativism (in all its guises) and the related issues of moral objectivity and the methodology of moral theory construction. I contend that if Marx, Engels, and other Marxists had been aware of the crucial distinctions between descriptive ethical relativism, normative ethical relativism, meta-ethical relativism, and (what I refer to as) metaevaluative relativism, they would at least have rejected normative ethical relativism (which is the only genuinely pernicious form of ethical relativism). I argue that descriptive ethical relativism is true but trivial. In addition, I maintain that no matter what position is taken on meta-ethical and metaevaluative relativism, these positions weigh no more against the Marxist's normative moral judgments than anyone else's and thus are irrelevant for purposes of deciding between them.

It is my contention, in other words, that all of the objections to the compatibility of Marxism and morality taken up in chapters 4 through 7 can be met. These objections, it seems to me, are primarily the result of Marx and later Marxists either ignoring or taking mistaken positions on such metaethical issues as the nature of morality, the logical structure of moral discourse, the nature of moral argument, and the possibility of justifying moral judgments, principles, and theories. However, in fairness to Marx, Engels, and other nineteenth- and early twentieth-century Marxists (and thinkers in general), it should be pointed out that most of the metaethical questions involved here had not even been properly formulated at that time, let alone answered. Thus they had a much better excuse for making such mistakes than do recent and contemporary Marxists. Some of the positions Marx and Engels take on these metaethical questions can, in fact, be seen as basically healthy reactions to the excessively metaphysical views of morality prevalent in their time. That the conceptual tools necessary to solve these philosophical problems or puzzles (e.g., the method of linguistic or conceptual analysis) had not yet evolved at that time insured, however, that many of the positions they came to endorse were inperspicuous or worse.

Since it is precisely these questions that the analytic-linguistic tradition of philosophy has examined and, to a certain extent, answered over the last several decades, my strategy is to utilize the theoretical advances of this tradition[2] to clarify and solve (or dissolve) the problems that Marxists tend to have with morality and moral theory and to answer objections concerning the relation between Marxism and morality. I shall also utilize the advances made within Analytic Marxism, a more recently developed school within the analytic-linguistic tradition.[3] This school or movement

[2] In particular, I have in mind such contemporary Anglo-American analytic-linguistic moral and social philosophers as R. M. Hare, Phillipa Foot, G. J. Warnock, Kurt Baier, William Frankena, Richard Brandt, Isaiah Berlin, John Rawls, Ronald Dworkin, Brian Barry, Thomas Scanlon, Thomas Nagel, Armatya Sen, H.L.A. Hart, Joel Feinberg, Jeffrie G. Murphy, Richard Wasserstrom, Alan Gewirth, Henry Shue, Rolf Sartorius, Bernard Williams, Robert Paul Wolff, Stephen Lukes, Kai Nielsen, Richard Norman, Norman Daniels, Allen E. Buchanan, and Andrew Levine. (Although Alasdair MacIntyre and Charles Taylor are important figures in contemporary Anglo-American moral and social philosophy, it would probably not be accurate to describe them as analytic philosophers.) (See references in the bibliography.)

[3] This school includes such social scientists as John Roemer, Robert Brenner, Eric Olin Wright, Claus Offe, Adam Przeworski, Pranab Bardhan, and Phillipe van Parijs, and such philosophers as G. A. Cohen, Jon Elster, Richard Miller, Allen W. Wood, Milton Fisk, Derek P. H. Allen, George Brenkert, Jeffrey Reiman, John McMurtry, William H. Shaw, Frank Cunningham, Daniel Little, Robert Ware, Norman Geras, Anthony Skillen, Andrew Collier, David Schweickart, Iris Marion Young, Roger Gottlieb, Lawrence Crocker, Julius Sensat, Gary Young, Nancy Holmstrom, Richard Arneson, and George Panichas. (Wolff, Lukes, Nielsen, Daniels, Buchanan, and Levine could also, I think, be classified as Analytic Marxists on the rather broad definition of the term I have in mind.) (See references in the bibliography.)

While I'm not sure all of these individuals would classify themselves as Analytic Marxists, they all seem to share (to a greater or lesser extent) the characteristics of being (1) grounded in the analytic-linguistic tradition of philosophy, (2) scholars of Marx and Marxism, and (3) basically sympathetic to Marxism or at least socialism. Since I utilize the writings of all these authors, the present work might almost be considered a joint effort of this school. Needless to say, the members of this school of thought are often at odds with one another over particular issues, and none of the above-listed authors can be expected to agree with all the positions taken in this work. Moreover, it will be seen that I have strong disagreements with a number of these figures. In fact, large parts of this work can be seen as a polemic against those philosophers propounding "Marxist anti-moralism" positions: particularly Wood, Miller, Skillen, and Collier.

Excellent review articles on Analytic Marxism are Miller's "Marx in Analytic Phi-

seeks to apply the methods and techniques of analytic philosophy in order to interpret, clarify, reconstruct, and/or critique both the empirical and normative components of Marxism. Analytic Marxists have done much to reconstruct and critique historical materialism and Marx's other empirical theories. They have also attempted to clarify the relation between Marxism and morality in general and between Marxism and concepts and theories of justice and/or human rights in particular. (As we shall see, however, one of the major issues dividing Analytic Marxists is whether Marxism is genuinely compatible with theories of justice and/or rights.)

In my opinion, the synthesis of these traditions is an extremely important development. It will serve as a corrective to the dogmatic and/or obscurantist philosophical traditions with which Marxists have often been involved, e.g., Soviet-sponsored and developed "diamat." Whatever criticisms one might have of the analytic tradition, it does not lack clarity, precision, or logical rigor. On the other hand, Anglo-American moral and social theory has often been overly complacent and guilty of failing to come to grips with social reality. Whatever criticisms one might have of Marxist and socialist moral and social theory, it has not lacked substance or social relevance.

In any case, if my arguments and analyses are correct, there is no difficulty in either admitting that Marx's worldview has a moral component or in entering into the enterprise of constructing an explicit Marxist moral theory. But it has been argued that even if this is true, a Marxist moral theory cannot be based on the concepts of social justice and/or human rights because Marx rejects these concepts and moral theories even more vehemently than morality in general. Chapter 8 examines these contentions and concludes that most of Marx's criticisms of concepts and theories of justice and rights parallel his criticisms of morality and moral theories in general and are based on the same sorts of conceptual muddles. I argue for three theses. First, Marx (and Marxists) need theories of social justice and/or human rights insofar as they are concerned to claim that socialism—as opposed to full-fledged communism—is morally preferable to capitalism, and that the government of a socialist society has legitimate political authority to which the political obligations of its citizens correspond. Second, contrary to much recent literature on the subject, Marx implicitly

losophy" and Buchanan's "Marx, Morality, and History." Representative anthologies are: *Marx, Justice, and History* (Marshall Cohen et al., eds.); *Marx and Morality* (Kai Nielsen et al., eds.); and *Analytical Marxism* (John Roemer, ed.).

espouses principles of justice that are to govern social arrangements in societies embodying what Hume and others have called the circumstances of justice (i.e., moderate scarcity and moderate egoism). Third, there is no contradiction between being committed to advancing the class interests of the proletariat (i.e., advancing the cause of socialism), on the one hand, and the demands of social justice, on the other. In fact, if what I have to say in the remaining portion of the work is basically correct, justice demands that we attempt to advance the interests of the proletariat (and other oppressed classes), especially, the cause of socialism.

To make these points clear, however, Marx's conception of socialism must be distinguished from his conception of communism, on the one hand, and from contemporary post-capitalist societies, on the other. Full-fledged communist society—what Marx calls the "higher stage of communism" in "Critique of the Gotha Program"—is a stateless, coercionless society based on the social ownership of productive property. It presupposes material abundance (as opposed to moderate scarcity) and the spontaneous and willing cooperation of the new, "fully socialized" or "fully humanized" persons who apparently are able to reach a consensus on all social and economic questions. It is a society that has gone beyond the "narrow horizon or bourgeois right," a society that has transcended Hume's famed circumstances of justice (moderate scarcity and moderate egoism). Thus it is a society with no need for such juridical concepts as distributive justice or human rights since such concepts are needed (and, indeed, intelligible) only within the circumstances of justice.

On the other hand, socialism—what Marx calls the "first stage of communism"—is characterized by the socialization of productive property, the elimination of profit as the basic motive of production, and by the fact that the working class and its allies (i.e., other oppressed and exploited classes) have been raised to the position of the ruling class (or classes). It is, however, still characterized by moderate scarcity, the incomplete socialization (or humanization) of the individual, and, thus, by the continuing existence of the state—albeit a democratic state—whose function is to adjudicate between conflicting claims put forward by individuals or groups of individuals and to coordinate the pursuit of the general welfare.

Though Marx, Engels, and the other major figures of Classical Marxism (Lenin, Luxemburg, Trotsky, and Gramsci) thought that the socialization of productive property and the elimination of pri-

11

vate profit as the dominant motive in economic decision-making processes were absolute prerequisites for the development of a better society, they also characterized socialism (i.e., the first stage of communism) as being more democratic than the most democratic bourgeois societies and thought that freedom (both negative and positive) would be more extensive. Furthermore, they believed that—except in the most severe circumstances—democracy and self-determination ought to apply to decision-making processes in both the political and economic realm. As a result, they found the notion of privileged bureaucracies monopolizing such decision-making processes entirely noxious. Marx, in fact, takes the state bureaucracy to task in *The Eighteenth Brumaire of Louis Bonaparte*, where he describes it as exploiting not only the working class and other subordinate classes but the bourgeoisie and landed aristocracy as well. In *The Civil War in France* he goes into considerable detail in describing safeguards against the bureaucratization of post-capitalist societies, including direct representational democracy, the right of immediate recall, and—most importantly— the requirement that no representative or person holding public office earn more than an average worker.

Once these distinctions are made, it is clear—it seems to me— that presently existing post-capitalist societies (i.e., so-called "communist countries") not only fail to be communist societies, according to Marx's definition, but also fall short of being socialist societies; they are not even societies that have reached the first stage of communism, as defined by Marx and the Classical Marxists. Although the nature of these societies is still much in dispute even among Marxists—who variously classify them as communist, state-capitalist, state-socialist, or even bureaucratic-centralist—I shall, for purposes of this work, classify them as *state-socialist*. This is meant to indicate that while they have eliminated capitalism, they are as yet still too repressive, bureaucratic, and undemocratic to be classified as socialist.[4] From a Marxist point of view, however, it would seem that so long as one classifies them as post-capitalist societies, one must be committed to opposing the resto-

---

[4] It should be noted that the Gorbachev regime in the Soviet Union is currently pushing programs of liberalization and economic reform (*glasnost* and *perestroika*). However, it should also be noted that even if these programs were fully implemented, they would constitute a *liberalization* but not a full-fledged *democratization* of Soviet society along the lines envisioned by the Classical Marxists. Although such liberalizations are much to be desired, they would not, in and of themselves, mean that such contemporary post-capitalist societies fulfill all the requirements for being a genuine socialist—let alone communist—society.

ration of capitalism no matter what other criticisms one might have of these societies. This is because, from the Marxist point of view, such counter-revolutions would presumably constitute a retrogression of world-historical importance in the development of an international federation of democratic, self-managing socialist societies to which all Marxists are seemingly committed.

Notice, however, that the way "socialism" has been defined leaves open the choice between a socialist command economy and a socialist market economy (such as exists in Yugoslavia). Whichever economy turns out to be more efficient, more compatible with democratic social and political institutions, or—generally speaking—more in line with the principles of an adequate theory of social justice is the economy that should be chosen. Although admitting that the market could play a dominant role in a socialist society is a major revision of the Marxist perspective, the historical fact that market-socialist Yugoslavia is arguably the most democratic and self-managing as well as—in certain ways—the most productively efficient post-capitalist society in existence obviously makes this revision a live option within the Marxist tradition.

If my analysis has been correct so far, then it seems clear that the following three theses should be accepted: (1) only socialism—as opposed to full-fledged communism—is a practical historical possibility at least in terms of the near and medium future; (2) thus it is *socialism*—and not communism—that Marxists should be most concerned to argue for; and (3) since socialism is characterized by both moderate scarcity and a state, Marxists need a theory of right (e.g., a theory of social justice and/or human rights) and must face up to all of the problems found in traditional social and political philosophy.

Once we have accomplished what Kai Nielsen has referred to as a "metaethical and methodological clearing of the decks"[5] concerning the relation between Marxism and both morality in general and theories of justice and rights in particular, the stage is set for analyzing Marx's implicit theory of distributive justice. This, in turn, will set the stage for constructing an adequate theory of social justice, which, in turn, is a necessary component of an adequate Marxist moral and social theory.

In chapter 9 I consider ten Marxist and left-leaning objections to John Rawls' theory and argue that though his theory requires certain modifications to be adequate, these are not nearly so sweep-

---

[5] Nielsen, "Introduction," *Marx and Morality*, p. 17.

ing as most of Rawls' Marxist and leftist critics assume. The modifications require the inclusion of a minimum floor principle explicitly stipulating that no one will be allowed to fall below a certain level of well-being (or have one's subsistence or security rights violated), the demand for at least approximate equality in the worth of liberty as well as strict equality of liberty, and the demand for social and economic as well as political democracy.

In the first part of chapter 10 I put forward a modified version of Rawls' theory of social justice that I take to be adequate. Its principles, listed in order of lexical priority, are:

(1) Everyone's basic security and subsistence rights are to be met: that is, everyone's physical integrity is to be respected and everyone is to be guaranteed a minimum level of material well-being including basic needs, i.e., those needs that must be met in order to remain a normally functioning human being.

(2) There is to be a maximum system of equal basic liberties, including freedom of speech and assembly, liberty of conscience and freedom of thought, freedom of the person along with the right to hold (personal) property, and freedom from arbitrary arrest and seizure as defined by the concept of the rule of law.

(3) There is to be (a) equal opportunity to attain social positions and offices, and (b) an equal right to participate in all social decision-making processes within institutions of which one is a part.

(4) Social and economic inequalities are justified if and only if they benefit the least advantaged, consistent with the just savings principle, but are not to exceed levels that will seriously undermine equal worth of liberty or the good of self-respect.

To show the theory's viability I compare it to Rawls' and Kai Nielsen's theories of social justice as well as to my reconstruction of Marx's moral theory and his principles for distribution under socialism. In the second part of chapter 10, I attempt to delimit the minimal set of Marxist empirical theses that must be true if its basic normative political positions are to be justified on the basis of the theory of social justice put forward. Finally, I argue that it is of primary importance that a theory of social justice be applied from an international and diachronic point of view—something that

Rawls pointedly fails to do. I argue that an adequate theory of social justice, when applied in this manner, will lead to the conclusion that we have—as a corollary of our natural duty to support and promote just social institutions—a duty to support and promote those organizations and/or movements that have a reasonable chance to lead eventually to a worldwide federation of democratic, self-managing socialist societies.

I would like to clarify two points before proceeding to the main body of the text. The first concerns the breadth of the moral and social theory being put forward, the second whether or not the theory can be classified as Marxist.

It should be kept in mind that I do not claim to provide a comprehensive moral theory. I am offering only the outlines of what I take to be an adequate Marxist moral and social theory. And its moral component is a theory of social justice, not a theory of every aspect or level of morality. In particular, I do not offer a full-fledged theory (or vision) of the good life. I do analyze Marx's theory of the good life when I examine his concept and theory of alienation; his values of freedom (as self-determination), human community, and self-realization; and his vision of communist society. But I do not attempt a full-scale reconstruction of his theory of the good life or offer such a theory on my own. This is because I am primarily concerned with what we minimally owe one another as free and equal moral beings in a social context, i.e., in terms of considerations of social justice and/or the rights of people.

Moreover, I am not offering a theory of the virtues or even an ethic of interpersonal relationships. Like Rawls, I am concentrating on the basic social structure: first and foremost, on the economic system and the political constitution. This is justified by the fact that precisely these structures determine people's life prospects to a very large degree. Thus, if we are committed to the notion that people have a right to equal concern and respect, this means the right extends to the design of basic social institutions and, secondly, to the design of governmental policies and programs.

Such a theory does not completely ignore the virtues since it seeks to justify or at least presupposes one virtue: that of justice or citizenship, i.e., the propensity or disposition to abide by the principles and dictates of social justice. What I and many others do assume, however, is that it is possible to develop a theory of social justice without at the same time developing a complete theory of the virtues or an ethics of individual action. This is not to say that a theory of social justice is a complete moral theory, only that it is relatively autonomous. What this view does deny, of course, is the thesis that a theory of the virtues in any sense holds primacy over an ethics of principles, in general, or a theory of social justice in particular. Although I do not have the space to argue the point here, I believe that the autonomy of an ethics of principles, in general, and theory of social justice, in particular, can and should be maintained. In treating basic social institutions, these theories are ultimately more important than an ethics of virtue or individual action, and agreement among rational moral persons seems more readily attainable on this "minimal" set of moral views.

Another way in which the breadth of this project may seem restricted is that it does not attempt a detailed analysis of all significant social inequalities or forms of oppression. For example, it does not consider in detail the oppression of women or minorities. This is in part because the nature of such forms of oppression—in particular, the link between them and the class oppression and exploitation characteristic of capitalism—is difficult to establish. Although Marxists are prone to claim that there is such a link, in view of the fact that such forms of oppression predated capitalism and have not been completely eliminated in contemporary postcapitalist societies, this is far from clear.

The socialist movement, of course, has generally aligned itself with the demand that all such forms of inequality and oppression be eliminated. Most socialists also hold the empirical view that it is possible to accomplish this only in a democratic socialist society. In any event, the theory of justice I am putting forward in this book makes this same demand. At least to the extent that such inequalities and forms of oppression can be ameliorated by altering social institutions, programs, or policies, I believe that the implementation of the principles of social justice I have proposed in the context of a democratic, self-managing socialist society would almost certainly lead to the elimination or amelioration of these inequalities and forms of oppression.

As to the second point, some will question the Marxist pedigree of the views put forward in this work. Ultimately, it is of little concern to me whether these views are classified as Marxist or non-Marxist, but it seems to me that it would be more than a bit disingenuous to deny that they are Marxist since they are explicitly designed to defend the basic normative political positions of Classical Marxism. But a few remarks on this issue are perhaps in order.

First, some will claim that the views propounded in this work cannot be classified as Marxist because I do not accept the dialectical method, or because they do not conform to the tenets of dialectical materialism. My response to this is twofold. First, as Marx makes clear in "Afterword to the Second German Edition" of volume I of *Capital*, the dialectical method—as he employed it—is simply viewing social formations and processes diachronically as opposed to synchronically. This is something I also stress. As for dialectical materialism, it should be pointed out that as a logical, epistemological, and/or metaphysical system it is not native to Marx's mature thought. As Robert Tucker notes:

> Marx has no "dialectical materialism" as a doctrine of nature apart from history. . . . "Dialectical materialism" as a theory of nature apart from human history is a development of the later scholastic period of Marxism. . . . Engels . . . sought to supplement Marx's "modern materialism" . . . with a doctrine of dialectics in nature that was a *melange* of Hegel at his worst and the materialism of such 19th-century writers as Haeckel.[6]

Moreover, many versions of "dialectics" and "dialectical materialism" are virtually incoherent from the start since, following Hegel, they deny the logical laws of noncontradiction, identity, and the excluded middle (usually without even adverting to the difficulties these laws may run into at the quantum level of physical reality). Therefore, if in order to be classified as Marxist a work has to reject these logical laws or accept the crude metaphysical and epistemological doctrines proffered by Engels, Stalin, Mao, and Soviet-sponsored "diamat," then this work proudly fails to qualify.

Second, against those Marxists who insist that "dialectics" is the distinctive method of Marxism and/or the only sound method for doing philosophy and/or social science, I agree with John Roemer that

> there is [no] specific form of Marxist logic or explanation. Too often, obscurantism protects itself behind a yoga of special terms and privileged logic. The yoga of [traditional] Marxism is 'dialectics'. Dialectical logic is based on several propositions

[6] Robert Tucker, *Philosophy and Myth in Karl Marx*, pp. 183–184.

which may have a certain inductive appeal, but are far from being rules of inference: that things turn into their opposites, and quantity turns into quality, [and all things are "internally" or "systematically" connected]. In Marxian social science, dialectics is often used to justify a lazy kind of teleological reasoning.[7]

Jon Elster concurs. He claims that "there is no 'dialectical reason' that separates Marxists from ordinary mortals"[8] and that "there is no specifically Marxist form of explanation [such as dialectics] . . . no commitment to any specific methods of analysis, beyond those that characterize good social science generally."[9] According to Elster, this means that Marxian social-scientific theory will rely on three types of explanation of social phenomena: (1) causal explanation (i.e., explaining a phenomenon by citing the antecedently occurring—but nonintentional—psychological and socioeconomic causes of the phenomenon); (2) intentional explanation (i.e., explaining a phenomenon by citing the intentions—or antecedently intended consequences—of the agents involved); and (3) consequence explanation (i.e., citing the subsequent consequences of a phenomenon in order to explain it). The most important variety of intentional explanation is rational-choice explanation (including game theory) which, according to Elster, "is becoming a central, perhaps even dominant view in the social sciences."[10] The most important variety of consequence explanation is functional explanation; i.e., explaining a phenomenon by citing the beneficial consequences that, supposedly, function to bring about the phenomenon.

Some parts of Marxist empirical theory—e.g., theories of ideology and preference formation—will probably be straightforward causal explanations citing both psychological and socioeconomic causes. Other parts, however, require intentional explanation. Almost all Analytic Marxists concede that rational-choice theory—especially, game theory—must be employed in those areas of Marxist theory involving strategic interaction: specifically, exploitation, class struggle, class alliances, and questions concerning reform and revolution. (This, of course, does not mean that the institutional constraints on people's behavior are left out of the

[7] Roemer, " 'Rational Choice' Marxism," p. 191.
[8] Elster, *An Introduction to Karl Marx*, p. 21.
[9] Elster, "Further Thoughts on Marxism, Functionalism, and Game Theory," p. 220.
[10] Elster, *An Introduction to Karl Marx*, pp. 25–26.

causal picture; from a Marxist point of view, such constraints are especially relevant to explanations of social phenomena.)

Functional explanation, however, has been the subject of vigorous debate within Analytic Marxism, especially between G. A. Cohen and Jon Elster.[11] The consensus that has emerged is, first, that functional explanation (in either biology or social science) is not an autonomous form of explanation since in order to be sound it must be provided with a causal story connecting the phenomenon to be explained with the beneficial consequences that follow it in time. (Such a causal story usually involves a feedback mechanism of some sort. The search for such feedback mechanisms is also referred to as "the search for microfoundations.") The second part of the consensus, however, is that sometimes functional explanations are extremely plausible even in the absence of known causal mechanisms and that such functional explanations ought to be provisionally accepted while the search for microfoundations proceeds. (G. A. Cohen offers an illuminating example of such a situation when he argues that it probably was reasonable for most natural historians who immediately preceded Darwin to be convinced that the traits of biological organisms are generally explainable by the beneficial consequences they have for such organisms, even though these theorists did not yet have Darwin's theory of natural selection to provide the microfoundations for this explanation.[12] Similarly, it may well be reasonable to accept one formulation or another of the laws of historical materialism—which are functional laws—even though we are not now able to articulate the social-psychological microfoundations of these laws.)

Perhaps the most vigorous methodological debate still taking place within the Analytic Marxist tradition concerns the related issue of methodological individualism. According to Elster, "Methodological individualism is the view that all institutions, behavioral patterns, and social processes can in principle be explained

[11] See G. A. Cohen, *Karl Marx's Theory of History* (chaps. 9 and 10), "Functional Explanation: Reply to Elster," "Functional Explanation, Consequence Explanation, and Marxism," "Reply to Elster on 'Marxism, Functionalism, and Game Theory,' " "Reply to Four Critics," and "Reconsidering Historical Materialism." See Elster, *Making Sense of Marx* (chap. 1), *An Introduction to Karl Marx* (chap. 2), "Review of G. A. Cohen: Karl Marx's Theory of History," "Marxism, Functionalism, and Game Theory," "Reply to Comments," and "Further Thoughts on Marxism, Functionalism, and Game Theory." See also Phillipe van Parijs, "Functionalist Marxism Rehabilitated," and Johannes Berger and Claus Offe, "Functionalism vs. Rational Choice?"

[12] See G. A. Cohen, "Functional Explanation: Reply to Elster," pp. 133–134.

in terms of individuals only: their actions, properties, and relations."[13]

Against this view Johannes Berger and Claus Offe maintain that "in spite of the potential helpfulness of game theory it has a limited reach because 'social structures' remain irreducible to individual acts of decision."[14] They further note that

> Logically, the game starts only after the actors have been constituted, and their order of preferences has been formed as a result of processes that cannot themselves be considered as part of the game. Instead, such limits as the resources available to the actors, their learning capacity, their priorities, and the payoffs of alternative modes of strategic behavior must be accounted for in a conceptual framework other than that of "rational choice."[15]

But this is not something that such Analytic Marxists as Elster and Roemer would wish to deny. It is not their position that all social phenomena are to receive intentional/rational choice/game theoretic explanations. As previously mentioned, the formation of preferences and explanations of similar constraints on behavior are precisely the sort of phenomena that require causal—as opposed to intentional—explanations. They insist only that *in principle* all social phenomena—including social structures—can be explained in terms of individuals. Elster holds that

> adherence to methodological individualism should not blind one to the dangers of premature reductionism. . . .
>
> The [claim] is not that there already exists a social psychology or sociology that has effectuated a complete reduction. Rather, it is that there is no objection in principle to such a reduction being carried out, even though it may remain impracticable for the foreseeable future.[16]

Elster attempts to preempt other possible objections to methodological individualism by specifying that

> first the doctrine has no implications about the kind of individual-level explanation that is needed to carry out the reduction. In particular, the assumption that individuals are rational

---

[13] Elster, *An Introduction to Karl Marx*, p. 22.
[14] Berger and Offe, "Functionalism vs. Rational Choice?" p. 521.
[15] Ibid., p. 525.
[16] Elster, *An Introduction to Karl Marx*, p. 23.

and selfish is not part of the doctrine, although compatible with it. Second, it does not assume that individuals are "atoms" that have a presocial existence before they come together to form society. Relations between individuals must be let in on the ground floor of social explanation. Third, it does not extend to what goes on inside people's heads. In the phrase "The United States fears the Soviet Union," the first collective noun is subject to reduction but not the second, because what the individual Americans fear may well be a nebulous collective entity.[17]

How ever this debate is resolved, it is clear that none of these controversies or forms of explanation has anything to do with "dialectics." It should be noted, however, that while these three types of explanation—causal, intentional, and functional—provide Marxism (and social science in general) with a rather broad range of explanatory alternatives, much of traditional Marxist explanatory theory is eliminated if one limits oneself to them. Certainly, the teleological explanations of historical phenomena in which Marx and Marxists sometimes indulge must be expunged. The notion that history is inherently tending toward communism because it is inherently tending toward the self-actualization of human species-being—in particular, the maximization of human freedom—is simply leftover Hegelian baggage having no scientific value whatever. There are other elements that must be jettisoned as well. As Elster argues:

> The Marxist methodology that [we ought] emphatically to reject is an amalgam of three elements. The first is methodological holism, the view that in social life there exist wholes or collectivities, statements about which cannot be reduced to statements about the member individuals. The second is [unconstrained] functional explanation, the attempt to explain social phenomena in terms of their beneficial consequences for someone or something, even when no intention to bring about these consequences has been demonstrated. The third is dialectical deduction, a mode of thinking that is derived from Hegel's Logic and that does not lend itself to brief summary.[18]

[17] Ibid.
[18] Elster, *An Introduction to Karl Marx*, p. 21. In addition to the articles cited in n. 10, see Roemer, " 'Rational-Choice' Marxism"; Levine, "Review of *Making Sense of Marx*"; Levine, Sober, and Wright, "Marxism and Methodological Individualism";

Therefore, if in order to be classified as Marxist a work must accept—without appropriate caveats—these questionable methodological assumptions or accept the obscurantist Hegelian thesis that social reality is to be explained by specifying which social and economic categories "sublate" (as in Hegel's *Aufhebung*) which other categories in a "systematic" or "dialectical" manner, then, again, this work proudly fails to qualify.

Although more sophisticated versions of dialectics and dialectical materialism have been offered by such Marxist theorists as Colletti, Schaff, Somerville, Cornforth, and Marković, to the extent that they go beyond Marx's original thesis that social phenomena must be viewed diachronically, they can—for purposes of this work—be safely ignored.[19]

Second, perhaps some will claim that the moral and social theory I develop and defend cannot be considered Marxist because I

van Parijs, "Why Marxist Economics Needs Microfoundations" and *Evolutionary Explanation in the Social Sciences*; Anthony Giddens, *A Contemporary Critique of Historical Materialism*, University of California Press, Berkeley, 1981 and "Commentary on the Debate," *Theory and Society*, vol. 11, no. 4 (July 1982); Schmitt, *Introduction to Marx and Engels* (chap. 2) and "Methodological Individualism, Psychological Individualism and the Defense of Reason"; McCarney, "Elster, Marx and Methodology"; Little, "Marxism and Popular Politics: The Microfoundations of Class Conflict"; and Cunningham, "Community, Tradition, and the 6th Thesis on Feuerbach."

[19] See Lucio Colletti, "Marxism and the Dialectic," *New Left Review*, no. 93 (Sept.– Oct. 1975); Adam Schaff, "Marxist Dialectics and the Principle of Contradiction," *Journal of Philosophy*, vol. 57, no. 7 (March 31, 1960); John Somerville, "Ontology, Logic and Dialectical Materialism," *Dialogues on the Philosophy of Marxism* (John Somerville and Howard Parsons, eds.); Maurice Cornforth, *Marxism and the Linguistic Philosophy* (pp. 267–302) and *The Open Society and the Open Philosophy* (pp. 60–128); and Mihaelo Marković, "Humanism and Dialectic," *Socialist Humanism* (Erich Fromm, ed.).

For Marxian attempts to synthesize "dialectics" with Marx's theory of alienation, see Lukács, *History and Class Consciousness*, and Ollman, *Alienation*.

For a critique of dialectical materialism by analytic-linguistic philosophers—some sympathetic and some not—see Roy Wood Sellars, "Reflections on Dialectical Materialism," *Neglected Alternatives: Critical Essays by Roy Wood Sellars* (W. Preston Warren, ed.), Bucknell University Press, Lewisburg, Pa., 1973, and "Three Levels of Materialism," *Soviet Studies in Philosophy*, vol. 1, no. 3 (Winter 1962–1963); Herbert Feigl, "Critique of Dialectical Materialism: A Few Points Regarding Epistemology, Ontology, and the Philosophy of Science," *Dialogues on the Philosophy of Marxism* (John Somerville and Howard Parsons, eds.); Sidney Hook, "Dialectic in Society and History," *Reason, Social Myths and Democracy*, John Day Co., 1940; Karl Popper, "What is Dialectic," *Conjectures and Refutations*, Harper & Row, N.Y., 1963; H. B. Acton, "Dialectical Materialism," *The Encyclopedia of Philosophy*, vol. 2 (Paul Eduards, ed.), Macmillan, N.Y., 1976; and Antony Flew, "A 'Linguistic Philosopher' Looks at Lenin's *Materialism and Empiro-Criticism*," *Praxis*, vol. 3 (1967).

For a contemporary assessment by Analytic Marxists, see A. Wood, *Karl Marx*, pp. 187–216; Elster, *Making Sense of Marx*, pp. 37–48; and Richard Norman and Sean Sayers, *Hegel, Marx and Dialectic: A Debate*.

do not accept certain basic or crucial Marxist empirical views. But this will depend not only on which views I accept or reject but also on which of Marx's many empirical theories are taken as canonical. While I do not accept all of Marx's empirical theories as true, I do accept a great many as being approximately true or true in a slightly modified form. Here I shall briefly summarize what I take to be Marx's major empirical theories and indicate whether I find them acceptable. (I shall have more to say about most of these views as this work progresses.)

Let us first break down Marx's empirical theories into three interrelated but distinguishable sets of views, each more general and abstract than the next. The first is his theory of history—historical materialism—which attempts to explain epochal social change by appeal to the concepts of productive forces (i.e., raw materials, instruments of production, and the productive knowledge and skill of producing agents), relations of production (i.e., the economic structure of society as determined by effective ownership rights over persons and productive forces), and the social-political-legal superstructure (i.e., all noneconomic social institutions).

At the next level of abstraction we have Marx's theory of classes and class struggle, which puts forward theses about the nature of socioeconomic classes, the struggle of these classes over the social surplus product, the state as the agent (albeit sometimes independently minded agent) of the ruling class, the subordination of the intelligentsia and intellectual life in general to the ruling class and its interests, etc.

At the lowest level of abstraction or generality, we find Marx's analysis and critique of capitalism and his projections concerning post-capitalist societies. But here it should be noted that what might be called Marx's *general* labor theory of value or, more simply, his theory of surplus value—belongs to his theory of classes and class struggle. However, the two pillars of his economic theory—namely, the *specific* labor theory of value (which equates abstract, homogeneous, socially necessary labor time with the prices of commodities in equilibrium market conditions) and the theory of the falling rate of profit—both belong to his analysis and critique of capitalism.

But statements of Marx's empirical views are always open to two questions. First, is the statement of the view a correct interpretation of Marx? Second, is the view, as stated, true? Consider his theory of historical materialism. On what I shall call the standard (or technological determinist) interpretation—which is based primarily on Marx's famous preface to *A Contribution to the Critique of Political Economy*—historical materialism postulates two very general historical 'laws': (1) the 'law' of technological determinism (the forces of production determine the relations of production) and (2) the 'law' of economic determinism (the mode of production or socioeconomic base determines the social-political-legal superstructure). (The word is here put in scare quotes to indicate that these so-called 'laws' may be only law-like tendencies. Popper's objections to Marx's 'laws' are taken up in chapter 5.) G. A. Cohen puts forward this interpretation of historical materialism in his groundbreaking work, *Karl Marx's Theory of History: A Defense*. However, Richard Miller (in *Analyzing Marx: Morality, Power, and History*) and Jon Elster (in *Making Sense of Marx*) both take issue with this interpretation.

Miller and Elster contend that even though this is a fair reconstruction of Marx's general formulations of historical materialism, it is not consistent with his concrete historical analysis of epochal transformations. Miller argues for a "mode of production" interpretation of historical materialism on which "basic, internal economic change arises (whenever it does, in fact, take place) on account of a self-transforming tendency of the mode of production as a whole, that is, the [social] relations of production, the forms of cooperation and the technology through which material goods are produced."[20] This means that epochal change can—and usually does—occur as a result of changes in the relations of production, i.e., these relations sometimes determine forces of production rather than the other way around. Elster agrees with Miller on this point, but what of the veracity of these interpretations? Elster, for example, attacks the standard interpretation of historical materialism for lacking social-psychological microfoundations to explain the proposed "laws" and for thus being irreducibly teleological or functionalistic. Furthermore, according to Elster, the standard theory is "inherently less plausible than an alternative account, according to which property relations are determined by their tendency to promote or hinder surplus maximization [as opposed to maximizing the rate of innovation or optimizing the forces of production]."[21]

The debate recorded so far primarily concerns the thesis of technological determinism. But similar questions can be raised con-

[20] Miller, *Analyzing Marx*, p. 172. Also see Brenner, "The Social Basis of Economic Development."
[21] Elster, *An Introduction to Karl Marx*, p. 193.

cerning the thesis of economic determinism. In fact, when it comes to interpreting Marx on this issue, one can find in his writings at least three models concerning the relation of the mode of production or economic substructure—i.e., the forces and relations of production, taken together—to the social-political-legal superstructure. The first posits that the substructure (mode of production) strictly determines the superstructure. The second posits that the substructure determines the superstructure, but "only in the final analysis." The third—often referred to as the organic or "dialectical" model—claims that the substructure and superstructure are "mutually determining."[22]

As to the question of which version of historical materialism (as a whole) is most adequate, I shall not take a position. My rationale is that the empirical theses I take to be centrally important to the formulation of an adequate Marxist moral and social theory are drawn from Marx's theory of classes and class struggle and his analysis of capitalism and projections concerning post-capitalist society. Thus, which formulation of historical materialism is most true to Marx or most nearly correct is not a major concern of this work. In fact, although I believe that the theses of some versions of historical materialism are highly plausible, it would not defeat the purpose or project of the present work if, strictly speaking, no version of historical materialism turned out to be true. Consequently, it is not imperative for purposes of the present work to take a position on every point of difference among the sophisticated reconstructions of this theory currently to be found in the works of Cohen, Miller, Elster, and others.

Let us now turn to Marx's (transhistorical) theory of classes and class struggle, which I take to be of crucial importance. This is, of course, where Marx's theory of economic exploitation comes into play: each historical form of class society is most perspicuously viewed as a struggle by the major socioeconomic classes over the social surplus product. The key to such a society lies in understanding how surplus labor (or surplus product or value) is pumped out of the productive classes by the nonproductive class (or classes) and in understanding the "laws of motion" of that mode of production. (In capitalism, for example, the capitalist class pumps surplus social product out of the working class, and the basic law of motion is that of the maximization of exchange value or, more loosely, profit.) In accord with these basic facts,

[22] See Rader, *Marx's Interpretation of History*, pp. 3–27, 56–70, 129–136.

Marxist theory attempts to explain class behavior on the basis of (objective) class interests and (subjective) class consciousness and to account for the nature of the state, the nature of the dominant ideologies, etc.

Marx's even more concrete analysis of capitalism and his projections concerning post-capitalist societies are equally important for developing an adequate Marxist moral and social theory. Although certain of Marx's theses and predictions—for example, his theory of the falling rate of profit and his prediction that a stateless, conflict-free communist society inevitably will come into existence—are surely false, many of his theses concerning the economic and social dysfunctions of capitalism and his predictions concerning the rise of revolutionary movements and appearance of post-capitalist societies are just as surely true. (I shall have more to say on these matters as this work proceeds.)

I do reject the specific version of Marx's labor theory of value and—as just mentioned—his theory of the falling rate of profit under capitalism. Since the latter is taken up in detail in chapter 5, I shall not pursue it here, but my rejection of the former requires further comment. The *popular doctrine* of the labor theory of value is that the value of a commodity is determined by the amount of labor that went into creating it. But this version of the theory is false even according to Marx, who held that the value of a commodity is determined by the amount of labor socially necessary to create it, given current technology. (Following G. A. Cohen, I shall call this the *strict doctrine*.)[23]

Marx then relates the labor value of a commodity to its price. More specifically, the value of a commodity (which supposedly is determined by the labor socially necessary to make it) determines the price of that commodity in equilibrium market conditions. Jon Elster summarizes the objections to this theory that are accepted by many contemporary Marxist economists and by most Analytic Marxists as follows:

> The labor theory of value is intellectually bankrupt. The very concept of the labor content of a commodity is ill defined in the presence of heterogeneous labor or heterogeneous work tasks. Even assuming that the concept could be defined, it has no useful role to perform. The equilibrium prices and rate of profit can be determined without invoking labor values. If any

[23] See G. A. Cohen, "The Labor Theory of Value and the Concept of Exploitation."

connection obtains, it is rather the other way around: Prices must be known before we can deduce labor values. The labor theory of value does not provide a useful criterion for the choice of socially desirable techniques, nor does it explain the actual choice of technique under capitalism. It vitiates the otherwise important theory of fetishism and detracts from the otherwise effective criticism of vulgar economy. Nor does the labor theory of value offer any useful insights into the possibility of stable exchange rates and of surplus.[24]

But this does not vitiate Marx's theory of exploitation as the expropriation of surplus value. As Allen E. Buchanan points out, all we need for Marx's sociology of economics to make sense is the distinction between necessary labor-time (i.e. the time it takes direct producers to produce the bundle of goods they consume) and surplus labor-time (i.e., the time they work that produces goods beyond those they consume).[25] Furthermore, as G. A. Cohen puts it: "What raises a charge of exploitation is not that the [nonproducing class] gets some of the value the worker produces, but that [it] gets some of the value *of what* the worker produces. Whether or not workers produce value, they produce the product, that which has value."[26]

Of course, if one takes as canonical the labor theory of value and/or the theory of the falling rate of profit, then the moral and social theory advanced in this work cannot be considered Marxist. It is not clear, however, that these views must or should be accepted as canonical. Although it is difficult to say with any degree of certainty which of Marx's many views are canonical, I would assert that any perspective that accepts substantial parts of (1) Marx's theory of classes and class struggle, (2) his analysis of the social and economic dysfunctions of capitalism, and (3) his projections concerning at least the first (or "lower") stage of communism, and that, in addition, accepts the basic normative political positions of Marxism, ought to be labeled "Marxist." In fact, I would assert—with some qualifications—that the sine quo non of Marxism is its normative component. As Elster states:

---

[24] Elster, *An Introduction to Karl Marx*, p. 192. See also Roemer, *A General Theory of Exploitation and Class*, pp. 148–151 and 168–173; *Value, Exploitation, and Class*, pp. 5–22; and *Free to Lose*, pp. 47–51; Elster, *Making Sense of Marx*, pp. 127–141; Sen, "On the Labour Theory of Value"; and Wartofsky, "Karl Marx and the Outcome of Classical Marxism."

[25] See Buchanan, *Marx and Justice*, p. 46.

[26] G. A. Cohen, "The Labor Theory of Value," p. 354.

Marxism is defined mainly by two . . . features. First, the belief that alienation and exploitation interfere with the good life
for man and that their suppression is not only desirable but
feasible. Or at the minimum, the unfeasibility of suppressing
them has not been proven. Secondly, Marxism is characterized by a few fundamental theoretical assumptions about the
structure and development of societies, with emphasis on the
interrelation between property rights, technical change and
class struggle. Of these, the first, normative element constitutes the *sine qua non* of Marxism. The second, explanatory
element can to some extent be modified and revised without
loss of identity. Only to some extent however, since the normative theory itself would have to be given up if it were to be
shown that the Marxist proposals are radically unfeasible, either in the sense that [even the first stage of] communism
would not be viable or in the sense that capitalism will never
produce a communist revolution [or transition].[27]

In order to elucidate and refine this normative content it is, in
my opinion, essential to bring recent and contemporary analytic
political philosophy to bear. We should not even be surprised, I
think, to find that there is considerable overlap in the ethical views
espoused by contemporary left-liberal moral and social philosophers within the analytic-linguistic tradition and Analytic Marxists
(or, indeed, Marxists in general). As John Roemer puts it:

To demonstrate the nature of [the] injustice [of class-divided,
exploitative societies] political philosophy must be called
upon. . . . These are not questions of positive history, but of
philosophy concerning what constitutes a desirable or just society. The sharpest form of the political debate on this question [of what constitutes a desirable or just society] is between
Marxists and libertarians on questions of self-ownership, in-
heritance, and various kinds of rights. [But] it is not at all clear
how analytical Marxists will differ [on these questions] from
non-Marxist philosophers like Ronald Dworkin, John Rawls,
and Amartya Sen . . . the lines drawn between contemporary
analytical Marxism and contemporary left-liberal political philosophy are fuzzy. This indicates there is a common core, yet
to be elucidated.[28]

[27] Elster, ''Further Thoughts on Marxism, Functionalism, and Game Theory,'' p.
220.
[28] Roemer, '' 'Rational Choice' Marxism,'' pp. 199–200.

(It is my hope that the present work will go a long way toward elucidating this common core.)

Another challenge to the Marxist pedigree of the moral and social theory developed in the present work would be one that challenged the analysis of contemporary post-capitalist societies offered here and/or the claim that political revolutions to democratize such societies might be justified on a Marxist point of view. Few, if any, Marxists and Marxologists will dispute my description of the Marxist's basic normative political positions: socialism—i.e., democratic self-managing socialism—is morally preferable to any form of capitalism and any other form of society possible in the present historical epoch; and revolution, if necessary and sufficient to effect the appropriate transformations, is *prima facie* morally justified. However, many Marxists will reject my characterization of contemporary post-capitalist societies as state-socialist, i.e., as not even meeting Marx's criteria for the first stage of communism. Although to some extent this may be an empirical dispute concerning how democratic and open (i.e., nonrepressive) contemporary post-capitalist societies are, for the most part it is a verbal dispute concerning the terms "socialism" and "communism." My only claim is that the definitions given these terms by the Classical Marxists prevent existing post-capitalist societies from being classified as either socialist or communist.

What flows from this claim, however, depends on what additional empirical assumptions one accepts. If one adduces that so-called communist societies are not post-capitalist societies at all but—as some Marxists claim—state-capitalist societies, then one presumably does not look upon them as historically progressive, in the sense of being steps toward a world socialist society, and thus would not necessarily care if they were transformed into more traditionally recognizable forms of capitalism. If, on the other hand, one holds that such societies have eliminated capitalism and are at least a halting step toward a worldwide democratic socialist society (or federation of such societies), then one would view them as historically progressive in the above sense and thus presumably would be opposed to their being transformed again into capitalist societies. Although I will not argue for it here, it seems abundantly clear that the latter position is the one in accord with the tenets of Classical Marxism.

An even more controversial position I assume to be in line with the tenets of Classical Marxism is that political revolutions are *prima facie* morally justified if necessary and sufficient to transform

29

contemporary post-capitalist societies into democratic, self-managing socialist societies. Some Marxists—for example, those who accept the proclamation that the U.S.S.R. passed from the first to the highest stage of communism in the late 1950s—presumably would claim that such revolutions are not necessary because these societies are already democratic and self-managing. Although this hardly seems a tenable position, it should be pointed out that the revolutions called for are not *social* revolutions designed to change the mode of production or class power but, rather, *political* revolutions designed to make political and social institutions more democratic and less repressive. In fact, from the perspective of the Classical Marxists, there is always a *prima facie* case to oppose a social revolution designed to return such post-capitalist societies to capitalism since such counter-revolutions would be viewed as severe blows to the long-term process of creating a world socialist society. In addition, since peaceful evolution is (all things being equal) always preferable to violent revolution, proponents of the position I am attributing to Classical Marxism will advocate such political revolutions only if there is no viable reformist alternative.

Finally, a challenge to the Marxist qualifications of the moral and social theory put forward in this work might be based on the rejection of my claim that market socialism may ultimately be preferable to any other form of post-capitalist as well as capitalist society. Note, however, that my definition of "democratic, self-managing socialism" does not automatically decide in favor of either a command or a market socialist economy. Thus one could accept the moral and social theory propounded in this work and simply reject the claim that market socialism is a feasible alternative.

However, a growing number of Marxists—having observed the historical experience of Yugoslavia's market socialist society, which has existed since the early 1950s—have come to the conclusion that market socialism is a viable and perhaps preferable historical alternative.[29] Since Marx emphasized that actual historical

[29] For a critique of command economy systems and a defense of self-managing market socialism by Marxian economists, see Horvat, *Toward a Theory of Planned Economy* and *The Yugoslav Economic System*; Vaneck, *The General Theory of Labor-managed Market Economies*, *The Labor-managed Economy*, and *The Participatory Economy*; Nove, *The Economics of Feasible Socialism*. See also Leslie Evans, "The Limits of Planning," *Against the Current*, 12–13 (Jan. 1988).

On the philosophical plane, self-managing market socialism is ably defended by Stojanović, Marković, Petrović, Supek, and other members of the *Praxis* school of Yugoslavian Marxists. Perhaps the most sophisticated attempt at integrating both

developments will illuminate the structure of future post-capitalist societies, it is reasonable to suppose that he would have seriously considered the implications of the fact that market economy post-capitalist societies (i.e., Yugoslavia) have arguably proved more economically efficient, more democratic, and less repressive than post-capitalist societies having command economies.[30]

It is important to note, however, that there are two structural features of market socialism that add up to an answer to many of Marx's objections to capitalist market economies. First, economic enterprises are to a large degree democratically controlled by their workers. The consequence is that labor can no longer be considered exploited as it is under capitalism because, as Schweickart puts it, "labor is not another 'factor of production' technically on par with land and capital. Labor is not a commodity at all, for when a worker joins a firm, she becomes a voting member, and entitled to a specific share of the net revenue."[31] (The notion of "exploitation" will be defined and analyzed in the last section of chapter 3.)

---

economic and philosophical arguments in defense of this system is David Schweickart's *Capitalism or Worker Control?*

Two excellent anthologies containing articles by economists, sociologists, and philosophers are Horvat et al. (eds.), *Self-Governing Socialism* (2 vols.) and Vaneck (ed.), *Self-management: Economic Liberation of Man.*

An impartial analysis is offered by Buchanan in *Ethics, Efficiency, and the Market*, pp. 104–117. More critical accounts are given by Ellen Turkish Comisso in *Workers' Control under Plan and Market: Implications of Yugoslav Self-Management*, Yale University Press, New Haven, Conn., 1979; and N. Scott Arnold, "Marx and Disequilibrium in Market Socialist Relations of Production," *Economics and Philosophy*, vol. 3, no. 1 (1987). For the case against market socialism from a Marxist perspective, see Mandel, *Marxist Economic Theory*, *Marx's Theoretical Legacy* and "A Defense of Socialist Planning."

[30] It should be noted, however, that Yugoslavia is currently suffering its worst economic crisis of the post-war period. The figures are depressing. Foreign debt rose from $4 billion to $20 billion between 1972 and 1981. Inflation is currently running at 200 percent annually, with wage increases restricted to 139 percent. Unemployment stands at 15 percent, and the annual growth rate is currently less than 2 percent per year. How this downturn in Yugoslavia's economic fortunes is best analyzed is debatable. Some will claim it shows that market socialism is inherently unworkable. Others see it as a temporary setback or the result of Yugoslavia's economy being too closely tied to the world capitalist market. Of those who believe that Yugoslavia's current economic problems show an inherent weakness of market socialism, some see the solution as less economic planning and/or greater privatization of the economy (i.e., a return to capitalism), while others see the solution as more economic planning and less privatization (moving toward a socialist command economy). Perhaps only empirical evidence gathered from the further development of the current Yugoslavian experience and/or other future experiments in market socialism will answer these questions.

[31] Schweickart, *Capitalism or Worker Control?*, p. 51.

The second structural feature is that investment is democratically controlled by society. Thus, it is argued, market socialism contains the best of both worlds (or, in this case, economies). It is supposed to maintain the efficiencies of the market while eliminating or ameliorating the dysfunctions of capitalist systems. For example, social control of investment capital arguably eliminates or at least ameliorates the boom-and-bust cycles of capitalism since it eliminates the phenomenon of the "investment strike" by private owners of capital during economically pessimistic periods. Moreover, it is argued that other phenomena that can be characterized as dysfunctional (such as the sales effect, the denigration of the value of labor, and the rapid depletion of natural resources) can also be eliminated or ameliorated. The argument here is as follows: (1) many of the dysfunctions of capitalism depend upon the tendency of the capitalist market to expand (which is the only sure way to keep the investment climate healthy and thus prevent an "investment strike"); (2) a market socialist economy need not constantly expand to be healthy; therefore, (3) a market socialist economy need not suffer these dysfunctions.[32]

While it is true that this view will necessitate giving up some of Marx's arguments against capitalism, based on the evils of the market per se, the Marxist tradition will not lack strong arguments against capitalism. They will be based on such dysfunctions as those mentioned above, as well as on the fact that private ownership of productive property leads to extreme differentials of wealth and power. (I cite additional considerations in chapter 10.)

Although my theory leaves the question an open one, if market socialism can be shown by theoretical arguments and/or historical observation to fulfill best the principles of an adequate moral theory or, more precisely, an adequate theory of social justice, then Marxist orthodoxy must give way. If market socialism can be expected to meet the criteria of a just society more effectively, then the claim that it is preferable must be accepted whether or not the position can legitimately be classified as Marxist. After all, what is ultimately of importance is the correctness of a position or theory, not its pedigree.

[32] For a more detailed rendering of this argument, see chapters 2, 3, and 4 of Schweickart's *Capitalism or Worker Control?*

PART I
MARX'S MORAL PERSPECTIVE

O N E

THE DEVELOPMENT OF MARX'S
MORAL PERSPECTIVE

It is sometimes said that Marxism has no moral component or that Marx's works—at least, his later works—have no moral component. As will be seen in what follows, these claims are clearly and demonstrably false. Although Marx never developed the philosophical basis for a full-fledged moral theory, he did exhibit a moral perspective, which remained relatively constant—although somewhat eclectic—throughout his writings. The objective of this chapter is to demonstrate his moral views. The approach taken is basically historical: the development of Marx's moral views, as well as the most important components of his empirical views, is traced from his earliest journalistic writings in his period of Radical Liberalism (1841–1843) through his periods of Revolutionary Humanism (1843) and Original Marxism (1844–1845) to the works of the Transitional Period (1845–1847), his works of maturation (1847–1858), and—finally—his fully mature works (1858–1883). (For my classification of Marx's works by period, see the Appendix.)

Besides laying the groundwork for refuting the claim that Marx's worldview is devoid of normative value judgments in general or of moral judgments (and principles) in particular—a refutation developed in detail in chapter 4—the present chapter, together with chapters 2 and 3, takes up the issue of the nature of Marx's implicit moral views. Although these views have been given a great many divergent interpretations, I argue for the following theses. First, although Marx's concepts of alienation and exploitation are central to his moral perspective, they can be analyzed in terms of other, more basic moral values and principles. Second, the more basic values involved are freedom (as self-determination), human community, and self-realization. Third, Marx implicitly espouses a principle requiring an egalitarian (or relatively egalitarian) distri-

35

bution of these goods, especially the good of freedom. (Whether this principle is identical to the principles he proposes for the first and second stages of communism—namely, "from each according to their contribution" and "from each according to his ability, to each according to his needs"—will be discussed in later chapters.) Fourth, if these values and principles can be analyzed in terms of some even more fundamental notion, it is not the notion of utility nor the satisfaction of preferences or desires, but that of human dignity and the good of self-respect—notions with a distinctly "deontological" ring.

Marx's First Period: Radical Liberalism (1841–1843)

In his initial, radical liberal period—from the time he received his Ph.D. in philosophy from the University of Jena in Berlin (April 1841) until he resigned as editor of the *Rheinische Zeitung* (March 1843)—Marx found no problem in speaking of moral or ethical requirements or making explicit moral judgments. In this period we also find his only attempts at characterizing morality from an internal point of view as a realm of human discourse or theory. In his later, social-scientific works, he would characterize morality from an external point of view as a cultural or social phenomenon.

In one of his earliest articles, "Comments on the Latest Prussian Censorship Instructions," which was originally written in 1842 for Arnold Ruge's *Deutsche-Französische Jahrbücher* but published by Ruge in *Anekdota zur neuesten deutschen Philosophie und Publicistik* (1843) in Switzerland when the *Jahrbücher* was shut down by the Prussian censors, Marx condemns censorship on the grounds that "it violates the most universal of all religions: the sacredness and inviolability of subjective conviction."[1] The censorship instruction, Marx argues, puts forward no "objective norms" but instead relies on the judgment of censors as to whether or not "the tendency" of writings is "well-intentioned" or "harmful," and it must therefore be classified as "tendentious." "Such laws," he writes, "are based on a lack of character and on an *unethical* and materialistic view of the state. They are indiscreet *outcries of bad conscience*"[2] (emphasis added).

In a paragraph that clearly reveals his Kantian predilections in

---

[1] Marx, "Comments on the Latest Prussian Censorship Instructions," p. 81.
[2] Ibid., pp. 80–81.

his conception of morality at this time, Marx attacks those who fail to separate religion from morality:

> The specifically Christian legislator *cannot recognize morality* as an independent sphere sanctified in itself, for he derives the inner universal essence of morality from religion. Independent morality offends the basic principles of religion, and particular concepts of religion are opposed to morality. Morality recognizes only its own universal and rational religion, and religion only its own particular positive morality. Following the Instruction, censorship will have to repudiate *such intellectual heroes of morality as Kant, Fichte, Spinoza* for being irreligious and threatening the discipline, morals, and outward loyalty. All of these moralists proceed from a principled opposition between morality and religion, because *morality* they claim, is based on the *autonomy*, and *religion* on the *heteronomy* of the human spirit.[3]

The notion that morality can and must be an independent, autonomous realm that is not subordinate to religion also comes out at the end of his article "On a Proposed Divorce Law," one of Marx's contributions to *Rheinische Zeitung* and perhaps the essay of this period most replete with moral language and moral claims. There he contraposes "conscious subordination to ethico-natural forces" to "unconscious obedience to a supra-ethical and supernatural authority."[4] Although Marx does not—here or elsewhere—explain what he means by "ethico-natural forces," it is clear that he is primarily distinguishing the sort of morality that would be based on such considerations from one based on religious commitments or the commands of God. One might be tempted to interpret his phrase as indicating that Marx has—at this point in his development, at any rate—a naturalistic theory of the good or that his ethical views take our naturalistic inclinations as the basis for all moral judgments, but this interpretation would be wrong. The most important element in the phrase concerning obedience or duty is the part reading "conscious subordination," which indicates that the choice of moral principles must be made on the basis of one's own rational reflection and must not be subordinated to any outer authority. Such a belief coincides with other remarks he makes around this time—especially those employing

[3] Ibid., p. 78.
[4] Marx, "On a Proposed Divorce Law," p. 142.

the terms autonomy and heteronomy—indicating his deep concern with the Kantian notion of the individual as an autonomous chooser of ends. And to whatever extent he accepted Kant's characterization of morality—which appears to be quite considerable—he would, of course, have distanced himself from the view that we should take our naturalistic inclinations as a basis for moral judgments. For the Kantian, to do so is a failure in moral reasoning of the first order: it is to let morality (practical reason) be ruled by the heteronomy rather than the autonomy of the human will. (We will do well to keep this in mind when, in chapter 4, we consider Skillen's and Collier's "naturalistic inclination" interpretation of Marx's normative perspective.)

Further evidence can be found for the fact that Marx makes substantive moral judgments in this period and that his views of morality, as well as these substantive moral views, are firmly ensconced in the deontological and rational-will tradition of Kantian and post-Kantian German philosophy. In "On a Proposed Divorce law," for example, he asks:

> If a legislator considers spiritual sacredness and not *human ethics* as the essence of marriage, if he replaces *self-determination* by determination from above, *inner natural dedication* by a supernatural sanction, and loyal submission to the nature of the relationship by passive obedience to commandments—commandments transcending the nature of that relationship—can he be blamed for subjugating marriage to the church . . . ?[5] [emphasis added].

However, even though religion cannot decree what is right and wrong, neither can the human individual or the legislator. Marx claims that "no legislature can decree what is ethical."[6] Revealing his leaning toward the natural-law branch of the tradition of ethical rationalism at this time, he declares: "The legislator . . . must consider himself a naturalist. He does not *make* laws; he does not invent them; he only formulates them. He expresses the inner principles of spiritual relationships in conscious, positive laws."[7]

As to the substantive moral issue at hand, Marx writes, "The *Rheinische Zeitung* agrees with the bill in considering the present marriage law as *unethical*, the numerous and frivolous reasons for divorce inappropriate, and the procedure used so far not commen-

---

[5] Ibid., p. 137.
[6] Ibid., p. 138.
[7] Ibid., p. 140.

surate with *the dignity of the matter*"[8] (emphasis added). He goes on to condemn those who "take an eudaemonistic view" of marriage and divorce for not taking into consideration "the ethical substance of the relationship."[9] Furthermore, according to Marx, it should be the case that

> the legislator shows *reverence* for marriage and recognizes its *deeply ethical nature*. Compliance with the wishes of individuals would become harshness against their essential nature, against their *ethical rationality*, which is embodied in *ethical relationships*[10] [emphasis added].

A clearer declaration of kinship to the rational-will tradition of Rousseau and Kant could hardly be found. The requirements of morality stem from the autonomy of the will (i.e., reason) rather than from its heteronomy (desire or inclination). Individuals must attend (or, by law, be made to attend) to their "ethical rationality," i.e., to their *real, rational wills* rather than their empirical wills. As with most components of Marx's worldview in this period, however, his views on morality are mediated by those of Hegel—in particular, by Hegel's distinction between an ethical essence and its corresponding existence. In the same article on the proposed divorce law, Marx cites Hegel's distinction, claiming that "no ethical *existence* corresponds to its *essence*, or at least does not *have to* correspond to it."[11] Marx differentiates himself from Hegel's authoritarian political views, however, and indicates his own commitment to democracy when, in the next paragraph, he states: "The guarantee . . . that the *conditions* will be fairly substantiated under which the *existence* of an ethical relationship no longer corresponds to its *essence* . . . will be present only when law is the conscious expression of the will of the people, created with and through it."[12] Here Marx's view is closer to that of Rousseau—at least on those nontotalitarian interpretations of Rousseau in which autonomy and free consensual agreement are definitive of the general will.

Nevertheless, Marx at this time is basically a Hegelian in his view of society and history as well as in his normative political theory (with the exception noted above). He accepts Hegel's view

---

[8] Ibid., pp. 138–139.
[9] Ibid., p. 139.
[10] Ibid., p. 141.
[11] Ibid., p. 140.
[12] Ibid., p. 141.

that reason is progressively manifesting itself in history, as well as Hegel's concept of the state as the actualization of rational freedom. Tracing the historical development of this view, Marx writes:

> Machiavelli and Campanella earlier, and Hobbes, Spinoza, and Hugo Grotius later, down to Rousseau, Fichte, and Hegel began considering the state from the human viewpoint and developed its natural laws from reason and experience.[13]

> While the earlier philosophers of state law derived the state from drives of ambition and gregariousness, or from reason— though not reason in society but rather in the individual—the more ideal and profound view of modern philosophy derives it from the idea of the whole. It considers the state as the great organism in which legal, ethical, and political freedom has to be actualized and in which the individual citizen simply obeys natural laws of his own reason, human reason, in the laws of the state. . . . [14]

Nevertheless, since "no ethical *existence* corresponds to its *essence*, or at least does *not* have to correspond to it," it is the job of philosophy to make sure that the state realizes its essence to the greatest degree possible. As Marx puts it: "Philosophy interprets the rights of humanity. Philosophy demands that the state be the state of human nature."[15] (Here we should note that at least the very early Marx was not reticent to speak of human rights.)

But whereas Hegel interprets the freedom to be actualized by the state as merely the rationality of the bureaucracy which, in his view, is to run it, Marx interprets it as including not only such civil liberties as freedom of thought and of the press but the active and equal participation of the entire citizenry as well. While Hegel is a conservative who advocates monarchy, a limited franchise, and government by middle-class, professional bureaucracies, Marx is a democrat and, in many ways, a liberal. As a radical journalist writing for opposition newspapers in Germany, he defended freedom of the press and freedom of thought and, as we have seen, demanded that the state be subject to the will of the people rather than the reverse. "In an ethical state," Marx claims, "the view of the state is subordinated to its members, even if they oppose an organ of the state or the government."[16]

[13] Marx, "The Leading Article in No. 179 on the *Kölnische Zeitung*," p. 129.
[14] Ibid., p. 130.
[15] Ibid., p. 127.
[16] Marx, "Comments on the Latest Prussian Censorship Instructions," p. 80.

Marx's Second Period: Revolutionary Humanism (1843)

As I have divided Marx's work, this period takes up only the second half of 1843 and consists of *Critique of Hegel's Philosophy of Right*, on which he worked during the summer of 1843, and his contributions to the first and only issue of *Deutsche-Französische Jahrbücher* (namely, "On the Jewish Question," "Contribution to the Critique of Hegel's *Philosophy of Right*: Introduction," and "Letters to Arnold Ruge"). This issue was published by Ruge and Marx in January 1844. These works are most notable for (1) the change in his normative political position—Marx moves from being a supporter of the bourgeois democratic state to an advocate of some sort of more communal society along the lines of Rousseau's model of the good society—and (2) his modified views on the means of social change. From viewing philosophical and journalistic criticism as sufficient for social change, he comes to argue that political activity and even material force may be necessary. For the most part, these revised positions were the result of changes in his empirical rather than his moral views. From the beginning, Marx accepted the values of the Enlightenment and the French Revolution—enjoyment, liberty, equality, and fraternity—in addition to the Kantian value of moral autonomy and the value of self-realization as stressed by the German philosophical tradition. These values lie behind his demand for the "realization of philosophy."

The tremendous influence of French Enlightenment thought on both his descriptive-explanatory and evaluative views comes out most clearly perhaps in a somewhat later work: *The Holy Family* (1845). In a section entitled "Battle Against French Materialism," in which Marx defends the French Enlightenment philosophers from the attacks of the left-Hegelian Bruno Bauer and his school of Critical Criticism, he writes:

No great acumen is required to see the necessary connection of materialism with communism and socialism from the doctrines of materialism concerning the original goodness and equal intellectual endowment of man, the omnipotence of experience, habit and education, the influence of external circumstances on man, the extreme importance of industry, the justification of enjoyment, etc. If man forms all his knowledge, perception, etc., from the world of sense and experience in the world of sense, then it follows that the empirical world

41

must be so arranged that he experiences and gets used to what is truly human in it, that he experiences himself as man. If enlightened interest is the principle of all morality, it follows that men's private interests should coincide with human interests. . . . If man is formed by circumstances, then his circumstances must be made human. If man is by nature social, then he develops his true nature only in society and the power of his nature must be measured not by the power of the single individual but by the power of society.[17]

Marx also indicates the impact of Enlightenment thought on his moral views when he goes on in this section to present a number of excerpts from the ethical writings of Holbach, Helvetius, and Jeremy Bentham.

Given his acceptance of these Enlightenment values, it was an easy step to his new positions. He only had to reach the conclusion that bourgeois society does not allow for the "realization of philosophy," i.e., for the realization of these values, and that philosophical criticism is not an effective means to create social arrangements that realize these values. This is not to say that Marx's moral views were absolutely static or that the way in which they were expressed did not change at all. The third noticeable change in this period, in fact, is that Marx—under the impact of Feuerbach's writings—came to express his moral views increasingly in terms of the dignity or, conversely, the degradation or dehumanization of human beings. This, however, seems mostly a change in the manner in which his basic moral sentiments are expressed and cannot account for the changes in his normative political positions.

In Marx's first expressly theoretical manuscript, *Critique of Hegel's Philosophy of Right*, he both reaffirms his commitment to democracy and begins to doubt that bourgeois society, with its divisions between the state and civil society and between "man as citizen" and "man as egoistic individual," has the potential to become a genuinely democratic and "human" society. Consequently, he defends universal suffrage and participation of all in political processes against Hegel's view of limited suffrage and government by a middle-class bureaucracy: "The drive of civil society to become political or to make political society actual is evident as a drive toward participation in *legislative power* as *universal* as possible."[18] According to Marx, "Voting is the paramount polit-

[17] *Writings of the Young Marx* (Easton and Guddat, eds.), pp. 394–395.
[18] Marx, *Critique of Hegel's Philosophy of Right*, p. 199.

ical interest of civil society. Only in *unlimited voting*, active as well as passive, does civil society *actually* rise to an abstraction of itself, to *political existence* as its true universal and essential existence."[19]

In the same manuscript, however, Marx indicates that universal suffrage, i.e., "the idea that *all* as individuals should participate in deliberating and deciding on political matters of general concern,"[20] is not in and of itself sufficient. In a passage that is, again, reminiscent of Rousseau, he claims:

> In a really rational state one could answer, "It is not the case that *all as individuals* should participate in deliberating and deciding on political matters of general concern," for the "individuals" participate in deliberating and deciding on political matters of *general concern* as "all," that is, within society and as parts of society. Not all as individuals, but individuals as all.[21]

As with Rousseau's conception of the general will, this can be interpreted as a prescription that everyone accept the moral point of view, that is, that everyone vote on the basis of the common good rather than their individual good or, more precisely, that they come to think of the common good as their individual good. As we shall see, the prescription that all members of society ought to act on the basis of the common good as well as the associated empirical thesis that people could and, in general, would act on this basis in a rationally constructed society, occurs in one form or another, in all the rest of Marx's works. In "On the Jewish Question," Marx refers to this thesis as the incorporation of the abstract, moral citizen into the egoistic individual of civil society. In the *Economic and Philosophical Manuscripts*, the thesis comes out in what he variously calls "universal," "social," "communal," or "species" consciousness. Persons who embody this sort of consciousness are called "species-beings." And although he does not often explicitly refer to this type of consciousness in his fully mature works, it is nevertheless presupposed by his vision of communism as a stateless, conflict-free society in which everyone lives in perfect harmony.

Furthermore, in "On the Jewish Question" Marx condemns the "acquisitive spirit" of "Judaism" or—as he makes clear—the system of private property and egoistic bourgeois civil society. He

[19] Ibid., p. 202.
[20] Ibid., p. 197.
[21] Ibid.

again distinguishes the state and the role of the citizen from civil society and the role of the egoistic individual and, consequently, political emancipation from human emancipation. *Political* emancipation releases members of society from the political repression of the state; it is the guaranteed recognition of their political rights. Mere political emancipation does not, however, free the member of civil society from the separated, isolated, individualistic, and egoistic condition of civil society itself. Realization of the various proposed "rights of man" is thus not sufficient for the attainment of a genuinely human or good society. Marx thus prescribes *human* emancipation, that is, "the emancipation of civil society." But a necessary condition for human emancipation is the incorporation of the abstract, *moral* citizen into the individual as a member of civil society.[22]

In terms of his empirical theory, Marx first links his normative political positions to the plight of the proletariat in "Contribution to the Critique of Hegel's *Philosophy of Right:* Introduction." Here Marx claims that human emancipation is tied up with the emancipation of a "universal" class, that is, a class whose "sufferings are universal"—in the case of modern industrial society, this is the proletariat. Furthermore, "the proletariat demands the negation of private property. . . ." and "just as philosophy finds its *material* weapons in the proletariat, so the proletariat finds its *intellectual* weapons in philosophy. . . . Philosophy can be realized only by the abolition of the proletariat, and the proletariat can be abolished only by the realization of philosophy."[23]

As to the evolution of his views on the means of social change, in a September 1843 letter to Arnold Ruge, Marx still sees philosophical criticism as the way to social change. However, this criticism must be a *"relentless criticism of all existing conditions,* relentless in the sense that criticism is not afraid of its findings and just a little afraid of the conflict with the powers that be."[24] By the end of this very short period, however, Marx claims: "Criticism is no longer an end in itself, but simply a means; *indignation* is its essential mode of feeling, and *denunciation* its principal task."[25] And, more importantly, "It is clear that the arm of criticism cannot re-

[22] See Marx, "On the Jewish Question," p. 31.
[23] Marx, "Contribution to the Critique of Hegel's *Philosophy of Right*: Introduction," p. 59.
[24] Marx, "An Exchange of Letters," p. 212.
[25] Marx, "Contribution to the Critique of Hegel's *Philosophy of Right*: Introduction," p. 46.

place the criticism of arms. Material force can be overthrown only by material force. . . ."[26]

Marx's third change of this period—his acceptance of Feuerbach's humanistic moral terminology—is evident as early as a May 1843 letter to Ruge. Speaking about the manner in which society can be revitalized and improved, Marx states that "freedom, the feeling of man's dignity will have to be awakened. . . . Only this feeling . . . can again transform society into a community of men to achieve their highest purpose, a democratic state."[27] He claims that "despotism's only idea is contempt for man, dehumanized man. . . . A Despot only sees man as degraded"[28] and that "the principle of monarchy in general is man despised, despicable, dehumanized."[29] Furthermore, Marx speaks of entering "the human world of democracy" and of "an order of free mankind."[30]

To see that Marx's criticism of politics at this time is very similar to Feuerbach's criticism of religion, one need only substitute the word "religion" for the terms "despotism," "despot," and "monarchy" in the sentences above. When these substitutions are made we have Feuerbach's criticism of religion framed precisely in his terms. Feuerbach believed that religion—or, at any rate, the Judeo-Christian tradition in religion which hypostatizes a personal God —is a sign of the psychic or "spiritual" alienation of the human species. Religion of this sort arises from the human species' externalization and projection of its needs and values into an otherworldly, transcendent realm, in particular, into the person of God. Through this process of projection and reification, Feuerbach argues, human beings come to compare themselves to the perfect and all-powerful creature they have built up in their imaginations and thus come to look upon themselves as debased, despised, and despicable creatures. Religion "dehumanizes" man, and the Feuerbachian project is to make people conscious of this connection so that they will lose interest in religious illusions and become free of them. Only then, according to Feuerbach, will people become "rehumanized." Only then will they take "man" as the most important being for "man" and rejoice in the glory of the human species rather than in that of an illusory God. As Marx remarks in the September 1843 letter to Ruge quoted above: "Our entire pur-

---

[26] Ibid., p. 52.
[27] Marx, "An Exchange of Letters," p. 206.
[28] Ibid., p. 207.
[29] Ibid., p. 208.
[30] Ibid., pp. 208–209.

pose consists in nothing else (as is also the case in Feuerbach's criticism of religion) but bringing the religious and political problems into self-conscious human form."[31]

The classic formulation of Marx's revolutionary humanist morality, however, is contained in "Contribution to the Critique of Hegel's *Philosophy of Right:* Introduction":

> The criticism of religion ends with the doctrine that *man is the supreme being for man.* It ends, therefore, with the *categorical imperative to overthrow all those conditions* in which man is an abased, enslaved, abandoned, contemptible being—conditions which can hardly be better described than in the exclamation of a Frenchman on the occasion of a proposed tax upon dogs: "Wretched dogs! They want to treat you like men!"[32]

Although Marx is not a moral philosopher and thus makes no attempt to construct a systematic moral theory, it is clear from these remarks—at least in the early stages of the development of his thought—that he has moral views, and these are most fundamentally based on the concept of intrinsic human dignity or worth rather than on the satisfaction of human desires. In this respect, at least, they must be classified as "deontological" as opposed to utilitarian. These moral views, as I shall argue presently, appear throughout the rest of Marx's works, even though the terminology in which they are expressed changes somewhat and they become increasingly less explicit. They constitute for Marx what he refers to in another context as the "ideas won by our intelligence, embodied in our outlook, and forged in our conscience . . . chains from which we cannot tear ourselves away without breaking our hearts . . . demons we can overcome only by submitting to them."[33]

Marx's Third Period: Original Marxism (1844)

Even though Marx was beginning to have an impact somewhat earlier, it was not until 1844—after moving to Paris to escape the Prussian censors—that he came into his own as an original theorist. It was in this year, as a result of his critical study of classical

[31] Ibid., p. 214.
[32] Marx, "Contribution to the Critique of Hegel's *Philosophy of Right*: Introduction," p. 52.
[33] Marx, "Communism and the Augsburg 'Allgemeine Zeitung,' " p. 135.

political economy and his adaptation of Hegel's problematic of objectification, alienation, and the transcendence of alienation to the historical development of human nature through human productive activity, that he first formulated the doctrines constituting Original Marxism. These doctrines include Marx's critique of classical political economy as an explanatory theory, his critique of capitalism as a social system, a more detailed presentation of his humanist morality, and the beginnings of his materialist theory of history. Furthermore, it is in the *Economic and Philosophical Manuscripts* of 1844 (hereafter referred to as the *Paris Manuscripts* or, more simply, the *Manuscripts*) that he first explicitly espouses communism in his normative political theory and offers the beginnings of an empirical explanation of its possibility and, indeed—in Marx's view—inevitability. It is here also that his concept of alienation blooms into the central category of his implicit humanist morality.

In this period Marx generally does not use the terms "moral" or "ethical" to qualify his own evaluative judgments as he had previously. His moral judgments are now almost entirely implicit and, for the most part, are packed into such quasi-descriptive terms as "alienation" and—as he uses the term—"human," as well as into such other value-laden terms as "impoverishment," "misery," "well-being," "debasement," "degradation," "domination," "freedom," "enjoyment," "satisfaction," "servitude," "depravity," "unnatural," "inhuman," "cruel," "crude," and "malignant."

Not only has Marx stopped qualifying his evaluative judgments by the terms "ethical" and "moral" but he has also stopped speaking of morality as an autonomous realm and, in effect, has stopped trying to characterize what today we refer to as the "moral point of view." When he speaks of morality in this period—and from then on—it is from a descriptive, sociological point of view. He speaks of the morality of particular classes, groups, and individual theorists. That Marx now conceives of morality from an *external, sociological point of view* rather than from an *internal, evaluative point of view* is further borne out by his comment that "the bearing of political economy upon morals is either arbitrary and accidental and thus lacking any scientific basis or character, is a mere *sham*, or else it is *essential* and can then only be a relation between economic laws and morals."[34] His project concerning morality from this point on is to ascertain the relation of a mode of production

---

[34] Marx, *Economic and Philosophical Manuscripts*, p. 173.

and its economic laws and—by extension—the interests of its dominant socioeconomic class to the system or systems of mores (accepted moral values) it contains. In this sense Marx is one of the seminal figures in the sociology of morals.

Although Marx's worldview, in this period, is becoming more and more empirical and, in a broad sense of the term, scientific, it is still in some respects abstractly philosophical. These philosophical aspects involve the concepts of alienation and its transcendence, on the one hand, and the concepts of essence and existence, on the other. While these concepts are beginning to receive a descriptive, social-scientific content, Marx still assumes that whatever is alienated seeks to overcome (transcend or supersede) its alienation and that existences tend toward their essences. Nevertheless, it is clear that he is in the process of abandoning the Hegelian idealism that his earlier views approximated. In the section entitled "Critique of Hegel's Dialectic and General Philosophy" in the *Manuscripts*, Marx—who always had too much of a naturalistic inclination to be fully a Hegelian—attacks the idealistic aspect of Hegel's philosophy:

> When Hegel conceives wealth, the power of the state, etc. as entities alienated from the human being, he conceives them only in their thought form. They are entities of thought and thus simply an alienation of the pure (i.e., abstract) philosophical thought. The whole movement therefore ends in absolute knowledge. It is precisely abstract thought from which these objects are alienated, and which they confront with their presumptuous reality. . . . It is not the fact that the human being *objectifies* himself *inhumanly*, in opposition to abstract thought, but that he *objectifies* himself by distinction from and in *opposition* to abstract thought, which constitutes alienation as it exists and as it has to be transcended.[35]

> For Hegel, *human life, man*, is equivalent to *self-consciousness*. All alienation of human life is, therefore, *nothing* but *alienation of self-consciousness*. This alienation of self-consciousness is not regarded as the *expression*, reflected in knowledge and thought, of the *real* alienation of human life.[36]

Nevertheless, Marx for the first time in this period adopts the Hegelian problematic of objectification, alienation, and the tran-

[35] Ibid., pp. 200–201.
[36] Ibid., p. 204.

scendence of alienation. Ironically, he did not utilize this problematic in his initial periods of development when he was actually much closer philosophically and politically to Hegel. The acceptance of the problematic of alienation, however, goes hand in hand with his growing attachment to the new science of political economy and is perhaps to be attributed as much to his reading of Adam Smith and the other classical political economists as to his rereading of Hegel's works at this time. His first study of Hegel—"Critique of Hegel's Philosophy of the State" or, alternatively, "Critique of Hegel's Philosophy of Right"—which he worked on in 1842 and 1843, contains no hint of the importance he would a year later attach to the concept of alienation. Furthermore, "Hegel's standpoint," according to Marx, "is that of modern political economy. He conceives of labour as the *essence*, the self-confirming essence of man."[37]

> The outstanding achievement of Hegel's *Phenomenology* is, first, that Hegel grasps the self-creation of man as a process, objectification as a transcendence of this alienation, and that he, therefore, grasps the nature of *labour*, and conceives objective man (true, because real man) as a result of his *own labour*.[38]

> In short, Hegel conceives labour as man's act of *self-creation* (though in abstract terms).[39]

On Marx's adaptation of the Hegelian problematic, human beings objectify their natural powers and faculties by creating an objective world of material and cultural objects, and in this historical development of material and intellectual production, beings create themselves, create their own historical human natures. While there is a certain basic or essential human nature or, rather, set of natural powers and faculties common to all (normal) persons throughout history, human personality and identity are created by and through the production of systems of physical and cultural objects in each specific historical period and culture.[40]

This creation of historical human nature, of human identity and personality, is, however, dependent upon the creation of cultural objects as much as upon the creation of physical objects. Marx speaks of the "objects of natural science and art" as "man's spiri-

---

[37] Ibid., p. 203.
[38] Ibid., p. 202.
[39] Ibid., p. 213.
[40] See Ibid., pp. 162, 164, 166.

tual inorganic nature, his intellectual means of life, which he must first prepare for enjoyment and perpetuation,"[41] and claims:

> It is only through the objectively deployed wealth of the human being that the wealth of subjective *human* sensibility . . . is cultivated and created. For it is not only the five senses, but also the so-called spiritual senses, the practical senses (desiring, loving, etc.), in brief, human sensibility and the human character of the senses, which can only come into being through the existence of *its* object, through humanized nature. The cultivation of the five senses is the work of all previous history.[42]

However, in all societies that have existed thus far these material and cultural objects have been in some sense separated from the vast majority of human beings, taken out of the orbit of their utilization and control. Consequently, they have been perceived by the vast majority of persons as "alien" and "hostile." The vast majority, therefore, have not only been alienated from the objects or products of material and intellectual production but, according to Marx, from the process of production, other persons, nature, and their own selves, i.e., "human life," or their own "species-being." These forms of alienation will be transcended, in Marx's view, only when the vast majority regain control of these objects and their own lives. This is possible only when they become truly social beings, which, in turn, is possible only with the creation of communist society.

Although the philosophical language of objectification, alienation, and the transcendence of alienation is somewhat vague and confusing, Marx's use of these terms, unlike Hegel's, does not require any profound metaphysical assumptions. Of the three German terms—*"vergegenständlichung," "entäusserung,"* and *"entfremdung"*—generally lumped together under the English terms "alienation" and "estrangement," the first is almost entirely descriptive in nature, the second primarily descriptive and secondarily evaluative, and the third primarily evaluative and only secondarily descriptive. All three concepts enter into Marx's philosophical anthropology and are connected by him to the categories of political economy.

Marx claims that human beings, through their physical and in-

---

[41] Ibid., p. 126.
[42] Ibid., p. 161.

tellectual labor, *objectify* (in the sense of *"vergegenständlichung"*) their powers and faculties in material and cultural objects. In the modern system of the division of labor and private property, the greater part of humanity is—in the sense of *"entäusserung"*—divested of or alienated from the material and cultural objects they create. These objects, in other words, are alienated from the common, laboring human being in precisely the sense that one's property is alienated when one sells it to another: one loses control of it. Finally, this social system—like all social systems based on the opposition of dominant and subordinate classes, as the later Marx observes—alienates (in the sense of *"entfremdung"*) one from the process and product of production as well as from other persons and one's self (i.e., one's own human nature) because one feels separated and isolated from these objects and perceives them as hostile forces against which one feels powerless.

It is clear that part of the meaning of "alienation"—at least in the sense of *"entfremdung"*—is its negative evaluative connotation. Marx makes this clear, for example, when he speaks of "the sense of alienation" as "error, a defect, *that which ought not to be*"[43] (emphasis added). The moral content of the various forms of alienation Marx describes in the *Manuscripts*, the moral grounds upon which he condemns these forms of alienation, can, I think, be successfully reduced to three primary moral principles to which he implicitly subscribes in the *Manuscripts* and throughout the rest of his writings. These principles are freedom (as self-determination), human community, and self-realization. On this interpretation, alienation from the products of production primarily concerns the domination of the producer by alien powers and thus a lack of freedom. Similarly, alienation from the process of production has to do with the domination of the producer by alien powers and the resultant loss of meaningfulness in his work, which indicates not only a lack of freedom but a lack of genuine community as well. Alienation from other men (and women) is normally objectionable because it indicates the lack of genuine community and thus the opportunity to realize certain human potentialities having genuine human community as their precondition. Alienation from the species-being or from one's own "truly human" nature suggests that certain "human" potentialities cannot be realized under prevalent socioeconomic conditions, thus indicating that the values of self-realization and human community are being impugned.

[43] Ibid., p. 219.

51

Alienation is, in fact, the evaluative concept Marx employs most in his critique of "the system of private property," or what he later simply refers to as capitalism. Human beings are alienated in this social system because of (1) the detrimental conditions in which they must live and work (detrimental, that is, to their physical and mental health, their ability to realize their human potentialities, and—in general—their ability to flourish), and (2) the lack of control they are accorded concerning their lives and work situations. This much, on Marx's analysis, is confirmed by the principles of political economy:

(The alienation of the worker in his object is expressed as follows in the laws of political economy: the more the worker produces the less he has to consume; the more value he creates the more worthless he becomes; the more refined his product the more crude and misshapen the worker; the more civilized the product the more barbarous the worker; the more powerful the work the more feeble the worker; the more the work manifests intelligence the more the worker declines in intelligence and becomes a slave of nature.)

Political economy conceals the alienation in the nature of labour in so far as it does not examine the direct relationship between the worker (work) and production. Labour certainly produces marvels for the rich but it produces privation for the worker. It produces palaces, but hovels for the worker. It produces beauty, but deformity for the worker. It replaces labour by machinery, but it casts some of the workers back into a barbarous kind of work and turns others into machines. It produces intelligence, but also stupidity and cretinism for the workers.[44]

Marx now describes these nonoptimal, detrimental effects of a society based on private property, profit, and the division of labor in terms of various forms of alienation. By way of contrast, in his later works he is satisfied to illustrate these effects without subsuming them under this concept. Though the manner of description thus changes, the postulation of the empirical effects themselves, together with Marx's moral evaluation of them, is constant throughout his writings.

The concepts of "human" (or "truly human") and of "species-being" also figure into Marx's evaluative framework at this time

[44] Ibid., pp. 123–124.

and are thus linked to his concept of alienation. Although the term "human" may seem to be of a purely descriptive nature, Marx's use of it on some occasions is at least partially evaluative. In such phrases as "how far man's natural behavior has become *human*" and "the human nature of needs," it is clear that "human" means something like "that which is worthy of human beings." In turn, that which is worthy of human beings is that which allows for or promotes the realization of their essential or "truly human" capacities, namely, sociability and the capacity for free, conscious creative activity. Furthermore, it is these two capacities or powers that are definitive of transhistorical human nature or of what he calls man's "species-being," distinguishing human beings from the lower animals.

> Productive life is . . . species-life . . . in the type of life activity resides the whole character of a species, its species-character; and free, conscious activity is the species character of human beings. . . . The animal is one with its life activity. It does not distinguish the activity from itself. It is *its activity*. But man makes his life activity itself an object of his will and consciousness. . . . Conscious life activity distinguishes man from the life activity of animals. Only for this reason is he a species-being. Or rather, he is only a self-conscious being, i.e., his own life is an object for him because he is a species-being. Only for this reason is his activity free activity. Alienated labour reverses the relationship, in that man because he is a self-conscious being makes his life activity, his *being*, only a means for his existence.[45]

Thus, on Marx's view, one is alienated when one's essential human capacities are blocked or thwarted, when those potentialities that must be fulfilled for human wholeness, health, and happiness go unfulfilled. The system of private property and profit alienates human beings because it thwarts the fulfillment of these two essential human capacities. Underlying this view are a descriptive-explanatory thesis and an evaluative one. According to the former thesis, human beings are naturally communal and creative beings, with the result that—unless corrupted by social arrangements or other contingencies—they will spontaneously cooperate among themselves and enter into creative activities. The evaluative or, more specifically, moral thesis proposes that it is good for human

[45] Ibid., p. 127.

individuals to be whole and to flourish and, consequently, it is good for human beings to be allowed to develop what Marx alternately calls "social," "communal," "universal," or "species" consciousness and to indulge in free, creative activity. It is good, in other words, that people be allowed to realize their essential human nature or conform to their "species-being."[46]

Although it may be tempting to claim that Marx's theory of alienation and the associated values of freedom (as self-determination), human community, and self-realization make up his entire moral theory, this raises two problems. First, it would not be able to account for Marx's concern for how these goods—especially the good of freedom—are distributed (more on this in chapter 3). The second problem—from a Marxist point of view —is that without some sort of principle of distribution of the good, we could be saddling Marx with an untenable theory. In short, while his theory of alienation and associated values may go a long way toward portraying his theory of the good and his vision of the good life, it does not provide an adequate moral theory.

Nevertheless, communism (which is now the explicit goal in Marx's normative political theory) is to be preferred to capitalism precisely because it allows for the realization of these two essential human capacities, whereas capitalism (the system of private property) does not. In one of his more Hegelian passages in the *Manuscripts*, Marx claims:

> *Communism* is the *positive* abolition of *private property*, of *human self-alienation*, and thus the real appropriation of *human* nature through and for man. It is, therefore, the return of man himself as a social, i.e., really human being, a complete and con-

[46] For other reconstructions and/or analyses of Marx's concept and theory of alienation, see A. Wood, *Karl Marx*, pp. 1–59; Elster, *An Introduction to Karl Marx*, pp. 41–59 and *Making Sense of Marx*, pp. 74–78, 100–107; Buchanan, *Marx and Justice*, pp. 36–49; Ollman, *Alienation*; Richard Schacht, *Alienation*, Doubleday, Garden City, N.Y., 1970; Istvan Meszaros, *Marx's Theory of Alienation*, Harper & Row, N.Y., 1970; David McLellen, "Alienation in Hegel and Marx," *Dictionary of the History of Ideas*, vol. 1 (Phillip P. Wiener), Scribner, N.Y., 1973; Petrović: "Alienation," "The Human Relevance of Marx's Concept of Alienation," and "The Philosophical and Sociological Relevance of Marx's Theory of Alienation."

See also Irving Louis Horowitz, "On Alienation and the Social Order," *Dialogues on the Philosophy of Marxism* (John Somerville and Howard Parsons, eds.); Melvin Seeman, "On the Meaning of Alienation," *American Sociological Review*, vol. 24, no. 6 (Dec. 1959); Nicholas C. Tatsis and George V. Zito, "Marx, Durkheim, and Alienation: Toward a Heuristic Typology," *Social Theory and Practice*, vol. 3, no. 2 (Fall 1974); Bowles and Gintis "Capitalism and Alienation"; Kenneth A. Megill, "The Community in Marx's Philosophy," *Philosophy and Phenomenological Research*, vol. 30, no. 3 (March 1970); and C. Taylor, "Alienation and Community."

scious return which assimilates all the wealth of previous development. Communism as a fully developed naturalism is humanism and as a fully developed humanism is naturalism. It is the *definitive* resolution of the antagonism between man and nature, and between man and man. It is the true solution of the conflict between existence and essence, between objectification and self-affirmation, between freedom and necessity, between individual and species. It is the solution of the riddle of history and knows itself to be this solution.[47]

While it may be suggested that Marx's vision of communism obviates the need for principles of distribution because, arguably, it is a society beyond the conditions of justice—namely, moderate scarcity and moderate egoism—this is of no comfort to those who want to argue that socialism (i.e., the first stage of communism) is preferable to capitalism. In addition, that full fledged communism could ever exist is doubtful, to say the least.

It is interesting to note, however, that although Marx's concept of communism is still expressed here primarily in philosophical language, his emerging social and political realism is, by this time, also clearly in evidence. "In order to supersede the *idea* of private property," he writes, "communist *ideas* are sufficient, but *genuine* communist activity is necessary in order to supersede *real* private property. History will produce it, and the development which we already recognize in thought as self-transcending will in reality involve a severe and protracted process."[48]

Marx's Transitional Works (1844–1847)

Between Marx's early works (which are primarily philosophical) and his later works (which are primarily empirical) lie a group of transitional works, each of which is noticeably less philosophical and more scientific than its predecessor. The first two—*The Holy Family* (1844–1845) and *The German Ideology* (1845–1846)—together with the "Theses on Feuerbach" (1845), constitute a polemic against the Young Hegelians, Feuerbach, and German speculative philosophy in general. This polemic was meant to settle accounts with his (and Engels') "erstwhile philosophical conscience," but its most important part—*The German Ideology*—remained unpublished during their lives and was, as Marx says, "abandoned . . . to the

---

[47] Marx, *Economic and Philosophical Manuscripts*, p. 155.
[48] Ibid., p. 176.

gnawing criticism of the mice . . . since we had achieved our main purpose—self-clarification."[49] The final work of this period—*The Poverty of Philosophy* (1847)—is Marx's polemic against Proudhon's views as expressed in *The Philosophy of Poverty* and is, in Marx's view, his first genuinely scientific work: "The salient points of our conception were first outlined in [a scientific], although polemical, form in my *Misère de la Philosophie* . . . which was aimed at Proudhon [and] published in 1847."[50]

It is in this period that Marx first develops at least the fundamentals of all his empirical, social-scientific theories, the theories—whether ultimately correct or incorrect—that entitle his thought to be designated scientific. These can be divided into: (1) his general approach to accounting for sociohistorical phenomena; (2) his theory of sociohistorical transformations (historical materialism proper); (3) the somewhat less general and abstract set of theories surrounding his class analysis of society, which serves as the basis for (4) his analysis of capitalism and projections concerning post-capitalist society. (It is, by the way, only the truth of a subset of the last two sets of theories—which Popper refers to as "Marx's institutional theories"—that I take to be crucial to the justification of the Marxist's basic normative political positions.)

Even in *The Holy Family*—the first and most philosophical work of this period and his first collaboration with Engels—Marx's developing social-scientific theories are in evidence even though he and Engels are still enmeshed in Hegelian and Young Hegelian terminology, as they polemicize against Bruno Bauer (one of Marx's former associates in Germany) and his school of Critical Criticism. Consider the following passage in which Marx both condemns the social situation of the proletariat and gives the outlines of an empirical, social-scientific explanation of how and why the proletariat will abolish these oppressive social conditions and establish a better society.

> In the fully-formed proletariat the abstraction of all humanity, even of the *semblance* of humanity, is practically complete; since the conditions of life of the proletariat sum up all the conditions of life of society today in their most inhuman form; since man has lost himself in the proletariat, yet at the same time has not only gained theoretical consciousness of that loss, but through urgent, no longer removable, no longer dis-

---

[49] Marx, *A Contribution to the Critique of Political Economy*, p. 22.
[50] Ibid.

guisable, absolutely imperative *need*—the practical expression of *necessity*—is driven directly to revolt against this inhumanity, it follows that the proletariat can and must emancipate itself. But it cannot emancipate itself without abolishing the conditions of its own life. It cannot abolish the conditions of its own life without abolishing *all* the inhuman conditions of life of society today which are summed up in its own situation. . . . It is not a question of what this or that proletarian or even the whole proletariat, at the moment *regards* as its aim. It is a question of *what the proletariat is*, and what, in accordance with this *being*, it will historically be compelled to do. Its aim and historical action is visibly and irrevocably foreshadowed in its own life situation as well as in the whole organization of bourgeois society today.[51]

The last part of the paragraph foreshadows his materialist approach to history and his theory of historical materialism, but it is the first part that helps illuminate Marx's implicit moral views. Bourgeois society is "inhuman" or a form of "inhumanity" because it does not allow for the majority of its members to be treated as human beings should be treated. It does not allow people to realize the positive aspects of their human nature: sociability and free, conscious creative activity. Marx argues in *The Holy Family* that humanity is "abstracted" from the proletariat and that "man has lost himself in the proletariat" precisely because the proletarian's "species-being" is not allowed to flourish. The resulting poverty, misery, and abasement of the proletariat "arouse man's indignation."[52]

The German Ideology, which comes next, is the major work of this period and—along with the *Paris Manuscripts*, the *Grundrisse*, and *Capital*—certainly one of the most important of Marx's larger works. It is a polemic against Bruno Bauer, Max Sterner, Ludwig Feuerbach, and the Young Hegelians in general as well as against Karl Grun and True German Socialism. It contains much more systematic accounts of Marx's materialist view of history, his theory of sociohistorical transformations, and his institutional social-scientific theories, as well as more explicit statements of the humanist moral principles underlying his moral judgments. His normative political positions have stabilized by this point into his advocacy of communism and communist revolution. His vision of commu-

[51] Marx and Engels, *The Holy Family*, pp. 44–45.
[52] See Ibid., pp. 42–43.

nism is, however, still somewhat idyllic—as evidenced by his famous passage stating that communism would allow one "to do
one thing today and another tomorrow, to hunt in the morning,
fish in the afternoon, rear cattle in the evening, criticize after din-
ner, just as I have in mind, without ever becoming hunter, fisher-
man, shepherd, or critic."[53]

Although Marx claims in *The German Ideology* that morality is a
form of ideology, there is perhaps no other work in which his definitive moral views are expressed so clearly. He uses the term
"alienation" less than he did in earlier works and even ridicules
the notion of "estrangement" (a synonym for "alienation") as "a
term that will be comprehensible [only] to philosophers,"[54] i.e.,
comprehensible to the Young Hegelians and other contemporary
German philosophers. But he still uses the term "alienation" upon
occasion. Marx states, for example, that "with the abolition of the
basis of private property, with the communistic regulation of production (and, implicit in this, the destruction of the *alien relation*
between men and what they themselves produce), the power of
the relation of supply and demand is dissolved into nothing, and
men get exchange, production, the mode of their mutual relation,
under their own control again."[55]

The values underlying both the concepts of alienation and—as I
shall argue presently—exploitation in Marx's works are themselves brought into the open in *The German Ideology*. In addition,
Marx utilizes the hybrid concept of "self-activity"—hybrid because
it combines the notion of free (i.e., self-determined) activity with
that of creative (i.e., self-realizing) activity. An important empirical
notion that Marx introduces and emphasizes at this point is that
of the division of labor:

> Only the proletarians of the present day, who are completely
> shut off from all self-activity, are in a position to achieve a
> complete and no longer restricted self-activity, which consists
> in the appropriation of a totality of productive forces and in
> the thus postulated development of a totality of capacities. All
> earlier revolutionary appropriations were restricted; individu-
> als, whose self-activity was restricted by a crude instrument of
> production and a limited intercourse, appropriated this crude
> instrument of production, and hence merely achieved a new

[53] Marx and Engels, *The German Ideology*, p. 124.
[54] Ibid., p. 125.
[55] Ibid., p. 126.

state of limitation. Their instrument of production became their property, but they themselves remained subordinate to the division of labour and their own instrument of production. In all expropriations up to now, a mass of individuals remained subservient to a single instrument of production; in the appropriation by the proletarians, a mass of instruments of production must be made subject to each individual, and property to all. Modern universal intercourse can be controlled by individuals, therefore, only when controlled by all.[56]

Only at this stage does self-activity coincide with material life, which corresponds to the development of individuals into complete individuals and the casting-off of all natural limitations. The transformation of labour into self-activity corresponds to the transformation of the earlier limited intercourse into the intercourse of individuals as such. With the appropriation of the total productive forces through united individuals, private property comes to an end. Whilst previously in history a particular condition always appeared as accidental, now the isolation of individuals and the particular private gain of each man have themselves become accidental.

The individuals . . . are no longer subject to the division of labour.[57]

These passages are a veritable gold mine of Marx's moral views. The goal of humanity-in-society is (or should be) *self-activity*, i.e., activity not controlled by outside ("alien") forces but directed by one's own self. Realizing self-activity means that individuals are no longer "subservient to a single instrument of production" nor "subject to the division of labour" nor in the thrall of any of many possible "natural limitations," i.e., limitations that are not consciously planned and willed by individuals but that can be eliminated once they succumb to conscious planning and willing. These phrases manifest Marx's commitment to a standard or principle of freedom as self-determination. His commitment to the value of human community is manifested in his claim that the formerly divided and isolated individuals will, under communism, be "united individuals" who freely and cooperatively control social production, whose instruments are "made subject to each individual, and

[56] Ibid., p. 155.
[57] Ibid., p. 156.

59

property to all." Finally, his commitment to the value of self-realization comes out in the phrases concerning the "development of a totality of capacities" and "the development of individuals into complete individuals."

The most explicit statement invoking these three cardinal values (freedom as self-determination, human community, and self-realization), and showing their interrelation for Marx, occurs several pages later. He writes:

> The transformation, through the division of labour, of personal powers (relationships) into material powers cannot be dispelled by dismissing the general idea of it from one's mind, but can only be abolished by the individuals again subjecting these material powers themselves and abolishing the division of labour. This is not possible without the community. Only in community (with others) has each individual the means of cultivating his gifts in all directions; only in the community, therefore, is personal freedom possible. In the previous substitutes for community, in the State, etc., personal freedom has existed only for the individuals who developed within the relationships of the ruling class, and only insofar as they were individuals of this class. The illusory community, in which individuals have up till now combined, always took on an independent existence in relation to them, and was at the same time, since it was the combination of one class over against another, not only a completely illusory community, but a new fetter as well. In the real community the individuals obtain their freedom in and through their association.[58]

> With the community of revolutionary proletarians . . . who take their conditions of existence and those of all members of society under their control . . . it is as individuals that the individuals participate in it. It is just this combination of individuals (assuming the advanced stage of modern productive forces, of course) which puts the conditions of the free development and movement of individuals under their control— conditions which were previously abandoned to chance and had won an independent existence over against the separate individuals just because of their separation as individuals, and because of the necessity of their combination which had been

[58] Ibid., pp. 162–163.

determined by the division of labour, and through their separation had become a bond alien to them.[59]

Genuine personal freedom permits the individual to have available the (social) means of cultivating his or her gifts to their full
potential. But the social means of self-development are not available to individuals except in a genuine community because (though
Marx does not make these points plain here): (1) outside of the
establishment of a real community in advanced industrial societies
(i.e., outside communism), the vast majority of people will not
have access to the leisure time and the material and cultural resources requisite for genuine self-development; and (2) outside of
a genuine community it is impossible for individuals to realize one
of their most fundamental human potentialities—a potentiality
sought by all persons unless they are warped by pernicious social
conditions—namely, full community, i e , full universal, communal, social, or "species" consciousness. "In the real community
the individuals obtain their freedom in and through their association."

This view, of course, has nothing in common with the totalitarian view of the relation between the individual and society so often falsely imputed to Marx by his vulgar critics. That individuals
should be controlled in any way by outside forces rather than their
own self-determining consciousness or that they should become
bland and unthinking conformists are both views that could not
be further from Marx's thought. The whole problem for him was
how to make possible the "free development and movement of
individuals" or, as he puts it elsewhere, the "full and free development of every individual." To this end every humanly alterable
circumstance must be made to conform. The only form of society
capable of insuring this, according to Marx, is communism. The
only class with the motive and ability to create communism is the
working class. Once communism has come about, however, coercion or the threat of coercion will no longer be necessary to insure
the possibility of the "free development and movement of individuals" because the individuals themselves, having achieved communal consciousness, will ensure it.

Now whether or not Marx is correct in this last assumption is a
matter of considerable debate, both between Marxists and non-
Marxists and within the Marxist tradition itself. Those who assert
that this scenario is unrealistic often claim that the struggle be-

[59] Ibid., pp. 161–162.

tween individuals (and groups of individuals) over the distribution of scarce resources is not the only source of interpersonal conflict and thus argue that the state, as a public organ having a monopoly on legitimate coercive power, will always be necessary. Marx's critics may well be right on this point, but fortunately Marx's normative political positions do not stand or fall with the truth or falsity of this particular empirical thesis nor with the connected thesis that full-fledged communism is a genuine historical possibility. In his later works Marx distinguishes between what he calls the "first" and "higher" stages of communism. He asserts that the first stage is a transitional period in which productive property has been socialized and the economy brought under a common plan but still embodies the conditions of moderate scarcity and moderate egoism (i.e., the incomplete socialization or "humanization" of the individual). At this stage the state—with its functions of coordination and arbitration—is still a necessary institution.

Since Marx and Marxists clearly believe this sort of society to be vastly superior to any form of capitalism, they are seemingly committed to the overthrow of capitalism and the establishment of socialism whether or not communism is a real historical possibility. Thus, even if we accept as true the claim that the state will always be necessary and, therefore, by definition, full-fledged communism is not historically possible, this does not relieve us of the responsibility of judging between capitalism and socialism (as well as between socialism and state-socialism or—if one is cynical enough to think that state-socialism is the only historically possible alternative to capitalism—between state-socialism and capitalism). That is, the truth of this thesis does not relieve us of the responsibility to decide for or against what I have described as the Marxist's basic normative political positions (more on these choices in chapter 10).

Thus far I have shown only that Marx made moral judgments and implicitly utilized moral principles in his early and transitional works. The thesis I am defending, however, is that Marx's moral views inform both his early and his later work and remain substantially the same. In the next section I shall take pains to show that he makes moral judgments in his later as well as his early writings. But even if the later works are not devoid of moral content, as many would claim, there are a number of different ways of interpreting the moral judgments, and not everyone familiar with the matter agrees that these judgments evidence a fundamental continuity of moral principles or moral theory from the early to the later Marx.

It might be maintained, for example, that even though freedom (as self-determination), human community, and self-realization are the primary values to be found in Marx's early and transitional writings, they are not primary throughout his works, having been replaced in the later period by a more utilitarian evaluative framework and the concept of exploitation, neither of which is reducible to these three values. This position was perhaps not unreasonable in the days before the publication of *Grundrisse* in 1939, but since this work makes clear the continuity of Marx's moral perspective from his early to his later writings, this position no longer seems tenable. But even those Marxists and students of Marx who proclaimed before the publication of the *Grundrisse* that his later works are value free or that his moral values or principles are radically different in his later works cannot be fully excused because—for the attentive reader—these claims are falsified by *Capital* as well as Marx's other later works.

Morality in Marx's Later Works (1848–1883)

Marx's later works can be divided into two subperiods: that of his works of maturation (1847–1858) and that of his fully mature works (1858–1883). I shall consider the period as a whole because, in general, the reader will be more familiar with Marx's thought in this time period and because the changes that take place in his thought are, on the whole, less extensive than was the case earlier.

After settling accounts with the Young Hegelians and their own "philosophical consciences" in the polemical works of their transitional period (1844–1847), Marx and Engels spent the years from 1847 to 1850 involved in revolutionary political activities and participated directly in the great European upheavals that took place from 1848 to 1850. (Marx edited over 300 issues of the *Neue Rheinische Zeitung* in Cologne during the German Revolution of 1848–1849.) As a result, they concentrated on writing programmatic documents that had immediate value in terms of building the revolutionary movement and, in particular, the Communist League. These short works—Engels' first draft of the manifesto for the Communist League entitled *The Principles of Communism* (1847); the *Communist Manifesto* (1848), coauthored by Marx and Engels; and Marx's *Wage Labor and Capital* (1849), which was given as a series of lectures by Marx to communist workers in Brussels—represent the first formulations of their mature (though not fully mature) political and theoretical positions.

After the European revolutions of 1848–1850 were put down, Marx and Engels spent the next period of their theoretical activity reflecting upon and analyzing these events from their theoretical and political perspective. This resulted in the first detailed application of their mature theories and views to recent historical events and gave rise to Marx's *Class Struggles in France: 1848–1850* (1850) and *The Eighteenth Brumaire of Louis Bonaparte* (1852), and to Engels' *The Peasant War in Germany* (1850) and *Revolution and Counter-Revolution in Germany* (1852).

Between the end of this period and Marx's writing of the *Grundrisse* (1857–1858), both he and Engels took a hiatus from large-scale theoretical writing. During this time Marx was in London engaged in his monumental studies of political economy and the other social sciences, which culminated in the *Grundrisse* (written in 1857–1858), *A Contribution to the Critique of Political Economy* (1858–1859), *Theories of Surplus Value* (1862–1863), and *Capital*, the first volume of which was published in 1867. (Marx worked on the second and third volumes from 1867 to 1880. These volumes were edited by Engels from Marx's unfinished manuscripts and published by him in 1885 and 1893–1894, respectively. Also, *Theories of Surplus Value* actually consisted of notebooks 6 through 15 out of a total of twenty-one notebooks written by Marx from 1861–1863.)
1863.)

Marx's final period—that of his *fully* mature works—begins, according to my analysis, in 1858, when he finished the *Grundrisse* and began work on *A Contribution to the Critique of Political Economy*. The preface to the latter text is well known due to its review of the development of his theories and theoretical works up to that point and its definitive statement of a standard version of his theory of historical materialism. The line between Marx's works of maturation and his fully mature works is most perspicuously drawn here for two reasons. First, after the *Grundrisse*, he no longer extensively employs the philosophical language of alienation to make points about the pernicious effects of capitalism and how these effects are to be overcome (i.e., how alienation is to be transcended) in communist society. Second, starting with *A Contribution to the Critique of Political Economy*, he makes the important theoretical distinction between *labor* and *labor-power*. (Although this terminology appears in current editions of Marx's earlier economic writings—e.g., in *Wage Labor and Capital* written in 1849—it is present because Engels made this change in later editions of Marx's works.)

On Marx's mature view, the worker sells his labor-power to the capitalist at whatever this commodity is going for on the labor market, and it is the differential between what the capitalist pays for this commodity (i.e., *labor-power*) and the actual value that the worker's *labor* adds to the product in the process of production that generates surplus value and profits for the capitalist. This is a significant modification of his economic theory and, indeed, of classical political economy generally. According to Engels' speech at Marx's graveside, it constitutes one of Marx's two great scientific discoveries, the other being the materialist approach to history.[60]

Marx's fully mature works are generally less concerned with philosophical issues, make less use of the language of alienation and its transcendence, and make less explicit moral proclamations than his writings up to 1858. This does not mean, however, that his fully mature or later works in general are devoid of moral content, as is sometimes claimed by the orthodox proponents of the school known as Scientific Socialism and certain other scholastic Marxists and students of Marx. Although all of his later works—including *Capital*—contain at least implicit moral judgments, his moral views, as well as the continuity between his early and later works, can be seen most clearly in the *Grundrisse*.

The *Grundrisse*, the massive predecessor of *Capital*, was written from 1857 to 1858 but not published until 1939 (and not in English until 1953). It is primarily concerned with laying the foundations for a critique of political economy; but rather than being as narrowly economic as *Capital*, its discussions of economics are, as David McLellen notes, "inextricably linked with digressions of a much wider nature on such subjects as the individual and society; problems of increasing leisure and the abolition of the division of labour; the nature of alienation in the higher stages of capitalist society; the revolutionary nature of capitalism and its inherent universality, and so on."[61] And, as McLellen further remarks, "It is these digressions that give the *Grundrisse* its primary importance."[62]

---

[60] The claim that labor is a unique commodity in this respect has recently been challenged from within the Marxist tradition by John Roemer. See his *A General Theory of Exploitation and Class*, pp. 183–186, 284–287.

[61] McLellan, "Introduction," p. 8.

[62] Ibid.

Its importance lies in the fact that it shows the fundamental continuity of much of Marx's thought from the Original Marxism of 1844 to the Mature Marxism of *Capital*. Although his views on humanity-in-society and, in particular, humanity-in-capitalist-society were in the process of becoming less speculative and philosophical and more empirical and scientific during this entire period of maturation, his concerns as well as the values underlying them remained substantially the same.[63]

While the concept of alienation is rarely seen in most of his later works, it is utilized extensively in the *Grundrisse*. As in the *Paris Manuscripts*, Marx's theory of alienation of humanity-in-capitalist-society can be divided here into the categories of alienation of the product of production, alienation of the activity of production, alienation of the individual from other individuals, and alienation of the individual from his or her own self and/or his or her own (human) nature.

Both the product and activity of production are alienated from and alien to the individual producer. (Here the first expression can be taken to represent the objective, sociological dimension of alienation, and the second to represent its subjective, psychological dimension.) But we can deduce from Marx's writings that the concept of alienation—though it usually implies psychological estrangement—is primarily a matter of subordination or domination by something outside the individual's control. He writes, for example: "The individuals are subordinated to social production, which exists externally to them, as a sort of fate; but social production is not subordinate to individuals who manipulate it as their communal capacity."[64] Thus the conditions of alienation violate the principle of freedom (as self-determination).

Similarly, "The universal nature of production creates an alienation of the individual from himself and others,"[65] and thus contravenes the value of human community. The condition of alienation in capitalism also works against the self-realization of individuals. Capitalism prevents people from developing and realizing their individual talents and capacities spontaneously and cooperatively and becoming all-around, well-developed persons because

[63] For an excellent defense of this general position, see T. B. Bottomore's introductory essay to *Karl Marx: Early Writings*.

[64] Marx, *The Grundrisse*, p. 68.

[65] Ibid., p. 71.

Universal prostitution appears as a necessary phase of the development of the social character of personal talents, abilities, capacities, and activities. This could be more delicately expressed as the general condition of serviceability and usefulness. It is the bringing to a common level of different things, which is the significance that already Shakespeare gave to money.[66]

The concept of alienation, in other words, has all of the evaluative implications in the *Grundrisse* that it has in his earlier works. Perhaps the biggest difference between Marx's account of alienation in the *Manuscripts* and in the *Grundrisse* is that in the latter he more consciously attempts to integrate his emerging economic theory (or sociology of economics) into the framework of his theory of alienation. The entire world of products is "objectified labor," i.e., the result of labor as it has been objectified in material products. This world of material goods is, however, "alienated" from the producers in capitalist society because they have no control over the products of production. Wage-labor is *alien labor* because the worker has no control over it. Furthermore, capital is *"alien objectified labor"* because it is value (or surplus-value) that has been alienated from the direct producers (in a legalistic sense) by the capitalist class.[67] Nevertheless—and this is of the utmost importance for understanding Marx—*objectified* labor is not, under any and all social conditions, necessarily *alienated* labor. The identification of objectified and alienated labor, i.e., the fact that objectified labor is alienated, is "in no way an *absolute* necessity of production; it is, rather, ephemeral."[68]

Social relations in capitalism tend to distort and hide their real nature (in ways Marx was later to develop in his theory of the fetishism of capital, money, and commodities in the first and third volumes of *Capital*), so that everyone in that society tends to misperceive them. But according to Marx it is especially the "bourgeois economists" who "are so bogged down in their traditional ideas of historical development of society in a single stage that the necessity of the *objectification* of the social forces of labour seems to them inseparable from the necessity of its *alienation* in relation to living labour."[69] But this equivalence, Marx claims, holds only in

[66] Ibid.
[67] See Ibid., pp. 81, 97, 99.
[68] Ibid., p. 151.
[69] Ibid.

class-divided, commodity-producing societies such as capitalism. He notes that as the productive forces develop, objectified labor (i.e., fixed capital) grows in proportion to living labor (i.e., variable capital) in the process of production and, thus,

> *social wealth becomes, in ever greater and greater proportions, an alien and dominating force opposing the worker.* Stress is placed not on the state of objectification but on *the state of alienation, estrangement, and abandonment,* on the fact that the enormous objectified power which social labour has opposed to itself as one of its elements belongs not to the worker but to the conditions of production that are personified in capital. So long as the creation of this material form of activity, objectified in contrast to immediate labour power, occurs on the basis of capital and wage-labour, and so long as this process of objectification in fact seems to be a process of alienation as far as the worker is concerned, or to be the appropriation of alien labour from the capitalist's point of view, so long will this distortion and this inversion really exist and not merely occur in the imagination of both workers and capitalists[70] [emphasis added].

In communist society this identification of objectified labor and alienated labor is destroyed. "But as labor loses its *immediate,* individual character, whether subjective or entirely external, as individual activity becomes directly general or *social,* the objective elements of production lose this form of alienation. They are then produced as property, as the organic social body in which individuals are reproduced as individuals, but as social individuals."[71]

But what does Marx mean here by "directly general or social labour"? Labor, for Marx, is directly social or general if, and only if, the direct producers have control of the activity and products of labor (rather than being subservient to them). He assumes that if this were to occur, then workers would come to see themselves as being voluntarily part of what in reality already is an inherently social process of the production of the total product of society rather than an involuntary individual producer of exchange values. In a rational society,

> the social character of production would make the product from the start a collective and general product. The exchange

[70] Ibid., pp. 150–151.
[71] Ibid., p. 151.

originally found in production—which is an exchange not of exchange values but of activities determined by communal needs and communal aims—would from the start imply the participation of individuals in the collective world of products.[72]

In this sort of society,

the labour of the individual is established from the start as collective labour. But whatever the particular form of the product which he creates or helps to create, what he has bought with his labour is not this or that product, but a definite participation in collective production. Therefore he has no special product to exchange. His product is not an exchange value. The product does not have to change into any special form in order to have a general character for the individual. Instead of a division of labour necessarily engendered by the exchange of values, there is an organisation of labour, which has as its consequence the participation of the individual in collective consumption.[73]

Just like Marx's earlier account of alienation, his present characterization of nonalienated labor is rather obviously connected with his three primary values. Alienated labor is not free in the sense of being self-determined (i.e., determined by the worker) since "labor serves an alien will and an alien intelligence."[74] Moreover, it is not conducive to the establishment of either genuine human community or to self-realization. Nonalienated labor is labor that is *free* (i.e., self-determined or, in other words, both freely chosen and noncoerced) and therefore partially constitutive of both human community and self-realization. This comes out most clearly, perhaps, in Marx's comments on Adam Smith's view of labor, which is worth quoting at length.

"Thou shalt labour by the sweat of thy brow!" was Jehovah's curse that he bestowed upon Adam. A. Smith conceives of labour as such a curse. "Rest" appears to him to be the fitting state of things, and identical with "liberty" and "happiness." It seems to be far from A. Smith's thoughts that the individual, "in his normal state of health, strength, activity, skill and efficiency," might also require a normal portion of work, and

[72] Ibid., p. 74.
[73] Ibid., p. 75.
[74] Ibid., p. 117.

of cessation from rest. It is true that the quantity of labour to be provided seems to be conditioned by external circumstances, by the purpose to be achieved, and the obstacles to its achievement that have to be overcome by labour. But neither does it occur to A. Smith that the overcoming of such obstacles may itself constitute an exercise in liberty, and that these external purposes lose their character of mere natural necessities and are established as purposes which the individual himself fixes. The result is the self-realisation and objectification of the subject, therefore real freedom, whose activity is precisely labour. Of course he is correct in saying that labour has always seemed to be repulsive, and forced upon the worker from outside, in its historical forms of slave-labour, bond-labour and wage-labour, and that in this sense non-labour could be opposed to it as "liberty and happiness." This is doubly true of this contradictory labour which has not yet created the subjective and objective conditions (which it lost when it abandoned pastoral conditions) which make it into *attractive labour and individual self-realisation*. This does not mean that labour can be made merely a joke, or amusement, as Fourier naively expressed it in shop-girl terms. *Really free labour*, the composing of music for example, is at the same time damned serious and demands the greatest effort. The labour concerned with material production can only have this character if (1) it is of a *social nature*, and (2) it has a *scientific character* and at the same time is general work, i.e. if it ceases to be human effort as a definite, trained natural force, gives up its purely natural, primitive aspects and becomes the *activity of a subject controlling all the forces of nature in the production process*[75] [emphasis added].

Thus, according to Marx, labor in the process of material production should be and—in communist society—will be *free* (directed toward "purposes which the individual himself fixes") and at least partially constitutive of both human community ("it is of a social nature") and self-realization ("the result is the self-realization . . . of the subject").

But even though genuine self-realization can be found in the realm of material production, according to Marx, full self-realization requires a variety of activities, and material production is not even necessarily the main one. Marx seems willing to concede at

[75] Ibid., pp. 123–124.

this point that the individual's higher capacities will, in the main, be realized outside of material production (which he later calls the "realm of necessity") in the free time available for leisure and the pursuit of higher activities (i.e., in what he later calls the "realm of freedom"). He claims, for example:

> The less time society requires in order to produce wheat, cattle, etc., the more time it gains for other forms of production, material or intellectual. As with a single individual, the universality of its development, its enjoyment and its activity depends on saving time.[76]

> The theft of others' labour time upon which wealth depends today seems to be a miserable basis compared with this newly developed foundation that has been created by heavy industry itself. . . . The surplus labour of the masses has ceased to be a condition for the development of wealth in general, in the same way that the non-labour of the few has ceased to be a condition for the development of the general powers of the human mind. Production based on exchange value therefore falls apart, and the immediate process of material production finds itself stripped of its impoverished antagonistic form. Individuals are then in a position to develop freely. It is no longer a question of reducing the necessary labour time in order to create surplus labour, but of reducing the necessary labour of society to a minimum. The counterpart of this reduction is that all members of society can develop their education in the arts, sciences, etc., thanks to the free time and means available to all.[77]

On Marx's view, a rational society would seek to reduce labor time as much as possible and still provide for the needs and wants of the "socialized" individuals of which it is composed. This can actually be put into the form of a stronger argument in favor of socialism, for as such contemporary Marxists as G. A. Cohen have pointed out, this is one thing that capitalist societies cannot do: the way the profit motive operates in the economy, the way it directs the flow of capital and social resources, it is simply not possible for capitalist society to choose to work less (i.e., allow the producers more free time) rather than to produce more. Every time this choice is faced in capitalist society, it is automatically made in fa-

[76] Ibid., p. 75.
[77] Ibid., p. 142.

vor of producing more. This choice is not so crucial at this point in history, as there are very many people in even the most advanced industrialized societies who want and deserve a better (i.e., higher) standard of material well-being, and even more people in the Third World who are in desperate need of even the most basic material goods (food, potable water, clothes, housing, and basic health care—not to mention jobs and the chance for even a minimal education). However, it can be an extremely strong point in favor of the socialist organization of society in anticipation of a time when everyone is afforded the opportunity to have a decent standard of living.

On the other hand, if Marx and other Marxists are basically right in their analysis of the dysfunctions of capitalist economies, it is this type of economic and social organization that is even now preventing the production of greater material wealth as well as preventing its just distribution. (Those who object to imputing to Marx any concern for justice would do well to attend to his phrase concerning "the theft of others' labour time" quoted above. We will explore this controversy at greater length in chapter 8.) Here one need only recall that the U.S. government periodically pays American farmers *not* to produce foodstuffs at the same time that there are millions of people starving in the world. Marx seems to have both of the preceding points in mind when he writes of capitalism that

> although its tendency is always to create disposable time, it also converts it into surplus labour. If it succeeds too well with the former, it will suffer from surplus production, and then the necessary labour will be interrupted as soon as no surplus labour can be valorised from capital. The more this contradiction develops, the clearer it becomes that the growth of productive forces can no longer be limited by the appropriation of the surplus labour of others; the masses of workers must appropriate their own surplus labour.[78]

Post-capitalist society will not have these problems, according to Marx, because "when this is done," i.e., when workers appropriate their own surplus labor,

> disposable time ceases to have a contradictory character. Thus firstly, the labour time necessary will be measured by the requirements of the social individual, and secondly, social pro-

[78] Ibid., p. 144.

ductivity will grow so rapidly that, although production is reckoned with a view to the wealth of all, the disposable time of all will increase.[79]

Although Marx seems to have generally been overly optimistic in his projections concerning communist societies, he does indicate what seems to be necessary for the long-term solution to our economic problems. One necessary condition, if the Marxist economic analysis of capitalism is even close to being correct, is the replacement of capitalism with a planned socialist economy. (As noted previously, this leaves open the possibility that it could be a planned modified-market economy, such as exists in Yugoslavia, if it were ultimately to prove the most efficient type of economic organization open to a society based on the social ownership and control of productive property and production.) Another condition quite possibly necessary is that the individuals composing such societies develop a social consciousness to such an extent that they will insist on everyone's basic needs being met and, for themselves, having only what they really need to live a quality life. This would probably spell the end of conspicuous consumption as we know it in advanced capitalist countries. Furthermore, this is a place where the ecological (or environmental) movement seems to dovetail with the ideal of a socialist society: both see the cost to the natural environment (not to mention the human psyche) of production for the mere sake of greater production (and profits) as prohibitive.[80]

Be that as it may, Marx believed the reduction of necessary labor time to be, evaluatively speaking, an absolute necessity. He claims that real wealth is the developed productive force of all individuals. It is no longer the labor time but the disposable time that is the measure of wealth. And from a work published in 1821, entitled *The Source and the Remedy of the National Difficulties*, Marx ap-

[79] Ibid., pp. 144–145.

[80] For more on the debate concerning the connection between Marxism and ecology, see Howard Parsons, *Marx and Engels on Ecology*, Greenwood Press, Westport, Conn., 1977, as well as the following articles in the journal *Environmental Ethics*: Donald C. Lee, "On the Marxian View of the Relationship between Man and Nature," vol. 2, no. 1 (Spring 1980), and "Toward a Marxian Ecological Ethic: A Response to Two Critics," vol. 4, no. 4 (Winter 1982); Val Routley, "On Karl Marx as an Environmental Hero," vol. 3, no. 3 (Fall 1981); Charles Tolman, "Karl Marx, Alienation, and the Mastery of Nature," vol. 3, no. 1 (Spring 1981); and Hwa Yol Jung, "Marxism, Ecology, Technology," vol. 5, no. 2 (Summer 1983). See also Rudolph Bahro, *The Alternative in Eastern Europe*, New Left Books, London, 1978, and *From Red to Green: Interviews with New Left Review*, Verso, London, 1984.

provingly quotes the passage: "A nation is truly rich when, instead of working 12 hours, it works only 6. Wealth is not command over surplus labour time, but disposable time, beyond that used in immediate production, for each individual and for the whole of society."[81]

And this holds, for Marx, whether the individuals choose leisure and recreation or higher cultural activities or the alternative he certainly approved: a balanced life of both. Although he has great regard for higher cultural activities and thinks that involvement in them is perhaps the highest form of human self-realization, he does not think that they are the "be all and end all" of human existence. As he writes in the *Grundrisse*:

> Economising, therefore, does not mean the giving up of pleasure, but the development of power and productive capacity, and thus both the capacity for and the means of enjoyment. . . . To economise on labour time means to increase the amount of free time, i.e., time for the complete development of the individual. . . . Work cannot become a game, as Fourier would like it to be; his great merit was that he declared that the ultimate object must be to raise to a higher level not distribution but the mode of production. Free time—which includes leisure time as well as time for higher activities—naturally transforms anyone who enjoys it into a different person, and it is this different person who then enters the direct process of production.[82]

This passage and the others previously quoted raise a number of interesting questions concerning the nature of Marx's implicit moral theory or views. Does he hold a hedonistic theory of good? Should he be classified as a hedonistic utilitarian? An ideal utilitarian? A perfectionist? A consequentialist of some other sort? A consideration of these questions will be postponed, however, until chapters 2 and 3. But before we move on, we need to analyze one more quote lest one be misled into thinking that Marx utilizes the values or principles of freedom (as self-determination), human community, and self-realization to justify his vision of communism vis-à-vis capitalism only in the *Grundrisse* and previous works but not in works after the *Grundrisse*, i.e., not in his fully mature works. The quote to which I refer, of course, is Marx's famous par-

[81] Marx, *The Grundrisse*, p. 143.
[82] Ibid., p. 148.

agraph in "The Trinity Formula" in the third volume of *Capital* concerning the realms of necessity and of freedom.

> The realm of freedom actually begins only where labour which is determined by necessity and mundane considerations ceases; thus in the very nature of things it lies beyond the sphere of actual material production. Just as the savage must wrestle with Nature to satisfy his wants, to maintain and reproduce life, so must civilized man, and he must do so in all social formations and under all possible modes of production. With his development this realm of physical necessity expands as a result of his wants, but, at the same time, the forces of production which satisfy these wants also increase. Freedom in this field can only consist in socialized man, the associated producers, rationally regulating their interchange with Nature, bringing it under their common control, instead of being ruled by it as by the blind forces of Nature; and achieving this with the least expenditure of energy and under conditions most favourable to, and worthy of, their human nature. But it nonetheless still remains a realm of necessity. Beyond it begins that development of human energy which is an end in itself, the true realm of freedom, which, however, can blossom forth only with the realm of necessity as its basis. The shortening of the working day is its basic prerequisite.[83]

This passage is important for two reasons. First, it shows that Marx had grown more realistic and less idyllic concerning the nature of work, even work in communist society. Formerly he seemed to think that if only work were perceived as meaningful by the socialized individual, put under the workers' collective control, and made as tolerable as possible, it would be the major means of the individual's self-realization. Now he submits that though work can be an integral component of the individual's self-realization (under these conditions), it is only in one's free time, when one can pursue creative and leisure activities of one's own choosing, that human potentialities can be fully realized.

Second, to return to Marx's substantive moral views, this is perhaps the most morally pregnant passage in his later works. Here again we find Marx's values of freedom (as self-determination), human community, and self-realization. The value of human community is obviously satisfied because communist society consists

[83] Marx, *Capital*, vol. 3, p. 820.

of "socialized man" or the "associated producers"—terms we have previously shown to refer to human individuals who have so greatly come to identify their good with the common good that, for all practical purposes, the distinction has collapsed. Whether or not this is a practical possibility is, of course, a different question and one that, on empirical grounds, seems rather dubious— at least to the extent that we have in mind modern mass societies (*Gesellschaften*) as opposed to small communities (*Gemeinschaften*).

The value of freedom (as self-determination) is realized because the associated producers are "rationally regulating their interchange with nature, bringing it under their common control, instead of being ruled by it as by the blind forces of Nature." Although Marx does not here go into the manner of this collective control, what he has in mind seems to be the elimination of the forces of the market—particularly the periodic crises of overproduction that lead to recessions and depressions—together with the democratic (perhaps consensual) social control over the investment of capital and general regulation of the economy. On Marx's view, the (socialized) individuals are self-determining and thus, in this sense, free. Moreover, due to their "socialization" workers spontaneously do the work required to run the economy. Since no coercion or force is involved, the workers—i.e., everyone capable of working—are free in this sense as well. Needless to say, people are not coerced to do anything by the state because there is no state. He seems to assume, as well, that there will be no important social or interpersonal conflicts of a sort that would require coercion or force to settle. (That this scenario is utopian with respect to modern mass societies I take to be self-evident.)

The value of self-realization is realized because, first, individuals have become "socialized" and thus see the attainment of the common good as their own good in whatever socially productive work they perform. Second, their wants—those of *truly human beings*, and which thus lead to self-realization when satisfied— have expanded. Finally, the "realm of necessity" (i.e., the "sphere of actual material production"), and thus the "working day," has been reduced, allowing individuals more time for "that development of human energy which is an end in itself."

Although he rarely utilized the terminology of alienation in his later works, the values (as has been previously argued) underlying the concept of alienation—namely, freedom (as self-determination), human community, and self-realization—remain Marx's basic moral problematic. He now uses the concept of exploitation in many evaluative contexts, but this concept—so I shall argue—can also be reduced to one or more of the three primary values and an egalitarian principle of distribution.

Furthermore, although Marx does not directly refer to it here, also present in his later, as well as his earlier, works is what might be called his most general evaluative concept because it contains his three primary values. This is his ideal of the *fully developed human being*, i.e., "the fully developed individual, fit for a variety of labours, ready to face any change of production, and to whom the different social functions he performs are but so many modes of giving free scope to his own natural and acquired powers."[84] Correspondingly, his most basic political demand is for a society in which "the free development of each is the condition for the free development of all."[85]

It remains to be seen whether these concepts and principles provide an adequate ground for Marx's criticisms of capitalism and for the Marxist's basic normative judgments that communism (in either its lower or higher state) is morally preferable to capitalism (as well as to state-socialism), and that social and/or political revolution, if necessary and sufficient to bring such a society into being, is morally justified.

It should be noted, however, that Marx and the Classical Marxists all conceived of the first stage of communism (i.e., socialism) as an extremely democratic form of society. Although they certainly believed that the state in a newly formed socialist society would have the legitimate authority and indeed the duty to prevent counter-revolution, none of them thought that this would require either severe or long-term repressive measures. They believed that the majority of the population would be highly supportive of the new organization of social life since, as Marx puts it, the socialist revolution would be the first revolution in history that is made by a "movement of the immense majority in the interests of the immense majority."[86] Any attempt by the former classes or ruling elites to resume power and initiate a counter-revolution in property relations would, therefore, be spontaneously squelched by the armed majority; the state as a source of legitimate coercive power would hardly be needed. As Marx makes clear in *The Civil War in France*, he also believed that the population, through institutions of direct and representative democracy and

[84] Marx, *Capital*, vol. 1, p. 488.
[85] Marx and Engels, "Manifesto of the Communist Party," p. 353.
[86] Ibid., p. 344.

various measures to counter tendencies toward bureaucracy (such as officials receiving no more pay than an average worker), would be firmly in control of the state rather than vice versa.

Although Marx was also certainly in favor of what is sometimes called "negative freedom" (i.e., freedom *from* interference by other individuals with one's actions), it is not at all clear that he gives an adequate account of how freedom in this sense is to be preserved. He may also have overestimated the extent to which the elimination of market forces will be beneficial and the extent to which this form of self-determination depends upon the (problematic) transcendence of the distinction between the individual and common good. In addition, even though Marx puts forward different principles of distribution for each stage of communism—the first based on the notion of contribution and the second on ability and needs—it is not at all clear that either of them or both taken together add up to an adequate theory of social or even distributive justice. I shall take up these difficulties in later chapters.

In fairness to Marx and the Classical Marxists, however, it should be stressed that they thought that socialist revolution was bound to occur first in the most advanced capitalist countries, whose populations generally had a substantial democratic tradition. Marx only hazily conceived of the possibility of socialist revolution occurring first in underdeveloped (i.e., relatively nonindustrialized) societies or on an isolated basis. Furthermore, none of the Classical Marxists thought that a genuine socialist society could exist on anything but a worldwide basis—or at least on the basis of the socialization of the economies of all the advanced industrialized societies.

In a passage in *The German Ideology*—the only passage, to my knowledge, in which Marx speaks of the possibility of communism taking root (or rather failing to do so) in an underdeveloped and isolated area—he writes that the

> development of productive forces (which itself implies the actual empirical existence of men in their *world-historical*, instead of local, being) is an absolutely necessary practical premise because without it *want* is merely made general, and with *destitution* the struggle for necessities and all the old filthy business would necessarily be reproduced; and furthermore, because only with this universal development of productive forces is a *universal* intercourse between men established, which produces in all nations simultaneously the phenome-

non of the "propertyless" mass (universal competition), makes each nation dependent on the revolutions of the others, and finally has put *world-historical*, empirically universal individuals in place of local ones. Without this, (1) communism could only exist as a local event; (2) the *forces* of intercourse themselves could not have developed as *universal*, hence intolerable powers: they would have remained home-bred conditions surrounded by superstition; and (3) each extension of intercourse would abolish local communism. Empirically, communism is only possible as the act of the dominant peoples "all at once" and simultaneously, which presupposes the universal development of productive forces and the world intercourse bound up with communism.[87]

This passage forebodes the development of the socialist revolutions of this century which have so far occurred only on an isolated and "local" basis. Although Marx arguably would have supported all the socialist revolutions of the twentieth century, just as he supported all the popular revolutions of the nineteenth century, and would today probably support the post-capitalist societies to which they gave rise—at least as steps toward world socialism—it is clear that they do not (yet) meet the democratic standards upheld by Marx and the Classical Marxists. It is not clear, however, that Marx's theory has been refuted by these historical events since the conditions he laid down for the development of socialism (namely, the success of the world revolution and consequent abolition of all major capitalist powers) have not yet been fulfilled. Thus the Marxist's contention that democratic, nontotalitarian forms of post-capitalist society can—and will—evolve has not been definitively refuted. Whether or not and under what conditions such societies can exist is, of course, *the* political question of our time, and one on which I shall have more to say as this work progresses.

[87] Marx and Engels, *The German Ideology*, pp. 125–126.

TWO

CONSEQUENTIALIST INTERPRETATIONS OF MARX

Even if it can be shown that Marx's primary values are freedom (as self-determination), human community, and self-realization, this does not yet settle the question of what general sort of moral theory he actually holds. Depending on how these values are explicated and defended and how they are related to a theory of right (as applied to actions, general rules for action, and/or social institutions), Marx's implicit moral theory might turn out to be a species of any one of a number of moral theories. Is Marx a utilitarian, his objections to this school of thought and especially raking criticisms of Jeremy Bentham notwithstanding? If so, is he a hedonistic or eudaemonistic utilitarian? Or is his moral theory most plausibly interpreted as prefiguring contemporary utilitarianism, which takes the satisfaction of preferences (or considered preferences) to be the basic nonmoral good to be maximized? Is Marx, instead, a nonutilitarian consequentialist, for example, a perfectionist, a self-realization theorist, or a consequentialist who takes freedom to be the basic nonmoral good to be actualized without further giving a utilitarian justification of freedom? Or does he, instead, hold a deontological or mixed deontological moral theory? If so, is he a natural law theorist, a rational-will theorist, a Kantian, or a deontologist who takes principles of social justice and/or human rights as basic?

In the present chapter I argue against the claims that Marx is a straightforward utilitarian and that the three primary values are, in fact, reducible to considerations of utility in any sense, (e.g., pleasure, happiness, welfare, or the satisfaction of preferences). I also argue against the claim that he is a nonutilitarian consequentialist: he is not, I argue, a consequentialist of any sort. His moral theory, I suggest, is a *mixed deontological theory*, a theory of right action or obligation that recommends the promotion of one or more types of nonmoral good—freedom, human community, and self-realization in Marx's case—but holds that the criterion of right action is not simply the maximization of the nonmoral good. This type of moral theory holds that there are other right-making characteristics of actions, rules for action, and/or social policies and institutions, for example, treating people as ends in themselves or treating people fairly or respecting people's rights.

In this chapter and the next, I am primarily concerned with rationally reconstructing Marx's implicit moral theory (or set of moral views) rather than with arguing that Marx or Marxists should accept a certain moral theory. These two questions are distinct—the first is an exegetical question and the second a question of substantive moral theory—and it is quite possible for them to have divergent answers.

Consequentialism, Utilitarianism, and Deontological Moral Theory

Marx's moral perspective has been identified, at one time or another, with almost all of the types of moral theory mentioned above. In the late nineteenth and early twentieth centuries, such evolutionary socialists as Eduard Bernstein and Karl Vorlander found Marx to be a Kantian. While explicitly rejecting morality as "ideological" and "unscientific," such "scientific socialists" as Engels and Karl Kautsky can often be found to be implicitly espousing a rather unsophisticated brand of utilitarianism. Since Engels and Kautsky viewed their own work as a continuation and elaboration of Marx's views, it seems fair to surmise that they found him to be a proponent of the same approach though, of course, even to suggest that Marx was operating with a moral theory during the height of the era of Scientific Socialism would have been a faux pas of major proportions—at least among orthodox Marxists.

More recently, such disparate philosophers as Adam Schaff, Derek P. H. Allen, and Allen E. Buchanan have suggested that Marx's moral evaluations are basically utilitarian in nature. John Somerville, Richard Miller, and Hilliard Aronovitch, on the other hand, defend the view that Marx is a nonutilitarian consequentialist who demands the maximization of all or some of the following values: self-determination, self-realization, and mutuality, i.e., human community or solidarity. Those who take the latter position usually see important similarities between the moral views of Marx and those of Aristotle. However, all of these interpretations see Marx's moral views as consequentialist in nature. By "consequentialism" I mean a theory of moral obligation holding that those actions that maximize some specified nonmoral good (or goods) are morally right actions and, by extension, those rules for action, social policies, and social institutions that maximize the specified nonmoral good (or goods) are not merely morally good but morally "right" in the sense that one has a moral obligation to support and promote them.

"Utilitarianism," as I shall use the term, is a consequentialist theory that specifies pleasure, happiness, or the preferences people have as the nonmoral good to be maximized. There is, of course, a broader sense of utilitarianism in which it is "the view that the right act is the act which will actually or probably produce at least as much intrinsic good, directly or indirectly, as any other action open to the agent in question."[1] But this definition simply makes every form of consequentialism a form of utilitarianism and, by doing so, obscures certain distinctions that ought to remain clear. As William Frankena notes, "On this interpretation, traditional utilitarianism is one species of utilitarianism—that which regards pleasure as the good. Ideal utilitarianism, on the other hand, holds that other things besides pleasure are good."[2] I shall not utilize the category of ideal utilitarianism in this work: in my system of classification such a theory is a form of nonutilitarian consequentialism.

By restricting utilitarianism as above we can keep those (utilitarian) moral theories that are exclusively concerned with producing certain desirable *states of mind* (occurrent and/or dispositional) from those consequentialist theories that are not exclusively concerned with desirable states of mind but, instead, call for the maximization of such nonmoral goods as power, knowledge, wisdom, beauty, human perfection, the realization of human (or "truly human") potentialities, or freedom. Any form of consequentialism calling for the maximization of one or more of these nonmoral goods or of similar (nonmentalistic) nonmoral goods is—in the system of classification adopted here—a form of nonutilitarian consequentialism. There may, of course, be cases in which it is not clear under which category a nonmoral good falls. The nonmoral good of *love*—an item that, together with pleasure, knowledge, wisdom, and the sense of beauty, is intrinsically good in the "ideal

[1] William K. Frankena, *Dictionary of Philosophy* (Dagobert D. Runes, ed.), Littlefield, Adams, and Co., 1958, p. 327.
[2] Ibid.

utilitarian" theory of G. E. Moore—seems particularly troublesome in this respect.

"Maximization" may be interpreted as the maximization of the sum total nonmoral good, of the average nonmoral good (mean or median), or any weighted alternative thereof. This will make no difference for our purposes. The main points we shall be concerned with in judging the various consequentialist interpretations of Marx are: (1) the nature of the nonmoral goods to be maximized and (2) the strategy of maximization per se.

Contrary to this sort of interpretation, a number of recent and contemporary philosophers see Marx as holding a deontological or mixed deontological moral theory. Sidney Hook made this suggestion in *Towards the Understanding of Karl Marx* in 1933. Eugene Kamenka—while stressing Marx's acceptance of the values as freedom (as self-determination), human community, and self-realization—takes the same general position in a more recent work, *The Ethical Foundations of Marxism*. Even more recently, Marxist humanists of the Yugoslav Praxis group—such as Mihaelo Marković and Svetozar Stojanović—have stressed Marx's commitment to the concept of human dignity as well as to freedom (as self-determination) and self-realization and have concluded that Marx is not a utilitarian but some sort of deontologist. George Brenkert takes a similar position in various articles and in his book *Marx's Ethics of Freedom*. He argues that Marx is a mixed deontologist who takes freedom and human autonomy as his most fundamental values.

By a "deontological" moral theory I mean, with Frankena, any theory "which does not make the theory of obligation entirely dependent on the theory of value, holding that an action may be known to be right . . . even though . . . it does not by being performed, bring into being as much good as some other action open to the agent."[3] By a *"strict* deontological" theory I mean one that holds that "an action may be known to be right without consideration of the goodness of anything,"[4] i.e., without bringing under consideration the production of any sort of *nonmoral* good whatever. (This, I take it, is Kant's position even though in his detailed arguments for particular moral maxims he often brings the production of certain nonmoral goods under consideration.) Arguably, Robert Nozick is also a strict deontologist.

[3] Ibid., p. 76.
[4] Ibid.

By a "*mixed* deontological" theory I mean a moral theory that considers the production of the (specified) nonmoral goods as a relevant consideration but holds, nonetheless, that the right action may not be the one that maximizes the nonmoral good. The production of the nonmoral good may be constrained, for example, by principles of its distribution or by other principles of right that are not themselves validated on the basis of their production or maximization of the nonmoral good. John Rawls and William K. Frankena are examples of contemporary moral philosophers holding mixed deontological theories.

Sometimes it is difficult to decide how to classify a particular theory or theorist. For example, if we are to take his explicit proclamations as good coin, J. S. Mill is not a mixed deontological theorist even though his theory contains both principles specifying the nonmoral good to be maximized and principles (of justice and human rights) that seem to govern its distribution. According to Mill, his principles of justice and human rights are secondary moral principles that are validated by the fact that, if recognized and followed, they will in the long run maximize utility. Consequently, he is committed to the claim that if such principles of justice and human rights did not, in fact, maximize the nonmoral good over the long run, they would not be justified as moral principles and their "violation" would not be, as such, a moral wrong—a thesis, one suspects, that would be difficult for Mill to swallow, despite his explicit statements. Mill—like most sophisticated utilitarians—would, of course, insist that this question is purely academic since the requirements of utility and those of our commonsense notions of justice do not, in reality, diverge. Nevertheless, if one could get Mill (or any other consequentialist) to take the side of the requirements of justice over those of utility even in purely hypothetical situations, one would thereby prove that she or he is, in reality, a mixed deontologist rather than a true-blue consequentialist. Despite his explicit proclamations to the contrary, I believe a strong case can be made for the thesis that J. S. Mill is, in reality, a mixed deontologist in consequentialist clothing.

As long as we are on the subject of J. S. Mill—Marx's great contemporary —there are two observations worth making on the connection between these two figures. First, the utilitarianism that Marx criticized was not that of J. S. Mill but that of Bentham, James Mill, and the French Encyclopedists. Second, to the extent that Marx knew of J. S. Mill's views, he actually expresses considerable respect for certain of them. As to the first point, George Brenkert notes that

> Marx's criticism was made primarily against Holbach, Helvetius, Bentham, and James Mill. John Stuart Mill's work on utilitarianism, as well as his monograph entitled *Utilitarianism*, did not appear until long after Marx had settled his philosophical conscience with regard to utilitarianism. . . . the utilitarianism Marx had in view was hedonistic, quantitative, and dependent upon associationist psychology for its answer to egoism.[5]

As to the second point, Marx was not undiscerning in his assessment of the various utilitarians. In volume 1 of *Capital*, for example, after calling Bentham an "arch-Philistine" and "that insipid, pedantic, leather-tongued oracle of the ordinary bourgeois intelligence of the 19th century," Marx is quick to note that "it would be wrong to class [men like J. S. Mill] with the herd of vulgar economic apologists."[6] Marx makes this assessment after approvingly quoting the following passage from Mill's *Principles of Political Economy*: "The really exhausting and the really repulsive labours instead of being better paid than others, are almost invariably paid the worst of all. . . . The more revolting the occupation, the more certain it is to receive the minimum of remuneration. . . . The hardships and earnings, instead of being directly proportional, as in any just arrangements of society they would be, are generally in an inverse ratio to one another."[7] In terms of their moral perspectives the two are, in fact, in certain respects quite similar.

With these definitions and clarifications in mind, let us proceed to examine the claim that Marx is a utilitarian of one sort or another.

---

[5] Brenkert, "Marx's Critique of Utilitarianism," p. 199.

[6] Marx, *Capital*, vol. 1, p. 611ff.

[7] Ibid., pp. 610ff. A comparison of the moral and social theories of these two great thinkers is well worthwhile. For a review of their probable knowledge of one another's work, see Lewis S. Feuer, "John Stuart Mill and Marxian Socialism," *Journal of the History of Ideas*, vol. 10 (Apr. 1949). For a comparison and contrast of their moral and social theories, see Abram L. Harris, "John Stuart Mill's Theory of Progress," *Ethics*, vol. 66, no. 3 (Apr. 1956); Gerald Dworkin, "Marx and Mill: A Dialogue," *Philosophy and Phenomenological Research*, vol. 26 (Mar. 1966); Graeme Duncan, *Marx and Mill: Two Views of Social Conflict*, Cambridge University Press, N.Y., 1973; and Arneson, "Mill's Doubts about Freedom under Socialism."

Marx as a Utilitarian: A Critique

As mentioned previously, many writers take Marx to be basically a utilitarian. There does not, however, seem to be a consensus as to what type of utilitarian he is. Ignoring the differences between maximizing sum total utility, average utility, and so forth, the various types of utilitarianism are differentiated according to their specific theories of the good. Hedonistic utilitarianism takes pleasure to be the summum bonum, the intrinsic good to be maximized. Eudaemonistic utilitarianism considers happiness to be the highest good. Preference utilitarianism takes the satisfaction of preferences—regardless of their causal connections to pleasure and pain or happiness and unhappiness—to be the highest good.

Among contemporary writers, the Polish Marxist philosopher Adam Schaff takes Marx to be a eudaemonistic or perhaps even a hedonistic utilitarian. In the English-speaking world Derek P. H. Allen is one of the most tenacious defenders of the utilitarian interpretation of Marx. Although it is sometimes not clear whether Allen interprets Marx as a eudaemonistic or a preference utilitarian, he claims, of Marx and Engels, that "their arguments are the kind used by utilitarians although not expressed in utilitarian vocabulary. . . . the arguments which support their moral judgments are utilitarian in all but name."[8] Examples of these utilitarian arguments are, according to Allen, those in favor of free trade and of certain cases of colonialism. Marx and Engels were in favor of free trade (i.e., against national tariffs) because "the free trade system is destructive. It . . . pushes the antagonism of the proletariat and the bourgeoisie to the extreme point. In a word, the free trade system hastens the social revolution."[9] Similarly, they were in favor of British colonialism in India because, according to Allen, the question for them was, "Can mankind fulfill its destiny without a fundamental revolution in the social state of Asia? If not, whatever may have been the crimes of England she was the unconscious tool of history in bringing about the revolution."[10] Allen's reasoning seems to be that since Marx obviously believes that communism will satisfy more people's needs and/or preferences than capitalism does or can, his decision to support the long-term interests of the proletariat over its short-term interests is simply a piece of

[8] Allen, "The Utilitarianism of Marx and Engels," p. 189.
[9] Ibid., p. 192.
[10] Ibid., p. 196.

utilitarian reasoning. It is dubious, however, that these arguments in and of themselves prove that Marx is a utilitarian or, more generally, a consequentialist. As Brenkert points out in his article "Marx and Utilitarianism,"

> The simple appearance in Marx's writings of the consideration of consequences is not sufficient to establish that Marx is a utilitarian. The crucial point is in what way the consequences are regarded. . . . He may accept principles of efficiency which are subordinate to a non-consequentialist determination of moral ends.[11]

In a subsequent article ("Marx's Critique of Utilitarianism"), Brenkert explains that

> a non-utilitarian need not reject principles of efficiency—principles which approve of something being done because it promotes a certain end. The crucial point is that the end promoted is not itself justified simply on the basis of its consequences. This point can be illustrated by reference to Kant, whose ethics (I assume) is non-controversially non-utilitarian. In "Perpetual Peace" Kant argued that governments should be representative because such governments are less likely to make war. This is an argument which takes consequences into account; but it does not therefore follow that the ethical theory which underlies Kant's views on war, governments, human actions, etc., is a utilitarian one. So it is with Marx's views. True, he does consider the consequences of various actions. It would be absurd for him not to do so. But such considerations do not undercut the argument . . . that Marx was not a utilitarian.[12]

The mere fact that Marx considers consequences in his moral reasoning does not settle the issue of whether he is a consequentialist (e.g., a utilitarian) or a deontologist in his implicit moral views. Therefore, let us proceed with our examination of utilitarian interpretations of Marx. Allen E. Buchanan—while offering a number of important caveats—also gives Marx's moral theory a utilitarian interpretation. In considering how it is that Marx can condemn capitalism and commend socialism in his later works once he has given up the normative concept of "species-being" or "truly human nature" of his early works in favor of a purely

[11] Brenkert, "Marx and Utilitarianism," p. 427.
[12] Brenkert, "Marx's Critique of Utilitarianism," p. 218.

descriptive "Protean core concept" of human nature, Buchanan proposes:

> One initially plausible answer is that the Protean concept focuses on the idea that human history is basically the activity of *satisfying needs* and that Marx's sole criterion of evaluation is simply the extent to which this activity is successful. On this interpretation, capitalism is condemned not because it is unjust or immoral, or because it does not accord with human nature, but because it fails at the constitutive task of all human societies: it fails to satisfy needs. Communism, then, is not superior because it better measures up to principles of justice, or other moral ideals, or because it actualizes human nature, but simply because it better satisfies needs. And progress in history in general is to be gauged by the same simple criterion of satisfaction. . . . on this interpretation, success in the satisfaction of basic and nonbasic needs, or of needs and desires, is Marx's ultimate evaluative yard-stick.[13]

On this interpretation, in other words, Marx is best reconstructed as a preference utilitarian. Buchanan goes on to argue that Marx favored only the satisfaction of *undistorted* preferences, that is, preferences people would have in a nonexploitative society in which social relations are clear rather than opaque, as they are in capitalism. (We shall return to this issue presently.) There is, however, one more point we should note before leaving Buchanan's initial analysis and turning to Marx's explicit and nonexplicit (but reconstructable) criticisms of utilitarianism. Buchanan's interpretation is based on attributing to Marx the primary demand that human needs be satisfied and, as Buchanan notes,

> "needs" should not be interpreted narrowly as "subsistence needs," for Marx makes it clear that while communism will do a better job of discharging the first task of human society its superiority is not limited to this. The full satisfaction of basic needs is for Marx only the prerequisite for the pursuit and satisfaction of the need for creative production and for the all-around development of the autonomous, socially integrated individual.[14]

The important point here is that the concept of needs seems to imply a moral perspective on which it is more important to satisfy

[13] Buchanan, *Marx and Justice*, pp. 28–29.
[14] Ibid., p. 29.

needs than to satisfy desires or preferences that are not needs and, if one further distinguishes between basic and nonbasic needs, that it is also more important to satisfy basic rather than nonbasic needs. If it is the case that Marx—according to Buchanan's interpretation—does not merely give a somewhat greater weight to needs but, instead, gives to them an absolute preference over desires or preferences that do not qualify as needs, then it cannot be the case for Marx that (even) a great number of mere desires or preferences on the part of some people ought to be satisfied at the cost of not satisfying other people's needs. If this is a correct reconstruction of Buchanan's interpretation of Marx, then Buchanan may not—strictly speaking—be interpreting Marx as a utilitarian or a consequentialist because he is implicitly attributing to Marx a principle of distribution of the nonmoral good and not just a principle of maximization. (The reason I say "may not" is that one could claim that this principle of the priority of needs has the status of a secondary moral principle which, if followed, will maximize utility in the long run.)

Let us retrace our steps, however, and first examine the claim that Marx is a hedonistic or eudaemonistic utilitarian who takes happiness as the good to be maximized in a narrow sense of the term, the sense indicating only satisfaction or contentment rather than, say, human flourishing. Adam Schaff claims, for example, that "Marx's point of arrival, the object of his endeavors is man in general, the happiness of every human individual."[15] Marx is a humanist, Schaff claims, where "by humanism we mean a system of reflection on man which, regarding him as the supreme good, aims at providing in practice the best conditions for human happiness."[16] In *A Philosophy of Man*, Schaff writes that "Marxist theory . . . leads to the general position that may be called 'social hedonism'—the view that the aim of human life is to secure the maximum happiness for the broadest masses of the people, and that only within the compass of this aim, can personal happiness be realized. . . . socialist humanism is indeed a variety of 'social hedonism.' "[17]

However, whether or not someone who calls for the maximization of happiness is a eudaemonistic utilitarian, as I am using the term, depends on whether we give a broad or narrow interpretation to the term "happiness." On the narrow interpretation, eu-

[15] Schaff, "Marxist Humanism," p. 184.
[16] Ibid., p. 181.
[17] Schaff, *A Philosophy of Man*, p. 60.

daemonistic utilitarianism is very similar to hedonistic utilitarianism. They are both concerned to produce the most satisfying states of mind, but whereas hedonistic utilitarianism believes such states to consist solely of occurrent states of pleasure (and the absence of pain), the eudaemonistic utilitarian believes that other states of mind besides pleasure and pain are intrinsically valuable and usually takes into consideration dispositional as well as occurrent states. (Happiness is, after all, more of a dispositional than an occurrent property of persons.)

There is, however, a broader interpretation of "happiness," according to which to speak of human happiness is to speak of human well-being or human flourishing—concepts that are not completely cashable in terms of such states of mind. "Human flourishing" seems to indicate growth and development, satisfaction and successful or productive activity as well as desirable states of mind. That there is such a broader concept of happiness seems to be borne out by the fact that *eudaemonia*, the term used by Aristotle to refer to activity in accordance with human virtue or excellence, can be translated as "happiness," "well-being," or "flourishing."

The proposal that Marx is a hedonistic utilitarian or a eudaemonistic utilitarian in the narrow sense is perhaps the easiest to refute. As we have seen, he values freedom, self-realization, and human community and does not attempt to reduce them to the pleasure that the realization of these values tends to produce. Marx condemns Fourier, for example, for attempting to reduce "free labor" to the notion of play and claims, "Really free labor, the composing of music for example, is at the same time damned serious and demands the greatest effort."[18] Perhaps the hedonistic utilitarian could invoke the doctrine of psychological hedonism at this point and maintain that the composer or artist who suffers to create and even the stranger who rushes into a burning building to save a child's life are in pursuit of the greatest balance of pleasure over pain (once we calculate both physical and psychological pleasure and pain) and thus maintain that this quote from Marx doesn't prove that he rejects hedonism as a theory of the good. But there are two points to be made against this suggestion. First, the proponents of hedonistic psychological egoism can remain faithful to their doctrine in the face of the above counter-examples only on pain of emptying their "theory" of all empirical content.

[18] Marx, *The Grundrisse*, p. 124.

(What could possibly count as evidence against this theory if the example of the complete stranger rushing into a burning building in an attempt to save others does not?) Second, the interpretative question concerning Marx's substantive moral views does not hinge on whether or not the composer is really doing what is going to maximize the balance of pleasure over pain or happiness over unhappiness but, rather, on whether or not Marx would hold that the composer's activity is commendable or laudatory even though it does not maximize pleasure or happiness. It seems quite clear from our previous discussion that Marx would see the composer's labors as laudatory or "worthy of human dignity" even if they did not maximize pleasure and, indeed, even if they created a substantial deficit of pain over pleasure or dissatisfaction over satisfaction in the composer's life. We need only remember that in Marx's concept of human nature the two essential (and transhistorical) human capacities are those for free, conscious, creative activity and for human community and that Marx's characterization of human nature is not purely descriptive but also evaluative. That is, even in his later works Marx is not only claiming that human beings have these two capacities but is advocating they be realized. (One need only review such passages as the one on the realms of necessity and freedom in the third volume of *Capital* to see that this is true.)

Even the attempt to reduce Marx's three primary values, which provide the moral basis for his evaluative characterization of human nature (or his normative concept of the human individual) to secondary moral rules for the promotion of pleasure is implausible—and for the same reasons. It seems clear that he would remain faithful to these principles even if their acceptance and implementation would not produce the greatest balance of pleasure over pain in the long run. His very concept of human nature as a bundle of capacities or potentialities that can be objectified and realized only through activity or *praxis* seems to be the antithesis of the classical hedonistic utilitarian's view of human nature as a collection of appetites to be satisfied. Marx asks, for example, "What is life but activity?" and continues, "In the type of life activity resides the whole character of a species, its species-character; and free, conscious activity is the species-character of human beings."[19] The basic notions in Marx's vision of human beings are

[19] Marx, *Economic and Philosophical Manuscripts*, pp. 126–127.

activity and realization; the basic notions in the hedonistic utilitarian's vision are appetite and satiation.

A related reason to reject the utilitarian interpretation of Marx is that the utilitarian is generally committed to an individualistic, egoistic conception of the individual's interests vis-à-vis the general interest (or common good). As shown in chapter 1, Marx's value of human community, as incorporated in his normative concept of human nature, sees as possible and recommends the transcendence of the distinction between individual and social interests, and the private and public good. Now whether the total coincidence of the individual and social interest is possible is perhaps dubious, but it is clear that—to whatever extent this is possible—it is favored by Marx. Compare, for example, the following two passages, the first from an 1853 *New York Tribune* article in which Marx comments on the phenomena of desperation and suicide in the bourgeois societies of his era, and the second from the *Paris Manuscripts* in which he reflects upon what for him must have been a harbinger of future communist society:

> What sort of society is it, in truth, where one finds several millions in deepest loneliness, where one can be overcome by an irresistible longing to kill oneself without anyone discovering it? This society is not a society; it is, as Rousseau says, a desert populated by wild animals.[20]

> When communist artisans form associations, teaching and propaganda are their first aims. But their association itself creates a new need—*a need for society*—and what appeared to be a means has become an end. The most striking results of this practical development are to be seen when French socialist workers meet together. Smoking, eating, and drinking are no longer simply means of bringing people together. Society, association, entertainment which also has society as its aim, is sufficient for them; the *brotherhood of man* is not an empty phrase but a reality, and the *nobility of man* shines forth upon us from their well-torn bodies.[21]

That Marx held human community or mutuality to be intrinsically valuable seems beyond doubt. (We shall do well to keep the latter passage in mind when we consider the purported "problem" of revolutionary motivation at the end of chapter 4.)

[20] Cited in Eugene Kamenka, *The Ethical Foundations of Marxism*, p. 36.
[21] Marx, *Economic and Philosophical Manuscripts*, p. 176.

Proponents of utilitarianism may object, however, that their theory does not necessarily mitigate against such feelings. This is perfectly true. In fact, given that such feelings are perhaps essential to human happiness and well-being, the consistent utilitarian may well uphold this value and commend its adoption. But this does not get to the root of the Marxist criticism because, as Brenkert puts it:

> Whether I am a private individual who prefers to live emotionally and psychologically detached from others, who sees in the interests of others threats to my own interests, or a social individual who desires a close identification with others, who sees in the interests of others a fulfillment and realisation of my own interests, is not as such a question for utilitarianism. Whether one is closely identified with others or is only distantly, neutrally, abstractly related to others through their products, money, etc. is indifferent to utilitarianism. Utilitarian theory itself does not demand that people identify closely with others, that they experience each other such that they share enjoyments or share in the significance of their own creations.[22]

Utilitarians may be willing to accept human community as a secondary moral value or principle of efficiency in the real world because, as things happen to be, accepting this value tends to maximize utility (pleasure, happiness, preference satisfaction, etc.). Nevertheless, if this were not the case, then utilitarians would not accept this value. Human community is not intrinsically valuable for utilitarians, only instrumentally valuable (if at all). Whether or not Marx is right on this score vis-a-vis the utilitarians and whether the value of human community should enter into an adequate moral and social theory are, of course, completely different questions.

Marx and Marxists also tend to object to utilitarianism on the grounds that if—as a matter of contingent fact—people desire, get pleasure from, or are happy due to participation in antagonistic and exploitative social relationships, such relationships may well be morally justified on utilitarian grounds. Since exploited persons tend not to get pleasure or happiness from their subordinate social positions, this will be true only if the pleasure or happiness of those in the dominant positions outweighs the displeasure or un-

---

[22] Brenkert, "Marx's Critique of Utilitarianism," p. 202.

happiness of those in the exploited, subordinate positions (and no other alternative set of social arrangements offers a greater balance of pleasure over pain or happiness over unhappiness). But in this case such relationships of dominance and exploitation are—for the utilitarian—morally justified. This would obviously be an objectionable assessment to Marx and must therefore count against interpreting him as a utilitarian.

But why is this? Why is it that Marx would find such an assessment objectionable? As we have already seen in chapter 1, one reason is that he views such relations of dominance and exploitation as constituting violations of freedom, which is perhaps his most cherished and deeply held value. Another reason, I submit, is that Marx finds the fulfillment and, indeed, the very existence of desires for dominance and feelings of social superiority morally objectionable. He believes that such desires (for dominance, power over others, symbols of material wealth) are created, or at least promoted, by capitalism and will not be characteristic of the completely socialized and humanized individuals he believes will populate communist society. Although one might be tempted to go from this fact directly to the conclusion that Marx denies one of the utilitarian's basic theses—namely, that all desires are *prima facie* equally worthy of satisfaction—one must proceed carefully at this point. There are actually three different theses involved here: (1) every desire is *prima facie* equally worthy of satisfaction; (2) some desires are better than others; and (3) capitalism produces distorted desires, and socialism (or communism) will produce undistorted desires on the part of individuals.[23]

Let us examine these three theses in reverse order. It is clear that Marx holds the third thesis. He believes the structure of capitalist society gives rise to such "distorted" desires as those for dominance and of symbols of material wealth. He believes that the structure of capitalism gives rise to the fetishism of money, commodities, and capital and the associated desire to be materially— as opposed to "spiritually"—wealthy. In Marx's vision of communist society, on the other hand,

> in place of the *wealth* and *poverty* of political economy, we have the *wealthy* man and the plentitude of *human* need. The wealthy man is at the same time one who *needs* a complex of

[23] I would like to thank Allen E. Buchanan for pointing out these distinctions to me.

human manifestations of life, and whose own self-realization exists as an inner necessity, a *need*.[24]

While, for the most part, it is only Marxists and other opponents of capitalism who accept the third thesis, a great many more people accept the second one. Although there is not universal agreement on this point, it is my contention that Marx is among them. He writes, for example, "The pleasure of all hitherto existing classes and estates have inevitably been either juvenile and tedious, or else coarse because they have always been divorced from the over-all life-activity of individuals."[25] In his earlier works he also often distinguishes "animal" from "human" functions or desires and "civilized" from "crude" or "barbarous" needs.

> Within the system of private property . . . needs become an *ingenious* and always *calculating* subservience to inhuman, depraved, unnatural, and *imaginary* appetites. Private property does not know how to change crude need into *human* need. . . .[26]

> No eunuch flatters his tyrant more shamefully or seeks by more infamous means to stimulate his *jaded appetite*, in order to gain some favor, than does the eunuch of industry, the entrepreneur, in order to acquire a few silver coins or to charm the gold from the purse of his dearly beloved neighbor. . . . The entrepreneur accedes to *the most depraved fancies* of his neighbor, plays the role of pander between him and his needs, awakes *unhealthy appetites* in him, and watches for every weakness so that later on he may claim remuneration for his labour of love[27] [emphasis added].

In his later works as well it seems obvious that Marx holds that some desires are better than others (e.g., the desire to cooperate as opposed to the desire to dominate), but the question we must now ask is whether or not he holds the first thesis, that all desires are *prima facie* equally worthy of satisfaction. Although Marx disapproves of some desires, there is, to my knowledge, no evidence that he thought such "distorted" desires hadn't even a *prima facie* claim to being satisfied. Most of these desires, of course, should

[24] Marx, *Economic and Philosophical Manuscripts*, pp. 164–165.
[25] Marx and Engels, *Historisch-Kritische Gesamtausgabe, erste Abteilung*, vol. V, pp. 396–397, as cited in R. Tucker, *Philosophy and Myth in Karl Marx*, p. 17.
[26] Marx, *Economic and Philosophical Manuscripts*, p. 168.
[27] Ibid., p. 169.

not be allowed to be satisfied on Marx's view, because this would entail harm to others, e.g., a limitation on the freedom of those in subordinate social positions. Furthermore, he undoubtedly thought that people with undistorted as opposed to distorted desires are in some sense better or more worthy and that a society that produces individuals having undistorted desires is better than one that does the opposite. This does not mean, however, that he would have disagreed with William James' famous dictum—"Take any demand, however slight, which any creature, however weak, may make. Ought it not, for its own sole sake, to be satisfied? If not, prove why not"[28]—at least when applied exclusively to human beings.

If we assume that Marx accepts the first thesis, however, there are still two ways we can reconstruct his view, depending on what position he takes on the second thesis, i.e., that some desires are better than others. If we interpret Marx as not holding this position, if we take him to agree with Bentham that—all things being equal—pushpin is as good as poetry or, more to the point, the desire to dominate is as good as the desire to cooperate, then we could, as Buchanan notes,

> evaluate a given form of society according to the extent to which it succeeds in satisfying the desires which *it* engenders. We judge that there is progress in history if (in general) later social forms do a better job of satisfying the desires they engender than earlier forms did in satisfying the desires they engendered. On this reading, Marx criticizes capitalism only for its failure to satisfy, or to satisfy fully, the desires characteristic of capitalist man, while he praises communism for its ability to satisfy fully the distinctive desires of communist man.[29]

But in reality, of course, Marx does not think all desires are equally worthy but, rather, that some desires are better than others. "He recognized," writes Kamenka, ". . . that human demands are not ultimates: that we might as well judge a society by the demands it *creates* as by the demands it satisfies."[30] As Buchanan notes of the previous suggested strategy for evaluating societies:

[28] William James, "The Moral Philosopher and the Moral Life." In *Essays in Pragmatism* (Albury Castell, ed.). Hafner Publishing Co., N.Y., 1969, p. 73.
[29] Buchanan, *Marx and Justice*, p. 29.
[30] Kamenka, *The Ethical Foundations of Marxism*, p. 95.

This interpretation . . . cannot be right, for it overlooks Marx's emphasis on the qualitative differences between the desires of capitalist man and those said to be distinctive of communist man. The former Marx portrays as slavish, destructive, in conflict with one another, and grounded in a consciousness that is distorted by the alienated social relations of class-divided society.[31]

But this brings us to a perennial problem with utilitarianism, namely, that it leaves no room (or very little) for a critique of the preferences people happen to have. J. S. Mill tried to provide grounds for such a critique with his "choice criterion of value," but it is doubtful that this modification really solves the problem. After all, we may still condemn some of the Marquis de Sade's preferences and activities, even if he had experienced a broad range of desires and activities and thus had met the condition of Mill's choice criterion of value.

In an attempt to get around this criticism of utilitarianism and thus improve the chances of successfully interpreting Marx as a utilitarian, Buchanan goes on to claim:

A promising way of capturing Marx's emphasis on the qualitative differences between communist and capitalist desires might be, then, to understand it as corresponding to a distinction between *distorted* and *undistorted* desires. Marx describes communism as a form of society in which relations among persons are no longer distorted, but rather transparent and thoroughly intelligible. In communism the gap between the surface appearances of social life and the underlying reality— the chasm Marx strives to bridge in *Capital*—will no longer exist. Utilizing this distinction, we might then say that for Marx the superiority of communism is not simply that it makes possible the fullest satisfaction of the desires it engenders, but that . . . Communism, and only communism, makes possible the fullest satisfaction of those desires which persons at this state of history would have or would develop, were their consciousness, and hence their desires, not distorted by the positions they occupy in class-society.[32]

This maneuver is, of course, the familiar one of attempting to save utilitarianism by qualifying the desires whose satisfactions

[31] Buchanan, *Marx and Justice*, p. 29.
[32] Ibid., p. 30.

are to be maximized, but with a new, Marxist twist. The normal, non-Marxist version of this strategy is simply to qualify the desires to be maximized as *considered* or something of the sort. (This is more or less a rendition of J. S. Mill's choice criterion of value. It is also the sort of utilitarianism Derek P. H. Allen puts forward as being adequate to account for Marx's moral reasoning.) The Marxist twist added here is to demand, further, that these desires not be distorted by (distorting) social relations.

To say these desires are "distorted," of course, is to do more than describe them; it is also to evaluate them (negatively). In attributing the distinction between distorted and undistorted desires to Marx, we might have in mind Marx's normative conception of human nature so prevalent in his early works. On this view, *distorted* desires deviate from human nature, whereas *undistorted* desires conform to human nature and, by doing so, are "truly human." One might, on the other hand, attribute this distinction to Marx without invoking the notion of "truly human" as used in his early works. But if this is done, one must keep in mind that—on pain of attributing a particularly gross form of the naturalistic fallacy to Marx—one cannot merely say that distorted desires are those that appear in capitalism and undistorted desires are those that will appear in communism. It is clear that "distorted" and "undistorted" are evaluative terms in this context and that their (negative) evaluative meaning must come from something more than the mere fact that they are bound to appear in different forms of society.

Perhaps the force of this strategy actually derives from the fact that—if Marx's theory of fetishism in capitalist society and associated theories are correct—the desires that arise in communist society come closer to being the product of fully effective, deliberative rationality than do those that arise in capitalist society or, in general, in the context of "distorted" social relations. The former arise under conditions in which social relations are viewed clearly, and the latter arise under conditions in which the nature of social relations is obscured. Still—if one is assuming only a narrow, means-ends view of rationality—the fact that certain desires are arrived at more rationally than others cannot account for the fact that they are better, worthier, or more commendable—something Marx also clearly believes. Furthermore, Buchanan's strategy seems to put an immense burden on an empirical theory—the "materialist theory of consciousness," which is to "explain both the distortions of consciousness in pre-communist society and the evolution of undistorted consciousness in the transition from capitalism to communism"[33]—that has not even been developed. If this is the risk one must take in order to interpret Marx successfully along utilitarian lines, one naturally tends to wonder if there might not be better alternatives. Buchanan, for example, admits there is one that may even be "more promising":

> Either the superiority of communism and the radical defects of capitalism are to be gauged by the standard of the satisfaction of undistorted desires or by reference to a set of ideals, including autonomy and community, which are not reducible to the standard of satisfaction. The former strategy is unsatisfactory because it either commits us to the yet unsupported view that undistorted desires will turn out to be the very desires Marx attributes to the members of communist society or to the uninspiring claim that communism is superior simply because it maximizes satisfaction, where the qualitative character of the desires is itself of no significance. The second strategy, though more promising, is also not without difficulties: it leaves us with a set of distinctive normative ideals which can be and have been challenged. To say that these ideals are not adequately supported by Marx is not, of course, to say they are unsupportable.[34]

It is this second alternative that I am putting forward. It remains to be seen, however, how such moral ideals as autonomy or freedom (as self determination) and self-realization figure into an adequate interpretation of Marx as well as into an adequate Marxist moral and social theory if these two happen to diverge. Even if we agree that such moral ideals are to play the roles mentioned by Buchanan, there are still two ways they can be utilized in a theory of moral obligation or right action: (1) as nonmoral goods to be maximized or (2) as the basis for principles of right that are not dependent on the maximization of the nonmoral good. In the next section I hope to show that the former (maximization) strategy will not do as an interpretation of Marx's moral views and that a better interpretation is that they form a sort of mixed deontological moral theory. I shall argue, further, that an adequate Marxist moral theory cannot be a form of utilitarianism or (nonutilitarian) consequentialism because all forms of consequentialism have certain crucial faults.

[33] Ibid., p. 31.
[34] Ibid., p. 35.

99

Marx and Nonutilitarian Forms of Consequentialism

Even if I have shown that Marx is not a utilitarian, I have not yet demonstrated that he is not a consequentialist of any sort. I shall now argue against the thesis that Marx is a nonutilitarian consequentialist.

Most of those who interpret Marx's implicit moral theory as a form of nonutilitarian consequentialism see substantial similarities between Marx and Aristotle. John Somerville goes so far as to claim, "In a sense, Marx equals Aristotle *minus* aristocracy *plus* historical science."[35] Both Aristotle and Marx, according to Somerville, agree that "value arises out of the built-in needs, desires and potentialities of development of man"[36] but

> from Marx's standpoint . . . though Aristotle understood correctly the relation between ethics and politics, value and science, social theory and social practice, what Aristotle lacked was a significant theory of history, a theory about the causal dynamics of large-scale socio-historical changes, and the effect of these changes upon ethics, politics, value, science, theory and practice.[37]

Somerville also notes that for Aristotle "there is a word for the overall good that everyone wants: happiness."[38] From these comments we can presumably deduce that the following characterization of ethics is meant by Somerville to apply to both Marx and Aristotle:

> Ethics must be a theory of how to attain human happiness. What human happiness is and how man can attain it naturally depend on the kind of being man is, on how man is made, on his needs, wants and potentialities, all of which is empirically determinable. Two things stand out: man is a rational animal, and man is a political animal. So the attainment of happiness depends primarily upon two things: the full development and application of man's intelligence, and the setting up of a society whose institutions are deliberately geared to the attainment of maximum human happiness.[39]

[35] Somerville, "The Value Problem and Marxist Social Theory," p. 54.
[36] Ibid.
[37] Ibid.
[38] Ibid., p. 53.
[39] Ibid., p. 54.

Somerville, at first glance, appears to be giving a eudaemonistic utilitarian interpretation to Marx. This depends, however, on whether we give a broad or narrow interpretation to "happiness." On the narrow interpretation, happiness is simply contentment or satiation—a particular state of mind. But we must keep in mind that Aristotle's term *eudaemonia* can be interpreted as "well-being" or even "flourishing," as well as "happiness." The point is that if we interpret Somerville to be claiming that Marx and Aristotle are proponents of happiness in the broader sense, then it is no longer clear that he is classifying them as eudaemonistic utilitarians as opposed to nonutilitarian consequentialists. At any rate, I shall group Somerville's interpretation with those who see Marx as an Aristotelian, perfectionist, self-realization theorist, or some other sort of nonutilitarian consequentialist.

Alan G. Nasser sees Marx as wholly an Aristotelian in his ethical perspective and interprets him as having the position that the actualization of whatever is, in fact, the "end" or "function" of human beings is the ultimate criterion of value and thus the ultimate determinant of the good for human beings. According to Nasser, we

find both in Marx's early and mature writings a normative philosophical anthropology whose partial function is to provide a basis for his condemnation of the capitalist mode of production. This feature of Marx's critique of capitalism is firmly rooted in the naturalist tradition which recognizes an implication from human nature to morality. The form of reasoning employed by Marx, which I shall call "the *ergon* argument," is found in its pure form in Aristotle's *Nicomachean Ethics*, and is used by both Aristotle and Marx to support commendations and condemnations whose import is *functionally ethical*. . . . there is an undisputably ethical component to Marx's critical social theory, and . . . this ethical element is based upon a normative anthropology, a "concept of man which . . . serve[s] as a standard against which his present existence . . . [is] measured and criticized."[40]

But, Nasser continues,

the general notion of the human good, well-being or happiness, can be given a specific sense only if man's natural function or *ergon* is first identified. This can be accomplished, Ar-

---

[40] Nasser, "Marx's Ethical Anthropology," p. 485.

istotle thinks, by determining the kind of activity that the human species, and only the human species, can perform, taking into account its characteristic structural organization. The good for man will consist in the performance of his function, the exercise of his specifically human powers, throughout a complete life. This *form* of reasoning, the *ergon* argument, presupposes the following three claims: 1) that it makes sense, and is correct, to say that nature endows man qua man with a special function to perform, 2) that this function can be ascertained by determining the kind of activity that distinguishes *homo sapiens* . . . from every other species, and 3) that such activity is (the moral) *good* for man.[41]

Nasser concludes from this that Marx has "an *historically modified self-realization theory of ethics*. Self-realization involves the 'free' and 'creative' exercise of those powers that define man's *ergon*"[42] and, furthermore, that it is the fact "that the continued existence of capitalist relations of production precludes the actualization of his possibility [which] is the basis of Marx's *ethical* case against capitalism."[43]

Now there can be no doubt that Marx and Aristotle have a similar view of human nature as a bundle of capacities whose realization constitutes the proper functioning and, therefore, the happiness and flourishing of human beings. But it is altogether another question whether or not Marx's views on morality can be completely assimilated to Aristotle's. It seems especially suspect that Marx would have been amenable to all of the metaphysical and quasi-metaphysical assumptions outlined by Nasser in the second passage quoted above—especially in his later works in which he had gotten away from the Hegelian problematic of essence and existence and in which he explicitly condemns philosophical theories of the human essence. Of course, the mere fact that Marx would have rejected this way of speaking does not prove that his views are not actually best captured by it.

Perhaps the strongest reason for rejecting this strict Aristotelian interpretation of Marx's moral views is that the three assumptions outlined by Nasser above are not necessary to an adequate interpretation of them. They are, in fact, so much extra baggage. All one needs to do to reconstruct Marx's position adequately is to

[41] Ibid., p. 486.
[42] Ibid., p. 500.
[43] Ibid.

point out that the capacities for free, conscious, creative activity and for human community are attributed by Marx to human beings on a species-wide basis and are, in addition, approved or commended by him. This seems an adequate account of Marx's views without dragging into the fray the claims that "nature endows man qua man with a special function to perform," that "this function can be ascertained by determining the kind of activity that distinguishes *homo sapiens*," and that "such activity is"—ipso facto—"(the moral) good of man."

Furthermore, from the point of view of the adequacy of a moral theory, these particular assumptions and self-realizationist theory as a whole, may well be found wanting. In his classic article, "Alienation and Self-realization," Kai Nielsen points out that there is no one capacity or one small set of capacities that is distinctively human:

> Suppose . . . we mean by "realizing yourself" essentially what Aristotle meant, namely that to realize yourself is to develop those capacities which are distinctive of *homo sapiens*. . . . The rub is that man—if he can correctly be said to have any function at all—can be said to have many distinctive functions; that is to say, there are many things which are peculiar to man—that men and only men do. Even *if* being able to reason or more plausibly to carry on rational discourse and act in accordance with what is deliberated upon is distinctive of the human animal, so is having guilt feelings, the capacity for anguish and alienation, to drive automobiles, to slaughter one's fellow human beings and other creatures with complicated weapons, etc., etc. There are a multitude of things which are distinctive of man.[44]

Furthermore, it is of no avail to claim that the moral good of human beings consists in realizing their *essential* capacities or characteristics because "essential" here seems to be functioning as an evaluative term. This move thus begs the question. As Nielsen argues:

> In defending Aristotle, people may reply to the above argument by saying that to find the function of a thing we not only need to find what is distinctive of it but we also need to find its *"essential* characteristic". . . . With respect to this argument, it should be noted that "essential" in "essential char-

[44] Nielsen, "Alienation and Self-Realization," p. 23.

acteristic" itself functions evaluatively. Thus, in order to specify the function of man or self-realization, one must invoke
some unspecified but still more fundamental *normative* criterion to establish what counts as an *"essential* characteristic."
There are many activities which are distinctively and pecu-
liarly human but some are more important than others and
thus are more essential. . . . But then we still have not decided how we ascertain what is more or less valuable. Certainly we do not do it by appealing to a criterion of self-realization, for we have to know already what counts as a more
essential and hence more valuable characteristic in order to
know what would count as attaining or approximating self-
realization.[45]

Thus the self-realization cannot be the basic intrinsic good because it presupposes a more basic criterion by which human capacities can be judged as worthy or unworthy of being realized.
Some writers believe this objection can be met by specifying that
an "essential" capacity is a "fundamental" capacity, i.e., a capacity
whose fulfillment is a precondition for the fulfillment of other capacities. They assert that for human beings this is the capacity for
self-determination. But breathing and rationality are also fundamental in this sense, so one wonders if an evaluation is not really
being made in singling out self-determination as *the* capacity
whose fulfillment constitutes human self-realization.[46]
Furthermore, besides having "internal" faults, self-realization
theory has "external" faults as well. The main one is that a self-
realizationist moral theory cannot, in and of itself, account for considerations of justice. Interpreted as an egoistic theory, it is obliv-
ious to possible conflicts between one's own interests and those of
others. Interpreted as a universalistic consequentialist theory, it
gives us no criteria for resolving conflicts of interests that are
bound to occur between persons, each of whom is pursuing his or
her own self-realization. In fact, if self-realization theory is understood to call for the overall maximization of the realization of certain human capacities or potentialities, then it is bound to be open
to counter-examples from considerations of justice. Those possible
or actual situations where the maximization of the overall realization of human potentialities means that some individuals will not
be allowed to realize any of their particular potentialities or will be

[45] Ibid., p. 24.
[46] See Hilliard Aronovitch's article, "Marxian Morality."

allowed to realize (or have the means to realize) only what is clearly an unjustly small number of them are bound to run counter to considerations of justice and thus cast doubt on the viability of self-realizationist theory.

Finally—though I shall take this up in more detail later—a strict form of self-realizationist theory with no provisions for human autonomy or freedom (as self-determination) may turn out to be outrageously paternalistic. While it may be morally permissible for parents to force their children to take piano lessons, certainly it is not permissible for society to force an adult human being to engage in activities against his or her will on the grounds that by means of such activities the individual's—and thus society's—realization of "human" capacities will be maximized.

Hilliard Aronovitch, in his excellent article "Marxian Morality," also gives an Aristotelian (or quasi-Aristotelian) interpretation of Marx's moral views, but one more sensitive to Marx's commitment to freedom (as self-determination) and human autonomy.

A basis is . . . needed for arguing that a classless society together with its moral principles can be counted as morally superior alternatives.

Marx does provide such a basis. He does so with his conception of human nature. That conception serves as the foundation of a morality of self-realization, a morality centering on the principle . . . that calls for the full and free development of individuals.[47]

And furthermore:

Marx's philosophical anthropology, his conception of human nature, makes it possible for him to evaluate different social systems, patterns of social relations and even individual courses of conduct by reference to whether and how far they manifest the free and consciously directed shaping by men of their world and themselves: Marx's philosophical anthropology gives him the leverage on which to build a system of ethics. . . . the foundation for his theory [is] that the realization of human nature is the criterion of the good.[48]

Aronovitch sees Marx diverging from Aristotle, however, on two counts. The first is that "what warrants the demand that [some capacity] be realized by men is not that men must develop

[47] Aronovitch, "Marxian Morality," p. 361.
[48] Ibid., p. 364.

105

what is uniquely human in them but that they must develop that capacity without which they cannot pursue the development of any other capacity."[49] This capacity, according to Aronovitch, is the capacity to

> shape my circumstances and myself, [for] unless I realize my capacity for doing these things, I cannot set myself to realizing any other, further capacities; whether I get to develop any further capacities and which ones and to what extent—all these things are then subject to the vagaries of circumstance or the whims of others.[50]

"Another key difference between the Marxian and the Aristotelian kinds of self-realization," according to Aronovitch, is that "self-realization . . . is . . . as much a matter of making or constituting myself as it is of affirming a pre-given self. . . ."[51] A third divergence we might note is that Marx subscribes to the concepts of human dignity and the equal moral worth of all human beings and thus is committed to fundamental equality not only *within* classes but *between* classes. This presumably leads him to a principle of *equal* freedom (as self-determination) and thus casts considerable doubt on the interpretation of Marx as a nonutilitarian consequentialist as opposed to a strict or mixed deontologist.

These considerations lead naturally to a more detailed comparison between Marx and Aristotle. Even though Marx, as a champion of freedom and self-determination, would have had no truck with such paternalistic and (presumably) unjust social institutions as slavery—whereas Aristotle would and, in fact, did—there are still those who argue that both are nonutilitarian consequentialists. In "Marx and Aristotle: A Kind of Consequentialism," Richard Miller traces some of the similarities and dissimilarities in the moral theories (or perspectives) of these two great philosophers. "Marx, like Aristotle," Miller claims, "judges societies by the kinds of human lives they create."[52]

> As against rights-based morality, both judge institutions by the kinds of lives they promote and judge proposed rights by assessing the consequences of embodying them in institutions. At the same time, their general conceptions of the kinds of lives worth promoting are highly similar, and emphatically

[49] Ibid., p. 366.
[50] Ibid., pp. 365–366.
[51] Ibid., p. 373. See also chapter 1 of Charles Taylor's *Hegel*.
[52] Miller, "Marx and Aristotle: A Kind of Consequentialism," p. 326.

opposed to utilitarianism. In short, as political philosophers they are non-utilitarian consequentialists.[53]

Furthermore, Marx and Aristotle have similar notions of what is intrinsically (nonmorally) good. "Aristotle's main arguments appeal to the alleged superiority of self-sufficiency, intrinsic desirability, and humanity."[54] Marx sees "self-expression and mutuality . . . as goods of great intrinsic importance,"[55] and one of his central concerns is "the promotion of self-control (i.e., control over one's life) and allied goods of dignity, self-expression and mutual respect."[56]

Where Marx and Aristotle differ most is on the issue of *equality* between persons. Aristotle—as a result of the structure of the society in which he lived—was an *anti-egalitarian* . . . at least so far as *inter-class equality* is concerned. Although all persons within a particular class must be treated equally with respect to the division of social goods, even here Aristotle adds that this holds only to the extent people are equal in relevant respects. Applied to the inter-class division of goods, this means that the upper classes—being, on his view, inherently more capable of enjoying higher cultural goods and achieving higher levels of perfection—are to be given the proportion of social goods they need to lead the best lives they can, regardless of what this means for the lower classes. As Miller notes:

> Whether he is judging individual ways of life or whole societies, Aristotle employs fixed, hierarchical rankings of human capacities in which what is less than best should, so far as possible, contribute to the activity of the best. In the best life, he argues, a man subordinates everything else to the best activity, the contemplation of eternal truths, concerning things that do not change, engaged in without consideration of practical human concerns. . . . Very few, he concedes, can approach this ideal. A more feasible way of life is one in which non-intellectual activities, in particular perceptual activities and the fulfillment of appetites, serve as means for the greatest exercise of intelligence in a broad sense, i.e., the capacity for rational and insightful thinking. . . . In the *Politics*, when Aristotle turns from individual ways of life to whole city-states

[53] Ibid., p. 323.
[54] Ibid., p. 349.
[55] Ibid., p. 332.
[56] Ibid., p. 343.

he follows a similar pattern. He unhesitatingly ranks political arrangements according to the quality of the best lives they promote, quite apart from costs to the majority. For example, his ideal society is an aristocracy in which leisured philosophers, political leaders, and military men are provided for by the farming of their slaves and the handiwork of artisans and tradesmen who are excluded from politics. . . . The non-slave non-citizens are consigned to inferior lives, in part through their political exclusion, even though they are not innately incapable of leading good lives. . . . By contrast, Aristotle ranks as merely the best version of a bad arrangement a democracy of small farmers, all of whom can exercise significant moral virtues even though they lack sufficient leisure for the best sorts of lives.[57]

However Marx's commitment to equality between persons and to egalitarian social arrangements is ultimately analyzed, it is clear that he has such commitments. In volume 3 of *Capital*, for example, he states:

It is one of the civilizing aspects of capital that it enforces this surplus-labour in a manner and under conditions which are more advantageous to the development of the productive forces, social relations, and the creation of the elements for a new and higher form than under the preceding forms of slavery, serfdom, etc. Thus it gives rise to a stage, on the one hand, in which coercion and *monopolization of social development (including its material and intellectual advantages) by one portion of society at the expense of the other are eliminated*; on the other hand, it creates the material means and embryonic conditions, making it possible in a higher form of society to combine this surplus-labour with a greater reduction of time devoted to material labour in general[58] [emphasis added].

It is important to realize here that Marx is not merely *predicting* this sort of social equality but *advocating* it. Although—as we have seen with reference to "Critique of the Gotha Program"—he thinks that it is "in general a mistake to make a fuss about so-called *distribution* and put the principal stress on it,"[59] this is only because "any distribution whatever of the means of consumption

57 Ibid., p. 348.
58 Marx, *Capital*, vol. 3, p. 819.
59 Marx, "Critique of the Gotha Program," p. 388.

is only a consequence of the distribution of the conditions of production themselves"[60] and, consequently, according to Marx, "with the abolition of class distinctions all social and political inequality arising from them would disappear of itself."[61] Nevertheless, in this document he goes on to espouse a principle of distributive justice for the first stage of communism, namely, to each according to her or his labor contribution. His only regret is that this principle may not really ensure equality since it still gives advantages to those endowed with "natural privileges," which allow them to produce more and thus receive a greater share of the social wealth in return. Even more importantly, in the "Critique of the Gotha Program" Marx is primarily considering equality of distribution in the "means of consumption," not equality in the distribution of all social goods or all primary social goods (in Rawls' sense). He is not, for example, considering equality in the distribution of *freedom*. Had he been, there is no doubt that he would have called for its *equal distribution*. This is, in fact, borne out by Marx's call—in the *Communist Manifesto*—for "an association, in which *the free development of each is the condition for the free development of all*"[62] [emphasis added].

One important distinction between Marx and Aristotle, then, is that even though both are concerned with human activity, development, and self-realization, Aristotle is a *perfectionist* and Marx is not. Aristotle holds that human perfection is the intrinsic good that ought to be maximized (or at least vigorously pursued). Thus the realization of human perfection—even on the part of a few individuals—is of overriding importance. For Aristotle, the development of the highest human capacities to the highest possible level is to be promoted regardless of the detrimental effects this policy may have on anyone or everyone else. The overriding ideal is *excellence* or *perfection*, and all other considerations are to be subordinate to promoting this end.

Although Marx's ideal of full human development or realization can be understood only in light of his great regard for the higher human intellectual and artistic activities and the cultural products to which they give rise,[63] he is *not* a perfectionist in the above

---

[60] Ibid.

[61] Ibid., p. 392.

[62] Marx and Engels, "Manifesto of the Communist Party," p. 353.

[63] Among later Marxists, Trotsky expresses the same high regard for these sorts of cultural activities and products—as well as the human individuals who excel with regard to them—when, in a (somewhat utopian) passage concerning the nature of future communist society, he writes: "It is difficult to predict the extent of

sense since he does not hold human perfection as an *overriding* normative (or moral) ideal. To promote the perfection of a few at the expense of the many would, in fact, be absolutely anathema to Marx. One of his major criticisms of all past societies is that they allowed the promotion of human excellence on the part of a few (i.e., members of the ruling class and allied intellectuals and artists) at the expense of the many. This, for Marx, is quite simply intolerable. Whereas for Aristotle it is the development of human perfection per se that is of primary importance, for Marx it is the *human individual* who is of primary—indeed exclusive—importance. Furthermore, an essential part of his notion of the individual is the intrinsic *dignity* of each and every human being. This conception accords to each the respect due to him or her as a human individual and prohibits any conditions (e.g., inequalities in freedom or extreme inequalities of wealth) that would undermine human dignity or self-respect.

The main points to be made here are (1) that Marx is committed to the equal intrinsic dignity of human beings and thus to equality in the distribution of freedom, and (2) on these grounds he would reject any moral principle that would violate the principle of equal freedom on the part of all. This means, in particular, that he would reject unfettered self-realizationist or perfectionist theories that demand the maximization of self-realization or human perfection, since such a policy may benefit some at the expense of others and thus interfere with the latter parties' freedom.

Furthermore, this means that Marx would reject any paternalistic violation of freedom called for by such maximization principles. Derek P. H. Allen, in defending his interpretation of Marx as a preference utilitarian, makes the same point. Marx, he claims,

> believed self-development was one way of *being* free, not the only way of *becoming* free. Free activities would include, *inter alia*, those performed in the free time of post-capitalist society;

---

self-government which the man of the future may reach or the heights to which he may carry his technique. Social construction and psycho-physical self-education will become two aspects of one and the same process. All the arts—literature, drama, painting, music and architecture—will lend this process beautiful form. More correctly, the shell in which the cultural construction and self-education of Communist man will be enclosed, will develop all the vital elements of contemporary art to the highest point. Man will become immeasurably stronger, wiser and subtler; his body will become more harmonized, his movements more rhythmic, his voice more musical. The forms of life will become dynamically dramatic. *The average human type will rise to the heights of an Aristotle, a Goethe, or a Marx. And above this ridge new peaks will rise"* (emphasis added) (*Literature and Revolution*, p. 256).

110

and "free time . . . includes leisure time as well as time for higher activities." Activities proper to free time are those which individuals prefer: it is in just this sense that surplus-time is free. Freedom from socially necessary labor to do as a person desired was one thing for Marx, and free development another. Doubtless he hoped and expected they would coincide. But he did not require that they should do so for men to be free. He did think it would be best if free time were used "productively," in developing essential powers.[64]

Post-capitalist society will permit "the complete development of the individual"; but *free*, i.e., *self*-development, by creative activity, not development *simpliciter*, is the greatest good. This distinction is crucial because in their free time men will be able to choose between "higher" and "lower" activities. Better they should choose "lower" than that they be forced to choose "higher." Marx would think it less disutile that someone freely choose pushpin than be afflicted with poetry. Inflicted poetry might cause him to develop, but not to self-develop. Better the fool satisfied than forced to become a dissatisfied Socrates. The point of overthrowing capitalist conditions of enslavement in "lower" activities is not to substitute slavery in "higher." If anyone prefers idleness to education, and if there is no evidence that he will come to change his mind, then there is no utilitarian justification for setting him on the path to learning; nor, I suggest, would Marx think it justified. This is how overall Marx appears to reason. And it is how a consistent utilitarian must reason.[65]

Thus, Allen agrees that Marx's value of self-realization would not take precedence over his value (or principle) of freedom (as self-determination). But, perhaps contrary to initial appearances, I am not here bringing to bear Allen's arguments for interpreting Marx as an antipaternalist primarily for additional support of my own thesis that Marx is of an anti-paternalistic bent. Rather, I bring them under consideration at this point to provide the background for what shall be my final and—I hope—decisive argument that Marx cannot be interpreted as a utilitarian or a consequentialist of any sort. The point I want to make is that Allen's own anti-perfectionist argument (which he offers to shore up his utilitarian inter-

[64] Allen, "The Utilitarianism of Marx and Engels," p. 198.
[65] Ibid., p. 199.

pretation of Marx) can be decisively turned against his own and, indeed, against any utilitarian or consequentialist interpretation of Marx. While Allen is correct, I think, in asserting that Marx would not find it morally permissible to force someone to engage in higher cultural activities against his or her will, it is *not* because, as Allen asserts, "Marx would think it disutile." For what if doing so did maximize utility? What if forcing someone with an abundance of musical talent to develop that talent did make for that individual's greatest happiness or greatest satisfaction of preferences and/or for the greatest happiness or greatest satisfaction of preferences for society as a whole? Would Marx, under these conditions, claim that forcing someone to engage in such activities is morally permissible? If he really is a utilitarian, the answer must be yes! In fact, on the strict utilitarian's view, it would not merely be morally permissible but morally obligatory to force people to engage in such "higher" cultural activities against their will under these conditions! Anyone who has really read and understood Marx, however, knows that Marx would never have submitted to this moral judgment.

Similarly, Allen's claim that "better the fool satisfied than forced to become a dissatisfied Socrates" does not represent Marx's rationale behind his anti-paternalistic position. Marx does not object to interference with an individual's freedom under these circumstances because it produces dissatisfied (but more cultured) individuals, but because interference with an individual's freedom is a bad thing in and of itself. Again, we can ask "What if such a policy generally turned out a *satisfied Socrates*?" Would Marx, then, be in favor of such paternalistic intervention? Of course not! It can be deduced from these considerations, I take it, that Marx would not accept the moral principle that requires this moral judgment and is, *ipso facto*, not a utilitarian.

Now it might be suggested that Marx could still be a *rule* utilitarian who accepts the principle of freedom (as self-determination) as a general rule on the basis that doing so maximizes utility in the long run, but this is not plausible because exactly analogous counter-examples apply in this case. That is, we can construct a case in which accepting the principle of freedom (as self-determination) will not, even in the long run, maximize utility—however one wishes to define utility—and then ask ourselves if Marx would give up the principle of freedom (as self-determination) under these conditions. Again, I suggest that the answer for him would be an emphatic No! Furthermore, utilitarianism—in any form—

will have these sorts of counter-intuitive results from Marx's point of view.

One might attempt to salvage a consequentialist interpretation of Marx's moral views by suggesting that the sole nonmoral good he wishes to maximize is freedom, but this view will not work either. Although Marx is certainly in favor of more freedom rather than less, he also demands, as we have seen, *equal freedom*. This is where my analysis of Marx's moral perspective diverges from Brenkert's. Although Brenkert thinks Marx is a mixed deontologist who takes freedom (as self-determination) as his primary concern, he insists that "Marxist freedom is not something which can be unjustly distributed as can income, wealth, and the like. . . . it is mistaken to treat freedom as one among many social goods which require distribution."[66] But such passages as those already cited suffice to refute this view. As Norman Geras writes:

> Communist society is a better society in Marx's eyes and capitalism [is] condemned by him at least partly because of the way in which the former makes such "goods" [as freedom] available to all where the latter allots them unevenly and grossly so. . . . His critique in the light of freedom and self-actualization is *itself* in part a critique in the light of a conception of distributive justice, . . . though it is so in part only, since there is also an aggregative aspect involved.[67]

Richard Arneson concurs:

> Issues of fairness in distribution (whether or not we label them "justice" concerns) are at the center of all Marx's objections to capitalism. With regard to freedom, for example, what bothers Marx about capitalism is not simply that it supplies too little of this nice non-moral value. Rather, the problem is the skewed distribution of freedom which a market economy enforces, and the superiority which Marx claims for socialism is supposed to lie in socialism's tendency to correct this maldistribution. To my knowledge Marx never even begins to argue for the dubious claim that under socialism the aggregate of freedom (measured how?) will be greater than the aggregate of freedom under capitalism. Marx's claim in this regard is plainer and more plausible: under socialism the distribution

[66] Brenkert, *Marx's Ethics of Freedom*, p. 158.
[67] Geras, "The Controversy about Marx and Justice," p. 72.

of freedom will be more equal, hence better and (one may as well say) more fair.[68]

Thus, although Marx's concept of freedom is broader than Rawls', he can be interpreted, with Rawls, to be demanding a maximum system of equal liberties (or freedoms), but he cannot be interpreted as demanding the maximization of freedom simpliciter. The reason is that in some possible worlds the maximization of freedom will make for an unequal distribution of freedom. In the next chapter I shall offer a more detailed reconstruction of Marx's concept and theory of freedom and show how his notion of economic exploitation is related to it.

[68] Arneson, "What's Wrong with Exploitation?" pp. 220–221.

THREE

MARX'S THEORIES OF FREEDOM AND EXPLOITATION: A RECONSTRUCTION AND DEFENSE

In this chapter I shall first argue that Marx's concern for human dignity and his (implicit) demand for an equal distribution of the primary good of freedom make him a mixed deontologist. Then I shall attempt to reconstruct his concept and theory of freedom. I argue that freedom, on Marx's view, is to be interpreted as the opportunity for self-determination where this is taken to indicate both *negative freedom*, i.e., freedom from the undue interference of others, and *positive freedom*, i.e., freedom to determine one's own life to as great an extent as is compatible with a like opportunity for all. Since Marx is an egalitarian, he is also committed to an equal (or nearly equal) distribution of these social goods. Thus the demand for negative freedom must be interpreted as the demand for a maximum system of equal liberties. Similarly, the demand for positive freedom must be interpreted as including both the right to equal participation in all social decision-making processes that affect one's life and the right of equal access to the means of self-realization. Finally, in societies still characterized by moderate scarcity, the right of equal access to the means of self-realization must be interpreted as entailing, first, the right to an equal opportunity to attain social offices and positions and, secondly, the right to an equal opportunity to acquire other social primary goods (income, wealth, leisure time, etc.). (This is not to say that Marx explicitly takes these positions but only that it is a reasonable reconstruction of his views.) In the final section I shall analyze Marx's concept of exploitation with an eye toward its connection with freedom or other moral values or principles.

Some may object to this reconstruction of Marx's concept of freedom on the grounds that it relies on the concept of justice (namely,

115

a just or equal distribution of freedom) and the concept of rights, both of which he rejects. In response to this I refer the reader to chapter 8, wherein I take up Marx's objections to the notion of justice in the distribution of goods and his criticisms of human rights. I argue that his objections are, for the most part, based on misconceptions and fail as indictments against all theories of social justice and human rights, even though they are often telling against what Marx might have referred to as "bourgeois" theories of justice and rights. In addition, I argue that—contrary to his explicit proclamations—Marx is not only concerned with a just distribution of freedom but with a just distribution of social goods in general (i.e., income and wealth, offices and opportunities, leisure time, etc.). Others may object to this reconstruction of Marx's moral theory on grounds that Marx is better portrayed as a communitarian. In addition to sharing with communitarians a suspicion (or even hostility) toward the concepts of rights and social justice, Marx accepts the value of human community as one of his three primary values. One of the main ways in which communism is morally superior to capitalism, according to Marx, is that it is a genuine community. (Although Marx never explicitly defined "community" in his works, we can take it as designating a group of persons who have common ends, who know they have common ends, and who take deep satisfaction in this fact.)

My answer to this is twofold. First, while I admit that Marx is strongly committed to the value of human community, it seems to me that he is even more strongly committed to the value of freedom (as self-determination) such that if the two were in conflict he would choose to uphold the latter over the former. In fact, it seems plausible to suggest that insofar as Marx would have been willing to entertain a theory of the right—in addition to a theory of the good—he would have specified that the value of freedom (as self-determination) is the only basis for restricting people's behavior by means of coercive social sanctions (e.g., laws). It seems that just as he would not have been in favor of paternalistically forcing people to engage in activities by which they would achieve greater self-realization, he would not have been in favor of restricting people's overall freedom in order to achieve a more extensive or intensive human community.

Second, it seems clear that a communitarian moral theory that has no place for social justice or human rights is simply not adequate with respect to modern mass, pluralistic societies. If Marxists are cogently to defend the positions that socialism (i.e., the

116

first stage of communism) is morally preferable to any form of capitalism (as well as to any form of state-socialism) and the state/government of such a society has legitimate political authority (to which correspond moral obligations on the part of its citizens), they must develop a theory of right: in particular, a theory of social justice and/or human rights. But if democratic socialist societies should come into existence they will undoubtedly exist at the level of the nation-state (or a federation of nation-states) and, hence, will be mass, pluralistic societies. Under these circumstances we cannot expect there to be unanimous agreement among individuals as to the nature of the good (or the good life). Therefore, a purely communitarian moral theory is simply not going to be able adequately to defend these positions. Thus, it cannot be an acceptable moral theory for Marxists or for anyone else who wishes to defend the position that some sort of state and some system of law are morally legitimate in the context of modern mass, pluralistic societies. (I shall present further criticisms of contemporary communitarian moral and social theory—particularly, the theories of Alasdair MacIntyre, Charles Taylor, and Michael Sandel—in chapters 7 and 9.)

But if Marx had appreciated these facts it seems extremely likely that he would have been amenable to having his theory reconstructed in something like the way I propose. Actually, there is even textual evidence that to a limited extent he did appreciate the problem of achieving genuine community in modern mass, pluralistic societies and the consequent necessity of having rights as social norms (at least in pre-communist societies). As noted toward the end of chapter 1, in the third volume of *Capital*, Marx had given up on the claim that freedom was to be found in the work process itself (which he now calls the "realm of necessity") in favor of the view that freedom was to be found in people's "free" time (which he now calls the "realm of freedom") during which they could engage in both leisure and creative activities. Perhaps he also had begun to contemplate the view that the value of community could better be met during this time since people would spend significant portions of it within the smaller communities—families, friendship groups, clubs, associations, etc.—to which most of them belong. In any case, this position seems an extremely reasonable one. It certainly seems clear that modern societies will always be large—at least larger than the Greek city–states—and irreducibly pluralistic. Moreover, it seems certain that Marx's projection that all individuals eventually will transcend the distinction

117

between the individual and common good (even when voting or participating in governance of the society) or the view that a unanimous—or even "overlapping"—consensus on the nature of the good could be developed in such societies must be considered highly unrealistic. (This is presumably why most communitarian moral theorists—from Rousseau through MacIntyre—have been profoundly pessimistic concerning the human prospect.)

Finally, concerning the necessity or at least the desirability of concepts of rights and justice, it should be noted that in *The Eighteenth Brumaire of Louis Bonaparte* Marx strongly endorses and defends the political rights and civil liberties demanded by the French democrats during the Revolution of 1848. Moreover, he propounds norms of political and economic justice (for post-capitalist but pre-communist societies) in *The Civil War in France* and "Critique of the Gotha Program," respectively. In any case, in the present chapter I lay what I hope is a sound basis, first, for the legitimacy of couching Marx's implicit moral theory partially in terms of rights (namely, the rights to equal participation in social decision-making processes and to equal access to the means of self-realization) and, second, for the integration of the concepts of social justice and human rights into what I take to be an adequate Marxist moral and social theory.

Marx, Human Dignity, and Deontologism

If the analysis offered in chapter 2 is correct, Marx is not—as I have defined the terms—a consequentialist of any sort. He is, rather, a mixed deontologist. While he does think that the production of the nonmoral good is always a relevant consideration in moral reasoning—the primary (intrinsically valuable) nonmoral goods for Marx being freedom (as self-determination), human community, and self-realization—he does not think it is the *only* consideration.[1] He also implicitly holds a principle of the distribution of the nonmoral good or at least a principle of distribution of the most important nonmoral good, namely, freedom. Furthermore, the demand for equal freedom itself is not determined by consequentialist considerations (i.e., determined on the basis that the implementation of this principle will maximize some nonmoral good), but flows from

[1] The satisfaction of these values obviously depends on a satisfactory status in terms of human health and welfare. These goods (health and welfare) are, it would seem, instrumentally though not intrinsically valuable for Marx.

the nonutilitarian and nonconsequentialist notion of *human dignity*.

There is, in fact, much textual evidence that Marx accepted the evaluative notion of human dignity. As Eugene Kamenka writes, Marx "is simply not concerned to portray communism as a society of plenty; he is concerned to portray it as a society of human dignity: a society in which labour acquires *dignity* and becomes free because it is carried out by full and conscious participants in a community given over to co-operation and common aims"[2] (emphasis added).

As George Brenkert notes, the concept of human dignity is closely related to the Kantian tradition of treating individuals as ends in themselves: "Marx conceives . . . communism to consist of a society of men living as men, as ends in themselves. That is, a central feature of Marx's ethics is the notion of human dignity, of man as an end in himself."[3] Brenkert claims, further, that "Marx does indeed appeal to consequences to determine certain judgments. But the nature and context of this appeal is within Marx's mixed deontological theory, which is centered on the notion of treating man as an end in himself, as having human dignity."[4]

The notion of the *dignity* of human individuals can be traced throughout Marx's works. In a short essay entitled "Reflections of a Youth on Choosing an Occupation," which he wrote just before graduating from the Trier Gymnasium in 1835, he states, "*Dignity* elevates man most, bestows a high nobleness to all his acts, all his endeavors, and permits him to stand irreproachable. . . . Only that position can impart *dignity* in which we do not appear as servile tools but rather create independently within our circle. . . . a position without *dignity* lowers us. . . . Then we see no aid except in *self-deception*."[5] Marx adds: "The most natural result [of lack of dignity] is *self-contempt*, and what feeling is more painful?"[6] In a letter in 1843 he claims that "freedom, the feeling of *man's dignity*, will have to be awakened again"[7] (all emphases added).

In a passage written during his early polemic against religion as the enemy of humanism (which could be mistaken for one of Nietzsche's), Marx writes, "The social principles of Christianity

---

[2] Kamenka, *The Ethical Foundations of Marxism*, pp. 156–157.
[3] Brenkert, "Marx and Utilitarianism," p. 428.
[4] Ibid., p. 433.
[5] Marx, "Reflections of a Youth on Choosing an Occupation," p. 38.
[6] Ibid.
[7] Marx, "An Exchange of Letters," p. 206.

preach cowardice, self-contempt, debasement, subjugation, humility, in short, all the properties of the canaille, and the proletariat, which does not want to be treated as canaille, needs its courage, its consciousness of self, its pride and its independence, far more than its bread."[8] In a famous passage in "Contribution to the Critique of Hegel's *Philosophy of Right:* Introduction," he speaks of "the *categorical imperative to overthrow all those conditions* in which man is an abased, enslaved, abandoned, contemptible being."[9]

In the *Economic and Philosophical Manuscripts* he writes that "the more the worker produces, the less he has to consume, the more values he creates, the less value—the less *dignity*—he himself has"[10] (emphasis added). In *The Holy Family* he speaks of "an independent moral, based . . . on the consciousness of *human dignity*."[11] Furthermore, in his early and transitional works he utilizes the term "dehumanization" (and its cognates) a great deal and in his later works often speaks of not only the misery, oppression, and exploitation of the proletariat under capitalism but also of its *degradation*. These concepts are much more readily connected up with the concept of human dignity than with the strictly utilitarian conceptual framework of the maximization of desires or happiness.

Furthermore, Marx's concept of human dignity seems to be associated with the Kantian thesis that men ought to be treated as ends in themselves and never as means only. In "On the Jewish Question" Marx explicitly utilizes this Kantian terminology: "in *civil society* [man] acts simply as a *private individual*, treats other men as means, degrades himself to the role of a mere means, and becomes the plaything of alien powers."[12] Furthermore, "contempt for theory, for art, for history, and for man as an end in himself . . . is the *real, conscious* standpoint and the virtue of the man of money."[13] To treat all human beings as ends in themselves is, according to Kant, to be a universal and, consequently, free being. Marx seems to agree with this view.

Somewhat more surprising, perhaps, is that Marx even ex-

[8] Marx, *Marx-Engels Werke*, vol. 4, p. 200, as cited in Stojanović, "Marx's Ethical Theory," p. 163.

[9] Marx, "Contribution to the Critique of Hegel's *Philosophy of Right*: Introduction," p. 52.

[10] Marx, *Economic and Philosophical Manuscripts*, as cited in Kamenka, *The Ethical Foundations of Marxism*, p. 74.

[11] Marx and Engels, *The Holy Family*, p. 236.

[12] Marx, "On the Jewish Question," p. 13.

[13] Ibid., p. 37.

presses a certain admiration for the retributive theory of punishment as found in Kant and Hegel. Like them, he bases this admiration on the concept of human dignity and—it should be noted—human rights. In a *New York Daily Tribune* article printed February 8, 1853, Marx writes:

Punishment in general has been defended as a means either of ameliorating or of intimidating. Now what *right* have you to punish me for the amelioration or intimidation of others? And besides there is history—there is such a thing as statistics—which prove with the most complete evidence that since Cain the world has been neither intimidated nor ameliorated by punishment. Quite the contrary. From the point of view of abstract right, there is only one theory of punishment which recognizes *human dignity*, in the abstract, and that is the theory of Kant, especially in the more rigid formula given to it by Hegel. Hegel says: "Punishment is the right of the criminal. It is an act of his own will. The violation of right has been proclaimed by the criminal as his own right. His crime is the negation of right. Punishment is the negation of this negation, and consequently an affirmation of right, solicited and forced upon the criminal by himself"[14] [emphasis added].

But, as Jeffrie Murphy points out in his article "Marxism and Retribution," even though Marx appears to think the retributive theory of punishment is *formally* correct, he does not view it as *materially* correct, i.e., as acceptable for the type of society to which it was supposed to be applied in Marx's day—or in ours, for that matter. This judgment seems to be based on Marx's belief that capitalist societies—and probably class societies generally—breed crime and criminals in two ways. First, they cast many people into poverty and desperate circumstances so that it is small wonder that some of them turn to crime. Second, such societies do not allow all of their members to develop into fully rational, fully autonomous moral agents—a condition presupposed by the retributive theory. Marx's conclusion, of course, is that we ought to change society in such a way that crime and criminals are no longer bred by the system. Rather than concern ourselves with abstract theories of punishment, we ought to create a society (namely, communism) where punishment is not necessary. As Marx puts it:

[14] Cited in Murphy, "Marxism and Retribution," p. 217.

It is not a delusion to substitute for the individual with his real motives, with multifarious social circumstances pressing upon him, the abstraction of "free will"—one among the many qualities of man—for man himself? . . . Is there not a necessity for deeply reflecting upon an alteration of the system that breeds these crimes, instead of glorifying the hangman who executes a lot of criminals to make room only for the supply of new ones?[15]

This is but another illustration of Marx's affinity with Kant's moral framework and his commitment to the evaluative concept of human dignity. Kant, of course, was primarily concerned with freedom as freedom of the will in connection with his concept of *moral autonomy*. Moral autonomy is characterized, on Kant's view, by two sorts or aspects of freedom: the *negative* freedom from alien or illegitimate considerations in practical reasoning and the *positive* freedom to act in accordance with the principles we give ourselves as free and rational beings. Two demands flow from these two principles, on Kant's view. The first is that we bar from practical reasoning considerations not only of self-interest but those based on desire, want, and inclination generally, i.e., that we reason in accord with the *autonomy* rather than the *heteronomy* of the will. The second is that our principles must be *universal* not only in the sense that they apply to everyone but also that in adopting them we act as legislators not merely for ourselves but for humanity, i.e., that we act as legislators in and of the universal kingdom of ends.

While I am not trying to make Marx out as a strict Kantian—even in his early works—the claim that Marx was very much influenced by Kant can hardly be doubted. Even though, as we saw in chapter 1, Marx emphasizes the distinction between heteronomy and autonomy in the moral realm in his early journalistic writings, he did not, even then, seriously take to heart Kant's demand that moral reasoning be purged from all considerations based on desires, wants, inclinations, needs, etc. This is one important respect in which Marx—and almost every other thinker who has proffered opinions on the subject—differs from Kant. This is also why Marx cannot be classified as a Kantian or a strict deontologist as opposed to a mixed deontologist. Marx does not accept the first of Kant's demands mentioned above. He thinks that the pursuit of the non-moral good is a relevant moral consideration. That he takes Kant's second demand somewhat more seriously is borne out by such

[15] Ibid., p. 218.

122

quotes as man "treats himself as . . . a *universal* and consequently free being."[16]

But this does not constitute even the beginnings of an adequate account of Marx's concept of freedom (as self-determination) because freedom, as Kant conceives it in relation to moral autonomy, is a *moral* good, whereas most of what Marx has to say about freedom concerns freedom as a (distributable) *nonmoral* good, i.e., as a good whose description need not contain moral terms. It is this aspect of Marx's concept of freedom to which we now turn.

Marx's Concept and Theory of Freedom: A Reconstruction

As stated at the beginning of the present chapter, I wish to argue that Marx's theory of freedom can be rationally reconstructed as follows. (1) freedom is essentially the opportunity for self-determination and is based, in the final analysis, on the moral value of autonomy; (2) self-determination entails both negative freedom (i.e., freedom from the undue interference of others) and positive freedom (i.e., the opportunity to determine one's own life to as great an extent as is compatible with a like opportunity for all); and (3) the opportunity to determine one's own life entails both (a) the right to equal participation in all social decision-making processes that affect one's life and (b) the right of equal access to the means of self-realization.

Let us consider each of these claims in order. The claim that Marx identifies freedom with self-determination—or, more precisely, with the opportunity for self-determination—can be interpreted in two ways. By "self-determination" philosophers have meant either (1) determination of one's self in accordance with one's essential nature (as the sort of being one happens to be) or (2) the determination of one's self in accordance with the laws (or imperatives or plans) one legislates or chooses for one's self. (It is important to note that while the formulation of Rousseau, Kant, et al. that freedom can be defined as being determined in accordance with one's real, rational will seems to be a version of the second interpretation of self-determination, it is actually a version of the first since the dictates of real, rational will are not necessarily the same as the dictates of one's actual, empirical will.)

While views (1) and (2) can be combined, they are separate and distinct. Both views, I believe, are to be found in Marx's earliest

---

[16] Marx, *Economic and Philosophical Manuscripts*, p. 126.

works, while only the second interpretation, on which the *actual, empirical self* is the determining agent, is to be found in his later works. Consequently, Marx is not open to the charge of collectivism or totalitarianism so often put forward. In fact, Marx can be interpreted (or at least reconstructed) as a methodological individualist (as opposed to a methodological holist) in social science, and it is clear that he is an ethical individualist (as opposed to a collectivist) in moral theory.[17]

As concerns the first view, Kamenka points out that "the Young Marx, following a line laid down in Spinoza and Hegel, treats freedom as self-determination. To be free is to be determined by one's own nature. To be unfree is to be determined from without."[18] For Marx, or at least for the (very) early Marx, the essential nature of human beings is freedom. Thus, unless the notion of freedom as man's essential nature is analyzed further, we seem to be able to derive from these remarks only the unenlightening and tautologous claim that to be free is to be determined in accordance with freedom. As we have seen, however, we can analyze Marx's claim that humanity's essence is freedom into the claim that human beings have two essential capacities: the capacity for free, conscious, creative activity and the capacity for human community (or solidarity). Thus, for human beings—given the sort of beings they are—to be self-determining is to be determined in accordance with (or to realize) these two capacities. On this view, anyone who doesn't realize these two capacities is, ipso facto, not free even if subject to no constraints and in complete control of his or her life. But this, of course, is an abuse of the term "freedom"—at least on its common meaning.

The (very) early Marx, with his praise of Aristotle, Spinoza, and Hegel and his acceptance of the Hegelian problematic of essence and existence, in which existences tend toward their essences, seems to have been attracted to this view of freedom. However, the later Marx rejected the philosophical problematic of essence and existence and is probably best interpreted as holding only (1) the *empirical* thesis that human beings, when not diverted from doing so, tend to realize the two capacities in question and (2) the *evaluative* thesis that it is good for human beings to realize these capacities and, even more importantly, it is good for human beings to be able to (i.e., *to be free to*) realize these capacities. On the

[17] See D.B.F. Tucker, *Marxism and Individualism*; and Elster, *Making Sense of Marx*, pp. 5–8, 117–118, and *An Introduction to Karl Marx*, pp. 22–25.
[18] Kamenka, *The Ethical Foundations of Marxism*, p. 97.

view I am attributing to the Marx of the *Manuscripts* and later, the fact that a person doesn't realize these two capacities does not constitute a conclusive but only a *prima facie* reason for assuming that that he or she is not free. If the person were free—the reasoning goes—he or she, in all probability, would realize these capacities. The person has not realized these capacities. Therefore, in all probability, there is some liberty-limiting condition at work that prevents the person from realizing these capacities, i.e., in all probability, the person is not free.

Philosophers of the rational will tradition—particularly Rousseau and Kant—tended to identify the self in this context as one's "real, rational self," with the result that one is free (or "truly free") if, and only if, one is acting in accord with the laws that the "real, rational self" would legislate or if one is acting in accord with the choices that the "real, rational will" would make. This leads, of course, to the view that one's freedom is not violated if one is forced to do something one doesn't want to do, so long as it is what one's "real, rational will" would dictate: one can, as Rousseau claimed, *be forced to be free*. This, too, seems to abuse our common notion of freedom or liberty on which actions (or persons) are free if, and only if, they are both uncoerced and self-determined. But freedom or liberty is not the only value most of us accept, and it would be a mistake, I think, to pack all of our values into this concept. This is the point Isaiah Berlin makes when he writes:

> Everything is what it is: liberty is liberty, not equality or fairness or justice or culture, or human happiness or a quiet conscience. If the liberty of myself or my class or nation depends on the misery of a number of other human beings, the system which promotes this is unjust and immoral. But if I curtail or lose my freedom, in order to lessen the shame of such inequality, and do not thereby materially increase the individual liberty of others, an absolute loss of liberty occurs. This may be compensated for by a gain in justice or in happiness or in peace, but the loss remains, and it is a confusion of values to say that although my "liberal" individual freedom may go by the board, some other kind of freedom . . . is increased.[19]

On the other hand, one can accept the second interpretation of freedom as self-determination and take freedom to be a matter of being determined in accord with the decisions or choices of one's

[19] Berlin, "Two Concepts of Liberty," p. 338.

actual, empirical self. Marx seems to have been attracted to the Rousseau-Kant interpretation of freedom as self-determination in his earliest works; he even goes so far as to claim that "only when his actual actions have shown that he has ceased to obey the natural law of freedom, *does the State force him to be free*"[20] (emphasis added). But he moved away from these views after his very early, journalistic period and, in his later works, came to view self-determination as simply a matter of *having control over one's life*, i.e., having the effective power to determine the course of one's own existence (to the extent this is empirically possible).

Although we shall return to this matter presently, one might say that the main difference between the later Marx and the rational-will theorists on this issue can be expressed in the triadic definition of freedom offered by Gerald MacCallum as a difference concerning the *first* variable, i.e., the variable standing for the sort of agent one has in mind. MacCallum's formula is "x is (is not) free from y to do (not do, become, not become) z."[21] In the rational-will tradition, the x is taken to stand not for actual, empirical individuals but for the *real, rational will* of such individuals, which may and often does stand in opposition to their actual but "merely" empirical wills. This is the reasoning behind Rousseau's claim that in being forced to conform to the laws of a (just) state, citizens are merely being "forced to be free." But in all but his earliest works Marx seems to be speaking of the freedom (i.e., the self-determination) of actual, empirical individuals rather than the "real, rational will" of such individuals. In his later works, for example, he never speaks of forcing the bourgeoisie to be free by means of the expropriation of productive property but, rather, speaks of "despotic inroads on the rights of property, and on the conditions of bourgeois production."[22] While Marx certainly sees as justified "despotic inroads"—i.e., the use of the legitimate coercive power of the (new) state to effect this end—he does not seem to conceive of the situation as one of forcing the bourgeoisie to be free.

On the other hand, it is clear that it is the notion of freedom (as self-determination) in the second sense that informs Marx from the *manuscripts* to his latest works. An individual is free, according to Marx, only if he is *self-determining*; and he is self-determining only if he is in control of his own life. To be free in the latter sense is to

[20] Marx, "Debates on Press Freedom," *Marx-Engels Gesamtausgabe*, section I, vol. 1, subvol. i, p. 210, as cited in Kamenka, *The Ethical Foundations of Marxism*, p. 34.
[21] MacCallum, "Negative and Positive Freedom," p. 296.
[22] Marx and Engels, "Manifesto of the Communist Party," p. 352.

be autonomous, to be one's own master. "A being does not regard himself as independent," Marx claims, "unless he is his own master, and he is only his own master when he owes his existence to himself. A man who lives by the favor of another considers himself a dependent being."[23] But to be in control of one's own life entails *both* that one is not prey to the warranted interferences of other individuals and that one can, in addition, have a significant impact or effect upon the direction of one's own life and the circumstances under which one must live.

Self-determination, for Marx, thus entails both *negative* and *positive* freedom. By "negative freedom" I mean freedom from interference on the part of other persons or groups of persons, e.g., the state. By "positive freedom" I mean freedom in the sense of being able to determine or control one's life. Speaking of negative freedom or liberty in his classic essay, "Two Concepts of Liberty," Isaiah Berlin writes, "By being free in this sense I mean not being interfered with by others"[24] and "liberty in this sense means liberty *from;* absence of interference."[25] The value of negative liberty, he claims, is based on the conviction that "there ought to exist a certain minimum area of personal freedom which must on no account be violated"[26] and that "we must preserve a minimum area of personal freedom if we are not to 'degrade or deny our nature.' "[27] Socially speaking, "a frontier must be drawn between the area of private life and that of public authority."[28]

It is often claimed that Marx had no respect for negative freedom, as thus defined, but this is not true. There are two kinds of evidence that tend to refute this claim. The first is the occasional statement Marx makes in support of negative liberty, one of the more striking examples being his comment in the "Critique of the Gotha Program" that (of course!) "everyone should be able to attend to his religious as well as his bodily needs without the police sticking their noses in."[29] The second piece of evidence is the simple fact that self-determination in the sense of having control over one's own life obviously excludes such unwarranted interferences with one's person and privacy and one's actions and activities. (Deciding on what constitutes a *warranted* intrusion, however, is

[23] Marx, *Economic and Philosophical Manuscripts*, p. 165.
[24] Berlin, "Two Concepts of Liberty," p. 337.
[25] Ibid., p. 339.
[26] Ibid., p. 337.
[27] Ibid., p. 339.
[28] Ibid., p. 337.
[29] Marx, "Critique of the Gotha Program," p. 397.

one of the most important albeit most difficult issues in moral and social philosophy and an issue on which individuals greatly differ.)

This sort of (negative) liberty was so obviously required, on Marx's view, that he hardly thought it worth commenting upon. What he will *not* allow, however, is that this sort of liberty exhausts the category of freedom. It is the view that negative liberty *does* exhaust the category of freedom that Marx has in mind when he writes (disapprovingly), "This right to the undisturbed enjoyment, upon certain conditions, of fortuity and chance has up till now been called personal freedom."[30] It is also this narrow conception of freedom Marx is describing (and implicitly condemning) when—at the transition point between descriptions of the spheres of circulation and of production in the first volume of *Capital*—he claims:

> This sphere that we are deserting, within whose boundaries the sale and purchase of labour-power goes on, is in fact a very Eden of the innate rights of man. There alone rule Freedom, Equality, Property, and Bentham. Freedom, because both buyer and seller of a commodity, say of labour-power, are constrained only by their own free will. They contract as free agents, and the agreement they come to is but the form in which they give legal expression to their common will. Equality because each enters into relation to the other, as with a simple owner of commodities, and they exchange equivalent for equivalent. Property, because each disposes only of what is his own. And Bentham, because each looks only to himself.[31]

It may be argued that Marx's normative ideal of individuals as communal or "species-beings" contradicts the thesis that he was concerned with the negative freedom of individuals, but this is not so. He was not a collectivist or totalitarian in this sense. His normative ideal of the individual as a truly social being is combined with the utmost respect for a person's individuality. In the *Manuscripts*, for example, he attacks "crude communism . . . [which] is only the culmination of . . . envy and levelly down on the basis of a *preconceived* minimum"[32] on the grounds that "this communism

[30] Marx and Engels, *The German Ideology*, p. 162.
[31] Marx, *Capital*, vol. 1, p. 176.
[32] Marx, *Economic and Philosophical Manuscripts*, p. 153.

. . . negates the *personality* of man in every sphere."[33] He attacks capitalism on the grounds that "what I *am* and *can do* is . . . not at all determined by my individuality [since] . . . what I as a *man* am unable to do, and thus with all my individual faculties are unable to do, is made possible for me by *money*."[34]

Nor does Marx's view that rights to such liberties will be an outmoded concept in communist society refute the thesis that he was concerned with negative liberty. He believed that in a full-fledged communist society individuals will have become so humanized that there will be no occasions on which it is necessary for them to press claims to their rights to privacy, conscience, expression, etc. Therefore, the category or concept of rights (as well as justice) will quite simply be otiose. But this is *not* to say that the freedoms claimed by such rights would be violated or the persons populating communist society will be bland conformists or unthinking automatons. Marx believed quite the contrary.

Marx's concept of freedom is, however, broader than that of mere negative liberty. Although Hilliard Aronovitch uses the term "self-determination" more narrowly than I, since he identifies it only with positive freedom—whereas I take this term to apply to both negative and positive freedom—a perspicuous explication of Marx's notion of self-determination is given in his article "Marxian Morality":

> Self-determination . . . is the free and conscious shaping of
> the *conditions* of one's life, which makes possible the further
> free and conscious shaping of *oneself* through the develop-
> ment of this or that specific capacity; it is what has sometimes
> been called positive freedom, being able *to do* things—those
> things, including effecting one's will upon circumstances, that
> accord with self-consciously arrived at choices. Put in these
> terms . . . the capacity for self-determination or positive free-
> dom is fundamental in that without it one is not in a position
> to deliberately achieve or even aim at anything else.[35]

> Self-determination, the free and consciously directed shaping
> of the conditions of one's life, obviously connotes freedom,
> and individual freedom, of a certain basic kind. The kind
> counts for very much. What is especially important is that
> freedom is specified not just in terms of the absence of coer-

[33] Ibid.
[34] Ibid., pp. 191–192.
[35] Aronovitch, "Marxian Morality," p. 366.

cion but in the more positive terms of actually being able to effect one's will, and that circumstances are not treated as fixed things to which I must adapt my will and within which I must find some residual area of choice: rather, my freedom on this conception is to be measured in crucial part by the extent to which I can effect my will upon them.[36]

But this *positive freedom* (i.e., *the freedom to determine one's own life*) has, in turn, two components. The first is the *right to equal participation* in all social decision-making processes—political, educational, economic, etc.—that affect one's life. Since, according to Marx, many and perhaps most of the decisions that affect our lives are *social* as opposed to individual decisions, it is of the essence of the matter that these decisions be made on the basis of the equal participation of all—or at least *the right of* equal participation of all (since some might prefer not to participate in certain social decision-making processes). As opposed to the bourgeois parliamentary system of representational democracy, which he regards as a sham, Marx demands that the new society extend democracy into all realms of social activity (particularly the economic) and that it be made real or effective democracy. By the process of reaching a consensus or, if that is not possible, by the most democratic method available, individuals collectively ought to control social and economic processes rather than be controlled by them. The fact that, in his view, social and economic processes control the lives of human beings under capitalism, rather than vice versa, is of course a key phenomenon described by Marx's concept and theory of alienation as well as part of what underlies his concept and theory of exploitation (more on this presently).

Opponents of Marxism may well be tempted to point out that currently existing post-capitalist societies do not seem to give their citizens even as much control over their lives as some capitalist societies. Proponents of Classical Marxism, of course, will reply that such post-capitalist societies do not yet qualify as socialist or communist societies and will normally cite historical circumstances as being responsible for their divergence from Marx's vision. The most important point of contention between Marxists and their opponents, in fact, is whether or not a democratic form of socialism is historically possible (more on this in chapter 10).

Although right-libertarians (e.g., Robert Nozick) and many liberals deride the concept of positive freedom in the sense of self-

---

[36] Ibid., pp. 370–371.

determination, an interesting question arises from this fact: on what grounds do right-libertarians or such liberals defend political democracy? Speaking of negative liberty, Berlin writes:

> Liberty in this sense is not incompatible with some kinds of autocracy, or at any rate with the absence of self-government. Liberty in this sense is principally concerned with the area of control, not with its source. . . . there is no necessary connexion between individual liberty and democratic rule. The answer to the question "Who governs me?" is logically distinct from the question "How far does government interfere with me?" It is in this difference that the great contrast between the two concepts of negative and positive liberty, in the end, consists. For the "positive" sense of liberty comes to light if we try to answer the question, not "What am I free to do or be?", but "By whom am I ruled?" or "Who is to say what I am, and what I am not, to be or do?" . . . The desire to be governed by myself, or at any rate to participate in the process by which my life is to be controlled, may be as deep a wish as that of a free area for action, and perhaps historically older.[37]

Be that as it may, the second component of Marx's concept of positive freedom, according to my reconstruction of his position, is the *right of equal access to the means of self-realization*. Marx demands that "man . . . [be] free not through the negative power to avoid this or that but through the positive power to assert his true individuality."[38] Insofar as this means that people aren't free unless they have (approximately equal) access to the means of self-realization, this thesis will be even more noxious to the right-libertarian (and to many liberals) than the last. But this principle is obviously in need of further analysis. First, to simplify matters and make my reconstructed version of Marx's theory more plausible, I propose to take "means of self-realization" to include all social primary goods mentioned by Rawls except the good of negative liberty or freedom (which is covered by the above principle). The social primary goods, according to Rawls, are rights and liberties, powers and opportunities, income and wealth, leisure and the social bases of self-respect.[39] I shall also take this right to an equal access to the means of self-realization to entail the right to an equal

---

[37] Berlin, "Two Concepts of Liberty," pp. 340–341.
[38] Marx and Engels, *The Holy Family*, p. 154.
[39] Leisure is not listed as a primary social good in *A Theory of Justice* but is added by Rawls in his "Reply to Alexander and Musgrave."

opportunity to attain social offices and positions. Although the very notion of social offices and positions may be otiose in a full-fledged communist society, Marx certainly thought they would exist in socialist societies. In *The Civil War in France*, he calls for such positions to be democratically elected, subject to recall, and done at workman's wages. (This last provision was designed to prevent a privileged bureaucracy from forming. The suggestion by many later socialists to rotate such offices or positions on a regular basis is designed to accomplish this task and perhaps to give people a chance to realize themselves in this way as well.)

On the other hand, I have framed this right as a one of equal *access* to the means of self-realization rather than as a right to equal means of self-realization to indicate that—at least in the first stage of communism where it still makes sense to worry about principles for the distribution of scarce goods—individuals have a right to an equal opportunity to realize their selves (i.e., their life plans) and thus an equal opportunity to attain the means to do so. This does not, however, necessarily include a right to an equal amount of self-realization (if it makes sense to speak this way) or to an equal amount of the means to self-realization (i.e., an equal share of primary social goods). As Marx makes clear in the "Critique of the Gotha Program," there is not to be strict equality of distribution of material goods in the first stage of communism (or what today is commonly called "socialism"). Except for those unable to work, individuals are entitled only to what they can attain by their own efforts within the (presumably fair) rules of the new social arrangements. The primary rules, according to Marx, are (1) that one person cannot realize a profit from another's labor, and (2) individuals are to receive back from society a share of the social wealth proportional to the productive (or socially useful?) labor they contribute to society. Commenting on that part of the Gotha Program which asserts an equal right on the part of individuals to the proceeds of labor, Marx writes: "No one can give anything except his labour and . . . nothing can pass to the ownership of individuals except individual means of consumption"[40] and, further, that

> the individual producer receives back from society—after the deductions have been made—exactly what he gives to it. . . . The same amount of labour which he has given to society in one form he receives back in another . . . . In spite of this advance, this *equal right* is still constantly stigmatised by a

[40] Marx, "Critique of the Gotha Program," p. 387.

bourgeois limitation. The right of the producers is *proportional* to the labour they supply; the equality consists in the fact that measurement is made with an *equal standard*, labour.[41]

Thus, in societies that still embody Hume's conditions of justice —moderate scarcity, and moderate egoism—Marx's view of freedom entails that the individual have a right to equal access to the means of self-realization (i.e., an equal opportunity to attain the means of self-realization). It does not, however, entail guaranteed access to any and all goods, services, and opportunities an individual may require for complete self-realization since this may not be possible. This proviso also allows us to ground our moral intuition that while a person's freedom is not violated just because he cannot obtain a yacht or a year-long trip around the world under present social conditions, it is violated if he cannot obtain a high-school education because, let us say, high-school tuition is $5,000 per year, his family cannot afford this amount, and there are no government programs to provide financial aid.

Even though Marx does not fall into the category of a proponent of the rational will version of positive freedom, he does accept a broader set of conditions as liberty-limiting than do Classical Liberals and most modern liberals, and he gives a wider interpretation of those things people ought to be free to do (or become). The differences between these several positions can be perspicuously outlined—and futile debates over vaguely defined notions of "positive" and "negative" liberty can be avoided—if we utilize MacCallum's triadic formula of freedom. As MacCallum points out, there are actually three variables to be considered: the sorts of persons to whom we are ascribing freedom, the conditions that are to count as liberty limiting, and the sorts of things freedom can have as its end. Thus, in the formula x is (is not) free from y to do (not do, become, not become) z, "x ranges over agents, y ranges over such 'preventing conditions' as constraints, restrictions, interferences, and barriers, and z ranges over actions or conditions of character or circumstance."[42] The x may stand for ourselves as we really are (the empirical self) or for the "real," "true," or "essential" self of the rational-will tradition. The y may stand for the direct interference of other persons, or for this plus any and all social and economic (or even psychological) conditions that limit one's choices, or for anything in between these extremes. Finally,

[41] Ibid.
[42] MacCallum, "Negative and Positive Freedom," p. 296.

the z may stand for actions people wish to perform or for what people do as well as what they can become.

As we have seen, Marx—or at least the later Marx—takes the x variable to refer to the actual, empirical wills of individuals. In this he agrees with the vast majority of modern moral and social thinkers. But whereas right-libertarians and some liberals insist that the z variable pertains only to actions ("doings"), Marx seems to hold that people should be free not only to do things but to become things and, thus, that the z variable pertains to both "doings" and "becomings." Since in Marx's view, however, one only becomes something (e.g., an artist) by doing things (e.g., studying art, drawing, painting, etc.), it is not clear that there is really much of a difference here. The more important difference concerns the y variable.

Whereas the right-libertarian and some liberals insist that the parameters of the y variable extend only to the *deliberate interference of other individuals* (or groups of individuals) and thus contend that this sort of interference constitutes the only liberty-limiting condition, Marx and many others reject this as overly narrow. Although Isaiah Berlin is generally taken to be an opponent of the broader view of liberty-limiting conditions, a careful reading of his "Two Concepts of Liberty" reveals that even such a thorough-going modern liberal as he leaves room for the broader view. As Berlin points out:

> You lack political liberty or freedom only if you are prevented from attaining a goal by human beings. Mere incapacity to attain a goal is not lack of political freedom. This is brought out by the use of such modern expressions as "economic freedom" and its counterpart, "economic slavery." . . . if a man is too poor to afford something on which there is no legal ban—a loaf of bread, a journey round the world, recourse to the law courts—he is as little free to have it as he would be if it were forbidden him by law. If my poverty were a kind of disease, which prevented me from buying bread, or paying for the journey round the world or getting my case heard, as lameness prevents me from running, this inability would not naturally be described as a lack of freedom, least of all political freedom. It is only because I believe that my inability to get a given thing is due to the fact that other human beings have made arrangements whereby I am, whereas others are not, prevented from having enough money with which to pay for

it, that I think myself a victim of coercion or slavery . . . . this use of the term depends on a particular social and economic theory about the causes of my poverty or weakness. . . . *I begin to speak of being deprived of freedom (and not simply about poverty) only if I accept the theory.* If, in addition, I believe that I am being kept in want by a specific arrangement which I consider unjust or unfair, I speak of *economic slavery or oppression.* "The nature of things does not madden us, only ill will does," said Rousseau. The criterion of oppression is the part that I believe to be played by other human beings, directly or indirectly, with or without the intention of doing so, in frustrating my wishes. By being free in this sense I mean not being interfered with by others. The wider the area of non-interference the wider my freedom[43] [emphasis added].

There is, of course, no reason a Marxist cannot accept this analysis. If this is done, the difference between Marxist and most other modern political thinkers will not be that they accept different concepts of freedom or that they have different criteria of what constitutes a liberty-limiting condition but that they have different empirical views about what (alterable) social conditions are, in fact, liberty-limiting or—more precisely—what (alterable) social conditions are *unjustifiably* liberty-limiting. Marx can be interpreted as proposing that, in addition to the direct interferences of other persons, the parameters of the y variable include *any alterable social arrangement* that unjustifiably restricts freedom. Marx, of course, offers an explanatory theory and analysis of how it is that (alterable) social institutions and arrangements—and thus indirectly people—act as liberty-limiting conditions for the vast majority in capitalist society. In the history of modern thought there has been no shortage of people with this view of freedom: the importance of Marx lies in his social-scientific theories that explain how the social arrangements of capitalism and all class-divided societies unjustifiably limit or constrain the freedom of the vast majority of people and how these unjustifiable constraints can be eliminated.

But is Marx's moral theory, as I have reconstructed it—especially his concept of freedom as self-determination—adequate? Although it is a more *viable* theory than most people are willing to give it credit for, it is not completely adequate as it stands. For one thing, we need to know what would constitute a *warranted* or *justifiable* intrusion on personal or political freedom. Not all actions

---

[43] Berlin, "Two Concepts of Freedom," pp. 336–337.

can or should be permitted in a society. One is not free to maim others, for example, but the fact that society (or the state) attaches sanctions to maimings of human beings constitutes an intrusion on people's freedom. But most or all of us would agree that this intrusion is warranted. Such warranted intrusions may be based on preserving equal freedom (e.g., laws against selling oneself into slavery); on creating a maximum system of equal freedoms (e.g., laws prohibiting people from expressing themselves so loudly that others are disturbed in their private abodes and laws against slander and libel); or (possibly) on promoting or maximizing some other important moral value such as human well-being.

Most recent and contemporary moral and social theorists are willing to admit that in some cases liberty can be limited on the basis of considerations other than liberty itself. Berlin is worth quoting again: "Liberty is not the only goal of men. . . . To avoid glaring inequality or widespread misery I am ready to sacrifice some, or all, of my freedom. . . . I should be guilt-stricken, and rightly so, if I were not in some circumstances ready to make this sacrifice."[44] Although it is difficult to imagine concrete cases in which one would be morally obliged to give up *all* of one's liberty, it is commonly agreed that we are morally obliged to trade off some of our liberty if doing so is necessary to prevent pain and suffering or extreme deprivation on the part of others. Right-libertarians, such as Nozick, are among the few who refuse to admit that liberty can be justifiably limited on the basis of anything other than liberty.[45]

[44] Ibid., p. 338.

[45] I use the term "right-libertarianism" rather than simply "libertarianism" to describe this school of thought because—as Noam Chomsky points out in *Problems of Freedom and Knowledge* and elsewhere—the latter term is also used to designate the views of left-wing anarchists and socialists who stress the value of freedom. (Obviously, such anarchists and socialists have a broader conception of freedom and, as such, might be designated "left-libertarians.")

Paradigmatic works of right-libertarianism include Robert Nozick, *Anarchy, State, and Utopia*, Basic Books, N.Y., 1974; John Hospers, *Human Conduct*, Harcourt, Brace, and World, N.Y., 1961; Milton Friedman, *Capitalism and Freedom*, University of Chicago Press, 1962, 1982; Friedrich A. Hayek, *The Constitution of Liberty*, University of Chicago Press, Chicago, 1960; and Ayn Rand et al., *Capitalism: The Unknown Ideal*, New American Library, N.Y., 1966. (It should be noted, however, that Hayek is not a pure right-libertarian because he believes that liberty can be limited in order to provide a "welfare safety net" to prevent severe deprivation among the indigent.)

I shall not attempt a detailed analysis and refutation of right-libertarianism because, first, it is beyond the purview of this work and, second, this task—in my opinion—has already been accomplished. See Nielsen, *Equality and Liberty*, pp. 191–277; G. A. Cohen: "Robert Nozick and Wilt Chamberlain," "Capitalism, Free-

But Marx gives us no theory or criteria for deciding what could constitute a warranted intrusion. At the economic level, as Berlin points out, I speak of economic oppression or slavery or—we can add—economic *exploitation*, only "if . . . I believe that I am being kept in want by a specific arrangement which I consider unjust or unfair."[46] But if this is so—which I believe it is—Marx's theory, in order to be adequate, also needs a theory of social justice. But while the grains of a theory of social justice, at least as applied to the first stage of communism, are apparent in the "Critique of the Gotha Program" and elsewhere in Marx's writings, he regularly condemns such concepts and theories and thus leaves us with a paradox to be solved. In chapter 8 I shall attempt to show that Marx's reasons for rejecting all notions of justice and human rights are unfounded. The next issue I wish to take up is his concept and theory of exploitation. In particular, I shall attempt to determine whether Marx's concept of exploitation has moral (or normative) content or force and, if so, what principles or values undergird it.

Morality and Marxist Concept(s) of Exploitation

Marx never gives a clear-cut definition or explication of his concept (or concepts) of exploitation. Moreover, while he usually seems to be employing the term "exploitation" in a morally condemnatory fashion, there is considerable debate among interpreters of his work as to whether this negative moral import is a necessary characteristic of exploitation. One interpretation, in fact, asserts that exploitation is simply a matter of the transfer of surplus labor (or value or product) from one group or class of people to another and that, in and of itself, this cannot be assumed to be wrong. A similar interpretation in this respect is the distributional theory of exploitation as proposed by John Roemer. On his analysis, a group is exploited if, and only if, it would be economically better off if it could withdraw from society with its inalienable assets (i.e., work skills) and—in the case of capitalist exploitation—its per capita share of society's alienable assets (i.e., productive forces). Again, it is not clear that exploitation in and of itself is even *prima*

---

dom, and the Proletariat," "Freedom, Justice and Capitalism," "Illusions about Private Property and Freedom," "Nozick on Appropriation," and "Self-ownership, World-ownership, and Equality, Part II"; Reiman, "The Fallacy of Libertarian Capitalism"; van Parijs, "Nozick and Marxism"; Wolff, "Robert Nozick's Derivation of the Minimal State"; Fisk, "Property and the State"; O'Neill, "Nozick's Entitlements"; and Smith, "Robert Nozick's Critique of Marxian Economics."
[46] Berlin, "Two Concepts of Liberty," p. 336.

facie wrong in this analysis. The objective of the following analysis of exploitation is to determine whether it has moral content and, if so, the nature of this content. That is, we must answer two questions: what is exploitation and what—if anything—is wrong with it?

Those who contend that exploitation has moral content often disagree as to what this content is. Some emphasize Marx's purely descriptive, technical notion of the degree of exploitation (or rate of surplus value) and insist that his concept turns primarily on its connections with his analysis of the economic dysfunctions of capitalism and, ultimately, on the loss of utility exhibited by capitalism in comparison to (hypothetical) socialist societies. Others emphasize the fact that exploitation seems to contravene the value of freedom as self-determination either because force or coercion is somehow involved or because the exploited class (or classes) has no say over the dispensation of the surplus value it produces, or both. Still others claim that the moral wrongness of exploitation has to do with the fact that principles of social or distributive justice are being violated when people are being exploited. Moreover, even if an interpreter opts for a value-neutral definition of exploitation, any of these evaluative perspectives can be used to explain what is wrong with it in those particular instances of exploitation that are, in fact, wrong.

A further complication is that Marx has not only a concept of *economic* exploitation but also a *general* concept of exploitation that sees the state as well as economic classes able to exploit people, and—seemingly—the benefits in question need not even be economic in nature. Moreover, within his concept of economic exploitation one must distinguish between his *transhistorical* theory of exploitation and his theory of exploitation as applied to particular modes of production, for example, *capitalist* exploitation. Furthermore, to appreciate the recent literature on Marxian exploitation, one must distinguish *labor* theories from *distributional* theories, and *force-inclusive definitions* from those that do not include force or coercion as a defining characteristic.

By "labor theories of exploitation" I mean those that focus on the transfer of surplus labor (or product or value) between economic classes. By "distributional theories of exploitation" I mean those that focus on the distribution of income or property wealth among individuals or classes.[47] The paradigmatic distributional

---

[47] My use of "distributional theory of exploitation" differs somewhat from Jeffrey

theory is that of the contemporary Marxist economist John Roemer. He utilizes "withdrawal rules" such as those previously mentioned to determine who is exploited and who is exploiting. (Thus, this sort of theory is sometimes called a "counterfactual theory of exploitation.") We will first consider Marx's general concept of exploitation and then take up his concept or concepts of economic exploitation. In examining economic exploitation we shall examine several versions of the labor theory of exploitation and then compare what I take to be the most adequate labor theory to Roemer's distributional theory of exploitation. I shall argue in favor of a labor theory of exploitation and a force-inclusive definition as being both most faithful to Marx and most adequate. Along the way we shall briefly consider the issue of whether taxation can generally be classified as a form of exploitation.

There are two sorts of evidence for the claim that Marx had a general concept of exploitation. The first is provided by his view that the state as well as economic classes can be an exploiter. In the Asiatic mode of production, where the state owns all land and receives rent from the peasantry, the state is the primary exploiter, according to Marx. Moreover, in *The Eighteenth Brumaire of Louis Bonaparte*, he describes the French state as a parasite on the rest of society, a simile most naturally cashed in terms of exploitation. In *The Civil War in France*, Marx describes the state as a semi-autonomous power standing above all classes. He implies that the Bonapartist state exploits them all—even the capitalist and landlord classes.

But the benefits Marx speaks of in these contexts are primarily—if not exclusively—economic. Hence, it might be argued that even though these considerations prove that he thought that the state as well as economic classes can be an exploiter, it does not show that Marx had a general concept of exploitation in addition to his concept of economic exploitation. (These considerations might even be taken as indications that the state can, in certain cases, take on the role of a ruling economic class.) There is, however, more direct textual evidence for Marx's general concept of exploi-

---

Reimann's in "Exploitation, Force, and the Moral Assessment of Capitalism." Reimann contrasts distributional theories with force-inclusive theories of exploitation and thus includes the simple surplus-value theory of exploitation as a distributional theory. I count this surplus-value theory—what I shall later call "simple exploitation"—as a labor theory, not as a distributional theory. This difference in terminology is unimportant so long as one does not confuse the usages.

tation. Consider the following passage from *The German Ideology*, which contains one of Marx's first uses of the term "exploitation":

> In Holbach, all the activity of individuals in their mutual intercourse, e.g., speech, love, etc., is depicted as a relation of utility and utilization. . . . In this case the utility relation has a quite different meaning, namely that I derive benefit for myself by doing harm to someone else (*exploitation de l'homme par l'homme*). . . . All this actually is the case with the bourgeois. For him only one relation is valid on its own account—the relation of exploitation; all other relations have validity for him only insofar as he can include them under this one relation, and even where he encounters relations which cannot be directly subordinated to the relation of exploitation, he does at least subordinate them to it in his imagination. The material expression of this use is money, the representation of the value of all things, people and social relations.[48]

This passage clearly indicates that Marx had a broader concept of exploitation. As Allen Buchanan notes:

> What is most striking is the extreme generality of this characterization: exploitation is not limited to the labor process itself. It is not simply that the bourgeois exploits the worker *in the wage-labor relationship*. Nor is it simply a matter of the bourgeois exploiting the *worker*. The point, rather, is that, for the bourgeois, human relations *in general* are exploitative, and this includes not only his relations with the worker, but with his fellow bourgeois as well.[49]

Buchanan goes on to offer the following characterization: "Marx's general conception of exploitation includes three elements: first, to exploit someone is to *utilize* him or her as one would a tool or natural resource; second, this utilization is *harmful* to the person so utilized; and third, *the end* of such utilization is *one's own benefit*."[50] Therefore, according to Buchanan, "Exploitation occurs wherever persons are harmfully utilized as mere instruments for private gain."[51]

This definition of exploitation obviously has moral import.

[48] Marx and Engels, *The German Ideology*, in Marx and Engels, *Collected Works*, vol. 5, pp. 409–410.
[49] Buchanan, *Marx and Justice*, p. 38.
[50] Ibid.
[51] Ibid., p. 44.

Given this analysis of the concept, to characterize a set of social relations as exploitative is to imply that it is morally bad or wrong. In this respect, Buchanan's analysis of exploitation agrees with the dictionary definition, which would seem applicable to such situations, as well as with the definitions given by most Marx scholars. The relevant dictionary definition of "exploit" is usually something like "to make use of meanly or unjustly for one's own advantage." For "exploitation" it is usually something like "an unjust or improper use of another person for one's own profit or advantage." Among Marx scholars, Jon Elster writes that "being exploited is being 'taken unfair advantage of,' a much subtler form of suffering harm than being the object of physical coercion."[52] George Panichas distinguishes between what he calls simple exploitation and wrongful exploitation, where the former is simply "taking advantage of" and the latter involves a "taking advantage of" that is, in some measure, morally wrong.[53]

Given this sort of characterization of exploitation, almost any well-known moral theory will judge exploitation to be—at least *prima facie*—morally wrong. Consequentialists will tend to judge it wrong because it inflicts harm on the person who is exploited. However, whether or not the consequentialist will come to judge a particular form or example of exploitation to be—*all things considered*—morally wrong will depend upon both (1) the nonmoral good or goods he or she is committed to maximizing (and, conversely, the nonmoral harms he or she is committed to minimizing), and (2) the amount of benefit that accrues to the exploiter, since this benefit could conceivably overbalance the harm to the exploitee(s) on some consequentialist views. Deontological moral theorists, on the other hand, will tend to judge exploitation, as thus defined, morally wrong either on grounds that it is—*at least prima facie*—unfair to harm another in pursuit of one's own advantage or that it is morally not permissible to treat someone as a mere instrument, that is, to treat another person merely as a means rather than as an end. Again, whether deontological moral theorists will judge exploitation—all things considered—morally wrong will depend on all relevant considerations. It is at least logically possible that eliminating exploitation of a certain sort will result in a situation that is even more unfair or more violative of

[52] Elster, *Making Sense of Marx*, p. 167.
[53] See Panichas, "Vampires, Werewolves, and Economic Exploitation," pp. 223–224.

141

people's rights, or which treats more people as mere means (more on this presently).

Let us now proceed to Marx's concept and theory of *economic* exploitation. Here we need to distinguish his concept of the degree of exploitation from his concept of economic exploitation per se and, concerning the latter, labor theories of exploitation from distributional theories of exploitation. The degree of exploitation (*exploitationsgrad*) is equivalent to the rate of surplus value (which is calculated by dividing surplus labor by necessary labor). As such, it is a purely descriptive concept, except that Marx would presumably use only the rubric "rate of surplus value" to describe a nonexploitative society such as communism. But any importance it may have from a normative perspective derives from its incorporation into a technical, utilitarian interpretation of Marx. As Lawrence Crocker puts it,

> Ultimately this notion finds use in the analysis of capitalist competition, the tendency of the rate of profit to fall, and the genesis of economic crises.
>
> Occasionally commentators on these technical questions create the impression that the central thrust of Marx's critique of capitalism is that it is inefficient. . . . On such a portrayal Marx emerges as the calculating engineer of revolution, committed to increased output and egalitarian distribution, but lacking sensitivity to freedom, democracy, community and, in general, whatever is unquantifiable.[54]

However, it is much more natural to interpret the values undergirding Marx's concept and theory of exploitation as being freedom (as self-determination) and/or his commitment to an egalitarian (or nearly egalitarian) distribution of social goods. If true, this, of course, will dovetail with my interpretation of his general moral perspective. It should be noted, however, that there is a choice to be made here in interpreting Marx's concept of economic exploitation. The first alternative is to take exploitation to be basically a technical, nonevaluative notion and then bring the appropriate values into play when judging whether or not and under what circumstances exploitation is morally wrong. The second alternative is to take exploitation to be an evaluative term and then elicit the values that are already embodied in the concept. Both labor

---

[54] Crocker, "Marx's Concept of Exploitation," pp. 202–203.

142

and distributional theories of exploitation are open to either interpretation.

The simplest labor theory of exploitation defines it as the appropriation of surplus value or the workers not getting back the full
value of what they produce. Speaking in terms of "necessary" and
"surplus" labor, Marx explains this as follows:

> The labourer, during one portion of the labour-process, pro-
> duces only the value of his labour-power, that is, the value of
> his means of subsistence. . . . That portion of the working-day
> . . . during which this reproduction takes place, I call "neces-
> sary" labour-time, and the labour expended during that time I
> call "necessary" labour. . . . the second period of the labour-
> process, that in which his labour is no longer necessary la-
> bour, the workman, it is true labours, expends labour-power;
> but his labour, being no longer necessary labour, he creates
> no value for himself. He creates surplus-value which, for the
> capitalist, has all the charms of a creation out of nothing.[55]

While Marx is speaking specifically of capitalism in the above
passage, it is clear that his concept of surplus labor and thus economic exploitation is *transhistorical*. He writes:

> Capital has not invented surplus-labour. Wherever a part of
> society possesses the monopoly of the means of production,
> the labourer, free or not free, must add to the working-time
> necessary for his own maintenance an extra-working time in
> order to produce the means of subsistence for the owners of
> the means of production, whether this proprietor be the Athe-
> nian [aristocrat], Etruscan theocrat, civis Romanus, Norman
> baron, American slave-owner, Wallachian boyard, modern
> landlord or capitalist.[56]

The cogency of this view does not depend upon the truth of the
labor theory of value in the narrow sense i.e., the claim that socially necessary labor time determines the prices of commodities in
equilibrium market conditions. All that need be accepted is what
Jeffrey Reimann calls the "general labor theory of value," i.e., the
view that labor time is "what ultimately matters about a product."[57] This view is also suggested by Elster, who writes, "From a

---

[55] Marx, *Capital*, vol. 1, pp. 216–217.
[56] Ibid., p. 235.
[57] Reimann, "Exploitation, Force, and the Moral Assessment of Capitalism,"
p. 8.

normative point of view, one could argue that the amount of labour time expended is the only relevant fact, irrespective of the skill with which the labour is performed."[58]

The interesting and important questions at this point are, first, whether or not to include force in the definition of exploitation and, second, whether labor theories of exploitation should be taken to imply some sort of unfairness or injustice. For Marx's theory of economic exploitation, it would seem plausible to answer both of these questions in the affirmative. Consider the issue of adding "force" to the definition of exploitation as the extraction or appropriation of surplus value. The first thing to notice is that Marx's notions of ruling and ruled classes already contain the notion of force or coercion. The ruling class maintains a monopoly over the means of production and distribution, and in class-divided societies the direct producers—be they slaves, serfs, or proletarian workers—are in effect forced to sell their labor-power to this class. Although Marx often speaks of the labor of the proletarian being "free," this only means that the proletarian is generally free to sell it to any one of a number of different buyers—if he can sell it at all. It does not mean that the proletarian is free in any real or substantial sense to not sell his labor at all, or that the proletarian really has control over it. As Marx writes concerning the relation of capital and labor, "[Capital] obtains this surplus-labour without an equivalent [such that] . . . in essence it always remains *forced labour*—no matter how much it may seem to result from free contractual agreement"[59] (emphasis added). Thus exploited labor is *forced* labor (more on this presently).

The other point this quotation highlights is that Marx conceives of exploited labor as *unpaid* labor, i.e., "labor without equivalent." Thus exploited labor seems to be *forced, unpaid, surplus labor*. Is there anything else that must be added to this characterization? I think so. This is the condition that the direct producers do not have control over the surplus labor they expend or, in other words, the surplus product they produce. But this condition may be redundant. If the direct producers did have control over the surplus social product such that they could use it for their individual and collective benefit, then presumably their labor would not be unpaid. Nevertheless, since a number of Marxists and students of Marx have emphasized this as a condition of exploitation, it is

[58] Elster, *Making Sense of Marx*, p. 202.
[59] Marx, *Capital*, vol. 1, p. 819.

good to make it explicit. What I do want to deny, however, is that this is the only condition or a sufficient condition for exploitation, as such writers as Kolakowski and Crocker maintain.[60] If the labor in question is not forced but, rather, voluntary, then it seems to me that it is not exploited labor even if those who volunteered their work have no control over the product they produce. In fact, this is a fair characterization of members of a church or civic group who must pay membership dues or volunteer labor to remain a member of the group, and surely we would not under normal conditions, call this "exploitation."

Thus we have arrived at the conclusion that, as Nancy Holmstrom puts it, exploited labor is "forced, surplus, and unpaid labor, the product of which is not under the producers' control."[61] But we have not yet answered the second question: namely, whether exploitation implies unfairness or injustice. Setting aside for now the difficulty that Marx—as well as some contemporary Marxists—insists that justice is a notion that can only be applied internally to a particular society such that exploitation will not be judged unjust so long as it corresponds to the basic economic norms of its mode of production, I believe the answer to this is "yes." Moreover, I believe a strong case can be made that Marx implicitly held this view. That he thought it unjust—even though he may not have been amenable to characterizing it in this fashion—is borne out in the many passages in which he speaks of exploitation (or the relation between capitalist and worker) as "robbery," "embezzlement," "theft," and "slavery." In the *Grundrisse* he speaks of "the *theft of others' labour-time upon which [the present] wealth depends.*"[62] In *Capital*, volume I, he speaks of the "yearly accruing surplus product" as "embezzled because [it is] abstracted without return of an equivalent."[63] There he also states:

There is not one single atom of its value that does not owe its existence to unpaid labour. The means of production, with which the additional labour is incorporated, as well as the necessaries with which the labourer is sustained, are nothing but component parts of the surplus-product, of the tribute annually exacted from the working-class by the capitalist class. Though the latter with a portion of that tribute purchases the

[60] See Kolakowski, *Main Currents of Marxism*, vol. 1, p. 333; and Crocker, "Marx's Concept of Exploitation."
[61] Holmstrom, "Exploitation," p. 359.
[62] Marx, *The Grundrisse*, p. 142.
[63] Marx, *Capital*, vol. I, p. 611.

additional labour-power even at its full price, so that equivalent is exchanged for equivalent, yet the transaction is for all that only the old dodge of every conqueror who buys commodities from the conquered with the money he has robbed them of.[64]

Finally, in "Critique of the Gotha Program" Marx proclaims that "the system of wage-labour is a system of slavery."[65]

The injustice or unfairness of exploitation would seem to follow immediately from the fact that exploited labor is both *forced* and *unpaid*. So long as we add the caveat that we are speaking here of its being *prima facie* wrong or unjust as opposed to its being *all-things-considered* wrong or unjust, I don't see how such a situation could be judged otherwise. This leaves open as a logical possibility, however, that exploitation can be all-things-considered just, as it might be, for example, if it were absolutely necessary in order to insure other important moral values such as meeting the subsistence needs of everyone. (Needless to say, Marxists would regard this as highly unlikely.)

This distinction between exploitation that is *prima facie* wrong and exploitation that is all-things-considered wrong is of paramount importance. Most disagreements concerning the definition of "economic" exploitation are, I believe, the result of failing to distinguish the following three notions:

(1) *Simple Exploitation*: the appropriation of surplus value or the direct producers not getting back the full value of what they produce.

(2) *Exploitation Proper*: forced, unpaid, surplus labor, the product of which is not under the control of the direct producers.

(3) *All-things-considered Unjustified Exploitation*: exploitation (proper) that is not justified by its promotion of some other weighty moral concern.

Simple exploitation cannot be considered even *prima facie* wrong since it may be the result of a fair agreement for mutual benefit— for example, a mutually beneficial agreement between an actor and his or her agent.[66] *Exploitation proper* as forced, unpaid, surplus labor is always *prima facie* wrong but may or may not be all-

---

[64] Ibid., p. 582.
[65] Marx, "Critique of the Gotha Program," p. 392.
[66] This example is given by Panichas in his "Vampires, Werewolves, and Economic Exploitation," pp. 233–235.

things-considered wrong. Although capitalist exploitation is *prima facie* wrong (and, at this point in history, all-things-considered wrong on Marxist empirical assumptions), it would not be all-things-considered wrong if capitalist apologists were correct in asserting that capitalism is a necessary condition for meeting people's basic needs, maintaining political democracy and civil liberty, etc. But, as just said, if Marxist empirical assumptions are correct, then capitalist exploitation is now *all-things-considered unjustified exploitation*. Marx did not, of course, think that it is always immediately feasible to abolish such exploitative social relations, but he certainly held that they ought to be abolished as soon as it is historically possible to do so.

These distinctions are essential for clearing up a number of counter-examples offered against the force-inclusive analysis of the Marxist concept of exploitation. Consider, first, G. A. Cohen's counter-example to Allen Wood's analysis of exploitation as essentially coercive nonreciprocity—an analysis I take to be in line with the one I have offered here. Cohen argues against the inclusion of force or coercion in the definition of "exploitation" as follows:

> To see that it [i.e., coercion] is not a necessary condition [for exploitation] consider a rich capitalist, A, who, for whatever reason, voluntarily works for another capitalist, B, at a wage which is such that, were A a worker, he would count as exploited on my view, and also Marx's. A, though not forced to work for B, or for anyone else, is exploited by B.[67]

But since A is not *forced* to work for B, it seems clear that Cohen is confusing Simple Exploitation with Exploitation Proper, or at least begging the question against the force-inclusive definition. Although Marx does use the concept of Simple Exploitation, it is clear, I think, that he normally uses "exploitation" in the negative, evaluative sense, which can most easily be accounted for by interpreting it as the force-inclusive notion I have labeled Exploitation Proper.

Arneson's analysis of Marx's concept of exploitation also suffers from not recognizing these distinctions. For example, in his article "What's Wrong with Exploitation?" Arneson first defines "a technical sense of the term 'exploitation,' according to which exploitation is the appropriation by a class of nonworkers of the surplus

[67] G. A. Cohen, "Review of *Karl Marx*, by Wood" p. 444.

147

product of a class of workers,"[68] and he claims—quite correctly, I think—that this sense of exploitation (which I am calling "simple exploitation") does not necessarily have negative evaluative import. But a few pages later—after having described Holmstrom's analysis of exploitation as surplus, unpaid, forced labor, the product of which the producers do not control—he asserts that *"Holmstrom might be correctly explicating the technical sense of exploitation, but . . . the technical sense fails adequately to capture Marx's moral concerns"*[69] (emphasis added). Here Arneson clearly conflates Simple Exploitation with Exploitation Proper and thus fails to appreciate that Exploitation Proper *does have* negative evaluative import, at least in the sense of always being *prima facie* wrong.

Arneson goes on to describe what he calls "wrongful exploitation" as follows:

> Wrongful exploitation exists wherever technical exploitation exists together with the following two conditions: (1) the nonproducers have vastly more social power than the producers, and they employ this power to bring about technical exploitation; and (2) this technical exploitation establishes an extremely unequal distribution of economic advantages, and it is not the case that one can distinguish the gainers from the losers in terms of the greater deservingness of the former.[70]

If Arneson were claiming here only to provide Marx's criteria for deciding which cases of Exploitation Proper were All-Things-Considered Unjustified Exploitation, I would have no objection. Indeed, I agree with Arneson's claim that the ideas that "people should get what they deserve [and] . . . people should not force others to do their bidding"[71] both underlie Marx's evaluative concept (or concepts) of economic exploitation. I also agree that it is a reasonable supposition that "Marx believes that . . . what [people] deserve varies with their intentions and (under normal circumstances) with their efforts or sacrifices expended, rather than with the actual outcome of their intentions."[72] What I do not agree with is Arneson's claim that Marx's concept of economic exploitation is best thought of as encompassing these values as a matter of definition. If this were the case, it would seem almost inconceivable

---

[68] Arneson, "What's Wrong with Exploitation?" p. 203.
[69] Ibid., p. 206.
[70] Ibid., p. 212.
[71] Ibid., p. 205.
[72] Ibid., p. 213.

for Marx simultaneously to maintain that a particular society is exploitative but that this exploitation is justified. But, in a sense, this is precisely Marx's position with respect to early capitalism or any economic system that is both exploitative and—at that stage of its development—historically progressive in terms of spurring the expansion of the forces of production. Thus, all things considered, it seems more perspicuous to accept Exploitation Proper as Marx's primary concept of economic exploitation and to classify Arneson's "wrongful exploitation" as an attempt to provide the moral standards Marx and Marxists generally employ when deciding which cases of Exploitation Proper—which are always *prima facie* wrong—are all-things-considered wrong. While these two moral standards may be Marx's primary desiderata in determining whether a given situation of exploitation is an All-Things-Considered Unjustified Exploitative situation, they are not necessary conditions for Exploitation Proper, i.e., for "exploitation" as Marx normally uses the term.

Given this analysis, Arneson's purported counterexamples to the thesis that Marx's primary concept of economic exploitation is what I am calling Exploitation Proper can be rather easily dealt with. It usually turns out that the scenarios he puts forward are indeed examples of Exploitation Proper—and are thus *prima facie* condemnable—but, for one reason or another, are not All-Things-Considered Unjustified Exploitation.[73] Arneson's mistake is to insist that because they are not cases of All-Things-Considered Unjustified Exploitation, they would not count (for Marx) as exploitation in a negative evaluative sense.

Before moving on to distributional theories of exploitation, I want to return to the topic of the role force plays in what I have described as Marx's basic concept of exploitation, i.e., what I am calling Exploitation Proper. I also want to explore briefly whether taxation is a form of exploitation.

Although it seems clear that Marx conceived of exploitation as (at least) forced, unpaid, surplus labor, many people will simply deny that workers are forced to work under capitalism. But here we must make two distinctions. The first is between coercion and force. The second is between standard cases of force and structural force. Both coercion and force imply the limitation of choice—usually to one alternative. But, with Elster, I shall take "coercion to

[73] See Arneson's feudal scenario on p. 203, his Disabled-Robust scenario on p. 206, and his Lowlander-Highlander scenario on p. 211.

imply [an] intentional agent or coercer, while force need not imply more than the presence of constraints that leave no room for choice. I am forced to live in my native town if I cannot get a job elsewhere, but I am coerced to live there if I would be arrested were I to try to leave."[74] While slaves in slave societies are generally coerced to labor, the direct producers in capitalist societies are not normally *coerced* to labor or, more properly, sell their labor-power. But it seems that a strong case can be made for the view that they are *forced* to sell their labor-power. Proletarians, by definition, have only their labor-power to sell. They do not receive investment or property income like capitalists or landlords. They do not have their own small means of production or distribution like the petty bourgeoisie. Although it might be argued that in contemporary welfare-state capitalist societies proletarians have the option of relying on welfare, this would not show that the capitalist economic system does not force workers to sell their labor-power, but only that the external force of the state can sometimes "save" some people from being forced to do so. Moreover, this is rarely such an attractive option that rational persons would see it as a genuine alternative to a reasonably paying job. As Elster writes: "The existence of alternative courses of action that might allow him to survive is irrelevant if they are so unattractive that no man in his senses would choose them."[75] (Although not directly germane to the present issue, it should also be noted that the existence of welfare transfer programs is primarily the result of past class struggles and the ruling class's conscious attempts to preempt future ones.)

Another objection to the view that workers are forced to sell their labor-power under capitalism is the claim that they do have reasonable options, i.e., other than starving to death, becoming criminals, or going on the dole. The claim here is that workers have the opportunity to escape from the working class into the petty bourgeoisie or even the capitalist class. In its crudest form, this is the Horatio Alger myth: any person of normal abilities can rise to the top if she or he is hard-working and persevering. A slightly less crude version is the claim that *talented* individuals can escape the working class if they are hard-working and persevering. However, if we are speaking of individuals with a high degree of natural talent or ability, this ignores the fact that even if such

---

[74] Elster, *Making Sense of Marx*, pp. 211–212.
[75] Ibid., p. 215.

individuals did well in the "natural lottery," they may not have fared as well in the "social lottery." If born into poverty and an unstimulating social environment, even highly talented, working-class individuals will, in all probability, not be able to escape their fate of wage-labor or worse.

Nevertheless, even some Marxists are willing to concede this point. G. A. Cohen, for example, argues that workers are *individually free* to stop selling their labor-power because any of them can—if they are of normal abilities and are hardworking and per-severing—eventually save enough money to buy small means of production or distribution and thus escape into the petty bour-geoisie.[76] However, Cohen also claims that the proletariat as a class is *collectively unfree* because the slots open in the petty bour-geoisie and capitalist or landlord classes are limited: only so many proletarians can be absorbed. Certainly it would be impossible for *all* proletarians to escape wage-labor since it is impossible to have only capitalists and petty bourgeois—to the exclusion of workers—and still have capitalism.

It is my belief that Cohen is being overly charitable to capitalism when he claims that any worker can become at least a petty bour-geois and then concludes that no individual worker is forced to sell his labor-power. First, his claim that any given worker can save enough of her or his income over a five- or ten-year period to pro-vide the initial capital for a small business is simply not true. Many workers are simply not paid that much. Even in contemporary welfare-state, capitalist societies, many workers lacking the requi-site skills or connections work in low-paying (usually nonunion) jobs and in some countries—the United States, for example—are normally expected to pay outrageously high rents, medical care for themselves and their families, etc. (This is, of course, dispropor-tionately true of women and minorities in such societies.) Second, those workers who do save up the initial capital and have suc-ceeded in maintaining a good credit rating are not guaranteed suc-cess even if they do buy—or buy into—a small business of some sort. Far from it. It is well known that (literally) most small busi-nesses do not successfully make it through their first five years, let alone provide their proprietors a long-term source of economic se-curity. And when a business fails, the individual is often in a worse financial situation than he or she was before becoming a petty bourgeois. I conclude that escaping into the petty bourgeoi-

[76] See G. A. Cohen, "The Structure of Proletarian Unfreedom."

sie (or big bourgeoisie) is a reasonable alternative only for a tiny minority of workers. Thus the vast majority of working-class individuals *are* forced to sell their labor-power to earn a living.

But the notion of force involved here is best captured by utilizing a concept of *structural* force. As Jeffrey Reimann puts it:

> Unlike the usual strongarm stuff that singles out particular individuals as its targets, this force works on people by virtue of their location in the social structure (that is, for example, *qua* members of some class), and it affects individuals more or less "statistically." By this I mean that *such force affects individuals by imposing an array of fates on some group while leaving it open how particular individuals in that group get sorted, or sort themselves, into those fates.*[77]

> In the standard cases, the target of force has no real choice over his fate, either because all his alternatives save one are unacceptable, or because he has no alternatives at all (perhaps he has been bound or drugged). In structural force, by contrast, there is some *play*. Structural force works to constrain a group of individuals to some array of situations, leaving it to them or to other factors to determine how they are distributed among those situations.[78]

> As long as the group is constrained such that its members must end up distributed among all the situations in the array determined by the structure, all the individuals are "forced into" the particular situations in which they end up—even if they exercised some choice on the way. In short, structural force can operate through free choice.[79]

If this analysis is correct, then one can cogently say that workers are forced to work in a capitalist system. Thus their labor—also being partially unpaid labor—is exploited. But if labor is exploited because it is forced and unpaid, is not taxation a form of exploitation? Although exploitation in the sense of forced, unpaid, surplus labor being transferred from one class to another is always *prima facie* wrong from a Marxist perspective such that it should be eliminated if historically possible, what is not clear is that this arrangement should be judged even *prima facie* wrong when the partici-

[77] Reiman, "Exploitation, Force, and the Moral Assessment of Capitalism," p. 12.
[78] Ibid., p. 14.
[79] Ibid., p. 15. See also Zimmerman, "Coercive Wage Offers" and "More on Coercive Wage Offers."

pants are the state and its citizenry. In fact—Nozick's arguments not withstanding—very few of us are willing to judge any and all taxes morally wrong or unjust or even to label them forms of exploitation in the negative, evaluative sense of the term. But why is this, and what is its significance for the definition of exploitation just given?

It would be nice to be able simply to dismiss this difficulty on grounds, say, that taxes are not transfers of surplus labor and thus are not comparable to the exchanges that take place at the point of production, as in Marx's theory of exploitation. But this would be disingenuous. For one thing, I have claimed that surplus labor and surplus product are to be taken as equivalent expressions for our purposes, so the transfer of money in terms of taxes is equivalent to a transfer of labor. For another, we have already noted that Marx viewed the tax-collecting state of the Asiatic mode of production as the primary exploiter in that sort of society. One might argue that in this case—and conceivably in the case of state-socialism—the state, or (more perspicuously) the state bureaucracy, has become an economic class itself as opposed to an institution representing the interests of the ruling economic class in society. While I am not sure how to tell when a state bureaucracy becomes an economic class—especially a ruling economic class—I think this may be a plausible suggestion. Marx was primarily concerned with substructural phenomena such as economic classes and the laws of economic motion of a mode of production in his theory of economic exploitation. The state—which, for Marx, is a superstructural institution—did not usually enter into his theory of exploitation because normally it is not the social institution that is the primary recipient of the surplus value which it (admittedly) helps the ruling economic class pump out of the direct producers. Perhaps this ultimately reveals a weakness or at least a hiatus in Marxist empirical theory.

In the "normal" situation where the state bureaucracy is clearly not an economic class, it seems a bit misleading—at least from a Marxist perspective —to speak of the state economically exploiting its citizens, although it may be exploitative in the more general sense of this term elucidated toward the beginning of this section. In any case, several other considerations militate against speaking of taxation as economic exploitation—at least in the standard case. It is arguable, in fact, that given a relatively democratic state, the transfer of labor involved fails to meet three out of the four conditions of exploited labor. Although it must be surplus labor (un-

153

less the state is taxing its citizenry to the point of starving them), it may not be *unpaid* or *forced* in the same sense or to the same degree as exploited labor in Marx's standard model. Moreover, given a democratic state, the direct producers who are taxed may very well *have control* over the product of their labor (i.e., the tax revenues).

The labor transferred to the state through taxation may not be *forced* labor in the same sense that the labor transferred from the direct producers to the ruling class is forced labor. While the alternatives acceptable to most—if not all—direct producers are usually considered unacceptable, there is usually a minimum income level below which one is not taxed, which is usually above that of absolute poverty. Although where this cutoff point is set will obviously be a relevant consideration, it is at least arguable that making this much money but no more, and thus not paying taxes, is an acceptable alternative to paying taxes. (Given a progressive taxation scheme, of course, one who barely goes over this limit will have to pay very little in taxes.) Some may object that this alternative is not acceptable because a person would usually be much better off (materially speaking) if he both made more money and paid more taxes. But an alternative is not unacceptable just because it fails to optimize.[80]

It is also arguable that taxation does not involve *unpaid* labor. To the extent that citizens receive benefits—either directly, as in medical assistance, or indirectly, as in public goods (including the good of security)—they are recouping their losses. However, since the amount of taxes people pay and the amount of benefits they receive may not be proportional, all individuals will not recoup exactly what they pay in. Finally, to the extent that the state is democratic and its citizens have control over the use of state revenues, taxation fails to meet the fourth condition in our definition of exploitation.

But even if—after considering all relevant similarities and differences between the standard case of exploitation and taxation—we were to conclude that taxation is a form of exploitation, this would not settle whether it was just (or justified). Remember the analysis given in this section in which it is logically possible for exploitation to be *just* exploitation or at least *justified* exploitation. Nor, conversely, should we assume that simply because something is not unjust it cannot be classified as exploitation. This is why I must

[80] See Elster, *Making Sense of Marx*, pp. 214–216.

disagree with G. A. Cohen's assertion that "one reason why welfare recipients are not exploiters is that the relevant transfer payments are not unjust."[81] There are conceivable situations in which exploitation is just. For example, if the only way a group of people could ensure that their basic needs were met was to exploit other people, then this may well be just. In any case, it is probably best not to classify standard cases of taxation as exploitation.

Let us now consider another approach to exploitation. The major competitor to labor theories of exploitation is John Roemer's purely distributional theory of exploitation, which takes property relations rather than the transfer of surplus value (or product) as basic. Roemer's announced project is to utilize the tools of contemporary mathematical economic theory—especially general equilibrium theory and cooperative game theory—to provide a general (Marxian) theory of exploitation and class and to hook up these notions with Marx's theory of historical materialism. He usually begins his analyses with what he calls the concept of Marxian Exploitation. His interpretation of Marx's concept of exploitation is as follows:

> An exploited producer is one who cannot possibly command as much labor value, through the purchase of goods with his revenues, as the labor he contributed in production, and an exploiter is one who unambiguously commands more labor time through goods purchased no matter how he dispenses his revenues. This is a generalization of the classical Marxian definition that the worker is exploited because the labor he expends is greater than the labor embodied in the only bundle he can feasibly purchase (and stay alive), his subsistence bundle.[82]

This is, of course, what I am calling Simple Exploitation. But Roemer finds this concept wanting on a number of grounds. First of all,

> the surplus-labor theory of exploitation fails with heterogeneous labor, despite various attempts to save it. . . . The surplus-labor characterization is useful only when capitalism is seen as a system with one primary factor, labor, which is homogeneous and equally endowed to all. With the property-

---

[81] G. A. Cohen, "Review of *Karl Marx*, by Wood" p. 444.
[82] Roemer, "New Directions in the Marxian Theory of Exploitation and Class," p. 269.

relations characterization, Marxists are no longer forced to claim that capitalism actually looks like this special case, for the theory applies in a completely general environment. Thus, not only is the labor theory of value irrelevant as a theory of price, but its role in the theory of exploitation is superceded [sic].[83]

Another reason for rejecting the labor theory of exploitation is that it does not (according to Roemer) make clear the ethical implications of exploitation. He writes that "the true reason to be interested in exploitation is not that we are concerned with labor flows, but that we are concerned with the underlying inequality of the means of production."[84] He also writes that "exploitation is a misleading attribute if one's true interest is inequality in the distribution of wealth. There appears to be no reason for an interest in the technical measure of exploitation, calculated in the classical Marxist way."[85]

Roemer's third reason is that in this interpretation of Marx's concept of exploitation, there are some conceivable cases in which the poor exploit the rich. As Roemer writes, "It can happen that the asset-rich are exploited by the asset-poor: the flow of surplus value goes the wrong way."[86] This would be the case, for example, if a worker or petty bourgeois had enough money to hire a big bourgeois and made a profit from the big bourgeois' labor. (That this is a highly fanciful possibility is obvious!)

In any case, Roemer's analysis of exploitation begins with the idea that a group (or individual) is exploited if, and only if, there is a conditionally feasible alternative under which it would be materially better off. More formally,

a coalition S, in a larger society N, is exploited if, and only if:
(1)   There is an alternative, which we may conceive of as hypothetically feasible, in which S would be better off than in its present situation.
(2)   Under this alternative, the complement to S, the coalition $N - S = S'$, would be worse off at present.[87]

(It is interesting to note that in *A General Theory of Exploitation and Class*, Roemer adds a third condition: "S' is in a relationship of

---

[83] Ibid., p. 286.
[84] Roemer, *Value, Exploitation, and Class*, p. 67.
[85] Roemer, *Free to Lose*, p. 131.
[86] Roemer, "Should Marxists be Interested in Exploitation?" p. 54.
[87] Roemer, *A General Theory of Exploitation and Class*, p. 194.

dominance to S."[88] But in an article that came out shortly after this book, he repudiates this condition as "undefined" and "ad hoc."[89] As we shall see, Roemer's analysis would have been less objectionable if he had kept this condition.)

Roemer goes on to utilize withdrawal rules to give a game-theoretic characterization of this definition of exploitation. A different specification of the withdrawal rules is given for each type of exploitation. The different rules are supposed to reflect the different property relations found in the various modes of production. Thus exploitation in slave and feudal societies is defined in terms of property in other people or the rights some people have in the labor of others. Capitalist exploitation has to do with the unequal distribution of alienable productive assets, i.e. the unequal ownership of resources and means of production and distribution. Socialist exploitation, according to Roemer, has to do with the unequal distribution of inalienable productive assets (primarily skills). He thinks that the progression of societies in Marx's theory of historical materialism can be perspicuously characterized in terms of the types of property in which unequal ownership is allowed. Each successive society, in the progression from slave to feudal to capitalist to socialist to communist society, constricts the type of property that can be distributed (i.e., owned) unequally. (Roemer also defines concepts of "status exploitation" and "socially necessary exploitation," of which I will have more to say presently.)

A group of persons (or coalition) is *feudally* exploited if it could improve its lot by withdrawing from an economy and taking its *own productive endowments*, i.e., its own work skills and family plots. That serfs in actual feudal societies were exploited, according to this analysis of feudal exploitation, depends on such further assumptions as that serfs owned their family plots and that their lords did not provide any essential services that they couldn't provide for themselves or buy. But, as Roemer writes, "it can be maintained that large groups of serfs themselves possessed the requisite skill to organize military protection and to take advantage of other externalities and economies of scale accompanying manor life."[90] That feudal lords and their retinues would be worse off in this situation is obvious.

A coalition of agents is *capitalistically* exploited if it could im-

[88] Ibid., p. 195.
[89] See Roemer, "New Directions," p. 277.
[90] Roemer, "New Directions," p. 279.

prove its lot by withdrawing with its *per capita share of society's alienable productive assets*—and its complement class would be worse off. Roemer claims that under simple models this type of exploitation is equivalent to the Marxian surplus-value characterization of exploitation. He claims that "to characterize capitalist exploitation in terms of an alternative egalitarian distribution of private property in the means of production captures precisely what Marxists mean by exploitation."[91] (This, I believe, is debatable since Roemer's definition doesn't include the notion of force.)

Roemer goes on to offer a characterization of *socialist* exploitation:

> If capitalist exploitation were annihilated inequalities would continue to exist, due to differential inalienable assets possessed by individuals. This inequality I call socialist exploitation. A coalition is socialistically exploited if it could improve its lot by withdrawing with its per capita share of society's inalienable assets, once alienable assets are distributed equally. While carrying out such a redistribution of skills might be impossible, or at the least would involve formidable incentive problems, as a thought experiment the calculations can be made.
>
> Socialist exploitation is supposed to exist in socialism, where people are to be paid "according to their work" and thus not in an egalitarian manner. . . .
>
> If all individual endowments are of either the alienable or inalienable type, then a distribution of income is free of socialist exploitation when it is egalitarian.[92]

The idea here is that even if the means of production are socially—and thus equally—owned in a socialist society, the skilled could still exploit the unskilled in the sense that the former could make more money than the latter. Even if everyone were to be paid the same hourly wage, some could earn more than others because they are physically and/or mentally able to work more hours. As Marx puts it in "Critique of the Gotha Program," "One man is superior to another physically or mentally and so supplies more labour in the same time, or can labour for a longer time."[93] Thus the first stage of communism "tacitly recognizes unequal individual endowment and thus productive capacity as natural priv-

[91] Ibid.
[92] Ibid., p. 283.
[93] Marx, "Critique of the Gotha Program," p. 387.

ileges."[94] Although Marx regards this as an unsatisfactory situation that will be overcome in the "higher stage of communism," he thinks it is the best that can be done in the first stage. Roemer concurs. He claims that "socialist exploitation" exists in socialism but, by hypothesis, will not exist in communism.

But, as Roemer recognizes, the skilled exploiting the unskilled is not likely to be the only or even the most important source of inequality in a post-capitalist society.

There is another inequality in existing socialist societies that appears to be more pernicious than skill inequality, namely, inequality in the distribution of income due to differential status, or access to position. To the extent that occupying certain positions is a return to skill, then these status differentials are a reflection of skill differentials. But much status inequality of socialist societies seems to be due not to skill differentials but to the privileges that come with occupying certain positions. Political office often brings with it myriad material benefits, with respect to housing, automobiles, and consumer goods. Those of high status can shop in special stores and are not rationed with respect to the purchase of goods that are otherwise scarce. Status exploitation is the consequence of real income inequality due to differential status.[95]

Whereas socialist exploitation, due to private ownership of skills, is supposed to exist under socialism, status exploitation is an unintended and undesirable form of inequality.[96]

Feudal exploitation is eliminated by abolishing property in others; capitalist exploitation is eliminated by abolishing private ownership of the means of production; socialist exploitation is eliminated by abolishing differential remuneration for skilled labor; and status exploitation is eliminated by abolishing the privileges of bureaucracies. Since, according to Roemer, "status exploitation exists because of the large degree of central planning and the consequent growth of a bureaucracy capable of creating privileges for itself,"[97] the elimination of status exploitation in contemporary post-capitalist societies will probably require a "judicious use of markets."

Finally, Roemer introduces the notion of *socially necessary exploitation*. A type of exploitation is socially necessary if, and only if,

[94] Ibid.
[95] Roemer, *Free to Lose*, p. 141.
[96] Ibid., p. 143.
[97] Ibid., p. 146.

eliminating it would make society as a whole—including the producing class—worse off. This would usually be caused by a change in incentive schedules but could also be caused, Roemer claims, by a slowing of technological change. The notion of socially necessary exploitation is closely related to the Marxist notion of a progressive economic system: so long as a system, such as capitalism, is progressive in the sense of spurring rather than fettering economic development, the exploitation involved would seem to be socially necessary. Obviously this notion is related to my concept of "all-things-considered justified exploitation," in that this consideration is the primary reason why exploitation in a particular society would be justified.

This brings us to another point: Roemer's concepts of exploitation have a built-in theory of distributive justice. In fact, one might say that his theory of exploitation is little more than a surrogate for a theory of distributive justice and is thus, in principle, dispensable. Roemer writes, for example, that "the labor theory of exploitation just does not work as an analytically convincing theory of distributive injustice, and must be replaced by the property relations approach, which says a group or person is exploited if he does not have access to his fair share . . . of the . . . productive assets of society."[98] Furthermore, to determine whether exploitation exists in a certain society, we "compare the existing distribution of income with the distribution of income which would ensue were property in the alienable (nonhuman) means of production to be redistributed in an egalitarian way."[99] Finally, the principle of distributive justice proposed by Roemer seems to be that of strict equality. He says, for example, that "the recipe for ending Marxian exploitation . . . is to eliminate differential ownership . . . of the means of production."[100] When comparing his implicit principle of distributive justice to Rawls' difference principle, he writes: "Certain inequalities may be to the benefit of the exploited or the least well off. The Rawlsian theory views such inequalities as just. I think, however, that *justice entails that incomes to individuals are deserved*."[101] Since Roemer does not view any income derived from differential ownership of either productive forces or

[98] Roemer, *Value, Exploitation, and Class*, pp. 80–82.
[99] Roemer, "R. P. Wolff's Reinterpretation of Marx's Labor Theory of Value," p. 81.
[100] Ibid., p. 82.
[101] Roemer, "Property Relations vs. Surplus Value in Marxian Exploitation," pp. 309–310.

work skills as being deserved, it seems that he must reject as just any distribution that is not strictly equal, even one that benefits the least well-off segment of the population.

There are a number of points to be made here. The first is that there is at least a tension—if not an inconsistency—between his principle of strict equality of productive assets (which seems to underlie his concept of exploitation) and his claim that exploitation is socially necessary (i.e., justified) if abolishing it would make society as a whole worse off. If Roemer wholly commits himself to strict equality in productive assets, then he cannot justify an unequal distribution because it prevents society as a whole from being worse off. Conversely, if he stands firm on his notion of socially necessary exploitation (i.e., on justified inequalities in productive assets and hence incomes), he cannot wholly commit himself to strict equality. (Here it could be argued that he should accept Rawls' difference principle since it is a reasoned attempt to integrate these two distributive principles.)

Second, Roemer does not provide the full-blown theory of social—or at least distributive—justice his theory of exploitation requires if it is to be a useful tool of social criticism. It is not even clear exactly to what principles of justice he is committed. Moreover, he emphasizes *desert* but does not seem to distinguish it from entitlement or provide a justification for the primacy of the former over the latter. Similarly, he does not defend his assumption that income derived from differential ownership of property or skills is not deserved. (As Elster and others have pointed out, this assumption may run into problems when faced with hypothetical cases of "clean accumulation."[102])

Third, it is not clear why the inequalities Roemer cites are cases of exploitation. As Allen Buchanan expresses this point,

> Roemer does little to explain why inegalitarian distributions of property are wrong and nothing at all to explain why, even if they are morally wrong, they are *exploi[ta]tive*. No attempt is made to connect the inegalitarian distribution of property with practice or actions that are, according to ordinary usage, exploi[ta]tive. . . . [He] provides no clue as to why the alleged injustice in question should be called *exploitation* (not all injus-

[102] See Elster, *Making Sense of Marx*, pp. 177, 226–228. For a more detailed critique of the view that inequalities resulting from "clean accumulation" are automatically morally justified, see G. A. Cohen, "Robert Nozick and Wilt Chamberlain."

tices are cases of exploitation) rather than simply a violation of a right of distributive justice, for example.[103]

In connection with this point, it is not clear why a theory of exploitation is needed if its content boils down to a theory of distributive justice. Why not simply apply the theory of justice straightaway to property relations in various societies. To quote Buchanan again:

> Roemer's definition of "exploitation," like Wolff's, achieves clarity and precision at the price of emptying the concept of normative force. Without the required theory of justice, the concept of exploitation cannot serve as a tool for social criticism. If the theory is supplied, however, it is not at all clear that the theory of "exploitation" (as opposed to the concept of justice embodied in the theory) would have any role to play.[104]

Before leaving Roemer's theory of exploitation, let us consider (in reverse order) his three reasons for rejecting a labor theory of exploitation mentioned at the beginning of this analysis. It is my contention that the objections that work at all work only against Simple Exploitation and not against Exploitation Proper (which includes force in its definition).

The last of the three reasons cited was that labor theories of exploitation may result in the poor exploiting the rich. A simple example would be a big bourgeois working for a rather poor petty bourgeois. Here the big bourgeois does not get back all of the value, product, or labor he or she expends since—let us stipulate—the petty bourgeois makes a profit from the big bourgeois's labor. Thus, in terms of Simple Exploitation—which Roemer takes to be Marx's concept of exploitation—the petty bourgeois exploits the big bourgeois. There are two points to be made here. First, if one utilizes a force-inclusive definition of "exploitation" (or Exploitation Proper), then clearly the petty bourgeois is *not* exploiting the big bourgeois since the latter, being wealthy, is not forced to sell his or her labor. Secondly, Roemer's theory is open to precisely the same sort of counter-example, and this is much more devastating for his theory since he cannot fall back on the requirement that exploited labor is forced labor. Consider a society divided between the Able-Bodied and the Disabled, where part of what the Able-Bodied produce is distributed to the Disabled. If the Able-

---

[103] Buchanan, "Marx, Morality, and History," pp. 129–130.
[104] Ibid., p. 130.

Bodied withdraw from society with their per capita share of the means of production, they will be better off since they will not have to share with the Disabled. The Disabled—the complement class of the Able-Bodied—will be worse off. Thus the Disabled (capitalistically) exploit the Able-Bodied! Although, as we saw earlier, the question of whether taxation for such purposes is a form of exploitation is somewhat puzzling, I take it that any theory that decides immediately and decisively that this is a case of the Disabled exploiting the Able-Bodied has somehow gotten off the track.

The second reason cited earlier for Roemer's rejection of labor theories of exploitation is that they do not make clear the ethical implications of exploitation, namely, inequality in the distribution of wealth. But this seems to beg the question since it is arguable that Marx and most Marxists have taken the violation of workers' freedom under capitalism to be at least as much of a moral implication of exploitation—and at least as morally important—as inequalities in the distribution of wealth. Roemer constantly emphasizes the inequality in the ownership of the means of production, but no Marxist disagrees with this. The question is: is inequality in ownership of the means of production to be condemned primarily because it results in inequalities in the distribution of income and wealth or because it results in inequalities of power, with the further result that people's freedom (as self-determination) is violated. Although Karl Popper misinterprets Marx on a number of issues, he is squarely on the mark, I believe, when he claims:

Marx's condemnation of capitalism is fundamentally a moral condemnation. The system is condemned . . . because by forcing the exploiter to enslave the exploited, it robs both of their freedom. Marx did not combat wealth, nor did he praise poverty. He hated capitalism, not for its accumulation of wealth, but for its oligarchical character; he hated it because in this system wealth means political power in the sense of power over men. Labour power is made a commodity; that means that men must sell themselves on the market. Marx hated the system because it resembled slavery.[105]

Exploitation is wrong, I contend, not only because it violates principles of distributive justice but also—and more fundamentally—because it violates the value of freedom. More precisely, it

[105] Popper, *The Open Society and Its Enemies*, vol. 2, p. 199.

163

violates the principle of maximum equal freedom as explicated in my reconstruction of Marx's concept and theory of freedom. Although a system of exploitation of direct producers by nonproducers does not *directly* violate the *negative* freedom of the producers, it may do so indirectly through the use of the police power of the state to break strikes, maintain order, and prevent the producers from expropriating the means of production and distribution from the nonproducers. But certainly such a system directly violates people's *positive* freedom in the sense of both their right to equal participation in all social decision-making processes and their right to equal access to the means of self-realization. (The latter is also a principle of *distributive* justice, of course.) Although my reconstructed Marxian theory of freedom does not take as basic a right to own an equal share of the productive forces of society, the claim that productive property should be socially owned—at a certain stage in history—is entailed by this theory when it is conjoined with the Marxist's empirical claim that capitalism violates people's freedom in the above-mentioned ways.

Finally, let us consider Roemer's first objection: that labor theories of exploitation presuppose the labor theory of value. As pointed out earlier, this is simply false. For a labor theory of exploitation to make sense, one does not have to be able to calculate the labor content of goods. Thus all the problems of heterogeneous labor, etc., simply do not come up. As Reiman puts it, only the "general labor theory of value" need be accepted. Or, as Elster puts it, we need only assume that, from a normative point of view, there is something important about how much one labors—or what percentage of society's total labor time one contributes—and what percentage of society's total wealth one gets back. Buchanan concurs:

> To recognize that the labor process in capitalism is exploitative according to the general conception of exploitation one certainly need not subscribe to the labor theory of value. For the general conception of the harmful utilization of a person as a mere means to one's advantage is not tied to anything so specific as that theory. Further, even the special conception of exploitation in the labor process in capitalism can be captured without reliance on the labor theory of value. All that is needed for the special conception is a distinction between nec-

essary labor-time and surplus labor-time, not the claim that labor is the sole source of the value of the product.[106]

But if Marx's concept and theory of economic exploitation have a moral component and he implicitly holds a principle of maximum equal freedoms (both positive and negative), what are we to make of the claims that he held no moral views and that Marxism and morality are incompatible? It is to these issues that we now turn.

[106] Buchanan, *Marx and Justice*, p. 46.

F O U R

"MARXIST ANTI-MORALISM":
A CRITIQUE

Having to this point described and analyzed Marx's moral views
in considerable detail, I shall in the next four chapters consider
some supposed incompatibilities between Marxism and morality.
The issues involved here are primarily of a metaethical nature, and
it is through the use of recent and contemporary metaethical theory that I hope to solve (or dissolve) these purported difficulties
and thus show Marxism and morality to be compatible. Chapter 5
takes up the objection that morality is irrelevant because, according to Marxist theory, socialist revolution is inevitable. Chapter 6
discusses the objection that morality, on the Marxist view, is a
form of ideology and is thus, in some sense, illegitimate. Chapter
7 focuses on the objection that morality is relative to social classes
and/or historical epochs and, therefore, the task of grounding the
Marxist's normative political positions in an "objectively valid"
moral theory is hopeless.

The purpose of the present chapter is somewhat more general:
namely, to consider a number of objections to the claim that
Marx's thought, and thus Marxism, has a moral component. The
objection I want to consider is not that the (supposed) moral component is not explicit but that Marx's thought contains neither an
explicit nor an implicit moral component. Although this claim may
seem absurd, given all of the evidence to the contrary, this depends to a large degree on one's definition of "morality." As we
shall see, the more sophisticated versions of this claim do not
maintain that Marx lacks a normative theory or form of practical
reasoning but only that this theory or form of practical reasoning
cannot be classified as *moral*.

In the first section of the present chapter, however, I shall consider the more radical position—seemingly put forward by such
thinkers as Werner Sombart, Donald Clark Hodges, and Louis

Althusser—that Marx's thought has no normative component whatever. This position is normally coupled with the claim that Marxism is purely scientific, but the only way contemporary theorists such as Althusser can make this claim with any semblance of plausibility is by the sleight-of-hand maneuver of giving a stipulative definition of "Marxism." If this definition is not being given, the only interesting question that remains is how this thesis could have come to be put forward seriously in the first place. In chapter 6 I shall argue that various misconceptions of morality to be found in Marx's work have at least aided and abetted this view.

In the second section of the present chapter I take up another objection to the thesis that Marxism has a moral component: the objection that though Marx has a *normative* perspective or form of practical reasoning, it is not *moral* in nature. This thesis has recently been defended by Allen W. Wood and Richard W. Miller. According to Wood, Marx's normative views fail to be moral views on two grounds. First, they have as their basis only nonmoral goods (such as pleasure, happiness, freedom, or the realization of human capacities) as opposed to moral goods (such as "virtue, right, justice, and the fulfillment of duty"). Second, they are not connected with our "love of virtue" and "sense of guilt." Both Miller and Wood also argue that Marxism cannot contain moral views because moral judgments and principles must be impartial, and the judgments of Marxists are simply not impartial between classes. But I shall argue that Wood is wrong in attributing only concern for nonmoral goods to Marx since Marx harbors notions of human dignity and autonomy and is seemingly committed to constraints on how nonmoral goods should be distributed. More importantly, I shall argue that the Wood-Miller critique is based on a misunderstanding of impartiality in moral contexts and on an excessively personalistic and Kantian conception of morality.

In the third section of the present chapter I criticize the version of "Marx's anti-moralism" based on a Marxist interpretation of the Freudian or psychoanalytic conception of morality, in which morality is a system of dominance and oppression and thus a reactionary form of ideology: a debilitating disease with which the workers' movement ought not be infected. This, I shall argue, is a one-sided view of morality and, as such, does not defeat the possibility of Marxism incorporating a set of moral views or even adopting an explicit moral theory. Proponents of this view—e.g., Lewis Feuer as well as Anthony Skillen and Andrew Collier of the Radical Philosophy group in Great Britain—tend to claim that

Marx's theory of practical reasoning is based purely on considerations of self-interest. Thus I also take up the claim that although Marx's thought has a normative component, the judgments and principles constituting it are based wholly on considerations of the rational self-interest of individuals and, thus, it is not a *moral* component. Since it is clear from Marx's writings that his normative component or theory of practical reasoning *is* based on considerations of human goods and harms in general rather than on egoistic considerations of the rational self-interest of individuals, I shall attempt to show where Skillen and Collier go wrong when they assert the opposite.

In the final section I briefly consider the implications of the ethical egoist interpretation of Marx for class struggle and revolutionary motivation. If this interpretation were correct, there would be a serious prisoner's dilemma or free-rider problem, which would block concerted action on part of the proletariat. But I shall argue that this is not correct, and so no insoluble problems arise in this respect. This is because (1) persons engaged in the class struggle often act on moral grounds as well as on the basis of self-interest, and (2) revolutionary struggle will not always be judged unreasonable by individuals who act on the basis of moral considerations as well as self-interest. Therefore, revolutionary struggle will not always be judged unreasonable or irrational even by those who risk more personal losses than gains by entering into it.

Morality and the Scientific Status of Marxism

Let us first consider the claim that Marxism has no normative theory or form of practical reasoning. This position was seemingly expressed by Werner Sombart when he wrote: "Marxism is distinguished from all other socialist systems by its anti-ethical tendency. In all of Marxism from beginning to end, there is not a grain of ethics, and consequently, no more of an ethical judgment than an ethical postulate."[1] As Robert Tucker notes in commenting on this passage, "The underlying assumption was that 'scientific socialism' as its name suggests . . . was essentially a scientific system of thought. The moral content of Marxism . . . was thought to be nil."[2]

This view—which was quite influential in the late nineteenth

---

[1] *Braun's Archiv für Sociale Gesetzgebung und Statistik*, vol. 5, 1892, p. 489, as cited in R. Tucker, *Philosophy and Myth in Karl Marx*, p. 12.
[2] Ibid.

and early twentieth centuries—has its origin in statements by Marx and Engels: "The communists do not preach morality at all"[3] and "Communism is for us not a *state of affairs* which is to be established, an *ideal* to which reality will have to adjust itself. We call communism the *real* movement which abolishes the present state of things."[4] The roots of this view can also be found in Marx's objection (in 1875) to the introduction into the Gotha Program of "obsolete verbal rubbish . . . ideological nonsense about right and other trash so common among the democrats and French Socialists."[5]

More potential evidence of Marx and Engels' "anti-ethical tendency" consists of their response to the bourgeois objection to communism (as presented by them in the "Communist Manifesto"): "There are . . . eternal truths, such as Freedom, Justice, etc., that are common to all states of society. But Communism abolishes eternal truths, it abolishes all religion, and all morality, instead of constituting them on a new basis."[6] Instead of attempting to refute this objection and save a place for morality in their system, Marx and Engels merely respond that "the Communist revolution is the most radical rupture with traditional property relations; no wonder that its development involves the most radical rupture with traditional ideas."[7] Thus they seem to reject morality in general rather than only bourgeois morality or moral theories in particular.

Although one might object that the above-quoted passages could be interpreted as constituting only a rejection of moral theory rather than normative theory generally, it seems to be the case that such passages at least aided and abetted the latter view. The position that there is not a "grain of ethics" in Marx's writings or thought usually goes hand in hand with the view that Marxism is purely scientific, that is, the view that not only is Marxism scientific but that it is *nothing but* scientific theory. Both doctrines were, in fact, key pillars of Scientific Socialism, the orthodox school of Marxism developed in the last part of the nineteenth and first part of the twentieth centuries. Besides being generally a child of its times—when scientism was ascendant—Scientific Socialism re-

[3] Marx and Engels, *The German Ideology*, in Marx and Engels, *Collected Works*, vol. 5, p. 247.
[4] Marx and Engels, *The German Ideology*, p. 126.
[5] Marx, "Critique of the Gotha Program," p. 388.
[6] Marx and Engels, "Manifesto of the Communist Party," p. 351.
[7] Ibid., pp. 351–352.

ceived support from Marx's seeming commitment to the inevitability of the socialist revolution, as well as from the thesis that the revolution would come about largely or even entirely as a result of proletarians acting in their own self-interest. Both doctrines, in turn, received encouragement and support from Marx's collapse theory of capitalism, which holds that the capitalist system was bound to shatter eventually due to an incredible depression or else wind down and come to a standstill due to the falling rate of profit and the consequent unwillingness of capitalists to make the investments necessary to keep the economy going (more on this in chapter 5). Thus Marx's thought undeniably has elements that tend toward a purely scientific, "anti-ethical" approach.

The assertion that Marxism is purely scientific—or, better yet, purely descriptive and explanatory—is, however, to be distinguished from the more limited claim that Marxism is scientific. The latter claim merely asserts that the descriptive-explanatory component of Marx's worldview is scientific. The former asserts that the descriptive-explanatory component is scientific, *and* that it is the *only* component of his worldview. In other words, Marx's worldview contains no evaluative, normative, or—more specifically—moral assertions or claims. The thesis that Marxism is scientific—while itself debatable—is at least plausible. The claim that Marxism is *purely* scientific or descriptive-explanatory in nature is so implausible in view of Marx's writings that one wonders how it could have developed and makes one suspect that its proponents have either given scant attention to Marx's writings—and those of later Marxists—or that, through some confusion or other, they simply do not recognize a moral claim when they see one. Let us examine some of the arguments offered to support the view that Marxism is devoid of moral or normative content, a thesis I shall refer to as that of Marx's anti-moralism.

Sometimes the assertion that Marxism is purely scientific (or descriptive-explanatory) seems to rest on the Hegelian or quasi-Hegelian thesis that there is no real or tenable distinction between fact and value. The thought here is that if factual and evaluative judgments are not separable, then Marx's descriptions (and explanations) of various social arrangements already contain his evaluative judgments which are said, by others, to depend upon discernible and separable normative or, more specifically, moral claims and principles.

But here we must distinguish "practically separable" from "logically separable." Although, as Max Weber and others point out, it

173

may be exceedingly difficult and in some cases even impossible (as a matter of *practice*) to separate the factual or descriptive-explanatory elements of a theory or worldview from its evaluative or normative elements, it seems always logically possible to distinguish these elements. As R. M. Hare has shown, even in the case of words that (normally) have both descriptive and evaluative meaning or force, it seems always possible to distinguish the one from the other. If—as shall be assumed for purposes of this work—no evaluative conclusions can be derived from strictly descriptive premises, then a worldview that contains normative political positions must have both descriptive and evaluative components.

In other cases, the thesis that Marxism is purely scientific and, as such, devoid of normative content rests on a stipulative definition of Marxism. Louis Althusser seems to take this tack. He claims, for example, that "ethics . . . is in its essence ideology"[8] and also that Marxism admits of no ideological elements. This would seem to entail that Marxism contains no ethical or normative elements, something that—on the common understanding of the term—is simply not the case. However, what Althusser is really claiming, upon closer analysis, is not that Marxism, as commonly understood, is lacking in normative content but that Marxist theory or, more specifically, Marxist empirical, social-scientific theory is lacking in normative content. But this is a rather noncontroversial and uninteresting claim—especially since Althusser does not deny that the workers' movement (and thus the practical activity of Marxists) relies upon and is motivated by a set of normative principles or commitments. Having distinguished between humanism as the early Marx's theoretical framework and as the normative framework of the workers' movement, Althusser claims that "it is possible to define humanism's status, and reject its *theoretical* pretensions, while recognizing its practical function as an ideology."[9] Therefore, Althusser asserts, "The corollary of theoretical Marxist anti-humanism is the recognition and knowledge of humanism itself: as an ideology."[10]

Thus Althusser's claim that Marxism is value-free even though the workers' movement is inextricably wed to a set of (humanistic) normative or moral views—which is partially constitutive of the "ideology" of the workers' movement—is of little significance because it depends on an artificial separation of the descriptive-ex-

[8] Althusser, "Marxism and Humanism," p. 232.
[9] Ibid., p. 229.
[10] Ibid., p. 230.

planatory and normative components of Marx's thought and upon a stipulative definition of Marxism as only a body of descriptive-explanatory theories. The point is that if we take Marxism to refer to Marx's worldview as a whole rather than only to its descriptive-explanatory component, then it is not *purely* scientific. Even if its descriptive-explanatory component is scientific—an assertion that is itself in need of explication and defense—it does not consist solely of such descriptive-explanatory theses and theories but contains something more besides: namely, a set of normative principles or claims.

Perhaps reflecting upon the term "Marxist" will bring this point home. To correctly describe someone as a Marxist is to do more than ascribe certain empirical theories or beliefs to that person: it is also to ascribe to him or her certain values. No one will be regarded as a Marxist who does not condemn capitalism and endorse socialism and (if it should be necessary) socialist revolution, even if he or she accepts all of Marx's empirical theory. Consider the case of a thoroughly reactionary (and cynical) member of the capitalist class who accepts all of Marx's empirical theory—including the inevitability of socialist revolution—but, nevertheless, applies all of his wealth, power, and ability toward forestalling the revolution in hopes that it will not take place within his lifetime or that of his children. Would we even be tempted to call this person a Marxist? Of course not! Even believing that the dissolution of capitalism and development of socialism is absolutely inevitable does not require one to *endorse* or *commend* this sequence of historical events, though, in these circumstances, it might be irrational to claim that things *ought* to happen differently since it is normally thought, as Hume put it, that "ought" implies "can."

But that such an astute thinker as the non-Marxist, late nineteenth-century sociologist Werner Sombart could have reached the conclusion that Marxism is devoid of normative content is surprising, even in light of the fact that he and other writers of this period did not have access to most of Marx's early works. Even in his later, fully mature works (such as *Capital*) there is ample evidence that Marx is not merely describing and explaining social phenomena but is commending and condemning various social arrangements and prescribing courses of action in line with these commendations and condemnations. Even though Marx—as Henry David Aiken puts it—"formally . . . disdained morality and professed to speak only in realistic and in scientific terms [and] only about class interests and historical events,"[11] one has only to glance at such sections of *Capital* as "Machinery and Modern Industry," "The General Law of Capitalist Accumulation," and "Historical Tendency of Capitalist Accumulation"—where Marx employs such terms as "misery," "agony," "slavery," "ignorance," and "degradation" to describe and condemn the condition of the working class under capitalism—to ascertain that he makes normative and indeed moral judgments.

Nevertheless, there are those who even today continue to insist that Marxism is devoid of morality or of any normative content whatever. Donald Clark Hodges, for example, in a well-known article entitled "Historical Materialism in Ethics," published in 1962, claims that "few Marxian philosophers have accepted [Marxism's] full implications for the study of ethics."[12] He goes on to castigate those Marxist philosophers interested in developing and defending a Marxist moral theory for "their efforts to resurrect the dead dog of normative ethics."[13] Since Hodges' defense of the thesis of Marx's anti-moralism is one of the most trenchant to be found in recent and contemporary philosophical literature, we will do well to examine it in more detail.[14] Hodges offers the following defense of this thesis:

> Although one of the theses of historical materialism is the futility of ethical controversy about right and justice, many Marxist philosophers continue to affirm the possibility of a normative science. . . . their researches are blighted by: (1) a normative conception of ethics—the conviction that normative judgments can be true or false, whereas at best they have a scientific foundation without themselves being scientific; (2) the lack of a sociological theory and dynamic approach to ethical studies that does not wag a philosophical tail; (3) an irra-

[11] Aiken, "Morality and Ideology," p. 150.
[12] Hodges, "Historical Materialism in Ethics," p. 1.
[13] Ibid., p. 5.
[14] Although "Historical Materialism in Ethics" is not Hodges' last word on the topic, I will concentrate on this particular article because the positions he takes and the arguments he offers therein are paradigmatic of contemporary Marxians who wish to uphold and defend the thesis of Marx's Anti-Moralism. See also Hodges' "Socialists in Search of an Ethic," *Studies on the Left*, 1963; "Marxist Ethics and Ethical Theory," *Socialist Register* (1964); "Marx's Contribution to Humanism," *Science and Society*, vol. 29, no. 2 (Spring 1965); "The Value Judgment in Capital," *Science and Society*, vol. 29, no. 3 (Summer 1965); "Moral Progress from Philosophy to Technology," *Philosophy and Phenomenological Research*, vol. 28, no. 3 (Mar. 1968); "The Economic Basis of Marx's Humanism," and *Dialogues on the Philosophy of Marxism* (John Somerville and Howard Parsons, eds.).

tional belief in the possibility of a universal human ethic, and not merely a partisan one, founded on a sociological and psychological basis; and (4) a confusion between the purely theoretical and strategical grounds of normative judgments in a positive science of ethics.[15]

This defense of the thesis of ''Marx's Anti-moralism'' is flawed, however, by a number of confusions concerning the nature of morality and moral theory. By thesis 1, for example, Hodges seems to be attacking not merely cognitivist metaethical theories but the very notion that one normative view or principle can possibly be judged better or worse than another. Thus he seems to be committing himself to the untenable doctrine of normative ethical relativism. (I will have more to say on this subject in chapter 7.) This inference is confirmed by thesis 3, where the notions of the *universalizability* of one's moral principles and judgments, on the one hand, and the possibility of any particular set of moral or normative judgments being *universally accepted*, on the other, are conflated.

Furthermore, while his second thesis may be legitimate as a piece of advice for those interested in the sociology of ethics —the only study of ethics Hodges believes legitimate to begin with—his fourth thesis seems rather pernicious. Amplifying this view, Hodges claims that ethics may be needed on purely strategic grounds because ''to get men to act, even in their own self-interest, it is frequently necessary to make use of ideological arguments and techniques of moral suasion; hence the need, on purely practical grounds, of a socialist ethic of rights and duties continuous with the body of classical ethical thought.''[16] It may be thought that Hodges is here proposing only a strategic justification of moral or ethical *means*—as opposed to *ends*—but Hodges himself makes clear that this is not the case. He claims, for example, that

> normative judgments are nothing but technical devices for achieving given ends. But what about those ends themselves? Presumably, the science of social control governs ends as well as means: ends are themselves means for living, so that there is a difference in degree but not in kind between ends and means.[17]

[15] Hodges, ''Historical Materialism in Ethics,'' p. 1.
[16] Ibid., p. 18.
[17] Ibid., p. 19.

Setting aside the issue of whether any sense can be made of the claim that ultimate normative ends are "means of living," let us concentrate on his claim that the only sort of justification any ethical (or normative?) standard can achieve is a purely strategic one. If we interpret Hodges as asserting that this applies to all normative standards or principles whatever—rather than to only *moral* standards and principles—then this line of argument is either question-begging or circular: strategies are only intelligible as devices for achieving given ends and directives to pursue given ends *are norms*; thus "strategic" justifications of norms are themselves normative. If, on the other hand, we interpret Hodges as claiming that it is only the justifications of specifically *moral* or *ethical* standards and principles that are strategic in nature, then we can give a more plausible interpretation of his position, namely, that ethical standards are justified if, and only if, they constitute sound strategies for pursuing nonmoral (e.g., prudential) ends. According to this interpretation, the ends which the "science of social control" directs us to pursue constitute a *normative* but not a *moral* framework because the reasons given for the ends to be pursued are *prudential* rather than *moral*. (This is, in fact, precisely what is claimed by such philosophers as Feuer, Skillen, and Collier, whose views we shall consider presently.)

Although it is not clear whether or not Marx would have agreed with the thesis that ultimate normative ends can be deduced from "the science of social control"—whatever this is supposed to be— it is clear that *if* he had, he would have been open to the charge of indulging a particularly gross form of the naturalistic fallacy. What is clear, however, is that Marx was no Machiavellian with respect to the ends—or even the means—of politics. Although he did not put much stock in using moral discourse to achieve the end of replacing capitalism with socialism and thus greatly improving the human condition, one of the values to which he is especially committed, as we have seen, is that of freedom (as self-determination) and the connected ideal of persons as autonomous choosers of ends—a value and ideal that would seem to be at odds with what Hodges writes here. This defense of Marx's Anti-moralism is, therefore, not convincing. It repeats many of the mistakes Marx made about the nature of ethics, most of which, I believe, can be attributed to the underdeveloped state of ethical and metaethical theory in the nineteenth century. More importantly, there is nothing in these arguments to prove Marxism and morality incompatible.

Moral and Nonmoral Evaluation in Marx: A Critique of Wood and
Miller

Although they offer various caveats, Allen Wood and Richard
Miller put forward other arguments for the thesis that Marx's
worldview lacks a moral component. One argument expressed by
both of them concerns the supposed facts that morality must be
impartial and that Marx and Marxists are not impartial about the
interests of different classes. Before we consider this argument,
however, we shall first consider Wood's argument based on the
distinction between moral and nonmoral goods. However, since
both Wood and Miller admit that Marx has normative views aimed
at the promotion of such goods as freedom, human community,
and self-realization, the dispute between Wood and Miller, on the
one hand, and those—such as myself—who wish to argue that
Marx held *moral* views, on the other, may seem to be much ado
about nothing. Although there is more than a little truth to this
claim, both Wood and Miller are adamant in their views, which—
rather than settling for "Marx's Anti-moralism"—they label "Marxist *Immoralism*." Furthermore, it is clear from reading their works
that this is not merely an abstract point concerning the interpretation of Marx's texts but, rather, a position they believe Marxists
and the entire workers' movement ought to accept.

Wood, for example, chides "self-styled Marxist Humanism"[18] as
well as those Marxists who consider themselves "champions of
justice."[19] In his article "Marx's Immoralism," he writes: "The un-
questioned assumption that the highest values simply must be
moral ones, is indefensible, misguided, and unhealthy"[20]; "morality . . . is necessarily ideological in the characteristically perjorative
Marxian sense of that term"[21]; and "morality may be an enemy of
the human race, a subverter of our self-understanding and an obstacle to the fulfillment of our long-term best interests."[22] Finally,
Wood admonishes those "who want to burden Marx with moral-
istic fantasies which (as we know from the texts) would certainly
have disgusted him."[23]

[18] A. Wood, "Justice and Class Interests," p. 21.
[19] Ibid., p. 23.
[20] A. Wood, "Marx's Immoralism," p. 97.
[21] Ibid., p. 688.
[22] Ibid., p. 698.
[23] Ibid., p. 686.

179

Miller, somewhat less polemically, writes:

> What is important is that Marx attacks pervasive philosophical assumptions about morality, that his attack separates him much further from typical moral philosophers than they are separated one from another, and that his consequent outlook on basic social choices in unexpectedly close to outlooks that we would all be inclined to call non-moral.[24]

> . . . my main interest is to present plausible arguments for a radical departure from the moral point of view, at least as philosophers have conceived it. When its foundations are brought to light, Marx's rejection of morality as the basis for social and political choice turns out to be complex, well-argued, and humane, though, in an important sense, anti-humanitarian.[25]

Given the fact that these two intelligent, well-informed, and well-intentioned philosophers claim that Marx completely rejects morality and urge us to do the same, it is important that we examine their arguments—even if, in the final analysis, the dispute turns out to be primarily a verbal one.

Let us first consider Wood's main argument. While he doesn't go so far as to claim that Marx's practical reasoning is purely "naturalistic" and "self-interested" (i.e., prudential), Wood does claim that Marx's normative views are based wholly on considerations of *nonmoral* good and evil and, therefore, fail to be *moral* views. "Marx," according to Wood, "believes that judgments about the nonmoral good of men and women can be based on actual, objective (though historically conditioned and variable) potentialities, needs, and interests of human beings."[26] Wood goes on to argue that the "common idea" that Marx's views on alienation and self-realization constitute the "moral foundations" of Marxism is simply wrong. There are no "moral foundations" of Marxism.

> We may doubt whether Marx's views about alienation and self-actualization are *fundamental* moral views. But it is also questionable whether these are *moral* views. No doubt there is a sense in which any far-reaching views about human well-being count as "moral" views, and in this sense I would not deny that Marx's conception of self-actualization is a "moral"

---

[24] Miller, *Analyzing Marx*, p. 18.
[25] Ibid., p. 16.
[26] A. Wood, *Karl Marx*, p. 128.

conception. But there is a narrower and I think more proper sense of "moral" in which we distinguish *moral* goods and evils from *nonmoral* ones.[27]

Explicating this distinction, Wood claims:

We all know the difference between valuing or doing something because conscience or "moral law" tells us we "ought" to, and valuing or doing something because it satisfies our needs, our wants or our conceptions of what is good for us (or for someone else whose welfare we want to promote—desires for nonmoral goods are not necessarily selfish desires). This difference roughly marks off "moral" from "nonmoral" goods and evils as I mean to use those terms here. Moral goods include such things as virtue, right, justice, the fulfillment of duty, and the possession of morally meritorious qualities of character. Nonmoral goods, on the other hand, include such things as pleasure and happiness, things which we would regard as desirable and good for people to have even if no moral credit accrued from pursuing or possessing them.[28]

From these distinctions it follows, according to Wood, that Marx's normative views are "nonmoral" as opposed to "moral" since

Marx bases his critique of capitalism on the claim that it frustrates many important *nonmoral* goods: self-actualization, security, physical health, comfort, community, freedom.[29]

Marx's condemnations of capitalism are often based quite explicitly on its failure to provide people with the nonmoral goods listed above, together with the claim that the existing powers of social production could provide them to all members of society if production were organized more rationally and democratically (i.e. socialistically). But Marx never claims that these goods ought to be provided to people because they have a *right* to them, or because *justice* (or some other moral norm) demands it. . . . He is evidently persuaded that the obvious nonmoral value of the goods to which he appeals is sufficient, quite apart from appeals to our love of virtue or sense of guilt, to convince any reasonable person to favor the over-

[27] Ibid., p. 126.
[28] Ibid., pp. 126–127.
[29] Ibid., p. 127.

throw of a social order which unnecessarily frustrates them and its replacement by one which realizes them.[30]

But here we ought to separate very carefully the claim that Marx does not base his normative views on conceptions of *rights* or *justice* from the claim that he does not base his normative views on *any* moral norm or norms. Although I shall argue in later chapters that Marx's critique of rights and justice is unsound because of certain confusions he has concerning these concepts—just as his broader critique of morality as a whole is unsound because of certain misconceptions he has concerning the nature of morality and moral discourse—it should be noted that his rejection of justice and rights (so much commented upon by Wood and others in contemporary philosophical literature) is separate and distinct from his attacks on morality as a whole and must be considered as such. Even if Marx does not base his normative views on the former concepts, he may—though perhaps only implicitly—base them on some other moral norm or norms. But Wood would quite probably agree with this assessment. The bone I wish to pick with Wood concerns his claim that Marx is somehow so different from other philosophers who explicitly claim to be offering a moral theory that his form of practical reason must be designated "nonmoral."

First notice that if the analysis of Marx's moral perspective offered in previous chapters is basically correct, Marx is *not* exclusively concerned with the nonmoral good. Underlying his view that freedom (as self-determination) is the most important nonmoral good, as well as his view that this nonmoral good must be equally distributed, is his concern for what can only be described as a moral good: *human dignity*. In addition, the very fact that Marx implicitly demands *the equal distribution of freedom*—without assuming that such an equal distribution will *maximize* freedom or some other intrinsically valuable nonmoral good—would seem to indicate that he implicitly harbors some notion of fairness or justice. Although this contention is quite controversial, I shall argue for this thesis in more detail in chapter 8. If this is the case, then Wood's interpretation fails since he holds that fairness and justice are *moral* goods.

Second, we should notice that—at least at first glance—Wood's argument seems to rule out as moral views far too much. It apparently rules out, for example, the utilitarianism of Bentham and J. S. Mill as well as the normative views of Marx. Does not utilitar-

[30] Ibid., p. 128.

ianism—which prescribes the maximization of pleasure, happiness, considered preferences, or some other nonmoral good—fail (based on Wood's criteria) to be a *moral* view? Wood anticipates this objection and attempts to derail it by claiming that the utilitarianism of Bentham and Mill is distinguished from Marx's normative views in that the former—unlike the latter—contains a conception of the *moral good* and (even) an explicitly stated theory relating the moral and nonmoral good. Namely, the *moral good* consists in the maximization of the (designated) *nonmoral good*. Wood writes:

> The distinction between moral and nonmoral goods is certainly one of which moral philosophers have been aware. Kant is cognizant of it when he distinguishes the "moral" from the "natural" (or "physical") good, or the "good" (*Gut*) from "well-being" (*Wohl*). Mill acknowledges it when he distinguishes the "utilitarian theory of life" (a hedonistic theory of the nonmoral good) from the "utilitarian theory of morality" (which holds that the moral good consists in what is conducive to the greatest nonmoral good).[31]

But what does all of this prove except that Marx refused to speak in terms of moral (as opposed to nonmoral) goods or explicitly to frame his normative claims in terms of moral obligation or moral right? In short, what does this prove except that Marx refused to put forward an explicit moral theory something agreed to by all sides. What is the difference between (1) condemning a social system on the grounds that it "starves, enslaves and alienates people," that it "frustrates human self-actualization, prosperity, and other nonmoral goods," without using the word "moral" or having a philosophical theory about the relation of the moral and nonmoral good, and (2) condemning a social system on precisely the same grounds while making explicit use of this term or having an explicit theory relating the moral and nonmoral good? The answer to this, I submit, is none whatsoever so long as both sets of normative judgments and principles are: (1) prescriptive, (2) universalizable, and (3) based on considerations of human harm and good (in the broadest senses of these terms). It is certainly arguable that Marx's normative judgments and principles meet these criteria and are, ipso facto, a set of *moral* judgments and principles.

The point is that whether or not one has a philosophical theory

---

[31] Ibid., p. 129.

of the moral good is plainly irrelevant to whether or not one's normative judgments and principles are *moral* judgments and principles. Consider the hypothetical case in which Bentham and J. S. Mill expounded all of their views except that they did not explicitly state that they understood the *moral good* as consisting in whatever is conducive to the maximization of the nonmoral good. Would we have been justified, under these circumstances, in concluding that Bentham and Mill held no *moral* views? Of course not! Yet this is precisely what Wood recommends we do in the case of Marx! To show Marx is not a *moral philosopher* is not to show that he is not a *moralist*, i.e., one having or propounding moral judgments and views. I believe Marx differed from Bentham and perhaps Mill in that he held a (nonreducible) principle of the distribution of the nonmoral good as well as a view of what nonmoral good (or goods) ought to be pursued. But the point is that even if Wood were correct in asserting that Marx's normative views are based solely on the "nonmoral good of men and women"—i.e., on "actual, objective (although historically conditioned and variable) potentialities, needs, and interests of human beings"—we would not have grounds to conclude that they are *not moral views* but, rather, that for Marx, just as for J. S. Mill and others, *the maximization of the nonmoral good simply constitutes the moral good.*

But perhaps Wood would claim that we have not given sufficient attention to his distinction between "valuing or doing something because conscience or 'moral law' tells us we 'ought' to" and "valuing or doing something because it satisfies our needs, our wants or our conceptions of what is good for us (or for someone else whose welfare we want to promote . . .)." But what does this come to? What does it mean to say that "conscience" tells us we ought to do something? What does it mean to say that "moral law" tells us we ought to do something?

Let us consider the latter question first. Unless Wood is here taking the extremist Kantian position that the "moral law" requires that our moral judgments be based *exclusively* on the "autonomy" (as opposed to the "heteronomy") of the human will—which means that our practical reasoning can make no reference whatsoever to wants, needs, desires, inclinations, or (what Wood calls) the "nonmoral good"—he must admit that the utilitarian's moral judgments can be phrased in terms of conformance to "moral law" every bit as easily as those of the Kantian. This is precisely where the traditional distinction between "deontological" and "consequentialist" or "teleological" moral theory fails.

On the traditional account, the former holds that actions are right or wrong according to whether or not they conform to moral law and the latter that actions are right or wrong according to their consequences or effects. But unless we accept Kant's radical position that the "moral law," by definition, can have nothing to do with considerations of nonmoral goods and evils, the utilitarian— as Wood admits—can claim that maximizing utility does conform to moral law. The *supreme* moral law, according to the utilitarian, is to maximize utility, so to follow this dictate *is* to act according to and in conformance with moral law.

In contrast, the Kantian can equally well claim (if he or she has a mind to) that actions conforming to the moral law (as the Kantian defines it) are morally right precisely because they have the *consequence* or *effect* of upholding or conforming to moral law or, alternately, of avoiding or limiting the violations of moral law. Or, to take Kant's more substantive version of the categorical imperative, which asserts that one is to treat persons always as ends and never as means only, one could say that actions are right or wrong according to the effects they have insofar as people are treated as ends or as means only. The orthodox Kantian would no doubt object to this claim on grounds that the only thing in the world that is truly and unconditionally good is a *good will* and, therefore, what is really important is not whether people are in fact treated as ends rather than as means only, but the *intentions* or *motives* of the persons whose actions we are considering. But this only goes to show that Kant's moral theory is primarily meant to apply to *intentions*, *motives*, and the *moral qualities of individuals* as opposed to *actions* per se and, thus, is often found wanting when it comes to judging actions or social practices and institutions.

These considerations show that Wood's distinction between valuing or doing something because it conforms to moral law and valuing or doing something because it satisfies needs, wants, or our conceptions of what is good for us (or for someone else whose welfare we want to promote) is, to put it mildly, not very useful. Furthermore, his formulation seems to obscure the difference between two pairs of distinctions, namely: (1) the distinction between doing something because it conforms to moral law versus doing something because it satisfies needs or wants, and (2) the distinction between doing something because it satisfies *our* needs or wants versus doing something because it satisfies needs or wants (or our conception of the nonmoral good) as applied impartially to persons in general. That is, Wood seems to confuse the

185

distinction between deontological and teleological ethical theory (as traditionally conceived) with the distinction between *prudential* and *moral* evaluation.

This is why so much depends upon how we construe the phrase "someone else whose welfare we want to promote" in Wood's previously quoted statement. Even though Wood assures us that "desires for nonmoral goods are not necessarily selfish desires,"[32] if Wood means to limit the set of people whose welfare we want to promote to ourselves, our family, and our friends, then he is contrasting doing or valuing something because conscience or moral law tells us we ought to do it, with doing or valuing something from a *prudential point of view*. If, on the other hand, we construe the set of people whose welfare we want to promote to include all human beings or all rational, autonomous, and sentient beings, then Wood cannot be contrasting doing or valuing something because conscience or moral law tells us we ought to with doing or valuing something from a prudential point of view. So long as we give each person involved equal consideration and are willing to universalize our judgments, to value or do something on the basis that it satisfies wants or needs or in some other way achieves our conception of what is good for people *is to make a moral judgment*. The point is that even if Marx can be construed to be evaluating on the basis of needs, wants, and his conception of the nonmoral good, it is much more problematic to construe him as recommending a purely prudential form of practical reasoning.

Even his partisanship toward the working class and the oppressed does not prove that he was proposing that we take a prudential point of view as applied to classes rather than only to family and friends. He is partisan toward these groups not because he thinks we should favor their interests in the same prudential sense that we favor our own or those of our family and friends but *on moral grounds*. The working class and the oppressed, on Marx's view, are the groups who suffer most in society and are the least free, and—for humanistic reasons—their suffering and bondage ought to be alleviated and/or eliminated. Furthermore, it is only by an unwavering partisanship toward these groups, in Marx's view, that we can succeed in bringing about a society in which their sufferings are alleviated and in which everyone is on an equal basis with everyone else in the sense of eliminating social and economic relations of dominance.

[32] Ibid., p. 126.

Let us now consider the other side of Wood's claim that Marx is not valuing morally: namely, that he is not valuing or doing things on the basis of what "conscience" tells one to value or do. It is Wood's contention that Marx's normative judgments are not based on appeals to "our love of virtue" or "sense of guilt" and are not, therefore, *moral* judgments. Although Wood is correct in asserting that Marx does not appeal to either of these subjective feelings as bases for his normative claims, he is wrong, I submit, in taking such a connection to be definitive of *moral* propositions or views. First, let us note that though our sense of guilt and conceptions of virtue are strongly connected with moral judgments of a person-to-person nature, this connection is extremely weakened—if not eliminated—when we are judging social practices or institutions from the moral point of view. But even if this is the case, there seems little doubt that normative theories of government and society can properly be labeled *moral* so long as they meet the three criteria previously listed. Are not the social and political philosophies of Locke, Rousseau, Kant, Hegel, and J. S. Mill at least in part *moral* theories? Would they not remain so even if these philosophers had been similar to Marx in the sense of not offering explicit moral theories whose focus was direct, person-to-person relationships as opposed to less direct and intimate social relationships such as those that form economic systems and types of government? The answer to these questions would seem to be a resounding "yes!"

To take an appeal to "love of virtue" or "sense of guilt" as a defining characteristic of moral judgments falsely demarcates morality. Whatever one takes as the defining characteristics of moral judgments or views—prescriptivity, universalizability, social acceptance (either actual or hypothetical), or being based on considerations of human harm and good—one will *not* normally find "invariably connected with our love of virtue or sense of guilt" among them, even if we recognize such a connection as a natural concomitant of moral judgments of a person-to-person nature. To insist otherwise would seem to indicate that one is operating with an excessively personalistic and Kantian (or "Protestant") conception of morality.

Since Marx is primarily concerned with evaluating social arrangements as opposed to personal actions, motives, intentions, characteristics, etc., it is not surprising that he is so little concerned with people's "love of virtue" or "sense of guilt." This lack of concern for and even overt hostility toward this sort of moralizing on a personal basis is even more understandable when we take into consideration the fact that, on Marx's view, it is often precisely these sorts of mores or norms that legitimize oppressive social orders in the minds of both the oppressors and the oppressed and thus make significant social change difficult to achieve.

Nevertheless, any principle or standard by which social arrangements are to be judged which is (1) prescriptive, (2) universalizable, and (3) based on considerations of human harm and good is, ipso facto, a *moral* principle or standard regardless of whether those proposing them have an implicit or explicit conception of the *moral* good. Thus, rather than automatically taking Marx's claim that he is not making moral judgments or espousing moral principles as good coin, we ought to discern whether or not the normative judgments he (explicitly or implicitly) espouses conform to the defining characteristics listed above. If they do—and it is my contention that this is the case—then they are, ipso facto, *moral* judgments and principles.

But Richard Miller, as well as Wood, disagrees with this explication of morality. In *Analyzing Marx*, Miller gives the following description of morality:

> As a basis for resolving political questions, that is, for choosing among social arrangements and strategies for attaining them, morality, in the narrow sense, is distinct from self-interest, class interest, rational interest or purely aesthetic concerns. The bases for political decision that we most comfortably classify as moral tend to display three features:
>
> 1. *Equality.* People are to be shown equal concern or respect or afforded equal status. In the manner appropriate to choices of institutions and political strategies, everyone is to be treated as an equal. . . . some standard of equality is to be the ultimate basis for resolving conflicts among different people's interests.
>
> 2. *General norms.* The right resolution of any major political issue would result from applying valid general norms to the specific facts of the case at hand. These rules are valid in all societies in which there is a point to resolving political disputes by moral appeal, roughly, all societies in which cooperation benefits almost everyone but scarcity is liable to give rise to conflicts (Hume's and Rawls' "circumstances of justice").

188

3. *Universality.* Anyone who rationally reflects on relevant facts and arguments will accept these rules, if he or she has the normal range of emotions.

In portraying Marx as a critic of the moral point of view in politics, I mean that he argues against all three principles as inappropriate to choosing what basic institutions to pursue.[33]

While Miller admits that a moral principle or view might lack one or even two of these characteristics, he claims that one will always be present. He mentions no other defining characteristics. On a charitable interpretation, however, it can be argued that Miller's view of morality encompasses the three characteristics I adumbrate above. Prescriptivity is embraced because morality is a basis for "resolving political questions" and "choosing social arrangements and strategies for attaining them." Universalizability is entailed not by his requirement of universality but, rather, by the fact that the prescriptions are *general norms*. Being based on considerations of human harm and good seems entailed by the fact that his "equality" requirement applies to people's *interests.* Interests, by definition, have to do with human harm and good.

Although it would seem bizarre to label a principle "moral" if it met only Miller's third characteristic of universality, the primary problem with his explication of morality is not that it leaves out characteristics that ought to be included but, rather, that it includes characteristics that ought to be left out. Consider first the characteristic of universality, which demands unanimous intersubjective agreement among all persons who "rationally reflect on relevant facts and arguments" and have "a normal range of emotions." While this *may be* a requirement for a principle or view being *morally justified*, it can hardly be a requirement for its being a moral principle or rule. Consider the following two propositions: (1) Abortion is permissible within the first trimester at the discretion of the mother, and (2) Abortion is not permissible at any time except if necessary to save the life of the mother. I take it as obvious that both of these propositions or rules are moral propositions or rules, even though we have no reason whatever to believe that all persons who meet Miller's conditions will agree on which of the two (if either) is correct. Similar sets of propositions can be constructed at the social level of moral reflection. Consider the proposition "Property rights are basic liberties and cannot be overridden by

[33] Miller, *Analyzing Marx*, pp. 16–17.

such considerations as increases in the general welfare, political democracy, equal opportunity, or material equality." Isn't it obvious that this is a moral principle *regardless* of whether all persons as described by Miller will agree to accept it? Previewing a thesis I shall put forward in chapter 7, the most that can be said in this context is that we *invite* all others to agree with us when we assert moral propositions. But being capable of garnering a unanimous intersubjective consensus is not a defining characteristic of a moral proposition.

Next consider the characteristic of *equality*. Although most of us are certainly willing to accept the requirement that "people are to be shown equal concern or respect or afforded equal status" as a *substantive* moral principle, it does not seem to be a defining characteristic of moral propositions or principles per se. Miller is obviously speaking of *all* people in this context, and there are many propositions that seem to be *moral* propositions that do not afford all persons equal worth. Thus the contention of many ancient philosophers that the freeborn are worthy of a type of concern and respect that slaves are not is seemingly a *moral* proposition, even if it does not show all persons equal concern and respect and thus is not an acceptable one.

But once Miller further specifies what this equality requirement entails, it becomes objectionable for other, more important reasons. The crux of the matter is that when he claims that this principle "requires neutrality among different people's interests," he does not have in mind merely the interests all people have qua simply being human, i.e., those interests that correlate with people's basic needs or even with what Rawls designates as social primary goods. Rather, Miller means *all* of the interests a person has at any particular point in time, regardless of whether they correlate to genuine needs or merely to desires, and regardless of whether they are in some suitable sense legitimate.

When the purported fact that morality "requires neutrality among different people's interests" is conjoined with the stipulation that by "interests" we are to mean *all* the actual interests people have—which, for example, will include the interests of some people to maintain exploitative or unjust social arrangements, or even cruel and inhuman social practices—it immediately follows that Marxists cannot accept morality while remaining true to their normative political commitments. As Wood puts this point:

190

The proletariat movement as Marx depicts it lacks the disin-
terestedness or impartiality which normally goes along with
moral concerns. Morality is normally taken to involve in principle an equal concern and respect for the interests of all. . . .
The proletarian movement, however, gives primacy to the interests of the proletarian class, and shows little or no concern
for the interests of capitalists, landowners and other classes
whose fundamental interests are hostile to proletarian ones.[34]

But notice that this will be a problem not only for Marxists. It
will be a problem for almost anyone else who bothers to think
about it. If morality absolutely requires that we give equal weight
to all interests, no matter how perverse or unjust, then in some
cases we will not be able to side with one good person against two
or more villains. But under these circumstances, conscientious
people will have no choice but to reject "morality." But would not
the conscientious persons in question be rejecting Miller's sort of
"morality" on precisely *moral grounds*? Obviously something has
gone awry in Miller's analysis. (Miller might here take Wood's tack
and claim that we are employing an overly broad concept of morality in speaking of "moral grounds" above, but—for reasons
given in my earlier critique of Wood—I don't think such a tack
would be successful. In addition, I strongly suspect that most people's linguistic intuitions will go against Miller and Wood on this
point.)
Some Marxist-oriented writers have suggested that the fact that
there are such incompatible interests in class-divided societies
need not overly worry the Marxist since, for example, those who
are exploited are far more numerous than those who exploit (and
thus have an interest in maintaining exploitative social arrangements). As Kai Nielsen puts it when considering Wood's "class interest argument" and "Marxist immoralism" position:

The Marxist, rightly or wrongly, conceives the matter in such
a way that the class interests of proletarians will also, as a
matter of fact (though surely not as a matter of definition), be
the interests of the vast majority of humankind.
    In morality, when push comes to shove, numbers count.
. . . Where interests of the same type and of the same order
of importance intractably conflict and both interests cannot be

[34] A. Wood, "Marx's Immoralism," p. 693.

satisfied, morality requires that we satisfy the greater or more extensive interests where this can be ascertained. Thus where proletarian interests conflict with capitalist interests of the same order, the proletarian interests trump them: the interests of the proletariat are in fact the interests of the vast majority, while the interests of the capitalist are those of a very small minority.[35]

But even though this observation is both true and significant, I submit that it is not the only nor even the most important reason for supporting the interests of the proletariat and other oppressed and/or exploited classes or groups. The main reason to support their interests and oppose those of the capitalists, I submit, is that the interests of the proletariat are *legitimate* and those of the capitalist (in this respect) are not. The important point for present purposes is not whether the Marxist perspective on this issue is correct, but whether the fact that there are more exploited people than exploiters wards off the above criticism of the Miller-Wood thesis, i.e., that moral judgment must be absolutely impartial between people's actual interests. To see that it does not, all one need do is imagine that the numbers are reversed, i.e., that there are more exploiters than people exploited. Would we then automatically have to accept exploitative social arrangements because they conform to more people's interests? Perhaps certain sorts of consequentialists would feel compelled to do so, but it is by no means clear that all rational, humane persons must likewise feel compelled. One perfectly reasonable response that can be given *on moral grounds* is simply to reject the claim that we must give equal weight to all actual interests of all people. That is to say, being committed to the view that morality requires us to show people equal concern and respect is *not the same as* and does *not entail* that we must give equal weight to all *actual* interests of all people. As Allen Buchanan notes:

> Miller's conclusion that Marx rejects not only justice but also all morality as such (not just the bourgeois variety) rests on an implausibly narrow conception of morality. In fact, Miller's view of morality is so constricted that neither Aristotle's view, nor utilitarianism, nor John Rawls's theory, nor Kant's, nor any position that permits destruction of incorrigible, danger-

---

[35] Nielsen, "Arguing about Justice," p. 222.

ous criminals or of the enemy in a just war seems to count as a morality.[36]

Miller . . . says that Marx believed that the bourgeoisie and their allies are not to be accorded "equal status," that their interests are not to be taken seriously, and this, Miller thinks, shows that Marx rejected the Equality Principle. (He does concede, however, that for Marx the fact that something would be in someone's interest is a reason in favor of it.) Miller does not see that on this criticism, not only Rawls's theory and Kant's, but every deontological theory—every view which ascribes to the priority of the right over the good—fails to qualify as a moral view. For as Rawls points out, it is distinctive of deontological moral theories that they do not count all interests equally. Indeed, some interests—namely those that run contrary to principles of justice—are to be given no weight at all. It is true that such theories, at least if they are Kantian, nevertheless claim that all persons are to be treated with equal respect. But this is taken to be quite compatible with depriving the individual of his liberties and even his life if he is sufficiently evil or if he is an enemy in a just war—so long as we use no more force than is needed, avoid unnecessary suffering, and so on. (Indeed, Locke, that quintessential "bourgeois moralist," maintained that incorrigible criminals forfeit their rights and may be destroyed like dangerous beasts.)[37]

Moreover, if we accept Miller's views, it turns out that even a principle like "Don't kill innocent people for the sole reason that doing so affords you a small gain in utility" does not count as a *moral principle*. This is because whoever stands to gain even a small amount of utility by committing a murder has an interest in doing so. This interest is perhaps not a basic nor a legitimate interest, but it is an interest nonetheless. Hence, such a principle is not impartial as to everyone's interests. Arguably, it does not even show equal concern and respect for everyone's interests. Thus, in Miller's view, it fails to meet the equality requirement and, hence, is not a moral principle. But while Miller may be perfectly content with this conclusion, I think that it rather obviously does violence to the term "moral" as normally construed. To put it bluntly, if this is not a moral proposition or principle, then nothing is a moral

[36] Buchanan, "Marx, Morality, and History," p. 120.
[37] Ibid., p. 121.

proposition or principle. But we know there are such things as moral propositions and principles. Hence, Miller's analysis must be faulty. And the fault, I suggest, lies in taking "interests" in the equality requirement to denote all actual interests people have rather than their *basic* or *legitimate* interests. As Rodger Beehler puts it: "The only 'equal concern for the interests of all mankind' which is a coherent, valid, moral concern is an equal concern for just those interests which Marx urged on behalf of the working class: the basic human needs of each person, *qua* human being."[38]

If Miller does go wrong in the way I suggest, then he has not shown that Marxism and morality are incompatible. While it is true that Marxists view the interests of certain classes to be incompatible in class-divided societies, this does not mean they must reject morality. They need not do so because they need not accept Miller's version of the equality requirement. They can, instead, accept the equality requirement as applicable only to basic interests or legitimate interests and thus can deny that the interests of exploiters to maintain exploitative social arrangements need be accorded equal concern and respect. This means, of course, that one must provide a moral theory—probably a theory of social justice—that will distinguish "basic" or "legitimate" interests, but this is another matter altogether—one taken up in part III of the present work.

Thus far, neither Wood nor Miller seems to have successfully sundered morality from Marxism. Another of Wood's arguments meant to establish this conclusion—namely, that all of morality is ideological from the Marxist point of view—will be considered in chapter 6. Both Wood and Miller, however, have separate arguments aimed at establishing the more limited claim that *justice* is incompatible with Marx's views and thus with Marxism. Wood's contention that Marx's writings contain no semblance of a concern for justice and, in fact, are unalterably opposed to justice, as well as his "class interest argument" against Marxists accepting concepts or theories of justice, will be considered in chapter 8. Miller's objection to Rawls' theory of justice—which I believe makes the same sort of mistake when it comes to defining "interests" or "needs" and claiming that morality requires us to give all interests or needs equal weight—will be taken up in chapter 9. The next claim we shall consider, however, is that Marx's normative views

[38] Beehler, "Critical Notice of Richard W. Miller, *Analyzing Marx*," p. 215.

are actually a form of ethical egoism and are, for this reason, not moral views.

Marxism, Naturalistic Inclinations, and Rational Self-Interest

Another tack often taken by recent and contemporary defenders of the thesis of "Marx's Anti-moralism" is that of claiming that Marx and Marxists are committed to ethical egoism in practical reasoning. This view, in turn, is often defended by attempting to drive a wedge between Marxism and morality by adopting a Freudian or psychoanalytic view of morality. One proponent of this view is Lewis Feuer. In his well-known article, "Ethical Theories and Historical Materialism," published in 1942, he explains:

> From the psychological standpoint, ethical terms may be described as the terms of the "superego language." The superego is made up of social values which are derived through the conditioning influences of parents, nursemaids, teachers. Moral restrictions are external in origin, but they are subsequently "introjected" (in other words, "interiorized") within the child. The source of these restrictions is, in later years, repressed; the child is now swayed by "the man within the breast, the abstract and ideal spectator of our sentiments and conduct," as Adam Smith puts it. The superego, which takes over the parental function, holds aloft certain ideals, and criticizes our activities.
>
> The function of ethical terms as the vehicles of social manipulation now becomes clear. The person who uses such terms is trying to have you identify him with your superego. He addresses you with a vocabulary which touches off tensions and anxieties, a vocabulary which stirs the unconscious in ways with which you cannot cope. Disobedience to an ethical statement carries with it a sense of moral guilt, the outcome of a conflict between conscience and desire.[39]

The basic notion here is that morality, as Freud claims, is a means by which an individual's naturalistic inclinations are repressed in order to conform with social norms and is thus a form of social manipulation and control. In class-divided societies, the argument continues, it is the oppressed classes that are most deprived of the means and opportunities to fulfill their naturalistic

[39] Feuer, "Ethical Theories and Historical Materialism," p. 243.

inclinations. In these sorts of societies, morality functions to make the oppressed classes accept their oppression. Morality is a reactionary—or at least conservative—form of ideology (in the narrow, critical sense of the term) and ought to be opposed by Marxists and all revolutionary socialists.[40] Above all, morality should not be allowed entrance into one's scientific views of society or into one's ideology (in the global sense of the term).

Anthony Skillen and Andrew Collier also argue along these general lines. Skillen, for example, claims:

> Moral thought characteristically rests on an assumed "individualism"—egoism, selfishness, anti-sociability—at the core of human nature. Morality's function, then, is precisely to inhibit this natural selfishness and guide us in some sort of modus vivendi with "others". By virtue of our conscience we have a power to regulate our naturally rampant lower self.[41]

> It was left to Nietzsche and Freud to explore this intra-psychic subordination more deeply. . . . considered as authoritative Knower of Right and Wrong, the conscience is an illusion. Scientifically described, what we have here is an internalized, socially formed force funded by the spontaneous love and hate the little child feels for his needed but frustrating and humiliating parents.[42]

> Morality in this sense then, is a sort of suppression, rationalized as the necessary subjection by a higher power of what is base—whether the enemy is presented as "the flesh", "the self", "the false self", "impulse", or "petit-bourgeois tendencies". The moral "must" is the individualistic form of socially inculcated demands.[43]

Collier endorses a similar Freudian account of the inculcation of moral values and the function of morality. He then claims:

> Historical materialism must treat morality as an ideology with a function in any society based on class exploitation. Any ex-

[40] For a similar argument for the incompatibility of Marxism and morality based on the *good-reasons* concept of morality and a Marxist critique of bourgeois society and ideology, see Michael Lerner, "Marxism and Ethical Reasoning," *Social Praxis*, vol. 2, no. 1–2 (1974). Lerner's position seems open to many of the same objections cited here. See also Kai Nielsen's response to Lerner ("Class Conflict, Marxism and the Good Reason Approach") in the same volume.
[41] Skillen, "Marxism and Morality," p. 12.
[42] Ibid., p. 13.
[43] Ibid., p. 13.

ploiting class will benefit from the prevalence of an ideology which will reconcile the exploited to the deprivation of possible satisfactions which they will suffer as a result of their exploitation. Hence the required ideology must be antagonistic to natural values (happiness, the satisfaction of wants) and lead its adherents to be prepared to sacrifice them. Its function is thus negative, but it must make this negative aspect appear as in some way a positive value. Its imperatives must stand independently of and in opposition to naturalistic ones. Finally, it must persuade its adherents to change themselves—abandon wants they have in favor of ones which can be fulfilled in the context of the class society in which they are exploited.

A moral ideology must therefore (a) be independent of and antagonistic to naturalistic values; (b) be conducive to the attempt to change oneself rather than to change the world; (c) find a source of appeal other than that based on conduciveness to satisfaction.[44]

Assuming that Collier is taking all morality to be a form of ideology and is thus indicting morality as a whole rather than some subset of moral views or theories, this analysis is not adequate. First, although *most* moral theories, codes, etc., seem to meet conditions (a) and (c), some—e.g., strict forms of hedonistic utilitarianism—do not. Furthermore, neither of these would seem to be negative features of morality or features that make morality or moral theories ideological in the negative, critical sense of the term (more on this in chapter 6). But the most important difference between the moral theory Skillen and Collier are attacking and the form of practical reasoning they see Marx as utilizing seems to be that the latter is egocentric in nature and the former—as any *moral* theory—is not.

But it is actually quite fortunate from a Marxist point of view that people generally accept moral theories or codes that are at least to some degree antagonistic to natural values, which to some extent find a source of appeal to considerations other than personal satisfaction and are not egoistic. If this were not the case, there quite probably would be no socialist militants and no revolutionary heroes because acting purely out of self-interest and on prudential considerations calculated to maximize personal satisfaction or one's own naturalistic interests and needs—which both Skillen

[44] Collier, "The Production of Moral Ideology," p. 9.

and Collier endorse as an alternate (nonmoral) form of practical reasoning—would much more likely lead individuals *away from* rather than *toward* revolutionary political activity. (This issue will be taken up in greater detail in the last section of the present chapter.) However, we might note here, with Kai Nielsen, that even if one accepts the satisfaction of people's naturalistic inclinations as the summum bonum for purposes of practical reasoning, as well as the Marxist's empirical claim that socialism is more conducive to fulfilling this condition than capitalism,

> there is a further question Marxists need to face. That social-
> ism is in the *collective* interests of the working class does not
> establish that it is in the immediate *individual* interest of all
> members of the working class or that in all situations it is in
> the interests of a given member of the working class to sup-
> port or act in solidarity with their own class. In the struggle
> for socialism sacrifices will sometimes be necessary for some
> members of the working class and it will be necessary, in the
> attainment of class consciousness, for at least some individu-
> als, immersed in the culture of possessive individualism, to
> attain a sense of class solidarity and to move from a preoccu-
> pation with the egoistic "I" to a commitment to the "We".[45]

Finally, it is simply false that feature (b) Collier puts forward in the previously cited paragraph is a characteristic or, rather, a de-fining characteristic of morality. It is not the case that all moral theories, codes, etc., are "conducive to the attempt to change one-self rather than to change the world" or that in this or some other way they always reconcile the exploited to their deprivation. Marx and Engels both seem to have recognized this fact. Engels states, for example, that

> as society has hitherto moved in class antagonisms, morality
> was always a class morality; it has either justified the domi-
> nation and the interests of the ruling class *or* as soon as the
> oppressed class became powerful enough, *it has represented the
> revolt against this domination and the future interests of the op-
> pressed*. That in this process there has on the whole been prog-
> ress in morality . . . cannot be doubted[46] [emphasis added].

In connection with this point, Nielsen argues that though "Marxists and socialists are, and must remain, committed to a cer-

[45] Nielsen, "Marxism, Ideology, and Moral Philosophy," p. 4.
[46] Engels, *Anti-Dühring*, p. 105.

tain scheduling of values, to a certain moral picture of the world,"[47] accepting these moral values

> [does] not at all dampen down [the socialist's] will to take part in the class struggle. It is only when some conceptions, which are quite foreign to socialism, are attached to select parts of that moral picture that it has the pacifying effects of a moral ideology. . . . Claiming that Marxism views all moralizing, including all talk of justice, as ideological twaddle can only muddy the waters intellectually and humanly. It is bad theory and bad practice.[48]

It may well be the case that Skillen, Collier, and other proponents of this kind of Freudian-Marxist approach to "morality" are, in reality, using this term more narrowly than the rest of us. It may be that they do not take "morality" to be defined as *all* commendations, condemnations, prescriptions, etc., put forward in universalizable form and made on the basis of consideration of human harm and good (in the broadest senses of these terms). If so, their arguments—even if telling against the particular sort of morality or moral theories they have in mind—are not effective against morality or moral theory as a whole and certainly do not show Marxism and morality to be incompatible.

Let us now consider a related version of the claim that Marx may have normative principles and positions, but they are not *moral* in nature. It has been suggested in recent philosophical literature that though Marxism has a normative component or method of practical reasoning it cannot be said to be a *moral* form of practical reasoning because, rather than being "universalistic" and based on considerations of human harm and good, it is *individualistic* in the sense of having the individual as its focal point and based solely on considerations of the "natural" self-interest of the individual. Both Skillen and Collier, in the journal *Radical Philosophy* and elsewhere,[49] have argued that (1) Marx repudiates morality on grounds that it is a form of ideology; (2) morality—in order to function as conserver of an established repressive social order—must get the majority of individuals to renounce fulfillment of

[47] Nielsen, "Justice and Ideology," p. 166.
[48] Ibid., pp. 176–177.
[49] Skillen, "Marxism and Morality," "Workers' Interest and the Proletarian Ethic," and *Ruling Illusions*. See also Collier, "The Production of Moral Ideology," and "Scientific Socialism and the Question of Socialist Values." (In the latter essay, it should be noted, Collier adds several significant caveats to his position.)

their natural inclinations and desires; and (3) an alternate, preferable form of practical reasoning from a Marxist point of view is one that, as Collier puts it, "involves understanding one's own needs, developing them in such a way that their most satisfying form of satisfaction is possible, gaining knowledge of and therefore power over the world, selecting the best means for the satisfaction of needs, etc."[50] He adds that "practical reasoning in this sense is not universalistic in nature, i.e., it does not necessarily take 'the good of all' as its end."[51]

It is important to realize that Skillen and Collier are not just attributing to Marx the empirical thesis that—at least in capitalist society—people do act (for the most part) on the basis of (perceived) self-interest, or the thesis that the working class will be motivated primarily (if not exclusively) by considerations of self-interest to undertake revolutionary activity in order to overthrow capitalism and establish a post-capitalist society. Both of these claims, as interpretations of Marx, are relatively noncontroversial. Their controversial claim is that Marx endorses a form of practical reasoning based exclusively on self-interest or, in other words, that Marx's normative theory is essentially a form of ethical egoism.

The notion that the normative component of Marxism can and should be based on the naturalistic, rational self-interest of individuals qua individuals rather than on the moral point of view can be shown to be wrongheaded on two grounds. First, such a conception is radically at odds with Marx's own fundamental evaluative commitments and perspective, and, second, it simply cannot account for the Marxist's own evaluative judgments concerning social and economic conditions or political events.

As emphasized previously, the appeal to self-interest as a moral theory is at odds with Marx's ideal of the "truly human" or "truly social" individual who will, on his view, inhabit communist society in opposition to the egoistic, self-interested individuals who presently inhabit bourgeois society. While Marx believes that human individuals will fully embody this sort of social or communal consciousness only in communist society, it is nevertheless clear that he holds this sense of human community to be intrinsically good. While Marx is not really concerned to judge individuals in existing society as better or worse in proportion to the degree they espouse the value of human community, he is concerned to insist

[50] Collier, "The Production of Moral Ideology," p. 9.
[51] Ibid., p. 9.

200

that it is better for people to embody this value than not to embody it and that communism is to be preferred to capitalism (partially) because it allows this value to be more fully realized than capitalism can or does.

Marx's vision of "socialized man" may in some sense go "beyond morality" just as his vision of communism certainly goes beyond considerations of justice (since it hypothesizes the elimination of moderate scarcity, which is, as Hume pointed out, a necessary condition for questions of distributive justice cogently to arise). If so, however, it certainly goes in precisely the *opposite* direction to that preferred by the anti-moralist in interpreting Marx's normative views. Whereas the anti-moralist envisions individuals pursuing their own naturalistic inclinations and looking out only for their self-interest, Marx envisions individuals who have evolved to such a high level of social consciousness that they automatically (as if by second nature) act in accordance with the common good. There could hardly be two evaluative perspectives that are farther apart.

There is a second reason why a form of practical reasoning based on egoistic considerations of the rational self-interest of individuals fails as an interpretation of Marx's normative views. While it is clear that Marx and Marxists wholeheartedly endorse the self-realization of the human individual, they also realize that it is at times good and, indeed, essential that working-class individuals—and, in fact, all individuals who have committed themselves to the betterment of humanity—set aside the direct pursuit of satisfaction for the sake of the class struggle and advancement of socialism. Proletarians (and others) are often tempted by the system in which they live to abandon (or simply fail to accept) radical political goals and activities in exchange for a more favorable position in the social and economic status quo. If Marxists were to accept the naturalistic self-interest form of practical reasoning, as Skillen and Collier suggest, there would be no grounds for the Marxist's soundly entrenched judgment that people should not be co-opted in this way. In fact, the conclusion they would be forced to draw is the exact opposite: proletarians *should* allow themselves to be co-opted if it is to their advantage!

There is, however, a possible rejoinder to this objection, namely, that the kinds of personal gain (more wealth, leisure, status, prestige, etc.) potentially obtainable by the (co-opted) proletarian in capitalist society may fall short of the personal gains (true human community, all-around development, etc.) that are attainable only within a socialist or communist society. But this rejoinder to the above criticism of Skillen's and Collier's rather Hobbesian interpretation of Marx's normative views would not seem to be available to them. First, this claim seems to require a *qualitative* assessment of these various types of goods so that the appropriate comparison can be made. But to make such qualitative assessments would seem to require that moral principles of some sort be brought to bear since the mere satisfaction of our naturalistic inclinations seems to afford no grounds for making such qualitative judgments. If, on the other hand, one restricts oneself strictly to *quantitative* comparisons of the satisfaction of naturalistic inclinations—a view to which Skillen and Collier seem committed—it will be difficult to prove that the proletarian's satisfaction will be greater in future socialist or communist society than it will be if he or she allows himself or herself to be co-opted in a capitalist society. This is especially true if we are trying to convince the individuals in question that they actively ought to support the socialist movement in circumstances that may entail substantial self-sacrifice or even death *now* in order to realize higher gains *at a later period*, i.e., after a successful revolution and the establishment of socialism or communism. But what could possibly convince the egoistic individual concerned to maximize his own rational self-interest that the "higher goods" available in post-capitalist societies are so superior to the goods available to him in capitalist society that he ought to risk that which is, from the prudential point of view, the *ultimate* good (i.e., one's own life), not to mention the goods of liberty (e.g., staying out of prison), income, leisure, etc.

There are two possible answers to this question. The first is that the risk of substantial self-sacrifice turns out to be so low and the gains to be made by the individual (human community, all-around development, etc.) are so highly valued that the individual is willing to risk his or her life—not to mention the possible loss of other goods—in order to give active support to the socialist movement. This answer hardly seems viable in the real world, however, since the risk is often *not* of an extremely low order of probability and the preference structures of individuals in capitalist societies do not seem to rate very highly such goods as human community.

Another possible answer is that by one's failure to support the socialist movement actively one incurs a *greater* risk of death (or other hardship) than one would incur in doing so. This might be the case, for example, if revolutionary proletarians utilized coercion against other proletarians in order to gain their own ends, i.e., concerted working-class action to overthrow capitalism. It seems quite doubtful, however, that such a strategy could engender the type of commitment that is presumably necessary for the success of a mass revolutionary movement. Furthermore, as an attempt to save the rational self-interested interpretation of Marx, this seems to fail because, as Buchanan notes:

> Marx nowhere . . . even suggests that the threat of either imminent or post-revolutionary violence plays a role in motivating the proletariat to action. It is, of course, true that Marx predicts that violence will be used during the revolution against the bourgeoisie and against those *lumpenproletarians* whom it hires to fight its battles. Further, his doctrine of the *dictatorship* of the proletariat implies that for some time after it has come to power the proletariat will find it necessary to employ coercion against the remnants of the bourgeoisie or perhaps even against proletarians who are still infected with bourgeois attitudes. But Marx does not say or even suggest that coercion will be needed in order to spur the proletariat to action.[52]

Since neither of these answers is viable, there seems to be no good answer one can give to rational egoists who want to know why they should risk substantial self-sacrifice in order to give active support to the socialist movement. (Notice that on the assumption that people should do what is in their own self-interest, the Marxist lacks an answer to the proletarian who is in a position to be co-opted within bourgeois society as well as to any individual proletarian or nonproletarian who values tranquillity and finds the prospect of substantial self-sacrifice unappealing.) Yet it is obvious that Marx holds the normative position that proletarians (and others) *should* support the movement to overthrow capitalism and establish socialism. The rational self-interest interpretation of Marx simply cannot account for this fact.

Along similar lines, it is impossible on this view for the Marxist to account for his or her considered moral judgment that those who take part in the class struggle in a fashion *above and beyond the call of duty* have done something truly morally commendable. It is, in short, impossible to make room for acts of *supererogation*. As Peter Binns puts it:

[52] Buchanan, *Marx and Justice*, p. 93.

Within Collier's theory there is no room for acts of supererogation, and especially not when they lead to the agent's own
death. If all acts are to be judged by the mechanical operations
of . . . [Collier's] felicific calculus many of the courageous acts
which have inspired millions of workers, from the Paris Com-
mune to the 1905 Petersburg Soviet would have been mistakes
pure and simple. Yet in spite of the fact that from the point of
view of many individuals involved, "self-interest" could
never have justified their action, who could doubt [from a
Marxist point of view] the value and the correctness of what
they did.[53]

Although Marx is not a moralist in the sense that he preaches
morality or puts forward explicit moral proclamations, it can be
said that if one is operating with the concept of morality as we
have defined it—that is, the concept of morality wherein moral
principles and standards are construed as universalizable prescriptions (or condemnations, commendations, etc.) based on human
ill and well-being that are (at least under nonextreme conditions)
considered to be binding on one's conduct—then his thought is
absolutely and thoroughly imbued with moral judgments and
principles. Marx's demands that alienation and exploitation be
abolished and that a society embodying the values of freedom, human community, and self-realization be created are obviously
based on considerations of human ill and well-being. Furthermore, although he does not explicitly state the matter as such, he
thinks that all individuals *ought* to strive to implement these demands even though, according to his empirical theory, it is inevitable in a class-divided society that some individuals will not accept these moral principles and imperatives.

Collier and other proponents of "Marx's Anti-moralism" can,
however, point to such declarations on the part of Marx as:

The communists do not preach morality at all. . . . They do
not put to people the moral demand: love one another, do not
be egoists, etc.; on the contrary, they are very well aware that
egoism, just as much as selflessness, is under definite conditions a necessary form of the self-assertion of individuals.[54]

Does this not prove the anti-moralist's claim? To this, I think the
answer is *no*. In the first place, it shows only that here Marx is

[53] Binns, "Anti-Moralism," p. 20.
[54] Marx and Engels, *The German Ideology*, in Marx and Engels, *Collected Works*, vol.
5, p. 247.

utilizing an extremely limited conception of morality, in which morality is a matter only of principles of individual action (as opposed to a matter also of principles by which to judge social arrangements) and in which the claim that moral proselytizing can be a major source of social change seems to be presupposed. Second, to read this passage as an endorsement of egoism would, indeed, be an instance of selective perception: Marx does not here claim that one ought to be an egoist but only that egoism—*as well as selflessness*—is, under certain conditions, the necessary form of the individual's struggle for survival.

Morality, Self-Interest, and Revolutionary Motivation

This brings us to the topic of the Marxist theory of revolutionary motivation. The *interpretative* question is whether Marx believes that the revolutionary motivation of the proletariat is exclusively a matter of acting from self-interest or that self-interest is only the primary or most important element. The *substantive, empirical* question is which of these alternatives—if either—is a correct account of revolutionary motivation. Although it is clear that in Marx's mature works self-interest is the primary motivational factor in his causal story concerning social revolution, it is, it seems to me, by no means the exclusive factor on his view. In addition to the above quotation in which he mentions "selflessness," Marx writes in the preface to volume I of *Capital*: "*Apart from higher motives* . . . their own most important interests dictate to the classes that are for the nonce the ruling ones, the removal of all legally removable hindrances to the free development of the working class"[55] (emphasis added)

In such programmatic documents as his "Inaugural Address of the Working Men's International Association" and "General Rules of the International Working Men's Association," both written in 1864, Marx also reveals his belief that the moral views or commitments of individuals will play some part in their motivation for political action. Despite protestations to Engels in their private correspondence,[56] Marx found it necessary in the former document to

[55] Marx, *Capital*, vol. 1, p. 9.
[56] See *Marx–Engels: Selected Correspondence*, pp. 138–139. In a letter to Engels, dated Nov. 4, 1864, in which he reports on the ongoing efforts by socialists in London to write a declaration of principles and provisional rules for the founding of the Working Men's International Association, Marx writes that he "was really alarmed when I heard . . . an appallingly wordy, badly written and quite raw preamble, pretending to be a declaration of principles . . . the whole coated over with the vaguest scraps of French socialism." He reports further that after conniving to

cite the "simple *laws of morals and justice*, which ought to govern the relations of individuals,"[57] and in the latter to claim that "the struggle for the emancipation of working classes means not a struggle for class privileges and monopolies, but for *equal rights and duties*, and the abolition of all class rule."[58] He writes further that "all societies and individuals adhering to [the International Working Men's Association] will acknowledge *truth, justice, and morality* as the basis of their conduct toward each other and towards all men, without regard to colour, creed, or nationality"[59] (all emphases added).

Now these proclamations may well be rather bizarre exceptions to the overwhelming majority of Marx's remarks about morality, rights, and justice—which view them as "ideological nonsense," unhelpful in the revolutionary struggle, or at least headed for obsolescence in coming communist society—but it is most interesting that he chooses the occasions on which he has the most direct and immediate impact on the socialist movement to acquiesce and put them forward. Together with the other passages cited above does this not indicate that Marx actually put more store in such concepts or principles as motivating factors than he was willing to admit? It seems to me that it does.

But here we should carefully distinguish two questions. First, does Marx think that there are both self-interested and nonself-interested (or other-regarding) motives for revolutionary action? Second, does Marx think that purely self-interested motives are *sufficient* for successful revolutionary action? It may well be the case that he would have answered both questions in the affirmative but, be that as it may, the thesis that purely self-interested motives are sufficient for successful revolutionary action seems to me extremely dubious. Even in his day it seems doubtful that motives of self-interest would have been sufficient especially in light of the fact that the leadership of the workers' movement was then—as it is now—generally provisioned from the relatively priv-

be appointed to "edit" this material, he "altered the whole preamble, threw out the declaration of principles and finally replaced the forty rules by ten." He then states: "My proposals have all been accepted by the Subcommittee. But I was obliged to insert two phrases about 'duty' and 'right' into the Preamble to the Rules, and also about 'truth, morality and justice', but these are placed in such a way that they can do no harm."

[57] Marx, "Inaugural Address of the Working Men's International Association," p. 381.

[58] Marx, "General Rules of the International Working Men's Association," p. 19.

[59] Ibid.

ileged layers of society. (One need only remind oneself that Engels was a big bourgeois and that Marx, Lenin, Luxemburg, and Trotsky were all from middle-class or petty bourgeois backgrounds.) Furthermore, in our time—at least in the developed capitalist countries where the proletariat is, materially speaking, far better off than Marx ever imagined possible—this seems even more doubtful. It may be that, as Buchanan explains the scenario,

> Marx underestimated the resilience of capitalism and its potential for reform. Many workers have not become revolutionaries for the simple reason that their lot has improved significantly since Marx's day. The crushing contradictions of capitalism have given way to the tolerable tensions of the welfare state. The normative inadequacy of Marx's view [that proletarian revolution will be motivated solely by considerations of self-interest] seems to follow as a matter of course: granted the proletariat's improved condition, it is no longer obvious that revolutionary activity is rational [on this basis].[60]

Thus the necessity of an explanation of the *moral necessity* of the world socialist revolution seems even more essential. It may be that socialist revolutions—if they do occur in advanced capitalist societies—will be based at least as much on the moral outrage to which capitalism gives rise as on the self-interest of the proletariat and other oppressed classes.

Buchanan, however, thinks there is "a much more radical objection" to the view that self-interest is a sufficient condition for the rationality of revolutionary action among the proletariat.

> Stated in the baldest and boldest form, it is the charge that even if revolution is in the best interest of the proletariat, and even if every member of the proletariat realizes that this is so, so far as its members act rationally, this class will *not* achieve concerted revolutionary action. This shocking conclusion rests on the premise that concerted revolutionary action is for the proletariat a public good in the technical sense. By a public good is meant any object or state of affairs such that if it is available to anyone in a group it is available to every other member of the group, including those who have not shared in the costs of producing it. . . . [Therefore] provision of the public good . . . is threatened by the free-rider problem. Each member of the group, if rational, will reason as follows: "Re-

[60] Buchanan, *Marx and Justice*, p. 88.

gardless of whether I contribute or not, either enough of the others will contribute to provide good G or they will not. If the former, then the good will be available to me free of charge and my contribution would be wasted. If the latter, then my contribution would again be a loss to me. So rational self-interest requires that I not contribute and go for a 'free ride' on the efforts of others."[61]

For purposes of analysis, this problem can be broken down into an empirical and normative component. Let us first consider the empirical component and ask whether or not, in the real world, this gives rise to a *practical* problem from a Marxist point of view. That—in the case of revolutionary motivation—this is, for the most part, a theoretical rather than a practical problem is borne out by all historical cases of revolutionary movements. The vast majority of those activists who work incessantly to bring about a revolution, as well as the vastly greater number of individuals who are swept up by the rising revolutionary tide during the course of an actual revolution, almost undoubtedly do not act solely on the basis of a careful, rational calculation of their long-term and short-term self-interest. As an *empirical* assumption then, the claim that revolutionary motivation is *only* a matter of self-interest seems implausible, and thus the "free-rider" problem simply does not arise at the practical level.

The correct analysis of this may be the one Elster suggests. After stating that "explaining class consciousness amounts to explaining why members of a class choose the cooperative strategy in the Prisoner's Dilemma,"[62] Elster goes on to ask: "Assuming that the class members have a correct understanding of their interests as a class, what motivations are needed to generate collective action?"[63] Two possible options are:

On one account . . . which seems more adequate to working class collective action, cooperation reflects a transformation of individual psychology so as to include feelings of solidarity, altruism, fairness, and the like. A related, yet different account suggests that collective action ceases to become a Prisoner's Dilemma because members cease to regard participa-

---

[61] Ibid., pp. 88–89.
[62] Elster, *An Introduction to Karl Marx*, p. 129.
[63] Ibid., p. 132.

tion as costly: It becomes a benefit in itself, over and above the public good it is intended to produce.[64]

But if the empirical thesis that revolutionary motivation is purely a matter of self-interest is false and thus no *practical* problem arises along these lines, might it nevertheless be the case that there is a *normative* problem here—a problem of the *justification* of revolutionary action and motivation? A normative problem *would* arise *if* an ethic of rational self-interest were the most reasonable one for people to accept or the only one they were capable of being governed by, but this also is not the case. Although Buchanan sees severe problems for the "Marxian who wishes to rehabilitate Marx's theory of revolutionary motivation by conceding a significant role to moral principles,"[65] it must nevertheless be conceded that to act rationally is to pursue one's ends in an efficient manner and that, for those who accept moral as well as prudential ends, *to act morally*—to do what is morally required—*is*, all things being equal, *to act rationally*. This, I take it, is at least the starting point for procuring a solution to the public goods problem of revolutionary activity, considered as a normative rather than an empirical difficulty.

Be that as it may, it is interesting to note that the later Classical Marxists were more amenable than Marx to express the "necessity" of socialist revolution in moral terms, though they, like Marx, relentlessly pointed out the dangers of appealing solely to moral considerations or even of taking such considerations to be the primary motivating force for revolutionary action. Lenin, for example, in his "Address at Congress of Russian Young Communist League," asks:

> Is there such a thing as communist ethics? Is there such a thing as communist morality? Of course, there is. It is often made to appear that we have no ethics of our own; and very often the bourgeoisie accuse us Communists of repudiating all ethics. This is the method of shuffling concepts, of throwing dust in the eyes of the workers and peasants.[66]

> Morality serves to help human society rise to a higher level and get rid of the exploitation of labor.[67]

---

[64] Ibid.
[65] Buchanan, *Marx and Justice*, p. 101.
[66] Lenin, "Address at Congress of Russian Young Communist League," p. 272.
[67] Ibid., p. 274.

. . . morality is what serves to destroy the old exploiting society and to unite all laboring people around the proletariat, which is creating a new communist society.

Communist morality is the morality which serves this struggle, which unites the toilers against all exploitation.[68]

It should be noted that Lenin is not offering here a *definition* of morality when he says that morality is "what serves to destroy the old, exploiting society and unite all laboring people around the proletariat." Rather, he is claiming that the correct set of moral principles or views—when conjoined with Marxist empirical theory—entails that the old exploiting society ought to be destroyed and that everyone ought to support the movement to build a new communist (or socialist) society. This is made clear in another part of Lenin's address where he indicates the moral principle(s) that he perceives as underlying the socialist's commitment to socialism and to the proletarian movement. There he states that "the old society was based on the principle: rob or be robbed, work for others or make others work for you, be a slave-owner or a slave."[69] The society with which Lenin is implicitly contrasting this old society is obviously one that does not have these characteristics, one that is, rather, a society of equality, one in which the relationships of domination he speaks of no longer exist. And it is clearly Lenin's contention that we should support and promote the latter sort of society and not the former.

Though Marx—given his negative feelings toward morality—did not put it this way, it seems clear that the Marxist's considered moral judgment must be that we all have duties to defend and promote progressive social arrangements and that these duties at least sometimes override considerations of self-interest. Perhaps more importantly—at least from a tactical point of view—even if Marxists and socialists continue to have ambivalent feelings toward morality and/or moral theorizing, they cannot afford to abandon them. As Kai Nielsen puts it:

Whether socialists like it or not, such moral-talk will be in the air. A clear establishment of the moral viability of socialism will help in motivating intelligentsia into taking the standpoint of labour and it will provide, to the extent that these egalitarian moral claims can be seen to be justified, an impor-

[68] Ibid., p. 273.
[69] Ibid., pp. 273–274.

tant weapon in ideological battles with the bourgeoisie. To show the reasonableness and non-ideological nature of *such principles* of justice, if this can be shown, will strengthen the case for socialism in such ideological battles. This may well be important, given the bamboozlement of the working class. Moreover, it can and should be argued both that socialism is in the interests of the working class *and* that these principles of justice, embedded in socialism, are justified. There is no need at all to make a choice here and the separation of morality from questions concerning interests, particularly collective interests, should be viewed with suspicion.[70]

What remains then is to ascertain what it is about morality—as conceived by Marx—that made it anathema to him and, thus laid the groundwork for the myth of "Marx's Anti-moralism," as well as for the myth that the Marxist worldview is incompatible with conceptions or theories of justice and human rights. This is the concern of the next four chapters.

[70] Nielsen, "Justice and Ideology," p. 178.

211

F I V E

MARXISM AND MORAL HISTORICISM

Even though it is apparent that Marx's thought contains moral judgments and—at least implicitly—moral principles, there are yet those who claim that all of this is irrelevant because his most basic moral (or metaethical) view is that whatever social structures have evolved or whatever social structures will evolve are, ipso facto, morally justified. This is the doctrine of moral historicism. It seems clear, however, that if Marxism is committed to moral historicism, this commitment is paradoxical since, as shown previously, Marxism is also committed to moral criteria for judging social institutions, namely, the values of freedom, community, and self-realization, and an egalitarian distribution of these goods. These moral values and principles are logically independent of the actual course of history and could, under some conceivable circumstances, be at odds with it. But let us examine this supposed difficulty in more detail.

Karl Popper explicates moral historicism as follows:

I have mentioned *moral positivism* (especially that of Hegel), the theory that there is no moral standard but the one which exists; that what is, is reasonable and good; and therefore, that *might makes right*. The practical aspect of this theory is this. A moral criticism of the existing state of affairs is impossible, since this state itself determines the moral standard of things. Now the historicist moral theory we are considering is nothing but another form of moral positivism. For it holds that *coming might is right*. The future is here substituted for the present—that is all. And the practical aspect of this theory is this. A moral criticism for the coming state of affairs is impossible, since this state determines the moral standard of things.[1]

[1] Popper, *The Open Society and Its Enemies*, vol. 2, p. 206.

In the following paragraph, Easton and Guddat amplify the consequences of Marx's (supposed) acceptance of this position:

> Marx identified what "ought to be" with the dialectical movement of history. With this identification he not only deprived himself of the moral leverage for criticizing history which was implicit in his humanism, but also provided a justification for anything and everything that happens, no matter how cruel or inhuman.[2]

We should take the phrase "dialectical movement in history" with a grain of salt, since in his later works Marx meant to indicate by the term "dialectical" not the deterministic, philosophical Hegelian view of the development of things (i.e., the development of the *Weltgeist*) but, rather, the need for a *diachronic*—as opposed to a *synchronic*—analysis of the development of societies. Nevertheless, if Easton and Guddat are right about Marx being a moral historicist, some dire consequences are in the offing.

Since, as Popper points out, "it is clear enough that the theory depends largely on the possibility of correct historical prophecy,"[3] let us first examine the claim that Marx (and Marxists) are committed to a rigid sociological determinism (i.e., to the so-called "inevitability thesis" concerning the coming of socialism or communism) and then take up the claim that Marx (and Marxists) are and must be committed to the claim that whatever social structures

---

[2] Easton and Guddat, "Introduction," in *Writings of the Young Marx*, pp. 29–30. We might note here that some writers see this doctrine as characteristic not of Marx himself but only of a particular school or set of schools within the Marxist tradition. As a characterization of the Stalinist tradition, this is quite plausible and I am not arguing that *no* group of Marxists held these views, only that Marx and the Classical Marxists did not. As Alasdair MacIntyre writes: "The Stalinist identifies what is morally right with what is actually going to be the outcome of historical development. History is for him a sphere in which objective laws operate, laws of such a kind that the role of the individual human being is predetermined for him by his historical situation. The individual can accept his part and play it out more or less willingly; but he cannot rewrite the play. One is nothing in history but an actor and even one's moral judgments on historical events are only part of the action. The 'ought' of principle is swallowed up in the 'is' of history. By contrast the moral critic puts himself outside of history as a spectator. He invokes his principles as valid independently of the course of historical events. Every issue is to be judged on its moral merits. The 'ought' of principle is completely external to the 'is' of history. For the Stalinist the actual course of history is the horizon of morality; that what belongs to the future is progressive is made into a necessary truth. For the moral critic the question of the course of history, of what is actually happening and the question of what ought to happen are totally independent questions" ("Notes from the Moral Wilderness I," p. 91).

[3] Popper, *The Open Society and Its Enemies*, vol. 2, p. 205.

213

evolve are, ipso facto, morally justified. It is my contention that neither of these theses is, without qualification, correct.

The Inevitability Thesis

Support for Marx's prediction that capitalism will give way to communism (or let us say, for our purposes, socialism) can be found at each of several levels of his complex, multi-layered social-scientific theory. These levels are: (1) the theory of historical materialism proper (built around the concepts of the forces of production, relations of production, and the political and ideological superstructure and propounding the laws of technological and economic determinism); (2) the theory of classes and class struggle (i.e., the struggle of classes over the social surplus product and social powers, benefits, and opportunities generally); and (3) Marx's more specific theories concerning the economic and social dysfunctions of capitalism and his projections concerning post-capitalist societies.

On the standard (or technological determinist) interpretation of historical materialism, Marx posits two important causal (or nomological) relations holding between the categories listed above. The first is that the forces of production (machines, land, human labor power, etc.) in some sense determine the relations of production (whose legal analogue is property relations). In particular, whenever the production relations begin to inhibit or "fetter" the forces of production, they are "burst asunder," and new production relations—ones that do not fetter the productive forces—are established. The second nomological regularity asserted by Marx is that the forces of production and the relations of production (which together constitute the mode of production) determine, in some sense, the vast political, legal, and cultural (or ideological) superstructure. As Marx puts it in his famous "Preface," "with the change of the economic foundations the entire immense superstructure is more or less rapidly transformed."[4] This is known as the thesis of economic determinism.

At this level, the advent of communism is predicted once one assumes (as does Marx) both that communism is more productively efficient than capitalism and that it is the only historically possible alternative to capitalism that is more efficient. Since Marx's theory predicts that—at least in the long run—a less pro-

---

[4] Marx, *A Contribution to the Critique of Political Economy*, p. 5.

ductively efficient social system must give way to a more productively efficient social system, capitalism will eventually give way to
communism or, as we are supposing, at least to its first stage, socialism. (Again, for this claim in Marx's writings, we should note
the problem of the lack of social-psychological microfoundations
in terms of people's beliefs and intentions.)

As noted in the introduction, however, there is an alternative
interpretation of historical materialism, according to which property relations are determined by their tendency to promote or
hinder surplus maximization as opposed to their tendency to optimize productive forces. On this interpretation, capitalism is likely
to give way to socialism because people in general, and the working class in particular, will come to realize that the economic dysfunctions of capitalism prohibit it from maximizing the goods and
services that can be produced, given the current productive forces.
This view dovetails more readily with Marx's theory of classes and
class struggle and his more specific analysis and critique of capitalism.

At the level of Marx's theory of classes and class struggle, it is
nomologically necessary (or at least extremely probable) that capitalism will give way to socialism, given the following assumptions.
First, the bourgeoisie and the proletariat are the two remaining
major classes in capitalist society, i.e., the only two classes capable
of setting up a state that conforms to their historical interests. Second, the proletariat has the power, once it becomes organized and
motivated, to alter society to conform more to its own interests,
i.e., to affect the transformation to socialism. Third, classes that
are historically aligned with progressive economic forces generally
achieve—at least in the long run—the organization *and motivation*
necessary to promote their interests (i.e., the common interests of
their members) in the struggle over the surplus social product,
available leisure time, etc. Thus, just as the insurgent bourgeoisie
was eventually able to usurp the landed aristocracy as the ruling
class in the transformation from feudalism to the more productive
economic system of capitalism, the proletariat is bound (or at least
likely) to replace the bourgeoisie as the "ruling" class in the transformation from capitalism to the more productive economic system of socialism or communism.

Note, however, that a crucial difference between these two historical transformations is that the capitalist economic system developed on a large scale within feudal society, whereas it is impossible for the socialist economic system to develop on a large scale

215

within capitalist society. The greater efficiency and productivity of socialism (according to Marx and Marxists) comes into being only at the level of an entire society since an essential part of its efficiency depends on national or society-wide economic planning. In addition, the ruling capitalist class—being cognizant of its own historical interests—will try to derail the development of successful worker-owned and controlled enterprises that could serve as showcases for socialism. It will generally be able to do so since such an enterprise will still be tied to the capitalist economic system as a whole and will thus be dependent upon the advancement of capital and other financial dealings that are likely to be made difficult by the capitalist class (and the power elite serving its interests). Whereas all previous transformations from one sociohistorical epoch to another were basically invisible-hand processes, "the proletarian movement [must be] the *self-conscious*, independent movement of the immense majority, in the interest of the immense majority"[5] (emphasis added).

At the level of Marx's economic theories we find the negative effects of capitalism which give content to both the above theories: capitalism is inherently unstable and dysfunctional because it must suffer the cyclical crises of overproduction. Since a socialist economy need not be unstable and dysfunctional in this respect and—Marx implicitly assumes—has no other overwhelming dysfunction that would make it even less productively efficient than capitalism, socialism is more productively efficient than capitalism and will thus succeed it. Furthermore, since socialism will benefit the proletariat and all other subservient classes because of its greater productive efficiency and—Marx, again, implicitly assumes—its propensity toward a more egalitarian distribution of social benefits and decision-making power, the proletariat and its allies will come to strive for the abolition of capitalism and the creation of socialism and, in all probability, will be successful.

Marx actually went beyond these claims, however, with his view that the capitalist economy will eventually suffer a complete collapse due to the increasing severity of the crises of overproduction or—if it happens to survive these crises for a sufficient amount of time—will collapse due to the falling rate of profit (which is due to the increasing proportion of constant to variable capital). The question I now wish to take up is this: is Marx really committed at any of these levels of his theory to the *inevitability*—

---

[5] Marx and Engels, "Manifesto of the Communist Party," p. 344.

as opposed to the mere *probability*—of the abolition of capitalism and its replacement by socialism and, if so, is his position tenable?

At the level of his theory of historical materialism proper, what we want to know is whether we can deduce the inevitability of socialism from Marx's thesis of technical or economic determinism taken in conjunction with correct empirical descriptions of social and economic conditions. The first thing to notice, perhaps, is that in the famous Preface to *A Contribution to the Critique of Political Economy* (1858–1859), Marx describes this theory as only "a guiding thread for my studies" and does not claim that it is a wholly adequate or complete theory. Secondly, the deterministic base-superstructure model emphasized there is only one—albeit the dominant one—of several heuristic models at work in his writings. As Melvin Rader emphasizes, two other models can be detected in his works.[6] One is a modified, "dialectical" base-superstructure model in which there is considerable interaction between base and superstructure, although, as Engels puts it, the economic or material base is "the ultimately determining element in history." Another is an organic model that asserts only that "the economic movement" is "by far the strongest, most primeval, most decisive" among the various interacting economic, political, and ideological factors involved in historical explanation. This is not to say that the strict base-superstructure theory of the Preface is a priori untenable, only that Marx's overall approach to accounting for sociohistorical phenomena is much more complex and sophisticated than it is sometimes given credit for being.

Nevertheless, there are those who claim that Marx is committed to absolute laws of historical development and thus that his theory is not merely false but unscientific. It is on this basis, in fact, that Popper labels Marxism "the purest, the most developed and the most dangerous form of historicism."[7]

By "historicism" in this context, Popper means "an approach to the social sciences which assumes that *historical prediction* is their principle aim, and which assumes that this aim is attainable by discovering the 'rhythms' or 'patterns', the 'laws' or 'trends' that underlie the evolution of history."[8] Marx's theory of historical materialism is unscientific, according to Popper, because—like all historicist theories—it confuses *trends in history* with *laws of history*. "The central mistake of historicism," according to Popper, is that

[6] Rader, *Marx's Interpretation of History*, pp. 3–85, 184–186.
[7] Popper, *The Open Society and Its Enemies*, vol. 2, p. 87.
[8] Popper, *The Poverty of Historicism*, p. 3.

its *"laws of development" turn out to be absolute trends*; trends which like laws, do not depend on initial conditions, and which carry us irresistibly in a certain direction into the future. They are the basis of unconditional *prophecies*, as opposed to conditional scientific *predictions*.[9]

. . . historicists *overlook the dependence of trends on initial conditions*. They operate with trends as if they were unconditional, like laws. Their confusion of laws with trends makes them believe in trends which are unconditional (and therefore general); or, as we may say, in *"absolute trends"*; for example, in a general historical tendency towards progress—"a tendency towards a better and happier state."[10]

While it is true that Marx was most definitively a child of the Enlightenment and, as such, had a predilection to believe in the inevitable progress of humanity, it is not clear that he thought this progress was guaranteed by "absolute historical laws" as opposed to discernible trends dependent for their continuation on the continuing existence of certain initial conditions. Furthermore, even if Marx did make the mistake Popper suggests, it is even less clear that contemporary Marxists must continue to make it.

The passage in Marx's works that Popper seems to see as the key to proving Marx's historicism (since he quotes it as evidence to this effect in both *The Poverty of Historicism* and the second volume of *The Open Society and Its Enemies*) is: "When a society has discovered the natural law that determines its movement, even then it can neither overleap the natural phases of its evolution, nor shuffle them out of the world by a stroke of the pen. But this much it can do: it can shorten and lessen the birthpangs."[11]

Even though Marx often spoke of "inexorable laws" of social development and of the inevitability of certain historical transformations (e.g., the transition from capitalism to communism), it seems dubious that he thought these "laws" were absolute in the

[9] Ibid., p. 128.
[10] Ibid.
[11] Cited by Popper in *The Poverty of Historicism*, p. 51, and in *The Open Society and Its Enemies*, vol. 2, p. 86.
Interestingly enough, the Moore and Aveling translation of the same passage does not have nearly so deterministic a ring. Their translation is: "And even when society has got upon the right track for the discovery of the natural laws of its movement . . . it can neither clear by bold leaps, nor remove by legal enactments, the obstacles offered by the successive phases of its normal development. But it can shorten and lessen the birth-pangs" (*Capital*, vol. 1, p. 10).

sense of not depending on initial conditions. In the same breath that he affirms the "inevitability," for example, of "capitalist laws of production," he identifies these laws with tendencies or trends: "It is a question of these *laws* themselves, of these *tendencies*, working with iron necessity toward inevitable results"[12] (emphasis added). (Even though the phrase "iron necessity" seems to support Popper's absolutist interpretation, it is important to see that Marx may have been amenable to identifying these laws with tendencies or trends.) It seems wildly implausible that he thought these "laws" or tendencies or trends would continue no matter how initial conditions changed. Even his most abstract and general "laws" (namely, technical and economic determinism) are so obviously dependent upon such initial conditions as the continued existence of the human species, the continued existence of biological and psychological human needs that are fulfilled through human productive activity, and the continued invention of new technology that a person of Marx's intellectual stature could hardly have supposed that the postulated "laws" would continue to operate in their absence.

The fact of the matter is that Marx's theory of historical materialism can (and must) be thought of in terms of both the trends or tendencies he called "laws" and certain sorts of initial conditions. Therefore, they are not causal or nomological *laws* in the *absolute* sense. But this seems irrelevant to their scientific status. If Marx claims that the "law" of economic determinism is always applicable or that the transition from capitalism to socialism is "inevitable," he obviously ought to be understood as asserting that not only his posited "laws" but the initial conditions they depend upon are going to remain operational. The degree of probability that one invests in the continuation of these initial conditions is, of course, as important for purposes of prediction as the degree of probability one invests in the "laws" or trends themselves. For example, whereas for Marx—being happily ignorant of the possibility of the nuclear annihilation of humanity—the initial condition of the continued existence of the human species seemed assured, we unfortunately have reason not to assign the maintenance of this condition as great a probability. Even if Marx's theory is correct, his prediction of the "inevitable" advent of socialism will obviously not be borne out if humanity destroys itself.

Even Popper recognizes the legitimacy of explanations and pre-

---

[12] Marx, *Capital*, vol. 1, p. 8.

dictions based on historical trends and initial conditions. He states, for example:

> But what about those who see that trends depend on conditions, and who try to find these conditions and to formulate them explicitly? My answer is that I have no quarrel with them. On the contrary: that trends occur cannot be doubted.[13]

> . . . if we have reason to assume the persistence of the relevant initial conditions then, clearly, we can assume that these trends or "dynamic quasi-laws" will persist, so that they may be used, like laws, as a basis for prediction.[14]

But even if Marx thought the laws of historical materialism "absolute" in Popper's sense instead of being dependent on the continued existence of initial conditions (which can include other trends, of course), there is absolutely no reason that the contemporary Marxist cannot render the theory in terms of trends and initial conditions as Popper demands. There is no reason, therefore—at least at this level of Marx's theory—to accept the claim that the advent of communism (or socialism) is inevitable rather than merely possible, probable, or extremely probable. But how does the inevitability thesis fare at the other levels of Marx's theory?

At the level of Marx's class analysis of society, the inevitability thesis, as stated by Kautsky, is that though the advent of socialism is "certainly not necessary in the fatalistic sense, that a higher power will present [it] to us of itself," it is nevertheless "necessary [and] unavoidable" in the sense that it is inevitable that

> inventors improve technic and the capitalists in their desire for profit revolutionize the whole economic life, as it is also inevitable that the workers aim for shorter hours of labour and higher wages, that they organize themselves, that they fight the capitalist class and its state, as it is inevitable that they aim for the conquest of political power and the overthrow of capitalist rule. Socialism is inevitable because the class struggle and the victory of the proletariat is inevitable.[15]

This victory of the proletariat and advent of socialism, as stated previously, are predicted by Marx and Marxists on the basis that:

---

[13] Popper, *The Poverty of Historicism*, p. 128.
[14] Ibid., p. 126.
[15] Kautsky, *Ethics and the Materialist Conception of History*, p. 206.

(1) over the long run classes achieve motivation and organization necessary to promote their own interests in terms of promoting social arrangements that best answer their needs, and (2) once the working class—and other exploited classes in capitalist society—achieve the motivation and organization necessary to promote their own interests, they will affect the transformation to the proper social arrangements (in this case socialism). Now each of these premises and even Marx's theory of classes—which structurally defines classes in terms of their relation to production and, on this basis, assigns them certain "objective" interests—are challengeable. It seems, however, that a very strong case can be made for the prediction of the transition to socialism if these premises are true and if certain initial conditions (or trends)—like the continued existence of the human species—continue to be met.

While the series of successful anti-capitalist revolutions in this century would seem to indicate that—at least under some circumstances—the working class has the power to change society (in conjunction with the middle-class intellectuals who usually stock the leadership positions of revolutionary parties and, in some cases, with the peasantry), is it reasonable to claim that such anti-capitalist revolutions are *inevitable* and, thus, that the advent of socialism is *necessary* rather than merely *possible, probable, or extremely probable*? To claim justifiably that this is inevitable would mean that we can (justifiably) assign a 100 percent probability to the claim that the working class will come to perceive and pursue its own true or objective *class* interests as well as to the claim that it—together with other exploited classes—will achieve the organization necessary to affect the transition in question.

But is one justified in assigning a 100 percent probability to these claims? Consider the first claim: can we be 100 percent certain that the majority of members of the working class in, for example, advanced capitalist societies will come to perceive their objective interests and be motivated to pursue them? Furthermore, can we be 100 percent sure that they will come to accept the empirical belief that socialism is more stable, democratic, and egalitarian and less exploitative than the best capitalist societies and that this sort of socialism is historically possible? Can we be 100 percent sure that the working class by and large will develop what Marx calls "communist consciousness" or, in other words, develop from what Georg Lukács calls a *class-in-itself* into a *class-for-itself*? The answer to this, it seems to me, is no: even if one feels confident in making these predictions, it would be foolish to claim for them a *100 per-*

cent probability, i.e., to claim that it is *impossible* for these predictions *not* to come true.

For one thing, though capitalism does tend to radicalize the less well-off segments of a population as well as some more well-off sympathizers, and though revolutionary movements are periodically generated in most capitalist societies, Marx seems to have greatly underestimated the power and tenacity of such ideological rivals of communist consciousness as nationalism and religion. In *The German Ideology*, for example, we find Marx claiming that

> if this mass of men, [the proletariat] ever had any theoretical notions, e.g., religion, etc., those have now long been dissolved by circumstance.[16]

> . . . universal competition . . . forced all individuals to strain their energy to the utmost. It destroyed as far as possible ideology, religion, morality, etc., and where it could not do this, made them into a palpable lie.[17]

In the "Communist Manifesto" Marx claims of the proletarian that

> modern industrial labor, modern subjection to capital, the same in England as in France, in America as in Germany, has stripped him of every trace of national character. Law, morality, religion, are to him so many bourgeois prejudices, behind which lurk in ambush just as many bourgeois interests.[18]

The cruelest irony in these statements is that the age of nationalism—with all its horrors—was just beginning when they were written. Even today anyone who wants to approach an adequate understanding of the failure of socialist revolutions in the West must take into consideration the continuing strength of nationalism and other nonclass group identities, as well as the so-called "bourgeoisification" of the workers in advanced industrialized countries in the West. In addition, the psychological and ideological effects on working classes resulting from the identification of existing state-socialist societies with genuine socialism (by both sides in the East-West conflict) and the interest that the state-socialist bureaucracies and their associated parties around the world

---

[16] Marx and Engels, *The German Ideology*, p. 130.
[17] Ibid., p. 136.
[18] Marx and Engels, "Manifesto of the Communist Party," p. 344.

have often had in preserving the local status quo rather than altering it must also be considered.

Even the so-called bourgeoisification of the working class in the West (made possible by the super-exploitation of the Third World) and Marx's theory of the fetishism of capital, money, and commodities—which asserts that the true exploitative nature of capitalist society is hidden by the appearance of these surface phenomena—cannot account for the degree to which the proletariat around the world has failed to be transformed from a class-in-itself to a class-for-itself. But Marx's theories simply did not anticipate the degree to which proletarians and others are influenced by such ideological factors as nationalism, religion, and morality. The truth is that even the continuing economic and political crises of capitalism do not guarantee the development of communist consciousness among the proletariat and the oppressed to the degree Marx projected. (It is perhaps Antonio Gramsci's attempts to come to terms with this theoretical difficulty that have made his works so attractive to contemporary Marxists.)

One of the major modifications of Marxist empirical theory made by Lenin, in fact, is his claim that the working class will, in the normal course of events, develop only trade-union consciousness. Communist consciousness—since it includes the acceptance of some quite sophisticated theories—must be brought into the proletariat from the outside by intellectuals and professional organizers, who come largely from the middle classes. But for Lenin, Luxemburg, Trotsky, and other early twentieth-century revolutionary Marxists, even the fulfillment of the conditions of the continuing social, economic, and political crises of capitalism and the evolution of communist consciousness among large sections of the working class and other exploited classes are not sufficient for successful socialist revolutions. Another necessary condition on their view is the existence of a revolutionary socialist party with a correct political program, a correct strategy, and an astute sense of timing. Successful socialist revolutions occur, according to this view, only if both the "objective" condition of capitalist crisis and the "subjective" conditions of the evolution of communist consciousness among large numbers of the oppressed and the existence of the right sort of revolutionary movement are fulfilled at the same time—and even then it may take a not inconsiderable amount of luck.

But the thesis that socialism is inevitable even under all of these conditions is questionable on another ground. Even if a transformation from capitalist to post-capitalist society is inevitable under these conditions, this does not mean that the advent of *socialism* is inevitable. That is to say, not all possible societies that would be classified as post-capitalist (on the basis of having socialized productive property and introduced economic planning) will be classified as socialist societies if we take socialism (i.e., the "first stage of communism") to have the democratic characteristics attributed to it by Marx and the Classical Marxists. It may be the case that— for reasons Marxists have not explained—only bureaucratic state-socialist societies rather than genuinely socialist societies will come into being and persist even after the worldwide abolition of capitalism. Although Trotsky, for example, never gave up his belief that a worldwide, genuinely socialist society would eventually be brought about, he was not dogmatic enough simply to deny the possibility that all future post-capitalist societies would be bureaucratically deformed. He faced up to this disheartening possibility when, toward the end of his life, he stated:

> The historic alternative, carried to the end, is as follows: either the Stalin regime is an abhorrent relapse in the process of transforming bourgeois society into a socialist society, or the Stalin regime is the first stage of a new exploiting society. If the second prognosis proves to be correct, then, of course, the bureaucracy will become a new exploiting class. However onerous the second perspective may be, if the world proletariat should actually prove incapable of fulfilling the mission placed upon it by the course of development, nothing else would remain except only to recognize that the socialist program, based on the internal contradictions of capitalist society, ended as a Utopia. It is self-evident that a new "minimum" program would be required for the defense of the interests of the slaves of the totalitarian bureaucratic society.[19]

Finally, we must keep in mind another possibility Trotsky constantly stressed, namely, the possibility that the struggle between the two major contending classes in capitalist society (the bourgeoisie and the proletariat) may end in their mutual destruction and a return to barbarism rather than the advent of socialism. For these reasons we can conclude that though Marx's theory of class struggle may prove revolutionary upsurges under capitalism to be

[19] Trotsky, *In Defense of Marxism*, p. 9.

inevitable (assuming the continuation of certain initial conditions), it by no means proves that the advent of socialism is inevitable.

The Collapse Theory of Capitalism

Are there any better arguments for the "inevitability thesis" at the level of Marx's more specific analysis of the dysfunctions of capitalism as a socioeconomic system? Is the advent of socialism or (at least) the fall of capitalism inevitable due either to a complete and sudden collapse of the economic system because of increasingly severe crises of overproduction (i.e., depressions) or to a grinding halt in production due to lack of capital investment resulting from the tendency toward a falling rate of profit? Marx, Engels, and other early Marxists seem to have assumed that such an economic collapse or a complete economic stagnation is inevitable. This contention, however, began to be challenged by Marxists around the turn of the century as it became increasingly apparent that Marx had underestimated the overall resiliency of the capitalist system in terms of its ability to purge itself of excess goods as well as inefficient enterprises through recessions and depressions without suffering a complete collapse—though not, of course, without causing a great deal of suffering. As Rosa Luxemburg points out in "Reform or Revolution," though capitalist societies have undergone one economic crisis after another, they have also exhibited an amazing ability to rebound—an ability Marx did not foresee, and which monopolization, Keynesian economic theory, and government regulation of the economy have further reinforced. The reason usually given by contemporary Marxists for rejecting the collapse theory of capitalism is that Marx did not foresee or take sufficiently into account certain counteractive tendencies. As the contemporary Marxist (or "Neo-Marxist") economist Paul Sweezy puts it,

> Capitalist production normally harbors a tendency to underconsumption (or overproduction). . . . In principle this tendency may manifest itself in a crisis or in stagnation of production. Both are methods, the one sudden and perhaps temporary, the other steady and continuous, whereby accumulation is prevented from outrunning the requirements of the market for consumption goods.[20]

[20] Sweezy, The Theory of Capitalist Development, p. 216.

225

Up to this point we have neglected those forces which have the effect of counteracting the tendency to under-consumption, forces which evidently have been powerful enough to dominate the actual historical course of capitalist development. In order to reach an answer to the question which at present concerns us—is capitalism in fact headed for a state of chronic depression?—we must alter this procedure and focus our attention on the counteracting forces.[21]

Generally speaking, the counteracting forces may be grouped together into two main categories: those which have the effect of raising the rate of growth of means of production, and those which deprive a disproportionate growth in means of production of its economically disruptive consequences. In the latter category fall (1) new industries, and (2) faulty investment; in the former, (3) population growth, (4) unproductive consumption, and (5) state expenditures.[22]

On Sweezy's analysis, the last factor, state expenditures—especially the pump-priming of the economy with money that is not taken from anyone's income but is created either directly or by borrowing from banks—and altering the pattern of volume of taxation and expenditure can go a long way toward influencing total consumption and total accumulation and thus significantly help to counteract the tendency to underconsumption. "The tendency to underconsumption," according to Sweezy, "instead of translating itself into chronic depression at a certain stage of development, becomes merely a *tendency* to chronic depression which may be counteracted by a new force, the deliberate action of the state."[23] (Sweezy does not here go into the consequences of this sort of state intervention—namely, permanent structural inflation—but, so far as ameliorating the evil effects of capitalism goes, this may be a classic example of robbing Peter to pay Paul. The bourgeois economist's answer to this dilemma appears to be that of Keynes, who noted that we are all dead in the long run.)

Sweezy also challenges Marx's analysis, which leads him to the law of the falling rate of profit, which

to [Marx] possessed great significance. It demonstrated that capitalist production had certain internal barriers to its own

---

[21] Ibid., p. 217.
[22] Ibid., pp. 217–218.
[23] Ibid., p. 235.

indefinite expansion. On the one hand, a rising organic composition of capital is the expression of growing labor productivity; on the other hand, the falling rate of profit which accompanies it must ultimately choke up the channels of capitalist initiative.[24]

While not denying the existence of a trend for the rate of profits to fall under capitalism, Sweezy argues that Marx's deduction of the law is not sound. "The tendency of the rate of profit to fall," according to Sweezy, "is deduced by Marx on the assumption that the organic composition of capital rises while the rate of surplus value remains constant."[25] To this Sweezy responds: "There seems to be no doubt about the propriety of assuming a rising organic composition of capital. Is it justifiable, however to assume *at the same time* a constant rate of surplus value?"[26] And to this he answers:

> Marx was hardly justified even in terms of his own theoretical system, in assuming a constant rate of surplus value simultaneously with a rising organic composition of capital. A rise in the organic composition of capital must mean an increase in labor productivity, and we have Marx's word for it that higher productivity is invariably accompanied by a higher rate of surplus value. In the general case, therefore, we ought to assume that the increasing organic composition of capital proceeds *pari passu* with a rising rate of surplus value.
>
> If both the organic composition of capital and the rate of surplus value are assumed variable, as we think they should be, then the direction in which the rate of profit will change becomes indeterminate. All we can say is that the rate of profit will fall if the percentage increase in the rate of surplus value is less than the percentage decrease in the proportion of variable to total capital.[27]

> . . . there is no general presumption that changes in the organic composition of capital will be relatively so much greater than changes in the rate of surplus value that the former will dominate movements in the rate of profit. On the contrary, it would seem that we must regard the two variables as of roughly co-ordinate importance. For this reason Marx's for-

---

[24] Ibid., pp. 96–97.
[25] Ibid., p. 100.
[26] Ibid.
[27] Ibid., p. 102.

mulation of the law of the falling tendency of the rate of profit is not very convincing.[28]

This does not mean that there is no tendency for the rate of profit to fall. Not only Marx but classical theorists and modern theorists as well have all regarded a falling tendency of the rate of profit as a basic feature of capitalism. All I have tried to show is that it is not possible to demonstrate a falling tendency of the rate of profit by beginning the analysis with the rising organic composition of capital.[29]

Sweezy then goes on to argue that the causal mechanism behind this tendency toward a falling rate of profit is to be found in the process of capital accumulation. In addition, however, there are other social and economic forces that enter into the determination of the rate of profit which Marx did not adequately take into account.

These forces may be classified as those tending to depress the rate of profit, and those tending to elevate the rate of profit. Among the forces tending to depress the rate of profit we may mention (1) trade unions and (2) state action designed to benefit labor; among the forces tending to elevate the rate of profit we may mention (3) employers' organizations, (4) export of capital, (5) formation of monopolies, and (6) state action designed to benefit capital.[30]

Thus Marx's thesis that capitalist systems must either collapse or grind to an economic halt is not tenable.[31] His major complaint about capitalism as an economic system is not, of course, that it is bound to collapse but, in part, that it is dysfunctional in certain important respects (particularly in allowing productive forces to lie fallow during downturns in the business cycle) and that it generally functions to promote the interests of capital over those of labor (particularly in its constant propensity to increase the degree of exploitation of the laboring classes and, in general, to deprive them of any social benefit beyond those necessary to maintain an

[28] Ibid., p. 104.
[29] Ibid., p. 105.
[30] Ibid., p. 107.
[31] See, also, Elster, *Making Sense of Marx*, pp. 155–161; Roemer, "Technical Change and the 'Tendency of the Rate of Profit to Fall' "; van Parijs, "The Falling Rate of Profit Theory of Crisis"; and Weisskopf, "Marxian Crisis Theory and the Rate of Profit in the Postwar U.S. Economy," and "Sources of Cyclical Downturn and Inflation."

acquiescent and functioning labor force). For purposes of the present work, however, the important point is that even if Marx is wrong in asserting that the continuing crises of overproduction or the tendency of the rate of profit to fall must result, at some point, in the collapse or complete stagnation of the capitalist economic system, he may well have been correct in enough of his empirical theory and his analysis of capitalism to provide a reasonable ground for both the empirical belief that the transformation from capitalism to socialism is a genuine historical possibility (or even probability), as well as the evaluative contention that such a transformation is—on the assumption of any humanitarian moral theory—to be endorsed.

Morality and History

Having argued that no unquestionable arguments exist for the "inevitability thesis" at any of the levels of Marx's empirical theory, let us now turn our attention back to his supposed moral historicism and ask: even if the inevitability thesis were correct, would Marx (and Marxists) be committed to the thesis that whatever social formations evolve (or are destined to evolve) are, ipso facto, morally justified? The answer to this, again, seems to be no. As John Somerville points out:

> If the concept of inevitability can exist side by side with "ethical considerations" in Spinoza, the Stoics, and other philosophers, why not Marx?
> Are there not at least three possibilities involved? A thinker who believes that a further stage of society will inevitably develop might believe,
> 1) that this further stage will be ethically worse than the present;
> 2) that it will be neither better nor worse;
> 3) that it will be better.
> Marx clearly is in the third category.[32]

What Somerville is getting at here is that Marx and Marxists hold (or at least should hold) that socialism and communism are the best of all historically possible societies *not* because they are *destined to evolve* but because they *best meet certain criteria of goodness*

[32] Somerville, "An Open Letter to Bertrand Russell," p. 70.

or rightness (for example, they better achieve human liberation or are more just than any other historically possible society).

Furthermore, it is immediately obvious that if "destined to historically evolve" is to be taken as a *definition* of "morally good," it is—like any other naturalistic definition of this term—vulnerable to the open-question argument. If "morally good" *means* "that which evolves," then whether or not something that has evolved is morally good should not be an open question. It would be the same as asking whether what is morally good is morally good. But, since asking whether or not a social formation destined to evolve is morally good is a meaningful and disputable question, the proposed definition of "morally good" cannot be correct.

However, very few contemporary thinkers familiar with these difficulties would want to claim they are *defining* "morally good" here. Instead they will claim to be offering a *theory of moral goodness*: the theory that whatever social formations evolve are—as a matter of fact though *not* as a matter of logical truth—morally good. But as a theory of moral goodness this is obviously wrong. In order for a principle of moral goodness (or theory of the good) to hold up, it must be in agreement with our considered moral judgments concerning any case we can think of—both actual and possible. This being the case, it is easy to see that "whatever kind of social formation evolves is good" is not going to serve as an adequate criterion. It is logically possible that a world fascist society must inevitably evolve, but—obviously—very few people would claim that such a society is morally justified or morally good even if it should happen to be inevitable. Under these circumstances it may be incoherent to claim that such a society "ought not to evolve" (since, as Hume puts it, "ought implies can"), but this does not mean that one has to endorse it as morally justified or good.

The point is that even though Marx certainly thought that the evolution of a "truly human" (i.e., morally good) society is *nomologically* necessary (at least given the perpetuation of certain initial conditions such as the continued existence of the human species and continuing technological development), there is no evidence at all that he is committed to the thesis that this is *logically* necessary. Given his values, Marx naturally views socialism and communism (as he conceives them) as morally superior to capitalism or any other form of society he thought historically possible. Nevertheless, since it is at least logically possible for a world fascist society to evolve, it would be absurd for Marx or any Marxist to commit himself or herself to the doctrine of moral historicism. If the question were put to Marx in this way and after making these distinctions, it is inconceivable—assuming he understood what we were saying —that he would have accepted the doctrine of moral historicism.

Although Marx may be committed to the thesis that a particular society cannot be judged *just* or *unjust* by any but its own (internal) standards, as, for example, Robert Tucker and Allen Wood suggest, it is nevertheless clear that Marx can and did make moral assessments of both actual and possible sets of social arrangements and that these assessments are both transhistorical and logically independent of considerations as to which social arrangements have evolved or are bound to evolve.

Perhaps what has bothered Marx and Marxists is that if a certain state of affairs or set of social institutions is inevitable or, at any rate, unalterable, then it serves little purpose to condemn them as immoral. As George Panichas writes:

It serves little purpose, on Marx's view, to refer to a state of affairs (or set of relationships) as morally condemnable if that state of affairs is unalterable or unavoidable. While Marx's views on this matter are complicated and cryptic (especially his view on whether something is immoral even if it serves no purpose to describe it as such), it appears that Marx maintained the position (a Marxist variant of the Kantian "ought not" implies "might not") that it serves little if any purpose to morally criticize some state of affairs if, at the time when such a criticism is to be offered, that state of affairs cannot be reasonably expected to be alterable or avoidable (where avoidable does not preclude terminable).[33]

There is a problem, however, in deciding what is and what is not to count as "unalterable." While there are paradigmatic cases of alterable and unalterable states of affairs, there are many cases that are not so clear. If someone (for some bizarre reason) offers the moral judgment that "pigs ought to be able to fly" or that "human beings should not ever be required to suffer pain of any sort" or that "human beings ought to live in complete harmony and never come into conflict with one another," we would say that he or she is violating the "ought"-implies-"can" criterion because it is not possible to fulfill these prescriptions. On the other hand, such judgments as "abortions ought not to be allowed" or "infanticide

[33] Panichas, "Vampires, Werewolves, and Economic Exploitation," p. 238.

ought not to be allowed" or "slavery ought not to be allowed" clearly do not violate this criterion because they are concerned with states of affairs that are clearly alterable. (This does not mean, of course, that all cases of abortion, infanticide, or slavery can be prevented because there are social sanctions against them, but it certainly seems possible, by means of social sanctions, either to allow or not allow them to become general practices.)

But consider now the case of the claim "slavery ought not to be allowed" made, let's say, in Rome in 70 B.C. around the time of the Servile Wars. Does this moral judgment violate the condition that "ought" implies "can"? The answer to this question is far from clear since it is far from clear whether slavery at that time was alterable or unalterable as a social institution. It was not, of course, impossible for individuals to escape the social position of slavery. Many escaped and were able to live as nonslaves elsewhere, and some (such as the Stoic philosopher Epictetus) were legally elevated from this position. So if one interprets the claim "slavery ought not to be allowed" as entailing the claims that "slavery as a social institution ought to be abolished" and "individual slaves, wherever possible, ought to be freed," then whether or not slavery as a social institution was alterable one would still have an obligation to free slaves if and whenever one was in a position to do so.

But the primary question is whether or not slavery *as a social institution* was at that time alterable. Presumably most Marxists would hold that it was not alterable (i.e., not capable of being eliminated) at that time because the forces of production were not yet ripe enough to force or allow a change in the relations of production, which, of course, the elimination of slavery would be. But even if this were true at an international level, it does not seem impossible that if the slave rebellions had succeeded, a slavery-free enclave could have been carved out of part of the Roman Empire.[34] This is not, of course, to say that all relations of exploitation

---

[34] In reality, however, the slave revolts in the Ancient World were aimed at freeing the individuals involved but not at abolishing slavery as a social institution. As Elster notes, "One can imagine three forms of struggle among the slaves: struggle to improve the slave condition, struggle to escape the slave condition, struggle to abolish the slave condition. The only organized collective action by slaves in Classical Antiquity—the slave revolts—took the second form. Slaves, when they revolted, fought for a freedom that included the right to possess other individuals as slaves," ("Three Challenges to Class," p. 152). For a discussion of the Marxist analysis of classes in Classical Antiquity, see M. I. Finley, *The Ancient Economy*, Chatto and Lindus, London, 1973, and *Economy and Society in Ancient Greece*, Chatto and Windus, London, 1981; G.E.M. de Ste. Croix, *The Class Struggle in the Ancient World*, Duckworth, London, 1981; and Elster, *Making Sense of Marx*, pp. 318–342.

could have been abolished in such a society. No one perhaps would disagree with the Marxist's claim that a complex society under conditions of relative scarcity and a relatively low level of development of productive forces—such as that existing on the Italian peninsula around 70 B.C.—could not have become a classless society, i.e., a society without a ruling class which in some way extracted surplus value from a ruled (or exploited) class or group of classes. But whether or not one of the primary class relations had to be that of slavery seems at least debatable, perhaps indeterminable.

But *even if* slavery as a social institution was unalterable in Rome in 70 B.C. or for the next several hundred years thereafter, does this mean that the moral judgment made at that time that "slavery ought not to be allowed" violates the "ought"-implies-"can" maxim? After all, slavery was not an unalterable state of affairs under any and all historical conditions, as its elimination in later historical epochs has proven. What we need, it seems, is a number of distinctions concerning the ways in which states of affairs are unalterable. This would include states of affairs that are *logically impossible* to alter ("squares ought to be round"), those that are *physically impossible* to alter ("pigs ought to be able to fly"), those that are—for social-scientific reasons—impossible to alter in any historical epoch ("people ought to live in complete harmony and never come into conflict with one another"), and those that are—for socioeconomic reasons—impossible to alter only within a particular historical epoch or a particular existing set of social arrangements ("slavery ought not to be allowed," as said in Rome in 70 B.C. or earlier).

Although I do not pretend to have a completely worked out theory concerning this issue, it seems that given these distinctions the moral judgment "slavery ought not to be allowed," when made during an historical epoch in which it is not possible to abolish slavery as a social institution, would be a violation of Hume's "ought"-implies-"can" maxim if it were meant to apply to the immediate present or within the historical epoch generally. But such an utterance would not count as a violation if it were meant to apply to the indefinite future, i.e., not only to the current historical epoch but to future ones as well.

Be this as it may, even if "ought" implies "can" (as Hume puts it) or "ought not" implies "might not" (as Kant puts it), what follows is *not* that one cannot morally criticize or condemn an unalterable state of affairs but only that in so doing one is making an

233

aretaic judgment (i.e., a judgment of moral worth) as opposed to a *deontic* judgment (i.e., a judgment of moral obligation). We obviously cannot be obligated to change what cannot be changed, but we can judge a situation as morally good or bad, better or worse —at least in comparison to other *logically possible* worlds.

These distinctions seem to lead to the conclusion that the Marxist (or anyone else, for that matter) need not morally approve or disapprove of a society just because it is historically inevitable (which perhaps none are); but if he or she makes a deontic judgment that some society or other ought to exist (a judgment that presumably entails certain obligations), then in order not to violate the "ought"-implies-"can" maxim, the society in question must be historically possible. Conversely, to make the judgment that a particular society ought not exist, it must be possible for that society not to exist. Thus, if a right-libertarian like Robert Nozick were secretly convinced that some sort of post-capitalist society (state-socialist, socialist, or communist) is inevitable, then even though he can make the *aretaic* judgment that the coming of such a society would not be good, he cannot—on pain of violating the negative version of the "ought"-implies-"can" maxim—make the *deontic* judgment that it ought not come into being or that we ought to prevent it from coming into being.

Furthermore, to know whether or not one is violating this maxim, it must be made clear whether one is claiming that a particular society is possible in the present historical epoch or only in some future historical epoch. Thus if Spartacus had conceived of Marx's vision of communism in 70 B.C. and proclaimed that it ought to exist, he would be violating the maxim in the first case but not in the second. Naturally, some of the most important political disagreements we can have will be disagreements over precisely this issue, i.e., whether or not a particular sort of society is possible and, if so, whether it is possible in this historical epoch or only in some future historical epoch. Given the Marxist's perspective, the claim that we ought to have a worldwide federation of democratic, self-managing socialist societies in this historical epoch does not constitute a violation of Hume's maxim since, in the Marxist's view, it is possible to have such a society in this historical epoch. On the other hand, given the anti-Marxist perspective that it is impossible to have such a society in this or any other historical epoch, this moral judgment does constitute such a violation. That Hume's maxim is violated is, of course, not the important issue here. The important issue is the empirical, theoretical disagreement over whether or not such a society is historically possible. The answer to this question determines radically different sets of social and political obligations.

Before taking up Marx's critique of justice, however, we must first resolve two more issues having to do with the relation between Marxism and morality: (1) the claim that morality is ideology and, therefore, must be repudiated; and (2) the claim that Marx's social theory commits those accepting it to one form or another of moral relativism and that, therefore, Marxists cannot claim any sort of objectivity for their moral views or normative political positions.

SIX

MORALITY AND IDEOLOGY

A paradox in Marx's thought (and for Marxism in general) is that while his writings abound in moral judgments (i.e., in commendations, condemnations, prescriptions, etc., made on the basis of a concern for human ill and well-being), they contain, at the same time, the claim that *morality is ideology* or, to say the same thing slightly differently, that *morality is ideological*. In the present chapter I shall first distinguish between a global and nonglobal concept of ideology and then give a detailed analysis of Marx's nonglobal (critical) conception of ideology. I will make these distinctions in order to ascertain whether or not morality (i.e., *all* moral judgments, principles, theories, etc.) turns out to be ideological, according to his criteria. Finally, I shall explore Marx's objections to morality, which seem to have led him to view all morality as ideological (in the nonglobal, critical, negative sense of the term) and argue that regardless of his position on this issue, it is simply false that all morality is ideological in this sense.

To claim that morality is ideology is one thing; to say exactly what this means is altogether something else. On most interpretations of the Marxist concept of ideology, to say of some X that it is ideological is to impute to it the characteristic of being somehow illegitimate and constitutes at least a *prima facie* case for the conclusion that it cannot be part of a true theory or of a correct worldview. Beyond this point, however, things are less clear. A bewildering number of different characteristics are attributed to ideology, all of which supposedly account for the fact that every X that is ideological is, ipso facto, somehow illegitimate and ought to be eliminated from or not admitted to one's theory or worldview.

In the writings of Marx and Engels, as well as of later Marxists, one finds the following features of theories or sets of ideas spoken of as *defining* characteristics of ideology, i.e., as the necessary and sufficient conditions a theory or set of ideas must fulfill in order to be properly labeled "ideology" or "ideological": (1) that it is generated within a class society or by a member of a class or social group that is generally sympathetic to the ruling class and/or the social status quo; that it is (2) unscientific, (3) illusory, (4) an inverted ("upside-down" or "topsy-turvy") representation of reality, (5) a result or component of "false consciousness," (6) systematically misleading, or (7) socially mystifying. Other suggested characteristics are that a theory or set of ideas (8) represents the interests of a ruling class as the common interest of society, (9) serves to justify the social status quo and/or the interests of a ruling class, and (10) functions to maintain the social status quo and/or defends the interests of a ruling class. (Notice that characteristic 10 is broader than 9 because not all ways of maintaining the social status quo or defending the interests of the ruling class are ways that *justify* the social status quo or interests of the ruling class. More on this presently.)

The fact that Marxists and other writers are divided on the question of which of these features are defining (or "essential") characteristics of ideology, together with the fact that a similar ambiguity plagues the term "morality" in the literature, makes the claim that morality is ideology troublesome. The object of this chapter is to determine, on the supposition that Marxist empirical theory is basically correct, whether or not this claim is true. Obviously, such a determination will involve an examination and, possibly, a rational reconstruction of the Marxist concept of ideology. I will, in fact, be proposing another—altogether different—characteristic as being definitive of ideology in the negative, critical sense and will be arguing that certain of the ten characteristics listed above are to be subsumed under it.

Notice that, on the assumption that "X is ideological" entails "X is somehow illegitimate and ought to be eliminated from or not admitted to one's theory or world-view," the claim that morality is ideology (or ideological) has quite significant consequences for Marxism. If it is true, it necessitates that morality as a whole, i.e., *all* moral judgments, principles, theories, and codes—even moral discourse itself—be given up, repudiated, eliminated from the Marxist (or any adequate) worldview. If this is the case, and if we accept the standard conception of morality on which moral judgments and principles have the characteristics of (1) prescriptivity, (2) universalizability, and (3) being based on considerations of human ill and well-being, then it becomes impossible for the Marxist to condemn capitalism on grounds, say, that it perpetuates poverty, war, and other major social problems and thus perpetuates human misery or that it restricts human freedom, curtails human self-actualization, and makes the attainment of genuine human community and solidarity impossible. Similarly, it becomes impossible for the Marxist to commend or prescribe socialism and/or communism on grounds that these forms of society will eliminate poverty, war, and other major social problems, expand the boundaries of human freedom, be conducive to human self-actualization and the development of human culture, and make the attainment of real human community and solidarity a genuine possibility. It would become impossible for the Marxist consistently to make these claims for the simple reason that *they are moral claims*, i.e., claims that primarily function to evaluate and prescribe rather than describe or explain, that are universalizable in the sense that they must be taken to apply to all persons and situations that are relevantly similar, and that are based on considerations of human ill and well-being (in the broadest sense of these terms).

Some Marxists have just bitten the bullet at this point and accepted these consequences. But, as seen in previous chapters, this extreme position is neither in accord with the ethic of human freedom, community, and self-realization implicit in Marx's writings nor with Marxist practice. Marxist political practice does not rely simply on predicting the abolition of capitalism and the advent of socialism and/or communism nor in explaining how and why this is bound (or at least extremely likely) to occur. Nor does it rely solely on the above propositions plus appeals to the self-interest of workers and other oppressed segments of the population. Marxists, in addition to all of the above, also appeal to workers (and to people in general) on the basis that socialism is better (i.e., *morally* better) than capitalism: on the basis, for example, that in general it promotes freedom, community, self-actualization, and human well-being better than any form of capitalism or, for that matter, any form of state-socialism; or that it is more just or more likely to respect human rights.

The correct way out of this paradox of Marxist ethics, I shall argue, is to reject the claim that morality (as a whole) is ideology in the negative, critical sense of this term. It is my contention that a correct understanding (or interpretation) of the concepts of ideology and morality will make it clear that such is not the case. The claim that morality (as a whole) is ideology (or ideological) gains credence, I shall attempt to show, only when one is operating with muddled or bogus concepts or morality and/or ideology.

Global and Nonglobal Conceptions of Ideology

Before taking up the matter of deciding which of our several candidate characteristics (if any) are *defining* characteristics of ideology, it is important to distinguish between what I shall call the *global conception* of ideology and the *nonglobal conception*, both of which are to be found in the writings of Marx and other Marxists though they, unfortunately, do not generally distinguish between them. Briefly stated, the difference between these two conceptions is twofold: (1) the global conception is wider in its application than the nonglobal, and (2) the global conception is used as a purely descriptive expression, while the nonglobal conception is used as a (negatively) evaluative expression.

To make matters even worse, a third conception of ideology can be found in the literature, in which ideology is defined as *normative* discourse, claims, or theories. According to this concept of ideology, ideological claims and theories cannot be part of a causal theory but can be and, indeed, of necessity are part of an adequate overall worldview. This concept is the basis for Louis Althusser's claim in "Marxism and Humanism" that humanism (as a system of values) is ideology and thus must be expunged from historical materialism though it can be accepted as the "ideology" of the workers' movement. But since this is not a normal use of the term, and since we can use other terms to discuss the (normative) claims and theories Althusser has in mind, we can safely ignore this concept of ideology. (Recall my critique of Althusser in chapter 4.)

Plamenatz is describing the *global* conception of ideology as found in the writings of Marx and Engels when he states: "Sometimes, when they speak of ideology, they seem to have in mind the entire system of ideas which men use to describe the world and to express their standards, feelings, and purposes. This is so when Marx and Engels are most self-consciously materialistic, when they are concerned to show how men come to have ideas at all."[1] This conception of ideology is so general as to label all the contents of human belief and value systems "ideology." Unlike the more narrow, *nonglobal* conception of ideology, it denotes both ideas and theories concerning nonhuman events and affairs as well as those concerning specifically human (or "social") affairs; it denotes true theories and perspicuous views as well as theories

---

[1] Plamenatz, *Man and Society*, vol. 2, p. 323.

that are false and views that are misleading or inperspicuous; it denotes views and theories that promote social progress or human well-being as well as those that militate against social progress or human well-being.

This distinction between the global and nonglobal conceptions of ideology is most clearly brought to the fore by the term's adjectival form. The nominal form—"ideology"—serves indiscriminately to denote either (1) any general set of ideas and/or values (the global conception), or (2) some set of ideas and/or values that we wish to indict on one ground or another (the nonglobal conception). But the adjectival form—"ideological"—automatically communicates the fact that a negative assessment is being made.

The fact that the terms "ideology" and "ideological" differ in this respect has often puzzled people. Once one distinguishes between the global and nonglobal senses of the term "ideology," the puzzle disappears. The term "ideological" is the adjectival form of "ideology" in the nonglobal, critical sense and thus conveys that a negative assessment of some sort is being made. The global sense of "ideology" has no such adjectival form. Thus, though Classical Liberalism and Marxism are both ideologies on the global conception of ideology, Classical Liberalism is an ideology on the nonglobal, critical conception, while Marxism is not—at least, that is, if we assume Marxist empirical theory to be basically correct. On this assumption, although Classical Liberalism can properly be characterized as *ideological*, Marxism cannot be so characterized. The point is simply that we cannot properly call a system of ideas and/or values of which we intend no criticism "ideological," even though this system of ideas and/or values can be properly referred to as "ideology" in the global sense.

In deciding the issue of whether or not morality is a form of ideology, I shall be concerned only with ideology in the narrow, nonglobal sense for the simple reason that the claim that morality is ideology is significant only if the term "ideology" is being used in this sense. For if it is being used in the noncritical, global sense—in which any set of ideas and/or values can be properly described as an ideology—the claim that morality is ideology is trivially true and thoroughly uninteresting. The philosophically interesting claim is that morality is ideology in the critical, nonglobal sense of the term. This is the claim being made by Marxists and others when they attack morality as a form of ideology. Conflating these two senses of the term has, of course, engendered confusion, not least in the works of Marx and Engels.

240

One further caveat is that I am not here concerned with developing or even examining in detail the Marxist theory of ideology as an empirical theory designed to account for connections between social and economic structures, on the one hand, and belief and preference formation, on the other. Whether or not such a specifically Marxist theory can and should be developed is a much disputed issue, even among Marxists. I find myself in agreement with Jon Elster, however, when he claims that an interesting and successful theory of this sort can be developed only by incorporating the insights of cognitive psychology, including current theories about how motivational and cognitive processes can distort belief and preference formation.[2] But my concern is specifically with whether or not morality is a form of ideology in the negative sense of the term. My answer is that it is not. And part of the reason for this answer is that, in the final analysis, "ideology" (in this sense) is itself a normative and, more specifically, moral concept—or at least a concept with an irreducible moral content. (After all, even to say that a belief or, especially, a preference is distorted is to make a normative and, usually, a moral judgment.)

[2] According to Elster, *An Introduction to Karl Marx*, p. 199: "The theory of ideology is not particularly well and alive, but I believe it can and should be resurrected. Of all Marxist doctrines, this more than any other has been brought into disrepute by the arbitrary procedures adopted. Sometimes functional explanation has been the culprit, sometimes the even less intersubjectively valid method of looking for 'similarities' between economic and mental activities. The first step to remedy the situation must be to draw upon the rich insights of cognitive psychology and its accumulated evidence about the motivational and cognitive processes that distort belief formation and preference formation. In fact, there could potentially be a two-way influence. The Marxist tradition in the sociology of knowledge might be able to suggest some specific hypotheses that could be tested by rigorous experimental procedures. One might, for instance, try to specify in a testable way the idea that the economic agents' perception of economic causality depends on their location in the economic system. Similarly, some forms of hot ideology formation [i.e., the formation of attitudes as opposed to nonevaluative beliefs], such as the motivated preference for some economic theories rather than others, would not seem to be outside the reach of experimental research. These are proposals for the future. The immediate task is to achieve recognition for the fact that the theory of ideology must have microfoundations if it is to go beyond its present stage, which is partly anecdotal, partly functionalist, partly conspiratorial, and partly magical."

For further discussions of Marx's concept (and theory) of ideology, see Elster, *Making Sense of Marx*, pp. 459–510; Gottlieb, "Alienation, Ideology, and Personal Identity" and "A Marxian Concept of Ideology"; H. M. Drucker, "Marx's Concept of Ideology," *Philosophy*, vol. 47 (Apr. 1972); Lichtheim, *The Concept of Ideology and Other Essays*; Richard Lichtman, "Marx's Theory of Ideology," *Social Revolution*, no. 23 (Apr. 1962); Jorge Larrain, *The Concept of Ideology*, University of Georgia Press, Athens, Ga., 1979; Martin Seliger, *The Marxist Conception of Ideology: A Critical Essay*, Cambridge University Press, N.Y., 1977; A. Wood, *Karl Marx*, pp. 111–122, 141–156; Miller, *Analyzing Marx*, pp. 45–50, 253–268; and McMurtry, *The Structure of Marx's World-View*, pp. 123–144.

The Marxist Concept of Ideology

Three major positions can be taken on the issue of the relation between morality and ideology (in the negative sense of the term):

1. morality is ideology and therefore must be repudiated,
2. morality is ideology but need *not* be repudiated, and
3. morality is *not* ideology and therefore need not be repudiated.

It would seem possible to eliminate perfunctorily the second position from the competition and concentrate our attention on the first and third. This is so because it would seem possible to make sense of the second position only on the condition that the global, noncritical conception of ideology is being employed. If the non-global, critical conception of ideology is being used, the statement seems necessarily false. Since "X is ideological" entails, in its non-global meaning, "X is illegitimate and, therefore, ought to be repudiated," the statement "morality is ideology but need not be repudiated" would come to the necessarily false statement "morality is illegitimate and ought to be repudiated, but it need not be repudiated."

It might be thought that this objection to the second position can be circumvented by claiming that the Marxist perhaps means by this only that morality must be eliminated from Marxist empirical (i.e., scientific) theory but not necessarily from the Marxist world-view as a whole—a position taken by Althusser and some other Marxists. But one need only realize that if this is what is meant, then one is not claiming that morality is ideological, for the claim "X is ideological" entails, according to the analysis offered here, "X ought to be eliminated from one's empirical theories as well as one's normative theories." Why this is so becomes clear if one assumes, as will be argued below, that a characteristic of ideology that comes close to being a defining one is that ideology functions to maintain the social status quo and/or defend the interests of the ruling class (in class-divided societies). If this is true, then it is clear that both the empirical-theoretical component and the evaluative or normative component of a worldview can be ideological because it is clear that views taken from either of these components can perform this function. Therefore, those wishing to maintain that morality must be eliminated from Marxist empirical theory but

242

need not be eliminated from the Marxist worldview as a whole are not proponents of the second position but of the third.

Since we are interested only in those claims about the issue of morality and ideology that use the nonglobal, critical conception of morality, we are faced with choosing between the first and third positions.[3] The first position—that morality, as such, is ideology and therefore ought to be repudiated—is usually taken by Marx and Engels as well as by their more orthodox followers and, as documented in chapter 4 of the present work, by such recent and contemporary philosophers as Lewis Feuer, Donald Clark Hodges, Allen Wood, Andrew Collier, and Anthony Skillen. I shall refer to this position as the *orthodox Marxist position*.

The third position—that morality is not ideology and therefore need not, as a whole, be repudiated—though not often defended by Marxists in its explicit form, can be expected to find favor among those Marxists and left-leaning philosophers who wish to argue for a Marxist ethic or who wish to argue from a Marxist ethic or Marxist moral and social theory to other (e.g., practical or political) conclusions. I take it that this would include all Marxists once they really thought the issue through. At present, it includes those who view themselves as Marxist Humanists as well as most contemporary Analytic Marxists, as I have previously described this school. (Wood, Collier, and Skillen are important exceptions.)

Most arguments for the orthodox Marxist position are of the form:

1. X is the defining characteristic of ideology,

2. morality (i.e., all moral concepts, principles, theories, codes, etc.) has characteristic X, therefore,

3. morality is ideology.

On the assumption that the nonglobal, critical conception of ideology is being used, we could then conclude that morality must be

---

[3] In his 1980 essay, "Marxism, Ideology, and Moral Philosophy," Nielsen tentatively endorses position 2—morality is ideology but need not be repudiated—by (apparently) holding that "X is ideology" establishes only a *prima facie* case in favor of eliminating X from one's theory or worldview, a case that may be overridden by other considerations.

Though I readily admit this way of construing the concept of ideology is not totally implausible, it is not, I think, the best way to go, especially since I am not convinced that all moral ideologies (in the *global* sense of the term) are "touched by the distortion" that reflecting class interests (supposedly) involves. At any rate, Nielsen has since given up this tentative defense of position 2 in favor of position 3. His new position is recorded in his 1981 essay, "Justice and Ideology: Justice as Ideology."

eliminated from or refused entry into one's worldview on pain of its being judged inadequate. I would like to argue, however, that in all such arguments either the first or second premise is false and that the argument is therefore unsound.

A classic example of this form of argument with a false first premise appears in Feuer's "Ethical Theories and Historical Materialism." Feuer first quotes Engels' statement that "ideology is a process accomplished by the so-called thinker consciously, indeed, but with a false consciousness. The real motives impelling him remain unknown to him otherwise it would not be an ideological process at all."[4] Feuer uses this statement as a definition of ideology. He then gives the Freudian analysis of the function of ethical terms (i.e., of morality) quoted in chapter 4 of the present work and concludes that all ethical theories and views are ideological.

> It is important to bear in mind the social psychology of ethical terms because we are thus enabled to understand the ideological character of ethical theories. . . . such theories are elaborated within a "false consciousness," . . . they are propounded with an ignorance as to the underlying motives.[5]

Though Feuer hints at another characteristic that might be definitive of ideology when he speaks of "ethical terms" being "vehicles of social manipulation," the main thrust of his analysis of ideology is that it is a result of "false consciousness." Thus, for a view to be ideological, it is only necessary to be ignorant of one's underlying motives for having accepted it. Adopting a Freudian analysis of the inculcation of mores or moral values, Feuer argues, in short:

1. Being a result of false consciousness is the defining characteristic of ideology.

2. Morality ("ethical theory") has the characteristic of being a result of false consciousness, therefore,

3. morality is ideology.

But this argument is unsound. Being a result of "false consciousness" is not the defining characteristic of ideology. To say a characteristic is the defining characteristic of an X is to say that it con-

---

[4] Feuer, "Ethical Theories and Historical Materialism," p. 242. (This quote is from a letter to Franz Mehring dated July 14, 1893, which can be found in *Marx-Engels Selected Correspondence*, p. 434.)

[5] Ibid., p. 243.

stitutes the necessary and sufficient conditions something must fulfill in order to be properly labeled an X. But being a result of "false consciousness" is neither a necessary nor a sufficient condition for something being properly labeled "ideology" (or "ideological"). It is not a necessary condition because some views or theories are ideological even though they lack this characteristic. Since the Freudian theory of inculcation is primarily concerned with evaluative attitudes rather than factual beliefs, any descriptive-explanatory view or theory that is ideological (for example, "vulgar" economic theory or the Horatio Alger myth concerning the correlation of hard work with material success) seemingly would lack this characteristic.

Furthermore, it is at least logically possible for a person to be perfectly cognizant of all the underlying motives and psychological factors that cause him or her to accept a certain set of mores or moral values, so that it cannot be said that they are the result of "false consciousness," and yet for this set of mores or moral values to be ideological. On the Marxist view, this set of values would still be ideological if it were the same or similar to, say, Classical Liberalism, Right-Libertarianism, Burkeian Conservatism, or the "moral" ideology of fascism—all of which function to preserve the social status quo and defend the interests of the ruling class in capitalist society and thus militate against the amelioration and/or improvement of the human condition.

Nor is "being a result of false consciousness" in this sense a sufficient condition for an X being properly labeled "ideology." There are views that have this characteristic but seem, nevertheless, not to be ideological, for example, the view that property rights are not as important from the moral point of view as people's basic rights to well-being (e.g., their security and subsistence rights) and that, therefore, if the two are (in some situation) incompatible, the former consideration must give way to the latter. Even if it were a result of "false consciousness" in the above sense, this view is not ideological. I suggest this is because it does not function to maintain the social status quo and/or defend the interests of the ruling class nor militate against human well-being.

But even some Analytic Marxists disagree. In the following passages, Allen Wood suggests an analysis that is in important ways similar to Feuer's:

> The term "ideology" is used in several different ways in Marx's writings, but for our present purposes I think we may regard something as "ideological" in Marx's usual pejorative

sense if it possesses the following three features: 1) it is (or is part of) a system of beliefs, thoughts and feelings which is socially prominent or influential; and 2) it belongs to this system because of the way in which it serves to sanction a mode of production or to promote definite class interests; and 3) its content includes features which mask feature 2, that is, features which tend to make people disregard or deny the fact that its social prominence or influence is due to the economic or class function it serves.

Morality as Hegelian *Sittlichkeit* can be seen in the light of historical materialism to have all three of these features. 1) It is a system of beliefs and thoughts about what is supposedly universally rational and individually self-fulfilling, to which powerful feelings (closely related to self-worth) are attached. 2) The system serves to meet the demands of the existing social order. Its appeal to us, however, is presented in terms of our subjective freedom or autonomy, of which moral conduct promises to be the fulfillment. But 3) according to historical materialism such an appeal is necessarily a fraudulent one, which serves to mask the fact that moral norms are valid or "actual" because of the social or class interests served by the influence which moral beliefs, thoughts and sentiments have on us. Morality, therefore, is necessarily ideological in the characteristically pejorative Marxian sense of that term.[6]

Although I do not believe the three characteristics suggested by Wood are either individually necessary or jointly sufficient to regard something as ideological in the "pejorative" sense of the term, it is the third characteristic I want to concentrate on here. The characteristic that a set of ideas or beliefs must have features that *mask* their real significance in terms of how they function to sanction a mode of production or promote definite class interests is analogous to Feuer's claim that something is ideological if, and only if, it is the result of false consciousness (as Feuer explicates this concept). As such, Wood's analysis is open to the same objections as Feuer's.

I also have reservations about Wood's claim that morality as a whole meets all three of his requirements for calling something ideological. I find especially dubious his claim that moral systems of belief always "serve to meet the demands of the existing social order," at least if he means by this the existing social status quo

[6] A. Wood, "Marx's Immoralism," p. 688.

(as Marxists usually do). I believe that, at bottom, Wood's objection—and probably Marx's—is that morality is always conservative in this sense, but this is clearly false. (This will be discussed in more detail in the last section of the present chapter.) Similarly, I find dubious Wood's claim that "moral norms are valid or 'actual' because of the social or class interests served by [them]." If by "valid" he means "justified"—which he presumably does—this also is rather obviously false. (I will discuss this issue in more detail in chapter 8.)

In any case, it is my contention that none of the ten characteristics previously listed—except possibly the last—are defining characteristics of ideology because it is possible in each case to produce counter-examples to the claim that the characteristic is either a necessary condition or a sufficient condition for properly labeling something ideological. Furthermore, I see no reason to believe that any combination of them—to the exclusion of the last—is jointly sufficient for something to be ideological. The last characteristic listed—that X functions to maintain the social status quo and/or defend the interest of a ruling class—is, I contend, a good first approximation of a defining characteristic but, on further analysis, fails also. The rest of the characteristics, or at least those that are at all viable, prove to be ways in which ideas, theories, or views fulfill the function of maintaining the social status quo and/or defending the interests of the ruling class.

For purposes of analysis we can group characteristics 1 through 9, as listed above, into three sets. The first set consists only of characteristic 1, which is the least viable of any of the proposed defining characteristics of ideology and the easiest to eliminate from serious consideration. It can even be eliminated as a way in which ideas and theories are generally ideological, i.e., as a cause of ideas and theories meeting condition 10 and thus being ideological. The second set is composed of characteristics 2 through 7. These characteristics generally represent ways in which descriptive-explanatory ideas or theories (as opposed to evaluative ideas or theories) go wrong and, as a consequence, tend to lead away from a correct understanding of human beings and their societies. In turn, such wrongheaded views usually lead away from effective political action and thus function to maintain the social status quo. On the other hand, characteristics 8 and 9 are generally ways in which evaluative theories and views can be ideological.

The first characteristic—that X be generated within a certain class society or historical epoch or by a member of the ruling class or a member of a class or social group that is generally sympathetic to the ruling class and/or the social status quo—translates into the proposition that "an X is ideological if and only if it meets one of these conditions." The fact is, however, that these conditions are neither necessary nor sufficient for an X to be ideological and thus this is not a defining characteristic.

The thought behind the first part of this characteristic is that the ideas or theories generated within a particular class society or historical epoch will bear the mark of that society or epoch and be supportive of the existing status quo. Though Marx does sometimes speak loosely about such connections (especially when utilizing the global conception of ideology), he recognizes the fact that not all ideas and theories produced by a given society or historical epoch are supportive of the social status quo. The "communist consciousness," which, according to Marx, is produced among the working class or at least some of its members (and even among members of other classes "through the contemplation of this class"), together with his own theory and view of society (which, in part, embodies this "communist consciousness"), provides—at least for the Marxist—conclusive counter-examples to the thesis that all theories and views generated within a particular class society or historical epoch are supportive of the existing social status quo.

The second part of this characteristic is no more plausible than the first. Though there is certainly an empirical trend that views and theories produced, accepted, and supported by the ruling class and classes and social groups sympathetic to it are supportive of that ruling class and the social status quo, there is always a minority of theoreticians from these classes and social groups whose theories and views do not support the social status quo. Again, Classical Marxism affords a perfect example: among its progenitors, Engels was, according to Marx's structural criteria of class and class membership, a member of the middle bourgeoisie, and Marx, Lenin, Luxemburg, and Trotsky were all from petty bourgeois or "middle class" backgrounds. Nevertheless, their theories and views presumably do not function to maintain the social status quo or defend the interests of the ruling class. Thus characteristic 1 is neither a defining characteristic of ideology nor even a standard cause of theories being ideological.

Our second set of characteristics (2 through 7) is more important to our analysis. Though some of these are more useful or perspicacious than others, they all represent ways in which a theory or

view can have epistemic failings and, for this reason, be ideological. The presupposition here is that there is a strong tendency for
false or misleading descriptive-explanatory theories or views concerning our social world to serve the interests of the ruling class
and/or function to maintain the social status quo.

However, the fact that X is false or misleading is not absolute
proof that X is ideological. In order to fulfill the function of maintaining the social status quo and/or defending the interests of the
ruling class, X must be *importantly misleading*: it must either directly or indirectly have a significant impact on social and political
circumstances. A perfect example of a descriptive-explanatory
view about our social world that is false but—at least from the
Marxist point of view—not importantly misleading is the "vulgar"
interpretation of the labor theory of value, namely, the proposition
that the exchange value of a commodity (i.e., the price of a commodity in equilibrium market conditions) is determined by the actual amount of human labor that went into its production. This
proposition is false according to Marx and other proponents of the
labor theory of value, who claim that it is the *socially necessary labor
time*, at any particular point in the development of society's productive forces, that determines its value in the sense of its price as
a commodity in equilibrium market conditions. But this proposition is not ideological because it (presumably) does not meet the
requirement of functioning to maintain the status quo and/or defend the interests of the ruling class. The wide acceptance of this
proposition in a capitalist society, in fact, may even function to
destabilize the social status quo and work against the interests of
the ruling class. Furthermore, it is arguable that even the technically correct interpretation of the labor theory of value is false. If
so, then this theory also provides a counter-example to the claim
that something is ideological if it is false, even if it isn't importantly
misleading.

For the Marxist, paradigmatic examples of descriptive-explanatory views that are ideological because of their epistemic failings
(i.e., because they are false and importantly misleading) include:

1. Religious and "philosophical" (e.g., Hegelian) world-
   views that misrepresent our social world and the ways in
   which it can be changed;

2. Theories and propositions concerning society, history,
   human nature, etc., that are importantly misleading. For
   example:

249

a. "Bourgeois" economic theory or, at least, those "bourgeois" economic theories that manifest what Marx called the fetishism of capital (the claim that the investment of capital *by capitalists* is a necessary condition for carrying out production in an industrialized society)

b. The interest group/power-politics theories denying that the Marxist class analysis of society has any validity at all

c. The claim that the state in capitalist societies functions as a neutral arbitrator between socioeconomic classes

d. The claim that virtually anyone with a modicum of intelligence can make a "success" of himself or herself in a capitalist society if he or she has enough initiative and drive, i.e., the Horatio Alger myth.

If Marxist empirical theory is basically correct, all of these theories or views are not only false but importantly misleading. To the extent that they are accepted in a capitalist society, they can be expected to function to maintain the social (capitalist) status quo and—perhaps unintentionally—defend the interests of the ruling (capitalist) class.

Of the set of characteristics we are now examining (i.e., 2 through 7), the two worthy of special note are the sixth and the seventh: the characteristic of being *systematically misleading* and of being *socially mystifying*. These characteristics represent the two sorts of ideology Marx was most concerned to combat in his writings. The characteristic of being systematically misleading is especially applicable to religious and "philosophical" conceptions of humanity-in-society or humanity-in-the-world. Such theories or views not only radically misjudge human nature and mislocate the springs of social and political action but also eschew the scientific, empirical approach to theory and practice—an approach shared by Marxists and "bourgeois" social scientists and theorists alike.

Among those theories and views that are in this broad sense "scientific"—and thus not *systematically* misleading, though they may still be *importantly* misleading—Marx recognized as ideological theories that are socially mystifying and those that are importantly misleading but not socially mystifying. *Socially mystifying* theories or views hide the real nature of social relations within a society by cloaking them with a misleading or "mystifying" surface description or explanation. The fetishism of money and commodities, which, according to Marx, cloaks the fact that labor is the sole creator of exchange value, and the fetishism of capital, which cloaks the fact that the capitalist class extracts unpaid labor from the working class in the form of surplus value, are, for Marx, the paradigmatic examples of theories or views that are socially mystifying.[7] By hiding the real nature of social relations within a society, such theories and views obscure the vision that "subordinate," "ruled," or "exploited" classes have of their own self-interest, stop up the springs of social and political action on the part of these classes, and thus function to maintain the social status quo and defend the interests of the ruling (capitalist) class.

Thus the characteristics of being systematically misleading and socially mystifying—though not defining characteristics of the concept of ideology—indicate the major ways in which, based on Marxist theory, a descriptive-explanatory theory or view can be ideological. The rest of the characteristics in this set (i.e., characteristics 2 though 5) can either be discarded completely as not even good candidates for the ways in which descriptive-explanatory theories can be ideological or can be subsumed under the two above-named characteristics. Let us consider them in order.

Characteristic 2—that of being unscientific—may, at first glance, seem a viable candidate for an important way in which a theory or view can be ideological, but it must be rejected. The problem here is that the term "scientific" is often used in a peculiar way by Marxists to mean, approximately, "that which is in agreement with Marxism" or "that which is in agreement with my (or our) interpretation of Marxism." If this persuasive definition is being used, then the proposition "X is unscientific" is roughly equivalent to the proposition "X is not in agreement with (some interpretation or other of) Marxism," a most uninteresting claim.

On the broader, more legitimate definition, "scientific" is that which is based on or in accordance with the principles and methods of science. The "principles and methods of science" are those relying on empirical evidence as the basis for confirming or, more importantly, disconfirming theories and propositions. (But this is

---

[7] See Marx's chapter on the fetishism of money and commodities in *Capital*, vol. 1, and his chapter on the Trinity Formula in *Capital*, vol. 3. See also Norman Geras, "Essence and Appearances: Aspects of Fetishism in Marx's *Capital*," *New Left Review*, no. 65 (1971); John Mepham, "The Theory of Ideology in *Capital*," *Radical Philosophy*, no. 2 (1972); John Maguire, "Marx on Ideology, Power and Force," *Theory and Decision*, vol. 7 (1976); and chapter 5 of G. A. Cohen's *Karl Marx's Theory of History*. It should be noted that even if it is false that labor creates all exchange value of products, it may still be true that only labor creates products. (Capital is viewed by Marx as nothing more than embodied labor from the past.)

not to be interpreted so narrowly as to rule out all systematic theory concerning our social world on the basis that it is not directly testable or easily falsifiable.) On this broader definition, it must be allowed that a considerable number of theories that are ideological are also scientific. On the above definition of "scientific" and on the assumption that Marxist empirical theory is basically correct, it is the case that many systematic theories found in "bourgeois" social science are ideological (because they are false and, more importantly, seriously misleading) but, nevertheless, scientific. (On a slightly different definition, to say that X is unscientific is to say that X is a descriptive-explanatory theory or view that is not susceptible to rational empirical investigation and confirmation. But pseudo-scientific theories of this sort can best be subsumed under the characteristic of being systematically misleading.)

Similarly, to the extent that they are useful at all, the characteristics of being illusory (characteristic 3) and an inverted representation of reality (characteristic 4) can be subsumed under the characteristics of being either systematically misleading or socially mystifying.

When Marx is speaking of religious and "philosophical" illusion and, in particular, when he is polemicizing against the Hegelian and neo-Hegelian worldview or theory of history, the characteristic of being illusory is best subsumed under the characteristic of being systematically misleading. When he is speaking of political illusion or of illusion in the realm of the social sciences, the characteristic of being illusory is best subsumed under the characteristic of being socially mystifying. That Marx distinguishes between these two basic sorts of illusion is borne out in *The German Ideology*: "While the French and the English at least hold by the political illusion, which is moderately close to reality, the Germans move in the realm of 'pure spirit,' and make religious illusion the driving force of history."[8]

Such illusory and systematically misleading theories as the historical theory of the Hegelians tend to function to maintain the social status quo and/or defend the interests of the ruling class. According to Marx, seeing history as determined in accord with the (Hegelian) Idea or in accord with peoples' ideas or consciousness not only obscures the truth of social and political processes but leads to the conservative and misleading strategy of improving human consciousness in order to improve the human condition:

[8] Marx and Engels, *The German Ideology*, p. 130.

The Old Hegelians had *comprehended* everything as soon as it was reduced to an Hegelian logical category. The Young Hegelians criticized everything by attributing to it religious conceptions or by pronouncing it a theological matter. The Young Hegelians are in agreement with the Old Hegelians in their belief in the rule of religion, of concepts, of an abstract general principle in the existing world. Only, the one party attacks this dominion as usurpation, while the other extols it as legitimate.

Since the Young Hegelians consider conceptions, thought, ideas, in fact all the products of consciousness, to which they attribute an independent existence, as the real chains of men (just as Old Hegelians declared them the true bonds of human society) it is evident that the Young Hegelians have to fight only against these illusions of the consciousness. Since, according to their fantasy, the relationships of men, all their doings, their chains, and their limitations are products of their consciousness, the Young Hegelians logically put to men the moral postulate of exchanging their present consciousness for human, critical or egoistic consciousness, and thus of removing their limitations. This demand to change consciousness amounts to a demand to interpret reality in another way, i.e., to accept it by means of another interpretation. The Young Hegelian ideologists, in spite of their allegedly "world-shattering" statements, are the staunchest conservatives.[9]

(To this, of course, Marx responds: "The philosophers have only *interpreted* the world, in various ways; the point, however, is to *change* it."[10])

When Marx uses "illusion" language in talking about bourgeois economic and sociological theory, the characteristic of being illusory is best subsumed under the characteristic of being socially mystifying. Speaking of the fetishism of capital, he speaks of the "complete mystification of the capitalist mode of production," the "false appearance and illusion" and "the world of illusion" from which even the classical bourgeois economists such as Smith and Ricardo could not escape. This form of ideology—the mystification of social relations—is, for Marx, the most pernicious form because, on his view, it is the most difficult to "see through."

Finally, let us consider characteristic 5—that something is a re-

[9] Ibid., p. 113.
[10] Marx, "Theses on Feuerbach," p. 109.

sult or component of "false consciousness." As our earlier discussion of "false consciousness" in the context of Feuer's argument for the proposition that morality is ideology should have indicated, the characteristic of "being a result or component of false consciousness" is neither a defining characteristic of ideology nor an important way in which theories and views can be ideological. Being a result of "false consciousness," in the Freudian or quasi-Freudian sense Feuer and others intend, is not a good indication that a theory or view is ideological because all moral theories and views, or, at any rate, the moral values or evaluative attitudes underlying them, are a result of "false consciousness" in this sense. Yet a great many of them do *not* support the social status quo. Some systems of moral values and principles—such as that which is implicit in Marx's writings and even, I would argue, the core of Rawls' theory of social justice—actually function to promote the cause of socialism, at least when combined with Marxist empirical theory of society and analysis of capitalism (more on this presently).

Being a *component* of "false consciousness" is no more a sign that a theory or view is ideological than being a *result* of "false consciousness." In fact, for Marx and Engels—for whom the term "false consciousness" had no Freudian connotations—to say that a theory or view is a component of "false consciousness" is to say no more than that it is wrong or false.

To sum up our assessment of the second set of characteristics (2 through 7), we can state: (1) they usually involve epistemic failings of descriptive-explanatory theories or views that, purportedly, make such theories or views ideological; (2) none is a defining characteristic of ideology; and (3) only two—the characteristics of being systematically misleading and socially mystifying—are important ways in which a theory or view can be ideological.

Our last set of characteristics (8 and 9) represents ways in which evaluative theories or views can be ideological. Characteristic 8— that a theory or view represents the interests of the ruling class as the common interest—has its genesis in Marx's remark that

each new class which puts itself in place of one ruling before it, is compelled, merely in order to carry through its aim, to represent its interests as the common interest of all the members of the society, put in an ideal form; it will give its ideas the form of universality, and represent them as the only rational, universally valid ones.[11]

[11] Marx and Engels, *The German Ideology*, p. 138.

Since there are many theories and views that lack this character-istic but are, nevertheless, ideological, this is not a defining char-acteristic. It is, in fact, but a specific form of characteristic 9, that of justifying the social status quo and/or the interests of the ruling class. This characteristic is, I submit, a third major way in which theories or views can be ideological. Whereas the characteristics of being systematically misleading and socially mystifying are major ways in which a descriptive-explanatory theory or, better, the de-scriptive-explanatory component of a theory or view can function as ideology, characteristic 9 is the major way in which evaluative theories or views can function as ideology.

Besides a theory or view representing the interests of the ruling class as the common interest of society—of which a good example is the claim often made in capitalist society that the institution of private property is in everyone's interest—there are many other ways in which a theory or view can justify the social status quo and/or the interests of the ruling class. Such justifications can ap-peal either to prudential or to moral considerations. The claim that the interests of the ruling class are the common interests of society is a factual claim which, if accepted as true, functions to get people to accept that society as "justified," at least so far as one is judging from the prudential point of view. This judgment may, of course, be taken as grounds for judging a particular society morally justi-fied as well, but its primary thrust is based on considerations of self-interest.

But theories or views that provide moral justification for the cap-italist social status quo and/or the interests of the ruling capitalist class are multitudinous. The paradigm case of such theories is the moral and social theory of Classical Liberalism and its most back-ward twentieth-century descendant, Right-Libertarianism. The first is best represented by the theory of John Locke and the sec-ond by the works of Robert Nozick, John Hospers, Milton Fried-man, and, at the level of popular exposition, Ayn Rand.

Normative views or theories that justify the social status quo and/or the interests of a ruling class—whether they are as sophis-ticated as the view that property rights are indefeasible before any and all other moral considerations or as unsophisticated as the view captured by the phrase "my country, right or wrong"—ob-viously have a strong tendency to function to maintain the social status quo and/or defend the interests of the ruling class and thus to be ideological. Characteristic 9 is not, however, the *defining* characteristic of ideology because it is not a necessary condition for designating a theory or view as ideological. A theory or view can

255

also be ideological because its descriptive-explanatory component is importantly misleading.

To sum up our analysis of the concept of ideology, we can say—at least as a first approximation—that the defining characteristic of ideology is characteristic 10 (functioning to maintain the social status quo and/or defend the interest of the ruling class), and that the characteristics of being systematically misleading, socially mystifying, and justifying the social status quo and/or the interests of the ruling class (i.e., 6, 7, and 9) are the main ways in which theories or views meet this criterion and are thus ideological.

On further reflection, however, it is clear that this definition of the Marxist concept of ideology is still not wholly adequate. It is not the case, for Marx and Marxists, that a theory or view that functions to support the social status quo and/or defend the interests of the ruling class in the context of a *socialist* society is ideological. (The ruling class is, of course, the working class according to Marx's conception of socialism.) Though few Marxists consciously realize it, the real (but submerged) defining characteristic of the Marxist concept of ideology is, I submit, the characteristic of militating against human well-being or, more grandly, against the amelioration and/or the improvement of the human condition. (Let us call this eleventh characteristic the "normative characteristic." Note that I have phrased this characteristic at a very abstract level so as to be neutral between consequentialist and deontological moral views.)

I believe that the reason Marxists have not generally distinguished between characteristics 10 and 11 is that, in the Marxist's empirical theory concerning society and history, the way in which theories and views are ideological, that is, the way in which they militate against human well-being (or the amelioration and/or improvement of the human condition) in this historical epoch, is that they function to maintain capitalist societies and/or defend the interests of ruling capitalist classes. Assuming that Marxist empirical theory is basically correct—that, for example, Marx's analysis of the class dynamics of capitalist society and his theses that (1) planned socialist economies are more efficient (in terms of the utilization of available natural and human resources) than capitalist economies, and (2) civil liberty and political democracy are, under favorable circumstances, perfectly compatible with socialist property relations are basically correct—it would seem that socialism is preferable to capitalism on almost any major moral theory concerning social arrangements. The only notable exceptions that come to mind are Right-Libertarianism and the moral theory of fascism—if such can be said to exist. And if it is true that socialism is morally preferable to capitalism, and that this is so because socialism is much more conducive to human well-being (i.e., to the amelioration and/or improvement of the human condition), then those theories and views that function to maintain capitalist societies and/or defend the interests of capitalist classes (i.e., those theories and views conforming to characteristic 10) pretty much constitute the set of theories that are ideological. In short, from the Marxist point of view, characteristics 10 and 11 are virtually coextensive in presently existing historical circumstances. (Notice, however, that not all ideology that functions to maintain bourgeois society is "bourgeois" ideology. Though religious ideology functions to maintain the status quo in bourgeois societies, religious ideology is not bourgeois ideology. It seems as though the criteria of individuation for kinds of ideology—feudal, bourgeois, petty bourgeois, etc.—have to do with the conditions of their historical genesis or with their content or both.)

However, in the context of a genuinely socialist or communist society (should one exist), the empirical (nomological) link between characteristics 10 and 11 is broken. If Marxist empirical theory is basically correct, theories or views that function to maintain the socialist social status quo (against capitalism and other historically regressive forms of society) and defend the interests of the "ruling class" of a socialist society (i.e., the working class, which will eventually be the only class in a socialist society) are not ideological because it is not the case that such theories and views militate against the amelioration and/or improvement of the human condition.

Under these circumstances, however, it is easily understandable that characteristic 10 has generally been taken to be the defining characteristic of the Marxist concept of ideology (both by Marxists and non-Marxists) rather than the normative (or moral!) characteristic underlying it, characteristic 11. But the fact that theories and views exhibiting characteristic 10, in reference to a socialist society, do not—assuming Marxist empirical theory to be basically correct—qualify as "ideology" or as "ideological" disproves the thesis that characteristic 10 is the defining characteristic of the Marxist concept of ideology.

We can summarize this analysis of the Marxist concept of ideology by noting that characteristic 11 is the defining characteristic of that which is ideology or that which is ideological, but that characteristic 10 is the major way in which theories and views are ideological in this and other pre-socialist historical epochs. Furthermore, characteristics 6, 7, and 9 are the primary ways in which theories and views fulfill the conserving function put forward in characteristic 10. That is, (a) being systematically misleading, (b) being socially mystifying, and (c) justifying the social status quo and/or the interests of a ruling class are the main ways in which theories and views (d) function to maintain the social status quo and/or defend the interests of the ruling class. In turn, this is the main way, under present historical circumstances, that theories and views (e) militate against human well-being and the amelioration and/or improvement of the human condition.

Morality, Ideology, and Moral Theory

The question with which we are now faced is: does *morality as a whole* have characteristics 6, 7, or 9 or in some way conform to characteristic 10 and thus to characteristic 11? For the orthodox Marxist claim that morality is ideology to be correct, the answer to this question must be yes. There are several points to be made at this time. The first is that in this analysis of ideology it may be a priori impossible to show that all morality is ideological. This is because the ultimate (normative) criterion for doing so *presupposes morality*. The very notions of human well-being and the amelioration and/or improvement of the human condition are *moral* notions.

The second point to note is that to falsify position 1 (morality is ideology and therefore must be repudiated) and make position 3 (morality is not ideology and therefore need not be repudiated) the most reasonable to accept, there need be only one moral theory or view that does not meet these conditions. The most obvious candidate for a counter-example to position 1 is Marx's moral theory (or set of moral values and principles) as elucidated in part I of the present work.

The third point concerns the claim that—as Allen Wood puts it—"Marx was operating with . . . a conception of morality which assigns to morality an exclusively conservative social function."[12] But, as argued in some detail in the last section of chapter 4 of the present work, this position simply cannot be defended. While many moral theories or views clearly are conservative in nature in

[12] A. Wood, "Justice and Class Interests," p. 11.

that they defend the social status quo and/or the interests of the ruling class in class-divided societies, many others are not. Even Engels—and, I have argued, Marx—recognized this fact. In a passage worth quoting again, Engels writes:

> As society has hitherto moved in class antagonisms, morality was always a class morality; it has either justified the domination and the interests of the ruling class *or* as soon as the oppressed class became powerful enough, *it has represented the revolt against this domination and the future interests of the oppressed* [emphasis added].[13]

The obvious fact that the belief that one has a moral obligation to respect a picket line during a labor strike or to support the struggle for socialism is not conservative but, rather, progressive in nature would hardly require comment, except for the fact that certain Marxists incessantly—and at times vehemently—deny it.

But how then are we to account for the fact that theoreticians of the intellectual stature and sophistication of Marx and Engels took the position expressed by proposition 1, that morality is ideology and therefore must be repudiated? Assuming that Marx and Engels were, for the most part, operating with a concept of ideology similar to that which we rendered previously, we can only conclude that Marx and Marxists generally have been operating with concepts of morality that are, to one degree or another, in one way or another, muddled.

That this should be the case is, of course, no great mystery. It has been only relatively recently—the last several decades, in fact—that philosophers have begun to get a handle on the nature of morality, i.e., the nature and function of moral discourse and the structure of moral arguments. In Marx's day, the concept of morality must have still seemed puzzling and mysterious. Not only had the techniques and methods of analytic-linguistic philosophy that would prove to be fruitful in the analysis of morality not yet evolved, but the questions that constitute the subject matter of metaethics had not even been formulated. It is thus small wonder that Marx, Engels, and all other pre-twentieth-century philosophers and social theorists harbored somewhat muddled conceptions of morality.

One important misconception Marx and Engels exhibit has to do with the supposed fact that the use of moral discourse (i.e., the

[13] Engels, *Anti-Dühring*, p. 105.

259

making of moral judgments, etc.) commits one to unacceptable ontological or epistemological positions that are not in line with the sort of rational, scientific, and materialistic worldview to which they were committed. A second misconception is that the use of moral discourse commits one to the view that the propagation and inculcation of moral theories or principles is the primary or, at least, one of the most important ways to attain the amelioration and/or improvement of the human condition.

The first misconception of morality exhibited by Marx and Engels—that the use of moral discourse or making of moral judgments commits one to unacceptable ontological or epistemological positions—seems to have had to do with the fact that they could not find a place for evaluative discourse in their materialistic and scientifically oriented worldview. If a statement such as "X is good" does not refer to some observable property of X, does not describe or explain, then their assumption seems to have been that it is superfluous and ought to be eliminated.

If, on the other hand, a statement such as "X is good" does describe or explain, it must do so, they seem to have assumed, by means of the term "good" referring to some unobservable, nonmaterial entity, property, or principle. The term "good" would (purportedly) refer to some "eternal, immutable, entity" or to some "transcendent" moral principle (as in "the word of God" or "natural law"), or to some moral principle immanent in world history or the development of the World Spirit (as the Hegelians put it). Examples of each of these concerns can be found in the writings of Marx and Engels. The objection that to indulge in moral discourse is, ipso facto, to accept the existence of transcendent moral entities is found, for example, in the "Communist Manifesto" when they are considering "bourgeois" objections to their doctrines:

> "Undoubtedly," it will be said, "religious, moral, philosophical and juridical ideas have been modified in the course of historical development. But religion, morality, philosophy, political science, and law, constantly survived this change. . . . There are, besides, eternal truths, such as Freedom, Justice, etc., that are common to all states of society."[14]

Their answer to this, in part, is to claim that all past societies have one characteristic in common—"the exploitation of one part

[14] Marx and Engels, "Manifesto of the Communist Party," p. 351.

of society by the other"—and that this accounts for the similarities in moral ideology pointed out by their opponents. Another part of their answer consists in claiming that, like all ruling classes in the past, the bourgeoisie has been induced, by its selfish misconceptions, "to transform into *eternal laws of nature and reason*, the social forms springing from [its] present mode of production and form of property"[15] (emphasis added).

Later on, in the course of a polemic against the liberal humanist Heinzen, Engels writes:

> Herr Heinzen appears to be alluding . . . to the fact that Communists have made fun of his sternly moral demeanor and mocked all those sacred and sublime ideas, virtue, justice, morality, etc., which Herr Heinzen imagines form the basis of all society. We accept this reproach. The Communists will not allow the moral indignation of the *honourable* man Herr Heinzen to prevent them from mocking these *eternal verities*. The Communists, moreover, maintain that these eternal verities are by no means the basis, but on the contrary the product, of the society in which they feature.[16]

In *Anti-Dühring* Engels again attacks such "eternal verities or principles." There he claims that "We [communists] . . . reject every attempt to impose on us any moral dogma whatsoever as an eternal, ultimate, and forever immutable moral law on the pretext that the moral world too has its permanent principles which transcend history and the differences between nations."[17]

A large part of their worry here, of course, is of a political rather than a metaphysical nature. They undoubtedly are concerned that the view that moral truths are "eternal" and universally valid will play a conservative social and ideological role since the more well-established (and conservative) moral principles—such as the (supposedly) immutable right to private property (both personal and productive)—would seem to stand to gain more from its acceptance than less well-established and more radical moral principles and precepts. Nevertheless, there is still a strong hint of metaphysical concern. How can such nonmaterial entities exist to begin with, let alone be eternal and immutable? For the hardheaded nineteenth-century materialist there seems to have been no way to

[15] Ibid.

[16] Engels, "The Communists and Herr Heinzen," Marx and Engels, *Collected Works*, vol. 6, p. 301.

[17] Engels, *Anti-Dühring*, p. 103.

account for the timeless quality of moral principles, so they tended simply to deny their "existence" and hence their validity or applicability altogether. One can suppose that this objection to morality was at the back of many a Marxist's mind.

Moral principles that are supposedly *immanent* in history are treated, by Marx and Engels, with similar disdain. Hegel had proposed that Freedom, i.e., the ethical component of the Absolute Idea, had embodied itself in the state and, in particular, the constitutional monarchy. It is rare today to have this position seriously put forward. But since this was the view of Hegel and of many of his followers, it is not surprising to find Marx and Engels still combating it. Marx attacks another version of this position in *The Poverty of Philosophy*, his 1846 critique of Proudhon. According to Proudhon, society in all its historical manifestations is governed by what he variously refers to as "Social Genius," "General Reason," or "Human Reason," whose telos or goal is *equality*. For Proudhon, Marx claims,

> the good side of an economic relation is that which affirms equality; the bad side, that which negates it and affirms inequality. Every new category is a hypothesis of the social genius to eliminate the inequality engendered by the preceding hypothesis. In short, equality is the *primordial intention*, the *mystical tendency*, the *providential aim* that the social genius has constantly before its eyes as it whirls in the circle of economic contradictions.[18]

In a letter written just prior to *The Poverty of Philosophy*, Marx gives the following account of his objections to Proudhon's general approach:

> M. Proudhon sees in history a series of social developments; he finds progress realized in history; . . . he merely invents the hypothesis of the universal reason revealing itself. Nothing is easier than to invent mystical causes, that is to say, phrases which lack common sense. . . . In short, it is not history but old Hegelian junk, it is not profane history—a history of man—but sacred history—a history of ideas. From his point of view man is only the instrument of which the idea or the eternal reason makes use in order to unfold itself. The *evolutions* of which M. Proudhon speaks are understood to be evo-

[18] Marx, *The Poverty of Philosophy*, p. 119.

lutions such as are accomplished within the mystic womb of the absolute idea.[19]

Although Proudhon believed the Social Genius to demand equality and therefore the abolition of capitalism and the establishment of a communal society of petty commodity producers, Marx knew quite well that a Social Genius or any moral principles that it might postulate may just as easily—perhaps more easily—support the existence of capitalism and thus play a conservative rather than a progressive role in the class struggle. Moreover, he naturally regarded Proudhon's vision of socialism as a society of small craftsmen, shopkeepers, and farmers as utopian and reactionary. The only way forward, on Marx's view, was through expanding large-scale industry, not through abolishing it.

The point is that the existence of either transcendent or immanent moral principles of the eternal, immutable variety is obviously noxious to hard-nosed materialists like Marx and Engels. They must have thought that to accept morality or engage in moral discourse under these circumstances would be tantamount to accepting *systematically misleading* views into one's theoretical fold and thus indulging in *ideology*. Therefore, the most reasonable thing for them to do was to repudiate morality and moral discourse.

The misconception of morality involved here is the basic one of taking evaluative discourse to have the same structure and function as descriptive-explanatory discourse and, more specifically, of taking statements of the form "X is good" as attributing the property of being good to X, just as "X is red" attributes the property of being red to X. But the real function of statements such as "X is good" is not to describe but rather to commend or prescribe. For this reason, were Marx and Engels alive today and familiar with recent and contemporary metaethical theory, they would, I think, be much less likely to insist that morality is systematically misleading or ideological in this way, or that it must, on these grounds, be repudiated. If one distinguishes between description and evaluation as two logically separable modes of human discourse and repudiates the view that making moral judgments of the form "X is good" or "X is right" or "X is just" commits one to recognizing "eternal verities" or transcendent or immanent moral principles, there is absolutely no reason to continue to reject morality as a whole on the grounds that it is metaphysically dubious.

Though I am presupposing a noncognitivist or at least prescrip-

---

[19] Marx, "Letter to Annekov," *Marx-Engels: Selected Correspondence*, p. 180.

tivist metaethics, I don't think this affects the conclusions drawn here because contemporary cognitivist and descriptivist metaethical theories would, so far as I can see, reach the same conclusion; namely, that Marx was mistaken in thinking that moral judgments of the form "X is good" commit one to recognizing "eternal verities" or transcendent or immanent moral principles. That is to say, cognitivist/descriptivist metaethical theories no more commit one to a nonnaturalistic ontology than do noncognitivist/prescriptivist metaethical theories.

The second sort of misconception of morality—that making moral judgments entails one's acceptance of the notion that the propagation and inculcation of moral values and principles is an effective way to attain the amelioration and/or improvement of the human condition—seems to be behind Marx and Engels' claim in *The Holy Family* that "morality is '*impuissance mis en action*' [impotence in action]. . . . Every time it fights a vice it is defeated."[20] This misconception is also behind Marx's vehement attack on a passage in the Gotha Program, which speaks of a fair distribution of the proceeds of labor.

> What a crime it is to attempt . . . on the one hand, to force on our Party again, as dogmas, ideas which in a certain period had some meaning but have now become obsolete verbal rubbish, while again perverting, on the other, the realistic outlook, which it cost so much effort to instill into the Party but which has now taken root in it, by means of ideological nonsense about right and other trash so common among the democrats and French Socialists.[21]

The doctrine that moral preaching can cause fundamental social change and thus a fundamental betterment of the human condition was characteristic of the utopian socialists as well as of religious and other traditional moralists. As Sidney Hook once pointed out,

> All his life Marx . . . was compelled to take a stand against abstract ethical idealism, not only as a consequence of his social theories but as a necessity of revolutionary practice. In every country eloquent voices were preaching a new social evangelism in the name of *justice, love and brotherhood*. Weitling, Feuerbach and the *wahre Socialisten* in Germany, St. Si-

[20] Marx and Engels, *The Holy Family*, p. 236.
[21] Marx, "Critique of the Gotha Program," p. 388.

monians and Proudhonians in France, Owenites and Pre-Raphaelites in England, Christian Socialists everywhere—were making impassioned pleas for social reform. All the saints and rebels in the calendar of history were invoked in appeals to such diverse things as conscience, reason, mercy, social consciousness and God. . . . In combating the excesses of ineffective and sentimental "moralising" Marx leaned so far backward that, soon after his death, the myth became current that he had no place for any ethics in his philosophy of social activity.[22]

Marx thought this doctrine—which, following Svetozar Stojanović, I shall refer to as "moralism"—was importantly misleading and that its acceptance functioned to maintain the social status quo and therefore, defend the interests of the ruling class. As Stojanović says of Marx:

There are two principal characteristics of the moralism that Marx opposed:

1. the use of moral language which is independent from cognitive language and which achieves primary importance in comparison with cognitive language to criticize the existing morality and simultaneously to preach the new "true" morality;

2. the belief that significant moral change and reform can be effected in this way.[23]

. . . instead of putting his hopes into moral preaching, he insisted on the need of changing social conditions resulting in immorality; to acquire the knowledge for these conditions he plunged into the scientific investigation of the existing social reality, its supporting forces, its tendencies and laws, possibilities for and carriers of its eventual change and so forth. That was the only way of breaking into the causes of the existing immoral order. Utopian socialism tried to deal primarily with the effects instead of causes. That is why it was powerless, inefficient and naive.

Against this background it is not difficult to understand why cognitive language became of primary importance to Marx. In the forefront was his effort to show the necessity and lawfulness of replacing capitalism with socialism. The ethical

[22] Hook, *From Hegel to Marx*, pp. 50–51.
[23] Stojanović, "Marx's Theory of Ethics," pp. 165–166.

criticism of capitalist reality was only of secondary importance to him. And the explicit ethical justification of socialism as his cause was the least important for him. These have misled some of his interpreters who have come to the wrong conclusion that there necessarily was no place for ethical ideas in Marx's theory.[24]

However, the doctrine of moralism, when incorporated into the concept of morality, renders a misconception of morality. There is absolutely no contradiction in accepting morality (and utilizing moral discourse), on the one hand, and rejecting the doctrine of moralism, on the other. Therefore, the doctrine of moralism cannot be a part of the concept of morality or of a correct theory about morality or moral discourse. Though the doctrine of moralism is, in Marxist empirical theory, undoubtedly ideological, morality does not entail and need not accept this doctrine and thus is not (for this reason, at any rate) ideological. This does not mean, of course, that no moral theories, codes, principles, etc., are to be rejected as ideological. A great many—perhaps the vast majority of—moral theories will probably still turn out to be ideological based on the criteria developed in the previous section.

On the other hand, it is crucial that Marxists not reject moral theories simply because they have been developed by thinkers who are not Marxists or socialists. Furthermore, one must separate the moral component from the empirical component of moral and social theories in order to be able to judge the merits of each. It is not always the case that both components of a moral and social theory are ideological when that theory as a whole is ideological. Conversely, even if Marxist empirical theory is *not* basically correct, the Marxist concept of ideology—under the analysis I have given it—is not thereby vitiated. Although certain of the ways in which a theory or view can be ideological may be vitiated, and though the penultimate criterion of supporting and defending the social status quo may fail, the ultimate (normative) criterion of militating against the amelioration and/or improvement of the human condition will still remain. Thus, if Marxist empirical theory is wide of the mark, and capitalism is the best way of ameliorating and/or improving the human condition, then *Marxism* itself—as its bourgeois opponents have long contended—will turn out to be ideological and, indeed, a major, world-historical form of ideology (in the negatively critical sense of the term). That my analysis of

[24] Ibid., p. 166.

the Marxist concept of ideology allows for this possibility I take to be a strength rather than a weakness of the theory. Being *self-sealing* or *auto-justificatory* is certainly no theoretical virtue; in fact, it is a cardinal theoretical vice.

Although there is no reason to view morality as a whole as ideology in the negative sense of the term, nor any other reason discovered so far to accept the thesis that Marxism and morality are incompatible, it remains to be seen whether Marxism is committed to a pernicious form of moral relativism and whether it can claim some sort of objectivity for its normative political positions. It is to these questions we now turn.

SEVEN

MARXISM, MORAL RELATIVISM, AND MORAL OBJECTIVITY

The final issue concerning the relation between Marxism and morality I shall consider is whether Marx and Marxists are committed to some form or other of moral or ethical relativism. If so, it would seem that there are no "absolute" or absolutely objective moral principles (or standards) and, consequently, that no moral judgments—including those underlying the Marxist's normative political positions—are well-founded. I hope to show that though Marx and especially Engels sometimes speak as though they accept this thesis, once one distinguishes ethical relativism proper (i.e., *normative* ethical relativism) from *descriptive* ethical relativism, on the one hand, and *metaethical* and *metaevaluative* relativism, on the other, it is not clear that they do. (The concept of *metaevaluative* relativism is introduced in this chapter in order to distinguish between two forms of relativism that are usually both included under the term *metaethical* relativism. Both concepts will be explicated as we go along.)

What is clear, I hope to show, is (1) descriptive ethical relativism is true but uninteresting; (2) normative ethical relativism is an untenable position; and, most importantly, (3) no matter what position Marx and Engels can be construed as taking on the issue of metaethical or metaevaluative relativism, it does not vitiate their substantive moral critique of capitalism (and of exploitative, oppressive, inhumane social institutions in general) nor their substantive moral commendations of socialism and communism.

In the second section of the present chapter I shall take up the related question of the justification of moral judgments and principles, or what is sometimes called the question of "moral objectivity." This will necessarily lead us to a consideration of what is perhaps the most sophisticated recent attempt at an answer to this question, namely, to a consideration of John Rawls' two-pronged approach: (1) the method of reflective equilibrium and (2) the strategy of the original position (a hypothetical choice theory). Certain objections to both methods or strategies will be considered, and an attempt will be made to determine if either method (or both in conjunction) can assure the *objectivity* of our moral judgments and principles, where "objectivity" is interpreted as *unanimous intersubjective agreement or consensus*. Finally, the third section examines the implications of distinguishing the possibility of a theoretical (i.e., hypothetical) consensus from a practical (i.e., actual) consensus on such matters.

Much of the present chapter involves rather detailed discussions of recent and contemporary metaethical theories. I hope the relevance of these discussions to the assessment of Marxist moral and social theory will become apparent as we proceed. In large measure, the present chapter is designed to lay out a theory of moral justification and/or objectivity in general, not a theory of moral justification and/or objectivity for Marxism in particular. However, attention is paid to various positions on these issues taken (or seemingly taken) by Marx, Engels, and other Marxists, and an attempt is made to apply the metaethical theory that is developed to Marxist moral and social theory.

This chapter is also the first part of this work—but not the last—to pay a substantial amount of attention to the theories of John Rawls. Although no attempt is made to defend Rawls' theories at this point, or show exactly how they might fit in with an adequate Marxist moral and social theory, these matters are attended to in chapters 9 and 10 respectively.

Marx, Engels, and Moral Relativism

Is Marxism committed to some form of ethical relativism? If so, the argument goes, Marxists cannot claim that their moral judgments or the normative political positions they underlie and uphold are objective. And if these judgments or principles are not objective, the argument continues, there is no reason for any rational person to consider herself or himself bound by them.

To answer this objection is no simple matter. We shall first have to distinguish the various forms of ethical relativism and then ask: (1) to which forms (if any) is the Marxist committed; (2) which forms (if any) are viable; and, if any are viable, (3) which of these are really destructive of moral objectivity and thus destructive of the Marxist's (and presumably everyone else's) ability to justify his or her moral standards or principles? The answers to these questions will show that though there may be some form of metaethical or metaevaluative relativism that is ultimately irrefutable, this does *not* mean that our considered moral judgments and principles are necessarily irrational, subjective, or arbitrary. Perhaps more importantly for our purposes, the analysis given will show that accepting the Marxist's empirical theories and evaluative framework does not put one in an untenable position vis-à-vis defending one's moral judgments and principles.

The problem of ethical relativism is more obviously a difficulty for Marxism than for most other schools of social and political thought because Marxism seems committed to a strong deterministic relation between the moral views of a society and its socioeconomic structures. This relation between the socioeconomic base and social consciousness or ideology, in general, is alluded to in the "Communist Manifesto" when Marx asks, "Does it require deep intuition to comprehend that man's ideas, views, and conceptions, in a word, man's consciousness, changes with every change in the conditions of his material existence, in his social relations and in his social life?"[1]

Nevertheless, we should not make too much of this as a difference between Marxist and non-Marxist social theory. After all, virtually all schools of social theory recognize some sort of causal relation between social and economic structures, on the one hand, and ideologies or social consciousness, on the other.[2] Furthermore—as mentioned in previous chapters—there are in Marx's writings a number of distinguishable models of the relation between the socioeconomic base and political and ideological superstructure of societies. Sometimes it seems as though he accords morality an independent and even a causal role, as in the preface to the first German edition of *Capital*, where he claims that socialist

[1] Marx and Engels, "Manifesto of the Communist Party," p. 351.
[2] Marx was one of the key sources of these commonly accepted views. As Svetozar Stojanović notes: "Marx correctly stressed the influence of the economic, especially of the class-economic, position of man upon his morality. One's moral views often really are ideological rationalizations of his economic class interests. If today we try to penetrate and formally identify different contents expressing and rationalizing different social interests, it is at least partially due to the impact of Marx. His idea of the ruling morality as the ruling class morality may also be fruitful. All these ideas are, in my opinion, important for ethics and particularly for the sociology of morals. It may be that they are commonplace now. If they are, it is to Marx's credit." ["Marx's Theory of Ethics," p. 168].

270

revolutionaries will be driven by both self-interest and "higher motives." But it is the more commonly accepted view that Marx's theory of ideology applies to morality as well as other areas of human culture and cognition, and that this raises suspicions concerning its validity or objectivity. This view is put forward, among other places, in *Anti-Dühring*, where Engels states:

> If we have not made much progress with truth and error, we can make even less with good and bad. This antithesis belongs exclusively to the domain belonging to the history of mankind, and it is precisely in this field that final and ultimate truths are most sparsely sown. The conceptions of good and bad have varied so much from nation to nation and from age to age that they have often been in direct contradiction to each other. But all the same, someone may object, good is not bad and bad is not good; if good is confused with bad there is an end to all morality, and everyone can do and leave undone whatever he cares.[3]

In the next paragraph, he states that

> when we see that the three classes of modern society, the feudal aristocracy, the bourgeoisie and the proletariat, each have their special morality, we can only draw the conclusion, that men consciously or unconsciously, derive their moral ideas in the last resort from the practical relations on which their class position is based—from the economic relations in which they carry on production and exchange.[4]

Speaking for those who accept historical materialism, Engels concludes:

> We therefore reject every attempt to impose on us any moral dogma whatsoever as an eternal, ultimate, and forever immutable moral law on the pretext that the moral world too has its permanent principles which transcend history and the differences between nations. We maintain on the contrary that all former moral theories are the product, in the last analysis, of the economic stage which society had reached at that par-

---

[3] Engels, *Anti-Dühring*, p. 303.
[4] Ibid., p. 104.

ticular epoch. And as society has hitherto moved in class antagonisms, morality was always a class morality.[5]

But to what sort of ethical relativism—if any—does this commit Engels? Here we must distinguish four sorts of relativism: descriptive, normative, metaethical, and metaevaluative.

Descriptive ethical relativism is the doctrine that what people believe to be right or wrong differs from individual to individual, society to society, or culture to culture.

Normative ethical relativism is the doctrine that what *is* right or wrong differs from individual to individual, society to society, or culture to culture (*because* what people believe to be right or wrong determines what is right or wrong for them).

Metaethical relativism is the doctrine that there is no sure way to prove (to everyone's satisfaction) what is *morally* right or wrong. That is, even if everyone were perfectly rational, conceptually clear, fully informed of the facts, and *accepted the moral point of view*, this would not ensure that they would agree on one unique set of *moral* principles as correct—let alone agree on the relative weight of the moral principles or how to apply them in each concrete case.

Metaevaluative relativism is the doctrine that there is no sure way to prove (to everyone's satisfaction) what is right or wrong. That is, even if everyone were perfectly rational, conceptually clear, and fully informed of the facts, this would not ensure that they would agree on one unique set of *normative* principles as correct—let alone agree on the relative weight of the normative principles or how to apply them in each concrete case.

Although the differences between the mores (i.e., accepted moral norms) of different individuals, societies, or cultures are sometimes exaggerated, since different "surface" actions may express the same underlying moral norm (or rule), *descriptive* ethical relativism seems undoubtedly true. But admitting that different individuals, etc., have different views of right and wrong does *not entail* that what *is* right and wrong actually differs any more than the fact that different individuals have different views on the issue of whether or not the earth is flat *entails* that what *is* true about the shape of the earth actually differs. It makes perfect sense to say that although some individual, culture, or society *believes* that something is morally right or wrong, it is *not, in fact*, morally right or wrong (as the case may be).

Thus, even *if true*, the thesis of *descriptive* ethical relativism is

[5] Ibid., pp. 104–105.

trivial and, for purposes of moral philosophy or thinking, simply irrelevant. (None of this, however, entails an intolerant attitude toward the moral practices or rules of other individuals, cultures, or societies. We may well want to adopt a principle of moral tolerance that rules out interference with other individuals, societies, or cultures except, say, in cases of violations of basic rights of others.)

On the other hand, both normative ethical relativism and the two "meta" relativisms are significant and relevant, but of these only the first is especially pernicious. Even if metaethical or meta-evaluative relativism must ultimately be accepted, it may be that only a very few people who meet the requisite conditions would fail to agree on the correct set of moral or normative principles. Furthermore, regardless of the degree of consensus that could be expected in these hypothetical-choice situations, the acceptance of the doctrines of metaethical and/or metaevaluative relativism in no way prevents us from claiming that a certain moral principle (e.g., "slaughtering defenseless infants is *prima facie* wrong") is right and that any principle or action to the contrary is simply wrong.

The acceptance of *normative ethical* relativism, however, is pernicious because it would prevent us from sensibly claiming that certain moral principles are correct and actions that violate them are wrong. According to this doctrine, if some individual, culture, or society believes that slaughtering defenseless infants merely for fun is morally permissible, then it *is* morally permissible (for them).

But are Marx, Engels, or any other Marxist committed to *normative* ethical relativism? This doctrine, as said above, is the thesis that what *really is* right and wrong can differ between persons. Versions of the doctrine differ in terms of whether reference is made only to the criteria of moral goodness or rightness held by persons per se, or to the criteria of moral goodness or rightness accepted by the cultures or societies in which they live. In the first case, one and the same action (for example) can be right for one person and wrong for another even within the same culture or society, depending on the criteria of moral rightness or principles of moral relevance they happen to accept. In the second case, one and the same action can be right and wrong only with reference to persons belonging to different cultures or societies whose criteria of moral rightness or principles of moral relevance differ. Among contemporary Anglo-American philosophers, Gilbert Harman can be singled out as a proponent of the former position and members

273

of the so-called Swanzei School of ethical theory (D. Z. Phillips, H. O. Mounce, R. W. Beardsmore et al.) as proponents of the latter.[6]

Milton Fisk—a contemporary Marxian ethical theorist within the Anglo-American tradition—attempts to adapt the second perspective to Marxist social theory by substituting *classes* for cultures or societies. "Validity in general is relative to classes," writes Fisk. "One should, then, choose to realize the principle [of justice and morality] only if it is valid relative to one's class."[7] Thus what is morally right and wrong, good or bad is determined by the criteria accepted by the class to which one belongs—or at least by the criteria that are in accord with the objective interests of one's class such that they would be accepted by individuals of that class were they fully aware of the facts and not deluded by foreign class ideologies. There are certain difficulties with this thesis. First, as pointed out in chapter 5, one's own *personal* interests may not be in accord with one's *class* interests. Furthermore, to speak of a class's interests (even its "objective" interests) is already to make a moral or at least evaluative judgment. But the main difficulty is simply that Fisk endorses a form of ethical relativism that seems to prevent one from condemning the evil actions of persons so long as they are done in accordance with their own class interests. But if we cannot condemn a group of capitalists or their allies in the power elite for, say, ordering the torture or massacre of workers and peasants or the brutal suppression of their organizations, something seems amiss.

But the fatal flaw that all of these versions of normative ethical relativism have in common is the position that whether or not a moral principle is correct depends on one's point of view. The normative ethical relativist claims that a particular moral principle can be correct for some and not correct for others, and no one can meaningfully assert that one's principle is correct and one's opponent's principle is wrong. They are *both correct* in this view! Consequently, one and the same moral principle—for example, that causing innocent persons pain for no good reason is morally wrong or that property rights are indefeasible before any and all

---

[6] See Gilbert Harman, "Moral Relativism Defended," *The Philosophical Review*, vol. 84 (Jan. 1975), and *The Nature of Morality*, Oxford University Press, N.Y., 1977; R. W. Beardsmore, *Moral Reasoning*, Schocken Books, N.Y., 1969; and D. Z. Phillips and H. O. Mounce, *Moral Practices*, Schocken Books, N.Y., 1970.

[7] Fisk, *Ethics and Society*, p. 235. Even though I disagree with Fisk's position on this *metaethical* issue, I find myself in agreement with most of the normative positions he takes.

other moral considerations—can be both true and false, correct and incorrect. When portrayed in this fashion, this position is easily reduced to absurdity.

Consider, for example, the following argument:

1. If someone believes it is morally permissible for him to torture another person, then *it is* morally permissible for him.

2. If someone is doing something that is morally permissible for him to do, then we have a moral obligation not to interfere.

3. Therefore, so long as the torturer believes he is morally right, we have an obligation not to interfere with his actions.

The first premise is simply an application of the normative ethical relativist's position. The second premise is a necessary truth flowing from the definition of "morally permissible." The conclusion follows deductively from the premises but, presumably, none of us will find it acceptable since it claims that we cannot interfere with the torturer and save the victim from his heinous acts even if we could do so at no risk to ourselves! But if the conclusion is unacceptable (i.e., false), then—since the argument is valid—one or more of the premises must be false. Since we have already seen that the second premise is a necessary (or definitional) truth, we *must* conclude that the first premise is false. And since the first premise is merely an application of normative ethical relativism, it follows that normative ethical relativism is false. Thus this position has been reduced to absurdity.

Nevertheless, this position has been held by a great many theorists who were determined not to accept the view that portrays morality as eternal, transcendental, or in some sense beyond both nature and humanity. Among Classical Marxists, for example, Karl Kautsky seems to endorse this position when he states:

> As all morality is relative, that which is called immorality is simply a deviating kind of morality. . . . so far as moral standards are concerned, there is just as little an absolute morality as an absolute immorality. . . . It is thus nonsense to declare particular moral principles of any people or class which are recognized as such, to be immoral simply because they contradict our moral code.[8]

[8] Kautsky, *Ethics and the Materialist Conception of History*, pp. 192–193.

Although—as we shall see shortly—it does not seem that Marx or Engels subscribed to the doctrine of *normative* ethical relativism, if they did, we should have to say that they, like Kautsky, were mistaken: mistaken *not* because there exists a transcendent realm of eternal values that people intuit or in some way have access to, but because it is simply part of the logic of moral discourse that we cannot meaningfully claim that a moral judgment or principle is both correct and incorrect. This is simply a consequence of taking moral judgments to have the formal property that R. M. Hare and others call "universalizability."[9] As Bernard Mayo explicates this principle in *Ethics and the Moral Life*:

> A moral judgment must be universalisable, firstly, in the sense that it applies not to a particular action, but to a class of actions; this is involved in the meaning of "principle" or rule. Secondly, it must be universalisable in the sense that it applies not only to me but to you; not only to you but to me; not only to us but everybody; this is involved in speaking of *moral* principles as opposed to maxims or private policies. And thirdly, a moral judgment must be "universalisable" in the sense that others besides the speaker are assumed to share it. To illustrate: when I say "It was wrong of you to torment that animal," I must be prepared to extend my judgment to all cases of tormenting animals (universalisability 1); I must be prepared to apply the principle, not only to give a verdict on your action, but also upon my own, and to come to decisions in the light of it (universalisability 2); and I must expect, or at least invite, assent to the principle on your part, and on the part of an indefinite community of moral beings like ourselves.[10]

Thus, if we maintain that a certain sort of action is morally impermissible (or permissible but not obligatory, or obligatory) for someone, then we must maintain that that sort of action is morally impermissible (or whatever) for *anyone* in similar circumstances. But here a brief explanatory note concerning his "universalisability 3" is necessary. Although his "universalisability 3" may seem to add social acceptance as a defining characteristic of moral principles, a closer reading of this passage reveals that such is not the case: he is *not* claiming, as some do, that *social acceptance* is a defin-

[9] See chapter 7 ("Description and Evaluation") of *The Language of Morals*, chapter 2 ("Descriptive Meaning") of *Freedom and Reason*, and chapter 5 ("Descriptivism") in *Essays on the Moral Concepts*.
[10] Mayo, *Ethics and the Moral Life*, pp. 91–92.

ing characteristic of moral principles per se but only that when one makes a moral judgment or asserts a moral principle, one must "expect *or at least invite*" assent to the judgment or principle in question "on the part of an indefinite community of moral beings like ourselves," which is altogether different. According to Mayo's position, it still makes sense to speak of an idiosyncratic moral principle (i.e., one held by only one member of a community) as being, nevertheless, a moral principle and possibly even a *correct* moral principle. According to the position that takes social acceptance to be a defining characteristic of moral judgments or principles, it does not make sense. (This matter is taken up in more detail in the following section of the present chapter.)

The point to be noted here is that, according to the thesis of universalizability, when one makes an evaluative judgment, it must apply to all cases, both actual and possible, that are similar in the relevant respects, that is, to *all relevantly similar agents in relevantly similar circumstances*. Thus, if I judge a case of infanticide in a noncrisis situation to be morally wrong, then by the very logic of moral discourse I am required to judge all relevantly similar cases of infanticide as morally wrong. If I subscribe to the moral principle that economic exploitation of human beings (i.e., the economic domination of one class by another) is bad, then the principle applies, for me, in all relevantly similar situations, even if the people of that place or time do not see such situations as morally evil. And if a person asserts a contradictory principle, e.g., that it is morally good or at least morally permissible to exploit people economically, I am forced, by the logic of moral discourse—by the fact that moral statements are universalizable—to deny that his prin ciple is correct or true. The thesis of universalizability asserts that if I make a judgment I am *not* willing to universalize in the above sense, then, ipso facto, it is *not* a moral judgment: it is perhaps a report of my subjective preferences or the preferences of some other person or group of people, or the expression of a private maxim, but these things are quite different from moral judgments.

The point is that if the thesis of universalizability is true, if this is a correct characterization of the logical structure of moral discourse, then *normative* ethical relativism is ruled out. We simply cannot accept the statement that two contradictory moral judgments or principles are both true or correct. If we do, we are no longer playing the moral language game—we have left the realm of moral discourse. This conclusion, it should be noted, holds true for both cognitivists and noncognitivists, for both descriptivists and prescriptivists, so long as they accept universalizability as a formal property of moral judgments.[11]

To forestall a confusion that is bound to arise at this point, however, we should note that, contrary to what Hare claims, there is a distinction between the logical thesis of universalizability as just described and the thesis that in making a moral judgment one must take everyone's interests equally into consideration. While most of us will accept this latter thesis as a constraint on what we take to be *considered* or *well-founded* moral judgments, there is no

[11] It should perhaps be noted that such quasi-Hegelian/communitarian moral and social philosophers as Alasdair MacIntyre and Charles Taylor endorse a closely related form of normative ethical relativism when they assert that the validity of moral principles or values is dependent upon their agreement with the accepted principles or values of the community or, in any case, that they are dependent upon their agreement with the "objective morality" (Hegel's *Sittlichkeit*) embodied in the community in question. (See MacIntyre, *After Virtue* and Charles Taylor, *Hegel and Modern Society* and "Hegel: History and Politics.") This kind of view seems susceptible to the objections I have raised in this chapter against the more straightforward versions of normative ethical relativism proposed by Harman and the Swanzei School.

Although it is more difficult to saddle Michael Sandel (another contemporary communitarian moral and social philosopher) with this sort of normative ethical relativism, he seems to flirt with it when he claims that commitments that are (partially) constitutive of one's identity give rise to valid moral obligations. (See Sandel, *Liberalism and the Limits of Justice*, especially the last section of the book, "Character, Self-knowledge, and Friendship.") If one further accepts the thesis that one is "embedded in"—and, thus, derives one's identity from—one's community, it would seem but a short step to the view that the moral values or principles that are valid are those that are objectively found in the community; or, again, that *Sittlichkeit* determines the validity of *Moralitat* (i.e., personally held moral values or principles). But if different communities have different objective norms embodied in them—as they do according to Hegel, for example—then individuals in these different communities can have contradictory norms or principles, each of which is equally and absolutely valid (for each person in his or her respective community). But this is merely a restatement of normative ethical relativism. (This is not to say, of course, that differing social conditions and differing psychologies are utterly irrelevant to moral justification. What should be clear, however, is that we cannot maintain that whatever an individual happens to believe to be morally right or wrong is automatically—for that reason—morally right or wrong, even if everyone in his community or society agrees with that person or even if it is part of the "objective norms" of that community or society, whatever this is supposed to mean.)

Interestingly, some Marxists hold similar, quasi-Hegelian views on this matter. Allen Wood, for example, also claims that in order to be valid *Moralitat* must be in agreement with *Sittlichkeit*. But he gives this position a Marxist twist when he asserts that the *Sittlichkeit* of a society is determined by the objective, material needs of the socioeconomic system in question. Thus, he concludes that the moral values or principles one holds are only valid if they conform to the needs of the present socioeconomic system. So, for example, if economic exploitation is an objective need of capitalism, then it is not possible to claim that it is morally wrong! (I critique—and, I believe, refute—Wood's views on this issue in the last section of chapter 8.)

278

reason, it would seem, to conclude that taking every person's interests equally into consideration is a *defining* characteristic of moral judgments per se. After all, there are many judgments we would normally refer to as moral judgments that do not meet this condition. Here I have in mind the judgments made by racists (or bigots in general) that obviously exclude such an equal consideration of interests. The racist who claims that Blacks or other minorities do not deserve the same sort of treatment as whites, the Nazi who claims that Jews ought to be exterminated, and the religious fanatic who shouts "Death to infidels" or "Heretics to the stake" would all seem to be making moral judgments, albeit moral judgments that very few of us would consider either well considered or correct. We may appeal to role-reversal arguments in an effort to refute such judgments, but, nevertheless, they count as moral judgments.

Now we may want to endorse the principle that one ought to give equal consideration to everyone's interests when making moral judgments, but if we do, we are making a *substantive* moral judgment rather than merely elucidating the defining characteristics of morality or moral principles or—at the very least—we are designating what we take to be a *considered* or *well-founded* moral judgment rather than a moral judgment simpliciter. But even if the logical thesis of universalizability makes it impossible to admit that what one defines as exactly similar actions can be both right and wrong or what we define as exactly similar agents or intentions both good and bad, thus vitiating *normative ethical relativism*, does not the real problem yet remain? Do not different individuals, societies, or cultures accept different sets of fundamental moral principles or even different views on what constitutes a basic good-making or right-making characteristic in moral contexts? And is there any reason to believe that all rational persons, or even all rational persons who accept the moral point of view, will agree on what is the correct set of moral principles or moral judgments? Is there any irrefutable method by which to arrive at objectively correct moral principles? If not, then even if we have won the battle against normative ethical relativism, we may have lost the war so far as obtaining moral objectivity is concerned.

As we proceed, we will want to keep in mind the distinction I have made between metaevaluative and metaethical relativism. *Metaevaluative* relativism is the position that it is not necessarily the case that all rational persons who are conceptually clear and fully informed of the facts will agree on which moral (or, more broadly, normative) principles and judgments are correct. Notice that this formulation does *not* specify that the persons in question accept the moral point of view. *Metaethical* relativism, on the other hand, specifies that the persons in question accept the moral point of view. Thus metaethical relativism is the position that it is not necessarily the case that all rational persons who are conceptually clear and fully informed of the facts and who accept the moral points of view will agree on which moral (or normative) principles and judgments are correct.

Before examining the doctrines of metaevaluative and metaethical relativism in more detail, however, let us revert to Engels' treatment of morality in *Anti-Dühring* in order to assess whether or not he seems committed there to some form or other of ethical relativism. Although it is clear that some Marxists—like Kautsky— see the acceptance of historical materialism as committing them to normative ethical relativism, and it seems, at first glance, that Engels accepts the same conclusion since he states that one ought to reject all attempts to impose "any moral dogma as an eternal, ultimate, and forever immutable law," such is not the case. Although Engels, Marx, and most other Marxists are not at all clear about the issues involved, I know of no evidence that they, like Kautsky, see themselves bound to admit equal validity or correctness to any and all moral judgments. They certainly thought— whether or not they would have wanted to defend this position— that their moral judgments were correct and, for example, that those of their bourgeois opponents who did not view exploitation as a moral evil were wrong. Furthermore, in portions of the paragraphs in *Anti-Dühring* not yet quoted, we find Engels claiming:

> That . . . there has on the whole been progress in morality, as in all other branches of human knowledge, cannot be doubted. But we have not yet passed beyond class morality. A really human morality which transcends class antagonisms and their legacies in thought becomes possible only at a stage of society which has not only overcome class contradictions but has even forgotten them in practical life.[12]

Here Engels not only seems to reject *normative* ethical relativism but seems to offer a method or at least a criterion by which to judge between conflicting sets of moral principles and thus circumvent *metaethical* and *metaevaluative* relativism. He makes this

[12] Engels, *Anti-Dühring*, p. 105.

criterion explicit three paragraphs earlier in the text when, discussing the conflicting moralities of the feudal aristocracy, bourgeoisie, and proletariat, he asks: "Which is then, the true one?" His answer is: "Not one of them in the sense of having absolute validity; but certainly that morality which contains the maximum of durable elements is the one which, in the present, represents the future: that is, the proletarian."[13]

But is this criterion for deciding between differing sets of fundamental moral principles adequate? Is it correct to assume, as Engels seems to assume here, that the moral principles that will evolve to govern human relations in the future are, ipso facto, better than those that have governed human relations in the past? The answer to this is no. Here Engels seems to be confusing the evolution of a correct set of moral principles with the evolution of a society within which the correct set of moral principles can be fully implemented or realized. Furthermore, if he is really claiming that whatever moral principles evolve are, ipso facto, good or correct or justified, he is committing the error of moral historicism or, more precisely, moral futurism, which, as we have seen in chapter 5, is rather easily debunked.

But if this suggestion will not still the objection of metaevaluative or metaethical relativism, and thus the claim that all moral principles have an equal *lack* of objectivity or validity, is there a suggestion that will work? The answer, which cuts across the differences between Marxists and non-Marxists, is "no," I shall argue, in the case of *metaevaluative* relativism and a qualified "no" in the case of *metaethical* relativism.

Let us first consider *metaevaluative* relativism. The question is, essentially, will all rational beings, merely by the fact that they are rational, agree on the correct set of moral (or normative) principles and judgments? If we accept a "thin," means-ends characterization of rationality—which I feel we must if we are to avoid begging substantive questions—then metaevaluative relativism is undoubtedly correct. To see that this is so, we need only consider actual or potential creatures who are rational in this respect but do not accept any set of moral principles or judgments we would even be tempted to see as correct.

First, consider a sociopath who lacks all common moral sentiments or "natural sympathies" but is instrumentally rational, or, better yet, the giant crablike creatures as imagined by H.L.A. Hart.

[13] Ibid., p. 105.

These creatures are perfectly rational but totally self-sufficient and impervious to harm inflicted by members of their own species. Thus they are totally lacking in the necessary sort of moral affections required for a being to be capable of considering things from a moral point of view. If such creatures consciously choose what they perceive to be the most efficient means to desired ends, there would seem no reason whatever to deny that they are rational beings even if they are incapable of any sort of empathy and thus incapable of considering things from a moral point of view. Fortunately for us, of course, most people do have at least a modicum of moral sentiments.

Consider next the ethical egoist. Although there have been perennial attempts to show the ethical egoist to be irrational, they all, I believe, have failed. The argument normally employed is that it is in the ethical egoist's enlightened self-interest to be moral. But one can always think of situations in which this will not be the case. Furthermore, it seems that the most that can be shown is that it is in the self-interest of the ethical egoist to *appear* to be moral but not to abide by the moral rules whenever it is to his or her advantage not to do so. (An analogous difficulty plagues Hobbes' argument that self-interested individuals ought to contract out of the state of nature into civil society because it is in their self-interest to do so. Why would the rational ethical egoist not promise to obey the sovereign—or at least utter words or sign a document to that effect—but intend to break that promise if and when it is to his or her advantage to do so?) The point is that in the general, action-guiding sense of the word "ought"—in the sense in which accepting the judgment that one *ought* to do something entails, all things being equal, that one *will* do it—there is no certainty that all rational agents (even all conceptually clear and fully informed rational agents) will agree on what one *ought* to do or even on what are relevant sorts of considerations in making such decisions. After all, one can always ask, "Why should I be moral?"—a question to which, as such disparate moral theorists as John Hospers and Kai Nielsen have argued, there is no *adequate, noncircular* answer. As Phillipa Foot puts it, although we can convict amoralists or ethical egoists of *villainy*, we cannot necessarily convict them of *irrationality*.[14]

To relate this position to the problematic of the Kantian tradi-

[14] See Hospers, "Why be Moral?" and Nielsen, "Why Should I be Moral?" both reprinted in *Readings in Ethical Theory* (Wilfrid Sellars and John Hospers, eds.). See also Phillipa Foot, "Morality as a System of Hypothetical Imperatives."

tion, we can say that that part of the categorical imperative suggesting that moral laws or principles are incumbent upon all rational beings *merely by virtue of their rationality* must be given up, even though its metaethical component (i.e., the thesis of universalizability) and its normative component (i.e., the claim that we ought always to treat individuals as ends and never as means only) may well be required by an adequate moral theory.

But what of *metaethical* relativism? Once we specify that the individuals in question accept the moral point of view, can this sort of relativism be defeated? This depends on what we mean by "accepting the moral point of view." If we mean only that one accepts the proposition that the concept of morality has a certain material content such that we can rule out as *moral* principles such statements as "always act so as to create the sensation of red on green" or "never turn N.N.E. after facing S.S.W.," then metaethical relativism probably cannot be defeated. Some contemporary moral philosophers disagree with this, however, and claim that the material content of the concept of morality is sufficient to generate moral standards. G. J. Warnock, for example, writes that

> certain standards—that is, the relevance at least of a particular range of considerations—though they do not have to be accepted at all, must be accepted if the claim to be evaluating *morally* is to be seriously made.[15]

The idea is that since, for example, the causing of pain is always a relevant consideration for moral reasoning, such standards as "it is always *prima facie* wrong to cause pain" must be (analytically) true. The problem with this, however, is that it is logically possible for a person to recognize that pain is prototypically a human harm, and thus that it is always a relevant consideration in moral reasoning, but still reject the above-mentioned standard. It is logically possible, in other words, for a person to be both clear about the concept of morality and to be *evil*. The reason for this is that although the material content of the concept of morality distinguishes *nonmoral* from *moral* propositions, it does not distinguish *immoral* from *moral* (i.e., morally correct) propositions. Thus the claim that we ought to cause other people as much pain as possible is a moral as opposed to a *nonmoral* proposition, but, according to most of us, it is not a moral proposition as opposed to an *immoral* one. Therefore, the mere acceptance of this conceptual constraint

---

[15] Warnock, *Contemporary Moral Philosophy*, p. 68.

does not ensure intersubjective agreement on morality on the part of all rational persons. Some persons may simply be evil.

On the other hand, if by "accepting the moral point of view" we mean, in part, accepting common conceptions of human harm and human good such that certain facts like "action A causes people unnecessary pain" always *prima facie* count against undertaking action A, then metaethical relativism can be defeated. But this rather obviously begs the substantive question. Furthermore, even those who accept the moral point of view in this sense cannot be expected to agree on the *relative weight* of different sorts of morally relevant considerations. (Later in this chapter we shall consider, as an example of this, the right-libertarian's extremely strong commitment to property rights.)

That neither metaevaluative nor metaethical relativism can be soundly defeated is not necessarily a nihilistic or irrationalist point of view. It may not even mean that moral objectivity (in some sense) cannot be had. Furthermore, it certainly is not in conflict with the general Marxist view that members of different classes—even assuming they are perfectly rational—will, in all probability, accept different moral principles due to their different class positions and perspectives. The reason that a better society can and will evolve, according to Marx's empirical, social-scientific theory, is *not* because all rational persons can and will reach agreement on a common moral code or normative political perspective, but because enough members of the working class, other exploited groups, and the allies they attract from other classes will be motivated by a combination of both prudential and moral considerations to strive in an organized way for such a society, namely, socialism. To think that social change is mainly a function of a change of moral attitudes or beliefs is, according to Marx and other Marxists, a grave mistake. It is, in fact, precisely the grounds on which Marx and Engels labeled Owen, Fourier, and Saint-Simon "*utopian* socialists."

But—assuming Marxist empirical theory to be basically correct—are there not ways in which so-called bourgeois moral theorists, or supporters of capitalism in general, are prejudiced or deluded and the Marxist or proponents of socialism are not? Is there not some sense in which the Marxist's moral judgments or principles are more objective than those of his bourgeois opponents? These considerations lead to an examination of methods of moral-theory construction and, particularly, to an examination of what Rawls refers to as the method of reflective equilibrium. There is, however, one more matter we need to clear up before turning to the method of reflective equilibrium, namely, the nature or definition of *moral objectivity*. For while we have concluded that morality in general and Marxist moral views in particular are not susceptible to the criticism that they entail normative ethical relativism, we have not yet examined the concept of moral objectivity closely enough to decide precisely under what conditions we may call our moral judgments or principles "objective."

Marxism, Reflective Equilibrium, and the Original Position

Marx, Engels, and most other pre-twentieth-century thinkers seemed to picture the "objectivity" of moral judgments and principles as consisting in some sort of correspondence between these judgments and principles and some set of transcendent or immanent values or principles just as the *truth* of a statement was (and still is) often thought to be a matter of its correspondence to some set of facts. Recent and contemporary philosophers, however, have increasingly come to reject this model of moral objectivity in favor of a theory or model of moral objectivity based on *intersubjective agreement*.[16] In short, in order to avoid the metaphysical baggage of the old model and its other unattractive features, contemporary value theorists have tended to reduce *objectivity* to *intersubjective validity*. Marx and Engels, needless to say, never

[16] This move from "objectivity" defined as *correspondence to objective reality* to "objectivity" defined as *intersubjective agreement* has not been confined to moral or evaluative contexts nor to Anglo-American philosophy. The great Pragmatist philosopher C. S. Peirce held this view, and such contemporary philosophers as Wilfrid Sellars, Richard Rorty, and Hilary Putnam have taken the truth (of factual, empirical, or descriptive-explanatory propositions) to be primarily a matter of intersubjective agreement or an ideal consensus rather than correspondence to an "objective" (nonlinguistic) set of facts or reality. See Wilfrid Sellars, *Science, Perception, and Reality*, Humanities Press, N.Y., 1963; Richard Rorty, *Philosophy and the Mirror of Nature*, Princeton University Press, Princeton, N.J., 1979; and Hilary Putnam, *Reason, Truth and History*, Cambridge University Press, N.Y., 1981. See also Thomas Nagel: "The Limits of Objectivity," *Tanner Lectures on Human Values*, vol. 1 (S. McMurrin, ed.), Cambridge University Press, N.Y. 1980, and *A View from Nowhere*, Oxford University Press, N.Y., 1986.

Moreover, among contemporary Continental philosophers, Jürgen Habermas and Karl-Otto Apel have expressed similar views. Habermas appeals to an ideal consensus in explicating the notions of truth (and rationality) as a matter of the resolution reached during the course of a free dialogue. The work of Habermas is especially relevant for our present concern since his primary project is that of constructing a critical social theory capable of rationally describing and judging social institutions and arrangements. See Habermas, *Theory and Practice*, especially, "Introduction: Some Difficulties in the Attempt to Link Theory and Praxis."

thought of things this way. But if they had, they might have been agreeable to this strategy since the positing of otherworldly, transcendent "eternal verities" or immanent self-realizing moral principles is thereby avoided.

Although contemporary value theorists are still at odds over whether moral claims are objective in this sense, today there is broad agreement that this is the correct account of moral objectivity. Some have suggested that the intersubjective agreement needed is an *actual* intersubjective agreement on moral principles of the society or culture in which one lives and have drawn the unpalatable conclusion that whatever moral principles are accepted by one's society or culture are, ipso facto, correct—at least for individuals living in those societies or cultures. This position is taken by those who are proponents of what Frankena calls a *social morality*, a conception of morality that sees such an agreement as not only necessary for the justification of moral principles but also definitive of moral judgments and principles per se. Others hold that while this sort of actual intersubjective agreement is not a definitive characteristic of a moral judgment or principle, it is a necessary condition for the *justification* of any moral judgment or principle; that is to say, if such a consensus does not exist, then the judgment or principle in question is, ipso facto, not justified.

One of the major difficulties of either version of this view is that it makes moral innovation or the having of an idiosyncratic moral code—or at least a *justified* idiosyncratic moral code—impossible. But this just doesn't seem to make sense. There is no reason, for example, to think that a Kantian moral code uniquely held by a member of a utilitarian-oriented society is *not* a moral code or that—for these reasons, at any rate—it is not a *justified* moral code.

A more promising approach is to make the intersubjective consensus needed for the justification or objectivity of moral principles a purely hypothetical one. Frankena, for example, takes this position. He claims that "a basic moral judgment, principle, or code is justified or 'true' if it is or will be agreed to by everyone who takes the moral point of view and is clearheaded and logical and knows all that is relevant about himself, mankind, and the universe."[17] The only notion that may need clarification here is that of the "moral point of view." Although Frankena offers his own, somewhat more complex, characterization of the "moral point of view," for our purposes we can accept Kurt Baier's char-

[17] Frankena, *Ethics*, p. 112.

acterization. As Frankena summarizes it: "Baier . . . holds that one is taking the moral point of view if one is not being egoistic, one is doing things on principle, one is willing to universalise one's principles, and in doing so one considers the good of everyone alike."[18] (Notice that though Baier does not conflate the logical thesis of universalizability with giving equal consideration to everyone's interests, as does Hare, both factors—according to Baier and Frankena—enter into what it is to take the moral point of view and thus enter into the criteria a moral judgment must meet to be a *considered* moral judgment. Notice also that at this point we are giving a substantive content to the moral point of view and thus begging the substantive question against the immoralist. Our conclusions, in other words, will hold only for those who accept the moral point of view in this sense.)

But even if this is the proper view of moral "objectivity" and avoids all of the metaphysical baggage that Marx, Engels, and others so rightly object to, is there any reason to believe that our moral principles meet this condition? Is there any good reason to believe that any of our moral principles would be bound to garner this sort of unanimous intersubjective agreement under these hypothetical conditions? More specifically, is there any reason to believe—even assuming Marxist empirical theory to be basically correct—that the Marxist's moral and normative political judgments are any more objective or correct than those of, say, right-libertarian supporters of capitalism? These considerations necessarily lead to an examination of moral-theory construction and justification and, especially, to an examination of what is perhaps the most sophisticated and well-worked out example of such a theory: John Rawls' two-pronged approach (as presented in *A Theory of Justice*), which utilizes both the method of reflective equilibrium and a hypothetical choice method known as the strategy of the original position. Although these methods can be applied independently, they are intimately related in Rawls' theory. In *A Theory of Justice*, Rawls first explicates the strategy of the original position and then uses the method of reflective equilibrium to ascertain whether or not the constraints placed on the hypothetical choice situation are reasonable from a moral point of view.

Following the Classical Contract Theorists—Locke, Rousseau, and Kant—Rawls holds that

[18] Ibid., p. 113.

287

the principles of justice for the basic structure of society are the object of the original agreement. They are the principles that free and rational persons concerned to further their own interests would accept in an initial position of equality as defining the fundamental terms of their association. These principles are to regulate all further agreements; they specify the kinds of social cooperation that can be entered into and the forms of government that can be established. This way of regarding the principles of justice I shall call justice as fairness.[19]

In order to ensure "objectivity," however, Rawls stipulates several conditions that are to characterize the parties in the original position. Not only are the parties free, rational, mutually disinterested, and in an initial position of equality (as are individuals in Hobbes' and Locke's "state of nature"), but they are *nonenvious* as well. Finally, they are behind a "veil of ignorance," meaning that they have no knowledge of their own situation in the real world but only of general facts of society, history, and human nature. This last constraint on the decision-making procedure in the original position "ensures that no one is advantaged or disadvantaged in the choice of principles by the outcome of natural chance or the contingency of social circumstances. Since all are similarly situated and no one is able to design principles to favor his particular condition, the principles of justice are the result of a fair agreement or bargain."[20]

To this Rawls adds:

Both autonomy and *objectivity* are characterized in a consistent way by reference to the original position. The idea of the initial situation is central to the whole theory and other basic notions are defined in terms of it. Thus, acting autonomously is acting from principles that we would consent to as free and equal rational beings. . . . Also, these principles are *objective*. They are the principles that we would want everyone (including ourselves) to follow were we to take up together the appropriate general point of view. The original position defines this perspective, and its conditions also embody those of *objectivity*: its stipulations express the restrictions on arguments that force us to consider the choice of principles unencumbered by the singularities of the circumstances in which we find ourselves[21] [emphasis added].

[19] Rawls, *A Theory of Justice*, p. 11.
[20] Ibid., p. 12.
[21] Ibid., p. 16.

But what does Rawls mean by "objective" and "objectivity" in this context? In claiming that the principles reached in the original position are objective because they are "the principles that we would want everyone (including ourselves) to follow were we to take up together the appropriate general point of view," he would seem to be attributing to moral principles nothing more than the property of *being universalizable*. In a passage quoted previously, Mayo claimed that part of the notion of the universalizability of moral principles is that "I must expect, or at least invite, assent to the principle on your part and on the part of an indefinite community of moral beings like ourselves."[22] To simply meet this condition would not seem enough to be characterized as an "objective" principle.

If Rawls means by "objectivity" only that we must "consider the choice of principles unencumbered by the singularities of the circumstances in which we find ourselves," he would seem to be demanding nothing more than *impartiality*—something that was demanded by Ideal Observer theorists such as Roderick Firth and by many other moral theorists in the history of philosophy. But even if impartiality is somehow a requirement of objectivity, it surely is not—in and of itself—a sufficient condition for it. I will here leave aside the criticism that the Ideal Observer theory and similar theories are vacuous unless substantive moral principles are somehow incorporated into them. Rawls, for his part, avoids this criticism simply by freely admitting that he does incorporate substantive moral principles into the hypothetical choice situation in his choice of the proper constraints. This is precisely why he is so concerned that we achieve the correct characterization of the original position.

> The original position . . . unites in one conception a reasonably clear problem of choice with conditions that are widely recognized as fitting to impose on the adoption of moral principles. This initial situation combines the requisite clarity with the relevant ethical constraints.[23]

> Once we grasp this conception, we can at any time look at the social world from the required point of view. It suffices to reason in certain ways and to follow the conclusions reached. This standpoint is also *objective* and expresses our autonomy.[24]

[22] Mayo, p. 91.
[23] Rawls, *A Theory of Justice*, p. 584.
[24] Ibid., p. 587.

As mentioned previously, however, the "objectivity" of moral principles is today normally interpreted as (unanimous) intersubjective agreement, and this is what Rawls also seems to mean when using the terms "objective" or "objectivity" in this context. But, as Rawls points out, "From the standpoint of moral philosophy, the best account of a person's sense of justice is not the one which fits his judgments prior to his examining any conception of justice, but rather the one which matches his judgments in reflective equilibrium."[25] The method of reflective equilibrium and the strategy of the original position are fused in Rawls' theory because "justice as fairness is the hypothesis that the principles which would be chosen in the original position are identical with those that match our considered judgments and so these principles describe our sense of justice."[26]

It is important to realize, however, that these two methods are separate and distinct: one can accept the method of reflective equilibrium without accepting Rawls' strategy of the original position (or any other sort of hypothetical choice strategy) and vice versa. Joel Feinberg, for example, characterizes the general method of reflective equilibrium without reference to hypothetical choice situations as follows:

> The best way to defend one's selection of principles is to show to which positions they commit one on . . . issues. . . . General principles arise in the course of deliberations over particular problems, in the efforts to defend one's judgments by showing that they are consistent with what has gone before. If a principle commits one to an antecedently unacceptable judgment, then one has to modify or supplement the principle in a way that does the least damage to the harmony of one's particular and general opinions taken as a group. On the other hand, when a solid, well-entrenched principle entails a change in a particular judgment, the overriding claims of consistency may require that the judgment be adjusted.[27]

Although Feinberg does not mention it in this passage, this method can be made even stronger by demanding that the moral judgments taken into consideration be only our *considered* moral judgments. One interpretation of "considered moral judgments" is those that we are willing to universalize and that meet Baier's

---

[25] Ibid., p. 48.
[26] Ibid.
[27] Feinberg, *Social Philosophy*, p. 34.

other conditions. (This might be interpreted to include projecting ourselves—à la Hare—into the worst possible position with respect to the universalized judgments and seeing if we still agree with them.)

But the point is that moral theories, on this view, are to be constructed on the hypothetico-deductive model of explanation, utilizing our *considered* moral judgments as the data base. We hypothesize certain principles that seem to systematize and be in accord with our considered moral judgments and then seek to "confirm" or, more importantly, "falsify" the hypotheses by seeing if our considered moral judgments agree or disagree with them. If too many of our considered moral judgments disagree with the proposed principle, we must modify the principle or propose a new one. On the other hand, if we have a very powerful set of principles and then come across a rather mundane moral judgment or set of moral judgments that contradict it, we are likely to modify the moral judgments in question and maintain the principle. Finally, just as in science, there is the element of competition. We choose from among competing theories on the basis of which of them accounts best for the data (i.e., which is *most* in reflective equilibrium with our considered moral judgments) and which is the most comprehensive, economical, and elegant.

Given their materialist and naturalist predilections, Marxists might be receptive to this theory insofar as it rejects the direct (or indirect) apprehension of transcendent or immanent values and other idealistic baggage. But I suspect that they might also be tempted to reject it on the basis that it would seem to allow "bourgeois" philosophers or even fascists to construct theories in accordance with their moral intuitions or judgments that would be immune from criticism so long as they were internally coherent.

But Rawls is cognizant of this kind of difficulty, and in an attempt to avoid allowing biased or otherwise suspect moral judgments to enter into the process of reflective equilibrium, he suggests that we allow only our *considered* moral judgments as data where

> considered judgments [are] . . . those judgments in which our moral capacities are most likely to be displayed without distortion. Thus in deciding which of our judgments to take into account we may reasonably select some and exclude others. For example, we can discard those judgments made with hesitation, or in which we have little confidence. Similarly, those

given when we are upset or frightened, or when we stand to gain one way or the other can be left aside. All these judgments are likely to be erroneous or to be influenced by an excessive attention to our own interests. Considered judgments are simply those rendered under conditions favorable to the exercise of the sense of justice, and therefore in circumstances where the more common excuses and explanations for making a mistake do not obtain.[28]

The fact that some individuals and groups of individuals might emerge from the process of achieving reflective equilibrium with moral theories that, in reality, are merely rationalizations for unjust privileges and powers of those in socially dominant positions has led Marxist-oriented philosophers who reject foundationalist views of moral-theory construction in favor of coherence theories—and who are thus, attracted to the method of reflective equilibrium—to attempt to expand upon this suggestion made by Rawls. Norman Daniels, for example, argues that

> there must be more to moral justification of both judgments and principles than . . . simple coherence considerations, especially in the face of the many plausible bases for rejecting moral judgments; e.g., the judgments may only reflect class or cultural background, self-interest, or historical accident.[29]

> Once the foundational claim is removed . . . we have nothing more than a person's moral opinion. It is a "considered" opinion, to be sure, but still only an opinion. Since such opinions are often the result of self-interest, self-deception, historical and cultural accident, hidden class bias, and so on, just systematizing some of them hardly seems a promising way to provide justification for them or for the principles that order them.[30]

To alleviate this difficulty and help prevent the sort of tainted moral judgments he mentions from creeping into our moral theories, Daniels proposes that we allow general empirical considerations and theories to interact with our considered moral judgments at the level of the data base. The idea is that if we have good em-

---

[28] Rawls, *A Theory of Justice*, pp. 47–48.

[29] Daniels, "Wide Reflective Equilibrium and Theory Acceptance in Ethics," p. 257.

[30] Ibid., p. 265.

pirical reasons to think that our moral judgments, even our *considered* moral judgments, are suspect in one of the above listed ways, then we may well reject them as unreliable data. Following Rawls, Daniels puts forward what he calls the method of *wide* reflective equilibrium.

> Wide equilibrium closely resembles scientific practice. Neither in science nor in ethics do we merely "test" our theories against a predetermined, relatively fixed data. Rather, we continually reassess and reevaluate both the plausibility and the relevance of these data against theories we are inclined to accept. The possibility thus arises that these pressures for revision will free considered moral judgments from their vulnerability to many of the *specific* objections about bias and unreliability usually directed against them.[31]

Which judgments are thus deemed unreliable will differ according to the general empirical theories concerning moral-belief formation that are utilized. Psychoanalytic theory is, of course, one of the most commonly proposed. One application of this method by a contemporary Analytic Marxist, in an attempt to show that the Marxist's moral judgments are less likely to be biased in these ways than those of the supporters of capitalism, revolves around the use of psychoanalytic theory to diagnose the self-interested rationalizations so often found in the moral intuitions and theories of privileged classes and castes. In his excellent article, "Marxism and Moral Objectivity," William Shaw argues:

> Social consciousness reflects social existence, but it is not, according to Marx, necessarily ideological. Definitions of ideology vary; on one plausible view, though, an ideological belief is one (a) whose believer remains ignorant of the real reasons for (or causes of) his holding it and (b) which would not be held if the believer ceased to be ignorant of these reasons. A bourgeois, for example, who held that capitalism is just, not for the reason he thinks he holds that belief (viz. that capitalism is in everyone's best interest), but because his own class interests and social milieu have fostered this sectional prejudice in him, would have an ideological belief. This belief

[31] Ibid., p. 273.

293

would not survive his acquiring knowledge of the reasons for his maintaining his belief.[32]

Relying on the above definition permits one to distinguish in the moral realm—at least in principle—between ideological and non-ideological beliefs. On this basis one could construct a two-pronged argument to support the objective validity of the judgment that socialism is morally preferable to capitalism (assuming, again, that there is agreement on the facts and that they are as Marx says). First, objections to this evaluation would be indicted as resting on ethical claims that are ideological and, therefore, illegitimate. . . . Second, the moral principles underlying the case for socialism would be demonstrated to pass the litmus test for ideology. Those who endorse the relevant principles would have to be shown as not doing so for reasons the knowledge of which would lead them to cease believing those principles. The proletarian can affirm the moral perspective of his class while understanding how and why those ideals have arisen at this point in history.[33]

Whether or not we accept Shaw's argument will turn in large measure on our views of the scientific and epistemological status of psychoanalytic theory. Both Marxists and non-Marxists are often bitterly divided on precisely this issue. Such philosophers as Adolph Gruenbaum argue that psychoanalysis is a pseudo-science as opposed to a genuine science and point to facts such as that the remission rate for people with psychological problems is no better among those treated by psychoanalysis than among those who simply have someone to talk to about their problems. But, as Elster emphasizes, the (presumably) more scientifically well-grounded claims of cognitive psychology might be well fitted to fill this theoretical role.[34]

Among other Marxist-oriented thinkers who give psychoanalytic theory credence, members of the Institute of Social Research, or Frankfurt School, such as Max Horkheimer, Theodor Adorno, Erich Fromm, and Herbert Marcuse have—since the 1930s—suggested that a fusion of the Marxist and psychoanalytic traditions is

[32] Shaw, "Marxism and Moral Objectivity," pp. 36–37.

[33] Ibid., p. 37.

[34] See Adolph Gruenbaum, The Foundations of Psychoanalysis: A Philosophical Critique, University of California Press, Berkeley, 1984, and the following works by Elster: "Belief, Bias, and Ideology"; Logic and Society; Sour Grapes; Ulysses and the Sirens; Making Sense of Marx, pp. 459–510; and An Introduction to Karl Marx, pp. 168–185.

necessary for the development of a truly adequate critical theory of society. Although they did not apply this to moral theory construction in particular, they did mean it to apply to ideology in general, of which moral theories and codes are a part.[35]

Among the intellectual descendants of the Frankfurt School, Jürgen Habermas has developed a sophisticated version of the fusion of these two traditions. This theory has interesting parallels with both the theory of wide reflective equilibrium as an attempt to rid our considered moral judgments of biased or "ideological" elements and with John Rawls' theory of the original position as a hypothetical choice situation designed to reach a rational consensus on moral principles among free and equal individuals.[36]

According to Habermas, norms—including moral principles by which to govern social arrangements—are justified or valid if, and only if, they would attain a rational consensus of individuals as free and equal participants in a dialogue (or "discourse") under conditions constitutive of an "ideal speech situation." This last clause is designed to eliminate precisely those sorts of biased and illegitimate opinions or views that Daniels and Shaw are concerned to bar from entering the data base in the construction of moral theories.

> Practical questions . . . are posed with a view to the acceptance or rejection of norms, especially norms for action, the claims to validity of which we can support or oppose with reasons. Theories which in their structure can serve the clarifica-

[35] See Max Horkheimer, *Critical Theory*, Herder and Herder, N.Y., 1972; and Horkheimer and Theodor W. Adorno, *Dialectic of Enlightenment*, Herder and Herder, N.Y., 1972. Also see Herbert Marcuse: *Eros and Civilization: A Philosophical Inquiry into Freud*, Beacon Press, Boston, 1955; *Reason and Revolution: Hegel and the Rise of Social Theory*, Beacon Press, Boston, 1960; and *Negations: Essays in Critical Theory*, Beacon Press, Boston, 1968. See also Erich Fromm: *Man for Himself*, Fawcett Publications, Greenwich, Conn., 1947, and *The Sane Society*, Fawcett Publications, Greenwich, Conn., 1955.

For a concise history of the Frankfurt School's attempt at such a fusion, see Martin Jay *The Dialectical Imagination*, Little, Brown, and Co., Boston, 1973, especially chapter 2 ("The Integration of Psychoanalysis").

[36] See "On Systematically Distorted Communication," *Inquiry*, vol. 13 (Autumn 1970), and "Toward a Theory of Communicative Competence," *Inquiry*, vol. 13 (Winter 1970). For a critical appraisal of Habermas' social theory, see Julius Sensat, *Habermas and Marxism*: Funk "Habermas and Social Goods"; and Nielsen: "Radical Philosophy and Critical Theory: Examination and Defense," *Philosophical Exchange*, vol. 2, 1975; "The Political Relevance of Habermas," *Radical Philosophers Newsjournal*, vol. 7 (Aug. 1976); "Can There Be an Emancipatory Rationality?" *Critica*, vol. 8, no. 24 (Dec. 1976); and "Rationality, Needs, and Politics: Remarks on Rationality as Emancipation and Enlightenment," *Cultural Hermeneutics*, vol. 4 (1977).

tion of practical questions are designed to enter into communicative action. Interpretations which can be gained within the framework of such theories cannot, of course, be directly effective for the orientation of action; rather, they find their legitimate value within the therapeutic context of the reflexive formation of volition. Therefore they can only be translated into processes of enlightenment which are rich in political consequences, when the institutional preconditions for practical discourse among the general public are fulfilled. As long as this is not the case, the restrictive compulsions, that is, the inhibitions to communication . . . themselves become a problem to be clarified theoretically.[37]

Although Habermas takes a rational consensus to be the criterion of a "generalizable interest" and thus a valid or legitimate norm, he is concerned to distinguish a "true" from a "false" consensus. A false consensus is based on "nongeneralizable interests" resulting from the inauthenticity, deception, or self-deception of individuals. This is why Habermas is concerned to develop a theory of "communicative competence"—including a conception of the "ideal speech situation"—as well as a theory of "systematically distorted communication" designed to explain the prevalence of ideologies based on nongeneralizable interests that result in a false consensus. This is also the point at which the psychoanalytic tradition comes into play in Habermas' theory. As Julius Sensat puts it in his work *Habermas and Marxism*:

Institutionally secured deviations from the ideal speech situation produce systematic distortions in communication. For example, repressive socialization processes hinder self-expression and produce neurotic disturbances.[38]

Neurotic behavior patterns have objective power over their victims despite the fact that they are produced by the victims themselves. The neurotic individual does not understand his own actions, which spring from motives that, though they are his motives, have been banished from his consciousness. . . . The true meaning of his pathological behavior patterns differs from their apparent meaning, which is expressed in rationalizations. Rationalizations serve to conceal from him the true cause of his behavior; at the same time, they themselves result

[37] Habermas, *Theory and Practice*, pp. 3–4.
[38] Sensat, *Habermas and Marxism*, p. 28.

from and express the irrational state of affairs which is his illness. Not truly rational, rationalizations can be criticized and seen through. Psychoanalysis helps the patient to accomplish this task, by means of which he regains his rational powers and becomes the conscious author of his own actions.

Ideologies are rationalizations writ large. Instead of individual behavior patterns they serve to legitimate institutions which are not discursively justifiable. Such institutions, like neurotic behavior patterns, have objective power over individuals, in spite of the fact that they are produced by the reciprocal behavioral expectations of these individuals in their interactions with each other. These institutions express conditions which are social; they express the society's answers to practical questions and are thus in principle amenable to practical deliberation and control. That is to say, it is possible in principle for social institutions to be evaluated in discourse. Such an evaluative procedure would allow only *generalizable* interests—those interests that all persons, as fully competent subjects, would regard as legitimate—to be secured institutionally. It thereby would result in formation of a rational general will.[39]

At this point we find ourselves back to the idea of (unanimous) intersubjective agreement in hypothetical choice situations. Although Habermas wants ultimately to apply his criterion of consensual validation to factual as well as evaluative claims, if we limit our attention to the validation of *moral* claims and principles, this theory can be considered as a sort of synthesis of Rawls' strategy of the original position and Daniels' and Shaw's proposed constraints on what can be taken as a considered moral judgment or a legitimate interest. The similarities between Rawls' characterization of the original position and Habermas' characterization of the ideal speech situation are especially significant.

Whereas Rawls' original position is, *ex hypothesi*, populated by rational, free, nonenvious individuals in a situation of initial equality, Habermas' ideal speech situation is populated by rational, free and (presumably) nonenvious individuals in a situation of equality.

The *ideal speech situation* . . . is characterized formally by the symmetrical distribution of chances to assume dialogue roles,

[39] Ibid., pp. 28–29.

i.e., to select and employ speech acts. In particular, (1) all potential participants in discourse must have the same chance to initiate discourses and to perpetuate them through asking and answering questions, making and replying to objections, giving arguments and justifications, etc. This requirement insures that all opinions and norms are potentially subject to discursive examination. Furthermore, (2) all participants in interaction must have the same chance to express their feelings, intentions, attitudes, etc. This requirement is meant to insure the authenticity of the participants, i.e., the transparency of their inner natures to themselves and to each other. Finally, (3) all participants in interaction must have the same chance to give orders, to permit, to forbid, to give and receive promises, etc.; in short, there must be a reciprocity in behavior expectations which excludes all privileges in the sense of one-sidedly binding norms.[40]

Furthermore, although Rawls does not bring psychoanalytic theory to bear on this matter, it is clear that he is also concerned that the moral judgments of parties in the original position be autonomous and that the consensus they reach be a "true" or "objective" one. This comes out in certain passages in *A Theory of Justice* not often commented on. Rawls first invites us to

imagine . . . that someone experiences the promptings of his moral sense as inexplicable inhibitions which for the moment he is unable to justify. Why should he not regard them as simply neurotic compulsions? If it should turn out that these scruples are indeed largely shaped and accounted for by the contingencies of early childhood, perhaps by the course of our family history and class situation, and that there is nothing to add on their behalf, then there is surely no reason why they should govern our lives.[41]

This is why the individual in the original position would demand that "the psychological processes by which his moral sense has been acquired conform to principles that he himself would choose under conditions that he would concede are fair and undistorted by fortune and happenstance."[42] Such individuals would also demand that a "person's sense of justice is not a compulsive

[40] Ibid., pp. 27–28.
[41] Rawls, *A Theory of Justice*, p. 514.
[42] Ibid., p. 515.

psychological mechanism cleverly installed by those in authority in order to insure his unswerving compliance with rules designed to advance their interests."[43] Furthermore, according to Rawls, "It follows that in accepting these principles on this basis we are not influenced primarily by tradition and authority, or the opinions of others."[44]

The parallel here between Habermas and Rawls is evident. They are both very much concerned with the same sorts of problems in achieving a "genuine," "true," or "enlightened" consensus among individuals on intersubjectively binding norms by which to judge and regulate social arrangements and practices. One important difference, of course, is that while Habermas seeks to incorporate large parts of psychoanalytic theory into his critical theory of society, Rawls does no more than allude to the types of difficulties that psychoanalytic theory—or theories in cognitive psychology—might be helpful in solving. Perhaps the most important difference, though, is that whereas Rawls' proposed consensus is purely hypothetical, the consensus proposed by Habermas is one he believes could and would actually come about if we had social institutions conducive to promoting the type of "discourse" between individuals necessary to achieve it—social institutions that were, for example, transparent to individuals rather than opaque and that fostered autonomous personalities rather than the reverse.

This distinction between a hypothetical and an actual consensus brings up the point that in judging theories of moral justification we must determine how they fare in assuring an enlightened intersubjective consensus at both the theoretical and practical levels. This distinction is perhaps particularly important to Marxists since, even if they admit the possibility of such a (unanimous) consensus on a theoretical level, they have no illusions of reaching such a consensus on the practical level where class interests and perspectives are operative.

This brings us to a recent change in Rawls' theory or method of justification from which I explicitly wish to distance myself. Apparently in response to his communitarian critics—primarily Alasdair MacIntyre, Charles Taylor, and Michael Sandel—Rawls now eschews his former analysis on which such principles are justified if (and only if) they would be unanimously agreed to in the origi-

[43] Ibid.
[44] Ibid., p. 516.

nal position in favor of an analysis on which they are justified (i.e., worthy of being accepted) if (and presumably only if) they are able to capture the implicit norms of all segments of a democratic, liberal society and, thus, constitute what he calls an "overlapping consensus."[45]

Rawls' purpose in proposing this new theory of justification seems to be to avoid the charge that his strategy of the original position is infused with essentially contestable value judgments—in particular, that it begs the question of individualism versus communitarianism in favor of individualism—and, thus, to "provide a shared public basis of the justification of political and social institutions," which will "ensure stability from one generation to another."[46] Rawls does not propose, however, that this method of justification is appropriate to all societies; on the contrary, he claims that it is only appropriate to societies having democratic constitutional institutions and traditions. In particular, such a society must have a tradition based on the "basic intuitive ideas" that persons are to be conceived as free and equal moral beings and that people ought to participate in a "fair system of cooperation" in order to realize the numerous opportunities for gain that are possible within such a system. He further assumes that the political traditions of this sort of society contain the values of toleration, free and orderly public discussion, and disdain for the oppressive use of state power. Given these assumptions it is Rawls' hypothesis that an actual overlapping consensus can be achieved on principles of social justice within currently existing democratic liberal societies; in particular, he believes that such a consensus can be achieved on his substantive principles of social justice.

Here I must part company with Rawls and insist that we utilize only his strategy of the original position as originally conceived. It seems to me that this new method of justification is susceptible to insurmountable objections. In addition, it weakens the arguments Rawls formerly had against a number of opponents and realizes no appreciable off-setting gain. (Later in this chapter I shall note how Rawls' new strategy even seems to undercut his case against such right-libertarians as Nozick, and in chapter 9 I shall explain

---

[45] See Rawls, "Justice as Fairness, Political not Metaphysical" and "The Idea of an Overlapping Consensus." For a critical response to these articles, see Hampton, "Should Political Philosophy Be Done without Metaphysics?" For a more sympathetic response, see Doppelt, "Is Rawls' Kantian Liberalism Coherent and Defensible?"

[46] Rawls, "The Idea of an Overlapping Consensus," p. 1.

how it also undercuts a possible response on his part to one of Richard Miller's criticisms.)

One objection to Rawls' new method is that it fails at the task it is designed to accomplish, i.e., the task of eliminating contestable value judgments in the justification of principles of social justice. In stipulating that it applies only to democratic constitutional liberal societies and that all members or at least all major segments of these societies accept the liberal values of toleration, respect for free and orderly discussion, and disdain for the oppressive use of state power, he seems to be merely begging the question at another level. (When he goes on to claim that such a consensus can be reached within contemporary Western constitutional democracies he enters the realm of the empirical and is, thus, susceptible to empirical refutation. More on this shortly.)

Although at first glance this new method of justifying principles of social justice by achieving an actual overlapping consensus may seem capable of placating Rawls' communitarian critics, not even this much is clear. After all, wouldn't MacIntyre, Taylor, and Sandel object to this theory as well since: (1) it is still based on the notion of rights (which they tend to reject on grounds that it incorporates an individualistic bias), (2) it still accepts justice as the first virtue of social institutions (while they think of it as merely a remedial virtue that is needed only as long as we have not achieved genuine community), and (3) it presupposes a pluralistic society and sees the job of the state as merely adjudicating conflicting interests (whereas they hold that the good life cannot be achieved unless pluralism is eliminated and replaced by a genuine community in which there is a consensus on the nature of the good and in which one of the main functions of the state is to promote the good, partially by encouraging universal participation in the process of governing, i.e., by encouraging civic republicanism)? If so, this fact, in and of itself, would seem to indicate that Rawls' hope of achieving an overlapping consensus within a democratic liberal society without begging any substantive moral questions is in vain.

Another difficulty with Rawls' overlapping consensus theory would seem to be that persons who have democratic sentiments but who happen to live in an undemocratic, illiberal (but yet pluralistic) society are left in a theoretical lurch, so to speak. Since they cannot justify principles of social justice—say Rawls' principles—by uncovering the right sort of implicit overlapping consensus, how are they to justify such a theory? Certainly we don't want to say that no theory of justice can be justified in such a society. This would leave people no cogent grounds on which to claim that undemocratic or illiberal practices or institutions in such societies are unjust and ought to be altered. On the other hand, if Rawls were to grant such persons the privilege of justifying a theory of justice by means of the strategy of the original position—which would seem his only other alternative—then why is this not a valid method of justification for everyone regardless of the sort of society in which they happen to live?

Perhaps one reason Rawls is hesitant to grant this is that he has taken to heart the communitarian criticism that his theory of justice may not be appropriate to all societies in all historical periods. But this is something that Rawls (or a Rawlsian) can perfectly well admit within the context of the strategy of the original position. Since, by hypothesis, the participants in the original position have all general knowledge that is relevant for making decisions on basic principles by which to govern social arrangements, they would know if there are (or might be) some societies in which—due to the empirical facts—liberal principles of justice (or rights) are not the best to accept. Individuals within close-knit band and tribal level societies, for example, might be so community oriented that they would have no use for principles protecting individual liberal freedoms and may even be opposed to such principles if they had reason to believe that their acceptance or promulgation would lead to a destruction of the genuine community they value so highly, along with the satisfaction and fulfillment they may gain from having common ends and a shared understanding of the human condition. (Marx's utopian vision of full-fledged communism may fall into the same category, but since such a society is not historically possible—at least as a mass society—we needn't concern ourselves with it.)

There are, however, two points to be made here. First, even if such community-oriented individuals would want to reject the "individualistic" liberal freedoms (of free speech, private property, etc.), they almost certainly would still wish to ensure that they are not tortured, murdered, or unnecessarily starved to death or made to suffer great hardships. Whether or not they would want to phrase these assurances in terms of rights or merely affirm them in terms of such natural duties as the duty not to harm and the duty of mutual aid, from the perspective of the original position they would undoubtedly insist upon them. (That actual individuals in band or tribal level societies may not even have the con-

302

cepts of rights or duties is, of course, irrelevant; the point is that they would want to protect themselves against such contingencies whether or not they have these concepts and that this can best be articulated within the original position by the use of such concepts.) So even with respect to such societies as these there is still valuable work to be done within the original position.

The second (related) point is that a Rawlsian can "relativize" her theory to accord with such essential psychological and sociological facts and, thus, admit that Rawls' principles of social justice (on both his general and special conceptions) are meant to be applicable to only mass, pluralistic societies that instantiate Hume's conditions of justice. But then, of course, the Rawlsian would be free to point out that as a matter of empirical fact this is basically the only type of society that exists in modern times and, thus, that Rawls' substantive principles of justice should be taken to apply at least to all presently existing societies as well as all other mass, pluralistic societies that may come into existence. As compared to Rawls' move to demanding an actual overlapping consensus within a democratic liberal society, this move has the advantages that it applies to all mass, pluralistic societies rather than only to democratic liberal ones and that it is not refuted by the mere empirical fact that not all actually existing persons or groups of persons within such societies will agree on these principles of justice or even on the underlying liberal principle of toleration. Thus, it seems to assuage at least one of the concerns of Rawls' communitarian critics without running into all of the difficulties of Rawls' overlapping consensus method of justification.

This brings us to the most obvious—and, I believe, most devastating—objection to Rawls' new method of justification. It is precisely that even if such an overlapping consensus could be achieved under the conditions he outlines, there is not the slightest reason to believe that there is any presently existing society (or will be any society for the forseeable future) in which all of these conditions are met; i.e., in which all members of society— or even all major groups within society—accept all of the values that Rawls claims are part of "our" democratic political culture. In the United States, for example, there are not only isolated individuals but whole segments of society that repudiate one or more of these values. (Here one need only think of the religious fundamentalists in the United States, some of whom advocate that homosexuals ought to suffer the biblical punishment of being stoned to death.) Notice that while Rawls' strategy of the original position is not susceptible to the objection that not all actual people will agree on a set of principles—the answer is "Of course not! But what I am claiming is that they *would* agree if they met the conditions of my hypothetical choice situation and this situation is the epitome of what is fair"—his new overlapping consensus method is fatally susceptible to this objection. As Jean Hampton puts it, "Not only is there no consensus on Rawls's conception of justice in our society, but more disturbingly, there is no consensus on the idea that all human beings deserve equal respect."[47]

But why doesn't Rawls perceive this fact as a major obstacle to his overlapping consensus method, if so many others do? I would hazard the guess that this is an instance in which Rawls has let his (sometime) neoclassical inclination to conceive society as almost wholly cooperative—rather than as marked by conflict and relations of dominance and exploitation—run amok. Although a Marxist may well agree with Rawls that a society allowing for such a consensus is a noble ideal and even that such a society may be historically possible even in the form of a mass, pluralistic society (although even a democratic, self-managing socialist society might contain religious fundamentalists), she or he will surely not agree that there are now any capitalist societies or, for that matter, any post-capitalist societies that meet these conditions. If the Marxist analysis that even contemporary liberal welfare-state capitalist societies are class divided and shot through and through with serious conflict stemming from relations of dominance and exploitation (class and otherwise) is even close to the mark, then Rawls' implicit assumption that all major groups within such societies can actually reach a consensus (on his theory of justice or any other) becomes almost laughable. And one certainly need not be a Marxist to accept the view that there is enough serious conflict in contemporary societies to make such a consensus highly fanciful.

In short, if reaching an actual consensus is a necessary condition for a theory of justice being justified (in a democratic liberal or any other type of society), then it seems exceedingly likely that neither Rawls' theory nor any other theory will ever be justified within a modern mass pluralistic society. This seems a steep price to pay for getting rid of contestable normative assumptions (although, as previously argued, Rawls does not succeed even in doing that). Even though a unanimous consensus in the real world is not guar-

[47] Hampton, "Should Political Philosophy Be Done without Metaphysics?" (forthcoming).

anteed by Rawls' original method of justification, at least this theory allows it cogently to be said that some theory—e.g., Rawls' own theory of social justice—is, in fact, justified (at least for mass, pluralistic societies) even in face of the fact that probably no theory of social justice could achieve an overlapping consensus (especially as long as the societies in question remain either class divided or heavily bureaucratized).

A final difficulty with Rawls' overlapping consensus theory is that it is myopic in an extremely important respect: namely, it apparently demands a consensus only among persons within a particular society and this consensus may not take sufficiently into account the interests and/or rights of persons in other societies whose life prospects are importantly impacted by decisions made within the society in question. This is an especially relevant issue when we consider the relation in today's world between the advanced industrialized capitalist societies (or industrialized nations, in general) and the developing nations. Since, however, essentially the same criticism can be made of the substantive portion of Rawls' original theory—or at least his application of it—and since I consider this objection in the last section of chapter 9, we shall postpone discussion of it until then. But even without taking this objection into consideration, it seems that a strong case can be made for continuing to accept Rawls' strategy of the original position while rejecting the newfangled method of overlapping consensus.

Moral Objectivity, Class Struggle, and Intersubjective Agreement

Whether or not certain moral principles are objective in the sense that they would command unanimous intersubjective agreement among all rational persons who meet certain other conditions—for example, the conditions imposed upon individuals in Rawls' original position or in Habermas' ideal speech situation—is an issue still much in dispute among moral philosophers and theorists of value. Those who reject this contention may hold either (1) that there is no guarantee of unanimous agreement even among individuals who meet these conditions; (2) that such an agreement under these conditions is no reason to label the principles thus chosen "objective" because the constraints placed upon the hypothetical choice situations beg the question in favor of certain sorts of moral principles or values (e.g., the value of autonomy); or (3) the fact that individuals would agree on certain moral principles under these or any other conditions is simply irrelevant to the issue of whether or not such principles are justified and thus of no import in deciding whether or not such principles are objective. Although I will not attempt to sort out all of these issues, I will presently offer some considerations that, I think, ought to make us uneasy about assuming that such a consensus would be reached even among individuals who meet all of the conditions stipulated in Rawls' and Habermas' hypothetical choice situations.

But before we take up the question of intersubjective agreement at the theoretical level, let us first examine the possibility of achieving such intersubjective agreement at the practical level—the level at which political activity is determined in the real world. It seems clear that *even if* such hypothetical choice strategies may be ultimately decisive between opposing moral theories at the theoretical level, at the practical level they are bound to be much less decisive. There are individuals who are not even prepared to accept the rational, humanistic framework in which such debates can profitably be carried on. The fascist's irrational, intolerant commitment to "racial purity" or the "destiny of the nation" or the "fuehrer" may result from psychologically neurotic or socially ideological causes that they *would* be able to see through, and thus be "freed" of, *if* they were rational and nondogmatic enough to engage in what Habermas calls therapeutic discourse. But many in the real world are simply not willing or able to do this. It is simply impractical for a Marxist to expect to be able to rationally persuade a committed fascist that a democratic form of socialism is morally justified *even on the assumption that Marxist empirical theory is basically true*. As Andrew Collier notes:

> There have existed, and do exist, axiologies in which human powerlessness, submission, resignation, acceptance of what comes, renunciation of satisfaction, are made into values. These axiologies generally involve the ideal of submission to a superior will; to divine providence, or to a human fuehrer, or in some versions, to some supra-natural entity, supposedly endowed with an irreducible will of its own, such as nation or race. The consistent adherent of one of these axiologies will be untouched by socialist arguments that class oppression and the subordination of human wills to market forces could be abolished; here we really do reach a logical breakdown in the possibility of rational argument.[48]

[48] Collier, "Scientific Socialism and the Question of Socialist Values," pp. 151–152.

But even if we limit ourselves to those within the contemporary secular (or at least nontheocratic) and humanistic framework of practical reasoning about social arrangements (i.e., to modern liberals, libertarians, social-democrats, socialists, and most conservatives), it still seems problematic that we would reach unanimous intersubjective agreement on moral principles or on the best set of social arrangements. First, both the right-libertarian and the conservative are bound to have a falling out with modern liberals, social-democrats, and socialists even if it is assumed by all parties that Marxist empirical theory is basically correct. The right-libertarian's view that the right to own and control both personal and productive property is a basic liberty that is indefeasible before any and all other sorts of moral considerations, and the conservative's view that liberty can be constrained on grounds of conserving traditional values, will presumably both be anathema to humanist liberals and socialists. And even if it can be plausibly argued that neither of these views would be reached by parties in Rawls' original position or Habermas' ideal speech situation, it may be impossible *as a practical matter* to convince the right-libertarian or the conservative to give up these views.

It may seem as though I am being prejudicial here in setting up these oppositions since, it may well be pointed out, (1) liberals will differ from both social-democrats and revolutionary socialists on such issues as the right to productive property, while (2) liberals and social-democrats will normally differ from Marxists on the issue of the justifiability of socialist revolution. But I am here taking the liberty of assuming that these differences are primarily (if not exclusively) a matter of disagreements in empirical theory and belief. To see that this assumption is not totally implausible with reference to the first issue, one need only remember that the two greatest moral and social philosophers of the liberal tradition in the last two centuries—J. S. Mill and John Rawls—both readily admit that bourgeois property rights are neither morally fundamental nor indefeasible and that, given certain empirical assumptions in the realm of economics and political sociology, socialism (i.e., a democratic form of socialism) is morally preferable to capitalism.[49] At this point, the liberal will, in all probability, fall out with both the social-democrat and the revolutionary socialist as to whether a democratic form of socialism is a genuine historical possibility; but

[49] See J. S. Mill, *Principles of Political Economy*, pp. 203–217, 792; and John Rawls, *A Theory of Social Justice*, pp. 265–284. Albert Einstein's article, "Why Socialism?" (*Ideas and Opinions*, Dell Publishing Co., N.Y., 1954), is also interesting in this respect.

both this proposition and the assessment of the degree of confidence we are entitled to have in this and similar historical predictions are matters of empirical dispute rather than differences in moral evaluation.

The further claim that the differences between the liberal (and social-democrat) and the revolutionary socialist on the justifiability of socialist revolution are primarily differences in empirical theory and belief seems somewhat more problematic. But if a liberal or a social-democrat came to accept the Marxist's empirical views that (1) capitalism is the cause of the world's major social problems and the only way to eliminate war, oppression, human deprivation, extreme inequality, and the violation of human rights in general is to eliminate capitalism; (2) a post-capitalist society—once established on a worldwide scale—will not be an oppressive or totalitarian form of society; and (3) *an evolutionary path to socialism is not feasible*, it seems reasonable to assume that liberals or social-democrats would agree that socialist revolution—even *violent* socialist revolution—is morally justified.

But even if we assume that the differences between liberals, social-democrats, and revolutionary socialists are entirely factual, achieving a consensus about normative political positions at a *practical* level is still extremely problematic precisely because of the persistence of these differences in empirical beliefs. Achieving agreement on the truth of Marxist empirical theory (or even upon the reality of the class struggle) is, in fact, perhaps even more problematic than achieving agreement on basic moral principles. Agreement in the social sciences is extremely difficult to command.

Moreover, if Marx's theory of ideology is basically correct, we can expect the bourgeoisie (and privileged groups in general) to reject Marxist empirical theory even if it is true. This rejection of Marxist empirical theory and political program can range from the right-libertarian's claim that laissez-faire capitalism is the solution to all of modern society's economic woes to the welfare-state liberal's more benign but no less ideological claim that the state is basically a neutral arbiter between classes and, consequently, that it is not necessary to bring class struggle into the picture when designing strategies for social change. As emphasized in chapter 6, however, this must not be taken as a prophylactic against any and all opposing views, as is sometimes done by dogmatic Marxists. One must always leave open the possibility that it is Marxist empirical theory that is false. To make such a use of the Marxist theory of ideology results in Marxist theory being self-sealing, and thus not genuinely scientific.

But if we assume that Marxist empirical theory or at least the Marxist analysis of capitalism is basically correct, it will be included in the background information to which the individuals in Frankena's and Rawls' hypothetical choice situations have access and in the empirical propositions that individuals in Habermas' ideal speech situation come to accept as true. Given these empirical assumptions, the Marxist's normative political positions will be vindicated on almost all well-known moral theories to which humanist liberals, social-democrats, and revolutionary socialists find themselves committed. The utilitarian, the Kantian, the Rawlsian liberal, the self-realization theorist, the proponent of perfectionist ethics, etc., will all choose socialism (i.e., democratic, self-managing socialism) over any form of capitalism and over any other society possible in this historical epoch. As Collier puts it, "There is an extremely wide spectrum of axiological standpoints which when combined with a Marxist analysis of the workings of capitalism, would compel their adherents to adopt socialist politics."[50]

But the *theoretical* question is: utilizing the method of wide reflective equilibrium, will the incorporation of Marxist empirical theory into the "knowledge" of individuals in these hypothetical choice situations *necessarily* result in *unanimous intersubjective agreement* on the Marxist's basic normative political positions? Even assuming that we can rule out the views of fascists on grounds that such views will not be held by rational, nonenvious persons who have any respect for human autonomy, it still seems doubtful that such a unanimous consensus will be reached.

Take the case of a right-libertarian having a particularly intractable nature and you may come up with an individual who—even meeting all the conditions Rawls, Frankena, and others put forward and even accepting Marxist empirical theory as basically correct—may very well still hold that an individual's right to own and control *both personal and productive property* is a basic component of human freedom or liberty. Since, on this view, either liberty cannot be limited at all or can be limited only on the basis of a greater gain in liberty (narrowly interpreted), this right will be indefeasible before any and all other kinds of moral considerations, e.g., considerations of utility or social justice.

If we were to argue that this belief is an ideological rationaliza-

[50] Collier, "Scientific Socialism and the Question of Socialist Values," p. 146.

309

tion (in the sense explicated by Habermas and Shaw) on the part of the bourgeoisie and other privileged classes or groups in capitalist society, some right-libertarians might justifiably respond that this may be true of a great many individuals but not of them because they *know* the historical and even personal psychological origin of this belief or commitment and yet choose to stand by it (perhaps as a matter of "existential commitment"). They might further point out that—on the explication of ideology given in this work at least—what is or is not ideological is relative to the ultimate normative ends to which one is committed and, therefore, to label their views "ideological" is to beg the question in favor of the Marxist's or humanist's ultimate normative commitments and thus cannot be decisive. They might even point out to us—with considerable justification—that the cause or origin of a normative principle or belief has nothing to do with its validity and that to reject a normative principle on the basis of its historical or psychological genesis is to commit a gross form of the "genetic fallacy."

Furthermore, rather than being persuaded that their moral views are the result of selfish class interests, right-libertarians are more likely to respond, rightly or wrongly, that it is the Marxist's moral views that are to be indicted on the grounds that they are the result of envy. (This would, however, have to be a much more detailed story to be plausible since many Marxists have come from wealthy and/or well-placed families and social backgrounds.) Furthermore, while bringing psychoanalytic theory into the hypothetical choice situation—as Habermas, Shaw, and others recommend—may make the method more powerful at the theoretical level, it makes unanimous intersubjective agreement, if anything, more problematic since there are many writers (both Marxist and non-Marxist) who will question the validity of psychoanalytic theory or the specific applications made of it. (I presume that even the claims of cognitive psychology cited by Elster in this context are not beyond dispute.)

Descending from the methodological or metaethical level to the level of substantive moral argument, we might attempt to propose that a genuine respect for human freedom or liberty requires a recognition of freedom *to do or not do* certain sorts of things, which includes the freedom to earn an honest living and thus be able to feed oneself and not starve. But the right-libertarian would probably respond that respect for the liberty of persons entails *only* that people be free from force, theft, and fraud to do (or not do) as they like. We might argue that respect for persons entails concern for their well-being as well as for their freedom, but right-libertarians such as Nozick might claim that respect for persons means respecting the boundary lines of their "territories" as persons and that nothing more is *morally required*, though being charitable to the more disadvantaged may be *morally admirable*. Furthermore, they might claim, again with considerable justification, that since the concept or principle of respect for persons is—like the concept of ideology—essentially contestable, we will not be able to solve our disagreements on normative principles by appealing to it.

If we were to invoke Rawls' strategy at this point and claim that parties in the original position would not agree to such an unrestrained right to private property,[51] right-libertarians still have a number of plausible retorts. First, they may grant the legitimacy of the strategy of the original position but disagree with Rawls' interpretation that the parties would not agree to such a principle— presumably on the grounds that such a right must be placed on the list of basic liberties that people would give priority to protecting. (Rawls, of course, counts as a *basic* liberty only the right to own *personal* property, along with the traditional "civil liberties"

---

[51] Notice, however, that on Rawls' more recent overlapping consensus view of the justification of principles of social justice, although this appeal to what would be agreed to in the original position has heuristic value, it no longer serves to justify such principles. Therefore, even if it could be conclusively shown that the parties to the original position would not recognize an unrestricted right to private property as basic (but only a restricted right to own personal as opposed to productive property), this does not show that the libertarian's principle is not justified and the more limited principle is. Thus, Rawls' case against Nozick and other right-libertarians is weakened. Moreover, the fact that right-libertarians such as Nozick presumably must be counted among those claiming allegiance to a democratic constitutional society (even though they do not recognize political democracy to have anything but instrumental value), shows contrary to Rawls' assumption—that the overlapping consensus on basic principles of social justice is simply not forthcoming in such societies. It is clear that right-libertarians such as Nozick have an unshakeable commitment to the right to own and control productive property as basic and incontrovertible, while Rawls and most other denizens of democratic constitutional societies have an equally unshakeable commitment to the claim that there is no basic right to own productive property, although it may turn out to be a derivative right depending on the empirical evidence concerning matters of political sociology. (Rawls, of course, does recognize the right to own personal property as basic even though this right—like any other—can sometimes be overridden by other moral considerations if they are weighty enough.) Since this is an irreconcilable difference on a fundamental issue of social justice among those committed to a democratic constitutional society, there would seem to be no possibility of attaining the sort of overlapping consensus Rawls is after. (On the irreconcilability of the democratic-liberal and libertarian concepts or theories of freedom and the problem of justifying one over the other to the satisfaction of all rational persons, see Doppelt, "Conflicting Social Paradigms of Human Freedom and the Problem of Justification.")

such as freedom of expression, religion, and conscience and such traditional political rights as freedom of association, the right to vote, the right to run for and hold political office, etc.) This move would still leave quite a lot of common ground on which to argue since we could attempt to develop the criteria a liberty must meet in order to be considered a *basic* liberty by parties in the original position and then ask if the particular right in question meets these criteria.

Second, however, right-libertarians might maintain that whether or not the parties in the original position would agree to such an unfettered right to private property—or to any other right or principle—has no moral import. This move would seemingly leave very little common ground on which to argue. But there is one important rejoinder that proponents of hypothetical choice strategies have available, namely, that whatever set of principles or rules is agreed upon in such hypothetical situations, it is, ipso facto, a *fair* set of principles or rules and that to abide by such a procedure is to be fair, and to refuse to do so is the paradigm of what it is to be unfair. (This is precisely why Rawls calls his theory "justice as fairness.") The right-libertarian—or anyone else—can still, of course, refuse to recognize the moral import of rules or principles arrived at in such a manner but only at what would seem to be a terrible price: admitting they do not feel themselves obligated to be fair or to be bound in any way by considerations of fairness.

It is possible, of course, that the persons in question might dispute this as a criterion of fairness, but it is difficult to imagine how. It is even possible that they may simply bite the bullet at this point and claim that fundamental liberties—such as unrestrained property rights—take precedence over considerations of fairness. In this case, appealing back to what would be agreed to in the original position or other hypothetical choice situations would carry no weight with our imaginary interlocutors since the force of such appeals depends, in the last analysis, on a commitment to fairness. Thus any attempt to get someone to agree that we ought to be constrained by considerations of fairness because we all would agree to do so in such hypothetical choice situations is question-begging and circular. (This is why Rawls does not attempt to *justify* the principle of fairness: it, together with his commitment to the value of autonomy, is presupposed by his theory rather than justified by it.)

It seems to me that such considerations as these ought to make us a bit uncomfortable in assuming *even at the theoretical level* of hypothetical choice situations that all individuals who meet the conditions stipulated by Frankena, Rawls, and Habermas will necessarily agree on the correct set of moral principles. Still, even if we cannot claim that such principles are objective in the sense that they command unanimous intersubjective agreement even within such carefully crafted hypothetical choice situations, it would seem that if we each presented our case to all other individuals under these conditions, it is almost certain that the vast majority of thoughtful, humane individuals would agree with us and not with the right-libertarian. It may also be the case that most people in the real world would agree that the right-libertarian's views simply do not show the proper respect for persons and will wonder how right-libertarians could hold the positions they do.

In the final analysis, perhaps this is really all that we can expect in the way of moral "objectivity." But—it may well be asked—can we claim that our moral principles are *objective* under these circumstances and that those of the right-libertarian are not? If objectivity, as both Hare and Rawls seem to claim, is simply taking all relevant things into consideration and weighing them as impartially as possible, then we would have every right, under these circumstances, to claim such objectivity. On the other hand, right-libertarians—if they really had taken all that is relevant into consideration—could make precisely the same claim. This is perhaps a good reason for not speaking of "objectivity" in evaluative contexts even if we ought to maintain *unanimous intersubjective agreement* as a *regulative ideal*.[52]

Finally, it should be noted here that the Marxist is perhaps in a better position at this point than those who demand that moral principles be "completely objective," in the sense of being indubitable, or who see a nearly unanimous consensus on moral issues as a necessary condition for social change. While individuals entertaining these beliefs may be subject to despair, the Marxist will see here only the inevitable truth of class-divided societies, societies that will be changed by the conscious political action of the vast majority of the downtrodden and oppressed, together with their allies within the middle class, the radical intelligentsia, and even—in the extreme case—within the bourgeoisie itself, all of whom will be set in motion partly by self-interest and partly by the moral outrage to which the capitalist system itself gives rise.

[52] For recent work on moral relativism and moral objectivity, see David B. Wong, *Moral Relativity*, University of California Press, Berkeley, 1984; Bernard Williams, *Ethics and the Limits of Philosophy*; and Milo, *Immorality*.

PART III

MARXISM AND SOCIAL JUSTICE

EIGHT

MARXIST CRITIQUES OF JUSTICE AND RIGHTS

To this point I have argued that both Marx's writings and the Marxist tradition of politics have a moral component and that there are no insuperable difficulties in reconciling this fact with other components of Marxism. If my arguments have been basically correct, there is no insuperable difficulty in reconciling the existence of a Marxist moral component or even a Marxist moral *theory* with: (1) Marx's (supposed) moral historicism, (2) the deterministic features of Marx's theory of historical materialism, (3) Marx's concept and theory of ideology, and (4) the (supposed) Marxist commitment to moral relativism. But even if all of this is true, there is still the question of whether or not Marx's views are compatible with theories (or even the concepts) of social justice and human rights. If it is not, then the hopes of those who wish to develop an adequate Marxist moral and social theory may well be in vain. It is the project of this chapter to show that—contrary to what has been claimed in much recent philosophical literature on the subject—Marxism and concepts and theories of social justice and human rights *are* compatible.

As shown in chapter 1, the most pervasive moral values found in Marx's works from the *Paris Manuscripts* of 1844 onward are freedom (as self-determination), human community, and self-realization. In chapter 3 I argued that Marx is a mixed deontologist as opposed to a utilitarian or any sort of consequentialist, strictly construed, and that he is committed to an equal distribution of freedom or, more specifically, to a maximum system of equal freedom, both negative and positive. Marx's concept of positive freedom, it was argued, includes a right to equal participation in social decision-making processes and a right to equal access to the means of self-realization, where the latter is best construed as an equal opportunity to attain social positions and offices and a genuinely equal opportunity to acquire social primary goods.

But this way of rendering Marx's theory seems inconsistent with his critique of justice and rights, for I have claimed that Marx is not only committed to a general principle of *equal* freedom but that he can be interpreted (or reconstructed) as holding that *people have certain rights*. Furthermore, as Isaiah Berlin points out in a passage quoted in the same chapter, speaking of economic or social freedom makes sense only if we have a *standard of justice* by which to judge what people are entitled to, and thus of what they have been unjustly deprived. For it is only if we believe that individuals are being unjustly deprived of something that we speak of them as not being free to have or acquire it. If we accept this view, then the very fact that Marx is committed to notions of social and economic freedom requires us to account for his implicit commitment to principles of distributive justice as well as human rights.

There is, however, another reason for my giving an account of the compatibility of Marxism and the concepts of justice and rights. I have asserted that an adequate Marxist moral theory must be able to show that *socialism* is morally preferable to *capitalism*, since socialism—but not *communism*—can reasonably be considered a genuine historical possibility. This is so, it was argued, because the superabundance of material goods, which is a precondition for communism, is not likely to come about even if the world socialist revolution is completed. Furthermore, it may be doubted that a full-fledged communist society will come about *even if* the condition of a superabundance of material goods is realized because (1) people will not develop a communist consciousness even under these conditions, as Marx predicted they would, and/or (2) a correct understanding of the concept of material scarcity reveals that even people's time and cooperative behavior are goods; and since such goods must be rationed out in the pursuit of various goals, the condition of material scarcity can never be completely overcome (more on this in chapter 9). In any case, it seems that an adequate Marxist moral theory must contain criteria for deciding between different forms of society embodying the condition of moderate scarcity.

Furthermore, since according to Marx and virtually all other political theorists a *state* must continue to exist as a form of social organization in societies embodying this condition, an adequate Marxist moral theory must be able to provide a moral basis for political authority and political obligation, which, in turn, requires a theory of right and, I believe, a theory of social justice and/or human rights. It seems clear, then, that anyone who wishes to develop an adequate Marxist moral theory should supplement Marx's implicit moral theory with a more well-worked-out theory of right or, more specifically, a theory of social justice and/or human rights. (This does not beg the question against consequentialists, however, since utilitarians or consequentialists may provide such theories without repudiating their view that "the right" is derivable from "the good" and that principles of justice and rights are derivable from a commitment to maximize utility or some other good.)

The problem with this move, of course, is that Marx explicitly rejects it. He attacks concepts and theories of justice and rights on the basis that they are part and parcel of bourgeois ideology and (in "On the Jewish Question") as a sign of the sort of alienation whose elimination he sees as imperative. Furthermore, in his later works he explicitly rejects the thesis that capitalist exploitation is unjust to the workers and, at least implicitly, the notion that socialism is to be preferred to capitalism because it is more just or better able to observe people's rights. Finally, he believes that both concepts will become otiose in a communist society. This presents those wishing to base an adequate Marxist moral and social theory on justice and/or human rights with a dilemma. Either they must give up this attempt or they must show that Marx's criticism of these concepts and theories is in some way faulty. In the present chapter I grasp the second horn of the dilemma and attempt to show that Marx's criticisms of these concepts and of moral theories based on these concepts are not sound, and that there is no *prima facie* difficulty in either explicating Marx's moral views in terms of rights and justice or in basing what can legitimately be called a *Marxist* moral and social theory on these concepts.

But Marx's critique of justice and rights is not simple or unitary. It can, in fact, be broken down into several different kinds of criticisms. One set of criticisms consists in applying his objections to moral concepts and theories in general to the more specific concepts and theories of rights and justice. I shall adduce textual evidence to show this, but I shall not attempt to refute these criticisms since these issues were taken up in chapter 6 with regard to moral principles in general, and there is no essential difference in their application to principles of justice or rights in particular.

A second sort of criticism that can be found in Marx is based on the *specific* characteristics of justice and rights rather than on the

319

generic characteristics they enjoy as members of the moral community (so to speak). One of these specific criticisms is that justice is entirely an internal, juridical concept that is applicable only within the specific social formation of which it is an integral part. On this view, any attempt to apply an "external" principle of justice to a social formation is wrongheaded. Thus any attempt to condemn capitalism as unjustly exploitative is unsound because the standard of justice inherent in bourgeois society is the standard of laissez-faire. Allen W. Wood has recently defended this interpretation of the Marxist view of justice.

Another criticism Marx seems to have of the juridical concepts (i.e., the concepts of rights and justice) is that they are bound to become otiose with the advent of communism since the conditions on which their intelligibility depends—moderate scarcity and moderate egoism—will no longer hold. Robert Tucker was perhaps the first to emphasize this point. Because Tucker and Wood initially focused people's attention on these two Marxist criticisms of justice, the general claim that Marx does not condemn capitalism as unjust or commend socialism as just, and the related (implicit) claim that it is not consistent for Marxists to do so, has become known as the "Tucker-Wood thesis."[1]

In the present chapter I shall first consider Marx's generic criticisms of justice and rights. Then I shall take up his specific criticisms, especially as amplified by such contemporary writers as

[1] The debate over this general thesis has generated quite a lot of literature over the past decade or more. See Chapter 2 ("Marxism and Distributive Justice") in R. Tucker, *The Marxian Revolutionary Idea*; Hancock, "Marx's Theory of Justice"; van de Veer, "Marx's View of Justice"; A. Wood, "The Marxian Critique of Justice" and "Marx on Right and Justice: A Reply to Husami"; Husami, "Marx on Distributive Justice." These three articles can be found in *Marx, Justice, and History* (Marshall Cohen et al., eds.). See also McBride, "The Concept of Justice in Marx, Engels and Others"; Holmstrom, "Exploitation"; G. Young, "Justice and Capitalist Production"; van der Veen, "Property Exploitation, Justice"; Buchanan, "Exploitation, Alienation, and Injustice" and *Marx and Justice: The Radical Critique of Liberalism*; and G. A. Cohen, "Freedom, Justice and Capitalism."

See also the following articles in *Marx and Morality* (Kai Nielsen and Steven C. Patten, eds.): Allen, "Marx and Engels on the Distributive Justice of Capitalism"; G. Young, "Doing Marx Justice"; Buchanan, "The Marxian Critique of Justice and Rights"; and Reiman, "The Possibility of a Marxian Theory of Justice."

More recent contributions to this debate are: A. Wood, "Justice and Class Interests" and "Marx and Equality"; Miller, *Analyzing Marx*, pp. 78–97; Elster, *Making Sense of Marx*, pp. 216–233; Geras, "The Controversy about Marx and Justice"; G. A. Cohen, "Peter Mew on Justice and Capitalism"; and Nielsen, "On the Poverty of Moral Philosophy: Running a Bit with the Tucker-Wood Thesis," "Marx on Justice: The Tucker-Wood Thesis Revisited," "Arguing about Justice," and *Marxism and the Moral Point of View*.

Tucker and Wood. Finally, I shall consider Wood's most recent attempts to show Marxism and justice as incompatible, including his "class interests argument."

Marx's Generic Criticisms of Justice and Rights

As noted throughout this work, but most specifically in the last section of chapter 6, Marx has a number of misconceptions of morality. These include confusions about (1) the meaning of moral terms (taking them to refer to incorporeal entities, for example); (2) the nature of moral justification (assuming, for example, that the fact that people disagree over moral judgments or principles commits one to normative—in addition to metaethical and meta-evaluative—relativism); (3) the function of moral discourse and theorizing (taking them invariably to support the established order, for example); and (4) the relation between morality and moralism (i.e., the doctrine that moral suasion is the primary or an important method of improving the human condition). Note that the latter two views become *misconceptions* only when taken to be defining characteristics of morality. Marx (and Engels) were rightfully wary of morality and moral theorizing because they saw that such practices quite often *do* support the (often immoral) social status quo and that—when taken to be the sole or even an important method of affecting significant social change—they do become ideological in the sense of being importantly misleading. But all of these misconceptions of morality in general have their analogues in Marx's criticisms of justice and rights.

Consider the first misconception: namely, that moral terms refer to "eternal verities" and thus entail idealistic metaphysical assumptions. As shown previously, Marx takes this to be a fault of morality in general, so it is no surprise to find him castigating Proudhon for speaking of "*justice éternelle*." Marx illustrates his objection to this notion by comparing Proudhon's use of it to the use of what he takes to be similar metaphysical entities in the explanations of the natural sciences:

> What opinion should we have of a chemist, who, instead of studying the actual laws of the molecular changes in the composition and decomposition of matter, and on that foundation solving definite problems, claimed to regulate the composition and decomposition of matter by means of the "eternal ideas," of "*naturalité*" and "*affinité*"? Do we really know any

more about "usury," when we say it contradicts "justice *éter-nelle*," "*équité éternelle*," "*mutualité éternelle*," and other "*vérités éternelles*" than the fathers of the church did when they said it was incompatible with "*grâce éternelle*," "*foi éternelle*," and "*la volanté éternelle de Dieu*"?[2]

Part of Marx's criticism of Proudhon here is that he is putting the cart before the horse: he is attempting to explain the economic structure and laws of society in terms of the concept of justice, whereas (in reality) it is the latter that must be explained by the former. "*Justice éternelle*" is a juridical relation arising from the very economic structures he proposes to explain. In attempting to *explain* economic phenomena by moral principles, Proudhon has, on Marx's view, reversed cause and effect. Nevertheless, there seems little doubt that Marx also found such notions as "justice éternelle" *metaphysically* suspect and that this is, in fact, the primary reason that they cannot be part of a legitimate explanation of natural or social phenomena or even the basis of an evaluative theory.

The second sort of generic objection Marx has to justice and rights is based on his misconception concerning the nature of justification of moral judgments, principles, and theories. On this misconception, actual disagreement about which moral judgments, principles, or theories are justified makes untenable the view that some of them are justified, while others are not. During his polemic against the Lassalean demand that principles of justice be included in the Gotha Program, for example, Marx notes that not only do bourgeois and socialist theorists differ on the appropriate principles of justice but that socialist theorists differ among themselves. "What is 'a fair distribution?' " Marx asks. "Do not the bourgeois assert that the present-day distribution is 'fair?'. . . . Have not also the socialist sectarians the most varied notions about 'fair' distribution?"[3] The inference Marx seems to draw from such examples is that there is no sense in which one principle of justice can be better justified than another. As we have seen, however, this direct inference is no better than inferring that there is no sense in which the judgment that the earth is round (or an oblong spheroid) can be better grounded or justified than the judgment that it is flat. Mere disagreement in morals does not automatically preclude that some positions can, in some sense, be better justified than others. Furthermore, this line of reasoning would seem to lead to either ethical skepticism or normative ethical relativism,

[2] Marx, *Capital*, vol. 1, pp. 84–85
[3] Marx, "Critique of the Gotha Program," p. 385.

both of which are fatal for any political program. All political programs are based on normative political positions, which, in turn, are based both on empirical theories and moral (or at least normative) judgments and principles. Hence, it is not a line of reasoning a Marxist (or anyone else endorsing political positions) can consistently pursue.

Marx's third generic criticism of justice and rights is based on his misconception that *all* moral theories are ideological in the sense that they *invariably* and *necessarily* support the social status quo. This criticism can be found at various points in his works. For example, he describes the bourgeois description of the surface (exchange) structure of capitalism—which he sees as one of the most pernicious ideological defenses of the bourgeois social status quo—as "a very Eden of the innate rights of man. There alone rule Freedom, Equality, Property, and Bentham."[4] Although it can be quite plausibly maintained that, in fact, only certain (e.g., bourgeois) ideas of freedom, equality, property, and rights are ideological, Marx seems to believe that at least the *juridical* concepts (i.e., justice and rights) are inevitably ideological in this sense. As argued in chapter 6 of the present work, however, neither morality in general nor the notions of justice and rights in particular would inevitably seem to meet one or more of the characteristics that make views or theories ideological.

Turning to the fourth sort of misconception, we can observe in "Critique of the Gotha Program" that Marx believes the employment of such juridical concepts as a means of effecting significant social change has the same pernicious consequences as employing other moral concepts or principles in this way. He states that

> I have dealt . . . at length with . . . "equal right" and "fair distribution" . . . in order to show what a crime it is to attempt . . . to force on our Party again, as dogmas, ideas which . . . have now become obsolete verbal rubbish, . . . again perverting . . . the realistic outlook, which it cost so much effort to instill into the Party but which has now taken root in it, by means of ideological nonsense about right and other trash so common among the democrats and French Socialists.[5]

Although, again, it can be plausibly argued that it is only *some* concepts or theories of justice and rights that have the pernicious effects Marx was concerned to combat, he seems to indict *all* jurid-

[4] Marx, *Capital*, vol. 1, p. 176.
[5] Marx, "Critique of the Gotha Program," p. 388.

ical concepts—as well as moral concepts generally—on these grounds. But, as noted elsewhere, to assert that people have certain rights or that certain principles of justice ought to be implemented and upheld is not necessarily to commit oneself to the thesis that the promulgation of such principles can or will be effective instruments of social change. (On the other hand, if one seriously held this view, one would certainly not fight for including them in a political program—on grounds of efficient use of political resources, if no other.)

Having argued that Marx's *general* objections to moral principles as applied to justice and rights are not decisive, let us inquire into his second type of criticism: that certain unique features of the concepts of justice and rights make them especially objectionable. As noted above, a criticism Marx has of *both justice and rights* is that they will be otiose with the evolution of socialism into communism. A criticism he has of *justice* is that standards of justice are internal to societies, which therefore can be judged only by their own internal standards of justice, not by any other. A criticism he has of *rights* is that they embody or presuppose the model of man as the egoistic individual of civil society. Let us take up the last criticism first.

Marx on Rights as Part of the Egoistic Image of Man

Although sometimes Marx seems to be objecting to only *bourgeois rights* rather than all rights or the concept of rights in general, there is—at least in his early works—a more radical critique in which all rights are to be rejected. In his 1843 polemical essay against Bruno Bauer ("On the Jewish Question"), he writes:

> None of the supposed rights of man . . . go beyond the egoistic man, man as he is, as a member of civil society; that is, an individual separated from the community, withdrawn into himself, wholly preoccupied with his private interest and acting in accordance with his private caprice. Man is far from being considered, in the rights of man, as a species-being; on the contrary, species-life itself—society—appears as a system which is external to the individual and as a limitation of his original independence. The only bond between men is natural necessity, need and private interest, the preservation of their property and their egoistic persons.[6]

[6] Marx, "On the Jewish Question," p. 27.

Since rights are integrally related to the conception of man as the egoistic individual, according to Marx, even their complete realization (i.e., *political emancipation*) will not result in genuine *human emancipation*. Human emancipation is release *from* the condition of being an egoistic individual, not emancipation of some sort *within* this condition. This critique of rights is, of course, intimately related to another of his specific criticisms of juridical concepts listed above, namely, the claim that such concepts will become otiose with the evolution of communist society. The reason, on Marx's view, is, in part, precisely because the egoistic individual of capitalism will have become transformed into the autonomous but communal individual of communism. (The other reason is that Hume's second condition of justice—moderate scarcity—will also be eliminated.)

There are two problems with this general indictment of rights. The first is its relevance. It may be doubted that full-fledged communism and the communist individual as Marx conceives them will ever evolve. Even if it is thought that they will, or might, evolve, there is the problem that Marx seems to leave no room for the concept of rights in the societies in which human beings will exist until the advent of such an ideal society. The problem here is that since the first stage of communism (i.e., socialism) will bear the birthmarks of the old society for quite some time—as Marx admits—there is a need for rights principles during this period.

Second, by tying the concept of rights so closely to that of the egoistic individual, Marx may have misinterpreted the concept, or at least not have allowed for the possibility of a more attractive conception of rights. As Allen E. Buchanan notes:

> Put most simply, the main defect of Marx's attack on rights is that he fails to see that there can be a vital need for a concept [of rights] . . . even where egoism and class divisions are not the only or even the main sources of conflict.[7]

According to the radical interpretation, Marx thought of rights exclusively as boundary markers which separate competing egoists in circumstances of avoidably severe scarcity, which absolve them of responsibility for each other's good, and which, through the coercive guarantees of the state, keep class conflict from erupting into outright war, while at the same time helping to preserve the dominant class's control

[7] Buchanan, *Marx and Justice*, p. 165.

over the means of production. Marx apparently thought that these are the defining functions of rights and hence that a conception of rights is needed only to cope with such egoistic conflict in class-divided societies. . . . he failed to consider the need for a different—and more attractive—conception of rights, grounded in a broader understanding of the sorts of conflicts which are to be dealt with by the invocation of rights and which admits the possibility that there are different rights in different socio-historical circumstances.[8]

A more attractive conception of rights, from a Marxist point of view, might be one that would countenance all of the rights—or at least all of the *kinds* of rights—found in the United Nations' Universal Declaration of Human Rights. Although Classical Liberals and right-libertarians are sure to object to the "positive" rights contained in this document, since they maintain that only "negative" rights (i.e., rights not to be interfered with) are *genuine rights*, it is surely arguable that J. S. Mill is correct in his analysis:

> When we call anything a person's right, we mean that he has a valid claim on society to protect him in the possession of it, either by the force of law, or by that of education and opinion. If he has what we consider a sufficient claim, on whatever account, to have something guaranteed to him by society, we say that he has a right to it. . . . To have a right, then, is . . . to have something which society ought to defend me in the possession of.[9]

There is certainly nothing in this analysis of *rights* as *valid claims resulting in entitlements* that necessarily limits them to "negative" as opposed to "positive" rights. The question, in this analysis, is not what "rights" someone or other intuits as "natural," but which moral principles are to be used in the validation of claims. If modern humanists—liberals as well as socialists—are correct in asserting that justice demands more than simple protection from force, theft, and fraud, then it can be plausibly argued that we have positive as well as negative rights. It can be argued that we have rights to well-being (e.g., the right to a minimum standard of well-being even if we are incapable of earning a living) and procedural rights (e.g., the right to legal counsel during a trial even if

[8] Ibid., p. 163.
[9] J. S. Mill, "Utilitarianism," p. 238.

we cannot afford it), as well as rights to noninterference (e.g., the right to free speech).[10]

Be that as it may, in his later works many of Marx's criticisms of rights can be taken as criticisms not of rights in general but of *bourgeois* conceptions of rights. In *The Eighteenth Brumaire of Louis Bonaparte*, for example, Marx is *not critical* of "the . . . general staff of the liberties of 1848, personal liberty, liberty of the press, of speech, of association, of assembly, of education and of religion, etc."[11] In fact, he expresses regret that later in the course of the Revolution of 1848 "the right of association—one of the most essential of the political victories of the February days—was abolished."[12] Rather, he is critical of the fact that in reality "all those liberties [are] regulated in such a way that the bourgeoisie in its enjoyment of them does not come into collision with the equal rights of the other classes."[13]

Engels also attacks bourgeois conceptions of rights on the grounds that they are not realized:

> Nowadays . . . equality of rights is recognized—recognized in words, since the bourgeoisie, in its fight against feudalism and in the development of capitalist production, was compelled to abolish all privileges of estate, i.e., personal privileges, and to introduce the equality of all individuals before the law, first in the sphere of private law, then gradually also in the sphere of state law. But the urge toward happiness thrives only to a trivial extent on ideal rights. To the greatest extent of all it thrives on material means; and capitalist production takes care to insure that the great majority of those with equal rights shall get only what is essential for bare existence. Capitalist production has therefore little more respect if indeed any more, for the equal "right to the pursuit of happiness" of the majority than had slavery or serfdom.[14]

Some Marx scholars, in fact, have interpreted Marx's critique of rights as consisting *only* of this criticism. John Plamenatz, for example, claims:

---

[10] This is not to say that there are no problems with developing such a conception of rights. But for an initial defense of such a conception, see my "A Defense of Rights to Well-Being."

[11] Marx, *The Eighteenth Brumaire of Louis Bonaparte*, p. 447.

[12] Ibid., p. 468.

[13] Ibid., p. 447.

[14] Engels, *Ludwig Feuerbach*, p. 39.

As a matter of fact, Marx himself believed in the rights of man. If he had been asked whether men ought to enjoy these rights, or whether they would eventually come to enjoy them, he would have said that they ought and would.

He merely thought that, society being what it was in the eighteenth and nineteenth centuries, only the property-owning classes could in fact enjoy the rights. These classes, though often willing to concede that all men should enjoy the rights, were determined to preserve a system of property which, in Marx's opinion, made it impossible for most men to enjoy them. As he saw it, they falsely believed that these rights could be enjoyed by all classes in a class society, whereas the truth was that they could be enjoyed by all men only in a classless society.[15]

If these are Marx's only criticism of rights, it might be argued— at least in his later works—that he is not really opposed to rights per se but only to certain rights (e.g., the bourgeois right to property), and to what, paraphrasing Rawls, we might call the divergence between *equality of rights* and *equality in the worth of rights* (i.e., equality in the ability to utilize or enjoy rights). But one could easily agree with both theses without objecting to rights per se. One need only claim that certain purported moral rights (e.g., the right to own and control productive as well as personal property) are not moral rights at all and that though a conceptual distinction can be made between rights and the ability to enjoy rights, justice requires not only equality of rights but *at least approximate equality* in the opportunity of persons to enjoy the rights they have (more on this in chapter 9).

These alterations in the standard liberal conception and theory of rights would go a long way, it seems, toward embodying the Marxist's more radically egalitarian moral intuitions. They would also go a long way toward allowing one legitimately to reinterpret Marx's moral theory as being based on the right to a maximum system of equal freedoms (both positive and negative) and to ground the right to equal participation in social decision-making processes and the right to equal access to the means of self-realization.

[15] Plamenatz, *Man and Society*, vol. 2, p. 333. See also Betty A. Sichel, "Karl Marx and the Rights of Man," *Philosophy and Phenomenological Research*, vol. 32, no. 3 (March 1972).

Marx on the Dissolution of Juridical Notions with the Advent of Communism

Another of Marx's specific criticisms of justice and rights is that such notions are bound to become outmoded. He envisions the higher stage of communism as a stateless and coercionless form of social cooperation based on material abundance and the social ownership and control of productive property and providing for the all-around and full development of the individual. Marx apparently believes that conflict within such a society will be so minimized that the practice of individuals asserting claims against each other will become otiose: there simply will be no need for it. Since this is precisely the practice on which the very concepts of justice and rights are based, they, too, in Marx's view, will become otiose. As he puts it in "Critique of the Gotha Program":

> In a higher phase of communist society, after the enslaving subordination of the individual to the division of labour, and therewith also the antithesis between mental and physical labour, has vanished; after labour has become not only a means of life but life's prime want; after the productive forces have also increased with the all-around development of the individual, and all the springs of cooperative wealth flow more abundantly—only then can the narrow horizon of bourgeois right be crossed in its entirety and society inscribe on its banner: From each according to his ability, to each according to his needs![16]

The "narrow horizon of bourgeois right" can be crossed because Hume's conditions of justice—moderate scarcity and moderate egoism—will both be superseded. But what is the relevance of this view as a part of Marx's critique of juridical moral concepts (i.e., justice and rights)? The answer to this question is far from clear. One perfectly reasonable response to this claim, even from a Marxist point of view, would seem to be: "So what! For the foreseeable future we must deal with societies that have not yet crossed this 'narrow horizon,' for this includes even what you [Marx] call the 'first stage of communism' and what today we commonly call 'socialism'! The point is that *for all practical political purposes* this thesis is, quite simply, *irrelevant*." The belief that Hume's conditions of

---

[16] Marx, "Critique of the Gotha Program," p. 388.

329

justice would be transcended in the not-too-distant future may help explain why Marx had such disregard for the concepts of justice and rights, but it is far from clear that this is a decisive critique of these concepts. But since he thought the very concepts of justice and rights were soon to become completely obsolete, it is small wonder he held that concentrating on developing a theory based on these concepts was—at the very least—a misdirection of one's energies.

In part, of course, Marx's attitude toward these juridical concepts was the result of an overly optimistic assessment of the speed and degree with which the world socialist revolution would take place and, quite possibly, also the speed and degree with which conditions of scarcity can and will disappear, *even if* capitalist property relations give way to socialist property relations on a worldwide scale. Today, however, it seems that no matter what portion of Marx's empirical theory we accept, we are no longer in a position to accept the thesis that the condition of relative scarcity will cease to hold at some point in the *near* future *even if* the world socialist revolution succeeds. Furthermore, even if full-fledged communism is a utopian impossibility, would not Marxists want to claim that socialism (i.e., the first stage of communism) is superior to any form of capitalism? Would they not also want to have principles of justice and rights by which to judge such a society against other possible societies (e.g., capitalism), as well as by which to judge that society itself? The answer to these questions would seem to be yes!

Marxists presumably will want to claim, for example, that the government of a (democratic) socialist society is *legitimate* and ought to be supported, i.e., that except under exceptional circumstances we would have an obligation or duty to obey its statutes and laws. But how can one claim that a government or society is legitimate and deserves our loyalty (i.e., that it has *legitimate political authority*) without some sort of notion of justice (at least in those possible social worlds in which scarcity is still a problem).

But there is another point to be made here: a conception and theory of justice may be needed even in a society of material "superabundance" populated by individuals instantiating what Marx calls "social," "communal," "species," or "communist" consciousness. Allen E. Buchanan has some extremely insightful remarks on this topic. First he points out that competition and conflict may not necessarily be *completely eliminated* even in such a full-fledged communist society, though they may be greatly reduced.

There is no compelling reason to believe that significant divergences between the good of the individual and that of others or of society as a whole occur only as the result of egoistic interaction under conditions of class struggle for control over the means of production. Even in a society of thorough-going altruists in which no group has exclusive control over the means of production, there may be violent disagreements over what the common good is and over how it is to be achieved. And insofar as different individuals support or even identify with competing conceptions of the common good and of the path to its attainment, the interests of individuals will conflict, even though the conflict will not be egoistic or class-based.[17]

Buchanan, however, offers an even more radical thesis, namely, that Marxists have underestimated the problem of scarcity—and thus the need for juridical concepts and practices—because they have not realized the extent of the difficulty of allocating scarce social goods in the broadest sense of this term.

The concept of scarcity relevant to the comparison of social systems and to the idea of the circumstances of justice is the most general one imaginable. Scarcity exists wherever the choice of one line of individual or joint action precludes the pursuit of alternatives which are in any way valued. In this sense, not only coal and oil and foodstuffs are scarce but also cooperative activity and time itself. Hence so long as an individual or a group must decide to use some natural and social resources rather than others in pursuit of some ends rather than others, there is scarcity. In a word, the need to choose implies scarcity. The question then is not whether communism will abolish scarcity, but rather whether the problems of scarcity in communism will be radically different.[18]

The benefit of bringing Marxist moral theory into line with such commonly accepted concepts as social justice and human rights is, therefore, not to be underestimated. The incorporation of these concepts into the Marxist worldview is, in fact, essential. Furthermore, although you wouldn't know it by reading many of the contemporary commentaries on the relation between Marx's views and distributive justice, since they emphasize their supposed in-

---

[17] Buchanan, *Marx and Justice*, p. 167.
[18] Ibid., pp. 169–170.

compatibility, Marx does implicitly espouse a principle of distributive justice for governing the distribution of the consumable social product in a socialist society. Due to the fact that the initial or lower stage of communism has, *ex hypothesi*, not reached material abundance, together with the fact that, *ex hypothesi*, individuals have not been completely transformed into socially minded, "truly human" beings, the norm of distribution, according to Marx, is still the bourgeois norm of "equal pay for equal work."

> The individual producer receives back from society—after the deductions have been made—exactly what he gives to it. What he has given to it is his individual quantum of labour. For example, the social working day consists of the sum of the individual hours of work; the individual labour time of the individual producer is the part of the social working day contributed by him, his share in it. He receives a certificate from society that he has furnished such and such an amount of labour (after deducting his labour for the common funds), and with this certificate he draws from the social stock of means of consumption as much as costs the same amount of labour. The same amount of labour which he has given to society in one form he receives back in another.
>
> Here obviously the same principle prevails as that which regulates the exchange of commodities, as far as this is exchange of equal values. Content and form are changed, because under the altered circumstances no one can give anything except his labour, and because, on the other hand, nothing can pass to the ownership of individuals except individual means of consumption. But, as far as the distribution of the latter among the individual producers is concerned, the same principle prevails as in the exchange of commodity equivalents: a given amount of labour in one form is exchanged for an equal amount of labour in another form.
>
> Hence *equal right* here is still in principle *bourgeois right*, although principle and practice are no longer at loggerheads.[19]

Does Marx wax apologetic here, one might wonder, as he does in his letter to Engels concerning his proposed standards of equal rights and justice for the International Working Men's Association? There is no sign that he does. As a matter of fact, the only

[19] Marx, "Critique of the Gotha Program," p. 387.

thing that seems to bother Marx about this proposal is that it may not turn out to be *truly* equal or fair. He claims:

> In spite of this advance, this *equal right* is still constantly stigmatised by a bourgeois limitation. The right of the producers is *proportional* to the labour they supply; the equality consists in the fact that measurement is made with an *equal standard*, labour.
>
> But one man is superior to another physically or mentally and so supplies more labour in the same time, or can labour for a longer time; and labour, to serve as a measure, must be defined by its duration or intensity, otherwise it ceases to be a standard of measurement. This *equal* right is an unequal right for unequal labour. It recognises no class differences, because everyone is only a worker like everyone else; but it tacitly recognises unequal individual endowment and thus productive capacity as natural privileges. It *is, therefore, a right of inequality, in its content, like every right.* . . . Further, one worker is married, another not; one has more children than another, and so on and so forth. Thus, with an equal performance of labour, and hence an equal share in the social consumption fund, one will in fact receive more than another, one will be richer than another, and so on. To avoid these defects, right instead of being equal would have to be unequal.[20]

This standard of distribution, Marx claims, is not fair because it allows those with "natural privileges" to capitalize on them and thus garner a greater share of the social wealth. Notice, however, that Marx (or anyone else) would have such a worry only if they accepted the underlying principle that people are entitled only to what they deserve and that *no one deserves the natural advantages they are born with*. (Rawls makes a similar point when he speaks about the "natural lottery" and claims that the fact that one does better or worse in it is—or at least should be—morally irrelevant.)

Second, it is not fair according to Marx because it does not take into consideration *differentials of need*. This is presumably the point he is making in comparing one worker who has a family with another who doesn't. He claims that the worker without a family is "richer" even if both have the same income because the worker with a family has more "needs," namely, providing for the mem-

[20] Ibid., pp. 387–388.

bers of his family. Now this may not be a very plausible case for the point Marx is trying to make since it could very well be maintained that their "needs"—so long as they are both healthy, etc.— are *not* different and, further, that neither is "richer" than the other but, rather, that one has chosen to spend his income in one way (for a family) and the other in another. A better case to illustrate this concern would be one in which the two workers receive equal pay but one has a need or needs that are (1) vital to his wellbeing, (2) very expensive to meet, and (3) nonvoluntarily acquired. The case of two workers of equal income, one healthy and one having kidney disease requiring dialysis (for which he must pay), would serve as a good example in today's world.

Nevertheless, the concern Marx evinces here is a very common one in theories of justice: how to take differential need into consideration. The point is that he *is* concerned—very genuinely concerned—with *equality* and with what we would commonly call *distributive justice* in these passages. This would seem to prove that even Marx saw this critique of justice and rights as destined to be otiose in future communist society as an irrelevant objection for practical purposes of dealing with present-day and even socialist societies.

Marx's Conception of Justice as an Internal Standard of Social Systems

Even in the face of all this evidence (and more), there are still those who insist that Marx did not condemn capitalism as unjust or advocate socialism because it is more just than capitalism. On Robert Tucker's interpretation of Marx, "the only applicable norm of what is right and just is the one inherent in the existing economic system. Each mode of production has its own mode of distribution and its own form of equity, and it is meaningless to pass judgment on it from some other point of view."[21] Allen Wood concurs. In his seminal article on this issue ("The Marxian Critique of Justice") he attributes to Marx and defends the view that juridical practices and principles are "rationally valid" if, and only if, they correspond to (and thus stabilize and/or promote) the prevailing mode of production. Consequently, justice is not a standard by which human actions and social institutions can be measured: it is a standard by which each mode of production measures itself. This means that slavery is *necessarily* just in a slave society (but unjust

[21] R. Tucker, *The Marxian Revolutionary Idea*, p. 46.

in feudal or capitalist societies), and that capitalist exploitation is *necessarily* just in a capitalist society (and unjust in noncapitalist societies).

Although these consequences would seem to constitute a reductio ad absurdum of this view of justice, Wood and others have aggressively defended it both as a correct interpretation of Marx and as a correct analysis of justice and juridical moral concepts in general. In the present section, I shall concentrate on this view as an interpretation of Marx. In the following section, I shall take up Wood's attempts to defend this analysis of justice as correct.

The passages on which this interpretation of Marx is based are primarily of two sorts: (1) those in which he asserts that the exploitation of the worker by the capitalist is no injustice to the worker, and (2) those in which the thesis that one cannot use juridical concepts to critique the entire system of which it is a part is stated in abstract, general terms. Turning to the first group of passages, we find Marx claiming the following of the capitalist and worker as buyer and seller of labor-power in *Capital*:

> The circumstance, that on the one hand the daily sustenance of labour-power costs only half a day's labour, while on the other hand the very same labour-power can work during a whole day, that consequently the value which its use during one day creates, is double what he pays for that use, this circumstance is, without doubt, a piece of good luck for the buyer, but *by no means an injury to the seller* [emphasis added].[22]

> The capitalist maintains his *rights as a purchaser* when he tries to make the working-day as long as possible, and to make, whenever possible, two working-days out of one. On the other hand, the peculiar nature of the commodity sold implies a limit to its consumption by the purchaser, and the labourer maintains his *right as seller* when he wishes to reduce the working-day to one of definite normal duration. There is here, therefore, an antinomy, *right against right, both equally bearing the seal of the law of exchanges. Between equal rights force decides* [emphasis added].[23]

Let us ignore for the moment the possible contradiction between these two passages in that the first asserts that the nature of the relation between capital and labor is "by no means an injury" to

[22] Marx, *Capital*, vol. 1, p. 194.
[23] Ibid., p. 235.

335

the worker, and the second would seem to indicate that the relation *is* an injury to the worker in that the *worker's right* (presumably to receive back the full value of the products he produces)—though under the circumstances not an enforceable right—is violated by this relationship. Let us look, instead, at a few passages that make clear the general principle behind Marx's refusal to condemn capitalist production relations as unjust. In "Critique of the Gotha Program," he claims that "right can never be higher than the economic structure of society and its cultural development conditioned thereby."[24] This claim is further explicated in the third volume of *Capital*, where Marx claims that the content of the rules governing economic exchange "is *just* whenever it *corresponds, is appropriate to the mode of production*. It is *unjust* whenever it *contradicts that mode*. Slavery on the basis of capitalist production is unjust; likewise fraud in the quality of commodities" [emphasis added].[25]

How seriously we should take Marx to be making a *normative, moral* claim as opposed to a *factual, empirical* one is the key consideration here. While Tucker, Wood, and others see him as making a genuine normative claim—by disallowing the claim that capitalism is unjust on these grounds—this seems to me extremely dubious. It seems to me that rather than taking a normative position here, Marx is really taking an *internal point of view* with respect to capitalism, but an *external point of view* with respect to his own standards, and then *reporting* certain facts about how capitalism is to be judged from its own operational normative standards. He is really simply pointing out that by the rules of the game it has set up, so to speak, capitalism is not unjust.

To get at the distinction I am making here, let us consider an analogous case. In anthropology and ethnology, taking the internal point of view in reporting on a culture or society is called taking the "emic"—rather than the "etic"—point of view with respect to that culture or society. An analogous case, therefore, would be an anthropologist insisting that the Yanomamo Indians of the Amazon do nothing morally wrong to individuals in neighboring villages when they brutally ambush and murder them in the jungle, nor to their own wives when the husbands savagely beat them, since both sorts of activities are tolerated—rather than condemned—in Yanomamo society. Now, given the fact that many

[24] Marx, "Critique of the Gotha Program," p. 388.
[25] Marx, *Capital*, vol. 3, p. 340.

people—including many anthropologists and ethnologists—are not cognizant of the distinctions between the various forms of "ethical relativism"—descriptive, normative, metaethical, and (according to one, at any rate) metaevaluative—we might have an extremely difficult time convincing the anthropologist in question that he doesn't *really* believe that the Yanomamo do nothing morally wrong when they engage in these activities. However, if both of us were patient and persistent enough, I believe that we could convince him—assuming he is not a psychopath or a sociopath— that he doesn't *really* think that it is morally permissible for people to do such things to one another and, further, that what he is really doing in saying that the Yanomamo do no wrong when they engage in these activities is *taking the point of view of the Yanomamo in reporting on their activities rather than making a moral judgment.*

If we were able to explain in sufficient detail the distinctions between descriptive, normative, and (at least) metaethical relativism and convince the anthropologist that moral judgments and principles are *universalizable* and, thus, that one cannot *really* be a *normative* ethical relativist, then the anthropologist would come to see that he does not really want to claim that the Yanomamo men do nothing morally wrong when ambushing others or savagely beating their wives, as opposed to claiming that they do not *perceive themselves to be doing wrong.* It could then be pointed out to our anthropological interlocutor that the second claim is not equivalent to and does not entail the first: we do not, for example, accept the claim that a cold-blooded mass murderer has done nothing wrong simply because he is cold-blooded and thus does not perceive himself as having done anything morally wrong. (Whether or not and to what extent he should be punished for his moral wrongdoing is, of course, a separate issue involving other considerations, e.g., the person's sanity and, perhaps, moral "knowledge" and "ignorance.")[26]

---

[26] As Ronald Milo writes in his excellent work, *Immorality:* "Wickedness seems less reprehensible when we conceive of the agent as failing to believe that what he does is wrong and believing instead that it is right. For, in this case, although he willingly does something that is morally wrong, he does not willingly do something that he believes is morally wrong. Although he knowingly and intentionally does what he does (e.g., he steals or refuses to prevent a death) and although this is something that is morally wrong, he does not knowingly and intentionally do it under the description of its being a morally wrong act" (p. 251). "The most serious and blameworthy kind of wrongdoing consists in the agent's deliberately doing something that he himself believes to be morally wrong, either because he prefers this to sacrificing some other end or because he simply does not care if what he does is morally wrong" (pp. 256–257).

Once the anthropologist came to realize that he was judging the Yanomamo's practices from a point of view *internal* to them but *external to his own values*, and that only judgments made from the latter point of view are normative or moral judgments, he would be much less likely to claim that what the Yanomamo were doing to one another is not morally wrong. This is perfectly compatible, of course, with being a *metaethical* or *metaevaluative* relativist in the sense of holding the view that there may be no way to convince even a perfectly rational Yanomamo that what he is doing is morally wrong, as well as a "cultural liberal" in the sense of wanting to maintain a great degree of leniency and tolerance in dealing with other cultures.

In the same sense, I believe that if Marx were alive today and had the patience and good grace to go over these distinctions with us, he, too, would come to see that his claims—that the capitalist does the worker no injustice and that capitalism is not unjust—are being made from a point of view *internal* to the capitalist system but *external* to his own considered normative point of view. If this analysis is basically correct, however, the Tucker-Wood thesis is not nearly so serious as may have first appeared. At first glance it seemed to entail that Marx's considered normative judgment is that capitalism is not unjust; but if the above analysis is correct, Marx is not really making a *normative* judgment at all in the passages quoted. Given this fact, some interpreters of Marx assume that he must have been speaking in an ironic, tongue-in-cheek or inverted-comma sense whenever he speaks of capitalist exploitation being just. Ziyad I. Husami, for example, criticizes Wood for missing Marx's "ironic tone" in the passages in which he claims that capitalist exploitation is just.[27] Richard Arneson takes the same position:

> It is true that Marx occasionally seems to characterize as "just" aspects of capitalism that strike us and him as fairly horrible. But when Marx uses terms of moral evaluation he is often employing them in what has been called the inverted-comma use, and this is almost invariably so when characterizations of justice are being mooted: that is, Marx's "this is just" can almost always appropriately be rendered "this is what is called just."[28]

[27] See Husami, "Marx on Distributive Justice," pp. 52–53.
[28] Arneson, "What's Wrong with Exploitation?," pp. 217–218.

Nancy Holmstrom makes essentially the same point when she claims that, from a Marxist point of view, "calling [the exchange between capitalist and worker] a just exchange could only be done tongue-in-cheek, or to mean: 'This is [erroneously] taken to be just.' "[29]

In fact, Marx occasionally supplies the inverted commas himself—for example, around the word "fair" at certain points in "Critique of the Gotha Program." And, as Arneson notes, "In other places, context and sense make it plain that the inverted comma sense of a moral term is intended."[30] But it does not seem that Marx is being ironic in *all* of the passages in question. The presumption being made by proponents of the position that he is always ironic in such contexts is that since he did not really believe capitalism to be just, he must be speaking ironically when he says it is. But in order for Marx to have been making these claims in an ironic or tongue-in-cheek fashion, he would—by definition, I presume—have had to be conscious of doing so. Thus there is another possibility: he may not have been fully cognizant (or conscious) of this inconsistency. If this is so, then it is possible that he did not really believe capitalism just *and* that sometimes he was *not* speaking ironically when he claimed that it was. On this interpretation, as G. A. Cohen puts it, Marx "must be treated as someone who thinks capitalism is unjust, even if he does not realize that he thinks it is."[31] Norman Geras concurs with Cohen's assessment when he states that "Marx did think capitalism unjust but he did not think he thought so."[32]

Although we tend to give great thinkers the benefit of the doubt when faced with obvious inconsistencies in their writings and thus usually attempt to explain them away in one way or another, there are cases in which it is more reasonable to assume that they really are enmeshed in such obvious inconsistencies. I believe this is probably such a case. Due to his various confusions about morality in general and the juridical notions of justice and rights in particular, Marx seems to have explicitly held capitalist exploitation to be just while implicitly condemning it as unjust. And, as Jon Elster is fond of pointing out, Marx can at times be maddeningly inconsistent—perhaps more so than most great thinkers. As to the issue at hand, I agree with Elster that "no interpretation of Marx's vari-

---

[29] Holmstrom, "Exploitation," p. 368.
[30] Arneson, "What's Wrong with Exploitation?" p. 218, note.
[31] G. A. Cohen, "Review of *Karl Marx* by Allen W. Wood," p. 443.
[32] Geras, "The Controversy about Marx and Justice," p. 70.

ous remarks on justice and rights can make them all consistent with one another."[33]

But just because Marx was enmeshed in such confusions and inconsistencies does not mean that contemporary Marxists have to be. Above all, just because Marx explicitly refuses to condemn capitalism as unjust does not mean that contemporary Marxists ought to follow suit. Next, however, we shall consider some arguments by Allen Wood to the contrary.

Class Interests and Social Justice: A Critique of Wood

Allen Wood not only interprets Marx as unquestionably holding the position that capitalism cannot be condemned on grounds of justice (or rights) but insists that we should maintain the same position today. As to the interpretive issue, Wood states:

> It is simply not the case that Marx's condemnation of capitalism rests on some conception of justice (whether explicit or implicit), and those who attempt to reconstruct a 'Marxian idea of justice' from Marx's manifold charges against capitalism are at best only translating Marx's critique of capitalism, or some aspect of it, into what Marx himself would have consistently regarded as a false, ideological or 'mystified' form.[34]

But Wood also offers a number of arguments against accepting principles of justice, or at least against Marxists accepting such principles. Since in some ways his attack on justice is just an extension of his various criticisms of morality in general, I shall first briefly review these criticisms and what I consider to be their refutations (as expressed at earlier points in the present work). Then I shall consider Wood's main arguments against justice per se: (1) the argument stemming from his quasi-Hegelian conception of justice (which he imputes to Marx), and (2) his so-called "class interest argument." I hope to show that neither is sound.

Since justice—along with obligation, duty, fairness, and rights— is, for Wood, a moral good par excellence, it is open to all of his criticisms of morality per se. These are: (1) morality is ideological because (2) it subverts our self-understanding and understanding of social reality, and (3) it always serves the function of preserving the social status quo. Wood also holds that (4) morality demands an impartial treatment of everyone's interests, regardless of class,

---

[33] Elster, *Making Sense of Marx*, p. 230.
[34] A. Wood, "The Marxian Critique of Justice," p. 272.

and (5) morality can have no rational basis or justification outside of reference to its functional role in a particular social system.

Let us consider the first criticism. "Morality is a form of ideology,"[35] according to Wood. "Morality . . . is necessarily ideological in the characteristically Marxian sense of the term."[36] The first ground on which morality is ideological, according to Wood, is that "morality fundamentally subverts the self-understanding of every individual who follows it, whatever the class position of that individual may be."[37] Apparently this is, in part, because as "Nietzsche and Freud have helped us to realize . . . morality . . . is bound up with neuroses and self-destructive impulses."[38] More importantly, for Wood, even though "objective moral norms represent the demands of the current social order,"[39] they tend to be accepted by all classes within that order and thus "to the oppressed classes, morality represents as rationally fulfilling a course of conduct which is in fact directly opposed to their interests."[40] Thus members of the oppressed classes are misled concerning their own interests or at least how best to fulfill their interests. But

> even to the members of the ruling class, who benefit from the system of conduct the norms enjoin, the demands of morality are deceptive and subversive of rationality. For while these norms in fact represent the class interests of such people, morality claims to represent something quite different, something exalted and sublime, a universal interest to which each subject is bound not by ties of class interest or empirical solidarity, but solely by ties of impartial and objective rationality.[41]

(We shall consider Wood's "impartiality criticism" of morality presently.)

A second (and closely related) ground on which morality is ideological, according to Wood, is that "morality . . . is an essentially conservative institution,"[42] that is, "morality [serves] an exclusively conservative social function."[43] This is because "objective

[35] A. Wood, "Marx's Immoralism," p. 688.
[36] Ibid.
[37] Ibid., p. 687.
[38] Ibid., p. 698.
[39] Ibid., p. 687.
[40] Ibid.
[41] Ibid.
[42] A. Wood, "Justice and Class Interests," p. 10.
[43] Ibid., p. 11.

moral norms" (i.e., norms that are accepted by and large in a society) are those that "represent the needs of the prevailing mode of production."[44] This is especially true of juridical principles. Wood holds, in fact, that acts or institutions are just *only if* they support the social status quo (more on this presently).

Adverting to my criteria for being ideological in chapter 6, we can see that Wood is claiming that all morality is ideological on the grounds, first, that it is systematically misleading and socially mystifying and, second, that it represents the interests of the ruling class as the common interest of society; serves to justify the social status quo and/or the interests of the ruling class; and/or functions to maintain the social status quo and/or defends the interests of the ruling class. But, as shown in chapter 6, it is simply false that morality in general (i.e., all moral values, principles, and theories) always fulfills one or more of these criteria. Perhaps the most persuasive counterexample to Wood's claim in this context is Marx's own implicit moral values and theory. As I explicated and reconstructed it in chapter 3, Marx's theory demands a maximum system of equal freedoms, both positive and negative. Wood, of course, would disagree with this interpretation primarily because its formulation includes the term "equal," which, according to Wood, is a moral concept and therefore not to be allowed a place in Marx's (purportedly) immoralist worldview. But Wood is not adverse to the demand that such "nonmoral" values as freedom (as self-determination), community, and self-realization be pursued or even maximized. He writes, "Presumably when historical materialism 'breaks the staff of all morality,' it does not undermine the value of human emancipation, community, or development, values to which Marx himself often appeals."[45]

According to Wood, one cannot claim that pursuing or maximizing these goods is an *obligation* or *duty* since these, too, are forbidden moral concepts. But, as argued in detail in chapter 4, these distinctions are totally arbitrary and extremely misleading. Whether we interpret Marx as demanding an approximately equal distribution of these goods or merely recommending their pursuit (without regard to equal distribution), he is still—on any nonarbitrary definition of "moral"—proffering a moral principle or theory. More importantly, as argued in the last sections of chapters 4 and 6, Marx's theory and many other moral theories and theories of

[44] A. Wood, "Marx's Immoralism," p. 687.
[45] Ibid., p. 684.

justice do *not* function to preserve the social status quo and are not in any other way ideological.

Support for this view can be found even among the Classical Marxists. Although Engels, for example, claims that "justice is but the ideologised, glorified expression of the existing economic relations, now from their conservative, and now from their revolutionary angle,"[46] he also realizes that "the modern demand for equality is . . . a claim to equal political or social status for all human beings, or at least for all citizens of a state or all members of a society,"[47] and that, historically speaking,

the bourgeois demand for equality was accompanied by the proletarian demand for equality. From the moment when the bourgeois demand for the abolition of class privileges was put forward, alongside of it appeared the proletarian demand for the abolition of the *classes themselves*—at first in religious form, basing itself on primitive Christianity, and later drawing support from the bourgeois equalitarian theories themselves. The proletarians took the bourgeoisie at their word: Equality must not be merely apparent, must not apply merely to the sphere of the state, but must also be real, must be extended to the social and economic sphere.[48]

Engels claims, furthermore, that

The demand for equality in the mouth of the proletariat has therefore a double meaning. It is either . . . the spontaneous reaction against the crying social inequalities, against the contrast of rich and poor, the feudal lords and their serfs, surfeit and starvation. . . . Or, on the other hand, the proletarian demand for equality, drawing more or less correct and more far-reaching demands from this bourgeois demand [serves] as an agitational means in order to rouse the workers against the capitalists, on the basis of the capitalists' own assertion.[49]

In any case, it hardly seems that these juridical concepts do play a conservative role in the revolutionary movement. Almost every revolutionary socialist movement in existence expresses its program partially in terms of rights and justice, and rightfully so.

Wood's fourth criticism of morality is that it requires an impar-

[46] Engels, "The Housing Question," p. 365.
[47] Engels, *Anti-Dühring*, pp. 113–114.
[48] Ibid., p. 117.
[49] Ibid., pp. 117–118.

tial consideration of everyone's interests, regardless of what class
they are in.

> The proletarian movement as Marx depicts it lacks the disin-
> terestedness or impartiality which normally goes along with
> moral concerns. Morality is normally taken to involve in prin-
> ciple an equal concern and respect for the interests of all. . . .
> The proletarian movement, however, gives primacy to the in-
> terests of the proletarian class, and shows little or no concern
> for the interests of capitalists, landowners and other classes
> whose fundamental interests are hostile to proletarian ones.[50]

But, as shown in chapter 4, the mistake that both Wood and Miller
make in this regard is taking morality to demand that equal weight
be given to *all interests* of all persons rather than that equal weight
be given to the *basic* or *legitimate* interests of all persons. This is
also a key mistake to be found in Wood's "class interest argument." But since we shall take up this argument presently, I shall
not belabor the point here.

Wood's fifth criticism of morality is that it can have no rational
basis or justification outside of referring to its functional role in a
particular social system. This criticism depends upon Wood's acceptance of Hegel's distinction between morality as *Moralität* and
morality as *Sittlichkeit* (a distinction he also imputes to Marx without textual evidence). According to Wood,

> *Moralität* is the reflective attitude of an active self seeking to
> actualize the idea of autonomy or subjective freedom. . . .
> *Sittlichkeit* is the set of institutions and objective norms, sanc-
> tioned by custom, through which the members of a living and
> rational social order fulfill the demands of the social whole to
> which they belong.[51]

According to the Hegelian conception of morality, *Moralität* is
parasitic upon *Sittlichkeit*. As Wood puts it:

> Without the customary morality derived from the social order,
> the conscientious individual self would have no content, no
> specific duties through which to express itself. . . . *Sittlichkeit*
> supplies such a content because its norms represent to the in-
> dividual a rational or universal life and interest, while the ful-
> fillment of individual autonomy consists precisely in the ac-

[50] A. Wood, "Marx's Immoralism," p. 693.
[51] Ibid., p. 686.

tualization of the universal by the individual. Also, without the social order the individual will would be doomed to impotence and frustration in its attempts to realize the moral good.[52]

This means that the moral values, principles, or theories held by individuals (as part of their *Moralität*) will be "valid" or "rationally valid" if, and only if, they conform to the *Sittlichkeit*. In turn, the *Sittlichkeit* is "rationally valid" if, and only if, it conforms to, fits with, or supports the current social system. When we combine this Hegelian view of morality with Marxist empirical views, Wood observes, it turns out that "objective moral norms" are those that "represent the economic needs of the prevailing mode of production."[53]

But there is a problem with this argument. Whether "objective" and "valid" are taken in Wood's quasi-Hegelian descriptive sense or in an evaluative sense, this argument does not establish the conclusion that people in general, or Marxists in particular, must reject morality. If the proposition that a moral value, principle, theory, or code is "objective" or "valid" or "rationally valid" (within a certain type of society) is interpreted as a *descriptive* claim, it merely says that the moral value or principle is, in fact, accepted within a particular type of society or—more faithfully to Wood—that it "fits" and thus supports the economic substructure of that type of society. But this claim does not in the least conflict with rejecting these values or principles as guides to conduct or accepting conflicting ones. Even if one accepts them as guides to conduct, this would be a different and separate proposition from accepting the truth of the claim that they are "objective" or "valid" in the above explicated descriptive sense.

Although someone sympathetic to Wood's position—or the Hegelian position generally—may be tempted to claim that the values that "fit" a specific mode of production must be accepted if we are to accept any values at all, since only *those* values are *conceivable* in that sort of society, such a claim is clearly untenable. Even if one accepts Wood's quasi-Hegelian view of morality, one must still admit that moral values other than the accepted ones, or those that "fit" the requirements of the economic substructure, are *conceivable*. Egalitarian values are conceivable in inegalitarian societies, for example.

[52] Ibid.
[53] Ibid., p. 687.

345

On the other hand, the claim that a moral value or principle is "objective" or "valid" or "rationally valid" can be interpreted as an *evaluative* claim (or at least as a claim that directly entails one or more evaluative claims). On this interpretation, to say that a moral value or principle is "objective" or "valid" is to say that it is *true* or *correct* and thus that it *ought to be accepted as a guide to conduct*. But on this interpretation, Wood's contention that a moral value or principle is "objective" or "valid" if, and only if, it "fits" the prevailing mode of production is a blatant version of moral positivism and, more specifically, moral historicism. Since this position was examined—and, I believe, refuted —in chapter 5, I shall not bother marshaling arguments against it at this point. Suffice it to say that, first, it is a version of what G. E. Moore called the naturalistic fallacy and, as such, is susceptible to his open-question argument and, second, that to identify the morally correct values or principles with whatever values or principles are accepted by or "fit" with a particular mode of production is truly pernicious, since these values or principles may be morally abhorrent.

Wood might object at this point that we have no independent criteria to tell what is morally correct or morally abhorrent. My answer to this—as supplied in chapter 7—is that the method of wide reflective equilibrium provides the best basis for justifying moral values or principles, even though we can never escape our moral intuitions/commitments altogether to reach that ever elusive Archimedean point of absolute moral objectivity.

An exactly analogous problem plagues Wood's first major argument against specifically juridical moral concepts, i.e., against justice and moral rights. This argument is based on what he takes to be the Marxist analysis of justice and rights. (I shall forthwith refer only to justice, but whatever can be said in this context of this concept can be taken to hold for rights as well.) According to Wood,

A determination of the justice of transactions or institutions demands . . . an appreciation of their function in production. . . . Just transactions "fit" the prevailing mode, they serve a purpose relative to it, they concretely carry forward and bring to actuality the process of collective productive activity of human individuals in a concrete historical situation. The judgment whether a social institution is just or unjust depends, then, on a concrete comprehension of the mode of production as a whole, and an appreciation of the connection between this whole and the institution in question. . . . All juridical forms and principles of justice are therefore meaningless unless applied to a specific mode of production, and they retain their rational validity only as long as the content they possess and the particular actions to which they apply arise naturally out of and correspond concretely to this productive mode.[54]

If, as Wood suggests, standards of justice are "valid" or "rationally valid" within a certain society if, and only if, they correspond to or "fit" the mode of production of that society, then it might *seem* to follow that the principle of laissez-faire (and thus capitalist exploitation) cannot be condemned as unjust since it "fits" the economic substructure of the capitalist system. But the validity and significance of this argument depends on whether we take "just" to be a descriptive or evaluative term in this context.

Let us formulate the argument as follows:

1. A principle of distribution is *just* if and only if it corresponds to the mode of production within which it is being proposed.

2. The principle of laissez-faire (which rationalizes capitalist exploitation) corresponds to the mode of production in which it is being proposed (namely, capitalism).

3. Therefore, the principle of laissez-faire (and thus capitalist exploitation) is *just* (within capitalism).

Now let us distinguish the normal evaluative sense of "justice" from Wood's purely descriptive sense (which he imputes to Marx). Two quotes from Wood will suffice to exhibit this difference. In "Justice and Class Interests," Wood describes the *evaluative use* when he claims that "practical recognition of the class interest thesis positively excludes us from taking *justice, in the sense of evaluative principles of distribution* . . . as our fundamental object of concern"[55] (emphasis added). In the same article he explicates the purely *descriptive sense* of the term as follows:

> Standards of justice prevail because they serve an economic function within the prevailing mode of production. Hence whenever we are correct in calling an act or institution "just", what we are really saying about it is that *it serves a certain economic function*. It follows that when we say that an act or insti-

[54] A. Wood, "The Marxian Critique of Justice," pp. 258–259.
[55] A. Wood, "Justice and Class Interests," p. 19.

tution is "just", *we need not be giving it any commendation or positive evaluation* [emphasis added].[56]

If, in the previous argument, we take "just" in this descriptive sense, the conclusion that the principle of laissez-faire is just becomes: the principle of laissez-faire serves a certain (conservative) economic function (in capitalist societies). But this is trivial and uninteresting and does not accomplish Wood's purpose. To see this, we need only realize that this statement is not in the least inconsistent with the contention that the principle of laissez-faire and the type of (capitalist) exploitation it supports are *unjust* in an evaluative sense. But the purpose of Wood's attacks on justice is clearly to convince Marxists and the entire workers' movement to reject the *evaluative* notion of justice in general and the claim that capitalism is, evaluatively speaking, unjust in particular. Thus this way of construing the argument fails as an attack on the evaluative notion of justice. And it certainly does nothing to show that an evaluative notion of justice is impossible or incoherent.

If, on the other hand, Wood is using the evaluative sense of "just," then the first premise ends up proclaiming rather crude and, as I have previously argued, unacceptable forms of moral positivism and normative ethical relativism. With respect to the charge of moral positivism, it is clear that on this interpretation the argument is just a version of moral historicism (which is a type of moral positivism). It asserts that whatever moral norms—or, in this case, principles of justice—evolve within or correspond to a particular mode of production are, ipso facto, correct. But there is, of course, no reason whatever to accept this view and many reasons to reject it. (For a more detailed critique, see chapter 5.)

Although perhaps more debatable, this interpretation of the argument also seems open to the charge of normative ethical relativism, i.e., the doctrine that what *is* right or wrong varies from person to person or—in this case—society to society. As argued previously, however, all one need accept to refute this doctrine is the thesis that universalizability is a characteristic of moral judgments and that two or more modes of production can be similar in certain relevant respects, e.g., that people are needlessly suffering or needlessly exploited. (For a more detailed critique of normative ethical relativism, see chapter 7.) Whether or not it is possible to alter a particular unjust society at a particular point in time is, of course, an empirical question. (The topic of the relation between

[56] Ibid., p. 10.

moral judgments and historical possibility is touched on in the last sections of both chapters 3 and 5.)

In any case, Wood's first major argument against justice clearly fails. He has a second major argument, however: the "class interest argument." The conclusion of this argument is that "practical recognition of the class interests thesis positively excludes . . . us from taking justice, in the sense of evaluative principles of distribution which are to be justified from disinterested or impartial considerations, as our fundamental object of concern."[57] The class interest thesis, according to Wood, is that "our actions are historically effective only insofar as they involve the pursuit of class interests, and . . . the historical meaning of our actions consists in their functional role in the struggle between such interests."[58]

The question, of course, is how Wood gets from the relatively innocuous—if somewhat amorphous—class interest thesis to the conclusion that accepting it is absolutely incompatible with taking justice as one's fundamental concern. Justice and the class interest thesis are certainly not a priori incompatible. After all, one seemingly can take justice as one's fundamental concern and still admit that if the class interest thesis is true and one is serious about advancing the cause of justice in the world, then one should support those class interests that, if realized, will best meet the demands of justice. Given the truth of a number of other Marxist empirical theses, these interests will be those of the working class (and other oppressed classes) in this historical epoch. Thus, *on grounds of justice*, one will find oneself committed to the cause of socialism and to the working-class movements aimed at its establishment, i.e., committed to advancing the class interests of the proletariat.

But Wood seems to offer at least two distinct arguments for his conclusion that justice and the class interest thesis are incompatible. I shall first put forward and critique these arguments and then attempt to elicit and critique what I take to be Wood's underlying concern in all of this, namely, that considerations of justice never be allowed to interfere with the prosecution of proletarian revolutions or the policies of the revolutionary regimes that result when they succeed.

The first argument is similar to Wood's impartiality argument against morality in general. After stating that principles of justice "must be advanced on a certain sort of basis, namely one which is

[57] Ibid., p. 19.
[58] Ibid.

disinterested or impartial as regards the interests of those to whom the principle is supposed to apply,"[59] Wood claims that Marx refused to evaluate social institutions from an impartial or disinterested standpoint and that he consistently argues for communism solely from the standpoint of the proletariat and other oppressed classes. Although one may wish to challenge Wood on this point, given the fact that Marx often spoke of the benefit of communism to humanity as a whole, it is certainly true that Marx believed that the ruling-class interest to maintain an exploitative system should not be respected. "The interests Marx defends," writes Wood, "are to be sure regarded by him as the interests of the vast majority. . . . But he never confuses this with the common interest of all society. Marx knows that there are large groups of people (the bourgeoisie and the landed aristocracy) whose interests are going to be simply ignored or sacrificed by the revolution."[60]

The implicit argument Wood is offering here is the well-worn one that justice (as morality) is unacceptable to Marxists because it requires impartiality between people's interests, and Marxists are not impartial. As detailed in chapter 4, this argument is bogus. Principles of morality and justice do not necessarily maintain that *all interests* of all people must count equally: indeed, according to most deontological principles or theories, some interests—like interests to exploit others or rob or murder them—are not to be counted at all. Therefore, when Marxists claim that the interests of capitalists or landlords in continuing to hold and profit from productive property are not to be counted as legitimate, they are not necessarily riding themselves out of the realm of morality or justice: they may have perfectly sound *moral* arguments for denying that such interests should be respected. This is not to say, of course, that members of the capitalist or landlord classes have no legitimate interests that must be respected. There is absolutely no reason why a Marxist should not maintain that all their *basic* human interests must be respected on an equal basis with everyone else's. (The question of whether some legitimate interests of some people—e.g., their civil liberties—can be overridden under extraordinary circumstances will be taken up toward the end of this chapter.)

Wood's second major argument for the incompatibility of justice and the class interest thesis is difficult to state concisely. I shall,

[59] Ibid., p. 14.
[60] Ibid., p. 16.

therefore, take Wood's various statements of the argument in "Justice and Class Interests" as successive approximations and critique each as it appears. It should be noted, however, that, according to Wood, the argument is conditional: it applies only to those who are concerned with the historical efficacy of their actions and who accept the class interest thesis. Let us take the following passage as Wood's first approximation:

> If our primary concern in our actions is with their historical results, then this recognition will inevitably have an effect on our goals themselves. Since we will tend to choose projects that we regard as having some chance of success, we will tend to see our projects within the framework of the class interests which are prominent in our society and age. We will see our task as historical agents not as one of setting our goals according to abstract values or standards and then trying to find some means of achieving them, but rather of choosing between the goals of already existing historical movements, and pursuing the goals of the movement we choose by joining this movement and identifying ourselves with it.[61]

Although some minor questions may need to be answered here—such as, what happens if the correct sort of historical movement has not yet formed so there is not one to join, and what exactly does it mean to identify oneself with an historical movement?—the major question is *on what basis are we to choose* between the goals of historical/class movements? The two obvious bases would seem to be prudential considerations and, broadly speaking, moral considerations, including considerations of justice. It would seem that choosing to support the class interests of the proletariat on the basis of moral considerations is not only possible but, in many cases, actual. As argued in the last section of chapter 4, there is every reason to believe that moral commitments, including commitments to social justice, form an important part of revolutionary motivation for many people. In fact, from a pragmatic point of view, to rely solely on prudential considerations for revolutionary motivation is surely a losing proposition, especially in advanced capitalist societies in this day and age.

But Wood will not so easily allow a rapprochement between Marxism and justice. He offers two arguments against the view that Marxists can consistently choose between goals of different

[61] Ibid., p. 19.

351

class movements on the basis of justice. The first harks back to the impartiality thesis. Wood writes:

> According to the class interest thesis, these [class] goals are in no case determined by disinterested or impartial considerations: they are always the particular interests of one class struggling against other classes. To identify ourselves with a class movement is therefore to abandon the pretense to ourselves that our fundamental concern is with what is disinterestedly or impartially good.[62]

But this is a non sequitur. The fact that the actual goals or interests of classes are not impartially chosen—and, indeed, not *chosen* at all according to Marx's theory of classes and class interests—in no way entails that individuals qua individuals cannot choose to support class goals on the basis of an impartial theory of social justice.

The second argument against Marxists choosing which class goals to support on the basis of justice has to do with Wood's claim that—for reasons to be explained—it is *irrational* for a Marxist (or anyone who accepts the class interest thesis and is concerned with the historical efficacy of his or her actions) to do so. Wood writes:

> The class interest argument . . . claim[s] that once we as self-conscious historical agents affiliate ourselves with a given class, it would be irrational for us to continue to maintain justice as our primary concern. . . . The argument does not deny that it may be a concern for justice before one self-consciously adopts a class affiliation. But it does assert that it is irrational for a historical agent to remain aloof from class affiliation, and it also [a]sserts that it is irrational for a person who has assumed a class affiliation to accord justice (or anything else) a higher priority than the interests of the class with which one identifies.[63]

Although I think it false that it is *irrational*—as opposed to, say, *immoral*—for all people (even the egoist) to remain aloof from class affiliation, the more important issue for our purposes is whether it is irrational for someone who has assumed a class affiliation still to take justice as his or her most fundamental concern. Wood says it is. But why should we assume this? Of course, one could define "assuming a class affiliation" or "identifying with the interests of a class" as (in part) "accepting the promotion of the class's inter-

[62] Ibid., p. 21.
[63] Ibid., p. 24.

ests—regardless of concerns for justice—as one's most fundamental concern." In this case, it would be analytically true that no one can consistently assume a class affiliation and take justice as one's most fundamental concern. But barring this dubious device, on what ground can one say that the two are incompatible or that one is irrational in viewing the proletarian movement as a means for fulfilling the demands of social justice?

According to Wood,

> the irrationality is one which Hegel explored very insightfully in Chapter 5 of the *Phenomenology of Spirit*. It would be the same irrationality as that of the tail flattering itself that it was wagging the dog. In effect, what the class interest thesis tells us is that those who strive for justice in human history are, objectively speaking, always striving in behalf of the interests of some class or other, and that their striving must, from a historical point of view, be regarded in this light, whatever their private aims and intentions in the matter may be. We cannot accept this thesis and still pretend to view our own aims and intentions in the same light we did before. In the case of aims and intentions which are not directed specifically to class interests, it requires us to see them only as vehicles or masks of class interests, which are impotent on their own to accomplish anything in history.
>
> To see our commitment in this way, however, is incompatible with regarding ourselves as using the proletarian movement as a means to justice.[64]

Here Wood seems to be harking back to the claim that an individual's set of moral commitments (i.e., *Moralität*) is parasitic upon the "objective norms" of the social system (i.e., *Sittlichkeit*) and supposedly, as such, completely impotent to effect social change. He may also have in mind the claim sometimes made by Marx and Marxists that morality and justice are merely superstructural intellectual constructs that can have no effect on the substructure of a society. Again, the first point to notice is that these empirical-explanatory claims are extremely dubious and are not even uniformly accepted by the Classical Marxists. More importantly, to claim that it is irrational to take justice as one's fundamental concern *because*, "objectively speaking," those who strive for justice are always striving in behalf of the interests of a specific class

[64] Ibid., pp. 25–26.

353

seems to confuse the evaluative question of *why* one *ought* to support a particular class with an empirical-explanatory question of what the "objective" consequences of doing so are. Of course, the two are connected, at least if one is concerned with the historical efficacy of one's action. To see the distinction, however, one need only realize that the question "what class interests do your actions objectively support?" is different from the question "why should you support those class interests?" Two people could agree on the answer to the first question but disagree on the answer to the second: one person might support those class interests on purely prudential grounds, for example, while another might do so on moral grounds. And, of course, two people could agree on what class interests a certain type of action supports and still disagree—on either prudential or moral grounds—on whether or not to support them. Notice, also, that Wood's theory provides no reason for choosing to pursue one class's goals rather than another's. It is equally as rational to pursue the bourgeoisie's goals as the proletariat's. Wood's theory cannot even sensibly say that it is better to support the goals of the working class! Finally, there is a genuine question as to whether or not all "intentions which are not directed specifically to class interests"—especially all theories of social justice—ought to be taken as *only* "vehicles or masks of class interests" (more on this presently).

Let us take the following passage as Wood's last attempt to formulate a sound version of his class interest argument:

> Because we want (and rationally ought to want) a unified and harmonious conception of ourselves as historical agents, we will form (or at least revise) our aims and intentions in light of the historical meaning we understand them to have. We will adopt intentions which coincide with the historical meaning of what we do. Since we recognize that objectively speaking the pursuit of justice is only a vehicle or mask for the pursuit of class interest, we will no longer think of ourselves as pursuing justice, but will come to think of ourselves as pursuing the interests of a particular class. For only in this way can we harmonize our conscious intentions with our historical self-understanding and thus attain to self-conscious historical agency.[65]

[65] Ibid., p. 27.

354

But what is the "historical meaning" of our aims and intentions? Presumably, it is the objective consequences they will result in if fulfilled. Thus this version of the class interest argument seems open to all the objections the previous versions were open to. But what of the claim that "the pursuit of justice is only a vehicle or mask for the pursuit of class interest"—a claim that seems crucial to Wood's argument? The main point I wish to make here is that in some cases the pursuit of justice—even the pursuit of *social* justice—may have nothing to do with class interests. Therefore, the reduction of justice to the pursuit of class interests is unacceptably simplistic and crude. First, even within class societies, not all questions of social justice are questions of class. Although many Marxists exhibit a knee-jerk reaction toward making this reduction, it seems fairly clear that questions of racial and gender justice are not *wholly* reducible to questions of class interest. (This is not to deny that a reasonable argument may be made for the claim that such injustices stand a better chance of being resolved in a socialist rather than a capitalist society.) Even the more general question of how best to divide whatever funds the capitalist state decides to set aside for social programs is not specifically a class question, although *how much* is set aside for such programs, as opposed to programs or policies that directly benefit the capitalist class, certainly is. (Naturally, Marxists and other socialists will want to argue that the only way to have a government that will work for the benefit of the vast majority—as opposed to the ruling-class minority and its hangers-on—is to have a socialist government, i.e., a government of a socialist society. In addition, Marxists will want to argue that the basic change must take place at the point of the relations of production rather than at the point of distributive principles or government policies.)

Finally, as shown earlier in the present chapter, it is a mistake to think that questions of justice will disappear with the disappearance of class divisions. In a socialist society—or what Marx calls the first stage of communism—where material scarcity remains a fact of life, the question of how to divide up society's disposable income will be an extremely important one, even though class divisions no longer exist since there is only one class: the working class (more on this issue in the next chapter). Moreover, as noted earlier, even in a full-fledged communist society based on material abundance, questions of justice will still arise due to the perpetual scarcity of people's time and energy and conflicting

355

opinions about how social resources should be used. For all of these reasons, it is clear that the pursuit of justice is not merely a vehicle or mask for the pursuit of class interest. Thus Wood's argument fails on this ground as well. Furthermore, if this reductionistic thesis is a consequence of the class interest thesis, then the latter also must be rejected. Certainly there is nothing in this reductionistic thesis or the more general class interest thesis to indicate that they are canonical to Marxism, as Wood suggests.

But why is Wood so adamantly opposed to justice and to morality generally? The answer, I suggest, is that Wood believes that acceptance of justice or morality is inimical to a vigorous prosecution of the class struggle. According to Wood,

> Practical recognition of the class interests thesis begins to interfere with this course of action [of attempting to reconcile the pursuit of proletarian class interests with the pursuit of justice] only when our concern for justice threatens to interfere with or predominate over our concern for the interests of the proletariat. In such cases, recognition of the class interests thesis dictates that *we get our priorities straight and thus dampen our enthusiasm for justice, so that we may get on with what really matters* [emphasis added].[66]

This is a rather startling claim. Does Wood really mean to suggest that the vigorous prosecution of the class struggle ought not be bound by any constraints imposed by justice, even the requirements of a just war, e.g., bans on indiscriminate killing of civilians, the use of chemical or biological weapons, or the torture of prisoners? Perhaps this will be regarded as a red herring. It might be argued that Wood has in mind only the distribution of such goods as income and wealth when he speaks of justice. But it seems to me extremely important for Marxists to make clear that while they are in favor of utilizing virtually any means to effect the socialist transformation—up to and including popular revolution and civil war if absolutely necessary—they are *not* in favor of violating the Geneva Accords in such situations or in any way violating the constraints of just-war theory, even if doing so would increase the chances for success.

Let us assume that sensible Marxists (including Wood) would not commit themselves to such violations. Although this in and of itself refutes the position that Marxism and considerations of jus-

[66] Ibid., p. 22.

tice are incompatible, let us reformulate the question. It seems to me that what Wood really may be worried about is that the dictates of justice may not even allow the prosecution of the class struggle within the limits set out above, i.e., that justice may even rule out the "standard" methods of proletarian class struggle: militant strikes, the formation of workers' councils and workers' militias, revolutionary uprisings, and—if unavoidable—civil war. Whether or not, and under what circumstances, such methods can be legitimately employed will depend, of course, on what theory of justice, as well as on what empirical views, one accepts. But almost all theories of social justice leave room for the possibility of justified and, indeed, just revolutions. If we accept even a moderately egalitarian theory of social justice *and* accept Marxist empirical theory as being essentially correct, then socialist revolutions will be justified. In fact, a strong case can be made for the claim that even Locke's moral theory will result in some socialist revolutions being justified if one interprets his right to life as both a negative (i.e., security) right and a positive (i.e., subsistence) right (more on this in chapters 9 and 10).[67]

Some theorists have gone so far as to claim that, given these empirical assumptions, the pursuit of proletarian class interests will, in fact, *never* conflict with the demands of morality or social justice. This is Kai Nielsen's position, which he compares to Wood's as follows:

> Where Marxist immoralism most decisively comes in, Wood claimed, is in the belief (resulting in a commitment) that if there is ever a conflict between proletarian class interests and what is disinterestedly good, the proletarian interests trump those moral interests. This reverses the usual belief that moral considerations override any such conflicting considerations.
>
> The justicizing Marxist (the Marxist moralist) should reply that this is an unreal situation, a desert islandish, hypothetical situation. Given a realistic understanding of what proletarian class interests are, they cannot, as a matter of fact, conflict with what is disinterestedly good; therefore, a historical agent could not be faced with a situation where he or she must choose between struggling to realize proletarian class interests and supporting what is disinterestedly good. The Marxist, rightly or wrongly, conceives the matter in such a way that the class interests of proletarians will also, as a matter of fact

[67] See Bender, "World Hunger, Human Rights, and the Right to Revolution."

although surely not as a matter of definition, be the interests of the vast majority of humankind: proletarians and, as well, many other groups (farmers, lumpen-proletarians, petty bourgeoisie, and most intellectuals and professionals).[68]

The defender of the class interests thesis does not have to choose between pursuing class interests and pursuing what is disinterestedly good, for *by* pursuing [working] class interests he or she thereby pursues what is disinterestedly good.[69]

I would also assert that if Marxist empirical theory is basically correct, then the vigorous pursuit of proletarian class interests is almost always justified and almost never comes into conflict with what is disinterestedly good. But I cannot agree with Nielsen that they, as a matter of fact, will *never* conflict in the real world. As shown by the previous example of employing heinous means in order to increase the chances of winning a just revolutionary war, there are cases that are not only conceivable but historically possible in which justice and proletarian class interests may conflict. One might, of course, argue that the use of such heinous means would not be in the interest of the proletariat (and other oppressed classes), even if they increased the chances of winning a just revolutionary war, because the enemy would retaliate in kind, and such a precedent might end up undermining all civilization, etc. But even if it turns out that—given Marxist empirical assumptions—proletarian class interests and justice never diverge in the actual world, we must still distinguish the two because it is at least possible that the Marxist empirical assumptions will turn out to be wrong and, thus, that the pursuit of proletarian class interests may not lead to the best or most just society that is historically possible. And this could be true even if the class interest thesis, as originally stated by Wood, is taken to be true. It is at least *logically possible* that it is true that "our actions are historically effective only insofar as they involve the pursuit of class interests," but false that "the pursuit of proletarian class interests never diverges from the demands of justice." This would be the case, for example, if the pursuit of those interests were to result in a situation in which the

[68] Nielsen, *Marxism and the Moral Point of View*, pp. 235–236.
[69] Ibid., p. 237. It should be noted that although Nielsen sometimes identifies Wood's class interest thesis as propounding that proletarian interests always come first (or always trump other interests), this is not actually what Wood states and—so far as I can tell—isn't even entailed by Wood's original statement of the thesis. It is, of course, *a* thesis put forward by Wood in "Justice and Class Interests."

proletariat is materially better off, but grave injustices are perpetrated against other segments of the population from that point in time on. I am not claiming there is any reason to believe they will diverge, but we at least have to be able to talk about such possibilities. Nor am I suggesting that the discussion of such abstract possibilities is important to the actual class struggle. As Nielsen puts it, "Proletarian militants, particularly when they are not also theoreticians, need not engage in such complicated reasoning. In the midst of class struggle, furthering proletarian class interests should be their aim."[70]

Another concern I suspect Wood may have is that the demands of justice may interfere with the policies of a revolutionary socialist regime. In particular, he may be worried that taking justice as the fundamental concern would mean that no one's civil liberties could ever be limited, even if this were absolutely essential to the success of a revolution and to the stabilization of the new revolutionary regime. The charge that socialism will inevitably (and unjustifiably) violate people's civil liberties is often trumpeted by opponents of Marxism and socialism. Nielsen's response to this is:

> The vital interests of capitalists that center on what are usually called our civil liberties need not be affected in most situations. Where they would be affected, say in the unsettled aftermath of a bitter civil war, their free speech rights would indeed be overridden. But, or so a Marxist is perfectly and consistently at liberty to claim, they still (in the way Joel Feinberg has shown) remain inalienable. What happens in such a particular situation is no different than what happens in any bourgeois society when it is in a state of war (or something similar) where all sorts of censorship restrictions are routinely recognized as essential. Moreover, they are recognized to be essential from the perspective of what is disinterestedly good. (Leon Trotsky was surely right in pointing out in his *Their Morals and Ours* the hypocrisy of bourgeois critics of the communists on such issues.)[71]

Such claims are quite controversial and obviously depend on the empirical assumptions one makes, as well as on the moral principles one espouses. But the point is that Marxists can consistently take justice as their fundamental concern and still remain faithful

[70] Ibid., p. 270.
[71] Ibid., p. 236.

359

to their basic normative political positions. But this does mean that *if* a Marxist were to come to the conclusion that pursuing the interests of the working class (by trying to overthrow capitalism and establish a socialist society) would lead to greater injustice, rather than less, then it would be irrational—or at least immoral—for him or her to continue to pursue those interests. (Indeed, how could it be otherwise!) But it is important to keep in mind that here I am using the word "justice" to refer to the protection not only of negative liberties but of all the rights people have, including their basic rights to well-being, i.e., their security and subsistence rights. But to decide whether the result of pursuing certain class interests or creating certain social formations is more just or less, we obviously need a well worked out theory of social justice. To provide at least the outline of such a theory is the task of the remaining two chapters of this work.

NINE

MARXIST AND LEFTIST OBJECTIONS
TO RAWLS' THEORY OF JUSTICE:
A CRITICAL REVIEW

Assuming that the circumstances of justice—moderate scarcity and moderate egoism—will continue to pertain to human societies even if a world socialist society is established, it seems clear that any adequate moral and social theory requires a theory of social justice that will provide us with principles governing the distribution of the benefits and burdens of social cooperation, as well as with the moral grounds of legitimate political authority and political (or social) obligation. The question thus becomes: what theory of social justice ought we adopt? Given the problematic of the present work, this question becomes: what theory of social justice must be adopted by an adequate Marxist moral and social theory?

One suggestion might be that we simply adopt the principles of distribution advocated by Marx for the first stage of communism. As found in "Critique of the Gotha Program," these principles are:

1. One can receive remuneration only for one's own labor and can acquire only the "means of consumption," i.e., personal property and consumer goods.

2. An individual is to receive remuneration in exact proportion to the number of hours he or she works.

3. Except for those incapable of doing so, everyone is required to labor.

4. Those unable to work shall be provided with *at least* a minimally decent standard of living.

There are two reasons why adopting these principles won't work. The first is that there may be cogent objections to some of them, especially if we take them to apply to well-developed as well as developing societies. The second is that these principles are too narrow to constitute an adequate theory of social justice.

Although I shall not offer here a detailed analysis of these four principles, it is my contention that while the first and fourth are acceptable, the second and third are questionable, especially if applied to a well-developed socialist society. The first principle is simply an explication of the concept of *socialized property relations* and is thus acceptable just in case socialism is morally preferable to capitalism. Although I am (in this work) attempting to make such a case, the point is that this principle cannot be accepted in advance of some sort of case being made. The fourth principle— although rather vague—certainly seems acceptable. But the second principle runs into difficulties in specifying what sort of work must be done (materially productive? socially useful?), and in explaining how such a requirement is compatible with incentive schedules and thus economic efficiency in mass industrial societies. (As we have seen, Marx himself is not completely satisfied with this principle. He asserts that it is not egalitarian enough since some people are capable of working more hours than others, and some have more dependents than others.)

The third principle runs into a similar difficulty in specifying the type of labor one is required to perform. Certainly digging a hole and filling it in each day for no good reason would not count as having fulfilled one's obligation to labor, on Marx's view. But it is notoriously difficult to define either "materially productive labor" or "socially useful labor."[1] Is the labor of the humanities scholar or

---

[1] The debate between all of these various interpretations is carried out in the following works: Baran, *The Political Economy of Growth*, pp. 22–47, 90–92, 262–263; Sweezy, *The Theory of Capitalist Development*, pp. 226–231, 278–286; Mandel, *Marxist Economic Theory*, pp. 191–206, 305–317; J. Morris, "Unemployment and Unproductive Employment," *Science and Society*, vol. 22 (1958); J. Blake, "Jacob Morris on Unproductive Employment: A Criticism," *Science and Society*, vol. 24 (1960); I. R. Gough, "Marx's Theory of Productive and Unproductive Labour," *New Left Review*, no. 76 (Nov./Dec. 1972).

Also, John Harrison, "Productive and Unproductive Labour in Marx's Political Economy," *Bulletin of the Conference of Socialist Economists* (hereafter *CSEB*), vol. 2, no. 6 (Autumn 1973); Paul Bullock, "Categories of Labour Power for Capital," *CSEB*, vol. 2, no. 6 (Autumn 1973); Ben Fine, "A Note on Productive and Unproductive Labour," *CSEB*, vol. 2, no. 6 (Autumn 1973); Ian Gough, "On Productive and Unproductive Labour—A Reply," *CSEB*, vol. 2, no. 7 (Winter 1973); John Harrison, "The Political Economy of Housework," *CSEB*, vol. 2, no. 7 (Winter 1973).

Also, Paul Bullock, "Defining Productive Labour for Capital," *CSEB*, vol. 3, no. 9; Ian Gough and John Harrison, "Unproductive Labour and Housework Again," *CSEB*, vol. 4, no. 1 (Feb. 1975); Jean Gardiner, Susan Himmelweit, and Maureen Mackintosh, "Women's Domestic Labour," *CSEB*, vol. 4, no. 11 (June 1975); Michael A. Lebowitz, "The Political Economy of Housework: A Comment," *CSEB*,

the unappreciated artist materially productive? Who is to decide which types of labor are socially useful? Moreover, while there may be a *prima facie* case for asserting that every able-bodied person must perform socially useful labor, since this is one of the burdens of social cooperation that must be distributed, it is arguable that in a well-developed society the principle of maximum equal negative liberty would override this demand. As David Schweickart puts it, "Under worker control [i.e., democratic, self-managing socialism] people are free to seek work where they will, to change work associations if they come into conflict with its rules or personnel, not to work at all if they can find someone to support them."[2] In *Proposed Roads to Freedom*, Bertrand Russell even goes so far as to propose a "vagabond's wage" for those unwilling to work.

> When education is finished no one should be *compelled* to work, and those who choose not to work should receive a bare livelihood, and be left completely free; but probably it would be desirable that there should be a strong public opinion in favor of work, so that only comparatively few should choose idleness.[3]

Needless to say, such a proposal would be nothing but a cruel joke in developing societies. In such situations there may well be an all-things-considered coercible obligation to engage in materially productive or socially useful labor.

The second problem is that the scope of these principles is too narrow for them to constitute a general theory of social justice: they concern only the benefit of material income and wealth and the burden of labor, whereas a general theory of social justice will concern *all* major benefits and burdens of social cooperation. Although Marxists may balk at the phrase "the benefits and burdens of social cooperation," since they view at least class societies in terms of social conflict rather than social cooperation, such a reaction is not called for. This phrase is simply meant to designate the distributable goods of society and can thus be cogently applied to societies based on social conflict as well as societies based on co-

---

vol. 5, no. 13 (March 1976); Ben Fine and Laurence Harris, "Controversial Issues in Marxist Economic Theory," *The Socialist Register 1976* (Ralph Miliband and John Saville, eds.), Merlin Press, London; and Marc Linder and Julius Sensat, Jr., *Anti-Samuelson*, vol. I, Urizen Books, N.Y., 1977, pp. 195–199.

[2] Schweickart, *Capitalism or Worker Control?* pp. 143–144.

[3] Russell, *Selected Papers*, pp. 138–139.

operation, e.g., socialism or communism. As we shall see presently, Rawls himself fluctuates between a neoclassical view of capitalism as a cooperative society and a more radical view that sees capitalism as a society based on relations of dominance and subordination. What Marxists object to in capitalism and other class societies is precisely that the distributable goods made possible by social organization (i.e., "cooperation")—including the goods of freedom and power—are not fairly distributed.

For our purposes, we can take the *benefits* of social cooperation to be the social primary goods to which Rawls refers: liberty and opportunity, income and wealth, leisure time, and the social bases of self-respect. (To this list we might add power and the worth of people's liberties, but probably they are already implicitly included as components of the social bases of self-respect. More on this presently.) The *burdens* of social cooperation are, of course, the limitations placed on our behavior by the various obligations we incur as members of a (basically) just society. Presumably we have a general obligation to obey the laws of such a society, including obligations to pay taxes and to contribute to the common defense (by military or alternative service) if called upon to do so.

Moreover, beyond the obligations we owe one another as members of a "cooperative" scheme, we may also have natural duties vis-à-vis other persons, whether or not they are fellow members of such a social scheme. Rawls suggests, for example, that the parties in the original position would also recognize certain "natural duties," including the duty not to harm, the duty of mutual aid (i.e., to help those in dire straits if we can do so without great cost or risk to ourselves), the duty of mutual respect, and the duty of justice (i.e., to support and promote just social institutions). These constitute additional "burdens" we may be morally required to accept, even though they need not arise from social cooperation.

So it is easy to see that the principles of distribution proposed by Marx for the first stage of communism are not wide-ranging enough for an adequate theory of social or even distributive justice. It could be suggested that Marx's theory of freedom (as I have reconstructed it) is a better candidate for such an overall theory of social justice, but, as I shall argue in chapter 10, there are problems with this suggestion as well.

But then what theory of justice should we use? Although a number of objections to Rawls' theory of social justice have been raised by Marxist and left-leaning writers, it is my belief that this theory is essentially correct and that under the impact of egalitarian consistency and even a minimal set of Marxist empirical assumptions, it will justify the Marxist's basic normative political positions. In the present chapter, I shall consider ten objections to Rawls' theory. I shall argue that most fail, and those that do succeed can be accommodated within Rawls' theoretical framework. Subsequently, I shall argue that a somewhat modified version of Rawls' theory can best serve as the moral component of an adequate Marxist moral and social theory.

Rights and Justice

Before considering Rawls' theory in detail, however, I would like to make some comments on the relation between rights and social justice. Although some writers view rights with considerable suspicion,[4] it is my contention that, when formulated properly, concepts and theories of rights can and should play an important role in an adequate moral and social theory. Another view sometimes put forward is that the concepts—or at least the principles—of rights and social justice are either unconnected or positively opposed to one another. But such is not the case. As S. I. Benn points out, rights are

> canons by which social, economic, and political arrangements can be criticized. Human rights, in short, are statements of basic needs or interests. They are politically significant as grounds of protest and justification for reforming policies. They differ from appeals to benevolence and charity in that they involve ideas like justice and equality.
>
> Human rights are the corollary, then, of the equally modern notion of social justice.[5]

Furthermore, although rights can be said to be *basic* in the sense that they are more important than any other type of moral consideration, *they are not epistemically basic*. Contrary to what Nozick and

[4] This includes such Marxist and leftist philosophers as Richard Miller and Kai Nielsen. See Miller's "Rights or Consequences" and "Rights and Reality," and Nielsen's "Skepticism and Human Rights" and "Arguing about Justice." In terms of their plausibility, the grounds for this sort of doubt about rights range from the not totally implausible to the completely ridiculous. The reasons adduced by Miller and Nielsen fall into the former category, while Alasdair MacIntyre's claim that rights should be rejected because—like witches and unicorns—they don't "exist" falls into the latter. (See MacIntyre, *After Virtue*, pp. 64–68.)

[5] Benn, "Rights," pp. 198–199. The analyses of rights as valid claims and as entitlements have sometimes been counterposed. (Feinberg defends the former view in the article just cited, while McCloskey defends the latter view in his article "Rights.") It seems clear, however, that they are not only compatible with each other but are both essential for a proper understanding of rights—or at least "claim-rights." (See my "A Defense of Rights to Well-Being.")

certain other writers assert, the answer to the question of what rights we have is *not* intuitively obvious. That rights are not intuitively obvious is shown by the fact that even extremely intelligent, clear-thinking, knowledgeable persons often disagree over what rights we have and even over the thesis that we have any rights at all. Jeremy Bentham, for example, referred to rights as "nonsense on stilts" and simply refused to recognize any of them. (This is a position taken by some Marxists as well.)

But an analysis exists on which rights are not known by intuition but can still be rationally justified, namely, the analysis of rights as valid claims that result in entitlements. But if rights are valid claims, then obviously we must rely on other moral principles to decide which of the claims put forward are valid. As Feinberg puts it, "To have a right is to have a claim against someone *whose recognition as valid is called for by some set of governing rules or moral principles* (emphasis added).[6] So long as we are taking rights to be something more than convenient fictions or mere rules of thumb for maximizing utility, the most obvious candidates for such moral principles would seem to be principles of social justice. (Note, however, that this does not beg the question against right-libertarianism since it is possible that the only legitimate principle of social justice is a principle of negative liberty and, thus, that the only rights we have are rights to negative liberties.)

In fact, human rights can be seen to be intimately connected with social justice. Human rights and principles of social justice are similar in that they both: (1) are concerned with fundamental human needs or interests (as opposed to, say, "mere desires"); (2) issue in coercible obligations (i.e., obligations that the state or, in some cases, other individuals can legitimately force us to meet); (3) provide a basis for justifying our actions and, in some cases, invoking the protection or aid of others; and (4) provide grounds for justifying or criticizing social institutions, programs, or policies.

Thus, though I would prefer to use the term "epistemically" rather than the term "morally" in the first sentence of the following passage, it would seem proper to agree with J. G. Murphy that

> rights claims are *not* morally basic. Rather they are derivative from more general moral principles. "To have a right," Mill suggests, "is to have something which society ought to defend me in the possession of." The central idea here is that rights claims function, not to mark out some specially fine fea-

[6] Feinberg, "The Nature and Value of Rights," p. 257.

ture of persons, but rather to mark which of all moral claims *ought to be enforced by the state, ought to be law.* On this view, a creature may be said to have a right to X if and only if it is morally reasonable, all things considered, to guarantee X to that creature as a matter of law.[7]

If what I am saying here about the relation between human rights and social justice is correct, then the distinction between "rights-based theories" and "theories of social justice" is no longer clear or tenable. Rights can only be generated by principles of social justice, be they those of Rawls, Nozick, or Marx. Moreover, theories of social justice will generate rights because they will specify which claims put forward are valid and thus what entitlements we have, i.e., what activities and interests we should be empowered to pursue or free to pursue or are entitled to help in pursuing.

Although some moral theorists—e.g., Nozick—will certainly disagree with the following, it seems to me that Murphy is also correct in claiming that "an individual should be understood as having a right to X if and only if a law guaranteeing X to the individual would be chosen by rational agents in the original position"[8] or, we might add, in the constitutional or legislative stages in Rawls' scenario. This being the case, I will dispense with an attempt to formulate an independent theory of human rights in favor of attempting to give at least the outlines of an adequate theory of social justice from which the rights we have can be generated.

Marx and Rawls

John Rawls' special conception of justice consists of the following two principles:

First Principle
    Each person is to have an equal right to the most extensive total system of equal basic liberties compatible with a similar system of liberty for all.
Second Principle
    Social and economic inequalities are to be arranged so that they are both:

---

[7] Murphy, "Rights and Borderline Cases," p. 232.
[8] Ibid., p. 235. For a detailed attempt to derive various rights from Rawls' theory, see Rex Martin's *Rawls and Rights*.

a. to the greatest benefit of the least advantaged, consistent with the just savings principle, and
b. attached to offices and positions open to all under conditions of fair equality of opportunity.

When applied to well-developed societies, these principles are placed by Rawls in the following lexical order, such that the higher-rated ones cannot be traded off for greater realization of the lower-rated ones: the first principle takes precedence over both parts of the second principle, and part (b) takes precedence over part (a) within the second principle. It is common practice to refer to these principles as the Maximum Equal Liberty Principle, the Equal Opportunity Principle, and the Difference Principle respectively. Rawls argues that these principles will be unanimously chosen in the original position, i.e., in the hypothetical choice situation in which people are rational, nonenvious, and mutually disinterested, and in which they stand behind the "veil of ignorance." Standing behind the veil of ignorance means that the individuals know nothing of their personal attributes or social position in the real world and thus must choose, knowing that they could end up in any actual position, even the worst-off one. They do, however, have all general knowledge of human nature, society, and history that is relevant for choosing the basic moral rules for designing social institutions. These conditions are meant to ensure that the principles or rules are fairly chosen and thus fair. (See chapter 7 for a more detailed discussion of these aspects of Rawls' theory.)

Many Marxists and left-leaning writers will strongly object to the claim that this theory or even a Rawlsian-like theory of social justice can provide the normative component of an adequate Marxist moral and social theory. Such writers generally claim that Rawls' theory is part and parcel of bourgeois ideology because it defends welfare-state capitalism or accepts the existence of classes as inevitable (or at least acceptable) or contains other, more specific flaws that make it ideological. Others have objections to Rawls' theory that are strong enough to make them reject it even though they do not necessarily see it as ideological.

Before examining those objections to Rawls' theory that seem relevant from the perspective of attempting to develop an adequate Marxist moral and social theory, let us first review the *similarities* between Marx and Rawls in order to show that an attempt to synthesize their views is not totally wrongheaded.

1. Both are concerned with evaluating basic social structures.

2. Both are acutely aware of the role of social institutions in the formation of desires, motivation, and character.

3. Both are acutely aware that in all societies up to now an individual's life prospects are almost totally shaped by the "natural and social lottery."

4. Because of the views expressed in numbers 2 and 3, both contend that we can and must subject social structures and conditions to conscious control. (It is for these reasons that they both also reject "historical theories of justice" as, for example, construed by Nozick.)

5. Both are committed to the notion of the dignity and worth of the human individual and to autonomy as a fundamental value.

6. Both are egalitarians in the sense that they take "substantive" as well as "formal" equality as the *base line or starting point* of their moral deliberations concerning social policies and arrangements.

7. Both reject the thesis that there can be *complete* or *strict* equality in any society that embodies Hume's conditions of justice, i.e., moderate scarcity and moderate egoism.

8. Both believe socialism to be morally preferable to capitalism, *given certain (not totally implausible) empirical assumptions*.

While I do not intend to make of Marx "a common liberal" (to use Lenin's phrase) or of Rawls a revolutionary socialist, given these important similarities, it does not seem totally implausible that they will accept very similar sets of moral principles. Marx and Rawls seem to have extremely important disagreements, of course, on a number of points such as the "absolute" priority of liberty, the possibility that relatively large inequalities in material wealth might be justified, and the justifiability of the "dictatorship of the proletariat" and revolutionary violence. But it is my contention that once one really understands both Rawls and Marx, one realizes that their disagreements are based almost entirely on *empirical* rather than *evaluative* considerations. Furthermore, it seems to me that the vast majority of the objections raised against Rawls by his Marxist and left-leaning critics are based either on misinter-

369

pretations of his moral theory or else are the result of failing to keep his *moral theory per se* separate from his *empirical assumptions* and his *normative political positions* (which result from combining his theory of social justice with these empirical assumptions).

As we examine Rawls' theory, it is of the utmost importance to keep in mind this distinction between his core moral theory (i.e., his basic egalitarian assumption, his postulated natural duties, his principles of social justice, and his theory of political obligation) and the various empirical assumptions that lead him to the view that it is possible for class-divided capitalist societies to meet his proposed principles of justice. Obviously, in our attempt to develop at least the outlines of an adequate Marxist moral and social theory (and, specifically, an adequate theory of social justice), it will be Rawls' core moral theory rather than his empirical assumptions about capitalism (and post-capitalist societies) that we will find of use.

In this context let us consider the following objections to Rawls' theory from what initially appears to be a more egalitarian and/or Marxist perspective:

1. Rawls' methods of reflective equilibrium and the social contract (i.e., the strategy of the original position) are pervaded by bourgeois or individualistic assumptions concerning the nature of human individuals.

2. Agreement on Rawls' principles of social justice is impossible in class-divided societies because any such agreement will be beyond the "strains of commitment" of one class or another.

3. Rawls' theory is merely a defense of welfare-state capitalism.

4. It assumes that the division of society into social classes is inevitable or at least acceptable.

5. It asserts the absolute priority of negative liberty over all other demands of social justice.

6. It assumes that large socioeconomic inequalities are compatible with strict equality of liberty.

7. It assumes that the Difference Principle is sufficiently egalitarian.

8. Rawls' theory demands *political* democracy but not democracy in the *social and economic realm*, e.g., democracy in the workplace).

9. The theory is meant to be applied to individual societies (e.g., individual nation-states) rather than to the world as a whole.

10. Rawls provides no theory concerning the means of transition from unjust to just societies; therefore, his overall moral and social theory is utopian.

The first two objections concern Rawls' methodology of moral-theory construction. These issues were analyzed to some extent in chapter 7, so I shall not spend an inordinate amount of time on them here. Objections 3 through 8 concern the substantive portion of his moral and social theory and are therefore more crucial to my project of synthesizing the moral theories or perspectives of Marx and Rawls into what I consider an adequate theory of social justice.

Objections 9 and 10 concern how Rawls applies (or fails to apply) his theory of social justice—issues, I believe, that have more to do with one's empirical views than one's evaluative judgments. This does not, however, make these last two objections less important than the substantive objections listed above. In fact, the Marxist empirical views that lead one to believe that a correct theory of social justice can (and thus should) be applied both internationally and diachronically may ultimately prove to be the most salient point of dispute between Marxist and most non-Marxist proponents of moderate and/or radical egalitarian theories of social justice.

Objections to Rawls' Methodology

Objections concerning the bourgeois or individualistic assumptions of his basic approach usually go on to cite the supposed egoism of the individuals in Rawls' original position or the fact that they are (supposedly) utility-maximizers rather than realizers of human capacities (or autonomous choosers of ends) or that Rawls' contractarian model is biased against communitarianism and in favor of individualism. But Rawls does not assume individuals in the original position to be egoists or "mere" utility-maximizers. They are not egoists—even though they are described as "mutually disinterested"—because they do not know their vision of the good in the real world nor even what type of person they are. For all they know, they may be communitarians or altruists in the real world rather than egoists. More importantly, within the original

371

position they are to act as though they are Kantian legislators in the universal kingdom of ends and are thus to give equal consideration to the legitimate interests of everyone in deciding on moral principles by which to judge social arrangements—hardly an egoistic point of view.

Nor does Rawls assume individuals to be "mere" utility-maximizers. First off, they don't know what their substantive conception of the good is in the real world, so they don't know if they most resemble the utility-maximizer. Secondly, in line with his Kantian predilections, Rawls views individuals within the original position as most concerned to realize their "highest" capacities, namely: (1) the capacity for an effective sense of justice, and (2) the capacity to form, revise, and rationally pursue a conception of the good. Thus Rawls views the individual in the original position as *both* a realizer of certain human capacities *and* as an autonomous chooser of ends. (Obviously this view is quite similar to Marx's normative conception of human nature.)

Similarly, Michael Sandel objects to Rawls' theory on grounds that in assuming that (1) individuals in the original position are mutually disinterested and primarily concerned to advance their own conceptions of the good, (2) such individuals would choose principles establishing individual rights, and (3) it is the function of the state to adjudicate conflicts between persons and groups pursuing differing conceptions of the good, it is biased against communitarianism and in favor of individualism. But according to Allen Buchanan, with whose analysis I concur:

> What such critics [of Rawls as Sandel] have failed to grasp is that the contract method assumes only pluralism, not individualism.[9]

> If the parties know that participation in community is in fact an important ingredient in human flourishing and know that their own conceptions of the good may include a prominent role for participation in community, then they will take this into account in their choice of principles of justice. If, as I have argued, individual rights can play a valuable role in protecting communities then the parties will appreciate this fact and it will influence their choice. But if this is so, then in order to argue that parties in the original position would choose a prin-

[9] Buchanan, "Assessing the Communitarian Critique of Liberalism," forthcoming.

ciple establishing individual rights, one need not assume that the parties' conceptions of the good are *individualistic*. All one need assume—and all Rawls does assume—is pluralism: the parties know that different individuals or different groups may have different conceptions of the good; whether they be individualistic or communitarian conceptions of the good is not known. It appears, then, that communitarians who have criticized the hypothetical contract method have mistaken its assumption of pluralism for an individualistic bias.[10]

In addition, according to Sandel, liberalism in general and Rawls' theory in particular are to be faulted for conceiving the self as an autonomous chooser of ends, a "conception in which the self, shorn of all its contingently-given attributes, assumes a kind of supra-empirical status, essentially unencumbered, bounded in advance and given prior to its ends, a pure subject of agency and possession, ultimately thin."[11] The self thus conceived—the argument goes—is incapable of commitment and hence of community. The argument for this is that our most important commitments are neither chosen nor severable at will. Thus, if commitments are severable at will they are not *genuine* commitments. But if the self is an autonomous chooser of ends it can freely decide to detach itself from any or all ends or commitments it has at any particular time. Since genuine commitment to shared ends is a necessary condition for community, the argument continues, being an autonomous chooser of ends is incompatible with the value of community. But the answer to this is that it is simply false that this conception of the self makes genuine commitment impossible. As Buchanan notes:

> One can freely choose an attachment and yet not be free to sever it, if one binds oneself appropriately. Even if there is a sense in which community cannot be freely chosen (at least not *directly* freely chosen) individuals nevertheless can and do freely choose to bind themselves to courses of action which they expect to create conditions under which community will emerge. In that sense community can be freely chosen, though chosen indirectly.[12]

[10] Ibid.

[11] Sandel, *Liberalism and the Limits of Justice*, p. 94. For Rawls' brief response to Sandel's criticism, see n. 21 of his "Justice as Fairness: Political Not Metaphysical," p. 239.

[12] Buchanan, "Assessing the Communitarian Critique of Liberalism."

We can accomplish this in real life because we know that interacting with people in certain ways—e.g., cohabitating with them
and/or having children with them or forming associations with
them—is to one degree or another likely to result in genuine commitments. And we know that once such emotional commitments
are established they become deeply entrenched in us; so deeply
entrenched that we no longer are psychologically capable of simply choosing not to have them. (This is not to say that people are
incapable of abandoning their commitments or responsibilities,
but presumably for everyone this side of the psychopath or sociopath, doing so will involve considerable psychic trauma.) Thus,
according to Buchanan, the liberal conception of the self

> is quite compatible with there being some things, such as
> one's most fundamental commitments to others, which one
> does not and indeed perhaps could not regard as wholly sep-
> arate from one's self. Instead, if the commitments are suffi-
> ciently deep and stable, one may regard them as an element
> of one's identity. Thus if one has become deeply and fully
> committed to a marriage or other community—even if that
> commitment emerged from earlier free choices—one will not
> regard that commitment merely as an object of choice.[13]

Finally, it is important to realize that Rawls' theory—as well as
the theories of such liberal theorists as Ronald Dworkin and Joel
Feinberg—stresses both mutual concern and respect for persons
and is, thus, committed to the value of individual well-being as
well as the value of individual autonomy. Moreover, there is nothing in these theories that militates against the communitarian thesis that participation in human community is an essential component of individual well-being. If this is in fact the case, then (in
principle) these "liberal" moral and social theories can take this
into account and, thus, deflate this communitarian's objection.
Given this fact and the other considerations adduced here, it
seems that the attack launched against Rawls' hypothetical contract method of justification by Sandel and other communitarian
theorists can be deflected.[14]

[13] Ibid.
[14] The three most important contemporary Anglo-American communitarian
moral and social philosophers are probably MacIntyre, Charles Taylor, and Sandel.
(See chapter 7, n. 7, above, for references.) Although F. A. von Hayek takes some
of the same positions and uses some of the same arguments as the communitarians, he is better classified as a (quasi-libertarian) conservative. Socialist moral and

The second objection has been put forward, most notably, by Richard Miller.[15] The idea is that individuals in the original position know that the society in which they live may be divided into antagonistic social classes, and if they are a member of the ruling social class, they may have greater "needs" for, say, wealth and power. This knowledge, Miller argues, will preclude individuals from reaching an agreement on principles of justice in the original position. Any one principle may be beyond the "strains of commitment" for an individual, depending on the class to which he or she actually belongs. This is important because, according to Rawls, it is not reasonable to accept a moral principle that goes beyond the bounds of what an individual's commitment to just social institutions can bear.

This objection, however, is based on a misinterpretation of the function of Rawls' original position and his notion of the "strains of commitment." First, there is the question of whether or not the (supposed) greater "needs" of individuals in the ruling classes would be seriously taken into account by parties in the original position. While the parties are certainly to give consideration to the *genuine* needs and *legitimate* interests of all individuals in deciding on moral principles by which to judge social arrangements, Rawls makes clear that the parties are to consider some needs or preferences as "illegitimate" and thus not worthy of consideration.[16]

Furthermore, as explained in chapter 7, Rawls requires that "needs" and preferences and, more importantly, the moral sense one utilizes in choosing principles (as well as the moral principles one accepts in the original position) be "screened" to rule out the type of prejudices and distortions that can properly be called "ideological." As William Shaw and Jürgen Habermas have argued, this screening mechanism can be extended to include the

social theorist Michael Walzer also shares some positions with the communitarians but veers toward liberalism when it comes to the importance of human rights.

Although not communitarians, both Thomas Nagel (in "Rawls on Justice") and Adina Schwartz (in "Moral Neutrality and Primary Goods") had earlier argued that Rawls' theory begs the question against communitarianism and in favor of liberal individualism. For further reflections on these issues, see Sandel (ed.), *Liberalism and Its Critics*; Amy Gutman, "Communitarian Critics of Liberalism," *Philosophy and Public Affairs*, vol. 14, no. 3 (Summer 1985); and Will Kymlicka, "Liberalism and Communitarianism," *Canadian Journal of Philosophy*, vol. 18, no. 2 (June 1988), "Liberal Individualism and Liberal Neutrality," *Ethics*, vol. 99, no. 4 (July 1989), and *Liberalism, Community, and Culture*, Oxford University Press, N.Y., 1989.

[15] See Miller's "Rawls and Marxism."
[16] See Rawls, *A Theory of Justice*, p. 31, and "Justice as Fairness," pp. 243–244.

requirement that all needs and preferences of individuals in the original position pass muster with psychoanalytic theory (or cognitive psychology) in order to rule out prejudice and ideological distortion.

Secondly, as Allen Buchanan points out, individuals are to judge various moral principles and the "strains of commitment" to which their implementation will give rise "from the perspective of the attitude toward primary goods attributed to the parties [in the original position], not from the perspective of the attitudes that persons actually occupying those various [social] positions would have."[17] Finally, to place as a constraint on principles of justice that all persons who know their actual circumstances in society agree on them and accept them as not being beyond the "strains of commitment" is preposterous. As Buchanan notes, no moral theory would ever even get off the ground if we were to assume that such a theory "is inadequate unless it commands the allegiance of everyone, regardless of his position in society and regardless of how his interests are related to injustices which currently exist."[18]

These considerations are precisely why Rawls' recent move to substitute an "overlapping consensus" method of justification for the strategy of the original position ought, in my opinion, to be rejected. If we were to accept the thesis that basic principles of social justice are justified if (and only if) they are capable of achieving a consensus among all segments of a democratic liberal society, then Miller's criticism of Rawls' theory would be extremely powerful. Assuming that the implementation of Rawls' Difference Principle would require members of the ruling class to part with a large part of their wealth and power, they would not be able to accept—or, in any case, would not accept—this or any other egalitarian principle of distributive justice. On the other hand, members of the least well-off segments of society would not freely accept any principle of distributive justice that was not at least moderately egalitarian. Fortunately, this is not a problem on Rawls' original method of justification, which is the one adopted here.

Substantive Objections to Rawls' Moral Theory

The primary fault of the third objection—that Rawls' theory is a defense of welfare-state capitalism—is that it fails to distinguish

[17] Buchanan, *Marx and Justice*, p. 146.
[18] Ibid., p. 133.

his core moral theory from how he applies it, given his empirical assumptions about society. As previously noted, Rawls himself admits that the choice between socialism and capitalism is to be decided on the basis of our empirical knowledge, in particular, our knowledge of political sociology:

> So far I have assumed that the aim of the branches of government is to establish a democratic regime in which land and capital are widely though not presumably equally held. Society is not so divided that one fairly small sector controls the preponderance of productive resources. When this is achieved and distributive shares satisfy the principles of justice, many socialist criticisms of the market economy are met. But it is clear that, in theory anyway, a liberal socialist regime can also answer to the two principles of justice. We have only to suppose that the means of production are publicly owned and that firms are managed by workers' councils say, or by agents appointed by them. Collective decisions made democratically under the constitution determine the general features of the economy, such as the rate of saving and the proportion of society's production devoted to essential public goods. Given the resulting economic environment, firms regulated by market forces conduct themselves much as before. Although the background institutions will take a different form, especially in the case of the distribution branch, there is no reason in principle why just distributive shares cannot be achieved. The theory of justice does not by itself favor either form of regime. As we have seen, the decision as to which system is best for a given people depends upon their circumstances, institutions, and historical traditions.[19]

Now many Marxists and socialists will object to Rawls' characterization of a "liberal" socialist society since it leaves the market intact. But whether or not a society is socialist (or, at any rate, post-capitalist) is *not* primarily a matter of whether or not the market still operates as a pricing and distribution mechanism but whether or not (1) property has been socialized and (2) the laws of motion of capitalism—especially the law of the maximization of exchange value—have been overcome. (As mentioned in the introduction to this work, there seems reason to believe that government control over large-scale investment and general government regulation of a market socialist economy can function to substitute

---

[19] Rawls, *A Theory of Justice*, p. 280.

the law of the maximization of use value for the law of the maximization of exchange value in such an economy.)

Furthermore, the choice between market forms of socialism and socialist societies having command economies is *not* something automatically decided by Rawls' moral theory per se. The reason that Rawls thinks that the former but not the latter could possibly be just has to do with certain empirical assumptions he makes about the market, namely, that (a) it is more efficient than a command economy, and (b) it is consistent with the Principles of Equal Liberty and Fair Equality of Opportunity, whereas (presumably) command economies are not.[20] A further advantage of the market, according to Rawls, is that it allows the problem of distribution to be handled as a case of pure procedural justice. However, if it actually turned out that command economies were both more efficient than market economies (as many Marxists and socialists maintain) *and* as compatible with the Principles of Equal Liberty and Fair Equality of Opportunity (as well as the Difference Principle), Rawls would presumably be required to forgo this theoretical advantage and favor command economies on moral grounds.

At any rate, according to Rawls' theory, the choice between the various forms of socialism and capitalism is determined on the basis of which best conforms to the requirements of social justice. Although Rawls *presumes* that a democratic form of welfare-state capitalism will best conform to these requirements, this position is not a function of his moral theory per se but of his moral theory in conjunction with his empirical, social-scientific beliefs. As I shall argue presently, however, if even a minimal set of Marxist empirical theses are correct, Rawls' theory will choose socialism (i.e., a democratic form of socialism) over capitalism. Thus his core moral theory is not an ideological defense—nor, for that matter, even a nonideological defense—of welfare-state capitalism or capitalism of any sort.

The first thing to notice about the fourth objection—that Rawls' theory assumes that social classes are inevitable or at least acceptable—is that he uses the term "classes" to refer to *social strata* rather than to groups having different relations to the means of production and distribution. That is, Rawls adopts the view of mainstream, "bourgeois" social theory with respect to the term "class." Thus, while it may be true that he assumes classes to be inevitable and/or acceptable in this sense, we cannot conclude that

[20] See Rawls, *A Theory of Justice*, pp. 270–275.

Rawls' theory (or even Rawls) assumes that *social classes in the Marxist sense* are inevitable or acceptable.

Actually, the claim that Rawls believes classes in the Marxist sense to be inevitable is proven not to be the case by the fact that he believes the principles of justice adumbrated by his theory could be met by a socialist society. Such a society—even a socialist society with a modified-market economy—is, by definition, a classless society, at least in the sense of *antagonistic* social classes, i.e., those that are in direct conflict over the production and distribution of the social surplus product. Even though components of the petty bourgeoisie (small storekeepers, artisans, working farmers, etc.) may still exist alongside the working class (and possibly the peasantry) in a post-capitalist society, presumably there are no economically exploited and exploiting classes because there is no ruling class to pump surplus labor out of one or more ruled classes.[21]

[21] This claim, however, is contested even within Marxist circles. Among Marxist economists, Charles Bettleheim is the most adamant proponent of the view that classes and economic exploitation exist in what I am referring to as contemporary post-capitalist or state-socialist societies. Bettleheim, in fact, classifies such societies as the USSR as state-capitalist. See his *Class Struggles in the U.S.S.R.: First Period 1917–1923*, Monthly Review Press, N.Y., 1976, and *Class Struggles in the U.S.S.R.: Second Period 1923–1930*, Monthly Review Press, N.Y., 1978. For a critique of this position see Michael Goldfield and Melvin Rothenberg, *The Myth of Capitalism Reborn: A Marxist Critique of Theories of Capitalist Restoration in the USSR*, Line of March Communications, San Francisco, 1980; Mandel, *Marxist Economic Theory*, pp. 548–689, and "On the Nature of the Soviet State," as well as Miliband, "Bettleheim and the Soviet Experience."

John Roemer offers a somewhat equivocal analysis. See *A General Theory of Exploitation and Class*, pp. 212–216, 238–263, as well as *Free to Lose*, pp. 125–147.

Among Marxist philosophers, perhaps Svetozar Stojanović gives the most compelling rationale for accepting the existence of classes in such societies. Speaking of contemporary state-socialist societies, he writes: "Since members of the ruling class, as individuals, cannot dispose of the means of production, many people suppose that the means of production are not the property of the state apparatus. The observation that nepotism plays no significant role in the rejuvenation of the statist class, in contrast to other ruling classes in history, adds to this impression. Yet the state apparatus does, in fact, control production and dispose of surplus value (primarily in its own interest) and it is therefore the owner of the means of production, regardless of any formal decrees to the contrary.

"Many Marxists apply only the mildest analytical-critical term to this group, calling it a social *stratum*. But this procedure only plays into the hands of the ideological mystification of the ruling class. In state socialism one can indeed talk meaningfully about the working class and the stratum of its representatives, the state officials. But in Stalinist society, where there are concentrations of political and economic power, wealth, and social prestige on the one hand, and of subjugation and exploitation on the other, the real relations between the ruling group and the proletariat can only be seen in terms of the following categorical symmetry: statist class—working class" (*Between Ideals and Reality*, pp. 48–49).

Rawls does seem to believe, however, that the existence of classes (in the Marxist sense of the term) may be *acceptable*. After all, he believes that capitalist societies may be just, and it is clear that capitalist societies are divided into antagonistic social classes. But here again we must be careful to distinguish between what Rawls' moral theory entails in and of itself and what conclusions about social arrangements he draws from it.[22]

But given the truth of even a minimal set of Marxist empirical assumptions, it is arguable that capitalist society, and indeed any society divided between exploiting and exploited classes, is unjust and—unless there is no better alternative—unjustified. As Allen Buchanan writes:

> Rawls' well-ordered society may be immune to some of the most fundamental Marxian criticism[s] of class-divided society. The satisfaction of the Difference Principle, which requires that the prospects of the worst-off be maximized, and of the Principle of Equality of Fair Opportunity, which requires fair access to offices and positions regardless of one's social position, seem incompatible with the exploitation of the majority by the minority.[23]

But even if Rawls does not believe classes in the Marxist sense to be inevitable (though they may, on his view, be acceptable), he does seem to believe that *social strata* are inevitable. But here we must be careful to say exactly what we mean by "social strata." The fact that there are inequalities of income, status, authority, and prestige between individuals in a certain society does not necessarily mean that this society is divided into social strata. In a just society such inequalities could be the result of individual accomplishment rather than the result of individuals belonging to different *institutionally defined cohesive groups whose whole life prospects are importantly different*. It is only if a society contains such institutionally defined groups who generally pass on their advantages (or disadvantages) from one generation to the next that we can say that social strata exist, as opposed to saying that some identifiable groups of people (e.g., inventors or factory managers or coal miners) generally have more (or less) income, authority, status, or prestige than other groups.

But it may be that we haven't dug deeply enough into Rawls'

---

[22] See Nielsen, *Equality and Liberty*, p. 81, and "On the Very Possibility of a Classless Society," p. 201.

[23] Buchanan, *Marx and Justice*, p. 158.

theory here. It might be claimed, for example, that the objection is not that Rawls assumes social strata to be inevitable at the point of applying his theory to the real world but that this belief enters into the actual construction of his core moral theory as a presupposition of the Difference Principle. It might be maintained, for example, that there would be no point to adopting the principle of maximizing the prospects of the worst-off social group if one did not believe social inequalities to be inevitable or at least acceptable. But this way of framing the objection involves a misinterpretation of Rawls' Difference Principle. The principle, properly interpreted, does not claim that inequalities are justified *because* they meet the maximin criterion but, rather, that *if* any inequalities are justified, this is the case only because they meet this criterion.

Although Rawls sometimes formulates his Difference Principle in such a way that it seems logically to presuppose inequalities, this is not how he intends it to be interpreted. As Buchanan argues, the correct formulation of Rawls' Difference Principle is that the basic structure is to be arranged so as to maximize the life prospects of the worst-off group. But this formulation of the principle does not entail inequalities since it is possible that this principle can be best fulfilled by observing strict equality in the distribution of primary goods, i.e., wealth and income, liberties and rights, powers and opportunities, and leisure time and the social bases of self-respect.[24] Rawls argues, of course, that allowing a certain range of inequalities will benefit the worst-off segments of the population since incentive schedules will increase production, and at least part of this increase can then be distributed to the worst-off segments by means of taxation and welfare transfers. Thus, neither at the level of applying his moral theory to actual societies nor at the level of deciding upon the main principle concerned with distributing material goods—which for Rawls turns out to be the Difference Principle—does his moral theory per se hold that social classes (or even social strata) are either inevitable or acceptable. It is only in conjunction with certain empirical beliefs that his moral theory will reach any of these conclusions.

The fifth objection—that Rawls' theory asserts the absolute priority of negative liberty over all other demands of social justice—is also primarily a matter of misinterpretation. It is true, of course, that he asserts the lexical priority of the Principle of Maximum Equal Liberty in his *special conception* of social justice that is to ap-

[24] See ibid., pp. 129–130.

ply to well-developed societies.[25] Since the right to own property is included in his Maximum Equal Liberty Principle, this priority rule may seem to be a straightforward defense of capitalism: the sort of bourgeois theory or view that Marx chides when he writes, "There alone rule Freedom, Equality, Property, and Bentham."[26] But this priority rule does not turn Rawls' theory into a straight-forward defense of capitalism in this way because, as noted previously, Rawls does not include the right to own *productive* property on the list of basic liberties that the Maximum Equal Liberty Principle is designed to protect.[27] As Rawls puts it in "A Kantian Conception of Equality,"

> liberties not on the list, for example, *the right to own certain kinds of property (e.g., means of production)*, and *freedom of contract* as understood by the doctrine of laissez-faire, are not basic; and so they are not protected by the priority of the first principle [emphasis added].[28]

But the priority of liberty rule may still be objectionable from a Marxist or egalitarian point of view. Unqualified, Rawls' special conception of justice would be unacceptable to even a moderate egalitarian because it does not allow a trade-off between liberty and other social primary goods even under conditions of extreme deprivation. But egalitarians—even "moderate" ones—would agree with Isaiah Berlin that "liberty is not the only goal of men. . . . To avoid glaring inequality of widespread misery I am ready to sacrifice some, or all, of my freedom. . . . I should be guilt-stricken, and rightly so, if I were not, in some circumstances, ready to make this sacrifice."[29]

But Rawls seems committed to *at least* as strong a form of egalitarianism as Berlin. It is important to realize that the set of principles Rawls propounds for the special conception of justice is *not* meant by him to apply to all social and historical situations. The special conception of justice is to hold, in fact, *only* in those cases in which society has advanced to the state where (1) the equal liberties guaranteed by the first principle can be effectively exercised by all and (2) a minimum level of material wealth has been at-

[25] See Rawls, *A Theory of Justice*, pp. 302–303.
[26] Marx, *Capital*, vol. 1, p. 176.
[27] See Rawls, *A Theory of Justice*, p. 61.
[28] Rawls, "A Kantian Conception of Equality," p. 96.
[29] Berlin, "Two Concepts of Liberty," p. 338.

tained. The preference for liberty attributed to the parties in the original position is *conditional*:

The supposition is that *if the persons in the original position assume that their basic liberties can be effectively exercised*, they will not exchange a lesser liberty for an improvement in their economic well-being, *at least once a certain level of wealth has been attained*. It is only when social conditions do not allow the effective establishment of these rights that one can acknowledge their restriction. The denial of equal liberty can be accepted only if it is necessary to enhance the quality of civilization so that in due course the equal freedoms can be enjoyed by all. The lexical ordering of the two principles is the long-run tendency of the general conception of justice consistently pursued under reasonably favorable conditions. Eventually there comes a time in the history of a well ordered society beyond which the special form of the two principles takes over and holds from then on [emphasis added].[30]

Until these conditions are met, the *general* conception of justice applies. According to this conception,

All social primary goods—liberty and opportunity, income and wealth, and the [social] bases of self-respect—are to be distributed equally unless an unequal distribution of any or all of these goods is to the advantage of the least favored.[31]

As Rawls remarks:

Now this general conception imposes no constraints on what sorts of inequalities are allowed, whereas the special conception by putting the two principles in serial order (with the necessary adjustments in meaning), forbids exchanges between basic liberties and economic and social benefits. . . . roughly, the idea underlying this ordering is that if the parties assume that their basic liberties can be effectively exercised they will not exchange a lesser liberty for an improvement in economic well-being.[32]

These stipulations would seem to answer the claim made by Marxists and other egalitarians that the principle of the priority of liberty should not apply to societies that do not provide their pop-

[30] Rawls, *A Theory of Justice*, pp. 542.
[31] Ibid., p. 303.
[32] Ibid., pp. 151–152.

ulations with even a minimally decent level of material well-being. (Perhaps even the basic biological needs of individuals are not being met.) This description, it can be argued, applies to all presently existing capitalist countries in the Third World and to such societies as the USSR and the People's Republic of China at the time of their anti-capitalist revolutions. Indeed, even the basic biological needs of many individuals in such societies routinely go (or went) unmet. One need only consult the staggering statistics on world hunger, malnutrition, undernutrition, and starvation to see this. And whatever criticisms one might have of post-capitalist societies, they have generally been successful in meeting the basic needs of their populations (more on this in chapter 10). Whether revolutions to create post-capitalist societies are justified will, of course, depend on one's empirical beliefs on how well such revolutionary regimes or societies meet security rights as well as subsistence rights. Thus, it is possible to disagree with the Marxist's claim that such anti-capitalist revolutions are justified even if one agrees on the priority of guaranteeing people a minimum level of well-being.

But egalitarians and Marxists may still not be completely satisfied with Rawls' stipulations—or at least his phrasing of these stipulations—because in speaking of a society as a whole reaching a certain level of material wealth before the priority of liberty goes into effect, Rawls does not seem to commit himself to a *minimum floor principle* that explicitly states (at least) that the basic biological needs of *all* individuals of a society must be met, and that *this* requirement takes precedence over any other demand of social justice. Perhaps Rawls means to imply that a minimally decent standard of well-being will be guaranteed to all individuals, but the mere fact that a society as a whole has reached a certain level of material wealth does not seem to entail that all members of that society will be maintained at a minimally decent level of well-being.

One might argue that Rawls incorporates a minimum floor principle into his theory at the institutional level when he speaks of the functions of the transfer branch of government. While it is true that in discussing the background institutions for distributive justice he puts forward the demand for a "social minimum" to be guaranteed by the transfer branch of government, this demand seems to be the result of the application of the Difference Principle within the special conception of justice. Thus it is a demand that seemingly cannot impinge on the priority of the Maximum Equal Liberty Principle. Apparently his demand for a social minimum in

384

this context is *not* the same as the demand for a minimum floor principle, which holds that all individuals must be guaranteed a minimum level of well-being and that this has priority over any and all other considerations of social justice, including the demand for maximum equal liberty.

Yet it would seem that the parties in the original position would be concerned to guarantee themselves such a minimum level of well-being and, thus, that a minimum floor principle ought to be incorporated into both the general and special conceptions of justice. Actually, since the parties would be equally as concerned to protect themselves against murder, torture, rape, and brutal assaults as they would be to protect themselves against hunger, malnutrition, and debilitating poverty, we should interpret this minimum floor principle as demanding protection against both sorts of contingencies. When we put this in terms of rights, the principle becomes a *basic rights principle* asserting that the most fundamental principle of social justice is that everyone's *security rights* and *subsistence rights* must be respected. (If this is not possible, then we are not within the circumstances of justice.)

The sixth objection is that Rawls' theory assumes that large socioeconomic inequalities are compatible with strict equality of liberty. This thesis is common to liberal moral and social theory and has been roundly criticized by Marxists and other egalitarians on grounds that equal liberty in the context of large socioeconomic inequalities is "equal" in name only, since the more well-off individuals and classes can take advantage of such civil and political liberties to a much greater extent than those who are less well off. If this is the case, how can we say that the liberties in question are really equal? Since the reason such formally equal liberties are really not equal is the discrepancy in socioeconomic advantages allowed by society, the conclusion drawn is that socioeconomic inequalities (at least beyond a certain degree) are not compatible with strict equality of liberty. (Naturally, the incompatibility here is of an empirical rather than a logical nature.)

Rawls' reply to this criticism is that it confuses *equal liberty* with *equal worth of liberty*.

> *Liberty* is represented by the complete system of the liberties of equal citizenship, while the *worth of liberty* to persons and groups is proportional to their capacity to advance their ends within the framework the system defines. Freedom as equal liberty is the same for all; the question of compensating for a

lesser than equal liberty does not arise. But the worth of liberty is not the same for everyone. Some have greater authority and wealth, and therefore greater means to achieve their aims [emphasis added].[33]

But if we accept Rawls' terminology, it becomes clear that Marxists and many other egalitarians will not be satisfied with this answer since it is precisely this sort of inequality they were objecting to from the start. In his now classic article, "Equal Liberty and Unequal Worth of Liberty," Norman Daniels launches a two-pronged assault on this portion of Rawls' theory. The first is designed to show that refusing to accept such socioeconomic factors as poverty and ignorance as constraints on liberty is arbitrary, given that Rawls—like J. S. Mill—accepts other nonlegal factors such as social pressure and public opinion as liberty-limiting constraints. If this is so, Daniels argues, then Rawls' distinction between liberty and worth of liberty is also arbitrary.

The other, even more decisive prong of Daniels' attack consists of accepting Rawls' terminological distinction and then showing that a principle demanding equal (or at least approximately equal) *worth of liberty* is as morally justified as a principle demanding *equal liberty*. More specifically, Daniels argues that for reasons precisely analogous to those used in choosing a principle of equal liberty, the parties in the original position will also choose a principle of equal (or approximately equal) worth of liberty. According to Rawls, people will choose the Maximum Equal Liberty Principle because they want to ensure themselves the good of self-respect, which is ultimately the most important good on Rawls' view. According to Daniels,

> the core of Rawls argument . . . depends on three claims: that public affirmation of the equal liberties could act as a social basis of self-respect, that enhancement of self-respect would be equal because the liberties are equal, and that this arrangement, viewed from behind the veil of ignorance, minimizes the risk of having relatively low self-respect, making it rational to choose equal citizenship liberties.[34]

Daniels goes on to argue that equal *worth* of liberty is analogous to equal liberty in all three of these respects and thus will be chosen in the original position as well. Even Rawls agrees, for exam-

[33] Ibid., p. 204.
[34] Daniels, "Equal Liberty and Unequal Worth of Liberty," p. 275.

ple, that the realization that the more well-off can exercise their liberties more effectively than the less well-off may cause the latter to view themselves as holding a "subordinate ranking in the public forum," which "would indeed be humiliating and destructive of self-esteem."[35] Thus, in order to be judged adequate, Rawls' theory of social justice—or any other theory of social justice, for that matter—must demand at least *approximate equality* in the worth of liberty as well as strict equality of formal liberty. This will be one of the modifications of Rawls' theory I take to be justified.

But choosing a principle of maximum equal (or approximately equal) worth of liberty as well as a Principle of Maximum Equal Liberty may have radical consequences for judging allowable differentials of wealth. This is because, as Daniels writes,

> worth of liberty is especially sensitive to *relative* differences in the index of primary social goods and is not a simple monotonic function of it. . . . worth of liberty is affected by comparative access to those resources and institutions such as qualified legal counsel or the mass media, which are needed for the effective exercise of liberty.[36]

If this is true, then it seems probable that large socioeconomic inequalities are destructive of the requirement that everyone be able to exercise their basic liberties effectively. As Daniels notes, an extremely important consequence of this fact is that

> many inequalities which might have been justified by the Second Principle taken in isolation will probably fail the test of compatibility with the First Principle.
>
> In a sense, a more far-reaching egalitarianism may be forced on us as a result of the two principles of justice than we at first expected, and certainly one more far-reaching than Rawls' examples indicate. Rawls, being primarily interested in the argument for the principles themselves, might be willing to roll with the punch. All this means is that his system is not compatible, as a matter of empirical fact, with as diverse a set of social systems as he might have hoped.
>
> But even if Rawls is willing to accept this result, there remains something of a surprise in it. . . . it is the First Principle, even more than the Second, which is likely to force strong

[35] Rawls, *A Theory of Justice*, pp. 544–545.
[36] Daniels, "Equal Liberty and Unequal Worth of Liberty," p. 271.

egalitarianism with regard to primary social goods other than liberty.[37]

It should be noted, however, that Daniels' proposed modification of Rawls' theory does not demand *strictly equal* but only *approximately equal* worth of liberty. Daniels proposes only that we refuse "to allow any Second principle inequalities which undermine the First Principle by making worth of liberty unequal"[38] and believes that we can accomplish this by "ruling out all such *significant* inequalities" (emphasis added).[39] As Allen Buchanan maintains, it would, in fact, be unreasonable to require *strictly* equal worth of liberty because "whether a given right will be of equal effectiveness or worth for different individuals will depend upon many different factors, some of which it is neither possible nor desirable to subject to social control or regulation."[40] It may not be *possible*, for example, to eliminate such differentials to the extent that they are due to differentials in natural talents and abilities. Moreover, it may not be desirable to eliminate all such differentials if doing so requires the elimination of the family as a social institution.

In light of these considerations, objection 7—that Rawls assumes the Difference Principle to be sufficiently egalitarian—may not be as important as one may have originally assumed. Nevertheless, it deserves our consideration. I shall consider two forms of this objection. The first is that the Difference Principle does not allocate sufficient resources to individuals with natural disabilities. The second is that the inter-group inequalities allowed by the difference principle are too severe because they will undermine people's self-respect or violate their moral autonomy.

The first objection is put forward by such writers as Armatya Sen and Ronald Dworkin. In "Equality of What?" Sen argues that the Difference Principle is inadequate because it will give those with natural disabilities neither more nor less than those who are not disabled; it will, in fact, leave them "severely alone."[41] Dworkin concurs with this assessment. In "What Is Equality? Part 2," he writes:

The difference principle is not sufficiently fine-tuned in a variety of ways. . . . In particular, the structure seems insuffi-

---

[37] Ibid., p. 280.
[38] Ibid., p. 274.
[39] Ibid.
[40] Buchanan, *Marx and Justice*, p. 151.
[41] Sen, "Equality of What?" p. 217.

ciently sensitive to the position of those with natural handicaps, physical or mental, who do not themselves constitute a worst-off group, because this is defined economically, and would not count as the representative or average member of any such group.[42]

According to Sen, the main problem with the Difference Principle is that it concentrates on the provision of primary goods per se rather than on the basic capabilities Rawls supposes these primary goods to ensure. Thus Sen proposes an equality of basic capabilities, which is, however, not a strict equality but an equality rendered in terms of a maximin or (the even more egalitarian) leximin principle ranging over basic capabilities. Quite frankly, I think that Sen may be right on this point, but, as he realizes, this does not constitute a major modification of Rawls' theory. As Sen puts it, "The focus on basic capabilities can be seen as a natural extension of Rawls' concern with primary goods, shifting attention from goods to what goods do to human beings"[43] (more on this in chapter 10). In any case, this modification probably will not make much of a difference when it comes to choosing between basic social institutions, especially between capitalism and socialism.

According to Dworkin, the main problem with the Difference Principle is that it applies to *groups* rather than to *individuals*. His proposed alternative is a type of Equality of Resources Theory designed to enforce "the fundamental requirement that only an equal share of social resources be devoted to the lives of each of [society's] members, as measured by the opportunity cost of such resources to others."[44] Dworkin argues that a market is the only way to measure opportunity costs and, thus, that just societies must have markets. His theoretical arguments also utilize markets and market transactions in hypothetical choice situations—especially an original market situation of complete equality—as means for arriving at an initially just distribution of resources and just distributions thereafter. (Welfare transfers are justified on grounds of hypothetical insurance contracts people would be willing to enter into behind a sort of veil of ignorance. Taxes are justified as premiums on such insurance contracts.)

Although many Marxists and socialists will have a knee-jerk reaction to condemn this theory because it utilizes hypothetical mar-

---

[42] Dworkin, "What is Equality? Part 2: Equality of Resources," p. 339.

[43] Sen, "Equality of What?" pp. 218–219.

[44] Dworkin, "What is Equality? Part. 2," p. 338. See, also, his "What is Equality? Part 1: Equality of Welfare."

kets and demands actual ones, such a reaction is not justified. As argued previously, a market form of socialism may well be preferable to either capitalist or command-economy post-capitalist societies. The use of hypothetical markets is also innocuous, especially since it is logically possible for a theory using hypothetical markets to end up demanding severe restrictions on actual markets or even their complete abolition.

From the perspective of the adequacy of Rawls' theory, however, the main line of defense consists of pointing out that other parts of his theory can potentially deflect Dworkin's criticism. In particular, Rawls' Fair Equality of Opportunity Principle and the Principle of Redress tend to obviate Dworkin's criticism that Rawls' theory does not allocate a fair amount of social resources to those with natural disabilities because it focuses on classes of individuals rather than on individuals per se. Dworkin mentions Rawls' Principle of Redress as a possible defense but dismisses it, apparently because he (mistakenly) sees it as being primarily tied up with Rawls' Difference Principle rather than with his Fair Equality of Opportunity Principle.[45] According to Rawls, the Principle of Redress is

> the principle that undeserved inequalities call for redress; and since inequalities of birth and natural endowment are undeserved, these inequalities are to somehow be compensated for. Thus the principle holds that in order to treat all persons equally, *to provide genuine equality of opportunity*, society must give more attention to *those with fewer native assets* and to those born into the less favorable social positions. . . . In pursuit of this principle greater resources might be spent on the education of the less rather than the more intelligent, at least over a certain period of life, say the earlier years of school.[46]

Similarly, it might be a reasonable interpretation or extension of Rawls' theory to demand, for example, that persons of equal intelligence but unequal physical abilities have approximately equal chances of gaining offices and positions for which the primary requirement is intelligence or other mental skills. This would mean that many persons having natural physical disabilities would receive a greater proportion of social resources than they would have received merely on the basis of the Difference Principle. Even

[45] Ibid., p. 339.
[46] Rawls, *A Theory of Justice*, pp. 100–101.

though Rawls differentiates his Principle of Fair Equality of Opportunity from the liberal version of fair equality of opportunity by subjecting it to the maximin criterion, he also stresses that the positions and offices in question must truly be open if we are not unjustifiably to deprive some "[of] experiencing the realization of self which comes from a skillful and devoted exercise of social duties . . . [which is] one of the main forms of the human good."[47] For these reasons, Dworkin's claim that Rawls' theory is insufficiently egalitarian with respect to those with natural disabilities seems unconvincing. Whether Dworkin's Equality of Resources Theory is ultimately more viable than Rawls' Difference and Fair Equality of Opportunity Principles is still a matter of debate. But, for purposes of this work, I shall assume that Rawls' position on the distribution of material wealth is at least as viable as Dworkin's.[48]

The second left-leaning objection to Rawls' difference principle is that it allows inequalities that are great enough to undermine self-respect or moral autonomy. In *Liberty and Equality*, Kai Nielsen puts forward this objection in the following passages:

> Rawls argues that in sufficiently favorable but still only moderately affluent circumstances, where his two principles of justice are taken to be rational ordering principles for the guidance of social relations, it could be the case that justice, and indeed a commitment to morality, would require the acceptance as just and as through and through morally accept-

[47] Ibid., p. 84.
[48] For further dicussions of this set of issues, see Dworkin, "What Is Equality? Part 3: The Place of Liberty"; Scanlon, "Equality of Resources and Equality of Welfare: A Forced Marriage?" Roemer, "Equality of Resources Implies Equality of Welfare" and "Equality of Talent"; Alexander and Schwarszchild, "Liberalism, Neutrality, and Equality of Welfare vs. Equality of Resources"; Arneson, "Equality and Equal Opportunity for Welfare"; and G. A. Cohen, "The Currency of Egalitarian Justice."
Another objection sometimes raised against Rawls' Difference Principle is that it will not allow even a tiny worsening of the position of the worst-off group in society, even if this is a necessary condition for preventing a dramatic worsening of the position of everyone else such that it becomes almost as bad as that of the worst-off group. (See Dworkin, "Equality of What? Part 2," pp. 339–340.) One possible response is that such situations are highly fanciful. But so long as they are possible, a theory of justice is required to handle them. Two substantive responses to this objection are that (1) justice must be upheld and the Difference Principle must prevail and (2) in situations such as these, justice can sometimes be overridden by considerations of immense utility. Although the second position seems more reasonable to me, since this objection is not claiming that Rawls' theory is insufficiently egalitarian, we can ignore it for our purposes.

able a not inconsiderable disparity in the total life prospects of the children of entrepreneurs and the children of unskilled laborers, even when those children are equally talented, equally energetic, and so on. If conditions are of a certain determinate sort, a just society, he claims, could in such circumstances tolerate such disparities.[49]

These conditions, of course, are that such inequalities are to the advantage of the worst-off segments of the population. But Nielsen concludes that

> one can still be inclined to say that such inequalities remain unfair, indeed even somehow grossly unjust. We have two children of equal talent and ability and yet in virtue of their distinct class backgrounds their whole life prospects are very different indeed. One can see the force of the utilitarian considerations which would lead the parents of such children or the children themselves to be resigned to the inequalities, to accept them as the best thing they could get under the circumstances, but why should we think they are *just* distribution?[50]

But here Nielsen may be mistaken in claiming that Rawls would (or even could) view this scenario as one in which his Fair Equality of Opportunity Principle is met. After all, Rawls explicitly demands that equality of opportunity be equal in a substantive as well as a purely formal sense, such that

> those who are at the same level of talent and ability, and have the same willingness to use them, should have the same prospects of success regardless of their initial place in the social system, that is, irrespective of the income class into which they are born. In all sectors of society there should be roughly equal prospects of culture and achievement for everyone similarly motivated and endowed. The expectations of those with the same abilities and aspirations should not be affected by their social class.[51]

In well-developed societies, of course, the requirement of fair equality of opportunity cannot be implemented by restricting any of our basic liberties, according to Rawls' theory. Moreover, we cannot expect this demand to be perfectly carried out "so long as

[49] Nielsen, *Equality and Liberty*, pp. 82–83.
[50] Ibid., pp. 88–89.
[51] Rawls, *A Theory of Justice*, p. 73.

the institution of the family exists."[52] Nevertheless, we can and should—within these restrictions—prevent social and economic inequalities that will undermine the Principle of Fair Equality of Opportunity. Where Rawls and Nielsen most disagree, it would seem, is on the *factual question* of whether or not social and economic inequalities can be so limited and fair equality of opportunity so insured within class-divided societies in general and capitalist societies in particular. Although Rawls at one point writes, "As these institutions presently exist . . . they are riddled with grave injustices,"[53] he more characteristically asserts that "there presumably are ways of running them compatible with their basic design and intention so that the difference principle is satisfied consistent with the demands of liberty and fair equality of opportunity. It is this fact which underlies our assurance that these arrangements can be made just."[54] Thus, once again, it appears that even if the objection in question is cogent, it may not tell against Rawls' basic moral theory as opposed to the empirical assumptions he makes in applying it.

This brings us to a second difficulty with Nielsen's scenario taken as an argument against the Difference Principle, namely, that in framing the case in terms of an opposition between the children of unskilled laborers and the children of *entrepreneurs*, he has not clearly distinguished between (a) the issue of the acceptability of the Difference Principle and (b) the issue of whether or not Rawls' principles of social justice can be satisfied by a class-divided society in general or a capitalist society in particular. As we have seen in our analysis of objections 3 and 4, above, Rawls assumes that his principles can be satisfied by class-divided and capitalist societies. But this conclusion is not something endemic to his moral theory. It results only when it is combined with certain empirical assumptions he happens to make. Nielsen acknowledges this, in fact, when he writes that one reply to such objections to Rawls' application of the Difference Principle consists in maintaining that class division and the resultant inequalities are inevitable.[55] Nielsen, of course, rejects the notion that classes and class-based inequalities are inevitable. Furthermore, like most socialists, he holds that the Difference Principle can be much better met in post-capitalist societies than in capitalist societies and thus

[52] Ibid., p. 74.
[53] Ibid., p. 87.
[54] Ibid.
[55] See Nielsen, *Equality and Liberty*, p. 86.

that—*ceteris paribus*—this part of Rawls' theory of social justice will choose the former sort of society over the latter. Nevertheless, the question of the justifiability of the Difference Principle can and should be separated from these empirical issues. We need to ascertain in abstraction from any empirical information regarding socialism, capitalism, etc., whether the Difference Principle or a principle calling for a more strict form of equality should be adopted. Nielsen—like most of us perhaps—has ambiguous leanings on the Difference Principle considered in and of itself. He recognizes the force of the "utilitarian reasoning" behind the Difference Principle in cases like this. If the least well-off people will be better off under a system of inequalities—even substantial inequalities—why not choose this system? Why trade off happiness or preference satisfaction of the least well-off people for greater equality between groups? But, Nielsen writes,

> Still I am also inclined to come back against such "utilitarian reasoning" concerning such a case with something (vague as it is) about *fairness, human dignity*, and being in a better position to control one's own life (*effective moral autonomy*) [emphasis added].[56]

> Even when it is to their advantage, the working class people in such a circumstance, both children and adults, have had, by the very existence of this extensive disparity, *their moral persons assaulted and their self-respect damaged* [emphasis added].[57]

But, as Nielsen realizes, these remarks point to another reply available to Rawls. Rawls generally speaks of the Difference Principle as being concerned with *material goods* such as income and wealth. But he also holds that the primary good of the *social bases of self-respect* must be taken into consideration in applying the Difference Principle if, as a matter of empirical fact, differentials in material wealth and/or social power have a significant effect on people's self-respect. He writes that "the confident sense of their own worth should be sought for the least favored and this limits the forms of hierarchy and the degrees of inequality that justice permits,"[58] and that "eventually in applying the difference principle we wish to include in the prospects of the least advantaged the

56 Ibid., pp. 89–90.
57 Ibid., p. 84.
58 Rawls, *A Theory of Justice*, p. 107.

primary good of self-respect."[59] While he believes that equal self-respect (or self-esteem) is primarily—if not exclusively—a function of having equal liberties and the status of equal citizenship, he admits that

> it is quite possible that this idea cannot be carried through completely. To some extent men's sense of their own worth may hinge upon their institutional position and their income share. If, however, [my] account of social envy and jealousy is sound, then with the appropriate background arrangements, these inclinations should not be excessive, at least not when the priority of liberty is effectively upheld. But theoretically we can if necessary include self-respect in the primary goods, the index of which defines expectations. Then in applications of the difference principle, this index can allow for the effects of excusable envy; the expectations of the less advantaged are lower the more severe these effects. . . . when necessary the expectations of the less advantaged can be understood so as to include the primary good of self-esteem.[60]

Thus it seems that rather than rejecting the Difference Principle as insufficiently egalitarian, we ought to accept it with the qualification that it is to include the social bases of self-respect among the goods to be maximized for the least advantaged, which—as a matter of empirical fact—will probably make reference to acceptable differentials in both material goods (income and wealth) and social decision-making power.[61] But if Marxist empirical theory is basically correct, Rawls' assumption that a Difference Principle that takes self-respect into consideration can be fulfilled in a capitalist (or any class-divided) society seems questionable, to say the least. If self-respect can be negatively affected by vast or even relatively large inequalities in wealth and income—a proposition that does not seem implausible, especially since such differences also

---

[59] Ibid., p. 39.

[60] Ibid., p. 546.

[61] At one point, Rawls suggests that the plurality of associations in a complex society might reduce the "visibility" or at least the "painful visibility" of social and economic inequalities that might otherwise undermine people's self-respect. (See *A Theory of Justice*, pp. 536–537.) But this deceptive (or self-deceptive) way of blocking from people's consciousness what might otherwise be characterized as "acceptable envy" seems to run counter to much of the rest of Rawls' moral theory, which emphasizes full disclosure of all facts relevant for deciding on social arrangements and rules at the various stages of his decision-making scenario. (See *A Theory of Justice*, p. 547. Also see Nielsen, *Equality and Liberty*, pp. 49–53; and Keat and Miller, "Understanding Justice.")

may affect the worth of our liberties and the amount of control we have over our lives—then such inequalities will not be justified on this version of the Difference Principle. But just as it may be unreasonable to demand strict rather than approximate equality in the worth of liberty, it may similarly be unreasonable to demand strict rather than approximate equality of material wealth and social power. This is especially true since (1) in all probability, self-respect will only begin to be undermined when the differentials in wealth, income, and/or power reach certain levels; and (2) even in a socialist society, income differentials may well be necessary to stimulate production, which may well benefit everyone, or at any rate the least advantaged.

This brings us to objection 8: Rawls' theory demands *political* democracy but not democracy in the *social and economic realm*, e.g., in the workplace. Rawls seems to take an equivocal position on this issue. Unlike many traditional liberals, he does *not* positively and unequivocally reject social and economic democracy. In fact, he admits that his theory may well be compatible with a democratic or "liberal" form of socialism within which "firms are managed by workers' councils say, or by agents appointed by them."[62] Assuming that these workers' councils are to be democratically elected—which seems likely to be Rawls' view—what we have here is *democracy in the workplace*, the major form of social and economic democracy most Marxists and socialists are concerned to ensure. So even though Rawls apparently is not opposed to social and economic democracy, he does not advocate it. Moreover, although one might have expected him to agree that there is a *prima facie* case for social and economic democracy on his theory since—along with political democracy—it would seem to be a natural extension of his concern for autonomy and his ideal of the person as an autonomous chooser of ends, not even this much is clear. For if he did perceive there to be a *prima facie* assumption in favor of social and economic democracy, one would expect him to take the time to explain why and how this assumption is overridden in welfare-state capitalist societies. But this he fails to do.

To come to terms with this perplexity, we need to answer two questions: (1) Is there reason to believe that Rawls *does*—or at least *should*—perceive there to be a *prima facie* assumption in favor of social and economic democracy? And (2) if so, on what grounds—

[62] Rawls, *A Theory of Justice*, p. 280.

if any—is this *prima facie* assumption overridden according to his theory.

Some have argued that Rawls should accept the view that there is a *prima facie* case for social and economic democracy since he accepts the value of autonomy in the original position. Although there seems to be something to this argument, we must be careful not to confuse the notion of *moral autonomy*—strictly construed— with that of autonomy as *freedom (as self-determination)*. On the explication of the notions of "moral good" and "nonmoral good" given in chapter 4, moral autonomy (like virtue, right, justice, and the fulfillment of duty) is a moral good, while autonomy in the latter sense (like physical health, pleasure, happiness, security, comfort, community, and self-realization) is a nonmoral good. *Moral autonomy*, according to both Kant and Rawls, concerns binding oneself to moral laws, which are one's own laws, because they are the laws (or maxims) that one can (and should) will for all rational beings (including oneself) when one is taking the perspective of a legislator in the universal kingdom of ends.[63] Moral autonomy, according to Kant, involves positive and negative autonomy: the positive autonomy of being the genuine author of the moral rules one obeys (and of thus obeying one's self) and the negative autonomy of one's decisions being free of alien or "heterogeneous" causes or influences such as prudential concerns, irrational impulses, or natural inclinations.

As I pointed out in chapter 3 when explicating Marx's principle of freedom (as self-determination), autonomy in the second sense can be divided into the values of *negative freedom* (i.e., freedom from the undue interference of others) and *positive freedom* (i.e., the freedom to determine one's own life, especially the freedom to participate in social decision-making processes that affect one's life). Obviously, the aspect of autonomy or freedom (as self-determination) we are concerned with when discussing political and/or social and economic democracy is that of "positive freedom" or, as some writers call it, "participatory autonomy."

It is clear that Rawls' strategy of the original position is designed to ensure the *moral autonomy* of the parties. But if we construe moral autonomy as above, then there is no basis to assume that Rawls would be inconsistent in *not choosing* participatory autonomy as a value or principle. This is because morally autonomous

[63] See Kant, *Foundations of the Metaphysics of Morals*, pp. 49–59, as well as Rawls, "A Kantian Conception of Equality," and "Kantian Constructivism in Moral Theory."

agents are not logically required to recognize any particular moral value or principle, even the value or principle of autonomy in the nonmoral sense. It is even logically possible that morally autonomous agents in a hypothetical choice situation would choose a principle of subordination of the individual (to the Church, state, or whatever) and endorse a hierarchical, authoritarian form of society as just or morally best. (Indeed, on one interpretation of Rousseau, morally autonomous individuals choose to commit themselves to a social contract that completely subordinates them to the state—a state that may even be authoritarian in nature.)

But Rawls' critics can still argue that even though there is no direct contradiction between Rawls' concern for moral autonomy and his apparent indifference to the value of participatory autonomy, there *is* an inconsistency involved between *Rawls' normative conception of persons as autonomous choosers of ends*—which is packed into his characterization of individuals in the original position—and his indifference to the value of participatory autonomy. One can also go on to argue that his commitment to *political* democracy (which seems based on the value of autonomy in the sense of freedom as self-determination) is inconsistent with his failure to endorse social and economic democracy. If we accept participatory autonomy as intrinsically good, then we must agree with Schweickart that "a social structure that permits individuals greater participatory autonomy will be judged (all else equal, of course) a better system."[64] If we further assume that there is no good reason to restrict the application of this principle to the political as opposed to the social and economic sphere, then—all things being equal—greater social and economic democracy will be preferred to less. T. M. Scanlon goes so far as to argue that

> one might claim, following Rawls' argument . . . that as soon as a certain level of basic well-being is attained it becomes and then remains irrational for persons to accept lesser control over the terms and conditions of their working lives "for the sake of greater material means and amenities." Indeed, such an appeal to [an] increasing preference [for various species of liberty] seems to me more satisfactory as an argument for industrial democracy than as an account of the priority of traditional constitutional liberties.[65]

[64] Schweickart, *Capitalism or Worker Control?* p. 139.
[65] Scanlon, "Rawls' Theory of Justice," p. 204.

Although one might hold that Rawls' concern for this sort of autonomy or self-determination provides *equal* justification for constitutional liberties and "industrial" (i.e., social and economic) democracy, or even that it will provide a stronger justification for the former, it seems clear that it is reasonable to make a *prima facie* assumption in favor of both. But if this is so, why and how does Rawls think it is overridden on his theory?

The answer to this, it seems to me, is twofold. First, it is important to realize that Rawls' commitment to *political* democracy is not as strong as one might assume. From this fact we can infer that even if he accepts participatory autonomy as intrinsically valuable, he does not see it as a particularly strong value. Second, although Rawls does not explicitly say so, he seems to suspect an incompatibility between certain other moral values—primarily negative liberty—and full-fledged social and economic democracy. Thus he may reject (or at least refuse to endorse) social and economic democracy because he believes that it conflicts with his Maximum Equal Liberty Principle and holds that social and economic value underlying it (i.e., participatory autonomy) must give way in case of such conflicts.

As to the first point, Rawls seems to demand political democracy not as a matter of principle but, rather, on grounds that adherence to it is the best way to ensure that other principles of social justice are met. According to his Principle of Participation, "all citizens are to have an equal right to take part in, and to determine the outcome of, the constitutional process that establishes the laws with which they are to comply."[66] This is to be exercised through the rights to vote and to stand for public office. But Rawls goes on to state that "the chief merit of the principle of participation is to insure that the government respects the rights and welfare of the governed."[67] Although he claims that "the grounds for self-government are not solely instrumental,"[68] he does so on the basis that certain benefits—greater self-respect, enlarged intellectual and moral sensibilities, and a greater sense of political competence—will accrue to individuals in societies allowing self-government.[69] But this itself is an *instrumental* justification of self-government and not a claim that self-government and the underlying value of "participatory autonomy" are intrinsically valuable.

[66] Rawls, *A Theory of Justice*, p. 221.
[67] Ibid., pp. 229–230.
[68] See ibid., p. 233.
[69] Ibid., p. 234.

However, since Rawls insists that "all should have a voice [in civic affairs, even though] the say of everyone need not be equal,"[70] he seems to assume, at some level, that self-government—or at least the value of autonomy or freedom (as self-determination) on which it is based—does have intrinsic value. Nevertheless, on Rawls' view, this value is not equal to that of negative liberty:

> One of the tenets of classical liberalism is that the political liberties are of less intrinsic importance than liberty of conscience and freedom of the person. Should one be forced to choose between the political liberties and all the others, the governance of a good sovereign who recognized the latter and who upheld the rule of law would be far preferable.[71]

Rawls agrees with this tenet. On his view, the "liberties of the ancients" (i.e., political liberties) are not nearly so important as the "liberties of the moderns" (i.e., negative liberties). He holds that since individuals in the original position do not value political democracy as highly as negative liberty, we must judge whether or not and to what extent we should implement it in the political and social and economic realms on the basis of the probable *a posteriori* consequences in relation to the even more fundamental value of negative liberty.

Finally, Rawls may also be making the empirical assumption that social and economic democracy will require socialism, and that a socialist form of society will, in all probability, violate one or more of his principles of justice in ways that a "liberal" capitalist society will not. This conjecture seems both to fit in with the general empirical assumptions he makes in applying his moral theory and to provide a good explanation of why he does not demand social and economic democracy. If this analysis is correct, we have here another example of a left-leaning objection to Rawls being based primarily on empirical—as opposed to evaluative—considerations.

However, some will insist that Rawls does not give sufficient emphasis to the value of autonomy (in the sense of autonomy as a nonmoral good) or, at any rate, to the value of *participatory autonomy*. It seems to me that although this criticism is correct, we should *not* put the value of participatory autonomy on a par with

[70] Ibid., p. 232.
[71] Ibid., p. 229.

the value of negative liberty. The thought experiment wherein we compare a society respecting the value of negative liberty, but not that of participatory autonomy, and a society respecting the value of participatory autonomy, but not that of negative liberty, seems quite convincing. All other factors being equal, almost all of us, I think, would prefer the former to the latter.

Nevertheless, we should, I contend, accept social and economic democracy as *prima facie* morally justified. First, social and economic as well as political democracy is valuable in that it satisfies the intrinsic value of participatory autonomy, or—more generally—freedom (as self-determination). Second, it seems likely that social and economic as well as political democracy—especially the equal right to participate in social decision-making processes—is instrumentally valuable in that it promotes the intrinsic good of self-respect. But what implications does this have for an adequate theory of social justice? I believe that Iris Young is correct when she argues that an adequate regard for the value of participatory autonomy issues in a Principle of Collective Self-determination.

> The basic content of the principle of self-determination is as follows. Justice requires that all institutionalized activities of social cooperation within a society be constituted so as to provide that all participants in the institution or activity also participate on an equal basis in the basic decisions regarding the organization and operation of that institution.[72]

> The principle of self-determination specifies that individuals participate equally in the making of the decisions which will govern their actions within institutions of social cooperation. Practically speaking, this means that no just institution of social cooperation which requires its members to obey rules and directives pertaining to their activity within that institution can permit a hierarchy in the organization of basic decision-making power. Justice requires that all institutions of social cooperation be democratically organized.[73]

Obviously, this Principle of Collective Self-determination is in accord with that part of Marx's implicit moral theory (on my interpretation) that demands the right to equal participation in social decision-making processes. But equally obviously, such a principle cannot sensibly demand complete direct democracy or a prohibi-

[72] I. M. Young, "Self-Determination as a Principle of Justice," p. 32.
[73] Ibid., p. 30.

401

tion on all hierarchical aspects of social organization. Young is well aware of this. She writes:

> It should be noted that while the principle specifies nonhier-archical structuring of decision-making within an institution of social cooperation, it does not preclude hierarchical differ-entiation of functions performed or privileges held within the institution. Nor does it even preclude a certain hierarchical or-ganization of executive authority. What the principle specifi-cally precludes is hierarchical authority in basic decision-mak-ing. Just what counts as a basic decision is again a matter which arises at the level of applying the principle in particular cases. It would include, however, such things as the determi-nation of the goals and priorities of the cooperative activity, and the rules and basic means guiding their enactment; the determination of how functions are to be differentiated, and what rights and obligations are to be accorded different posi-tions; as well as the appointment of individuals to positions of executive authority within the institution, where such posi-tions exist.[74]

And Young maintains that a society embodying this principle would be quite different from presently existing societies.

> In such a society particular establishments of social coopera-tion—such as particular schools, production centers, distri-bution centers, or community service centers—are organized in such a way that all persons who contribute through their actions directly to the operation and maintenance of the estab-lishment's activity, and all those persons whose actions or life circumstances are directly affected by the rules and poli-cies of the establishment, participate in making the basic de-cisions about the establishment's goals, rules and policies. Where possible, participation is direct, but sometimes it is necessary or desirable to have representatives who are re-sponsible to their constituencies. Within any establishment there is likely to be differentiation of tasks and responsibilities among different positions. The basic character of these re-sponsibilities, as well as the allocation of positions among persons, is determined democratically, and all persons in the establishment are ultimately answerable to the whole collec-tivity for their actions.

[74] Ibid., p. 33.

Cooperative interaction among individual establishments, or primary collectivities, within the society is also guided by the principle of self-determination. Primary collectivities send representatives to local community councils, which decide the goals, rules and policy relating to the cooperative interaction of all the establishments in the community. The society is organized into a series of such councils, each of which represents an increasingly broad segment of the total society. At every level membership in representative councils rotates and the higher councils are responsible to lower ones.[75]

Obviously, there are a number of issues that must be clarified and resolved concerning this principle and its application. For example, the question needs to be addressed of how exactly negative freedom (i.e., civil liberties) will be protected in face of the assertion that "all persons in the establishment are ultimately answerable to the whole collectivity for their actions [within the collectivity]." Further questions concern the possibility that persons will want to belong to authoritarian institutions, e.g., certain churches. Shouldn't they have the right to form or join such organizations? But what if a majority of people in such an organization decide they want to run it democratically? Could they then vote to transform it from an authoritarian to a democratic organization? If a minority wants to maintain it as an authoritarian institution but loses the vote—assuming this is allowed—are they entitled to a portion of the institution's accumulated resources or must they simply leave and start from scratch? Presumably, such questions can be adequately answered, but no attempt to do so will be made here.

It seems clear, however, that neither contemporary capitalist societies nor most contemporary post-capitalist societies come even close to this model. The only partial exception to this claim would seem to be Yugoslavia's form of self-managing socialism. Although Yugoslavia is not completely democratic by any stretch of the imagination and thus does not meet the principle of collective self-determination, it may be that the only form of large-scale society that can meet this criterion will be a genuinely democratic, self-managing socialist society.

To summarize: of the first eight objections to Rawls' theory we have considered, objections 1 through 4 are wholly off the mark; they are based on misinterpretations of Rawls' theory or else are

[75] Ibid., pp. 41–42.

objections only to certain of his empirical assumptions but not to his moral theory per se. Objections 5 through 8 are basically on the mark; although sometimes they have involved misinterpretations of Rawls' theory or have been applicable primarily to certain of the empirical assumptions he makes, all would seem to require modifications of his theory. In some of these cases, however, it is arguable either that Rawls already (at least implicitly) endorses the modifications or that there are elements in his theory that can quite easily be interpreted as supporting them. In any case, the modifications that seem required to answer objections 5 through 8 are:

1. There must be a minimum floor of well-being below which persons are not allowed to fall, and this principle must take precedence over any other principle of social justice. (This principle is meant to ensure that both the subsistence and security rights of people are protected.)

2. There must be at least approximate equality in the *worth of liberty* as well as strict equality of liberty per se. (Since equal worth of liberty is primarily a function of keeping social and economic inequalities within certain limits, this modification can be incorporated into the Difference Principle.)

3. The Difference Principle must take the social bases of self-respect—as well as material wealth—as a good to be maximized for the least advantaged.

4. Democracy must not be limited to the political realm but must be implemented in the social and economic realms as well, most especially in the workplace.

The theory of justice I shall offer in the following chapter will take these four modifications into consideration. The remaining objections (i.e., objections 9 and 10) have to do with Rawls' application of his theory and with certain empirical assumptions he does or does not make.

Objections to Rawls' Application of His Theory

The ninth objection to Rawls' theory is that it is applied only to individual societies—in particular, individual nation-states—rather than to the world as a whole. Given the fact that, although they are cognizant of general facts of human nature and history, participants in the original position know nothing about their real-life personal situation —not even what nation or part of the world or what time period they live in—it has seemed obvious to some of Rawls' critics that the original contractors would choose to apply at least the Difference Principle internationally. As Brian Barry puts it:

> Suppose that you were an embryo with a random chance of being any child conceived in the world in a certain period of twenty-four hours, what kind of world would you prefer? One, like the present one, which gives you about a fifty-fifty chance of being born in a country with widespread malnutrition and a high infant mortality rate and about a one-in-four chance of being born in a rich country, or a world in which the gap between the best and the worst prospects had been reduced? Surely, it would be rational to opt for the second kind of world; and this conclusion is reinforced if we accept Rawls's view that an element in rationality is playing safe when taking big decisions.[76]

> Although [the parties in the original position] do not know whether their own society is rich or poor, they can presumably know that, if they live in the twentieth century, there will be a minority of rich societies and a majority in which there is undernourishment or malnutrition or, even if these are escaped, very little over and above the bare minimum of food, clothing and shelter necessary. Surely, then, the arguments which are said to lead the participants in the original position to insist on maximizing the wealth of the worst-off within any given community would even more strongly lead to an insistence that what this minimum is should not depend capriciously upon the good luck of being born into a rich society or the ill luck of being born into a poor one.[77]

> Surely, viewing things from the "original position" one would at all costs wish to avoid this kind of poverty if one turned out to live in a poor state even if this meant being less well off than otherwise if one turned out to live in North America or Western Europe.[78]

[76] Barry, *The Liberal Theory of Justice*, pp. 132–133.
[77] Ibid., p. 129.
[78] Ibid., p. 130.

There are, however, within Rawls' problematic several arguments for the position that the Difference Principle should not be applied internationally. The first argument relies on the fact that Rawls explicitly states that his theory applies only to well-ordered societies where one of the criteria for such a "well-ordered society" is that it have a shared, public conception of social justice. This condition, it might be argued, is met only within individual nation-states. Therefore, his principles—including the Difference Principle—can apply only to such nation-states.

It should be noted, however, that nothing in his definition of a well-ordered society weighs against the possibility that such a society might be global in nature. Although such a fully integrated social and political entity does not now exist on a worldwide scale, one would be truly dogmatic to assert that it could not exist. If such a global society were to exist, then welfare transfers between its component parts (i.e., between the developed and developing "nations" or areas) *would* be justified according to Rawls' principles. Furthermore, besides being merely an empirical possibility, there may well be good arguments, either within Rawls' theory of social justice or on the basis of other moral principles, for the creation of such a society. (We shall return to this claim presently.)

A second argument against the international application of the Difference Principle involves Rawls' claim that principles of social justice apply only to "cooperative ventures for mutual advantage." Since independent nation-states are not involved in such a cooperative venture, the argument continues, these principles cannot be applied internationally nor can they be used as the basis for an argument that a socially and politically integrated global society should be brought into existence.

The major difficulty with this argument lies in the second premise because as nearly as can be determined by most students of *A Theory of Justice* and Rawls' subsequent work, he defines his notion of a "cooperative venture for mutual advantage" in such a way that all persons involved in the international economy (i.e., virtually everyone) *are* involved in such a cooperative venture. As Thomas Scanlon writes, "Whenever there is regularized commerce there is an institution in Rawls' sense, i.e., a public system of rules defining rights and duties etc. . . . . Thus the Difference Principle would apply to the world economic system taken as a whole as well as to particular societies within it."[79]

[79] Scanlon, "Rawls' Theory of Justice," p. 202.

Second, the way Rawls defines "cooperative venture," the contemporary nation-state cannot be considered much more of one than can international society. As Alan Gilbert has observed, Rawls seems to vacillate between a neoclassical social theory and one recognizing dominance and exploitation in social relations.[80] But not even in his most neoclassical moods does Rawls assume that real societies are genuinely and universally cooperative or that their arrangements are to the mutual advantage of all participants. He writes, for example, "No society can, of course, be a scheme of cooperation which men enter voluntarily in a literal sense; each person finds himself placed at birth in some particular position in some particular society, and the nature of this position materially affects his life prospects."[81] Thus, *in this respect* an individual nation-state is no more of a "cooperative venture for mutual advantage" than is an international society, since both are characterized by social and economic intercourse between individuals that is not entirely voluntary nor always mutually advantageous. Yet Rawls insists that principles of social justice apply to the former but not the latter. This position may not be tenable.

There is, in fact, reason to believe that Rawls ought to apply at least the Difference Principle both at a national and international level. He cites (1) the political constitution and (2) the principal economic and social arrangements as the major institutions (of the basic social structure) to which principles of justice apply. But since economic arrangements and transactions are one of the primary ways in which the benefits and burdens of social cooperation are actually distributed, it would seem that all systems of economic transactions must fall at least under his Difference Principle whether such systems are purely internal to a particular society (i.e., nation-state) or between such societies. As Robert Amdur states:

> Although it is not absolutely clear what Rawls means by a cooperative venture for mutual advantage, it would seem that by any sensible definition this term must encompass relations between the inhabitants of different states engaged in ongoing commerce. Sometimes Rawls himself seems to realize this. At one point, he implies that it will be necessary to extend the theory to deal with more difficult international questions,

[80] See Gilbert, "Equality and Social Theory in Rawls' *A Theory of Justice*."
[81] Rawls, *A Theory of Justice*, p. 13.

once the narrower, more manageable problems have been solved.[82]

Although applying all of his principles of social justice internationally may be difficult or even impossible in the absence of world government, since the application of the first principle presupposes a common constitution and political order, this consideration does not weigh against applying the Difference Principle internationally. But notice that even if there were a cogent argument for not applying the Difference Principle internationally, this would not mean that Rawls' *overall* theory would not endorse significant or even massive welfare transfers between the developed and developing nations. As Charles Beitz notes: "There is nothing in [Rawls'] reasoning to suggest that we can *only* have moral ties to those with whom we share membership in a cooperative scheme. It is possible that other sorts of considerations might come into the justification of moral principles. Rawls himself recognizes this in the case of natural duties."[83] With reference to questions of international redistribution, the duty of mutual aid, which, according to Rawls, would be one of the natural duties chosen in the original position, is of primary interest. Since the fulfillment of natural duties is *not* contingent upon persons being involved in a "cooperative venture of mutual advantage," and since the duty of mutual aid requires us to "help another when he is in jeopardy, provided that one can do so without excessive risk or loss to oneself,"[84] it seems clear that it is our duty to prevent starvation, malnutrition, or any sort of deprivation that is considered a serious harm. (Since this duty cannot possibly be fulfilled by any particular individual, however, it makes more sense to think of it as a collective duty that we should do our fair share to see implemented through our respective governments or by changing our respective governments and/or other social institutions.)

Furthermore, if world government is the only means of meeting either our duty of mutual aid or our obligation to ensure that the Difference Principle is applied on an international level, then, all things being equal, our natural duty to support and promote just social institutions will entail our working for world government. (Marxists and most other socialists, of course, will insist that world

[82] Amdur, "Rawls' Theory of Justice," p. 453.

[83] Beitz, *Political Theory and International Relations*, p. 141. See also Sterba, *The Demands of Justice* and "The Welfare Rights of Distant Peoples and Future Generations."

[84] Rawls, *A Theory of Justice*, p. 114.

government is possible only if capitalism is eliminated on a world-wide scale or, in other words, that the only sort of world government historically possible is a world socialist government. Ideally this would be a democratic, self-managing socialist society or a worldwide federation of such societies.) In either case, this will entail a substantial redistribution of wealth from the developed to the developing nations by way of monetary and trade reforms, cancellation or rescheduling of debts, massive development aid, etc. Although it is not clear that such a transfer would result in the complete "impoverishment" of the populations of developed nations, it seems clear that the amount of disposable income for most such individuals would be substantially reduced.

This brings us to a third argument against the international application of the Difference Principle, namely, that the above fact is a *reductio ad absurdum* of any argument in favor of such an application. There is even a basis within Rawls' theory upon which to make a case of this sort since he places as a constraint on the principles of justice chosen in the original position that people have good reason to believe they will be able to act on them in the real world. Since people in developed nations are not (supposedly) going to be willing to "impoverish" themselves in order to realize the Difference Principle on an international scale, they cannot choose to apply this principle internationally.[85] This argument is analogous to Richard Miller's "strains of commitment" argument and, as such, is subject to the same objections. Moreover, while it assumes a great degree of impoverishment of the populations of developed nations, this may not occur since there may be concomitant changes in social and economic policy or institutions (e.g., the partial or complete elimination of military expenditures, the rationalization of the economy, etc.) that would tend to mitigate the effect of international redistribution.

An additional argument sometimes offered is that such transfers will leave the worst-off groups of people in the developed societies in even worse circumstances, and this is not allowable. But the above-mentioned possibility, and the additional possibility that there might be a substantial redistribution from the wealthy (and upper middle class) to the worst-off *within* the developed nations, makes it unclear that an international application of the Difference Principle would be to the detriment of the worst-off classes in the

---

[85] See Peter Danielson, "Theories, Intuitions and the Problem of World-Wide Distributive Justice," *Philosophy of Social Science*, vol. 3 (1973), p. 337.

developed nations. Second, even if the sacrifice on the part of persons in the developed nations was quite substantial, they might be willing to undergo it if they had reason to believe that such sacrifices are necessary to avoid even greater evils such as warfare with peoples of the Third World who might otherwise fight for what they consider to be their fair share of the world's wealth. In any case, even if people in developed countries had to give up a great many luxuries, it may well be the case that they would come to develop new attitudes such that they would not resent this fact (unless it got to the point at which they were denied a minimally decent standard of living).

But what does Rawls' theory have to say on this matter? The most important consideration here is that, in setting up the situation in which persons are to choose principles of social justice, he stipulates that the contractors know themselves to be within the "circumstances of justice." According to Rawls, the primary *objective* circumstances of justice are the existence of moderate scarcity and the fact that people are "mutually disinterested." Although Rawls does not precisely define "moderate scarcity" in order to set it off from extreme scarcity, we can suppose that the latter is the condition that obtains when not everyone's basic needs (i.e., for security and subsistence) can be met. If extreme scarcity were to obtain in developed nations due to their "impoverishment" by the implementation of the Difference Principle on an international scale, then principles of social justice would simply no longer be applicable. But the implication seems to be that so long as we have not passed from the lower end of moderate scarcity into the condition of extreme scarcity, principles of justice should continue to apply and could presumably be accepted and acted upon by those individuals who have a sense of justice and who conceive of themselves as free and equal moral beings. Rawls argues that such persons are required to adjust their expectations to what the principles of justice demand. Although some individuals in the real world may not be able to bring themselves to accept and act on Rawls' principles of justice, this is not necessarily an indictment of these principles as opposed to an indictment of the persons who reject them.

The fact that some people in the real world would refuse to accept and act on the Difference Principle or its international application would not sway Rawls (or a Rawlsian) to abandon it. This can be seen by considering the fact that in the real world there will be persons who cannot bring themselves to accept and act upon *any moral principle that would cause them any loss whatsoever.* As Miller has pointed out, there will undoubtedly be members of the more favored strata of society who cannot bring themselves to accept even moderately egalitarian principles of distribution even when such principles are applied only within wealthy, developed societies, but this does not mean (so I argued, contrary to Miller) that the principles are illegitimate or that they somehow violate Rawls' "strains of commitment" constraint on the acceptability of moral principles. Finally, there is no reason to believe that we must be "moral supermen" (or "superwomen") to conform to them. We need only be persons who accept the moral point of view and have a sense of justice.

This does, however, bring out an important distinction that can and should be made between what is morally required of us as free and equal moral beings and what policies and programs a particular population will find acceptable at any particular time. Although the international application of Rawls' Difference Principle may require large transfers of wealth from the First and Second to the Third world, it is a practical political question as to how rapidly or to what degree such a program could be implemented, given a particular population in a particular developed society at a particular time. Although Rawls does not delve into this issue, since he does not spend much time on "partial compliance theory," as a practical political matter it may be necessary to implement such policies and programs more or less gradually and to do so in conjunction with extensive educational campaigns. However, if the Marxist perspective is correct, such an event will be occasioned only by socialist revolutions in developed nations. And if such revolutions actually occur, the egalitarian attitudes of these populations may be considerably reinforced. Therefore, under these circumstances the practical component of the "strains of commitment" issue may not be nearly so important as more conservative thinkers are generally prone to think.

Finally, before leaving this issue let us ask what reasons might underlie Rawls' failure to apply his theory (or at least the Difference Principle) internationally. According to Robert Amdur:

> It is not difficult to understand why Rawls focuses his attention on distribution within particular societies. Western political philosophers at least since Plato have assumed that the state is the appropriate unit for discussions of distributive justice. Because virtually no one has challenged this assumption,

411

no one has felt the need to defend it. The weight of precedent has made it appear perfectly natural to ignore global questions.[86]

While it is true that most Western political philosophers accept this view, it is probably only because of an underlying *empirical assumption* they have held in common. In the final analysis I strongly suspect that Rawls' failure to take up the international implications of his theory stems from the assumption that nation-states are a permanent or extremely long-term feature of human society on earth or, in other words, that there is no realistic chance of the creation of a world government that would more or less conform to the standards he puts forward. This is an assumption that Marxists and many other internationalists will strongly challenge. Although Marxists generally believe that the creation of such a global society and world government is contingent upon the elimination of capitalism and the completion of the world socialist revolution, belief in the realization of this possibility is certainly not completely beyond the pale. (I will have more to say on this topic in chapter 10.)

The tenth, and final, objection we shall consider is that Rawls provides no theory concerning the means of transition from unjust to just societies and that, therefore, his overall theory is utopian. As Allen Buchanan writes:

> [A] serious Marxian objection to Rawls is the charge that this theory is utopian: it includes no adequate account of how the transition from our unjust society to a Rawlsian well-ordered society will or even can be made. So far as Rawls provides even the barest elements of such an account, his approach is "idealistic"—it relies exclusively upon the individual's sense of justice, ignoring the dominant influence of material interests and, above all, of class interests. Marx's scathing criticism of utopian socialists, who rely on the motivating power of moral ideals, applies with undiminished force to Rawls. . . . Even if we acknowledge that Rawls' principles would be chosen by beings concerned to express their nature as free and equal moral beings, the motivational structure imposed by our social position will continue to govern our conduct. Rawls provides neither a theory of moral education nor a theory of how

[86] Amdur, "Rawls' Theory of Justice," p. 453.

socioeconomic transformations will produce, or at least make possible, the needed motivational shift.[87]

One reason why Rawls is not very concerned to speak to the issue of the means of creating a just society is that he apparently conceives of Western capitalist democracies as already being nearly just—although he does vacillate on this description, sometimes speaking of them as "rifled with grave injustices." Since these societies meet his first (and most important) Principle of Maximum Equal Liberty perhaps as well as can be expected of any real society, and since he seems to think that both parts of his second principle can be implemented either as the result of enlightened leadership or pressure from below (or a combination of the two), the issue of transitional means to a just society seems relatively unimportant. (The only way he can maintain this comfortable position, however, is by conveniently ignoring international distributive justice, which, if required, surely necessitates a theory of means other than charity or "enlightened leadership.") Nevertheless, it is important to see that any disagreement between Rawls and his leftist critics on this issue is *not* of a moral but, rather, an empirical nature and thus does not affect the acceptability of his core moral theory.

Other critics have accused Rawls of being a conservative on the issue of means for reaching a just society since the only form of active opposition he discusses in detail in his works is civil disobedience. But this is a false charge. Although he doesn't discuss in detail more radical forms of opposition, such as revolt or revolution, he does state that "when a society is regulated by principles favoring narrow class interests, one may have no recourse but to oppose the prevailing conception [of justice] and the institutions it justifies in such ways as promise some success."[88] If this is added to his statement that "in certain circumstances militant action and other kinds of resistance are surely justified,"[89] we have a recipe for revolt.

Another part of the explanation of why Rawls fails to put forward a theory of transition to a just society—a part that also bears out my claim that the dispute between him and his leftist critics is of an empirical rather than an evaluative nature—is that he often presupposes a neoclassical social theory on which the transition

---

[87] Buchanan, *Marx and Justice*, pp. 147–148.
[88] Rawls, *A Theory of Justice*, p. 353.
[89] Ibid., pp. 367–368.

from an unjust to a just society (at least for capitalist societies) will be seen to by the feeling of noblesse oblige among the well-off and "enlightened leadership" together, presumably, with invisible-hand processes spurred on by various forms of competition. But, as mentioned previously, Rawls seems at other times to be presupposing an alternate and incompatible social theory on which class relations are characterized by dominance and exploitation.[90] Naturally, which social theory is used has a direct bearing on the necessity of having a theory of transition and on what sort of theory one must have. Although the neoclassical social theory Rawls sometimes utilizes is, arguably, unrealistic, he is at least consistent on these occasions in ignoring the question of means of transition. But on those occasions when he utilizes the more realistic class domination theory it seems inconsistent (or at least the sign of an incomplete theory) for him to ignore this question. Furthermore, even if it were reasonable for him to ignore this issue with reference to contemporary democratic Western capitalist societies, it would still seem that a theory of the means of transition is required for other parts of the world.

But perhaps all of this is irrelevant as a criticism of Rawls' theory for, after all, he never claims to be offering a complete moral, social, and political theory replete with strategy and tactics for reaching stated goals. He is offering us a theory of social justice that can then be applied according to the best empirical theories and information available in order to reach practical, political conclusions. So long as these conclusions (e.g., the moral necessity of worldwide redistribution or of socialism) are genuine empirical possibilities, there is no a priori objection to them; if they are not, then they will not be generated as conclusions from Rawls' theory since, by hypothesis, parties in the original position know all facts relevant to making such decisions. Other than the empirical theories that enter into his description of the original position, it seems that his overall moral theory is not committed to any particular set of empirical assumptions or theories. Thus it is simply not his job to put forward or defend such theories.[91]

This is not a conservative stance, however. After all, he does claim that once the principles are chosen in the original position, we are required to follow them wherever they lead in the face of correct empirical theories. In fact, as noted previously, Rawls

[90] See Gilbert, "Equality and Social Theory in Rawls' *A Theory of Justice*."
[91] For a similar defense of Rawls, see Hampshire, "A New Philosophy of the Just Society."

states that "the principles of justice do not exclude certain forms of socialism and would in fact require them if the stability of a well-ordered society would be achieved in no other way."[92] It is not, therefore, necessary for those convinced that socialism is preferable to capitalism to undermine Rawls' theory. Given its strengths, a better strategy is to show that socialism can better conform to this kind of theory than can any form of capitalism or, more to the point, that a world socialist society is historically possible and is more just than a world in which major parts remain capitalist.

[92] Rawls, "Fairness to Goodness," p. 546.

TEN

TOWARD AN ADEQUATE MARXIST
MORAL AND SOCIAL THEORY

As outlined in the Introduction to this work, an adequate Marxist moral and social theory must have certain features. First, it must be based on a moral theory that is in wide reflective equilibrium with our considered moral judgments. Second, it must be informed by a correct set of empirical, social-scientific views. Third, it must account for the Marxist's basic normative political positions that (1) socialism is morally preferable to any form of capitalism (as well as to any other type of society possible under the historical conditions of moderate scarcity and moderate egoism), and (2) social and/or political revolution, if necessary (and sufficient) to effect the appropriate transformations, is *prima facie* morally justified.

That an adequate Marxist moral and social theory be in accord with Marx's implicit moral theory is another constraint we might be tempted to add, but this, I think, would be a mistake. First, while I believe my reconstruction of this theory in chapter 3 to be essentially correct, there is still considerable debate over the correct explication and interpretation of Marx's implicit moral theory. Second, and more importantly, whatever interpretation we give to Marx's theory, it may turn out that we find ourselves disagreeing with his implicit moral theory even though we are in agreement with his normative political positions. (As noted in chapter 7, however, most moral theories will lead to the acceptance of these positions once a number of Marx's empirical assumptions are accepted.) Even if my interpretation of Marx as a mixed deontologist most concerned with an equal distribution of freedom is correct, this is no reason for a Marxist with utilitarian intuitions to accept being in accord with such a theory as a criterion of adequacy for a Marxist moral and social theory. In the same vein, if a utilitarian interpretation of Marx's implicit moral theory were correct, this would not automatically count as a reason for someone with nonutilitarian convictions accepting being in accord with utilitarianism as a constraint on the construction of an adequate Marxist moral and social theory. For the same reasons I shall not count being in accord with Marx's principles of distribution as expressed in "Critique of the Gotha Program" as a constraint on the development of an adequate Marxist *theory of social justice*.

Nevertheless, it should be clear by now that I believe Marx's implicit moral theory to be essentially on the right track. On my reconstruction of this theory, you will recall, Marx espouses the principle of *maximum equal freedom (both negative and positive)*, which, in turn, can be explicated as the following set of principles:

There is to be a maximum equal system of:
1. *negative freedom* (i.e., freedom from the undue interference of others), and

2. *positive freedom* (i.e., the opportunity to determine one's own life), including:

    a. the right to equal participation in social decision-making processes and

    b. the right of equal access to the means of self-realization, which entails:

        i. the right to an equal opportunity to attain social offices and positions, and

        ii. the right to an equal opportunity to acquire other social primary goods (income, wealth, leisure time, etc.).

Many of us, perhaps, will find that these principles come rather close to being in wide reflective equilibrium with our considered moral judgments. Thus it is arguable that they (or something very much like them) would be chosen by free and equal moral persons in the original position. But this theory (i.e., this set of moral principles concerning social arrangements), as it stands, is simply too general and vague to be considered an adequate moral theory as opposed to the bare outlines of one. Even if it is generally in accord with our considered moral judgments, it needs to be tightened up: the various terms ("interference," "access," "opportunity," etc.) need to be given more precise definitions; the notion of a "maximum equal system" needs to be clarified; decisions need to be made on what priority rules (if any) are to be established, etc. Although, on this reconstruction, Marx's moral theory has already been rendered as a theory of social justice since its principles govern the distribution of the most important social primary goods, it seems to me that a clearer and more adequate theory of social justice can be constructed by starting with John Rawls' theory and modifying it where necessary.

A Theory of Social Justice

Taking into consideration the modifications to Rawls' theory as put forward in the previous chapter, I propose that the following principles—*listed in order of lexical priority*—make for an adequate, or at least more adequate, theory of social justice:

1. Everyone's security rights and subsistence rights shall be respected.

2. There is to be a maximum system of equal basic liberties, including freedom of speech and assembly; liberty of conscience and freedom of thought; freedom of the person along with the right to hold (personal) property; and freedom from arbitrary arrest and seizure as defined by the concept of the rule of law.

3. There is to be (a) a right to an equal opportunity to attain social positions and offices and (b) an equal right to participate in all social decision-making processes within institutions of which one is a part.

4. Social and economic inequalities are justified if, and only if, they benefit the least advantaged, consistent with the just savings principle, but *are not to exceed* levels that will seriously undermine equal worth of liberty or the good of self-respect.

To better judge the adequacy of this theory, let us briefly compare it to the theories of Marx, Rawls, and Nielsen.

I contend that my theory entails Marx's principles but is more complete and, therefore, more adequate. On my reconstruction, Marx's first (negative freedom) principle is covered by my second principle. His principles *2a* (the right to equal participation in social decision-making processes) and *2bi* (the right to an equal opportunity to attain social offices and positions) are combined in my third (equal opportunity) principle. Since 2 and *2b* are included for purposes of explication, this leaves only his principle *2bii* (the right

418

to an equal opportunity to acquire other social primary goods such as income, wealth, leisure time, etc.). This principle is inadequate, however, since it does not—in and of itself—demand a minimum floor of well-being nor does it give us explicit criteria by which to decide whether inequalities in material wealth are allowable and, if they are, to what degree. Neither does it explicitly demand that the social bases of self-respect as well as material wealth be taken into consideration, although it is arguable that this is Marx's intent. His theory must therefore be supplemented by my first and fourth principles. Finally, Marx's theory (or my reconstruction of it, at any rate) does not include the necessary priority rules, while my proposed theory does.

Rawls' special conception or theory of justice consists of the following two principles listed in order of lexical priority:

First Principle
Each person is to have an equal right to the most extensive total system of equal basic liberties compatible with a similar system of liberty for all.
Second Principle
Social and economic inequalities are to be arranged so that they are both:
  a. to the greatest benefit of the least advantaged, consistent with the just savings principle, and
  b. attached to offices and positions open to all under conditions of fair equality of opportunity.[1]

Although we have already spent considerable time discussing Rawls' theory, a brief comparison is in order. Recall first that the four modifications of Rawls' substantive moral theory argued for in the previous chapter are:

1. There must be a minimum floor of well-being below which persons are not allowed to fall, and this principle must take precedence over any other principle of social justice.
2. There must be at least approximate equality in the *worth of liberty* as well as strict equality of liberty per se.
3. The Difference Principle must take the social bases of self-respect—as well as material wealth—as a good to be maximized for the least advantaged.

[1] Rawls, *A Theory of Justice*, p. 302.

4. Democracy must not be limited to the political realm but must be implemented in the social and economic realms as well, most especially in the workplace.

The first principle of the theory of social justice I have proposed—the Basic Rights Principle—incorporates the first modification mentioned above. As explained previously, the minimum floor of well-being must be taken to include people's security rights as well as their subsistence rights. Security rights are the rights not to be tortured, executed, raped, brutally assaulted, etc. Subsistence rights are the rights to food, drinkable water, shelter, clothing, basic medical care, a livable environment, etc. Individuals in the original position would undoubtedly want to ensure that both of these kinds of rights are protected against the standard threats that undermine them or cause them to be violated, and would take this principle to have lexical priority over any other. Following Henry Shue, I shall refer to these as *basic* rights, both because they are intrinsically the most important rights we have and because, as Shue argues, their fulfillment is a necessary condition for the enjoyment of any other right. Also following Shue, I shall take these rights to entail three correlative duties: (1) the duty to *avoid* harming or depriving, (2) the duty to *protect* from harm or deprivation, and (3) the duty to *aid* the harmed or deprived.[2]

Although neither security nor subsistence rights are mentioned as liberties in Rawls' Maximum Equal Liberty Principle, it can be argued that these rights exist at least implicitly in Rawls' theory of natural duties, which espouses, among others, "the duty of helping another when he is in need or jeopardy provided that one can do so without excessive risk or loss to oneself; the duty not to harm or injure another; and the duty not to cause unnecessary suffering."[3] Although Rawls prefers to use the concept of coercible duties (i.e., duties which people justifiably can be coerced to fulfill) rather than the concept of rights to express these views, the end result is the same. It may not matter in the final analysis which terminology we use here, but it seems quite natural to include the right to life in a theory of social justice. The main difference between my theory and the traditional (e.g., Lockean) lists of rights is that I take the right to life to be both a negative and a

[2] See Shue, *Basic Rights*, pp. 52–53.
[3] Rawls, *A Theory of Justice*, p. 114.

positive right and, thus, to entail subsistence as well as security rights.

It may be objected that including a Basic Rights Principle or Rawls' coercible duties in the theory of social justice should be avoided since—on Rawls' definition, at any rate—theories of social justice have to do with the benefits and burdens of *social cooperation*, whereas these principles are usually taken to be applicable even outside the context of such institutions. The answer to this, I think, is first that, given the economic interdependence of today's world, the distinction between moral principles requiring and those not requiring institutions of social cooperation is probably moot. (As argued previously, this economic interpendence, itself, establishes the existence of social cooperation in the relevant sense.) Second, if we don't explicitly make these principles part of our theories of social justice, there is a tendency for people to overlook them or downgrade their importance when, in fact, they are arguably the most important principles of all. For these reasons I shall include the Basic Rights Principle in my theory of social justice.

The second principle of my theory is simply Rawls' Maximum Equal Liberty Principle minus the "political liberties," which are included in my third (equal opportunity) principle. It seems perspicacious to separate our negative liberties from our political liberties since—even on Rawls' theory—it is agreed that the former are both different in kind and stronger than the latter. In addition to the traditional political liberties such as the rights to vote and to run for and hold political office, the third principle includes the right to participate in decisions within all social and economic institutions of which one is a part. As required by the fourth modification of Rawls' theory listed above, the term "social," as used in my third principle, is to be taken to refer to *political, social,* and *economic* positions and decision-making processes. It should be noted, however, that although I do not follow Rawls' wording of "fair equality of opportunity" in framing my Equal Opportunity Principle, I agree with him that it is neither possible nor desirable to demand a *precisely equal* opportunity even for persons of equal talent, skill, and motivation. The most we can reasonably demand, it seems, is that such persons have an *approximately equal* opportunity. Two minimal conditions that seemingly must be fulfilled in order to accomplish this are (1) providing everyone with a quality education from early childhood on, and (2) eliminating discrimination in all of its guises.

My fourth principle is, obviously, Rawls' Difference Principle after the incorporation of the second and third modifications listed above. Although I have not previously spoken of the Just Savings Principle, following Rawls I include it here. Since persons behind the veil of ignorance must not be biased in any way, they do not know at what point in history they actually exist. It is therefore reasonable for them to agree to a Just Savings Principle to ensure that the generation to which they belong will not inherit a completely impoverished and/or polluted environment. Although there is considerable controversy over the issue of justice between generations, I shall accept Rawls' analysis as being essentially correct.[4]

Kai Nielsen's radical egalitarian theory of social justice (which he calls "justice as equality") is:

1. Each person is to have an equal right to the most extensive total system of equal basic liberties and opportunities (including equal opportunities for meaningful work, for self-determination and political and economic participation) compatible with a similar treatment of all. (This principle gives expression to a commitment to attain and/or sustain equal moral autonomy and equal self-respect.)

2. After provisions are made for common social (community) values, for capital overhead to preserve the society's productive capacity, allowances made for differing unmanipulated needs and preferences, and due weight is given to the just entitlement of individuals, the income and wealth (the common stock of means) is to be so di-

[4] Actually, as Schweickart points out, the way Rawls formulates this principle in terms of savings does not do justice to his underlying concern of conserving the natural as well as the social and cultural environment. "Rawls's concern is misplaced. He worries about insufficient savings—but the tendency of capitalism, especially Keynesian capitalism, is toward a high rate of savings. The tendency is for savings to outstrip investment, and this (as Keynes showed) causes the economy to contract—unless the government intervenes. Capitalism—especially Keynesian capitalism —is structured to save, to invest and to grow. But it is precisely this growth that poses the threat to future generations, not the lack of saving. Capitalist 'saving,' when balanced by investment, involves a channelling of workers and resources into activities that promise increased consumption later. 'Saving' does not involve a saving of resources or a reduction of the strain placed on the environment. This latter sort of 'saving' occurs when consumption is traded for leisure, or perhaps for less 'efficient' but more ecologically sound techniques, not for more consumption later. But . . . it is worker control and not capitalism that allows society to decide consciously the rate and structure of its investment, and on its labor-leisure tradeoff" (Schweickart, *Capitalism or Worker Control?* pp. 188–189). See also Weisskopf, "The Irrationality of Capitalist Economic Growth."

vided that each person will have a right to an equal share. The necessary burdens requisite to enhance human well-being are also to be equally shared, subject, of course, to limitations by differing abilities and differing situations. (Here I refer to different natural environments and the like and not to class position and the like.)[5]

Nielsen's theory, like my proposed theory of social justice, originated as a critique of Rawls' theory of justice as fairness. Our theories are also similar in that they both strive to be more consistently egalitarian than Rawls' theory; in fact, Nielsen's theory—in one way or another—seems to incorporate the four modifications of Rawls' theory previously suggested. The demand for a minimum floor of well-being, below which individuals are not allowed to fall, seems covered by that part of Nielsen's second principle demanding that "allowances be made for differing unmanipulated needs and preferences." The demand for approximate equality in worth of liberty is presumably entailed by the fact that Nielsen's first principle demands the most extensive total system of equal basic liberties *and opportunities* (including equal opportunities for meaningful work, for self-determination and political and economic participation). The fact that self-determination and political and economic participation are mentioned here also takes care of my demand for social and economic (as well as political) democracy. Finally, the demand that we take the social bases of self-respect as a good to be maximized seems to be covered by Nielsen's first principle, since he states that it is supposed to give "expression to a commitment to attain and/or sustain equal moral autonomy and equal self-respect."

There are, however, some significant differences between Nielsen's theory and mine. Although his first principle is basically a combination of my second and third principles, my theory does not assert an *equal right to equal opportunities for meaningful work*. One problem with such a demand is that what constitutes meaningful work may vary to some extent among individuals; in any case, the concept is not very precise. Presumably, however, there is a correlation between meaningful work and (a) how creative the work is, (b) how much autonomy the worker has in the work process, including the extent to which he or she can participate in decisions made in the workplace, and (c) the extent to which the worker identifies with and supports the society in which he or she

[5] Nielsen, *Equality and Liberty*, pp. 48–49.

lives and thus sees his or her activity as socially useful and valuable. Although all three conditions may very well be better met in a genuinely socialist society than in contemporary societies, it would seem almost impossible to provide everyone with equally meaningful work or even to guarantee everyone an equal opportunity for meaningful work. (This is especially true if Nielsen is demanding a *precisely* as opposed to only an *approximately* equal opportunity for meaningful work.)

Meaningful work is to be counted as a positive good on any Marxist or egalitarian view; and—subject to the demands of my Modified Difference Principle—greater equality in life prospects (including the prospect for meaningful work) is always to be preferred to less. However, it seems unnecessary (if not impossible) to guarantee a precisely equal opportunity to acquire this good, especially if we have in mind a *substantively* equal—as opposed to a merely *formally* equal—opportunity. (If we have in mind merely formal equality of opportunity this can be achieved simply by preventing discrimination; surely Nielsen has in mind a stronger form than this.) Perhaps the strongest form of substantive opportunity for equal work (or anything else) would be to distribute the opportunities by lottery. But considerations of both desert and efficiency weigh strongly against this solution. In fact, if we have any interest in efficiency at all we probably will not want to go beyond Rawls' interpretation of fair equality of opportunity as providing persons of approximately equal talents and abilities approximately equal chances of acquiring desired positions and offices: in this case, jobs or occupations that are viewed by individuals as meaningful (or at least more meaningful than most jobs or occupations). This does not mean, however, that society should not compensate persons who end up with the less meaningful or satisfying work or should not take measures to ensure diversity within jobs or mobility within the job market. Perhaps, as J. S. Mill suggests, those having less desirable jobs ought to be paid more than those having more desirable positions. Although this would not make such jobs any more meaningful, it might be demanded even by Rawls' Difference Principle if we were to specify that meaningful work or job satisfaction is a social primary good (which is not, it seems, a totally implausible suggestion).

Nielsen's second principle says that *after certain antecedent conditions are met*, income and wealth is to be so divided that each person is to have a right to an equal share. These conditions are that society provide for:

a. common social (community) values,

b. capital overhead to preserve the society's productive capacity,

c. differing unmanipulated needs and preferences, and

d. the just entitlement of individuals.

While provisos *a* and *b* would seem to be entailed *as empirical necessities* by my first and fourth (i.e., my Basic Rights and Modified Difference) Principles, there seems no reason to list them as *basic* moral principles. That part of proviso *c* concerning providing for people's *needs* would also seem to be entailed by my Basic Rights Principle. The part of this proviso about providing for people's unmanipulated *preferences* seems a bit mysterious, however, since it is not clear how this is to be integrated with the primary claim of his second principle, which he puts forward after listing these provisos, namely, the claim that "the income and wealth (the common stock of means) is to be so divided that each person will have a right to an equal share." If all the (unmanipulated) preferences of all persons are to be taken care of *before* the principle of strict equality of distribution goes into effect, what sense does it make even to have such a principle? Under conditions of moderate scarcity, of course, not all the preferences of all persons can be met. But if this is so, what set of criteria is to be used in deciding which preferences will be met? If we say "strict equality," then we are invoking the main principle on which the proviso we are now discussing is supposed to be a condition.[6]

There is a similar difficulty with proviso *d*, which concerns taking account of people's just entitlements. Since this proviso is a

---

[6] In his article "Liberal and Socialist Egalitarianism"—part of which is based on his "Reply to Rodney Peffer" (Canadian Philosophical Association, Windsor, Ontario, May 31, 1988)—Nielsen responds to this point as follows: "Peffer rightly finds fault with my proviso that our unmanipulated preferences be first taken into account before we make an equal division of resources. What, he quite properly asks, is left of strict equality of distribution if these differing preferences must be met before the rule of equal distribution goes into effect? The same applies for just individual entitlements. It is better to proceed, as I did in the last chapter of *Equality and Liberty* and writings subsequent to it, by a principle which prescribes that we are to first provide institutional conditions for the meeting of basic needs, where everyone's needs are to have equal consideration, then where that provision has been made, we are to move to a similar consideration of non-basic needs and finally, when provision for the meeting of non-basic needs has been made, we should move to a similar consideration of preferences (particularly preferences that adequate information would not extinguish). A *roughly* equal division of resources is meant to be a way of furthering that" ("Liberal and Socialist Egalitarianism," forthcoming).

condition of the main principle of strict equality in the distribution of income and wealth, there must be a set of criteria for just entitlements other than the economic distribution resulting from the application of the principle of strict equality. But so far as I can ascertain at any rate, Nielsen offers no such set of criteria. Nor *could* he offer such a set of criteria for ascertaining just entitlements *without* bringing in his main principle of distribution of income and wealth because what is considered a just entitlement will be whatever is gained *within the rules of the game* without the use of force, theft, or fraud. While Nozick can get away with not offering such a set of criteria because he denies that there are any other rules of the game than not to use force, theft, or fraud, neither Rawls nor Nielsen nor anyone else who accepts "patterned" or "end-state" principles of distributive justice can do so. While one may have a *prima facie* entitlement to all that one can get without the use of force, theft, or fraud, within societies governed by Rawls' or Nielsen's principles of distributive justice, one will not necessarily have an *all-things-considered* entitlement to that entire portion because some of it may be needed to ensure that the principles of social justice are met. (This is the justification for taxation and other procedures society uses to direct social wealth toward the accomplishment of social purposes.)[7]

There is, however, an even more fundamental objection to his second principle. Even after taking his provisos into account, his main claim calling for strict equality in the distribution of income and wealth is untenable. There are, it seems to me, cogent objections to that part of Nielsen's second principle reading "income and wealth (the common stock of means) is to be so divided that each person will have a right to an equal share," that parallel some of Marx's objections (in "Critique of the Gotha Program") to LaSalle's claim that "the proceeds of labor belong undiminished with equal right to all members of society." To this, Marx replies:

> "To all members of society"? To those who do not work as well? What remains then of the "undiminished proceeds of labour"? Only to those members who work? What remains of the "equal right" of all members of society?[8]

---

[7] To this criticism Nielsen responds: "There should be, as Peffer rightly argues, criteria for individual just entitlements which are not determined by a principle of strict equality. But that is exactly what I argue. *Prima facie*, I argue if someone acquires something, say a family farm or family restaurant, without force, theft or fraud she has a just entitlement to it; this entitlement is strengthened by desert."

[8] Marx, "Critique of the Gotha Program," p. 385.

Nielsen's phrasing of this part of his second principle has the unfortunate consequence of divorcing such factors as effort and contribution from the actual distribution of social primary goods or the "common stock of means." He attempts to get around this difficulty with his proviso concerning giving due weight to the just entitlements of individuals, but, as we have just seen, this does not seem to work.

Furthermore, as Marx notes in his criticisms of LaSalle, to speak of a right to an equal distributive share in this context seems rather bizarre. How are we to measure equal amounts of both income and wealth so we can make sure everyone gets a precisely equal share, especially in contemporary societies where much "wealth" comes in the form of public goods? It is especially troublesome to speak of a *right* to an equal (i.e., a precisely equal) share, for to say that someone has a right to something is to say that the state or society must protect him or her in the possession of it or make sure the person receives it. Thus to speak of a right in this context is to give people grounds for legitimate claims that the state or society may well find impossible to fulfill.

Actually Nielsen anticipates and attempts to answer this objection when, in reference to the proviso of his second principle concerning fulfilling people's unmanipulated needs and preferences, he states that "the differing preferences and needs should, as far as possible, have equal satisfaction, though what is involved in the rider 'as far as possible' is not altogether evident."[9] He also states:

> My second principle of justice is not the same as a principle which directs that a pie be equally divided, though it is like it in its underlying intent, namely that fairness starts with a presumption of equality and only modifies a strict equal division of whatever is to be divided in order to remain faithful to the underlying intent of equal treatment.[10]

But Nielsen compounds this problem when he endorses the interpretation of his second principle on which people do not merely have a right to an equal share of social primary goods or an equal share of the total overall wealth of society but actually and literally have a right to an equal share of each and every type of good in the entire world.

[9] Nielsen, *Equality and Liberty*, p. 54.
[10] Ibid., pp. 54–55.

People, if they are rational, will exercise their rights to shares in what Rawls calls the primary goods, since having them is necessary to achieving anything else they want, but they will not necessarily demand equal shares and they will surely be very unlikely to demand equal shares of all the goodies of the world. People's wants and needs are simply too different for that. I have, or rather should have, an equal right to have fish pudding or a share in the world's stock of jelly beans. *Ceteris paribus*, I have an equal right to as much of either as anyone else, but, not wanting or liking either, I will not demand my equal share.[11]

Since it is impossible for society or the state to guarantee everyone a precisely equal share of the total social wealth, it is certainly impossible to guarantee everyone an equal share—*even an approximately equal share*—of any particular good, let alone all types of goods in the world. And if this is so, then it is absurd to say that people *have a right* to an equal share—or even an approximately equal share—of any particular good or of all goods in the world. By definition, no one can have a right to something that it is impossible—under any realistic set of circumstances—to guarantee them. The most they can have is *permission* to attain those goods if they can do so within the rules of the social game.

All in all, it seems much more perspicuous *not* to speak of *rights* to *equal distributive shares* of particular goods nor even of income and wealth, as opposed to speaking of society being structured so that certain sorts of overall divisions of income and wealth can or cannot result from the activities of individuals. It is much better, it seems to me, to demand that persons have *equal access* to social primary goods or an *equal opportunity*—but a substantively and not merely formally equal opportunity—to attain social primary goods. And this, I think, is what Nielsen is really concerned about, and properly so.[12]

---

[11] Ibid., p. 55.

[12] Nielsen's response to this is: "I take Peffer's point about the mistake of saying that people should have precisely equal shares. What this would be we often cannot ascertain; moreover, a good bit of our wealth comes in public goods which cannot be so parcelled out. What I would argue is that in a society of abundance, where differing needs have been met, just entitlements honored as described above, [and] contribution and desert accounted for, those benefits and burdens [that are] not so hedged in [and, thus, that are capable of being] divided should be divided equally. Equal division is a deep underlying value rooted in our sense of fairness. Where we do not know anything about the individuals in question our sense of what is to be done is to make an equal division but where the differences

Furthermore, such an interpretation or extension of Rawls' theory seems perfectly natural. As Armatya Sen and Bernard Williams point out in the introduction to their anthology, *Utilitarianism and Beyond*:

> Rights-based moral theories differ from utilitarianism . . . in their concentration on *opportunities* rather than on the value of the exact *use* made of these opportunities. . . . the ultimate concern with opportunities can perhaps be made more direct in an extension of the Rawlsian system, focusing not on primary goods as such but on primary "capabilities" of people, e.g. the capability to meet nutritional requirements, or the capability to move freely. Such a formulation will be sensitive to differences in people's "needs," reflected in differences in the conversion of goods into capabilities (e.g. being sensitive to the greater nutritional needs of larger persons, or greater transport needs of disabled people, etc.).
>
> This is really one method of dealing with the so-called "positive" freedoms, and primary goods are treated just as the *means* of achieving such freedoms. The focus is not on primary goods as such, but on the actual capabilities that the primary goods provide. The question then arises of interpersonal variation in the transformation of primary goods into actual freedoms: e.g. of income into freedom from nutritional deficiency (taking note of variation of nutritional needs), or of the "social

---

that I have specified come under our cognizance we also recognize the rightness in certain circumstances of departing from an equal division. This, however, is not a departure from the structure of argument in *Equality and Liberty*, but a restatement of it.

"Egalitarians want a society of equals; they want a world in which, as far as this is possible, people will have the same life-prospects and have abundant life-prospects. They do not want a Spartan world where we share out the misery equally. They want a world in which people receive equal treatment though what this comes to is plainly a very contested matter. But I think it should entail that *ab initio* I have no greater or less right to one of the spare kidneys that just happen to be around than you do or anyone else [does]. In this way it seems to me each has a right—a *prima facie* right—to an equal share of each and every type of good (where it is feasible that they could be so distributed) in the entire world and that a just society, where it can, will protect that right" ("Liberal and Socialist Egalitarianism," forthcoming).

Thus, while Nielsen concedes some of my points, he is still unwilling to give up his claim that we have a right to an equal share of every type of good in the entire world. Notice, however, that the way he describes the right to spare kidneys makes it sound more like a permission-right than a claim-right. I am arguing only that we do not have claim-rights of this sort; that we have (*prima facie*) permission-rights to acquire by legitimate means any of the world's goods is uncontroversial.

basis of self-respect" into the actual capability to have self-respect (taking note of variation of personal characteristics).[13]

However, the most important difference between Nielsen's theory and mine has yet to be addressed. It is that his theory does not accept the Difference Principle in any form and thus would choose a situation of substantially less overall wealth so long as the wealth is divided more nearly equally, *even if* a feasible alternative distribution having much more overall wealth would not violate constraints concerning self-respect and equal worth of liberty.

Consider Table 1: four distributions of a society of 100 families of four, where 95 percent of the families receive a relatively low yearly income and 5 percent receive a relatively high income as indicated. Now make the following assumptions: (1) $20,000 is the minimally decent income level for a family of four in this society; (2) the self-respect of individuals and equal worth of liberty start to be undermined only when income differentials exceed a 1:2 ratio; and (3) there are no other noneconomic differences—such as one distributional state resulting in the society having greater liberty—which are relevant to deciding between them.

---

[13] Sen and Williams, "Introduction," *Beyond Utilitarianism*, pp. 19–20.

A completely adequate moral theory would have to clarify the notions of "equal," "opportunities," "primary capabilities," "primary goods," and "rights," as well as specify the relations between them. For some of the issues involved here, see Hart, "Are There Any Natural Rights?" Gregory Vlastos, "Justice and Rights," which is reprinted in A. I. Meldon, ed., *Human Rights*, Wadsworth, Belmont, Calif., 1970; McClosky, "Rights," Feinberg, "Duties, Rights, and Claims," "The Nature and Value of Rights," "The Rights of Animals and Unborn Generations," (all of which are reprinted in Feinberg's *Rights, Justice, and the Bounds of Liberty*), and *Harm to Others* (*The Moral Limits of the Criminal Law*, vol. 1).

See also Murphy, "Rights and Borderline Cases"; Peffer, "A Defense of Rights to Well-Being"; Samuel Scheffler, "Natural Rights, Equality, and the Minimal State," *Canadian Journal of Philosophy*, vol. 6 (1976); Phillip Montague, "Two Concepts of Rights," *Philosophy and Public Affairs*, vol. 9, no. 4 (Summer 1980); Mackie, "Can There Be a Rights-Based Moral Theory?" Alan Gewirth, "Why There Are Human Rights" and *Human Rights*; David Braybrooke, *Meeting Needs*; Nickel, "Are Human Rights Utopian?" and *Making Sense of Human Rights*; Buchanan, "What's So Special about Rights?" Shue, *Basic Rights*; Carl Wellman, *Welfare Rights*, Rowman & Allanheld, Totowa, N.J., 1985; Patricia H. Werhane et al. (eds.), *Philosophical Issues in Human Rights*, Random House, N.Y., 1986.

See, too, Dworkin, "What is Equality? Part 1: Equality of Welfare," "What is Equality? Part 2: Equality of Resources," and "What Is Equality? Part 3: The Place of Liberty"; Sen, "Equality of What?" "Utilitarianism and Welfarism," "Rights and Capabilities," and "Well-being, Agency, and Freedom"; B. Williams, "Persons, Character, and Morality" and "Utilitarianism and Moral Self-Indulgence"; Scanlon, "Rights, Goals, and Fairness" and "Preference and Urgency"; and Nagel, "Equality."

TABLE 1

	Yearly income of 95% of families	Yearly income of 5% of families	Yearly GNP (in millions of dollars)
A.	$25,000	$200,000	$3.375 mil.
B.	25,000	50,000	2.625 mil.
C.	25,000	30,000	2.525 mil.
D.	20,000	22,500	2.013 mil.

Given these assumptions, it seems clear that an unreconstructed version of Rawls' theory—as well as most utilitarian theories—will choose distribution A since it maximizes wealth and (presumably) preference satisfaction while meeting Rawls' Difference Principle. My theory will choose distribution B since it creates the most over-all wealth while conforming to the Difference Principle modified to ensure that the values of self-respect and (approximate) equal worth of liberty are not undermined.

Now let us consider which distribution Nielsen's theory would choose. For our purposes let us assume that each distribution meets all of the other provisions of his theory. Let us first consider only the first three distributions. Nielsen's theory would presumably choose C because it most closely approximates strict equality (of the first three, that is). But this, it seems to me, is unreasonable since (based on our assumptions) distribution B creates more over-all wealth and presumably preference satisfaction *without* under-mining people's self-respect or the principle of (approximately) equal worth of liberty. Why should we choose less rather than more social wealth when it will not violate these constraints? Even more telling against this part of Nielsen's theory, however, is that when all four distributions are considered, his theory will choose distribution D even though *everyone is worse off under this distribution*.

The first line of defense Nielsen could raise here is that in comparison to D, the other distributional states allow for unjustifiable differentials of power. Since such power differentials are a bad thing from an egalitarian point of view, the argument would go, we must choose D. While I agree that the existence of significant power differentials among people is a bad thing and to be avoided, I do not think that this, in and of itself, weighs in favor of choosing distribution D (or even C) over B in this hypothetical scenario, or that it weighs in favor of choosing Nielsen's theory over mine. As to the scenario, it is specified that there are no noneconomic differences relevant to deciding between the distributions so, by hypothesis, there are no (significant) differentials of power. More importantly, it is specified that distribution B has not equaled the 1:2 differential in income (and wealth) required for self-respect or equal worth of liberty to be seriously undermined. Since these goods—especially the good of equal worth of liberty—are undermined when there are significant differences in power, the scenario has been set up to show that no significant differences in power exist in any distribution but A. (However, we should keep in mind that it is only reasonable to require approximate as opposed to strict equality in the worth of liberty.)

In general, it seems to me that my theory is at least as effective as Nielsen's in terms of not allowing significant differentials of power. The demand for (approximately) equal worth of liberty and the demand that the good of self-respect not be seriously undermined already go a long way toward disallowing significant power differentials. In addition, my Substantive Equal Opportunity Principle—especially the part demanding social and economic as well as political democracy—also obviates the possibility of significant differentials of power.

Nielsen may reply that we must choose D because not to do so is to undermine equal *moral autonomy*.[14] But it is not clear what this notion of moral autonomy comes to. It is clear that Nielsen is not referring to the Kantian notion of moral autonomy having to do with the distinction between the autonomy and the heteronomy of the will. It is also clear that Nielsen's notion is not identical to the idea of participatory autonomy (or freedom as self-determination), i.e., the idea of having control of one's life in the sense of having a fair say in social decisions that affect one's life. Nielsen's notion of moral autonomy—with its allied talk of one's moral person being assaulted when it is not observed—is obviously closely tied to the notions of self-respect and the social basis of self-respect, but it is not clear (to me, at any rate) whether this is all his notion of moral autonomy comes to. If it is, then Nielsen and I would not seem to have a substantive disagreement, and it would seem that both our theories will choose distribution B. In other words, to the extent that his notion of moral autonomy has to do with the notion of self-respect, my theory already provides for it; to the extent that

[14] See Nielsen, *Equality and Liberty*, pp. 84, 88–92, and "Radically Egalitarian Justice."

432

his notion goes beyond the notion of self-respect, I see no reason to accept his demand for more material equality than is necessary to ensure that self-respect (and approximately equal worth of liberty) not be undermined by social conditions.[15]

One final difficulty with Nielsen's theory is that he refuses to arrange his principles in order of lexical priority. But it seems quite plausible that persons—within or without the original position—will be more concerned to assure themselves that their basic security and subsistence rights will be respected than with any other value and will prefer the value of negative liberty over that of participatory autonomy. Finally, it seems to me that they will hold all of these values more dear than that of equality as expressed in a Difference or Modified Difference Principle of distributive justice.

Although I have (naturally) concentrated on what I take to be the objectionable features of Nielsen's theory, I would like to stress the fact that our theories are more in agreement than not. Nielsen and I also agree that an egalitarian or even moderately egalitarian theory of social justice will choose socialism (i.e., a democratic, self-managing form of socialism) over any other form of society possible under historical conditions of moderate scarcity. It is, in fact, my view that socialism is preferable on this or any other egalitarian (or nearly egalitarian) theory of social justice, given the truth of only a minimal set of Marxist empirical theses. It is to this issue that we now turn.

Social Justice and Marxist Empirical Theory

It is obvious that the theory of social justice I am here putting forward is not a specifically Marxist moral theory. This should not be surprising. Not even Marx's implicit moral theory per se is a specifically Marxist theory. There is, in fact, no such thing as a specifically Marxist *moral theory*. There is, however, such a thing as a specifically Marxist *moral and social theory*, i.e., a theory which combines a moral theory with a set of empirical, social-scientific theses in order to judge alternative sets of social arrangements, pro-

---

[15] The position I am criticizing here is the one taken by Nielsen in his book *Equality and Liberty*. In some of his more recent writings he has modified his theory in ways that meet these objections or at least come close to meeting them. In the passage from his more recent "Liberal and Socialist Egalitarianism" (already quoted in n. 12) he claims that egalitarians "do not want a Spartan world where we share in the misery equally." However, a recent restatement of his principles of social justice, in his article "Autonomy and Justice," would still seem at least to allow (and possibly demand) the choice of distributions C and D over B.

grams, and policies. In fact, *any* moral and social theory that utilizes a recognizably Marxist set of empirical, social-scientific theses and supports a recognizably Marxist set of normative political positions qualifies as a *Marxist* moral and social theory.

Since there is no uniquely Marxist moral theory and no reason Marxists automatically ought to accept Marx's implicit moral theory as either definitive or correct, there will be as many different Marxist moral and social theories as there are moral theories that Marxists wish to combine with their empirical assumptions. Furthermore, there may be a considerable divergence among Marxists as to which empirical, social-scientific theses within the Marxist tradition are both relevant and true. But the real goal, of course, is not simply to develop a Marxist moral and social theory but to develop an *adequate* moral and social theory, i.e., one based on an adequate moral theory, on the one hand, and a true set of social-scientific theories, on the other. (Naturally, Marxists believe that the set of true social-scientific theories will be drawn largely from the Marxist tradition.)

If there is no set of Marxist empirical theses that meets these conditions, then, of course, the project of developing an adequate Marxist moral and social theory is doomed. The truly monumental political questions of the day, it seems to me, turn on the truth or falsity of the Marxist's analysis of capitalism and the present world situation. If this analysis is essentially correct, then the Marxist's basic normative political positions will be justified; if it is essentially incorrect, then in all probability these normative political positions will not be justified. These positions, you will recall, are that (1) socialism (i.e., democratic, self-managing socialism) is morally preferable to any feasible form of capitalism and to any other form of society possible in the present historical epoch (e.g., bureaucratic state-socialism), and (2) socialist revolution—if necessary and sufficient to effect the appropriate transformations—is *prima facie* morally justified. (Although there exist many kinds of capitalist society in terms of the type of government that prevails and there might be different types of state-socialist societies, at least in the sense that some of them will be more bureaucratic and/or repressive than others, I take these three forms of society—capitalism, state-socialism, and democratic, self-managing socialism—to be exhaustive of the *basic* types of society possible in this historical epoch.)

In what follows I shall first defend these normative political positions and then attempt to comment briefly on the empirical theses I have utilized in doing so. (That is, I shall delimit the minimal set of Marxist empirical assumptions of which I have previously spoken.) I shall not try to prove that these Marxist empirical theses are correct. Rather, I shall attempt to show which of them must be essentially correct in order for the Marxist's basic normative political positions to be justified. At this point I shall be painting a picture in fairly broad strokes: I shall not argue for the truth of the empirical theses put forward, nor shall I argue for the pedigree of the theses or the normative political positions I take them to support. Although it seems to me that they flow from the Classical Marxist tradition, I shall not argue the point here.[16]

Determining whether the first normative position is justified is simply a matter of determining whether democratic, self-managing socialism meets the four principles espoused by our theory of social justice better than any feasible form of capitalism or any form of state-socialism. One of the most important Marxist empirical theses I will be utilizing is precisely that a democratic, self-managing socialist society is a real historical possibility. However, since many will deny this, another important question is whether capitalism is morally preferable to state-socialism if these are the only real choices open to us. A further complication is that our judgments may vary depending on whether we are speaking of an advanced, industrialized society or a developing society. Therefore, in reference to advanced, industrialized societies I shall consider (A) the choice between democratic, self-managing socialism and capitalism; (B) the choice between democratic, self-managing socialism and state-socialism; and (C) the choice between capital-

---

[16] As noted in the introduction, I take the major figures of the Classical Marxist tradition to be Marx, Engels, Lenin, Luxemburg, Trotsky, and Gramsci. Contemporary Marxist political theorists whom I believe to be representative of the Classical Marxist tradition, and whom I believe would agree with much of what I say in the rest of this chapter, include Ernest Mandel, Ralph Miliband, Perry Anderson, Mihailo Marković, Svetozar Stojanović, and Roy Medvedev. (See references in the bibliography.) Although Alasdair MacIntyre probably never accepted enough of Marxist empirical theory to be classified as a Marxist, some of his early works are clearly sympathetic to the normative political positions of Classical Marxism. See *Marxism and Christianity*, and his essays on politics and political philosophy in part one of *Against the Self-Image of the Age*.

I suspect that Noam Chomsky also would agree with most of the basic normative political positions for which I argue in this chapter, even though he is a self-proclaimed libertarian (i.e., left-wing) anarchist and, as such, is opposed in principle to certain Marxist claims having to do with the long-term legitimacy of a socialist state (since the state, for anarchists, is inherently evil) and the justifiability of a democratic-centralist—i.e., Marxist-Leninist—political party. (Anarchists are highly critical of *any* form of centralized power, even one that proclaims itself to be both democratic and temporary.) But see the references to Chomsky's works below, all of which provide unrelenting critiques of both contemporary capitalist and contemporary state-socialist societies.

ism and state-socialism. With reference to the developing nations, I shall consider (D) the choice between revolutionary, post-capitalist societies (such as the People's Republic of China, Cuba, and—potentially—Nicaragua) and capitalism.

These issues cannot be intelligently decided, of course, unless we specify what sort of capitalist society we have in mind, as well as the severity of the violation of civil liberties and political rights in the state-socialist society we have in mind. Obviously, our choice will differ depending on whether we accept fascist Germany or contemporary Sweden as our model of capitalism, as well as on whether we accept Stalinist Russia of the 1930s or, say, contemporary Hungary as our model of state-socialism. In addition, these issues cannot be fully joined unless we bring both diachronic and international factors into consideration. Therefore, we shall have to consider variations of such societies along two parameters: (1) the tendencies of each of these types of society to change in certain ways over time, and (2) the relations of these types of societies to other societies that may exist (in particular, the developing societies of the Third World).

In attempting to come to terms with these issues within the framework of Classical Marxism, we will do well to keep in mind its claim that communism—or, for our purposes, democratic, self-managing socialism—can exist as a stable and continuing structure only on a worldwide scale, i.e., only in the absence of major capitalist powers that otherwise will attempt to undermine it economically and/or militarily. Thus the ultimate normative political position of Classical Marxism would seem to be that we are obligated to work toward the creation of a worldwide federation of democratic, self-managing socialist societies. After all, if democratic, self-managing socialism is to be preferred within an individual society then—barring any ill effects of their amalgamation—a worldwide system of such societies is to be preferred to any other historically possible world scenario. And far from having ill effects, Marxists maintain that a worldwide system of such societies will be the only insurance the world has against incessant war, international distributive injustices, the lack of cooperation in solving environmental and demographic problems, etc.

A. Democratic, Self-Managing Socialism vs. Capitalism

Given the theory of social justice advanced in the present chapter, it seems quite clear that a truly democratic, self-managing socialist society will be preferable to any historically possible form of capitalist society, even a capitalist society such as Sweden, which most of us, I think, will agree meets the principles of our theory of social justice as well or better than any capitalist society now extant and perhaps as well as any capitalist society can be expected to meet them. In brief, the reason a democratic, self-managing socialist society would be judged morally preferable is that while both sorts of society would meet the first two principles (the protection of basic rights to well-being and maximum equal liberty), a socialist society would quite probably better meet principles three and four. In reference to the third (equal opportunity) principle, though Swedish government-owned corporations like Volvo have introduced a certain amount of worker participation into the labor process, even these industries do not allow for genuine workers' democracy or, arguably, even as much of it as currently exists in many self-managed enterprises in Yugoslavia. Since a genuinely democratic, self-managing socialist society presumably will have a much greater degree of workers' self-management than present-day Yugoslavia, it would seem, based on this criterion, superior to Sweden or any "Swedenized" capitalist society.

As to the fourth principle, it must be kept in mind that while income differentials will exist in a socialist society, such a society— by hypothesis —will not be one in which systems of bureaucratic privilege exist. Since property is socially owned, neither will there exist the great differences in investment wealth (and income) that exist in capitalist societies. Although Sweden probably meets principle four as well or better than any other capitalist society, due to its extremely progressive taxation scheme and extensive welfare transfer programs, the investment wealth and, to a lesser extent, income are still severely skewed toward the Swedish capitalist class and, in particular, the famous "fifteen families."[17]

---

[17] For some relevant data and analyses concerning contemporary Sweden on this point, as well as the degree of social and economic democracy existing there, see the articles collected in *Limits of the Welfare State: Critical Views on Post-War Sweden* (J. A. Fry, ed.). According to the endnotes of Lennart Bernston's "Post-War Swedish Capitalism," in recent years, "The accumulation and concentration of wealth in the hands of Sweden's top fifteen families has continued and with government approval and support the number of annual mergers has increased. The position of finance capital in the Swedish economy has always been strong with the fifteen leading families clustered around three major banks [two of which have recently merged]. During recent years these financial institutions have extended their control over the most expansive sectors of industry both in monopoly and non-monopoly . . . controlled branches" (*Limits of the Welfare State*, p. 87).

According to Stig Larsson and Kurt Sjöström in "The Welfare Myth in Class Society," "In general, no . . . income levelling [between social classes] has occurred in Sweden (with the exception of temporary phenomena). Even those who earlier tried to conceal class cleavages have been forced to concede their continued exis-

Since such a democratic, self-managing socialist society meets the first two principles as well as the best capitalist societies and meets the last two principles better, it must be judged morally superior. It does not, however, immediately follow that socialist revolution would be justified to transform a capitalist society like Sweden into a democratic, self-managing socialist society since, presumably, revolutions are justified only if the injustices of a society surpass certain limits (more on this presently). We should also keep in mind, of course, that the Swedish capitalist economy is part and parcel of the international capitalist economy and, as such, participates in the super-exploitation of the Third World.[18]

But even if a democratic, self-managing socialist society is morally preferable to any form of capitalism, the choice, many will maintain, is between such historically existing societies as the United States and the Soviet Union, and—it is argued—we must decide in favor of democratic capitalism over "totalitarian communism." The answer to this, it seems to me, is (1) this is not the choice facing us; (2) even if it were, the choice of a democratic cap-

---

tence in spite of decades of social democratic rule. . . . income levelling has stagnated during the post war period. The levelling effect of the taxation has been low—'approximately 90 per cent of inequality prior to tax remains after taxation' " (*Limits of the Welfare State*, p. 171). "Riches grow on one side and poverty spreads on the other. While the number of millionaires grows by a couple of hundred per year, the number of individuals who must seek social assistance . . . increases by about 50,000 annually. . . . 5 per cent of the population owns 50 per cent of the wealth . . . nearly one-half of the wage earners have an annual income of less than five thousand dollars (ibid., p. 172).

The income and wealth differentials within a less egalitarian advanced capitalist society such as the United States are, of course, even more severe. See Ferdinand Lundberg, *America's Sixty Families*, Vanguard Press, 1937, and *The Rich and the Super-Rich: A Study in the Power of Money Today*, Lyle Stuart, 1968; and David Kotz, *Bank Control of Large Corporations in the United States*, University of California Press, Berkeley, 1978. Conversely, see Michael Harrington, The Other America: Poverty in the United States, Macmillan, N.Y., 1962, 1964, and *The New American Poverty*, Holt, Rinehart, and Winston, N.Y., 1984. The differentials in *power* resulting from the structures that create such wealth and income differentials are documented by William Domhoff in: *Who Rules America?* Prentice-Hall, Englewood Cliffs, N.J., 1967; *The Higher Circles: The Governing Class in America*, Random House, N.Y., 1970; *Fat Cats and Democrats: The Role of the Big Rich in the Party of the Common Man*, Prentice-Hall, Englewood Cliffs, N.J., 1972; *The Bohemian Grove and Other Retreats: A Study in Ruling Class Cohesiveness*, Harper & Row, N.Y., 1974; *Who Really Rules? New Haven and Community Power Re-examined*, Transaction Books, New Brunswick, N.J., 1978; *The Powers That Be: Process of Ruling Class Domination in America*, Random House, N.Y., 1979; *Who Rules America Now?: A View of the Eighties*, Prentice-Hall, Englewood Cliffs, N.J., 1983.

[18] See the following articles in *Limits of the Welfare State* (J. A. Fry, ed.): Lennart Bernston, "Post-War Swedish Capitalism"; Karl Anders Larsson, "The International Dependence of the Swedish Economy"; and Jan Annerstedt, "The Swedish Arms Industry and the Viggen Project."

italist society such as the U.S.A. would be incontrovertible *only* if we failed to take diachronic and international factors into consideration. (This issue is discussed later in this chapter.)

B. Democratic, Self-Managing Socialism vs. State-Socialism

Democratic, self-managing socialism is also quite obviously morally preferable to state-socialism. Even if they both were to meet the first principle concerning the protection of basic rights to well-being, a democratic, self-managing socialist society would almost undoubtedly better meet principles two, three, and four. By definition, democratic, self-managing socialist societies protect civil liberties and instantiate not only political but also social and economic democracy; by definition, state-socialist societies do not. Thus the former will better meet principles two and three. Furthermore, while the former, by hypothesis, will *not* have a privileged bureaucracy, the latter—as a matter of both definition and empirical fact—do.[19] Thus democratic, self-managing socialism will probably better meet principle four as well.

[19] For documentation of the rather extensive privileges of the political-military-managerial-technocratic bureaucracies of state-socialist societies, see Walter D. Connor, *Socialism Politics, and Equality: Hierarchy and Change in Eastern Europe and the USSR*, Columbia University Press, N.Y., 1979; Mervyn Matthews, *Privilege in the Soviet Union*, Allen & Unwin, London, 1978; Murray Yanowitch, *Social and Economic Inequality in the Soviet Union*, Myron Sharpe, N.Y., 1979; P. Wiles, *Distribution of Income: East and West*, North Holland Press, Amsterdam, 1974; Frank Parkin, *Class Inequality and Political Order: Social Stratification in Capitalist and Communist Societies*, Praeger, N.Y., 1971; and Victor Zaslavsky, "The Regime and the Working Class in the USSR," *Telos*, vol. 42 (1979–80), and "Socioeconomic Inequality and Changes in Soviet Ideology," *Theory and Society*, vol. 9, no. 2 (1980). Also, Trotsky's *The Revolution Betrayed* contains valuable information concerning the initial formation of a privileged bureaucracy in the Soviet Union.

Although this phenomenon is most well studied and well documented with respect to the Soviet Union and other Eastern European post-capitalist societies, it is clear that such privileged bureaucracies also exist (to one degree or another) in the People's Republic of China and other Third World post-capitalist societies. Cuba and Nicaragua, however, may be the least bureaucratized of all presently existing post-capitalist societies. One reason for this might be that they are among the most recently created post-capitalist societies. Perhaps an even more important reason, however, is that their anti-capitalist revolutions were not led by (already) Stalinized Communist Parties but by indigenous revolutionary socialist parties that either absorbed the smaller Communist Party after the revolution (as in the case of Castro's July 26th Movement in Cuba) or simply ignored it (as in the case of the Sandinista Party in Nicaragua). (These factors also may help account for the fact that both the leadership and the general population of these societies seem to exhibit the highest degree of revolutionary fervor to be found among presently existing post-capitalist societies. This, in turn, may account for the U.S. government's special antipathy toward them.)

The more interesting question concerns the view that the Classical Marxist tradition would (or should) take of presently existing post-capitalist societies. This is certainly one of the most controversial and divisive issues within the Marxist tradition as a whole. As pointed out previously, various Marxists describe these societies as communist (i.e., the higher stage of communism), as socialist (having reached the first stage of communism), as a bureaucratic-centralist, as state-capitalist, and as state-socialist. As expressed throughout this work, it is my contention that these societies should be described as *state-socialist*. Such societies are quite obviously not stateless, coercionless societies based on material superabundance. Therefore, they are not communist societies. Neither are they democratic enough to be classified as socialist societies (or, in Marx's words, as the first stage of communism). It would be inperspicuous to classify them as "state-capitalist" societies because they do not have classes of capitalists who can transfer investment wealth to their descendants, nor do such societies operate according to capitalist economic law of motion (i.e., according to the law of the maximization of exchange value). Finally, it would be misleading to classify them (along with fascist societies like Nazi Germany) as "bureaucratic-centralist" societies because this description ignores the fact that—unlike fascist societies—they have abolished capitalist production relations and successfully substituted the maximization of use value for the maximization of exchange value as the dominant economic law of motion.

More important than the label we attach to such societies are the normative political positions that seem to flow from the above descriptions. If the Marxist tradition is correct in its assertions that (1) capitalism is the chief cause of the world's social and economic problems and thus that capitalism must be eliminated on a worldwide scale in order to solve these problems and (2) the USSR and other so-called "communist countries" have eliminated capitalism,

---

Actually, since the process of socializing large-scale productive property has not to date been completed in Nicaragua, it is not quite accurate to classify it as a post-capitalist society. But it seems clear that barring the success of the U.S. policy of overthrowing the Sandinista government or completely bankrupting the Nicaraguan economy in order to ferment massive popular discontent and, thus, an internal revolt against the Sandinistas, Nicaragua eventually will complete the process of socialization of large-scale productive property and, thus, become a full-fledged post-capitalist society. (This does not mean that the Sandinista government will not let *some* productive enterprises remain in private hands or that they will not continue to rely on market mechanisms to some extent but, as I argued in the Introduction to this work, this would not necessarily count against classifying such a society as post-capitalist or even socialist.)

then whatever their drawbacks might be it would seem likely that a reversion to capitalism within such societies would be a major blow to the goal of developing a worldwide federation of democratic, self-managing socialist societies. Hence, it would seem that even though proponents of the tradition of Classical Marxism ought consistently to explain that state-socialist societies are not yet truly socialist and ought to call for implementation of democratic political, social, and economic institutions in such societies by evolutionary or, if necessary, revolutionary means, they ought also consistently to explain why such post-capitalist societies must be defended against the ideological, political, economic, and military attacks of the capitalist world. (Note that the revolutions in question would change the political and other decision-making superstructures rather than production relations—i.e., the economic substructure—and thus are classified by the Classical Marxist tradition as *political* rather than *social* revolutions.)[20]

[20] At the present time, as I am going over the copy edited version of this work, the student-led movement for greater freedom and democracy and less corruption on part of the privileged bureaucracy in China has just been brutally suppressed by the Chinese government. UPI has reported that the Red Cross in China has estimated that 1400 people were killed and thousands wounded when the 27th Army cleared Tiananmen Square of demonstrators and retook Beijing, which had effectively been under the control of the students and the local population, who had surrounded and convinced numerous army units not to participate in the repression in the previous days. (Other estimates in the Western press range from 400 to 3,000 deaths.) Presently hundreds of students and workers who had supported them are being rounded up, imprisoned, beaten, forced to recant, and—in some cases—executed. There are reports that at least two generals and fifty officers from other army units that refused to participate in the bloody crackdown have also been executed.

Chinese government officials are now attempting to convince their own citizens (and anyone in the outside world willing to listen to them) that this mass movement on the part of students and workers was, in fact, a counterrevolutionary movement aimed at the overthrow of both the Communist Party and socialist property relations. The evidence, however, shows rather convincingly that this movement was not aimed at a social revolution to change property relations—i.e., at a reversion to capitalism—but, rather, at a political revolution to establish socialist democracy. (Actually, it is probably somewhat misleading to say that it was aimed at *any* sort of revolution, since the movement demanded only a dialogue with top government officials, publication of government leaders' assets and salaries, greater freedom of the press and other democratic rights, and price controls on consumer goods in the face of high inflation.) Assuming this analysis is basically correct, this is precisely the type of movement that Marxists and all those in favor of democratic socialism ought to advocate and support.

Not surprisingly, many capitalist politicians and ideologues in the West have hypocritically shed crocodile tears over Tiananmen Square while simultaneously supporting such brutally repressive, anti-democratic governments as those in Taiwan, South Korea, Chile, Guatemala, Honduras, and El Salvador. These figures, together with much of the bourgeois media in the West, have also trumpeted these

In light of these considerations, it seems necessary to add two further positions to our list of the Classical Marxist's basic normative political positions, namely, that (3) *political* revolutions are justified in contemporary post-capitalist societies *if*, and only if, they are both necessary and sufficient to achieve genuinely democratic forms of socialism in those societies, and (4) contemporary post-capitalist societies—even though they, by no stretch of the imagination, meet the criteria of the Classical Marxists for being socialist societies in that they lack democratic institutions of workers' self-management—must be supported and defended in their struggles with capitalist and especially imperialist powers—except perhaps under extremely unusual circumstances.

C. State-Socialism vs. Capitalism

To decide between a capitalist and a state-socialist society we must specify what form of capitalism we have in mind as well as the degree of repression that exists in the state-socialist society. While this may seem to beg the question against state-socialist societies on the issue of the existence of repression, it is merely a definitional point: if a post-capitalist society is neither undemocratic nor repressive, then it is a genuinely socialist rather than a state-socialist society.

Since choosing between the worst-known form of capitalism

---

events as signaling the "revolt against communism" and the "demise of socialism" rather than describing them as attempts to establish a more democratic and, therefore, more viable form of socialism. (That most of these individuals would not support pro-democracy movements in state-socialist societies if they really thought they would succeed can presumably be deduced from the fact that if such movements did succeed in transforming state-socialist societies into democratic, self-managing socialist societies, then these capitalist politicians and ideologues would lose their main argument for the superiority of capitalism—namely, that socialist property relations are incompatible with freedom and democracy—as well as their main rationale for savagely repressing anti-capitalist movements and/or installing pro-capitalist dictatorships around the world.) I would argue that while there is no evidence for the view that these events forebode a return to capitalism, they do seem to confirm the hypothesis that the entrenched bureaucracies in most state-socialist societies are not about to give up their privileges and their monopolies on political power without a serious struggle. (For an analysis of the political bureaucracy in China, see P'eng Shu-tse, *The Chinese Communist Party in Power*, Pathfinder Press, N.Y., 1980; Tom Kerry, *The Mao Myth and the Legacy of Stalinism in China*, Pathfinder Press, N.Y., 1977; and Leslie Evans, *China After Mao*, Pathfinder Press, N.Y., 1978. For a brief analysis of the recent events in China from the perspective of those Marxists in favor of democratic socialism, see Cliff DuRand, "Only through Socialism Can Full Democracy Be Realized: China's Socialists Have One Last Chance," *The Guardian* [N.Y.], June 21, 1989.)

(say, Nazi Germany of the 1930s and 1940s) and the worst form of state-socialism (say, Stalinist Russia of the late 1920s and the 1930s) is neither palatable nor enlightening, I shall for the present limit my discussion to presently existing forms of capitalism and state-socialism (both of which, I will assume, meet the first principle). It seems clear that *so long as this choice is made in isolation from diachronic and international factors*, a Swedenized form of advanced, industrialized capitalism is morally preferable to a state-socialist society because it better meets the second (maximum equal liberty) principle and at least the second part of the third principle, i.e., the part calling for political democracy. Similarly, in a decision between less egalitarian democratic capitalist societies (e.g., the contemporary U.S.A.) and state-socialist societies (e.g., the contemporary USSR), one would have to choose the former on precisely the same grounds—again, so long as the decision is made in isolation from diachronic and international considerations.

Attending to such diachronic and international considerations will quite probably not substantially weaken the case for preferring Sweden to state-socialist societies. Even though Swedish capital is, in part, international capital, Sweden has a relatively nonaggressive, egalitarian, and humanitarian foreign policy. However, attending to these factors will almost undoubtedly weaken the case for preferring such capitalist societies as the United States to state-socialist societies. Any such decision would also, of course, be contingent upon an analysis of the international and diachronic dimensions of contemporary state-socialist societies, in particular, their relations with other countries and their own potential for change toward a democratic form of socialism.

As to the first (diachronic) factor, it is an assumption of the Classical Marxist tradition that class struggle in capitalist societies is inevitable (or at least highly likely) and that capitalist societies such as the United States may well degenerate into dictatorial forms of government during the future course of this struggle. Although the claim that even hitherto stable capitalist democracies will quite possibly become authoritarian may at first seem outlandish, the historical evidence concerning the rise of fascism—as analyzed by Trotsky and others—points in another direction.[21]

---

[21] See Trotsky's *The Struggle Against Fascism in Germany* and *The Spanish Revolution (1931–39)*; Daniel Guerin, *Fascism and Big Business*, Pathfinder Press, N.Y., 1973; Poulantzas, *Fascism and Dictatorship*; Rupert Palme Dutt, *Fascism and Social Revolution*, Proletarian Press, N.Y., 1936; Franz Neumann, *Behemoth: The Structure and Practice of National Socialism (1933–1944)*, Harper & Row, N.Y., 1944; and David

In fact, the Marxist assessment of fascism as the ultimate defense of capitalism is an important empirical thesis in Marxism's defense of its normative political positions. Although this analysis is much disputed, it seems quite plausible that at least certain components of the capitalist class and the power elite that serves its interests will fight fervently for such a "solution" (i.e., a military dictatorship or fascist regime) if a revolutionary workers' movement actually begins to develop into a significant 'threat.' And Marxists—as opposed to some other sorts of socialists—are generally in agreement that not even the most prosperous and/or powerful capitalist society can keep the lid on the class struggle indefinitely. The logic of capitalism, so it is argued, will eventually lead to the capitalist class attempting to drive down the relative (and perhaps absolute) proportion of the surplus social product consumed by the working class and other subordinate classes, and this—conjoined with all of the other economic, social, and political crises of capitalism—will eventually lead to the radicalization of at least significant parts of these subordinate classes.

Furthermore, as pointed out in the previous discussion of the choice between democratic, self-managing socialism and state-socialism, another thesis of the Classical Marxist tradition is that there can be a democratic, self-managing form of socialism. A correlative thesis is that presently existing state-socialist societies—as well as presently existing capitalist societies—can by either evolutionary or revolutionary means be transformed into democratic, self-managing socialist societies. On this analysis, post-capitalist societies can, in the long run, also be expected to meet the second and third principles better than capitalist systems. Thus our theory of social justice will choose them as morally preferable. Ultimately, of course, the Marxist tradition demands that any real comparison be made on a world scale since it is assumed that capitalist and post-capitalist societies are incompatible and cannot indefinitely coexist. But if the above analysis is correct, the choice facing the human species is *not* between bourgeois parliamentary democracy and "totalitarian communism," as many bourgeois polemicists and ideologues maintain, but—in the final analysis—between some form (perhaps, in time, an extremely democratic form) of socialism and some form (perhaps an extremely undemocratic or even a totalitarian form) of capitalism.

Schoenbaum, *Hitler's Social Revolution: Class and Status in Nazi Germany (1933–39)*, W. W. Norton, N.Y., 1980.

As to the second (international) parameter, it is an assumption not only of the Marxist tradition but of many non-Marxists as well that capitalism, in general, and such capitalist societies as the United States, in particular, are the major cause of the underdevelopment of the Third World and are thus responsible for the starvation, malnutrition, and abject poverty and misery of hundreds of millions of people.[22] Since the Marxist's view is that there is no chance of capitalism reforming itself to meet these problems, the conclusion is that the only way to solve the problems of the Third World is to transform both Third World societies and such advanced capitalist societies as the United States into socialist (or at least post-capitalist) societies. Therefore, post-capitalist societies are to be preferred to capitalist societies on a world scale because only the former will be able to ensure people's subsistence rights. This is assuming, of course, that there would be no comparable violations of security rights by such post-capitalist societies (due to mass torture, executions, slave-labor camps, etc.). Moreover, based on these assumptions even a worldwide state-socialist society may be morally preferable to a world that still contains major capitalist powers, since the principle providing for the protection of basic rights to well-being takes precedence over all other principles of social justice. (Fortunately, this is *not* the only alternative to capitalism if the Marxist tradition is correct.)

Opponents of Marxism often claim that post-capitalist soci-

---

[22] For a defense of these claims, see Sweezy, *The Theory of Capitalist Development*; Baran, *The Political Economy of Growth*; Magdoff, *The Age of Imperialism*; Andre Gunder Frank, *Capitalism and Underdevelopment in Latin America*, Monthly Review Press, N.Y., 1967, and *Dependent Accumulation and Underdevelopment*, Monthly Review Press, N.Y., 1978; Immanuel Wallerstein, *The Capitalist World Economy: Essays*, Cambridge University Press, N.Y., 1979; Samir Amin, *Unequal Development: An Essay on the Social Formations of Peripheral Capitalism*, Monthly Review Press, N.Y., 1976, and *Imperialism and Unequal Development*, Monthly Review Press, N.Y., 1977; and Weisskopf, "Imperialism and the Economic Development of the Third World."
See also Ronald H. Chilcote, *Theories of Development and Underdevelopment*, Westview Press, Boulder, Colo., 1984; Gabriel Kolko, *The Roots of American Foreign Policy*, Beacon Press, Boston, 1969; Robert Rhodes (ed.), *Imperialism and Underdevelopment*, Monthly Review Press, N.Y., 1970; Robert Owen and Bob Sutcliffe, *Studies in the Theory of Imperialism*, Longman, London, 1972; Michael Barratt-Brown, *The Economics of Imperialism*, Longman, London, 1973; Charles Wilber (ed.), *The Political Economy of Development and Underdevelopment*, Random House, N.Y., 1973; and Richard Barnet and Ronald Muller, *Global Reach: The Power of Multinational Corporation*, Simon & Schuster, N.Y., 1974.
See also Michael Harrington, *The Vast Majority: A Journey to the World's Poor*, Simon & Schuster, N.Y., 1977; the Brandt Commission, *North-South: A Program for Survival*, MIT Press, Cambridge, Mass., 1980; Teresa Hayter, *The Creation of World Poverty: An Alternative View to the Brandt Report*, Pluto Press, London, 1981; and Castro, *The World Crisis*.

eties—and especially a global post-capitalist society—will violate more basic rights to well-being than their capitalist counterparts due to torture, executions, and slave-labor camps. If this were true, then capitalism would be morally preferable to such post-capitalist societies. Abuses often cited are from 1930s Stalinist Russia: the massacre of millions of rich peasants and forced collectivization of the peasantry, the ruthless elimination of all political opposition both inside and outside the Communist Party, the Gulag Archipelago, etc. Although it is beyond the purview of this work to attempt a systematic assessment of the development of the Soviet Union and other post-capitalist societies, some relatively plausible assertions made by non-Stalinist Marxists are: (1) such policies have no basis within the tradition of Classical Marxism, and it is of the utmost importance to distinguish Stalin and Stalinism from Marx and Marxism;[23] (2) the grain strike against the state, which led to Stalin's "liquidation" of the kulaks in the early 1930s, could in all probability have been avoided if the left opposition's program of gradual, voluntary collectivization and the prevention of the formation and solidification of a class of rich peasants had been accepted in the 1920s; (3) the abhorrent policies of the Soviet Union and other post-capitalist societies have largely

[23] The claim that the violence against the Soviet population perpetrated by the Stalinist regime can be laid at the door of Marxist theory or values is debatable, to say the least. The Classical Marxists—including Lenin and Trotsky—never thought that the Soviet Union could, by itself, achieve a lasting democratic form of socialism but, rather, pinned their hopes on the spread of the socialist revolution to the industrialized West, especially to Germany. They neither thought necessary nor advocated the pernicious policies or methods here mentioned. Trotsky puts this in perspective when he writes: "Stalinism . . . [is] an immense bureaucratic reaction against the proletarian dictatorship in a backward and isolated country. The October Revolution abolished privileges, waged war against social inequality, replaced the bureaucracy with self-government of the toilers, abolished secret diplomacy, strove to render all social relationships completely transparent. Stalinism reestablished the most offensive forms of privileges, imbued inequality with a provocative character, strangled mass self-activity under police absolutism, transformed administration into a monopoly of the Kremlin oligarchy and regenerated the fetishism of power in forms that absolute monarchy dared not dream of.

". . . Stalinist frame-ups are not a fruit of Bolshevik 'amoralism'; no, like all important events in history, they are a product of the concrete social struggle, and the most perfidious and severest of all at that: the struggle of a new aristocracy against the masses that raised it to power.

"Verily boundless intellectual and moral obtuseness is required to identify the reactionary police morality of Stalinism with the revolutionary morality of the Bolsheviks" (*Their Morals and Ours*, p. 25).

On the phenomenon of Stalinism, see Trotsky, *The Revolution Betrayed*; R. Medvedev, *Let History Judge* and *On Stalin and Stalinism*; Ali (ed.), *The Stalinist Legacy*; and R. Tucker (ed.), *Stalinism*.

resulted from the process of modernization and industrialization, which economically advanced capitalist societies had already undergone over a longer period of time, though not necessarily at less expense in terms of human misery;[24] (4) it was precisely the economic and political backwardness of the Soviet Union that resulted in its eventual degeneration into a totalitarian society; and (5) despite continued violation of civil rights and lack of democracy in the Soviet Union and other (now industrialized and modernized) post-capitalist societies, the past practices of mass executions, torture, and slave-labor camps have either been eliminated or severely curtailed.[25] Furthermore, it is arguable that capitalist rather than post-capitalist societies are today the worst violators of human rights.[26] Thus, rather than "communism" or Marxism being the primary cause of human-rights violations, as is often claimed, a strong case can be made for the view that today capitalism is the primary cause (more on this presently).

Although there is much talk of the "imperialism" of post-capitalist societies (as in "Soviet-socialist imperialism"), it is arguable that whatever state-socialist societies do to further their geopolitical interests, these interests are qualitatively different from those of capitalist societies. The geopolitical interests of capitalist powers like the United States (or, more precisely, the interests of the ruling classes and their allies within such societies) lie in maintaining what Noam Chomsky and others describe as a "favorable investment climate." This is because the laws of motion of capitalism demand an ever-expanding increase of capitalist investment and thus an ever-increasing penetration of the developing countries. Post-capitalist societies, however, are not subject to the same economic law of motion (namely, that of the maximization of exchange value or, more loosely, profit) and do not have the same

---

[24] See Marx's description, in the first volume of *Capital*, of the plight of the emerging proletariat and dispossessed peasantry in England during and after the Industrial Revolution, or E. P. Thompson's account in *The Making of the English Working Class*, Vintage, N.Y., 1963, 1966.

[25] See, however, Sidney Bloch and Peter Reddaway, *Psychiatric Terror*, Basic Books, N.Y., 1977; and Zhores Medvedev and Roy Medvedev, *Questions of Madness*, W. W. Norton, N.Y., 1979.

[26] According to the American Friends Service Committee pamphlet, "Questions and Answers on the Soviet Threat and National Security" (Philadelphia, 1981): "The top ten recipients of US military and economic aid, according to Amnesty International, are also the world's top ten dictatorships or violators of human rights: South Korea, The Philippines, Indonesia, Thailand, Chile, Argentina, Uruguay, Haiti, Brazil, and formerly, Iran" (p. 16). (Needless to say, all of these countries are capitalist.)

447

economic interests or relations with developing countries. Although presently existing post-capitalist societies are interested in striking the best economic deals possible with such countries and often in supporting "friendly regimes," and—to a limited extent—supporting anti-capitalist movements around the world, they are not forced to maintain a favorable investment climate on an international scale. In short, unlike the imperialist capitalist powers, they are not compelled to undertake the role of maintaining a favorable economic status quo in every far-flung quarter of the world.

In addition, while we in the West (and especially in the United States) are told virtually every day of the "Soviet threat" and "international communist conspiracy," it is arguably the case that it is the United States that is committed to massive war expenditures and active military intervention around the world in order to protect "American interests" and "American security," i.e., to protect the right of the Western capitalist economy to have at its disposal favorable investment opportunities. It is also arguable that it is not the "international communist conspiracy" but the conditions of abject poverty and permanent misery engendered by capitalism in almost all (capitalist) developing countries that lead to the *indigenous* revolutionary movements. In short, it is arguably capitalism rather than "communism," and the United States rather than the USSR that is the main instigator of the arms race, the basic cause of revolutionary movements, and the primary aggressor in the world today.[27]

[27] In addition to the American Friends Service Committee pamphlet quoted above, see Robert Aldridge, *First Strike: The Pentagon's Strategy for Nuclear War*, South End Press, Boston, 1983, and *The Counterforce Syndrome: A Guide to U.S. Nuclear Weapons and Strategic Doctrine*, 2nd ed., Institute for Strategic Studies, Washington, D.C., 1979; Seymour Melmen, *Profits without Production*, Knopf, N.Y., 1983, and *The Permanent War Economy*, Touchstone, 1985; Daniel Ellsberg, "Call to Mutiny," *Protest and Survive* (E. P. Thompson and Dan Smith, eds.), Monthly Review Press, N.Y., 1981; Richard Barnet, *Roots of War: The Men and Institutions Behind U.S. Foreign Policy*, Penguin Books, N.Y., 1981; Noam Chomsky, *Towards a New Cold War: Essays on the Current Crisis and How We Got There*, Pantheon, N.Y., 1982; and Michael T. Klare and Peter Kornbluh (eds.), *Low Intensity Warfare: Counterinsurgency, Proinsurgency, and Antiterrorism in the Eighties*, Pantheon, N.Y., 1987. See also the following books by Micheal T. Klare: *War without End: American Planning for the Next Vietnams*, Knopf, N.Y., 1972; *Beyond the Vietnam Syndrome: U.S. Intervention in the 1980's*, Institute for Policy Studies, Washington, D.C., 1981; and *The American Arms Supermarket*, University of Texas Press, Austin, 1984.

For a Marxist defense of the view that the two superpowers are equally responsible for the arms race, however, see E. P. Thompson, "Notes on Exterminism, the Last Stage of Civilization," *New Left Review* 121 (May–June 1980); "Letter to America," *The Nation*, Jan. 24, 1981 (reprinted in *Protest and Survive*); *Exterminism and Cold War*, Schocken, N.Y., 1982; and *The Heavy Dancers*, Merlin Press, London, 1985. For

D. Capitalist vs. Post-Capitalist Societies in the Third World

Similar arguments can be offered in favor of choosing revolutionary, post-capitalist regimes over capitalist regimes in developing countries. Moreover, these arguments are sound whether or not a full-fledged democratic, self-managing socialist society is a real historical possibility on either a national or international scale. On what basis is this claim made? First, there is copious evidence that the only way for a developing nation to ensure the subsistence rights of all of its population is to overthrow capitalism and institute policies aimed at national food self-sufficiency.[28] Whereas some will argue that fulfilling subsistence rights by these means will result in violations of equally basic security rights due to unwarranted execution and/or torture of numerous individuals, the truth seems quite the opposite. There is also copious evidence that it is not post-capitalist societies in the Third World nor revolutionary movements aimed at creating such post-capitalist societies that are the major violators of the basic security rights of their populations but, rather, the right-wing capitalist dictatorships that are directly and indirectly supported by world capitalism and especially by the United States (the preeminent imperialist power of our age).[29] The measures that the United States and other capitalist

a Marxist response to this position, see Roy Medvedev and Zhores Medvedev, "A Nuclear Samizdat on America's Arms Race," *The Nation*, Jan. 16, 1982.

[28] See Bender, "World Hunger, Human Rights, and the Right to Revolution"; Frances Moore Lappe and Joseph Collins, *Food First: Beyond the Myth of Scarcity*, Ballantine Books, N.Y., 1977; Medea Benjamin, Joseph Collins, and Michael Scott, *No Free Lunch: Food and Revolution in Cuba Today*, Institute for Food and Development Policy, San Francisco, 1984; Joseph Collins et al., *Nicaragua: What Difference Could a Revolution Make?* Institute for Food and Development Policy, San Francisco, 1985; Suzan George, *How the Other Half Dies: The Real Reasons for World Hunger*, Allanheld, Osmun & Co., Montclair, N.J., 1977; and *Who Shall Eat?: Report on an Inquiry into U.S. Food Policy Options*, American Friends Service Committee, N.Y., 1977.

[29] Of course, one can easily be (mis)led to the opposite conclusion. If one read and/or watched only American mainstream news sources, one might think that the Sandinista government indulges in torture and execution of political opponents on a massive scale, while such U.S.-supported governments as those in El Salvador, Guatemala, and Honduras, and U.S.-supported movements like the Contras have a relatively good record in this respect. (After all, President Reagan called the Contras the "moral equivalent of our Founding Fathers," while Secretary of State George Schultz characterized the Sandinista government as the closest thing to Nazi Germany we now have!) But if one bothers to consult the reports of Amnesty International or any other well-known, neutral human rights monitoring group, one will find that the truth is quite the opposite. While there have been a few isolated cases of Sandinista security forces torturing and killing suspected Contra

powers are willing to take in order to preserve the world capitalist order and a favorable investment climate in the Third World hardly need be mentioned. In addition to direct military intervention, such powers use their control of the International Monetary Fund and World Bank to deny offending countries needed loans (and prop up right-wing dictatorships and friendly Third World "democracies"); engage in economic boycotts; give tactical and material support to the military and the secret police (and thus the right-wing death squads) of "loyal" countries; and directly employ their own secret police (e.g., the CIA) to fix elections, undermine economies, assassinate offending parties, etc.

Thus anti-capitalist revolutions in developing countries may be

---

sympathizers in the war zones and while prisoners are sometimes beaten or isolated in dark cells in present-day Nicaragua, there is no evidence of the systematic use of torture against political prisoners by the Sandinistas. But there is copious evidence of the most brutal forms of torture being systematically utilized against political opponents by the above-named U.S.-backed regimes. Similarly, while these U.S.-backed regimes systematically extrajuridically execute or "disappear" political opponents, the Sandinista government does not. In fact, the Sandinistas abolished the death penalty when they took power and refused to execute even known torturers among Somosa's national guardsmen whom they took prisoner. The U.S.-backed Somosa dictatorship, which was overthrown by the Sandinistas had, of course, an abysmal record on both scores. Moreover, the torture and extrajuridical executions now reported by human rights groups in Nicaragua are almost exclusively carried out by the Contras rather than the Sandinistas. (Most of the isolated incidents mentioned above have been investigated by the Sandinista government with the result that a number of Sandinista army officers and soldiers have been found guilty in these incidents and are now serving up to thirty years in prison.)

Turning to the other revolutionary regime in the Western Hemisphere, although one may well be justified in decrying the some three hundred summary executions that took place after the Cuban revolution, this pales in comparison to the hundreds of "disappearances" and extrajuridical executions *per week* perpetrated upon the Salvadoran people in the 1980s by the United States-funded and trained military and police, and the right-wing death squads they, in turn, organize and support. (In the early 1980s Salvadoran right-wing death squads killed or "disappeared" up to eight hundred people per week.)

See Amnesty International Yearbooks. See also Edward S. Greenberg, "In Order to Save It, We Had to Destroy It: Reflections on the United States and International Human Rights," *Human Rights and American Foreign Policy* (Fred E. Baumann, ed.), Kenyon College, Gambier, Ohio, 1982; A. J. Langguth, *Hidden Terrors: The Truth about U.S. Police Operations in Latin America*, Pantheon, N.Y., 1978; Michael T. Klare, *Supplying Repression: U.S. Support for Authoritarian Regimes Abroad*, Institute for Policy Studies, Washington, D.C., 1977; Noam Chomsky and Edward Herman, *The Washington Connection and Third World Fascism* (The Political Economy of Human Rights, vol. 1), South End Press, Boston, 1979, and *After the Cataclysm: Post War IndoChina and the Reconstruction of Imperial Ideology* (The Political Economy of Human Rights, vol. II), South End Press, Boston, 1979; Noam Chomsky, *Turning the Tide: U.S. Intervention in Central America and the Struggle for Peace*, South End Press, Boston, 1985; and Noam Chomsky (ed.), *Radical Priorities*, Black Rose Books, Montreal, 1981.

the only effective way to ensure the subsistence rights of all of the people as well as the only way—at least in many cases—to eliminate the wholesale violation of basic security rights. Even among Third World capitalist countries that currently have democratic governments, there is no guarantee that they will remain democratic: if installing right-wing dictatorships comes to be in the interest of the national oligarchy and/or the world capitalist system (and its component capitalist classes and associated power elites), then it is quite likely that such right-wing dictatorships will be installed, or at least that there will be an attempt to install such dictatorships. (Here one need only recall the overthrow of the democratically elected Allende government in Chile and its replacement by the United States-backed Pinochet dictatorship.) Even when civilian governments are formally in power, it is commonly conceded that the military oligarchy holds the real reins of power and that it unflinchingly supports the interests of that society's capitalist class and landed aristocracy.

If post-capitalist societies are the only type of societies that can guarantee subsistence rights in the Third World and, in many cases, the only way to stop the massive violation of security rights carried out by such right-wing dictatorships, then they are morally preferable to capitalist societies in the Third World. Furthermore, since we are dealing with the *basic* human rights here, anti-capitalist revolutions are justified in such countries.[30]

Although some will argue that such post-capitalist societies are *not* morally preferable because they violate the second (maximum equal liberty) principle and also the second half of the third principle (concerning political democracy), the answer to this is that (1) fulfillment of the first principle takes precedence over any of the other principles; (2) the violations of these principles by revolutionary regimes in the Third World are often overestimated and, in fact, the vast majority of the populations of such Third World

[30] The only exception might be in a case like the anti-capitalist revolution in Kampuchea, which apparently led to the Pol Pot regime's direct and indirect killing of a substantial portion of its own populace. It should be noted, however, that some writers claim that the number of Cambodians who died by execution or starvation due to Pol Pot's policies is substantially less than reported by most Western writers. See François Ponchaud, *Cambodia: Year Zero*, Holt, Rinehart, and Winston, N.Y., 1978; and Noam Chomsky and Edward Herman, *After the Cataclysm* (previously cited). In any event, the crimes of Pol Pot can hardly be laid at the door of Classical Marxism since they were the result of insane (and non-Marxist) policies carried out by a thoroughly Stalinized party in the context of the United States' massive and prolonged imperialist war, which engulfed and disrupted the entire region of Southeast Asia.

451

nations as China, Cuba, and Nicaragua now have much more control over their lives than they did when they lived in a capitalist system;[31] (3) as these societies continue to develop, and the military and economic pressure of the imperialist capitalist powers eases, they will probably make even more progress toward democratization; and (4) the only realistic alternatives to such post-capitalist societies in many cases are right-wing regimes whose violation of the second and third principles—not to mention the first—are much worse.

In summary, given the truth of the above empirical views: (1) democratic, self-managing socialism is morally preferable to any form of capitalism and any form of state-socialism, and thus we should strive toward the creation of a worldwide federation of democratic, self-managing socialist societies; (2) although democratic welfare-state capitalist societies are morally preferable to state-socialist societies if the diachronic and international dimensions of the situation are not taken into consideration, once these dimensions are taken into consideration, this is not so clear; (3) although presently existing post-capitalist societies are in need of democratization, their reversion to capitalism would be a horrendous blow to the world socialist revolution, and thus they ought to be defended in face of the aggression of capitalist powers; and (4) anti-capitalist revolutions in the Third World are morally justified even if democratic, self-managing forms of socialism are not historically possible.

Revolution and Marxist Empirical Theory

Before setting out the minimal set of Marxist empirical theses upon which I believe an adequate Marxist moral and social theory should be based, I would like to make a few brief comments concerning the second basic normative political position I have attributed to Classical Marxism, namely, that socialist revolution—if necessary and sufficient to effect the appropriate transformations—is *prima facie* morally justified. I should make clear from the start that I am

[31] See Marc Blecher, "Consensual Politics in Rural Chinese Communities: The Mass Line in Theory and Practice," *Modern China*, vol. 5, no. 1 (Jan. 1979); John P. Burns, "The Election of Production Team Cadres in Rural China: 1958–74," *China Quarterly*, no. 74 (June 1978); Victor C. Falkenheim, "Political Participation in China," *Problems of Communism*, vol. 27, no. 3 (May–June 1978); Maurice Zeitlin, *Revolutionary Politics and the Cuban Working Class*, Princeton University Press, 1967; Lee Lockwood, *Castro's Cuba, Cuba's Fidel*, Vintage Books, NY, 1969; and the previously cited works by Joseph Collins.

content to accept what might be called the standard view concerning the justifiability of social (and political) revolution. This is the view that people have a right to revolt against a government or make a revolution to transform socioeconomic arrangements if the government or socioeconomic arrangements in question are sufficiently unjust or sufficiently violative of people's actual rights. This standard is vague, and its application will, of course, differ, depending on the principles of justice and/or the rights one recognizes. For purposes of this work, the standards are the four principles of social justice (and their associated rights) stated in the previous section.

Although I do not have room to argue the point here, it seems to me that the justification of revolutions grows progressively weaker as we advance through our set of lexically ranked principles. I take it as fairly obvious that any system or government that by intentional action or negligence allows widespread violations of the first principle (which states that everyone's basic rights to well-being must be guaranteed) can legitimately be overthrown if there is a reasonable chance of replacing it with a system or government that will meet this principle. Similarly, I take it that systematic violations of the second (maximum equal liberty) principle give rise to a right to rebel unless they are justified by other extremely weighty moral considerations, e.g., meeting the first principle. And although justifications of revolution based on violations of the third and fourth principles are correspondingly weaker, if the violations of these principles were severe, unnecessary, and unending, then revolution might be justified (if it were both a necessary and sufficient condition to correct this situation).

I take it that this analysis accounts for my earlier claim that revolution would not be justified in present-day Sweden simply because it does not fulfill the third and fourth principles as well as a democratic, self-managing socialist society would. The same holds for my claim that socialist revolution is justified in both Third World capitalist societies and such advanced capitalist societies as the United States if such revolutions are necessary to guarantee that people's basic subsistence and security rights are upheld in the Third World. The most controversial claim of this sort, at least within Marxist circles, is that political revolutions are justified in state-socialist societies—and, in particular, presently existing post-capitalist societies—if such revolutions are both necessary and sufficient to transform these societies into democratic, self-managing socialist societies. Such revolutions would be justified, in the view put forward here, because state-socialist societies systematically violate the second and third principles. Those who object to this position may do so because they do not realize that the revolutions (as described) would not change basic production relations or cause a reversion to capitalism but would simply democratize the political and economic institutions of such societies. Or they may do so because they do not believe that such political revolutions are necessary (and/or sufficient) to reach these goals.[32] If this last claim is true, then of course such revolutions would not be justified. All things being equal, peaceful evolution is always preferable to violent revolution.

Similarly, objections to the Marxist position in favor of socialist revolution in capitalist countries are sometimes based on misinterpretations of what Marxists are advocating. In this connection it is important to realize that for Marx and other Classical Marxists the means that advance socialist revolution are only those that advance the *mass* movement of the proletariat and its allies. (This is the empirical ground on which all Classical Marxists opposed terrorism as a means of social change.) The Classical Marxist view of revolution is one in which the majority of the population—or at least the majority of the working class and other oppressed segments of the population—is actively committed to radical social change and is forced into the use of violent means to protect themselves and their organizations (e.g., trade unions, workers' parties, and—in revolutionary situations—the popular organs of "dual power" that have begun to function as an alternate government) against the reactionary violence of the official police and military forces and/or fascist gangs or death squads. On this scenario the justification for workers' self-defense of their movements and organizations is essentially of the same sort as the justification that can be given for workers not allowing scabs to cross picket lines during a just labor strike.[33]

An adequate moral theory will certainly prohibit any violence not absolutely essential to a just struggle and may, besides, prohibit certain forms of violence (e.g., torture) under *any* circum-

[32] For a discussion of whether democratic, self-managing socialism can be achieved by evolutionary means in the Soviet Union and like societies, see R. Medvedev, *On Socialist Democracy*, and Coates (ed.), *Détente and Socialist Democracy: A Discussion with Roy Medvedev*.

[33] See Trotsky, *Transitional Program for Socialist Revolution*; James P. Cannon, *Socialism on Trial*, Pathfinder Press, N.Y., 1970; Luxemburg, "The Mass Strike, the Political Party, and the Trade Unions"; and Gintis and Bowles, "Socialist Revolution in the United States: Goals and Means."

stances. But the means proposed by the Classical Marxists—demonstrations, strikes, picket lines, the active and direct defense by workers and their allies of their organizations and movements, and (in extreme circumstances) rebellion and war—do not differ from the means most liberals (or most other people, for that matter) find permissible when essential for the successful prosecution of a just war or just struggle against oppression.[34] Although Marxists and non-Marxists may well disagree on the correct set of moral principles and/or the correct set of empirical theses involved in making such decisions, the point is that if a relatively egalitarian moral theory and a minimal set of Marxist empirical theses are essentially correct, then the Marxist position on socialist revolution is justified.

I wish now to discuss the minimal set of Marxist empirical theses I have utilized in justifying the Marxist's basic normative political positions. Previously I described three levels of Marx's empirical theories. In decreasing order of abstraction or generality they are: (1) historical materialism, (2) Marx's theory of classes and class conflict, and (3) Marx's more specific economic and sociological theories, including his analysis of the dysfunctions of capitalism and his projections concerning socialism. The theory of historical materialism seeks to account for epochal social transformations by relating the categories of forces of production, relations of production, and the political-legal-ideological superstructure by means of two laws (or statements of lawlike regularities). The 'law' of *technological determinism* states that the forces of production in some sense determine the relations of production. The 'law' of *economic determinism* states that the mode of production (i.e., the forces and relations of production taken together) in some sense determines the political-legal-ideological superstructure.

[34] Although this form of reasoning is sometimes decried as crude consequentialism, it is not "consequentialist" in the strict philosophical sense of the term, since one can take human rights or principles of social justice as morally basic and make such judgments on the basis of minimizing the violation or maximizing the observance of such rights or principles. Such a mixed deontological view might be called a "teleology of rights."

For further philosophical discussions of these issues, from a leftist perspective, see Marcuse, "Ethics and Revolution"; Marković, "Violence and Human Self-Realization"; Petrović, "Socialism, Revolution and Violence"; Stojanović, "Revolutionary Teleology and Ethics"; Wolf, "On Violence"; Honderich, *Three Essays on Political Violence* and "Four Conclusions about Violence of the Left"; Harris, "The Marxist Conception of Violence"; and the following articles by Nielsen: "On the Choice Between Reform and Revolution," "On Justifying Revolution," "On the Ethics of Revolution," "On Justifying Violence," "Political Violence," "Capitalism, Socialism, and Justice," and "On Terrorism and Political Assassination."

At the next level of abstraction comes Marx's theory of classes and class struggle. Some of the more important claims here are that (1) all societies having a significant surplus social product are divided into dominant and subordinate (or ruling and ruled) classes on the basis of how these classes of individuals are related to the means of production, (2) the economic interests of these classes are diametrically opposed to one another, and (3) the political-legal-ideological superstructures of such societies almost always support the interests of the dominant class. At the lowest level of abstraction we find the Marxist analysis of such dysfunctions of capitalism as depression, recession, inflation, imperialist wars, and (today) the problem of pollution and environmental destruction.

It is my contention that although historical materialism and Marx's theory of classes and class struggle (as applied to all surplus social product societies) can be given quite plausible interpretations, it is his theory of classes and class struggle *as specifically applied to capitalism*, together with the Marxist's analysis of the social and economic dysfunctions of capitalism and possibilities for post-capitalist societies, that composes the minimal set of Marxist empirical theses necessary to justify the Marxist's basic normative political positions. While the acceptance of the more abstract components of Marx's overall empirical theory may well give us more confidence in the lower-level claims, they are in principle dispensable for the justificatory purpose we have in mind.

Some writers hold that at least the "rational kernel" of historical materialism is relevant to or even necessary for the justification of these normative political positions since, the argument goes, this rational kernel is needed to show that socialism is possible.[35] But

[35] See Levine, *Arguing for Socialism*. Although we disagree on this point, I find that we are in basic agreement on most others. The only other major disagreement I see us as having is that I believe a stronger case can be made for choosing socialism over capitalism. Levine argues that since only a weak case can be made for socialism at an abstract, theoretical level, and since these are not the sorts of beliefs in which we can have a great deal of confidence to begin with, it is best to conceive of the choice situation as a Pascalian wager and thus choose the more attractive alternative, namely socialism. It seems to me that we can make a much stronger case for socialism once we descend from the abstract level on which we compare capitalism and socialism in terms of Pareto optimality, etc., and begin to compare them on their impact and potential future impact on the rights of people in developing nations, etc. In relation to this point, I do not understand how Levine can claim, in the last paragraph of his work, "Capitalism is not Hell on earth; and socialism, even in its most radically democratic forms, would not be Heaven" (p. 225). While I agree with the latter part of this statement, it seems to me that even cursory knowledge of capitalism's impact on people in the Third World falsifies the

my answer to this is that (1) historical materialism does not show that socialism is possible (at least if we take "socialism" to mean democratic, self-managing socialism) and thus does not ensure that the Marxist's basic normative political positions are justified, and (2) since 1917 we haven't needed the theory of historical materialism to show us that at least some stable, ongoing form of post-capitalist society is possible. The point is that we may well have good reason to believe that post-capitalist societies in general and democratic, self-managing socialist societies in particular are historically possible, whether or not some formulation of historical materialism (or of its rational kernel) is tenable.

Similarly, whether Marx's theory of classes and class struggle can be successfully applied to *all* specified societies seems irrelevant for our present justificatory purposes. I would venture the opinion that it may not even matter whether Marx's structural view or Max Weber's stratification view of classes (or some combination of the two) is ultimately correct so long as it is admitted that, on either account, it is reasonable to speak of dominant and subordinate classes and, in particular, of a ruling class. In fact, if Richard Miller's analysis is correct, asking whether there is a ruling class is not so much an abstract theoretical question as a practical and strategic political one. If we answer no, we seem to be implying that the less well-off segments of the population can pursue their interests and garner for themselves a fair share of the social wealth by legal and 'proper' means, while if we answer yes we seem to be implying the opposite view.[36]

Finally, this minimal set of theses will *not* include certain parts of Marx's less abstract economic and sociological theory either because they are demonstrably false or because, though plausible, they are irrelevant. The labor theory of value clearly falls into the first camp, while the thesis that there can be a completely classless

---

former part. Capitalism may not be hell on earth for everyone, but it *is* hell on earth for the hundreds of millions of persons who are unnecessarily starving to death or going hungry and who must watch their loved ones suffer and die in the same way.

[36] See chapters 3 and 4 of Miller, *Analyzing Marx*. For other contemporary Marxist analyses of classes, see G. A. Cohen, *Karl Marx's Theory of History*, chapter 3; McMurtry, *The Structure of Marx's World-View*, chapter 3; Elster, *Making Sense of Marx*, chapter 6; Roemer, *A General Theory of Exploitation and Class*; Miliband, *Class Power and State Power* and "State Power and Class Interests"; Poulantzas, *Classes in Contemporary Capitalism* and *Political Power and Social Classes*; Laclau, "The Specificity of Political"; Therborn, *What Does the Ruling Class Do When It Rules?*; and the following works by Wright: *Class, Crisis and the State*; *Class Structure and Income*; *Classes*; and "Class Boundaries in Advanced Capitalist Societies."

and *stateless* society under modern conditions would seem to fall into the latter.

Under present historical circumstances this set of assumptions should, I think, include the following sociological and economic claims:

1. As a result of the logic of the maximization of exchange value, all capitalist societies—developed or developing, partially planned or completely unplanned—exhibit and will continue to exhibit certain economic and social problems (inflation, depression, recession, unemployment, poverty, failure to regulate environmental pollution sufficiently, etc.) that can be solved only by the institution of a planned (but not necessarily command) socialist economy.

2. Even the mixed, welfare-state capitalist societies of advanced, industrialized nations of the West exhibit severe social inequalities and—if sufficiently threatened by mass working-class movements for social equality—will almost undoubtedly exhibit severe repression.

3. The world capitalist system causes in the Third World both extreme inequality and suffering, on the one hand, and (often) extremely repressive regimes, on the other.

4. So long as it is dominant or codominant on an international scale, the capitalist system will not allow the massive transfers of capital, technology, and knowledge necessary to solve the Third World's major social and economic problems.

5. Such conditions in the Third World make for perpetual social instability since those who are severely oppressed and/or deprived will organize and, if necessary, fight to better their condition or "the condition of their peoples."

6. The predictable response from the most powerful nations at the capitalist "center" (primarily the United States at this point in history and for the foreseeable future) is first to install and/or aid those Third World regimes or military cliques that can best suppress these mass movements for radical social change and, second, if that strategy fails, to intervene either directly with its own military forces or indirectly through proxy armies and "low-intensity warfare."

458

7. However else we may characterize contemporary post-capitalist societies, it seems clear that they are not the primary cause of the many indigenous revolutionary movements in the Third World and do not bear the primary responsibility for the nuclear arms race.

8. The bureaucracies of such post-capitalist societies genuinely want to reduce or eliminate arms expenditures in order to better satisfy the consumer appetites of their own populations.

9. Without the economic, diplomatic, and military pressure of the Western capitalist powers, such post-capitalist societies may well achieve significant democratization (by either evolutionary or revolutionary means).

10. Socialist transformations can occur in the advanced industrialized countries of the West, and such transformations can lead to democratic forms of socialism; thus a worldwide federation of democratic, self-managing, socialist societies is a genuine historical possibility.

I am not saying that all of these claims are necessary for justifying the Marxist's basic normative political positions, although I would assert—barring extremely implausible counter-assumptions—that they are jointly sufficient. I put them forward as examples of the sorts of (seemingly plausible) claims that must be true in order for the Marxist's positions to be justified on any fairly egalitarian theory of social justice. If the vision of the present world social order expressed by this set of claims is not tenable, then, in all probability, neither are the Marxist's basic normative political positions.

As to the responsibilities of individuals, I here have very little to say. If both a relatively egalitarian theory of social justice (such as the one put forward here) and a minimal set of Marxist empirical assumptions are essentially correct, then our natural duty to support and promote just social institutions (on both a national and international level) would seem to require us to do our fair share in supporting and promoting various working-class and progressive causes within our own societies and, if possible, on an international scale. (Perhaps the most efficient way to support such causes on an international scale is to monitor and, if necessary, alter our own societies' foreign policy, investment and aid policies, etc.)

In any case, this would seem to include supporting the struggles of workers and labor unions, the struggles of poor people (and nations) for a just share of the world's wealth, the struggles of oppressed minorities, and the struggle for the liberation of women, as well as environmentalist movements, anti-nuclear and anti-interventionist movements, and organizations and movements committed to the protection of human rights. If Marxist political theory is correct, however, the most important sorts of movements and organizations we can (and should) support are *political parties* explicitly committed to eliminating capitalism and bringing into being a world federation of democratic, self-managing socialist societies.

The simple truth is that if a relatively egalitarian theory of social justice (and human rights) and the Marxist's vision of contemporary social reality are essentially correct, then the only way we can respect other persons as free and equal moral beings—and, consequently, respect ourselves—is to do our fair share in supporting such movements, organizations, and struggles.

APPENDIX

STAGES IN THE DEVELOPMENT OF MARX'S THOUGHT

Period	Works[1]	Date Written	Date Published[2]
I.	Early Works (1841–1844)		
	A. Radical Liberalism (1841–1843)		
	Anekdota articles	(1842)	(1843)*
	Rheinische Zeitung articles	(1842–1843)	(1842–1843)*
	B. Revolutionary Humanism (1843)		
	Critique of Hegel's Philosophy of Right	(1843)	(1927)
	"On the Jewish Question"	(1843)	(1844)*
	"Contribution to the Critique of Hegel's *Philosophy of Right*: Introduction"	(1843)	(1844)*
	C. Original Marxism (1844)		
	Economic and Philosophical Manuscripts	(1844)	(1932)
	Economic Notebooks	(1844–1845)	(1932)
II.	Transitional Works (1844–1847)		
	The Holy Family (M/E)	(1844–1845)	(1845)
	"Theses on Feuerbach"	(1845)	(1888)
	The German Ideology (M/E)	(1845–1846)	(1926–1932)
	The Poverty of Philosophy	(1847)	(1847)
III.	Works of Maturation (1847–1858)		
	A. First Formulations of Mature Positions (1847–1850)		

[1] (M/E) means written by both Marx and Engels: (E) means written by Engels. All other works were written by Marx.

[2] An asterisk (*) after the Date Published indicates that the work was first published in article form.

Period	*Works*[1]	*Date Written*	*Date Published*[2]
	The Principles of Communism (E)	(1847)	(1914)
	The Manifesto of the Communist		
	Party (M/E)	(1848)	(1848)
	Wage Labor and Capital	(1849)	(1849)*
	"Address of the Central Commit-		
	tee to the Communist League"		
	(M/E)	(1850)	(1850)*
B.	Application of Mature Positions to		
	Historical Events (1850–1852)		
	Class Struggles in France: 1848–1850	(1850)	(1850)*
	The Peasant War in Germany (E)	(1850)	(1850)*
	The Eighteenth Brumaire of Louis		
	Bonaparte	(1851–1852)	(1852)
	Revolution and Counter-Revolution		
	in Germany (E)	(1851–1852)	(1851–1852)*
C.	Further Development of Marx's Critique of Capitalism		
	(1853–1858)		
	Grundrisse (*Foundations of the*		
	Critique of Political Economy)	(1857–1858)	(1939–1941)
IV.	Mature Works (1858–1883)		
	A Contribution to the Critique of		
	Political Economy	(1858–1859)	(1859)
	Theories of Surplus Value (3 vols.)	(1861–1863)	(1905–1910)
	"Inaugural Address of the		
	Working Men's International		
	Association"	(1864)	(1864)*
	Results of the Immediate Process of		
	Production	(1865)	(1933)
	Wages, Price and Profits	(1865)	(1898)
	Capital (vol. 1)	(1864–1867)	(1867)
	Capital (vol. 2)	(1865–1878)	(1884)
	Capital (vol. 3)	(1864–1875)	(1893–1894)
	"General Rules of the		
	International Working Men's		
	Association"	(1871)	(1871)*

[1] (M/E) means written by both Marx and Engels: (E) means written by Engels. All other works were written by Marx.

[2] An asterisk (*) after the Date Published indicates that the work was first published in article form.

Period	Works[1]	Date Written	Date Published[2]
	The Civil War in France	(1871)	(1871)
	"Critique of the Gotha		
	Program"	(1875)	(1891)
V.	Engels' Later Works of Popularization		
	(1872–1888)		
	"The Housing Question"	(1872)	(1872)
	Anti-Dühring	(1877–1878)	(1877–1878)*
	Dialectics of Nature	(1872–1882)	(1927)
	"Speech at the Graveside of		
	Marx"	(1883)	(1883)*
	The Origin of Family, Private		
	Property, and the State	(1884)	(1884)
	Ludwig Feuerbach and the Outcome		
	of Classical German Philosophy	(1886)	(1886)*
	The Role of Force in History	(1887–1888)	(1895–1896)*
	The Tactics of Social Democracy	(1895)	(1895)*

[1] (M/E) means written by both Marx and Engels: (E) means written by Engels. All other works were written by Marx.

[2] An asterisk (*) after the Date Published indicates that the work was first published in article form.

BIBLIOGRAPHY

If an article is part of an independently cited anthology, only the author and short title of the anthology are given after the author and title of the article.

Journals with multiple citations and more than one word in their names are abbreviated as follows:

A&K   *Analyse & Kritik*
AERPP *American Economic Review, Papers, and Proceedings*
AP   *Acta Politica*
APQ   *American Philosophical Quarterly*
APSR   *American Political Science Review*
CJE   *Cambridge Journal of Economics*
CJP   *Canadian Journal of Philosophy*
E&P   *Economics and Philosophy*
E&S   *Economy and Society*
IPSR   *Indian Political Science Review*
JHI   *Journal of the History of Ideas*
JP   *Journal of Philosophy*
JVI   *Journal of Value Inquiry*
MR   *Monthly Review*
MSP   *Midwest Studies in Philosophy*
NGC   *New German Critique*
NLR   *New Left Review*
NR   *New Reasoner*
NYRB *New York Review of Books*
OR   *The Occasional Review*
P&S   *Politics and Society*
PAAPA *Proceedings and Addresses of the American Philosophical Association*
PAS   *Proceedings of the Aristotelian Society*
PF(B)   *Philosophical Forum (Boston)*
PhS   *Philosophical Studies*
PI   *Praxis International*
PPA   *Philosophy and Public Affairs*
PPR   *Philosophy and Phenomenological Research*
PR   *Philosophical Review*

PS	*Political Studies*
PSS	*Philosophy of the Social Sciences*
PT	*Political Theory*
QJE	*Quarterly Journal of Economics*
RIP	*Revue Internationale de Philosophie*
RP	*Radical Philosophy*
RPNS	*Radical Philosophers News Journal*
RRPE	*Review of Radical Political Economics*
S&S	*Science and Society*
SAJF	*South African Journal of Philosophy*
SP	*Social Praxis*
SPP	*Social Philosophy and Policy*
SST	*Studies in Soviet Thought*
STP	*Social Theory and Practice*
T&S	*Theory and Society*

Works by Marx

Marx, Karl. "Address to the Central Committee of the Communist League." In *The Marx-Engel Reader*.
———. *Capital* (3 vols.). International Publishers, N.Y., 1967.
———. *The Civil War in France*. In *The Marx-Engels Reader*.
———. *Class Struggles in France: 1848–1850*. In *Karl Marx and Friedrich Engels: Selected Works*, vol. 1.
———. "Comments on the Latest Prussian Censorship Instructions." In *Writings of the Young Marx on Philosophy and Society*.
———. "Communism and the Augsburg 'Allgemeine Zeitung.' " In *Writings of the Young Marx on Philosophy and Society*.
———. "Contribution to the Critique of Hegel's *Philosophy of Right*: Introduction." In *Karl Marx: Early Writings*.
———. *A Contribution to the Critique of Political Economy*. International Publishers, N.Y., 1970.
———. "Critique of Hegel's Philosophy of the State." In *Writings of the Young Marx on Philosophy and Society*.
———. "Critique of the Gotha Program." In *The Marx-Engels Reader*.
———. *Economic and Philosophical Manuscripts*. In *Karl Marx: Early Writings*.
———. *The Eighteenth Brumaire of Louis Bonaparte*. In *The Marx-Engels Reader*.

———. "An Exchange of Letters." In *Writings of the Young Marx on Philosophy and Society*.

———. "General Rules of the International Working Men's Association." In *Karl Marx and Friedrich Engels: Selected Works*, vol. 2.

———. *The Grundrisse* (David McClellan, ed.). Harper & Row, N.Y., 1971.

———. "Inaugural Address of the Working Men's International Association." In *The Marx-Engels Reader*.

———. *Karl Marx: Early Writings* (T. B. Bottomore, ed.). McGraw-Hill, N.Y., 1964.

———. "The Leading Article in No. 179 on the *Kölnische Zeitung*: Religion, Free Press, and Philosophy." In *Writings of the Young Marx on Philosophy and Society*.

———. "On a Proposed Divorce Law." In *Writings of the Young Marx on Philosophy and Society*.

———. "On the Jewish Question." In *Karl Marx: Early Writings*.

———. *The Poverty of Philosophy*. International Publishers, N.Y., 1963.

———. "Reflections of a Youth on Choosing an Occupation." In *Writings of the Young Marx on Philosophy and Society*.

———. "Theses on Feuerbach." In *The Marx-Engels Reader*.

———. *Wage Labor and Capital*. In *Karl Marx and Friedrich Engels: Selected Works*, vol. 1.

———. *Wages, Price and Profits*. In *Karl Marx and Friedrich Engels: Selected Works*, vol. 2.

———. *Writings of the Young Marx on Philosophy and Society* (Lloyd D. Easton and Kurt Guddat, eds.). Doubleday, Garden City, N.Y., 1967.

Works by Marx and Engels

Marx, Karl, and Friedrich Engels. *Collected Works*. International Publishers, N.Y., 1975.

———. *The German Ideology*. In *The Marx-Engels Reader*.

———. *The Holy Family*. Progress Publishers, Moscow, 1956.

———. *Karl Marx and Friedrich Engels: Selected Works* (3 vols.). Progress Publishers, Moscow, 1969.

———. "Manifesto of the Communist Party." In *The Marx-Engels Reader*.

———. *The Marx-Engels Reader* (Robert Tucker, ed.). W. W. Norton, N.Y., 1972.

Marx, Karl, and Friedrich Engels. *Marx-Engels: Selected Correspondence*. Progress Publishers, Moscow, 1963.

Works by Engels

Engels, Friedrich. *Anti-Dühring*. International Publishers, N.Y., 1939.
———. "The Housing Question." In *Karl Marx and Friedrich Engels: Selected Works*.
———. *Ludwig Feuerbach and the Outcome of Classical German Philosophy*. International Publishers, N.Y., 1941.
———. *The Origin of Family, Private Property, and the State*. In *Karl Marx and Friedrich Engels: Selected Works*, vol. 3.
———. *Principles of Communism*. In *Karl Marx and Friedrich Engels: Selected Works*, vol. 1.

Other Works

Acton, H. B. *The Illusion of an Epoch: Marxism-Leninism as a Philosophical Creed*. Routledge & Kegan Paul, Boston, 1955.
Aiken, Henry David. "Morality and Ideology." In *Ethics and Society* (DeGeorge, ed.).
Alexander, Larry, and Maimon Schwarzschild. "Liberalism, Neutrality, and Equality of Welfare vs. Equality of Resources." *PPA*, vol. 16, no. 1 (Winter 1987).
Ali, Tariq, ed. *The Stalinist Legacy: Its Impact on 20th-Century World Politics*. Penguin, N.Y., 1984.
Allen, Derek P. H. "Does Marx Have an Ethic of Self-Realization? Reply to Aronovitch." *CJP*, vol. 10, no. 3 (Sept. 1980).
———. "Is Marxism a Philosophy?" *JP*, vol. 71 (1974).
———. "Marx and Engels on the Distributive Justice of Capitalism." In *Marx and Morality* (Nielsen and Patten, eds.).
———. "Reply to Brenkert's 'Marx and Utilitarianism.' " *CJP*, vol. 6, no. 3 (Sept. 1976).
———. "The Utilitarianism of Marx and Engels." *APQ*, vol. 10, no. 3 (July 1973).
Althusser, Louis. "Ideology and Ideological State Apparatus." In *Lenin and Philosophy*. Monthly Review Press, N.Y., 1971.
———. "Marxism and Humanism." In *For Marx*. Pantheon Books, N.Y., 1969.

Amdur, Robert. "Rawls' Theory of Justice: Domestic and International Perspectives." *World Politics*, vol. 29 (Apr. 1977).

Anderson, Perry. *Arguments within English Marxism*. New Left Books, London, 1980.

———. *Considerations on Western Marxism*. Verso, London, 1976.

———. *In the Tracks of Historical Materialism*. Verso, London, 1983.

———. "Trostky's Interpretation of Stalinism." *NLR*, no. 139 (May–June 1983).

Apel, Karl Otto. *Towards a Transformation of Philosophy*. Routledge & Kegan Paul, Boston, 1980.

Arendt, Hannah. *The Human Condition*. Doubleday, Garden City, N.Y., 1959.

———. *On Revolution*. Viking Press, N.Y., 1965.

Arneson, Richard. "Equality and Equal Opportunity for Welfare." *PhS*, no. 54 (1989).

———. "Marxism and Secular Faith." *APSR*, vol. 79 (1985).

———. "Mill's Doubts about Freedom under Socialism." In *New Essays on John Stuart Mill and Utilitarianism* (Cooper, Nielsen, and Patten, eds.). *CJP*, supplemental vol. 5, 1979.

———. "What's Wrong with Exploitation?" *Ethics*, vol. 91 (Jan. 1981).

Aronovitch, Hilliard. "Marxian Morality." *CJP*, vol. 10, no. 3 (Sept. 1980).

———. "More on Marxian Morality: Reply to Professor Allen." *CJP*, vol. 10, no. 3 (Sept. 1980).

Arthur, John, and William H. Shaw, eds. *Justice and Economic Distribution*. Prentice-Hall, Englewood Cliffs, N.J., 1978.

Avineri, Shlomo. "Aspects of Freedom of Writing and Expression in Hegel and Marx." *STP*, vol. 4, no. 3 (Fall 1977).

———. *The Social and Political Philosophy of Karl Marx*. Cambridge University Press, N.Y., 1971.

Baier, Kurt. *The Moral Point of View*. Random House, N.Y., 1965.

Ball, Terence, and James Farr, eds. *After Marx*. Cambridge University Press, N.Y., 1984.

Baran, Paul. *The Political Economy of Growth*. Monthly Review Press, N.Y., 1957.

Baran, Paul, and Paul M. Sweezy. *Monopoly Capital: An Essay on the American Economic and Social Order*. Monthly Review Press, N.Y., 1966.

Bardhan, Pranab. *Land, Labour and Rural Poverty: Essays in Development Economics*. Columbia University Press, N.Y., 1984.

Bardhan, Pranab. "Marxist Ideas in Development Economics: An Evaluation." In *Analytical Marxism* (Roemer, ed.).

Barry, Brian. *The Liberal Theory of Justice*. Clarendon Press, Oxford, 1973.

————. *Sociologists, Economists and Democracy*. University of Chicago Press, Chicago, 1978.

Bauer, Otto. "Marxism and Ethics." In *Austro-Marxism* (T. B. Bottomore et al., eds.). Oxford University Press, N.Y., 1978.

Beehler, Rodger. "Critical Notice of Richard W. Miller, *Analyzing Marx: Morality, Power, and History*." *CJP*, vol. 17, no. 1 (Mar. 1987).

Beitz, Charles R. *Political Theory and International Relations*. Princeton University Press, Princeton, N.J., 1979.

Bender, Frederic L. *The Betrayal of Marx*. Harper & Row, N.Y., 1975.

————. "World Hunger, Human Rights, and the Right to Revolution." *SP*, vol. 8 (1981).

Benn, S. I. "Rights." *The Encyclopedia of Philosophy*, vol. 7 (Paul Edwards, ed.). Macmillan, N.Y., 1976.

Berger, Johannes, and Claus Offe. "Functionalism vs. Rational Choice? Some Questions Concerning the Rationality of Choosing One or the Other." *T&S*, vol. 11, no. 4 (July 1982).

Berlin, Isaiah. *Karl Marx: His Life and Environment*. Oxford University Press, N.Y., 1978.

————. "Two Concepts of Liberty." In *Political and Social Philosophy* (J. Charles King and James A. McGilvray, eds.). McGraw-Hill, N.Y., 1973.

————. "Rationality of Value Judgments." *Nomos*, VII (Carl J. Friedrich, ed.). Atherton Press, N.Y., 1964.

Binns, Peter. "Anti-Moralism." *RP*, no. 10 (Spring 1975).

Blackburn, Robin. "Inequality and Exploitation." *NLR*, no. 42 (March–April 1967).

————. "Marxism: Theory of Proletarian Revolution." *NLR*, no. 97 (May–June 1976).

Blackburn, Robin, ed. *Ideology in Social Science*, Vintage, N.Y., 1973.

Borge, Tomas et al. *Sandinistas Speak: Speeches, Writings, and Interviews with Leaders of Nicaragua's Revolution*. Pathfinder Press, N.Y., 1982.

Bottomore, T. B. *Classes in Modern Society*. Vintage Books, N.Y., 1966.

————. "Industry, Work, and Socialism." In *Socialist Humanism* (Fromm, ed.).

———. "Karl Marx: Sociologist or Marxist?" *S&S*, vol. 30, no. 1 (Winter 1966).

———, ed. *A Dictionary of Marx's Thought*. Harvard University Press, Cambridge, Mass., 1983.

———. *Karl Marx* Prentice-Hall, Englewood Cliffs, N.J., 1973.

———. *Karl Marx: Early Writings*. McGraw-Hill, N.Y., 1964.

Bowles, Samuel, and Herbert Gintis. "Capitalism and Alienation." In *The Capitalist System* (Edwards et al., eds.).

———. "The Power of Capital: On the Inadequacy of the Conception of the Capitalist Economy as 'Private.' " *PF(B)*, vol. 14, nos. 3–4 (1983).

———. "Socialist Revolution in the United States: Goals and Means." In *The Capitalist System* (Edwards et al., eds.).

———. "Structure and Practice in the Labor Theory of Value." *RRPE*, vol. 12, no. 4 (1981).

Brandt, Richard. *A Theory of the Right and the Good*. Clarendon Press, Oxford, 1979.

———. *Ethical Theory*. Prentice-Hall, Englewood Cliffs, N.J., 1959.

Braverman, Harry. *Labor and Monopoly: The Degradation of Work in the Twentieth Century*. Monthly Review Press, N.Y., 1974.

Braybrooke, David. *Meeting Needs*. Princeton University Press, Princeton, N.J., 1987.

Brenkert, George. "The Alien and the Alienated." *Southern Journal of Philosophy*, vol. 13 (Summer 1975).

———. "Cohen on Proletarian Unfreedom." *PPA*, vol. 14, no. 1 (Winter 1985).

———. "Freedom and Private Property in Karl Marx." *PPA*, vol. 8, no. 2 (Winter 1979).

———. "Marx, Engels and the Relativity of Morals." *SST*, vol. 17 (1977).

———. "Marx and Utilitarianism." *CJP*, vol. 5, no. 3 (Nov. 1975).

———. "Marx's Critique of Utilitarianism." In *Marx and Morality* (Nielsen and Patten, eds.).

———. *Marx's Ethics of Freedom*. Routledge & Kegan Paul, Boston, 1979.

Brenner, Robert. "Agrarian Class Structure and Economic Development in Pre-Industrial Europe." In *The Brenner Debate* (T. H. Ashton and C.H.E. Philpin, eds.). Cambridge University Press, N.Y., 1985.

———. "The Origins of Capitalist Development: A Critique of Neo-Smithian Marxism." *NLR*, no. 104 (July–Aug. 1977).

Brenner, Robert. "The Social Basis of Economic Development." In *Analytical Marxism* (John Roemer, ed.).

Buchanan, Allen E. "Assessing the Communitarian Critique of Liberalism." *Ethics*, vol. 99, no. 4 (July 1989).

————. "The Conceptual Roots of Totalitarian Socialism." In *Marxism and Liberalism* (E. F. Paul, ed.).

————. "Deriving Welfare Rights from Libertarian Rights." In *Income Support* (P. G. Brown et al., eds.). Rowman & Allanheld, Totowa, N.J., 1981.

————. *Ethics, Efficiency and the Market*. Rowman and Allanheld, Totowa, N.J., 1985.

————. "Exploitation, Alienation, and Injustices." *CJP*, vol. 9, no. 1 (1979).

————. "The Fetishism of Democracy: A Reply to Professor Gould." *JP*, vol. 77 (1980).

————. "John Rawls' Theory of Justice: An Introduction." In *John Rawls' Theory of Social Justice* (G. Blocker and E. Smith, eds.). Ohio University Press, Columbus, 1980.

————. *Marx and Justice: The Radical Critique of Liberalism*. Rowman and Littlefield, Totowa, N.J., 1982.

————. "Marx, Morality, and History: An Assessment of Recent Analytical Work on Marx." *Ethics*, vol. 98 (Oct. 1987).

————. "Marx on Democracy and the Obsolescence of Rights." *SAJF*, vol. 2, no. 3 (1983).

————. "The Marxian Critique of Justice and Rights." In *Marx and Morality* (Nielsen and Patten, eds.).

————. "Revolutionary Motivation and Rationality." *PPA*, vol. 9, no. 1 (1979).

————. "Review of Allen W. Wood: *Karl Marx*." *JP*, vol. 80 (1983).

————. "The Right to a Decent Minimum of Health Care." *PPA*, vol. 13, no. 1 (Winter 1984).

————. "Revisability and Rational Choice." *CJP*, vol. 5 (1975).

————. "What's So Special about Rights?" *SPP*, vol. 2, no. 1 (Autumn 1984).

Carter, Alan R. *Marx: A Radical Critique*. Westview Press, Boulder, Colo., 1988.

Castro, Fidel. *Fidel Castro: Nothing Can Stop the Course of History (Interview by Jeffrey M. Elliot and Mervyn M. Dymally)*. Pathfinder Press, N.Y., 1986.

————. *In Defense of Socialism*. Pathfinder Press, N.Y., 1989.

————. *The World Crisis: Its Economic and Social Impact on the Under-*

developed Countries. Maroon Publishing House, Morant Bay, Jamaica, 1984.

Chavance, Bernard, ed. *Marx en Perspective*. Editions de l'Ecole des Haute Etudes en Sciences Sociales, Paris, 1985.

Chomsky, Noam. "Anarchism." In *Essays on Socialist Humanism* (Ken Coates, ed.).

———. *Language and Responsibility*. The Harvester Press, Sussex, 1978.

———. *Problems of Freedom and Knowledge*. Pantheon Books, N.Y., 1971.

———. *For Reasons of State*. Vintage Books, N.Y., 1973.

Clark, Barry, and Herbert Gintis. "Rawlsian Justice and Economic Systems." *PPA*, vol. 7, no. 4 (Summer 1978).

Coates, Ken, ed. *Can the Workers Run Industry?* Sphere Books, London, 1968.

———. *Détente and Socialist Democracy: A Discussion with Roy Medvedev*. Monad Press, N.Y., 1976.

———. *Essays on Socialist Humanism*. Spokesman Books, Nottingham, 1972.

Cohen, G. A. "Are Workers Forced to Sell Their Labor Power?" *PPA*, vol. 14, no. 1 (Winter 1985).

———. "Are Disadvantaged Workers Who Take Hazardous Jobs Forced to Take Hazardous Jobs?" In *Moral Rights in the Workplace* (Gertrude Ezorsky, ed.). State University of New York Press, Albany, 1987.

———. "Are Freedom and Equality Compatible?" In *Alternatives to Capitalism* (Elster and Moene, eds.).

———. "Bourgeois and Proletarians." In *Marxist Socialism* (Shlomo Avineri, ed.). Lieber-Atherton, N.Y., 1973.

———. "Capitalism, Freedom, and the Proletariat." In *The Idea of Freedom* (Alan Ryan, ed.). Oxford University Press, N.Y., 1979.

———. "Forces and Relations of Production." In *Analytical Marxism* (Roemer, ed.).

———. "Freedom, Justice and Capitalism." *NLR*, no. 126 (1981).

———. "Functional Explanation: A Reply to Elster." *PS*, vol. 28, no. 1 (1980).

———. "Functional Explanation, Consequence Explanation, and Marxism." *Inquiry*, vol. 25 (1982).

———. *History, Labour, and Freedom: Themes from Marx*. Oxford University Press, N.Y., 1988.

———. "Illusions about Private Property and Freedom." In *Issues in Marxist Philosophy* (Mepham and Ruben, eds.), vol. 4.

473

Cohen, G. A. "Karl Marx's Dialectic of Labour." *PPA*, vol. 3, no. 2 (Spring 1974).

———. *Karl Marx's Theory of History: A Defense*. Princeton University Press, Princeton, N.J., 1978.

———. "Labor, Leisure, and a Distinctive Contradiction of Advanced Capitalism." In *Markets and Morals* (G. Dworkin et al., eds.). Hemisphere Publishing Co., Washington, D.C., 1977.

———. "The Labor Theory of Value and the Concept of Exploitation." *PPA*, vol. 8, no. 4 (Summer 1979).

———. "More on Exploitation and the Theory of Value." *Inquiry*, vol. 26 (1983).

———. "Nozick on Appropriation." *NLR*, no. 150 (1984).

———. "On Some Criticisms of Historical Materialism." *PAS*, supplemental vol. 44 (1970).

———. "On the Currency of Egalitarian Justice." *Ethics*, vol. 99, no. 4 (July 1989).

———. "Peter Mew on Justice and Capitalism." *Inquiry*, vol. 29, no. 3 (Sept. 1986).

———. "Reconsidering Historical Materialism." *Nomos*, vol. 26 (1983).

———. "Reply to Elster on 'Marxism, Functionalism, and Game Theory.' " *T&S*, vol. 11, no 4 (1982).

———. "Reply to Four Critics." *A&K*, vol. 5 (1983).

———. "Restricted and Inclusive Historical Materialism." In *Marx en Perspective* (Chavance, ed.).

———. "Review of *Karl Marx*, by Allen W. Wood." *Mind*, vol. 92 (1983).

———. "Robert Nozick and Wilt Chamberlain: How Patterns Preserve Liberty." In *Justice and Economic Distribution* (Arthur and Shaw, eds.).

———. "Self-Ownership, World-Ownership, and Equality, Part II." In *Marxism and Liberalism* (E. F. Paul, ed.).

———. "The Structure of Proletarian Unfreedom." *PPA*, vol. 12, no. 1 (Fall 1983).

———. "The Workers and the Word: Why Marx Had the Right to Think He was Right." *Praxis*, vol. 4, no. 3–4 (1968).

Cohen, Joshua. "Reflections on Rousseau: Autonomy and Democracy." *PPA*, vol. 15, no. 3 (Summer 1986).

———. "Review of *Karl Marx's Theory of History: A Defense*, by G. A. Cohen." *JP*, vol. 79, no. 5 (1982).

Cohen, Joshua, and Joel Rogers. *On Democracy*. Penguin Books, Middlesex, England, 1983.

Cohen, Marshall, Thomas Nagel, and Thomas Scanlon, eds. *Marx, Justice, and History*. Princeton University Press, Princeton, N.J., 1980.

Colletti, Lucio. *From Rousseau to Lenin: Studies in Ideology and Society*. Monthly Review Press, N.Y., 1972.

―――. *Marxism and Hegel*. N & B, London, 1973.

Collier, Andrew. "The Production of Moral Ideology." *RP*, no. 9 (Winter 1974).

―――. "Positive Values." *PAS*, supplemental vol. 57 (1983).

―――. "Scientific Socialism and the Question of Socialist Values." In *Marx and Morality* (Nielsen and Patten, eds.).

Collinicos, Alex. *Marxism and Philosophy*. Oxford University Press, N.Y., 1985.

Connolly, William E., and Glen Gordon, eds. *Social Structure and Theory*. Heath, Lexington, Mass., 1974.

Cornforth, Maurice. *Marxism and the Linguistic Philosophy*. Lawrence and Wishert, London, 1965.

―――. *The Open Society and the Open Philosophy*. International Publishers, N.Y., 1968.

Crocker, Lawrence. "Equality, Solidarity, and Rawls' Maximin." *PPA*, vol. 6, no. 3 (Spring 1977).

―――. "Marx's Concept of Exploitation." *STP*, vol. 2, no. 2 (Fall 1972).

Cunningham, Frank. "Community, Tradition, and the 6th Thesis on Feuerbach." In *Marx Analyzed* (Nielsen and Ware, eds.).

―――. *Democratic Theory and Socialism*. Cambridge University Press, N.Y., 1987.

―――. "Practice and Some Muddles about Historical Materialism." *CJP*, vol. 3, no. 2 (Dec. 1973).

Daniels, Norman. "An Argument about the Relativity of Justice." *RIP* (1989).

―――. "Equal Liberty and Unequal Worth of Liberty." In *Reading Rawls* (Daniels, ed.).

―――. "Merit and Meritocracy." *PPA*, vol. 7, no. 3 (Spring 1978).

―――. "Moral Theory and the Plasticity of Persons." *Monist*, vol. 62, no. 3 (July 1970).

―――. "On Liberty and Equality in Rawls." *STP*, vol. 3, no. 2 (Fall 1974).

―――. "On Some Methods of Ethics and Linguistics." *PhS*, no. 37 (1980).

―――. "Reflective Equilibrium and Archimedean Points." *CJP*, vol. 10, no. 1 (March 1980).

Daniels, Norman. "Two Approaches to Theory Acceptance in Ethics." In *Morality, Reason, and Truth* (David Copp and David Zimmerman, eds.). Rowman and Allanheld, Totowa, N.J., 1985.
——. "Wide Reflective Equilibrium and Theory Acceptance in Ethics." *JP*, vol. 76, no. 5 (May 1979).
Daniels, Norman, ed. *Reading Rawls*. Basic Books, N.Y., 1976.
DeGeorge, Richard T., ed. *Ethics and Society*. Doubleday, Garden City, N.Y., 1966.
Deutscher, Isaac. *Marxism in Our Time*. Ramparts Press, San Francisco, 1971.
Doppelt, Gerald. "Conflicting Social Paradigms of Human Freedom and the Problem of Justification." *Inquiry*, vol. 27 (1984).
——. "Is Rawls' Kantian Liberalism Coherent and Defensible?" *Ethics*, vol. 99, no. 4 (July 1989).
——. "Rawls' System of Justice: A Critique from the Left." *Nous*, vol. 15 (1981).
Dworkin, Ronald. "In Defense of Equality." *SPP*, vol. 1 (Autumn 1983).
——. *A Matter of Principle*. Harvard University Press, Cambridge, Mass., 1985.
——. "The Original Position." In *Reading Rawls* (Daniels, ed.).
——. *Taking Rights Seriously*. Harvard University Press, Cambridge, Mass., 1977.
——. "What Is Equality? Part 1: Equality of Welfare." *PPA*, vol. 10, no. 3 (Summer 1981).
——. "What Is Equality? Part 2: Equality of Resources." *PPA*, vol. 10, no. 4 (Fall 1981).
——. "What Is Equality? Part 3: The Place of Liberty." *Iowa Law Review* (1987).
——. "Why Liberals Should Believe in Equality." *NYRB* (Feb. 1983).
Easton, Lloyd, and Kurt H. Guddat. "Introduction." In *Writings of the Young Marx on Philosophy and Society* (Easton and Guddat, eds.). Doubleday, Garden City, N.Y., 1976.
Edwards, Richard C., Michael Reich, and Thomas E. Weisskopf, eds. *The Capitalist System: A Radical Analysis of American Society* (2nd ed.). Prentice-Hall, Englewood Cliffs, N.J., 1978.
Einstein, Albert. "Why Socialism?" In *Ideas and Opinions*. Dell Publishing Co., N.Y., 1954.
Elster, Jon. "Belief, Bias, and Ideology." In *Rationality and Relativism* (Martin Hollis and Steven Lukes, eds.). MIT Press, Cambridge, Mass., 1982.

———. "Clearing the Decks." *Ethics*, vol. 91, no. 4 (July 1981).

———. *Explaining Technical Change*. Cambridge University Press, N.Y., 1983.

———. "Exploitation, Freedom, and Justice." *Nomos*, vol. 26 (1983).

———. "Exploring Exploitation." *Journal of Peace Research*, vol. 15 (1978).

———. "Further Thoughts on Marxism, Functionalism, and Game Theory." In *Analytical Marxism* (Roemer, ed.).

———. "Historical Materialism and Economic Backwardness." In *After Marx* (Ball and Farr, eds.).

———. *Logic and Society*. John Wiley, N.Y., 1978.

———. *An Introduction to Karl Marx*. Cambridge University Press, N.Y., 1986.

———. *Making Sense of Marx*. Cambridge University Press, N.Y., 1985.

———. "The Market and the Forum." In *Foundations of Social Choice Theory* (A. Hylland and Jon Elster, eds.). Cambridge University Press, N.Y., 1986.

———. "Marxism, Functionalism, and Game Theory." *T&S*, vol. 11, no. 4 (1982).

———. "A Paradigm for the Social Sciences? (Review of van Parijis: *Evolutionary Explanation in the Social Sciences*)." *Inquiry*, vol. 25 (1982).

———. "Rationality, Morality, and Collective Action." *Ethics*, vol. 96 (1985).

———. "Reply to Comments." *T&S*, vol. 12, no. 1 (1983).

———. "Roemer vs. Roemer." *P&S*, vol. 11, no. 3 (1982).

———. "Review of G. A. Cohen: *Karl Marx's Theory of History*." *PS*, vol. 28 (1980).

———. "Self-Realization in Work and Politics: The Marxist Conception of the Good Life." In *Marxism and Liberalism* (E. F. Paul, ed.).

———. *Sour Grapes*. Cambridge University Press, N.Y., 1983.

———. "The Theory of Combined and Uneven Development." In *Analytical Marxism* (Roemer, ed.).

———. "Three Challenges to Class." In *Analytical Marxism* (Roemer, ed.).

———. *Ulysses and the Sirens*. Cambridge University Press, N.Y., 1979.

Elster, Jon, and Karl O. Moene (eds.). *Alternatives to Capitalism*. Cambridge University Press, N.Y., forthcoming.

Feinberg, Joel. "Duties, Rights, and Claims." *APQ*, vol. 3, no. 2 (Apr. 1966).

———. *Harm to Others* (*The Moral Limits of the Criminal Law*, vol. 1). Oxford University Press, N.Y., 1984.

———. "The Nature and Value of Rights." *JVI*, vol. 4, no. 4 (Winter 1970).

———. *Rights, Justice, and the Bounds of Liberty*. Princeton University Press, Princeton, N.J., 1980.

———. "The Rights of Animals and Unborn Generations." In *Philosophy and Environmental Crisis* (William T. Blackstone, ed.), University of Georgia Press, Athens, Ga., 1974.

———. *Social Philosophy*. Prentice-Hall, Englewood Cliffs, N.J., 1973.

Feuer, Lewis S. "Ethical Theories and Historical Materialism." *S&S*, vol. 6, no. 3 (1942).

Fisk, Milton. "The Concept of Primacy in Historical Explanation." *A&K*, vol. 4 (1982).

———. *Ethics and Society*. Harvest Press, N.Y., 1980.

———. "Freedom and Historical Materialism." *Nous*, vol. 20 (1986).

———. "The Human Nature Argument." *SP*, vol. 5 (1979).

———. "History and Reason in Rawls' Moral Theory." In *Reading Rawls* (Daniels, ed.).

———. "Property and the State: A Discussion of Robert Nozick's *Anarchy, State, and Utopia*." *Nous*, vol. 14 (1980).

———. "Property Rights." In *The Main Debate: Capitalism versus Communism* (Tibor Machan, ed.). Random House, N.Y., 1987.

———. "Why the Anti-Marxists Are Wrong." *MR*, vol. 38, no. 10 (Mar. 1987).

Foot, Phillipa. "Moral Arguments." *Mind*, vol. 67 (Oct. 1958).

———. "Moral Beliefs." *PAS*, vol. 59 (1958–1959).

———. "Morality as a System of Hypothetical Imperatives." *JP*, vol. 81, no. 3 (July 1972).

———. "When Is a Principle a Moral Principle?" *PAS*, vol. 28 (1954).

Frankena, William K. *Ethics*. Prentice-Hall, Englewood Cliffs, N.J., 1963.

———. "Recent Conceptions of Morality." In *Morality and the Language of Morals* (Hector-Neri Castenada et al., eds.). Wayne State University Press, Detroit, 1963.

———. "Under What Net?" *Philosophy*, vol. 48 (Oct. 1973).

Fromm, Erich. *Marx's Concept of Man*. Frederick Ungar Publishing Co., N.Y., 1961.

—————. *May Man Prevail*. Doubleday, Garden City, N.Y., 1961.

Fromm, Erich, ed. *Socialist Humanism*. Doubleday, Garden City, N.Y., 1961.

Fry, J. A., ed. *Limits of the Welfare State: Critical Views on Post-War Sweden*. Saxon House, Farnborough, Eng., 1979.

Funk, Nanette. "Habermas and Social Goods." *Social Text*, no. 18 (1988).

Geras, Norman. "Classical Marxism and Proletarian Representation." *NLR*, no. 123 (Jan.–Feb. 1981).

—————. "The Controversy about Marx and Justice." *NLR*, 150 (Mar.–Apr. 1985).

—————. *The Legacy of Rosa Luxemburg*. New Left Books, London, 1976.

—————. *Marx and Human Nature: Refutation of a Legend*. New Left Books, London, 1983.

—————. "Marx and the Critique of Political Economy." In *Ideology in Social Science* (Blackburn, ed.).

Gewirth, Alan. *Human Rights: Essays on Justification and Applications*. University of Chicago Press, Chicago, 1982.

—————. "Rights and Virtues." *A&K*, vol. 6 (1984).

—————. "Why There Are Human Rights." *STP*, vol. 11, no. 2 (Summer 1985).

—————. *Reason and Morality*. University of Chicago Press, Chicago, 1978.

Gilbert, Alan. "An Ambiguity in Marx's and Engels' Account of Justice and Equality." *APSR*, vol. 76 (1982).

—————. "Democracy and Individuality." In *Marxism and Liberalism* (E. F. Paul, ed.).

—————. "Equality and Social Theory in Rawls' *A Theory of Justice*." *OR*, no. 8/9 (Autumn 1978).

—————. "Historical Theory and the Structure of Moral Argument in Marx." *PT*, vol. 9 (1981).

—————. "Marx on Internationalism and War." *PPA*, vol. 7, no. 4 (Summer 1978).

—————. "Marx's Moral Realism: Eudaimonism and Moral Progress." In *After Marx* (Ball and Farr, eds.).

—————. *Marx's Politics: Communists and Citizens*. Martin Robertson, Oxford, 1981.

Gottlieb, Roger. "Alienation, Ideology, and Personal Identity." *RPNJ* (Spring 1978).

Gottlieb, Roger. *History and Subjectivity: The Transformation of Marxist Theory*. Temple University Press, Philadelphia, 1987.

———. "A Marxian Concept of Ideology." *PF*(B), vol. 6, no. 4 (Summer 1975).

Gramsci, Antonio. *Selections from the Prison Notebooks*. International Publishers, N.Y., 1971.

Guevara, Che. *Che Guevara and the Cuban Revolution: Writings and Speeches of Ernesto Che Guevara*. Pathfinder Press, N.Y., 1987.

Habermas, Jürgen. *Communication and the Evolution of Society*. Beacon Press, Boston, 1979.

———. *Knowledge and Human Interests*. Beacon Press, Boston, 1971.

———. *Legitimation Crises*. Beacon Press, Boston, 1975.

———. "On Systematically Distorted Communication." *Inquiry*, vol. 13 (Autumn 1970).

———. *Theory and Practice*. Beacon Press, Boston, 1974.

———. *The Theory of Communicative Action, Vol. I: Reason and the Rationalization of Society*. Beacon Press, Boston, 1984.

———. *The Theory of Communicative Action, Vol. II: Lifeworld and System: A Critique of Functionalist Reason*. Beacon Press, Boston, 1984.

———. *Toward a Rational Society: Student Protest, Science, and Politics*. Beacon Press, Boston, 1970.

———. "Toward a Theory of Communicative Competence." *Inquiry*, vol. 13 (Winter 1970).

Hampshire, Stuart. "A New Philosophy of the Just Society." *NYRB*, vol. 18, no. 3 (Feb. 24, 1972).

Hampton, Jean. "Should Political Philosophy Be Done without Metaphysics?" *Ethics*, vol. 99, no. 4 (July 1989).

Hancock, Roger. "Marx's Theory of Justice." *STP*, vol. 1, no. 3 (Spring 1971).

Hare, R. M. *Essays on the Moral Concepts*. University of California Press, Berkeley, 1973.

———. *Freedom and Reason*. Oxford University Press, N.Y., 1963.

———. *The Language of Morals*. Oxford University Press, N.Y., 1952.

Harrington, Michael. *Socialism*. Saturday Review Press, N.Y., 1972.

———. *The Twilight of Capitalism*. Simon & Schuster, N.Y., 1976.

Harris, Abram L. "The Social Philosophy of Karl Marx." *Ethics*, vol. 58, no. 3 (Apr. 1948).

———. "Utopian Elements in Marx's Thought." *Ethics*, vol. 60, no. 2 (Jan. 1950).

Harris, John. "The Marxist Conception of Violence." *PPA*, vol. 3, no. 2 (Winter 1974).

Hart, H.L.A. "Are There Any Natural Rights?" *PR*, vol. 64, no. 2 (1955).

———. *Concept of Law*. Oxford University Press, N.Y., 1961.

———. "Rawls on Liberty and Equality." In *Reading Rawls* (Daniels, ed.).

Hegel, G.W.F. *The Philosophy of Right*. Oxford University Press, N.Y., 1967.

Heilbroner, Robert L. *An Inquiry into the Human Prospect: Updated and Reconsidered for the 1980s*. W. W. Norton, N.Y., 1980.

———. *Between Capitalism and Socialism: Essays in Political Economy*. Peter Smith, Gloucester, Mass., 1983.

———. *Marxism: For and Against*. W. W. Norton, N.Y., 1980.

———. *The Nature and Logic of Capitalism*. W. W. Norton, N.Y., 1986.

———. *The Worldly Philosophers: The Lives, Times, and Ideas of the Great Economic Thinkers* (6th ed.). Simon & Schuster, N.Y., 1987.

Heller, Agnes. *The Theory of Needs in Marx*. Allison and Busby, London, 1976.

Hobbes, Thomas. *Leviathan* (C. B. Macpherson, ed.). Penguin Books, Baltimore, Md., 1968.

Hodges, Donald Clark. "The Détente between Marxism and Linguistic Philosophy." *Praxis*, vol. 3, no. 4 (1967).

———. "Historical Materialism in Ethics." *PPR*, vol. 23, no. 1 (Sept. 1962).

Holmstrom, Nancy. "Exploitation." *CJP*, vol. 7, no. 2 (1977).

———. "Marx and Cohen on Exploitation and the Labor Theory of Value." *Inquiry*, vol. 26 (1983).

Honderich, Ted. "Democratic Violence." *PPA*, vol. 2, no. 2 (Winter 1973).

———. "Four Conclusions about Violence of the Left." *CJP*, vol. 9, no. 2 (June 1979).

———. *Three Essays on Political Violence*. Basil Blackwell, Oxford, 1976.

Honderich, Ted, ed. *Morality and Objectivity*. Routledge & Kegan Paul, London, 1985.

Hook, Sidney. *From Hegel to Marx: Studies in the Intellectual Development of Karl Marx*. Reynal & Hitchcock, N.Y., 1936.

———. *Towards an Understanding of Karl Marx*. Victor Gollancz, London, 1933.

Horvat, Branko. *The Political Economy of Socialism*. M. E. Sharpe, Armonk, N.Y., 1982.

———. *Towards a Theory of Planned Economy*. Yugoslav Institute of Economic Research, Beograd, 1964.

———. *The Yugoslav Economic System: The First Labor-Managed Economy in the Making*. International Arts and Sciences Press, White Plains, N.Y., 1976.

Horvat, Branko, Mihailo Marković, and Rudi Supek, eds. *Self-Governing Socialism* (2 vols.). International Arts and Sciences Press, White Plains, N.Y., 1975.

Howe, Irving. "On the Moral Basis of Socialism." *Dissent* (Fall 1981).

———. *Socialism and America*. Harcourt, Brace, Jovanovich, San Diego, Calif., 1985.

Hume, David. *An Inquiry Concerning the Principles of Morals*. Bobbs-Merrill, Indianapolis, Ind., 1957.

———. *A Treatise of Human Nature*. Clarendon Press, Oxford, 1888.

Husami, Ziyad I. "Marx on Distributive Justice." *PPA*, vol. 8, no. 1 (Fall 1978).

Kamenka, Eugene. *The Ethical Foundations of Marxism* (2nd ed.). Routledge & Kegan Paul, Boston, 1972.

———. "Review of Stephen Lukes, *Marxism and Morality*." *New York Times Book Review* (Feb. 2, 1986).

Kant, Immanuel. *Critique of Practical Reason*. Bobbs-Merrill, Indianapolis, Ind., 1956.

———. *The Doctrine of Virtue*. Harper & Row, N.Y., 1964.

———. *Foundations of the Metaphysics of Morals*. Bobbs-Merrill, Indianapolis, Ind., 1959.

Kautsky, Karl. *The Class Struggle*. Charles A. Kerr, Chicago, 1910.

———. *The Dictatorship of the Proletariat*. University of Michigan Press, Ann Arbor, Mich. 1964.

———. *Ethics and the Materialist Conception of History*. Charles H. Kerr & Co., Chicago, 1914.

Keat, Russell, and David Miller. "Understanding Justice." *PT*, vol. 2, no. 1 (1974).

Kolakowski, Leszek. *Main Currents of Marxism* (3 vols.). Oxford University Press, N.Y., 1978.

———. *Toward a Marxist Humanism*. Grove Press, N.Y., 1968.

Kólakowski, Leszek, and Stuart Hampshire, eds. *The Socialist Idea*. Weidenfeld and Nicolson, London, 1974.

Kurtz, Paul, and Svetozar Stojanović, eds. *Tolerance and Revolution:*

A Marxist–Non-Marxist Humanist Dialogue. Philosophical Society of Serbia, Beograd, 1970.

Laclau, Ernesto. "The Specificity of the Political: Around the Poulantzas–Miliband Debate." *E&S*, vol. 5, no. 1 (Feb. 1975).

Lebowitz, Michael A. "Is Analytical Marxism Marxism?" *S&S*, vol. 52, no. 2 (Summer 1988).

———. "Social Justice Against Capitalism." *MR*, vol. 40, no. 1 (May 1988).

Lenin, V. I. "Address at Congress of Russian Young Communist League." In *Reader in Marxist Philosophy* (Selsam and Martel, eds.).

———. *Selected Works* (3 vols.). International Publishers, N.Y., 1967.

———. "Imperialism: The Highest Stage of Capitalism." In *Selected Works*, vol. 1.

———. "Left Wing Communism: An Infantile Disorder." In *Selected Works*, vol. 3.

———. "State and Revolution." In *Selected Works*, vol. 2.

———. "The Three Sources and Component Parts of Marxism." In *Selected Works*, vol. 1.

———. "What Is to Be Done?" In *Selected Works*, vol. 1.

Levin, David S. "The Moral Relativism of Marxism." *PF*(B), vol. 15, no. 3 (Spring 1974).

Levine, Andrew. *Arguing for Socialism: Theoretical Considerations.* Routledge & Kegan Paul, Boston, 1984.

———. *The End of the State.* Verso, London, 1987.

———. *Liberal Democracy: A Critique of Its Theory.* Columbia University Press, N.Y., 1981.

———. *The Politics of Autonomy: A Kantian Reading of Rousseau's Social Contract.* University of Massachusetts Press, Amherst, 1976.

———. "Review of *Making Sense of Marx*, by Jon Elster." *JP*, vol. 83, no. 12 (1986).

———. "What Is a Marxist Today?" In *Marx Analyzed* (Nielsen and Ware, eds.).

Levine, Andrew, and Erik Olin Wright. "Rationality and Class Struggle." *NLR*, no. 123 (Sept.–Oct. 1980).

Levine, Andrew, Elliott Sober, and Erik Olin Wright. "Marxism and Methodological Individualism." *NLR*, no. 162 (March/April 1987).

Lichtheim, George. "Alienation." In *International Encyclopedia of the Social Sciences*, rev. ed. (David A. Sills, ed.). Macmillan, N.Y., 1968.

Lichtheim, George. *The Concept of Ideology and Other Essays*. Random House, N.Y., 1967.

————. "Historical and Dialectical Materialism." In *Dictionary of the History of Ideas*, vol. 2 (Phillip Wiener, ed.). Scribner, N.Y., 1973.

————. "On the Interpretation of Marx's Thought." In *Marx and the Western World* (Lobkowicz, ed.).

————. *Marxism: An Historical and Critical Study*. Frederick A. Praeger, N.Y., 1961.

Little, Daniel. "Marxism and Popular Politics: The Microfoundations of Class Conflict." *Marx Analyzed* (Nielsen and Ware, eds.).

————. *The Scientific Marx*. University of Minnesota Press, Minneapolis, 1986.

Lobkowicz, Nicholas, ed. *Marx and the Western World*. University of Notre Dame Press, Notre Dame, Ind., 1967.

Lock, G. "G. A. Cohen and the Crisis of Marxism." *AP*, vol. 16, no. 3 (1981).

Locke, John. *Two Treatises of Government*. Cambridge University Press, N.Y., 1960.

Lukács, Georg. *History and Class Consciousness: Studies in Marxist Dialectics*. MIT Press, Cambridge, Mass., 1971.

Lukes, Stephen. "Alienation and Anomie." In *Social Structure and Theory* (Connolly and Gordon, eds.).

————. "Can a Marxist Believe in Human Rights?" *PI*, vol. 1, no. 4 (1982).

————. "Can the Base Be Distinguished from the Superstructure?" In *The Nature of Political Theory* (D. Miller and L. Siedentop, eds.). Oxford University Press, N.Y., 1983.

————. "Marxism and Dirty Hands." In *Marxism and Liberalism* (E. F. Paul, ed.).

————. *Marxism and Morality*. Clarendon Press, Oxford, 1985.

————. *Power: A Radical View*. Macmillan, N.Y., 1974.

————. "Socialism and Equality." In *The Socialist Idea* (Kolakowski and Hampshire, eds.).

Luxemburg, Rosa. "Leninism or Marxism?" In *The Russian Revolution and Leninism or Marxism?* University of Michigan Press, Ann Arbor, Mich., 1961.

————. "The Mass Strike, the Political Party and the Trade Unions." In *Rosa Luxemburg Speaks* (Waters, ed.).

————. "Reform or Revolution." In *Rosa Luxemburg Speaks* (Waters, ed).

———. "The Russian Revolution." In *Rosa Luxemburg Speaks* (Waters, ed).

MacBride, William L. "The Concept of Justice in Marx, Engels and Others." *Ethics*, vol. 85, no. 3 (Apr. 1975).

———. "Marxism and Natural Law." *The American Journal of Jurisprudence*, vol. 15 (1970).

———. "Rights and the Marxian Tradition." *PI*, vol. 4, no. 1 (1984).

———. "Social Theory *Sub Specie Aeternitatis*: A New Perspective." *Yale Law Journal*, vol. 81, no. 5 (Apr. 1972).

MacCallum, Gerald C., Jr. "Negative and Positive Freedom." In *Concepts in Social and Political Philosophy* (Richard E. Flathman, ed.). Macmillan, N.Y., 1973.

McCarney, Joe. "Elster, Marx and Methodology." In *Marx Analyzed* (Nielsen and Ware, eds.).

———. *The Real World of Ideology*. Harvester Press, Brighton, England, 1980.

———. "Recent Interpretations of Ideology." *E&S*, vol. 14, no. 1 (1985).

McCloskey, H. J. "Rights." *Philosophical Quarterly*, vol. 15 (1965).

MacIntyre, Alasdair. *After Virtue: A Study in Moral Theory*. University of Notre Dame Press, Notre Dame, Ind., 1981.

———. *Against the Self-Image of the Age: Essays on Ideology and Philosophy*. University of Notre Dame Press, Notre Dame, Ind., 1978.

———. "Breaking the Chains of Reason." In *Out of Apathy* (Thompson, ed.).

———. "Ideology, Social Science and Revolution." *Comparative Politics*, vol. 5, no. 5 (Apr. 1973).

———. *Marcuse*. Viking Press, N.Y., 1970.

———. "Marx." In *Western Political Philosophers* (Maurice Cranston, ed.). Capricorn Books, N.Y., 1964.

———. *Marxism and Christianity*. Schocken Books, N.Y., 1968.

———. "Notes from the Moral Wilderness I." *NR*, no. 7 (Winter 1958–1959).

———. "Notes from the Moral Wilderness II." *NR*, no. 8 (Spring 1959).

Mackie, J. L. "Can There Be a Rights-Based Moral Theory?" *MSP*, vol. 9, no. 4 (1978).

———. *Ethics: Inventing Right and Wrong*. Penguin Books, N.Y., 1977.

———. *Persons and Values*. Clarendon Press, Oxford, 1985.

McLellan, David. "Introduction." In *The Grundrisse* (McLellan, ed.). Harper & Row, N.Y., 1971.

————. *Karl Marx, 1818–1883*. Oxford University Press, 1977.

————, ed. *Marx: The First Hundred Years*. St. Martin's Press, N.Y., 1983.

McMurrin, Sterling M., ed. *The Tanner Lectures on Human Values*, vol. 1. University of Utah Press, Salt Lake City, 1980.

McMurtry, John. "How to Tell the Right from the Left." *CJP*, vol. 9, no. 1 (Sept. 1979).

————. "Is There a Marxist Personal Morality?" In *Marx and Morality* (Nielsen and Patten, eds.).

————. "Making Sense of Economic Determinism." *CJP*, vol. 3, no. 2 (Dec. 1973).

————. *The Structure of Marx's World-View*. Princeton University Press, Princeton, N.J., 1978.

Macpherson, C. B. "Class, Class Consciousness and the Critique of Rawls." *PT*, vol. 6, no. 2 (May 1978).

————. *Democratic Theory: Essays in Retrieval*. Clarendon Press, Oxford, 1973.

————. *The Political Theory of Possessive Individualism*. Oxford University Press, N.Y., 1977.

————. "Rawls on Man and Society." *PSS*, vol. 3, no. 4 (Dec. 1973).

Magdoff, Harry. *The Age of Imperialism: The Economics of United States Foreign Policy*. Monthly Review Press, N.Y., 1969.

————. "Socialism, Democracy, and Planning." *MR*, vol. 33, no. 2 (June 1981).

Mandel, Ernest. "A Defense of Socialist Planning." *NLR*, no. 159 (Sept.–Oct. 1986).

————. *The Formation of the Economic Thought of Karl Marx*. Monthly Review Press, N.Y., 1971.

————. *From Class Society to Communism*. Ink Links, London, 1977.

————. "How to Make No Sense of Marx." *Marx Analyzed* (Nielsen and Ware, eds.).

————. *An Introduction to Marxist Economic Theory*. Pathfinder Press, N.Y., 1970.

————. *Late Capitalism*. New Left Books, London, 1975.

————. *Marxist Economic Theory*. Merlin Press, London, 1962.

————. *Marx's Theoretical Legacy: Restating the Case for Socialism at the End of the Twentieth Century*. Verso, London, 1987.

————. "On the Nature of the Soviet State." *NLR*, no. 108 (Mar.–Apr. 1978).

Mandel, Ernest, and George Novack. *The Marxist Theory of Alienation*. Pathfinder Press, N.Y., 1970.

Marcuse, Herbert. *An Essay on Liberation*. Beacon Press, Boston, 1969.

———. "Ethics and Revolution." In *Ethics and Society* (DeGeorge, ed.).

———. *One Dimensional Man*. Beacon Press, Boston, 1964.

———. "The Realm of Freedom and the Realm of Necessity: A Reconsideration." *Praxis*, vol. 5, no. 1–2 (1969).

———. "Socialist Humanism?" In *Socialist Humanism* (Fromm, ed.).

———. *Soviet Marxism: A Critical Analysis*. Columbia University Press, N.Y., 1958.

Marković, Mihailo. "Basic Characteristics of Marxist Humanism." *Humanist*, vol. 29 (Jan.–Feb. 1969).

———. *The Contemporary Marx*. Spokesman Books, Nottingham, England, 1974.

———. "Critical Social Theory in Marx." *Praxis*, vol. 6, no. 3–4 (1970).

———. *Democratic Socialism: Theory and Practice*. St. Martin's, N.Y., 1982.

———. *From Affluence to Praxis*. University of Michigan Press, Ann Arbor, Mich., 1974.

———. "Philosophical Foundations of the Idea of Self-Management." In *Self-Governing Socialism* (Horvat et al., eds.).

———. "Possibilities of Evolution to Socialist Democracy." In *Détente and Socialist Democracy: A Discussion with Roy Medvedev* (Coates, ed.).

———. "Marxist Humanism and Ethics." In *Dialogues on the Philosophy of Marxism* (Somerville and Parsons, eds.).

———. "Self-Government and Planning." In *Self-Governing Socialism* (Horvat et al., eds.).

———. "Socialism and Self-Management." In *Self-Governing Socialism* (Horvat et al., eds.).

———. "Stalinism and Marxism." In *Stalinism* (R. Tucker, ed.).

———. "Violence and Human Self-Realization." In *Essays on Socialist Humanism* (Coates, ed.).

Marković, Mihailo, and Gajo Petrović. *Praxis: Yugoslav Essays in the Philosophy and Methodology of the Social Sciences*. D. Reidel, Dordrecht, 1969.

Martin, Rex. *Rawls and Rights*. University Press of Kansas, Lawrence, 1986.

Mayo, Bernard. *Ethics and the Moral Life*. St. Martin's, N.Y., 1958.

Medvedev, Roy. *Leninism and Western Marxism*. Schocken Books, London, 1982.

————. *Let History Judge: The Origins and Consequences of Stalinism*. Macmillan, N.Y., 1972.

————. *On Socialist Democracy*. W. W. Norton, N.Y., 1975.

————. *On Stalin and Stalinism*. Oxford University Press, N.Y., 1979.

————. "Problems of Democratization and Détente." In *Detente and Socialist Democracy* (Coates, ed.).

Mepham, John, and David-Hillel Ruben, eds. *Issues in Marxist Philosophy, vol. 4: Social and Political Philosophy*. Humanities Press, Atlantic Highlands, N.J., 1981.

Miliband, Ralph. "Bettleheim and Soviet Experience." *NLR*, no. 91 (May–June 1975).

————. *Class Power and State Power*. Verso, London, 1983.

————. "The Capitalist State: Reply to Nicos Poulantzas." *NLR*, no. 59 (Jan.–Feb. 1970).

————. *Marxism and Politics*. Oxford University Press, N.Y., 1977.

————. *Parliamentary Socialism: A Study in the Politics of Labour*. Allen and Unwin, London, 1961.

————. "Socialist Democracy." In *Détente and Socialist Democracy* (Coates, ed.).

————. *The State in Capitalist Society: An Analysis of the Western System of Power*. Basic Books, N.Y., 1969.

————. "State Power and Class Interests." *NLR*, 138 (Mar.–Apr. 1983).

Mill, John Stuart. "On Liberty." In *The Essential Works of John Stuart Mill* (Max Lerner, ed.). Bantam, N.Y., 1961.

————. *Principles of Political Economy* (Sir William Ashley, ed.). Augustus M. Kelley, Clifton, N.J., 1909, 1973.

————. "Utilitarianism." In *The Essential Works of John Stuart Mill* (Max Lerner, ed.). Bantam, N.Y., 1961.

Mills, C. Wright. "Alienation and Social Structure." In *Social Structure and Theory* (Connolly and Gordon, eds.).

————. *The Power Elite*. Oxford University Press, N.Y., 1956.

Mills, C. Wright, ed. *The Marxists*. Dell Publishing Co., N.Y., 1962.

Miller, Richard W. *Analyzing Marx: Morality, Power, and History*. Princeton University Press, Princeton, N.J., 1984.

————. "The Consistency of Historical Materialism." *PPA*, vol. 4, no. 4 (Summer 1975).

———. "Democracy and Class Dictatorship." In *Marxism and Liberalism* (E. F. Paul, ed.).

———. "Marx and Aristotle: A Kind of Consequentialism." In *Marx and Morality* (Nielsen and Patten, eds.).

———. "Marx and Morality." In *Marxism* (Pennock and Chapman, eds.). [*Nomos*, vol. 26 (1983).]

———. "Marx in Analytic Philosophy: The Story of a Rebirth." *Social Science Quarterly*, vol. 64, no. 4 (Dec. 1983).

———. "Productive Forces and the Forces of Change: A Review of G. A. Cohen's *Karl Marx's Theory of History: A Defense*." *PR*, vol. 40, no. 1 (Jan. 1981).

———. "Rawls and Marxism." *PPA*, vol. 3, no. 2 (Winter 1974).

———. "Rights or Consequences." *MSP*, vol. 7 (Peter French et al., eds.). University of Minnesota Press, Minneapolis, 1982.

———. "Rights and Reality." *PR*, vol. 90 (1981).

Milo, Ronald D. *Immorality*. Princeton University Press, Princeton, N.J., 1984.

Moore, Stanley. "A Consistency Proof of Historical Materialism." *PPA*, vol. 5, no. 3 (Spring 1976).

———. *A Critique of Capitalist Democracy: An Introduction to the Theory of the State in Marx, Engels, and Lenin*. Paine-Whitman Publishers, N.Y., 1957.

———. "Marx and Lenin on Historical Materialism." *PPA*, vol. 4, no. 2 (Winter 1976).

———. *Marx on the Choice between Socialism and Communism*. Harvard University Press, Cambridge, Mass., 1980.

———. *Three Tactics*. Monthly Review Press, N.Y., 1963.

Murphy, Jeffrie G. "Marxism and Retribution." *PPA*, vol. 2, no. 3 (Spring 1973).

———. "Rights and Borderline Cases." *Arizona Law Review*, vol. 19, no. 1 (Winter 1978).

Nagel, Thomas. "Equality." *Mortal Questions*. Cambridge University Press, N.Y., 1979.

———. "Moral Conflict and Political Legitimacy." *PPA*, vol. 16, no. 3 (1987).

———. "Rawls on Justice." In *Reading Rawls* (Daniels, ed.).

Nasser, Alan G. "Marx's Ethical Anthropology." *PPR*, vol. 35 (June 1975).

Nell, Edward. "Understanding the Marxian Notion of Exploitation: The 'Number One Issue.' " In *Samuelson and Neo-Classical Economics* (George R. Feiwell, ed.). Kluwer-Nijhoff, Hingham, Mass., 1982.

Nell, Edward, and Onora O'Neill. "Justice under Socialism." In *Justice: Alternative Political Perspectives* (James P. Sterba, ed.). Wadsworth, Belmont, Calif., 1980.

———. *Making Sense of Human Rights: Philosophical Reflections on the Universal Declaration of Human Rights*. University of California Press, Berkeley, 1987.

Nielsen, Kai. "Alienation and Self-Realization." *Philosophy*, vol. 48 (1973).

———. "Arguing about Justice: Marxist Immoralism and Marxist Moralism." *PPA*, vol. 17, no. 3 (Summer 1988).

———. "Autonomy and Justice." *Proceedings of the 18th World Congress of Philosophy*, Brighton, England, 1988.

———. "Capitalism, Socialism, and Justice." *SP*, vol. 7, no. 3–4 (1980).

———. "Class and Justice." In *Justice and Economic Distribution* (Arthur and Shaw, eds.).

———. "Class Conflict, Marxism and the Good Reason Approach." *SP*, vol. 2, no. 1–2 (1974).

———. "Coming to Grips with Marx's Anti-Moralism." *PF(B)*, vol. 19 (1987).

———. "Cultural Pessimism and the Setting Aside of Marxism." *A&K*, vol. 7, no. 1 (1985).

———. *Equality and Liberty: A Defense of Radical Egalitarianism*. Rowman and Allanheld, Totowa, N.J., 1984.

———. "Impediments to Radical Egalitarianism." *APQ*, vol. 18, no. 2 (Apr. 1981).

———. "Justice and Ideology: Justice as Ideology." *Windsor Yearbook of Justice*, no. 1 (1981).

———. "Liberal and Socialist Egalitarianism" *Social Philosophy* (forthcoming).

———. "Marxism and Ideology." *African Philosophical Inquiry*, vol. 1, no. 1 (Jan. 1987).

———. *Marxism and the Moral Point of View*. Westview Press, Boulder, Colo., 1988.

———. "Marxism, Ideology, and Moral Philosophy." *STP*, vol. 6 (1980).

———. "Marx, Morality and Egalitarianism." *Ratio*, vol. 28, no. 1 (1986).

———. "Marx on Justice: The Tucker-Wood Thesis Revisited." *University of Toronto Law Journal*, vol. 38 (1988).

———. "Morality, Marxism, and the Ideological Functions of Morality: *A Theory of Justice* as a Test Case." *OR*, no. 8/9 (Autumn 1978).

490

————. "On Justifying Revolution." *PPR*, vol. 37, no. 4 (1977).

————. "On Justifying Violence." *Inquiry*, vol. 24, no. 1 (Mar. 1981).

————. "On Taking Historical Materialism Seriously." *Dialogue*, vol. 22 (1983).

————. "On Taking Human Nature as the Basis of Morality." *Social Research*, vol. 29, no. 2 (Summer 1976).

————. "On Terrorism and Political Assassination." In *Assent/Dissent* (J. P. White, ed.). Kendall-Hunt, Dubuque, Iowa, 1984.

————. "On the Choice between Reform and Revolution." In *Philosophy and Political Action* (Virginia Held et al., eds.). Oxford University Press, N.Y., 1973.

————. "On the Ethics of Revolution." *RP*, no. 6 (Winter 1973).

————. "On the Poverty of Moral Philosophy: Running a Bit with the Tucker-Wood Thesis." *SST*, vol. 33 (1987).

————. "Political Violence." *IPSR*, vol. 16, no. 2 (July 1982).

————. "The Priority of Liberty Examined." *IPSR*, vol. 11 (Jan. 1977).

————. "Radical Egalitarian Justice: Justice as Equality." *STP*, vol. 5, no. 2 (Spring 1979).

————. "Radically Egalitarian Justice." In *Legal Theory Meets Legal Practice* (Anne F. Bayefsky, ed.). Academic Printing and Publishing, Edmonton, Canada, 1988.

————. "Rawls and the Left: Some Left Critiques of Rawls' Principles of Justice." *A&K*, vol. 2 (1980).

————. "The Rejection Front and the Affirmation Front: Marx and Moral Reality." *Journal of Indian Council of Philosophical Research*, vol. 4, no. 1 (Autumn 1986).

————. "The Role of Radical Philosophers in Canada." *Socialist Studies*, vol. 1, no. 1 (1979).

————. "Skepticism and Human Rights." *Monist*, vol. 52, no. 4 (Oct. 1968).

Nielsen, Kai, and Steven C. Patten, eds. *Marx and Morality*. [*CJP*, supplementary vol. 7 (1981).]

Nielsen, Kai, and Roger Shiner, eds. *New Essays on Contract Theory*. [*CJP*, supplementary vol. 3 (1977).]

Nielsen, Kai, and Robert Ware. *Marx Analyzed: New Essays in Analytical Marxism*. [*CJP*, supplementary vol. 15 (1989)]

Noone, John B., Jr. *Rousseau's Social Contract: A Conceptual Analysis*. University of Georgia Press, Athens, 1980.

Norman, Richard. "Does Equality Destroy Liberty?" In *Contempo-*

rary Political Philosophy (Keith Graham, ed.). Cambridge University Press, Cambridge, 1982.

———. *Free and Equal: A Philosophical Examination of Political Values.* Oxford University Press, N.Y., 1987.

———. *The Moral Philosophers.* Oxford University Press, N.Y., 1984.

———. "Moral Philosophy without Morality." *RP*, no. 6 (Fall 1973).

———. "What Is Living and What Is Dead in Marxism?" In *Marx Analyzed* (Nielsen and Ware, eds.).

Norman, Richard, and Sean Sayers. *Hegel, Marx, and Dialectic: A Debate.* Humanities Press, Atlantic Highlands, N.J., 1980.

Novack, George. *Humanism and Socialism.* Pathfinder Press, N.Y., 1973.

———. *Uneven and Combined Development in History.* Merit Publishers, N.Y., 1966.

———. "The Permanent Revolution in Latin America." *Intercontinental Press*, vol. 8 (Nov. 16, 1970).

———, ed. *Existentialism versus Marxism: Conflicting Views on Humanism.* Dell Publishing Co., N.Y., 1966.

Nove, Alec. *The Economics of Feasible Socialism.* Allen & Unwin, London, 1983.

Nozick, Robert. *Anarchy, State, and Utopia.* Basic Books, N.Y., 1974.

Offe, Claus. "Structural Problems of the Capitalist State, Class Rule and the Political System: On the Selectiveness of Political Institutions." *German Political Studies*, vol. 1 (1973).

———. "Political Authority and Class Structure: An Analysis of Late Capitalism." *International Journal of Sociology*, no. 2 (1972).

Offe, Claus, and V. Ronge. "Theses on the Theory of the State." *NGC*, vol. 6 (1975).

Offe, Claus, and H. Wiesenthal. "Two Logics of Collective Action: Theoretical Notes on Social Class." *Political Power and Social Theory*, vol. 1 (1980).

Ollman, Bertell. *Alienation: Marx's Conception of Man in Capitalist Society.* Cambridge University Press, N.Y., 1971.

———. "Marxism and Political Science: Prolegomena to a Debate on Marx's Method." *P&S*, vol. 3, no. 4 (Summer 1973).

———. "Marx's Vision of Communism: A Reconstruction." In *Radical Visions of the Future* (Seweryn Bialer, ed.). Westview Press, Boulder, Colo., 1977.

O'Neill, Onora. "Nozick's Entitlements." *Inquiry* (Winter 1976).

Ortega, Daniel et al. *Nicaragua: The Sandinista People's Revolution (Speeches by Sandinista Leaders)*. Pathfinder Press, N.Y., 1985.

Panichas, George. "Vampires, Werewolves, and Economic Exploitation." *STP*, vol. 7, no. 2 (Summer 1981).

———. "Marx's Moral Skepticism." In *Marx and Morality* (Nielsen and Patten, eds.).

Parsons, Talcott. "Some Comments on the Sociology of Karl Marx." In *Sociological Theory and Modern Society*. Free Press, N.Y., 1967.

Pateman, Carol. *Participation and Democratic Theory*. Cambridge University Press, N.Y., 1970.

Paul, Ellen Frankel, ed. *Marxism and Liberalism*. [*SPP*, vol. 3, no. 2 (Spring 1986).]

Paul, Jeffrey, ed. *Reading Nozick*. Rowman and Allanheld, Totowa, N.J., 1981.

Peffer, R. G. "A Defense of Rights to Well-Being." *PPA*, vol. 8, no. 1 (Fall 1978).

———. "Morality and the Marxist Concept of Ideology." In *Marx and Morality* (Nielsen and Patten, eds.).

Pennock, J. Roland, and John Chapman, eds. *Marxism*. New York University Press, N.Y., 1983. [*Nomos*, no. 26 (1983).]

Petrović, Gajo. "Alienation." In *Encyclopedia of Philosophy*, vol. 1 (Paul Richard, ed.). Macmillan, N.Y., 1967.

———. "The Human Relevance of Marx's Concept of Alienation." In *Self-Governing Socialism* (Horvat et al., eds.).

———. *Marxism in the Mid-Twentieth Century: A Yugoslav Philosopher Reconsiders Karl Marx's Writings*. Doubleday, Garden City, N.Y., 1967.

———. "Marxism versus Stalinism." *Praxis*, vol. 3, no. 1 (1967).

———. "The Philosophical and Sociological Relevance of Marx's Theory of Alienation." In *Marx and the Western World* (Lobkowicz, ed.).

———. "Socialism, Revolution and Violence." In *The Socialist Idea* (Kolakowski and Hampshire, eds.).

Plamenatz, John. *German Marxism and Russian Communism*. Longman, London, 1954.

———. *Ideology*. Praeger, N.Y., 1970.

———. *Karl Marx's Philosophy Man*. Clarendon, Oxford, 1975.

———. *Man and Society*, vol. 2. Longman, London, 1963.

Popper, Karl. *The Open Society and Its Enemies*, vol. 2. Harper & Row, N.Y., 1962.

———. *The Poverty of Historicism*. Harper & Row, N.Y., 1957.

Poulantzas, Nicos. "The Capitalist State: A Reply to Miliband and Laclau." *NLR*, no. 95 (Jan.–Feb. 1976).

———. *Classes in Contemporary Capitalism*. New Left Books, London, 1975.

———. *Fascism and Dictatorship: The Third International and the Problem of Fascism*. New Left Books, London, 1974.

———. *Political Power and Social Classes*. Verso, London, 1978.

———. "The Problem of the Capitalist State." *NLR*, no. 58 (Nov.–Dec. 1969).

———. *State, Power, Socialism*. New Left Books, London, 1978.

Przeworski, Adam. "The Ethical Materialism of John Roemer." *P&S*, vol. 11, no. 3 (1982).

———. "From Proletariat into Class: The Process of Class Formation from Kautsky's *The Class Struggle* to Recent Contributions." *P&S*, vol. 7, no. 4 (1977).

———. "Material Interests, Class Compromise, and the Transition to Socialism." In *Analytical Marxism* (Roemer, ed.).

———. "Social Democracy as a Historical Phenomenon." *NLR*, no. 122 (July–Aug. 1980).

Przeworski, Adam, and Michael Wallerstein. "The Structure of Class Conflict in Democratic Capitalist Societies." *APSR*, vol. 76 (1982).

Rader, Melvin. *Marx's Interpretation of History*. Oxford University Press, N.Y., 1979.

Rawls, John. "The Basic Liberties and Their Priority." In *Tanner Lectures on Human Values*, vol. 3 (Sterling M. McMurrin, ed.). University of Utah Press, Salt Lake City, 1982.

———. "The Basic Structure as Subject." *APQ*, vol. 14, no. 2 (Apr. 1977).

———. "Fairness to Goodness." *PR*, vol. 84 (Oct. 1975).

———. "The Idea of an Overlapping Consensus." *Oxford Journal for Legal Studies*, vol. 7, no. 1 (1987).

———. "The Independence of Moral Theory." *PAAPA*, vol. 47 (1974–1975).

———. "Justice as Fairness: Political Not Metaphysical." *PPA*, vol. 14, no. 3 (Summer 1985).

———. "A Kantian Conception of Equality." *Cambridge Review* (Feb. 1975).

———. "Kantian Constructivism in Moral Theory." *JP*, vol. 77, no. 9 (Sept. 1980).

———. "The Priority of the Right and Ideas of the Good." *PPA*, vol. 17, no. 4 (Fall 1988).

———. "Reply to Alexander and Musgrave." *QJE* (Nov. 1974).

———. *A Theory of Justice.* Belknap Press of Harvard University Press, Cambridge, Mass., 1971.

———. "Social Unity and Primary Goods." In *Utilitarianism and Beyond* (Sen and Williams, eds.).

———. "Some Reasons for the Maximin Criterion." *AERPP,* vol. 64 (May 1974).

Reimann, Jeffrey. "An Alternative to 'Distributive' Marxism: Further Thoughts on Roemer, Cohen, and Exploitation." In *Marx Analyzed* (Nielsen and Ware, eds.).

———. "Exploitation, Force, and the Moral Assessment of Capitalism: Thoughts on Roemer and Cohen." *PPA,* vol. 16, no. 1 (Winter 1987).

———. "The Fallacy of Libertarian Capitalism." *Ethics,* vol. 92 (Oct. 1981).

. *In Defence of Political Philosophy.* Harper & Row, N.Y., 1972.

———. "The Labor Theory of the Difference Principle." *PPA,* vol. 12, no. 2 (Spring 1983).

———. "The Marxian Critique of Criminal Justice." *Criminal Justice,* vol. 6, no. 1 (Winter–Spring 1987).

———. "The Possibility of a Marxian Theory of Justice." In *Marx and Morality* (Nielsen and Patten, eds.).

———. *The Rich Get Richer and the Poor Get Prison: Ideology, Class, and Criminal Justice,* 2nd ed. John Wiley, N.Y., 1984.

———. "Why Socialists Should Support Individual Natural Rights." *Against the Current,* no. 10 (Sept.–Oct. 1987).

Richards, D.A.J. *A Theory of Reasons for Acting.* Clarendon Press, N.Y., 1971.

Riley, Patrick. "Marx and Morality: A Reply to Richard Miller." In *Marxism* (Pennock and Chapman, eds.).

Roemer, John. *Analytical Foundations of Marxian Economic Theory.* Cambridge University Press, N.Y., 1981.

———. "Are Socialist Ethics Consistent with Efficiency?" *PF(B),* vol. 14, no. 3–4 (1983).

———. "Equality of Resources Implies Equality of Welfare." *QJE,* vol. 101 (1986).

———. "Equality of Talent." *E&P,* vol. 1 (Fall 1986).

———. "Exploitation, Alternatives, and Socialism." *Economic Journal,* vol. 92 (1982).

———. *Free to Lose: An Introduction to Marxist Economic Philosophy.* Harvard University Press, Cambridge, Mass., 1988.

Roemer, John. *A General Theory of Exploitation and Class*. Harvard University Press, Cambridge, Mass., 1982.

———. "Methodological Individualism and Deductive Marxism." *T&S*, vol. 11, no. 4 (1983).

———. "New Directions in the Marxian Theory of Exploitation and Class." *P&S*, vol. 11, no. 3 (1982).

———. "Property Relations vs. Surplus Value in Marxian Exploitation." *PPA*, vol. 11, no. 4 (Fall 1982).

———. "R. P. Wolff's Reinterpretation of Marx's Labor Theory of Value: Comment." *PPA*, vol. 12, no. 1 (Winter 1983).

———. " 'Rational Choice' Marxism: Some Issues of Method and Substance." In *Analytical Marxism* (Roemer, ed.).

———. "Reply." *P&S*, vol. 11, no. 3 (1982).

———. "Second Thoughts on Property Relations and Exploitation." In *Marx Analyzed* (Nielsen and Ware, eds.).

———. "Should Marxists Be Interested in Exploitation?" *PPA*, vol. 14, no. 1 (Winter 1985).

———. "Technical Change and the 'Tendency of the Rate of Profit to Fall.' " *Journal of Economic Theory*, vol. 16 (Dec. 1977).

———. "Unequal Exchange, Labor Migration, and International Capital Flow: A Theoretical Synthesis." In *Marxism, Central Planning and the Soviet Economy: Economic Essays in Honor of Alexander Erlich* (P. Desai, ed.). MIT Press, Cambridge, Mass., 1983.

———. *Value, Exploitation, and Class*. Harwood Academic Publishers, N.Y., 1986.

———. "What is Exploitation?: Reply to Jeffrey Reimann." *PPA*, vol. 18, no. 1 (Winter 1989).

Roemer, John, ed. *Analytical Marxism*. Cambridge University Press, N.Y., 1986.

Roemer, John, and Roger E. Howe. "Rawlsian Justice as the Core of a Game." *AERPP*, vol. 71, no. 5 (1981).

Roemer, John, and Herve Moulin. "Public Ownership of the External World and Private Ownership of Self." *Journal of Political Economy*, vol. 97 (Apr. 1989).

Rousseau, Jean-Jacques. *The Social Contract and Discourse on the Origin of Inequality* (Lester G. Crocker, ed.). Simon & Schuster, N.Y., 1967.

Russell, Bertrand. *Selected Papers of Bertrand Russell*. Random House, N.Y., 1955.

Ryan, Cheyney C. "Socialist Justice and the Right to the Labour Product." *PT*, vol. 8, no. 4 (Nov. 1980).

Sandel, Michael. *Liberalism and Its Critics*. Basil Blackwell, London, 1984.

———. *Liberalism and the Limits of Justice*. Cambridge University Press, N.Y., 1982.

Sartorius, Rolf E. "Benevolence, Collective Action, and the Provision of Public Goods." In *The Limits of Utilitarianism* (H. B. Miller and W. H. Williams, eds.). University of Minnesota Press, Minneapolis, 1982.

———. *Individual Conduct and Social Norms*. Wadsworth, Belmont, Ca., 1975.

———. "The Limits of Libertarianism." In *Liberty and the Role of Law* (Robert L. Cunningham, ed.). Texas A & M University Press, College Station, Texas, 1979.

Sayers, Sean. "Analytical Marxism and Morality." In *Marx Analyzed* (Nielsen and Ware, eds.).

Scanlon, Thomas. "Equality of Resources and Equality of Welfare: A Forced Marriage?" *Ethics*, vol. 97, no. 1 (Oct. 1986).

———. "Nozick on Rights, Liberty, and Property." *PPA*, vol. 6, no. 1 (Fall 1976).

———. "Preference and Urgency." In *The Tanner Lectures on Human Values*, vol. 1 (McMurrin, ed.).

———. "Rawls' Theory of Justice." In *Reading Rawls* (Daniels, ed.).

———. "Rights, Goals, and Fairness." *JP*, vol. 76, no. 9 (Sept. 1979).

Schaff, Adam. *A Philosophy of Man*. Dell Publishing Co., N.Y., 1963.

———. "Alienation as a Social and Philosophical Problem." *STP*, vol. 3, no. 1 (Spring 1974).

———. "Marx and Contemporary Humanism." *Diogenes*, no. 64 (Winter 1968).

———. *Marxism and the Human Individual*. McGraw-Hill, N.Y., 1965.

———. "Marxism and the Philosophy of Man." In *Socialist Humanism* (Fromm, ed.).

———. "Marxist Humanism." In *Dialogues on the Philosophy of Marxism* (Somerville and Parsons, eds.).

———. "Marxist Theory of Revolution and Violence." *JHI*, vol. 34, no. 2 (April–June 1973).

Schmitt, Richard. *Alienation and Class*. Schenkman, Cambridge, Mass., 1983.

———. *Introduction to Marx and Engels: A Critical Reconstruction*. Westview Press, Boulder, Colo., 1987.

Schmitt, Richard. "Methodological Individualism, Psychological Individualism and the Defense of Reason." In *Marx Analyzed* (Nielsen and Ware, eds.).

———. "What Classes Are: Bolshevism, Democracy and Class Theory." *PI*, vol. 2 (Jan. 1983).

Schwartz, Adina. "Moral Neutrality and Primary Goods." *Ethics*, vol. 83 (July 1973).

Schweickart, David. "Capitalism and Work: Some Utilitarian Considerations." *Philosophical Forum*, vol. 10, no. 2–3–4 (1980).

———. *Capitalism or Worker Control? An Ethical and Economic Appraisal*. Praeger, N.Y., 1980.

———. "On the Exploitation of Cotton, Corn and Labor." In *Marx Analyzed* (Nielsen and Ware, eds.).

———. "Review of *Understanding Marx: A Reconstruction and Critique of Capital*, by Robert Paul Wolff." *JP*, vol. 83, no. 12 (1986).

———. "Should Rawls Be a Socialist?" *STP*, vol. 5, no. 1 (Fall 1978).

———. "Workers Controlled Socialism: A Blueprint and Defense." *RPNJ*, no. 8 (Apr. 1977).

Sellars, Wilfrid, and John Hospers, eds. *Readings in Ethical Theory*. Prentice-Hall, Englewood Cliffs, N.J., 1970.

Selsam, Howard, and Harry Martel, eds. *Reader in Marxist Philosophy*. International Publishers, N.Y., 1963.

Sen, Armatya. *Choice, Welfare and Measurement*. MIT Press, Cambridge, Mass., 1982.

———. *Collective Choice and Social Welfare*. Holden-Day, San Francisco, 1970.

———. *Commodities and Capabilities*. Reidel, Amsterdam, 1985.

———. "Equality of What?" In *The Tanner Lectures on Human Values*, vol. 1 (McMurrin, ed.).

———. *On Economic Inequality*. W. W. Norton, N.Y., 1973.

———. "On the Labour Theory of Value: Some Methodological Issues." *CJE*, no. 2 (1978).

———. *Poverty and Famines*. Oxford University Press, N.Y., 1981.

———. "Property and Hunger." *E&P*, vol. 4, no. 1 (1988).

———. "Rights and Capabilities." In *Resources, Values and Development*. Harvard University Press, Cambridge, Mass., 1984.

———. *The Standard of Living*. Cambridge University Press, N.Y., 1987.

———. "Utilitarianism and Welfarism." In *The Tanner Lectures on Human Values*, vol. 1 (McMurrin, ed.).

———. "Well-Being, Agency, and Freedom." *JP*, vol. 82, no. 4 (Apr. 1985).

Sen, Armatya, and Bernard Williams, eds. *Beyond Utilitarianism*. Cambridge University Press, N.Y., 1982.

Sensat, Julius. "Exploitation." *Nous*, vol. 17, no. 1 (Mar. 1984).

———. *Habermas and Marxism: An Appraisal*. Sage Publications, Beverly Hills, Calif., 1979.

Shaw, William H. "Historical Materialism and the Development Thesis." *PSS*, vol. 16 (1986).

———. "Marxism and Moral Objectivity." In *Marx and Morality* (Nielsen and Patten, eds.).

———. "Marxism, Revolution, and Rationality." In *After Marx* (Ball and Farr, eds.).

———. *Marx's Theory of History*. Stanford University Press, Stanford, Calif., 1978.

———. "Marx's Historical Materialism: The Traditional Interpretation and Its Critics." *SAJP*, vol. 2 (1983).

———. "Ruling Ideas." In *Marx Analyzed* (Nielsen and Ware, eds.).

Shue, Henry. *Basic Rights: Subsistence, Affluence, and U.S. Foreign Policy*. Princeton University Press, Princeton, N.J., 1980.

———. "The Burdens of Justice." *JP*, vol. 80, no. 10 (Oct. 1983).

———. "The Current Fashions: Trickle-downs by Arrow and Close-Knits by Rawls." *JP*, vol. 71 (June 13, 1974).

———. "Liberty and Self-Respect." *Ethics*, vol. 85 (1974–1975).

Singer, Peter. *Marx*. Hill and Wang, N.Y., 1980.

Skillen, Anthony. "Marxism and Morality." *RP*, no. 8 (Summer 1974).

———. *Ruling Illusions: Philosophy and the Social Order*. Harvester Press, Sussex, England 1977.

———. "Workers' Interest and the Proletarian Ethic: Conflicting Strains in Marxian Anti-Moralism." In *Marx and Morality* (Nielsen and Patten, eds.).

Smith, A. Anthony. "Robert Nozick's Critique of Marxian Economics." *STP* vol. 8, no. 2 (Summer 1982).

Somerville, John. "Adam Schaff and Contemporary Marxism." *PPR*, vol. 34, no. 2 (Dec. 1973).

———. "An Open Letter to Bertrand Russell." *Philosophy of Science*, vol. 13, no. 1 (Jan. 1946).

———. "Marxist Ethics, Determinism and Freedom." In *Dialogues on the Philosophy of Marxism* (Somerville and Parsons, eds.).

———. "Marx's Theory of Value." *PPR*, vol. 33, no. 2 (Dec. 1972).

Somerville, John. *The Philosophy of Marxism*. Random House, N.Y., 1967.

———. "The Value Problem and Marxist Social Theory." *JVI*, vol. 2 (Spring 1978).

———. "Violence, Politics and Morality." *PPR*, vol. 32, no. 2 (Dec. 1971).

Somerville, John, and Howard Parsons, eds. *Dialogues on the Philosophy of Marxism*. Greenwood Press, Westport, Conn., 1974.

Sterba, James. *The Demands of Justice*. University of Notre Dame Press, Notre Dame, Ind., 1980.

———. "The Welfare Rights of Distant Peoples and Future Generations: Moral Side-Constraints on Social Policy. *STP*, vol. 7 (Spring 1981).

Stojanović, Svetozar. *Between Ideals and Reality: A Critique of Socialism and Its Future*. Oxford University Press, N.Y., 1973.

———. "Freedom and Democracy in Socialism." *Praxis*, vol. 1, no. 2–3 (1965).

———. "From Post-Revolutionary Dictatorship to Socialist Democracy." *Praxis*, vol. 9, no. 4 (1973).

———. "Marx's Ethical Theory." In *Marx and the Western World* (Lobkowicz, ed.).

———. "The Morality of the Revolutionary Avant-Garde as the Historical Presupposition of Socialism." *Praxis*, vol. 2, no. 1–2 (1966).

———. "Prospects of Socialist Revolution in the Present Time." *Praxis*, vol. 5, no. 1–2 (1969).

———. "Revolutionary Teleology and Ethics." In *Tolerance and Revolution* (Kurtz and Stojanovic, eds.).

———. "Social Self-Government and Socialist Community." *Praxis*, vol. 10, no. 1–2 (1974).

———. "Stalinist 'Partinost' and Communist Dignity." *Praxis*, vol. 10, no. 1–2 (1974).

———. "The Statist Myth of Socialism." *Praxis*, vol. 3, no. 2 (1967).

———. "Power and Socialism." In *Self-Governing Socialism* (Horvat et al., eds.).

———. "Some Contradictions and Insufficiencies of Yugoslav Self-Managing Socialism." *Praxis*, vol. 7, no. 3–4 (1971).

Sweezy, Paul. "Capitalism and Democracy." *MR*, vol. 32, no. 2 (June 1980).

———. *The Theory of Capitalist Development: Principles of Marxian Political Economy*. Monthly Review Press, N.Y., 1942.

Sweezy, Paul, and Charles Bettleheim. *On the Transition to Socialism*. Monthly Review Press, N.Y., 1971.

Swingewood, Alan. *Marx and Modern Social Theory*. John Wiley & Sons, N.Y., 1975.

Taylor, Charles. "Alienation and Community." *Universities and Left Review* (Autumn 1958).

————. *Hegel*. Cambridge University Press, N.Y., 1978.

————. *Hegel and Modern Society*. Cambridge University Press, N.Y., 1979.

————. "Marxism and Empiricism." In *British Analytic Philosophy* (Bernard Williams and Alan Montefiore, eds.). Humanities Press, N.Y., 1966.

————. "On Social Justice." *Canadian Journal of Political and Social Theory*, vol. 1 (Fall 1977).

————. *Philosophy and the Human Sciences: Philosophical Papers*, vol. 2. Cambridge University Press, N.Y., 1985.

————. "Socialism and Weltenschaung." In *The Socialist Idea* (Kolakowski and Hampshire, eds.).

Taylor, Michael, ed. *Rationality and Revolution*. Cambridge University Press, N.Y., 1988.

Therborn, Göran. "The Prospects of Labour and the Transformation of Advanced Capitalism." *NLR*, no. 145 (May–June 1984).

————. *What Does the Ruling Class Do When It Rules?* New Left Books, London, 1978.

Thompson, E. P. *Poverty of Theory*. Monthly Review Press, N.Y., 1979.

Thompson, E. P., ed. *Out of Apathy*. Stevens-New Left Books, London, 1960.

Trotsky, Leon. *The Challenge of the Left Opposition*. Pathfinder Press, N.Y., 1975.

————. *History of the Russian Revolution* (3 vols.). Sphere Books Ltd., London, 1967.

————. *In Defense of Marxism*. Pathfinder Press, N.Y., 1973.

————. *Literature and Revolution*. University of Michigan Press, Ann Arbor, 1960.

————. *The Permanent Revolution*. Merit Publishers, N.Y., 1969.

————. *The Revolution Betrayed*. Pathfinder Press, N.Y., 1972.

————. *Transitional Program for Socialist Revolution*. Pathfinder Press, N.Y., 1973.

Trotsky, Leon, John Dewey, and George Novack. *Their Morals and Ours*. Merit Publishers, N.Y., 1969.

Tucker, D.B.F. *Marxism and Individualism*. St. Martin's Press, N.Y., 1980.

Tucker, Robert. "Marx as a Political Theorist." In *Marx and the Western World* (Lobkowicz, ed.).

———. *The Marxian Revolutionary Idea*. W. W. Norton, N.Y., 1969.

———. *Philosophy and Myth in Karl Marx*. Cambridge University Press, N.Y., 1961.

Tucker, Robert, ed. *The Marx-Engels Reader*. W. W. Norton, N.Y., 1972.

———. *Stalinism: Essays in Historical Interpretation*. W. W. Norton, N.Y., 1977.

van de Veer, Donald. "Marx's View of Justice." *PPR*, vol. 33, no. 3 (Mar. 1973).

van der Linden, Harry. "Marx and Morality: An Impossible Synthesis?" *T&S*, vol. 13, no. 1 (Jan. 1984).

van der Veen, Robert J. "Property, Exploitation, Justice." *AP* vol. 13 (1978).

Vanek, Jaroslav. *The General Theory of Labor-Managed Market Economies*. Cornell University Press, Ithaca, N.Y., 1970.

———. *The Labor-Managed Economy*. Cornell University Press, Ithaca, N.Y., 1977.

———. *The Participatory Economy*. Cornell University Press, Ithaca, N.Y., 1977.

Vanek, Jaroslav, ed. *Self-Management: Economic Liberation of Man*. Penguin, Baltimore, Md., 1975.

van Parijs, Phillipe. *Evolutionary Explanation in the Social Sciences*. Rowman and Littlefield, Totowa, N.J., 1981.

———. "The Falling Rate of Profit Theory of Crisis: A Rational Reconstruction by Way of Obituary." *RRPE*, vol. 12 (1980).

———. "Functionalist Marxism Rehabilitated." *T&S*, vol. 11 (1982).

———. "In Defense of Abundance." In *Marx Analyzed* (Nielsen and Ware, eds.).

———. "Marxism's Central Puzzle." In *After Marx* (Ball and Farr, eds.).

———. "Nozick and Marxism: Socialist Responses to the Libertarian Challenge." *RIP*, no. 146 (1983).

———. "What (If Anything) is Intrinsically Wrong with Capitalism?" *Philosophica*, vol. 34 (1984).

———. "Why Marxist Economics Needs Microfoundations." *RRPE*, vol. 156 (1983).

Walzer, Michael. *Just and Unjust Wars: A Moral Argument with Historical Illustrations*. Basic Books, N.Y., 1977.

———. "Political Action: The Problem of Dirty Hands." *PPA*, vol. 2, no. 2 (Winter 1973).

———. *Spheres of Justice: A Defense of Pluralism and Equality.* Basic Books, N.Y., 1983.

———. "What's Left of Marx: A Review of *Making Sense of Marx*, by Jon Elster." *NYRB* (Nov. 21, 1985).

Ware, Robert. "Marx, The Division of Labor, and Human Nature." *STP*, vol. 8, no. 1 (Spring 1982).

———. "Habermas's Evolutions." *CJP*, vol. 12, no. 3 (1982).

Warnock, G. J. *Contemporary Moral Philosophy.* St. Martin's Press, N.Y., 1967.

Wartofsky, Marx. "Karl Marx and the Outcome of Classical Marxism, or: Is Marx's Labor Theory of Value Excess Metaphysical Baggage?" *JP*, vol. 80, no. 11 (Nov. 1983).

Wasserstrom, Richard. *Philosophy and Social Issues: Five Studies.* University of Notre Dame Press, Notre Dame, Ind., 1980.

Wasserstrom, Richard, ed. *War and Morality.* Wadsworth, Belmont, Calif., 1970.

Waters, Mary-Alice, ed. *Rosa Luxemburg Speaks.* Pathfinder Press, N.Y., 1970.

Weisskopf, Thomas E. "Imperialism and the Economic Development of the Third World." In *The Capitalist System* (Edwards et al., eds.).

———. "The Irrationality of Capitalist Economic Growth." In *The Capitalist System* (Edwards et al., eds.).

———. "Marxian Crises Theory and the Rate of Profit in the Postwar U.S. Economy." *CJE*, vol. 3 (1979).

———. "Sources of Cyclical Downturns and Inflation." In *The Capitalist System* (Edwards et al., eds.).

Williams, Bernard. "The Idea of Equality." In *Moral Concepts* (Feinberg, ed.).

———. *Ethics and the Limits of Philosophy.* Harvard University Press, Cambridge, Mass., 1985.

———. "On Social Justice." *The Listener* (June 3, 1976).

———. "Persons, Character, and Morality." In *Identities of Persons* (A. Rorty, ed.). University of California Press, Berkeley, 1976.

———. "Utilitarianism and Moral Self-Indulgence." In *Contemporary British Philosophers* (H. D. Lewis, ed.). Allen & Unwin, London, 1976.

Williams, Raymond. "Beyond Actually Existing Socialism." *NLR*, no. 120 (Apr.–May 1980).

Wolff, Robert Paul. "A Critique and Reinterpretation of Marx's Labor Theory of Value." *PPA*, vol. 10, no. 2 (Spring 1981).

———. *In Defense of Anarchism*. Harper & Row, N.Y., 1970.

———. "On Violence." *JP*, vol. 66 (Oct. 1969).

———. "The Rehabilitation of Karl Marx." *JP*, vol. 80, no. 11 (Nov. 1983).

———. "Reply to Roemer's 'R. P. Wolff's Reinterpretation of Marx's Labor Theory of Value.'" *PPA*, vol. 12, no. 1 (Winter 1982).

———. "Robert Nozick's Derivation of the Minimal State." In *Reading Nozick* (J. Paul, ed.).

———. *Understanding Marx: A Reconstruction and Critique of Capital*. Princeton University Press, Princeton, N.J., 1984.

———. *Understanding Rawls*. Princeton University Press, Princeton, N.J., 1977.

Wood, Allen W. "Historical Materialism and Functional Explanation." *Inquiry*, vol. 29 (Mar. 1986).

———. "Justice and Class Interests." *Philosophica*, vol. 33, no. 1 (1984).

———. *Karl Marx*. Routledge & Kegan Paul, Boston, 1981.

———. "Marx and Equality." In *Issues in Marxist Philosophy, vol. 4* (Mepham and Ruben, eds.).

———. "Marx and Morality." In *Darwin, Marx and Freud* (Arthur L. Caplan and Bruce Jennings, eds.). Plenum Press, N.Y., 1984.

———. "Marx on Right and Justice: A Reply to Husami." *PPA*, vol. 8, no. 3 (Spring 1979).

———. "The Marxian Critique of Justice." *PPA*, vol. 1, no. 3 (Spring 1972).

———. "Marx's Immoralism." In *Marx en Perspective* (Chavance, ed.).

———. "Marx's Immoralismus." In *Ethik und Marx* (Emil Angehern and G. Lohmann, eds.). Hain, Konigstein, 1986.

Wood, Ellen Meiksins. "Marxism and the Course of History." *NLR*, no. 147 (Sept.–Oct. 1984).

———. "The Separation of the Economic and Political in Capitalism." *NLR*, no. 127 (May–June 1981).

Wright, Eric Olin. "Capitalism's Futures." *Socialist Review* (1970).

———. "Class Boundaries in Advanced Capitalist Societies." *NLR*, no. 98 (July–Aug. 1976).

———. *Class Structure and Income*. Academic Press, N.Y., 1979.

———. *Classes*. Verso, London, 1985.

———. *Class, Crisis, and the State*. New Left Books, London, 1978.

———. "Giddens's Critique of Marxism." *NLR*, no. 138 (Mar.–Apr. 1983).

———. *The Politics of Punishment: A Critical Analysis of Prisons in America*. Harper & Row, N.Y., 1973.

———. "What is Middle about the Middle Class?" In *Analytical Marxism* (Roemer, ed.).

Young, Gary. "Doing Marx Justice." In *Marx and Morality* (Nielsen and Patten, eds.).

———. "The Fundamental Contradiction of Capitalist Production." *PPA*, vol. 5, 1976.

———. "Justice and Capitalist Production: Marx and Bourgeois Ideology." *CJP*, vol. 8 (Spring 1978).

Young, Iris Marion. "Self-Determination as a Principle of Justice." *PF(B)*, vol. 11, no. 1 (Fall 1979).

———. "Toward a Critical Theory of Justice." *STP*, vol. 7, no. 3 (Fall 1983).

Zimmerman, David. "Coercive Wage Offers." *PPA*, vol. 10, no. 2 (Spring 1981).

———. "More on Coercive Wage Offers: A Reply to Alexander." *PPA*, vol. 12, no. 2 (Spring 1983).

INDEX

absolute idea, 262, 263
abundance, material, 318, 330, 332, 355
activity, 97, 105, 134; creative, 53–58,
71, 75, 103, 107, 111, 124; cultural,
109; free, 53, 54, 57, 58, 110, 111, 124;
higher, 74, 111, 112; lower, 111; self-,
58, 59, 103; social, 68. *See also* pro-
duction
Acton, H. B., 22
"Address at Congress of Russian
Young Communist League" (Lenin),
209
Adorno, Theodor, 294, 295
Aiken, Henry David, 175
Aldridge, Robert, 448
Alexander, Larry, 391
Ali, Tariq, 446
alienation, 50, 51; Hegel's theory of, 47;
Marx's concept of, 5, 15, 28, 45, 48,
50–54, 58, 64–69, 76, 97, 130, 180,
204, 319
"Alienation and Self-Realization"
(K. Nielsen), 103
Allen, Derek P. H., 9, 81, 86, 98, 110,
111, 112, 320
Allende government (Chile), 451
Althusser, Louis, 170, 174, 239, 242
altruism, 331, 371
Amdur, Robert, 407, 411
American Friends Service Committee,
447, 448
Amin, Samir, 445
Amnesty International, 447, 449
Analyzing Marx (Richard Miller), 24,
188
anarchism, left-wing, 136, 435
Anderson, Perry, 435
*Anekdota zur neuesten deutschen Philoso-
phie und Publicistik*, 36
anthropology (ethnology), 336–338
Anti-Dühring (Engels), 261, 271, 280
Apel, Karl-Otto, 285
Argentina, 447
Aristotle, 81, 90, 100–103, 105–110, 124,
192
Arneson, Richard, 9, 85, 113, 147–149,
338, 339, 391

Arnold, N. Scott, 31
Aronovitch, Hilliard, 81, 105, 129
art (artists), 49, 71, 90, 109, 110, 120,
134, 363
Asia, 86, 451. *See also* mode of production: Asiatic
authoritarianism, 398, 443. *See also* bureaucracy; repression; totalitarianism
authority, 380, 386; executive, 402. *See
also* political authority
autonomous choosers of ends: persons
as, 38, 88, 121, 178, 371–373, 396, 398
autonomy, 170, 246, 288, 289, 298, 299,
305, 309, 312, 344, 369, 374, 396–400,
423; moral, 37–41, 122, 123, 184, 186,
388, 391, 394, 397, 398, 422, 423, 432;
negative, 122, 397; nonmoral, 99,
105, 397, 398, 400; participatory, 397–
401, 432, 433; positive, 122, 397. *See
also* autonomus choosers of ends;
freedom (as self-determination)

Bahro, Rudolph, 73
Baier, Kurt, 9, 286, 287, 290
band and tribal level societies, 302,
336–338
Baran, Paul, 362, 445
Bardhan, Pranab, 9
Barnet, Richard, 448
Barry, Brian, 9, 405
base-superstructure models, 217, 270
basic liberties, 309, 311, 383, 392; effective exercise of, 383, 387; equal, 395,
404; priority of, 369, 381–385. *See also*
freedom (Marx's theory of); maximum equal liberty
basic rights principle, Peffer's, 385,
420, 421, 425, 437, 439, 453
basic social structure, 15, 369, 381, 389,
407
Bauer, Bruno, 41, 56, 57, 324
Beardsmore, R. W., 274
Beehler, Rodger, 194
Beitz, Charles, 408
Bender, Frederic, 357, 449
benevolence, 365
Benjamin, Medea, 449